RENEWABLE ENERGY

LAW, POLICY AND PRACTICE

■ ■ ■

Troy A. Rule
Professor of Law
Arizona State University Sandra Day O'Connor College of Law

AMERICAN CASEBOOK SERIES®

WEST
ACADEMIC
PUBLISHING

American Casebook Series is a trademark registered in the U.S. Patent and Trademark Office.

© 2018 LEG, Inc. d/b/a West Academic
     444 Cedar Street, Suite 700
     St. Paul, MN 55101
     1-877-888-1330

West, West Academic Publishing, and West Academic are trademarks of West Publishing Corporation, used under license.

Printed in the United States of America

ISBN: 978-1-68328-142-9

For Amy, Kiersten, Peyton, and Preston

PREFACE

This is the first hardcover law school casebook devoted solely to the legal, policy, and practical issues associated with renewable energy. The publication of this book is yet another milestone in the historic and long-awaited emergence of an industry that is already transforming economies and benefiting billions across the world. The dawn of a new age for energy has arrived, and this casebook is yet another manifestation of it.

Advancements in energy technologies have been raising complex new issues for courts and policymakers more than a century. The excellent "Energy Law" casebooks already on the market are expertly designed to educate law students on this pattern, covering everything from courts' early adoption of the "rule of capture" for oil and gas to more modern debates about clean coal policies and restrictions on hydraulic fracturing. However, as valuable as the historical perspective of general energy law casebooks may be for today's aspiring energy lawyers, it is increasingly evident that the energy law work they will encounter most over their careers is not likely to revolve around fossil fuels or nuclear power plants. Instead, most next-generation energy lawyers will spend their years of practice grappling with various legal and policy questions and challenges befitting the unique and often-perplexing characteristics of renewable energy resources. The U.S. Department of Energy reported that, in 2015 alone, more than two-thirds of all new electric generating capacity added in the U.S. took the form of wind turbines and solar panels. Lawyers' contributions to the development of legal constructs governing to these and other renewable energy strategies will have profound impacts on the long-term well-being of the human family. An ideal law school energy law curriculum for the twenty-first century should be equipped to consciously prepare law students for this important challenge.

Although existing energy law casebooks aptly acquaint law students with the general legal topics and policy questions surrounding renewables, the broader scope of those books prevents them from delving very deeply into renewable energy law and policy issues. This book does not seek to replace conventional energy law casebooks, which will unquestionably continue to have tremendous value in legal pedagogy for many more decades to come. Rather, its primary intended purpose is to make it easier for law professors to offer a separate renewable energy law course—one that has more policy and practice elements and could thus serve as a capstone for the growing legion of law students interested in this fascinating and rewarding area of practice. That said, in regions of the country where renewable energy already dominates the energy law landscape, some professors might find it justifiable and worthwhile to use this book as the primary course materials for a general energy law course.

This casebook assumes that its readers have minimal familiarity with energy law. It begins with a chapter designed to introduce law students to the complex energy industry within which renewable energy law operates, with an emphasis on issues and concepts that are the most likely to arise when representing clients on renewable energy-related matters. The book focuses most heavily on the property and land use questions associated with renewable energy development and on the retail-level utility regulatory issues arising from the growth of distributed renewable energy markets. One reason for this emphasis is that these tangible and relatable issues tend to retain student interest better than weedy discussions of federal utility regulatory topics, many of which are incidentally covered in more detail in conventional energy law or utilities law courses. A separate course may thus be warranted for students with particularly strong interests in FERC regulation, power purchase agreements, wholesale markets, RTOs/ISOs, and the like.

Today's budding energy lawyers are likely to face a formidable barrage of complicated, unsettled, and highly controversial issues over their storied careers. How can law schools better prepare them to effectively represent clients in these matters and to help shape sensible laws in a field where there are so few precedents? As this book emphasizes at multiple points, policy approaches that seek to analogize wind and solar resources to other resources such as water, wild animals, minerals, or oil & gas often produce inefficient or inequitable outcomes. Crafting distinctive new and innovative rules and theories to suit the unique attributes of renewable energy resources will therefore be crucial going forward. This book seeks to nurture the creative inquiry and innovative policymaking that future energy lawyers will need as the transition toward a more sustainable energy industry progresses in the coming decades.

I never could have produced this book without the generosity and support of Arizona State University—an institution that has repeatedly proven through its actions that it is genuinely committed to advancing environmental sustainability in all its forms. Dean Douglas Sylvester particularly deserves recognition for his willingness to support this daunting project over two summers and a sabbatical. I am also indebted to my research assistant, Jordan Brunner, for his invaluable help in getting the book into publishable form.

As with any first-time casebook in an emerging field, there are surely numerous gaps in coverage and other shortcomings in the pages that follow. Please be forthright in sending your suggestions to me so that I can address them in subsequent editions. I look forward to hearing your comments and to improving upon this first edition in the years to come.

TAR

November 2017

ACKNOWLEDGMENTS

Ana Isabel Baptista & Kumar Kartik Amarnath, *Garbage, Power, and Environmental Justice: The Clean Power Plan Rule*, 41 Wm. & Mary Envtl. L. & Pol'y Rev. 403 (2017).

Sara C. Bronin, *Building-Related Renewable Energy and the Case of 360 State Street*, 65 Vand. L. Rev. 1875 (2012).

Sara C. Bronin, *Curbing Energy Sprawl with Microgrids*, 43 Conn. L. Rev. 547 (2010).

Edith Brown Weiss, *In fairness to Future Generations and Sustainable Development*, 8 Am. U. Intl. L. Rev. 19 (1992–93).

Dallas Burtaw & Karen Palmer, *The Environmental Impacts of Restructuring: Looking Back and Looking Forward*, 1 Envt'l & Energy L. & Pol'y J. 171 (2005).

Charles Cicchetti, *Residential Demand Charges: Bad Choice,* 154 No. 12 Pub. Util. Fort. 34 (2016).

Ryan Cook & Lawrence Susskind, *The Cost of Contentiousness: A Status Report on Offshore Wind in the Eastern United States*, 33 Va. Envtl. L.J. 204 (2015).

Kimberly E. Diamond, *Wake Effects, Wind Rights, and Wind Turbines: Why Science, Constitutional Rights, and Public Policy Issues Play a Crucial Role*, 40 Wm. & Mary Envtl. L. & Pol'y Rev. 813 (2012).

Figure 1, Chapter 2, Texas Electricity Generation, Robert Fares, *Texas Sets New All-Time Wind Energy Record*, Sci. Am. (Jan. 14, 2016), https://blogs.scientificamerican.com/plugged-in/texas-sets-new-all-time-wind-energy-record/. Reprinted with Permission.

Elisabeth Graffy & Steven Kihm, *Does Disruptive Competition Mean a Death Spiral for Electric Utilities?*, 35 Energy L. J. 1 (2014). Reprinted with permission from the copyright holder, Energy Law Journal.

Todd J. Griset, *Harnessing the Ocean's Power: Opportunities in Renewable Ocean Energy Resources,* 16 Ocean & Coastal L.J. 395 (2011).

Lakshman Guruswamy, et al., *Model Law on Lighting for Developing Countries*, 44 Denv. J. Int'l L. & Pol'y 337 (2016).

Victor Hanna, Felix Mormann & Dan Reicher, *A Tale of Three Markets: Comparing the Renewable Energy Experiences of California, Texas, and Germany,* 35 Stan. Envtl. L.J. 55 (2016).

Keith H. Hirokawa & Andrew B. Wilson, *Local Planning for Wind Power: Using Programmatic Environmental Impact Review to Facilitate Development*, 33 No. 1 Zoning and Planning Law Report 1 (2010).

Kevin B. Jones, et al., *The Urban Microgrid: Smart Legal and Regulatory Policies to Support Electric Grid Resiliency and Climate Mitigation,* 41 Fordham Urb. L.J. 1695 (2014).

Alexandra B. Klass, *The Electric Grid at a Crossroads: A Regional Approach to Siting Transmission Lines*, 48 U.C. Davis L. Rev. 1895 (2015).

Alexandra B. Klass & Andrew Heiring, *Lifecycle Analysis and Transportation Energy*, 82 Brook. L. Rev. 485, 511–21 (2017).

Felix Mormann, *Beyond Tax Credits: Smarter Tax Policy for a Cleaner, More Democratic Energy Future*, 31 Yale J. on Reg. 303 (2014).

Elias L. Quinn & Adam L. Reed, *Envisioning the Smart Grid: Network Architecture, Information Control, and the Public Policy Balancing Act*, 81 U. Colo. L. Rev. 833 (2010).

David Raskin, *Getting Distributed Generation Right: A Response to "Does Disruptive Competition Mean a Death Spiral For Electric Utilities?"*, 35 Energy L.J. 263 (2014). Reprinted with permission from the copyright holder, Energy Law Journal.

Arnold W. Reitze, Jr., *Biofuel and Advanced Biofuel,* 33 UCLA J. Envtl. L. & Pol'y 309 (2015).

Jim Rossi, *The Common Law "Duty to Serve" and Protection of Consumers in an Age of Competitive Retail Public Utility Restructuring,* 51 Vand. L. Rev. 1233 (1998).

Troy A. Rule, *Airspace in a Green Economy*, 59 UCLA L. Rev. 270 (2011).

Troy A. Rule, *Buying Power: Utility Dark Money and the Battle over Rooftop Solar,* 5 LSU J. Energy L. & Res. 1 (2017).

Troy A. Rule, *Shadows on the Cathedral: Solar Access Laws in a Different Light,* 2010 U. Ill. L. Rev. 851 (2010).

Troy A. Rule, *Solar Energy, Utilities, and Fairness,* 6 San Diego J. Climate & Energy L. 115 (2015).

Troy A. Rule, Solar, Wind and Land: Conflicts in Renewable Energy Development (Routledge-Earthscan, 2014)

Troy A. Rule, *Unnatural Monopolies: Why Utilities Don't Belong in Rooftop Solar Markets,* 52 Idaho L. Rev. 387 (2016).

Troy A. Rule, *Wind Rights under Property Law: Answers Still Blowing in the Wind*, 26-DEC Prob. & Prop. 56 (2012).

David Schraub, *Renewing Electricity Competition*, 42 Fla. St. U. L. Rev. 937 (2015).

Shannon J. Skinner, *A Practical Guide to Title Review (with Form)*, 21 No. 4 Prac. Real Est. Law. 35 (2005).

Amy L. Stein, *Distributed Reliability*, 87 U. Colo. L. Rev. 887 (2016).

Amy L. Stein, *Reconsidering Regulatory Uncertainty: Making a Case for Energy Storage*, 41 Fla. St. U. L. Rev. 697 (2014).

Stoel Rives LLP, *Solar Project Property Rights: Securing Your Place in the Sun*, The Law of Solar: A Guide to Business and Legal issues (5th Ed. 2017). © Stoel Rives LLP. All rights reserved.

Ben Tannen, *Capturing the Heat of the Earth: How the Federal Government Can Most Effectively Encourage the Generation of Electricity from Geothermal Energy*, 37 Environs Envtl. L. & Pol'y J. 133 (2014).

David Tarasi, et al., *18,000 Americans Without Electricity: Illuminating and Solving the Navajo Energy Crisis*, 22 Colo. J. Int'l Envtl. L. & Pol'y 263 (2011).

Jeffrey Thaler, *Fiddling as the World Floods and Burns: How Climate Change Urgently Requires a Paradigm Shift in the Permitting of Renewable Energy Projects*, 41 Envtl. L. 1101 (2012).

Morgan Walton, *A Lesson from Icarus: How the Mandate for Rapid Solar Development has Singed a Few Feathers*, 40 Vt. L. Rev. 131 (2015).

Gina Warren, *Hydropower: It's a Small World After All,* 91 Neb. L. Rev. 925, 928–37 (2013).

Gina Warren, *Small Hydropower, Big Potential: Considerations for Responsible Global Development,* 53 Idaho L. Rev. 149 (2017).

Racheal White Hawk, *Community Solar: Watt's In It for Indian Country?,* 40 Environs Envtl. L. & Pol'y J. 1 (2016).

EDITOR'S NOTE

This book adopts most of the stylistic conventions commonly used in law school casebooks to enhance cleanliness and readability. Nearly all of the book's case and article excerpts are heavily edited to make them more digestible for law students. Deletions are indicated with ellipses. Most footnotes are omitted and those that remain retain their original numbering. Most parallel case citations and references to evidentiary records are also cut to reduce the choppiness of the text and ease reading.

SUMMARY OF CONTENTS

TABLE OF CONTENTS

_____

TABLE OF CASES

The principal cases are in bold type.

RENEWABLE ENERGY
LAW, POLICY AND PRACTICE

CHAPTER 1

INTRODUCTION AND BACKGROUND

■ ■ ■

Shortly before his death in 1931, Thomas Edison—one of the fathers of modern electric power—made a prophetic statement about the long-term trajectory of the industry he helped to create. In a conversation with Henry Ford and Harvey Firestone about the future of the energy industry, Edison declared:

> I'd put my money on the sun and solar energy. What a source of power! I hope we don't have to wait until oil and coal run out before we tackle that.[1]

Edison recognized the energy potential in wind resources as well and sketched futuristic drawings of windmills powering small clusters of homes. He even designed an energy self-sufficient home powered with 27 battery cells and hoped to eventually connect the home to a windmill to supply its electricity needs.[2]

More than 85 years later, Thomas Edison's futuristic vision of modern energy is increasingly becoming a reality. As President Barack Obama noted in his final State of the Union address in 2016, renewable energy technologies "have reached an important tipping point in a number of markets in the world. . . . They are now, in a growing number of locations, becoming cost competitive."[3] Although some believed that the election of President Donald Trump would reverse the nation's embrace of renewable energy, no such reversal had materialized nearly a year into his presidency. Instead, utilities and energy users throughout the country—including some of the nation's most politically conservative states—continued to invest heavily in renewable energy development, often finding it to be the most economical available means of supplying additional electric power to homes and businesses.[4]

---

[1] Heather Rodgers, *Current Thinking*, N.Y. TIMES MAG. (June 3, 2007), http://www.nytimes.com/2007/06/03/magazine/03wwln-essay-t.html?mcubz=3.

[2] *See id.*

[3] Chris Mooney, *Why Clean Energy Is Now Expanding Even When Fossil Fuels Are Cheap*, WASH. POST (Jan. 14, 2016), https://www.washingtonpost.com/news/energy-environment/wp/2016/01/14/why-clean-energy-is-now-expanding-even-when-fossil-fuels-are-cheap/?utm_term=.45cfe30 49978.

[4] *See generally* Justin Gillis & Nadja Popovich, *In Trump Country, Renewable Energy Is Thriving*, N.Y. TIMES (June 6, 2017), https://www.nytimes.com/2017/06/06/climate/renewable-energy-push-is-strongest-in-the-reddest-states.html?mcubz=3.

As the nation shifts toward renewable energy sources, today's energy lawyers are encountering vastly different issues than their predecessors encountered even one generation ago. The energy industry is rapidly transitioning on multiple fronts. Technological innovation and shifting attitudes about how we produce and consume energy are compelling energy industry stakeholders and policymakers to rethink longstanding business models, question existing policy approaches, and swiftly adapt in what have historically been relatively stable and predictable markets.

As the energy industry transforms itself, many of the topics and issues that law students have traditionally studied in energy law courses no longer reflect what lawyers are most frequently encountering in practice. The U.S. coal industry is on the decline, with coal-fired power plants closing across the country and very few new plants opening or under construction. Although a few states have begun subsidizing their aging nuclear power plants to keep them in operation, as of 2017 only two major nuclear power reactors were under construction in the United States and even the future of those projects was uncertain. And although advancements in hydraulic fracturing techniques have increased domestic oil and gas extraction over the past decade, renewable energy development has continued to be the country's fastest-growing energy strategy. In 2015, roughly two-thirds of all new electric generating capacity in the United States was attributable to wind and solar energy. Renewable energy technologies are predicted to account for nearly half of all electricity generated annually in the United States by as early as 2030.

The country's pivot toward renewable energy technologies raises numerous new legal and policy questions that have yet to be fully resolved. For instance, to what extent should governments subsidize renewable energy development? How should the law delineate property interests in wind and solar energy resources among neighbors? And how should regulators respond as competition from rooftop solar and distributed energy storage companies increasingly threatens electric utilities' long-term stability? These types of complex questions comprise much of the next great frontier for energy law—a field that, since its earliest beginnings, has demanded that lawyers frequently adapt to new technologies and shifting policy priorities.

A general familiarity with the historical backdrop and principles that undergird today's law and policy issues involving renewable energy is prerequisite to effectively studying these issues. This Chapter's background materials seek to provide readers with that familiarity, laying the groundwork for the more topical subject matter that follows in subsequent chapters. Part A of this Chapter examines the distinction between renewable and non-renewable energy and considers whether this distinction is justifiable in law and policy. Part B provides general introductory information about the nation's current energy system and the regulatory structures that govern it. Part C outlines the primary factors that are driving today's transition toward more sustainable energy sources. Part D then highlights some concepts that recur multiple times in the study of renewable energy law.

A. WHAT IS RENEWABLE ENERGY?

The term *renewable energy* describes just one narrow class of energy strategies. Engineers and physicists generally define *energy* as the capacity to do work. Humans have long relied upon various natural resources to supply the energy necessary to survive on this planet and to build and operate productive economies. Energy exists in a variety of well-documented forms, ranging from thermal heat to kinetic energy to chemical energy. However, whether a given energy source warrants classification as *renewable* is an entirely different question and is not always clear. Crafting rules to distinguish renewable energy strategies from nonrenewable ones is thus an inherently imperfect exercise with significant consequences.

1. DISTINGUISHING RENEWABLES FROM NON-RENEWABLES

On a few occasions, vigorous debates have arisen in recent years over whether a certain type of energy strategy should qualify as "renewable" energy and thus be eligible for special government subsidies or other benefits. Some common energy resources, such as coal and crude oil, are obviously *non*renewable because they are formed only through processes occurring over thousands or millions of years. For example, the energy stored in coal typically originates from swamp forest plants and ferns that lived millions of years ago and were compressed and heated over time. Oil and natural gas are formed through a similar process. Because they develop over such lengthy periods, coal, oil, and natural gas are often referred to as *fossil fuels*.

Fossil fuels are perpetually forming at various locations below the earth's surface, so in a broad sense one might conceivably characterize them as renewable resources. However, in practical terms, the planet's supplies of these resources are finite because the pace at which humans are depleting known, extractable fossil fuel reserves far exceeds the pace at which new reserves are forming. Accordingly, fossil fuels are the prototypical example of a nonrenewable energy source.

On the other end of the spectrum, some energy sources are undisputedly renewable. Solar energy resources fit into this category. Abundant quantities of solar radiation constantly penetrate the earth's atmosphere, providing enormous amounts of light and heat. Existing technologies could theoretically convert enough of that radiation to supply all of the planet's electricity needs without diminishing the amount of sunlight the planet continues to reliably receive each day. See RICHARD SCHMALENSEE ET AL., THE FUTURE OF SOLAR ENERGY (2015), http://mitei. mit.edu/futureofsolar. Sunlight is a decidedly renewable resource because humankind can use it in practically limitless quantities today without thereby reducing the amounts of it available for use tomorrow or even centuries into the future.

Unfortunately, distinguishing renewable resources from nonrenewable ones is not always as straightforward as it is for sunlight or coal. Policymakers have long struggled to craft standards that effectively differentiate renewable energy resources from all others. Consider, for example, *woody biomass*, a type of biomass resource that is burned to generate electric power. Woody biomass is generally derived from trees that take decades to grow and store energy, and when a power plant burns a woody biomass pellet that energy is released in a matter of seconds. Relying solely on the burning of woody biomass to meet the planet's electricity demand would quickly deplete the earth's precious forests, but woody biomass does regenerate within a few dozen years as new trees grow—a timetable far shorter than that of coal or petroleum. Because some attributes of woody biomass straddle the line between renewable and nonrenewable resources, it is debatable whether policymakers should treat it like coal or like sunlight when crafting renewable energy policies.

In some instances, policymakers have resorted to crafting lengthy statutory definitions to distinguish renewable energy from nonrenewable energy. The Texas legislature has adopted this definition:

> "renewable energy technology" means any technology that exclusively relies on an energy source that is naturally regenerated over a short time and derived directly from the sun, indirectly from the sun, or from moving water or other natural movements and mechanisms of the environment. Renewable energy technologies include those that rely on energy derived directly from the sun, on wind, geothermal, hydroelectric, wave, or tidal energy, or on biomass or biomass-based waste products, including landfill gas. A renewable energy technology does not rely on energy resources derived from fossil fuels, waste products from fossil fuels, or waste products from inorganic sources.

TEX. UTIL. CODE ANN. § 39.904(d) (West 2007).

By contrast, the following definition for renewable energy resources appears in a federal statute:

> the term "renewable energy resource" means any energy resource which has recently originated in the sun, including direct and indirect solar radiation and intermediate solar energy forms such as wind, ocean thermal gradients, ocean currents and waves,

hydropower, photovoltaic energy, products of photosynthetic processes, organic wastes, and others.

42 U.S.C. § 7372 (2016).

––––––––––

QUESTIONS

1. The distinctions between renewable and nonrenewable energy resources drawn in the statutory definitions excerpted above have some subtle differences. Consider, for instance, how these definitions would treat geothermal generating facilities, which generate electricity using geothermal heat sources found below the surface of the earth. Would geothermal energy qualify as renewable energy under the Texas statute?

2. Would geothermal power, which is generated from heat originating deep inside the earth, qualify as renewable energy under the federal statutory language above?

3. Which definition above (the Texas statutory definition or the federal statutory definition) do you think is more defensible from a public policy perspective, and why?

4. Suppose you represent a dairy farm in Texas that uses a methane digester—a large device that essentially harvests methane gas from manure—and burns its harvested methane to generate electric power that meets most of the farm's electricity demand. The dairy farm has approached you and expressed concern that its operation may not qualify as a renewable energy facility under the Texas definition set forth above. Draft proposed revisions to the Texas statutory definition aimed at resolving your client's concern.

––––––––––

POLICY PROBLEM

Should electricity generated from burning trash qualify as "renewable energy"?

Like many statutory definitions, the definitions of "renewable energy" excerpted above reflect numerous embedded policy decisions. When drafting the definitions, the drafters had to make difficult choices about which specific types of energy strategies should qualify for special subsidies or incentives and which should not. Proficient drafters of statutory provisions also identify and address potential ambiguities when drafting to reduce legal uncertainty and the likelihood of future litigation over a statute's meaning. The following hypothetical problem illustrates the importance of conscious policy choices and careful drafting in these contexts.

Suppose that TrashLight Corporation, a new start-up company, has plans to build a new power plant with a boiler designed to generate electricity from the burning of trash—the smelly waste trash collectors gather each week from curbside bins in front of homes and businesses. The legislature in TrashLight's home state is currently drafting legislation that, if enacted, would provide large state tax credits for renewable energy. The tax credits subsidize all forms of "renewable energy," but the current draft of the statute provides no statutory definition of that term. TrashLight executives know that the company would benefit tremendously if its new waste-to-energy power plant were to qualify as a renewable energy facility under the proposed statute.

Suppose that executives at SolarCo—a major solar energy company operating in the same state—are also aware of the state's new legislative effort to create a state-level renewable energy tax credits. SolarCo's executives recognize that, if TrashLight's power plant facility qualifies as a renewable energy facility under the proposed legislation, the tax credits will be less effective at generating additional demand for the company's solar energy products.

1.   Suppose you represent TrashLight in its policy advocacy efforts aimed at ensuring that its planned trash-burning power plant qualifies as a renewable energy facility under the state's tax credit program.

a.   Craft a detailed argument for why power plants that burn only trash should be included within the definition of "renewable energy" under the tax credit statute.

b.   Draft a proposed statutory definition of "renewable energy" that would accomplish your client's goals.

2.   Suppose instead that you represent SolarCo in its advocacy campaign to ensure that state legislators draft the new tax credit statute so as *not* to include electricity generation from trash burning in its definition of renewable energy.

a.   Craft a detailed argument for why trash-fired electricity generation should *not* be included within the definition of "renewable energy" under the tax credit statute.

b.   Draft a proposed statutory definition of "renewable energy" that would accomplish your client's goals.

3.   Suppose instead that you are a state legislator serving on the drafting committee for the state's new renewable energy tax credit bill.

a.   Brainstorm possible ways of structuring the state's renewable energy tax credits to create some incentive for trash-to-power companies such as TrashLight to build their power plants and yet provide even greater incentives for solar energy development.

b.   Do you think it should make a difference if TrashLight's power plant burns only old newspapers and other *paper* waste and burns no plastic or other types of waste? Why or why not? What if the plant burns only yard waste (grass clippings, etc.)?

4.   Do you think TrashLight's power plant would qualify as a renewable energy facility under the Texas or federal statutory definitions set forth above? Why or why not?

For those curious enough to look ahead: more detailed coverage of the *waste-to-energy* issues raised in this Policy Problem follows in Chapter 8.

2.   RENEWABLE VS. NONRENEWABLE: A USEFUL POLICY DISTINCTION?

All else equal, renewable energy resources seem to have some clear public policy advantages over nonrenewable ones. One disadvantage of fossil fuels is that burning them depletes global supplies, which increases their scarcity and thereby imposes costs on future generations. By contrast, using renewable energy resources has little or no impact on the planet's long-term supplies of them and thus imposes no such costs. On that basis alone, distinctions between renewable and nonrenewable energy arguably warrant some attention in energy policy.

However, the renewable-versus-nonrenewable distinction in energy policy is clearly far from perfect. One downside of focusing on "renewableness" in energy policy is that it can lead to underinvestment in some environmentally-beneficial and sustainability-promoting energy strategies that do not directly involve renewables. Consider, for instance, laws that provide special tax credits to citizens and businesses that purchase certain specified types of renewable energy systems such as wind turbines or rooftop solar panels. Although these policies promote renewable energy development, they do nothing to incentivize utilities to convert coal-fired power plants into cleaner-burning natural gas-fired plants or to make other changes to coal-fired plants to reduce their adverse environmental impacts. Nor do they incentivize citizens to invest in various energy efficiency features in buildings and vehicles that could also provide significant environmental and other benefits.

Recognizing that several nonrenewable energy strategies also have significant environmental and other benefits, policymakers in some jurisdictions have found ways to incentivize private investment in those nonrenewable energy strategies as well. Consider for instance, the following excerpts from a statute creating a "Clean Energy Portfolio Standard" program in Indiana—a state with abundant coal resources. The program is carefully designed to boost investment in the specific types of energy projects falling within the statutory definition below.

INDIANA CLEAN ENERGY PORTFOLIO STANDARD, IND. CODE §§ 8–1–8.8–2 & 8–1–8.8–3

(2011)

§ 8–1–8.8.2: "Clean energy projects" defined

As used in this chapter, "clean energy projects" means any of the following:

(1) Any of the following projects:

(A) Projects at new energy production or generating facilities that employ the use of clean coal technology and that produce energy, including substitute natural gas, primarily from coal, or gases derived from coal, from the geological formation known as the Illinois Basin.

(B) Projects to provide advanced technologies that reduce regulated air emissions from or increase the efficiency of existing energy production or generating plants that are fueled primarily by coal or gases from coal from the geological formation known as the Illinois Basin, such as flue gas desulfurization and selective catalytic reduction equipment.

(C) Projects to provide electric transmission facilities to serve a new energy production or generating facility or a nuclear energy production or generating facility.

(D) Projects that produce substitute natural gas from Indiana coal by construction and operation of a coal gasification facility.

(E) Projects or potential projects that enhance the safe and reliable use of nuclear energy production or generating technologies to produce electricity.

(2) Projects to develop alternative energy sources, including renewable energy projects or coal gasification facilities.

(3) The purchase of fuels or energy produced by a coal gasification facility or by a nuclear energy production or generating facility.

(4) Projects described in subdivisions (1) through (2) that use coal bed methane.

§ 8–1–8.8–3: "Clean coal technology" defined

As used in this chapter, "clean coal technology" means a technology (including precombustion treatment of coal):

(1) that is used in a new or existing energy production or generating facility and directly or indirectly reduces or avoids airborne emissions of sulfur, mercury, or nitrogen oxides or other regulated air emissions associated with the combustion or use of coal; and

(2) that either:

(A) was not in general commercial use at the same or greater scale in new or existing facilities in the United States at the time of enactment of the federal Clean Air Act Amendments of 1990 (P.L.101–549); or

(B) has been selected by the United States Department of Energy for funding or loan guaranty under an Innovative Clean Coal Technology or loan guaranty program under the Energy Policy Act of 2005, or any successor program, and is finally approved for such funding or loan guaranty on or after the date of enactment of the federal Clean Air Act Amendments of 1990 (P.L.101–549).

――――――――――

QUESTIONS

1.   Why do you think the Indiana state legislature opted to enact policies that incentivize the broader list of "clean energy projects" defined above rather than a more limited list of renewable energy projects? What types of stakeholder groups were likely to have lobbied in favor of this policy approach?

2.   What are some advantages and disadvantages of categorizing all the energy strategies described in the Indiana statutory provisions excerpted above together and affording them identical policy treatment?

3.   Suppose you were an attorney hired to advocate on behalf of wind energy developers in Indiana. What arguments would you make against Indiana's policy approach to promoting clean energy? How would the coal industry likely respond to your arguments?

――――――――――

Perhaps recognizing the deficiencies of laws centered on the "renewableness" of energy resources, some have advocated instead for a greater policy focus on deterring emissions of carbon dioxide (CO_2)—a gaseous byproduct of fossil fuel-fired electricity generation that is widely believed to contribute to global warming. Many policies aimed at reducing CO_2 emissions make no distinction between renewable and nonrenewable energy strategies. For example, some policymakers have advocated for a simple tax on all carbon dioxide emissions. Such a tax would certainly encourage renewable energy development, but it would also motivate citizens and businesses to invest in energy efficiency, energy conservation, and conversions of coal-fired plants to run on natural gas. Many of these other activities are often not incentivized through policies focused solely on promoting renewable energy. Regardless, carbon tax proposals have historically proven politically infeasible in the United States. The ongoing policy debate over carbon taxation proposals is explored in greater detail later in this Casebook.

Despite their shortcomings, statutes and regulations distinguishing between renewable and non-renewable resources have become a common fixture in energy policy. Accordingly, this Casebook perpetuates the concededly imperfect renewable-versus-nonrenewable distinction by incorporating the term "renewable energy" into its title. However, this book does not limit its coverage solely to legal and policy issues associated with renewable energy generation. Subsequent chapters consciously expand beyond renewable energy resources themselves to cover legal issues associated with cogeneration, energy storage, smart grids, and numerous other modern energy strategies that are consonant with the overarching aims of renewable energy policies.

B. AN INDUSTRY IN TRANSITION

Regardless of whether we call them "clean", "sustainable", "renewable" or something else, technologies that make use of renewable energy resources are transforming today's energy industry. A common refrain among energy industry stakeholders is that the industry is rapidly "transitioning" toward greater reliance on renewable energy resources. This historic transition is progressing rapidly in communities and nations across the globe.

It is worth acknowledging that humans have been relying upon many renewable resources for energy for thousands of years. Renewable energy resources such as wind, solar radiation, water currents, and biomass have been furnishing valuable energy to humankind since long before the dawn of the Industrial Revolution. Humans have relied on solar radiation as an important source of indoor lighting for millennia and have likewise used it for centuries to dry food, heat water, and warm homes. Owners of windmills and sailboats have similarly been harnessing the powerful energy in wind for hundreds of years. Even various forms of wood and grass products that qualify as "biomass" under many modern renewable energy policies have long served as vital energy sources in stoves and other settings across the globe.

Still, today's transition toward renewables is distinct and historic because it involves a conscious departure from the fossil fuel-centric models that have powered developed nations for more than a century. Until very recently, the electrification of modern economies—which the National Academy of Engineering has called the greatest engineering achievement of the twentieth century—has depended almost entirely upon unsustainable levels of nonrenewable energy consumption. Enormous coal mines, vast pipeline systems, and seemingly endless webs of wires and cables have helped to ensure the nation's lights stay on, our phones stay charged, and buildings constantly remain climate-controlled. Renewable energy and related technologies could ultimately render some of that infrastructure investment obsolete by enabling the global economy to function on entirely different energy sources. Massive amounts of new infrastructure investment and creative regulatory and business models will be needed to support this cleaner, more sustainable energy system.

1. TODAY'S FOSSIL FUEL-POWERED SOCIETY

Of course, the "transition" toward renewables described above is clearly still in its earliest stages. Meanwhile, fossil fuels and nuclear power continue to serve as the world's primary energy sources. For more than a century, developed countries have heavily relied upon these rich energy sources to power most of their activities and humankind has been extremely dependent on them. If coal, petroleum, and nuclear fuel supplies were to suddenly run out tomorrow, the global economy would instantly plunge into its most severe economic depression in recorded history. In many regions across the globe, food and medical care would quickly become unavailable and water supplies would soon become unsafe for drinking. Millions of families across the planet would shiver from the cold or suffer heat exhaustion in their own homes. Manufacturing activity would plummet, transportation would be far more restricted and expensive, and most humans' quality of life would precipitously decline. Of course, humankind has not always been as dependent upon fossil fuels and nuclear energy as it is today. The following is a brief overview of how the nations of the world became so hooked on coal, oil, gas, and nuclear power.

a. The Rise of Fossil Fuel Energy

Humankind's use of fossil fuels dates back thousands of years. Archeological evidence suggests that some Chinese communities may have used coal for household energy purposes as early as 3,000 B.C. *See* Colin Barras, *Coal Fueled China Long Before Industrial Revolution*, New Scientist (Apr. 2, 2014), https://www.newscientist.com/article/mg22229632 -600-coal-fuelled-china-long-before-industrial-revolution/. Coal served as an indoor heating fuel in some regions controlled by the Roman Empire. *See* BRUCE G. MILLER, COAL ENERGY SYSTEMS 30 (2005). Coal was likewise a valuable and regularly-traded commodity in medieval Europe. *See id.* at 31. Multiple ancient civilizations are also believed to have burned petroleum for lighting.

However, during the eighteenth and early nineteenth centuries, new technologies and diminishing supplies of timber propelled the demand for fossil fuels in Western society to levels that were unprecedented until that time. Improvements in hearth designs made in-home stoves less smoky, spurring greater reliance on coal as a household energy source in parts of Europe during the early industrial age. Meanwhile, coke—a refined fuel derived from coal—became an important fuel source for the iron blast furnaces used to make the steel that helped drive the Industrial Revolution. The world's dependence on coal only further intensified through the late 1800s as coal-powered steam locomotives and steamboats revolutionized the transportation of passengers and cargo across the planet.

Petroleum similarly rose to prominence during the 19th century. As the whale populations shrank due to overexploitation during that era, whale oil became an increasingly valuable commodity. Those changes and innovations in the manufacture of kerosene and lamp oil from petroleum developed in the mid-1800s helped petroleum to emerge as an attractive alternative to whale oil during that period. Shortly after Edwin Drake garnered significant attention for using a steam engine to drill a shallow oil well in Pennsylvania in 1859, U.S. oil production steadily increased. *See* Rob Wile, *153 Years Ago Today, An Unemployed Sick Man Drilled the First Modern Oil Well*, Bus. Insider (Aug. 27, 2012), http://www.businessinsider. com/edwin-drake-first-modern-oil-well-153-years-ago-2012-8. Advancements in internal combustion engine and automobile technologies in the years that followed only further boosted oil demand, solidifying petroleum's role as the world's most important transportation energy source within just a few decades.

b. Electrification

Although petroleum-powered automobiles are a major contributor to the world's dependence on nonrenewable energy, the electrification of the world's economies has increased the planet's reliance on fossil fuels more than anything else. In 1882, Thomas Edison opened New York's coal-fired Pearl Street Power Station—the first central power plant in the United States. Many more power plants soon followed, bringing electric power to customers first in cities such as Buffalo, Pittsburgh, and Portland and eventually to every major city in the country. By the turn of the twentieth century, these developments and Edison's invention of the light bulb had already begun paving the way for a technological boom based on electric power technologies.

Further advancements in electricity technology throughout the twentieth century revolutionized the role of energy in society. For the first time in history, they made it possible to affordably generate and distribute electric current—an energy form so fungible and reliable that it could serve an extraordinarily diverse array of functions. A wide array of products and appliances soon emerged that used electric energy to heat, cool, wash, dry, illuminate, transmit, calculate, blend, toast, and perform countless other valuable tasks. As demand for electricity soared, vast webs of wires sprung up in cities throughout the world, delivering electric current directly into countless homes and businesses and improving living standards for billions across the globe.

Policymaking unquestionably played a role in promoting early electrification. The earliest electricity distribution grids served primarily urban areas where there were dense concentrations of potential electricity customers. Hoping to extend the enormous benefits of these technologies to nearly every American citizen, Congress enacted the Rural Electrification Act of 1936. The Act authorized subsidized federal loans for the development of electric transmission and distribution systems to bring electricity access to rural America. By the 1940s, most of the nation's homes and businesses had onsite access to fairly inexpensive, reliable electricity. Most of that electricity was generated through the burning of coal or natural gas to create steam and rotate large electromagnetic turbines. Eventually, nuclear energy—which is not typically classified as a fossil fuel energy source but is not renewable, either—emerged as a significant electricity source as well.

2. GENERATION, TRANSMISSION, AND DISTRIBUTION

As power plants and electricity lines spread out across America's landscape in the twentieth century, regulatory structures materialized to govern what was becoming an increasingly important industry. The distinct characteristics of the electricity industry compelled policymakers to craft multiple unique regulatory structures that largely still exist today. To effectively represent clients on renewable energy matters, lawyers must be familiar with the basics of the broader electricity industry, the regulatory structures that govern it, and the jargon that stakeholders use when discussing it. The following is a short primer intended to help bring students up to speed who have had minimal exposure to these issues.

The electricity industry's process of creating electric power and delivering it to customers generally consists of three main activities: (i) generation, (ii) transmission, and (iii) distribution. The simple graphics in Figure 1.1 below illustrate these three basic activities. *Generation* refers to the actual production of electric power by a power plant, wind farm, or other generating facility. *Transmission* refers to the long-distance transportation of electricity from centralized generation facilities to distribution systems, typically across high-voltage transmission lines. *Distribution* is the local delivery of lower-voltage power to individual homes and businesses.

**Figure 1.1. Generation, Transmission,
and Distribution of Electricity**

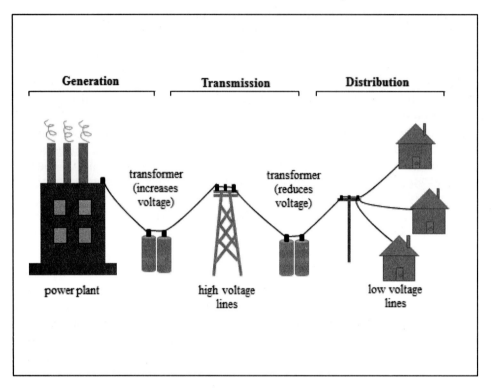

a. Electricity Generation

Although renewable energy technologies certainly impact electricity transmission and distribution in significant ways, they relate most directly to electricity *generation*. Generating electricity from wind, solar, or other renewable resources presents several unique challenges that seldom arise when a utility relies solely on nonrenewable power. For instance, consider the process of deciding where to site a new power plant. Utilities usually choose the locations of generating facilities that run on nuclear energy or fossil fuels based largely on convenience. These facilities are often found on the outskirts of cities, in close proximity to rail lines or pipelines capable of delivering regular supplies of fuel and near enough to water sources to conveniently access and use them to generate steam.

Of course, siting projects that generate electricity from renewable energy resources such as geothermal heat, wind currents, or moving water is considerably more difficult than siting fossil fuel-fired power plants. As described in detail later in this Casebook, many renewable energy resources are present in developable quantities in relatively few geographic locations across the planet and are not easily transported to other places. Accordingly, electric generating facilities relying on these types of resources—such as wind or geothermal steam—often must be sited at or near the specific locations where the resources naturally reside.

The primary function of nearly every coal-fired power plant, hydroelectric dam, wind farm, and other generating facility is the same: to generate electric power. The typical measure of a utility-scale generating facility's maximum electricity output is its *nameplate capacity*, which is usually expressed in megawatts (MW). One megawatt equals one million watts (W) or 1000 kilowatts (kW). To help put these measurements in perspective: one MW of electricity is an amount sufficient to power 10,000 100-watt incandescent light bulbs at the same time. Nameplate capacities of generating facilities and devices obviously vary widely. Most residential rooftop solar arrays have nameplate capacities or "ratings" of less than 10 kW. By contrast, Arizona's Palo Verde nuclear generating plant—the largest power plant in the country—has a nameplate capacity of roughly 4,000 MW. Based on simple math, this means that Palo Verde could theoretically produce 400,000 times as much power as a large residential solar array.

Wind and solar energy generating facilities and devices usually produce quantities of electric power far below their nameplate capacities. Consequently, the electricity industry uses a second measure known as a *capacity factor* to more accurately describe the actual energy productivity of a generating facility with a given nameplate capacity. The capacity factor of a generating facility is the ratio of the facility's *actual* electricity output to its nameplate capacity or *maximum potential* output.

A simple numeric example using wind turbines helps to illustrate this important concept. Most utility-scale onshore wind turbines have nameplate capacities of between 1.5 and 3 MW. However, they only generate that quantity of electric current when the wind is blowing at an optimal direction and speed—typically about 30 miles per hour (mph). Fortunately, capacity factors for specific turbine sites reflect the fact that wind conditions are rarely ideal at any site and thus provide a more accurate measure of a wind turbine's energy productivity if sited in a particular place. Suppose, for instance, that a wind turbine installed at a specific location near the top of a hill outside Golden, Colorado, has a nameplate capacity of 2 MW but only generates an annual average of 1.1 MW of electricity. Based on these two measures, the turbine's capacity factor at that site is

$$\frac{1.1 \text{ MW}}{2 \text{ MW}} = 55\%.$$

Put another way: suppose that the same model of wind turbine is anticipated to have a capacity factor of only 40% at a second proposed turbine site situated a two miles away from the first site. Based on this information, the expected average electricity generation at this second site is

2 MW × 40% = 0.8 MW.

Because the productivity of wind energy resources can vary significantly from one location to another, the capacity factors associated with potential turbine sites can also differ a lot from place to place. The careful siting of wind farm projects and *micro-siting* of wind turbines within those project areas is therefore a crucially important aspect of wind energy development. The capacity factors of photovoltaic solar panels and other solar energy generating devices and facilities likewise vary across regions of the country based on the amount of unshaded sunlight each location typically receives each year. In comparison, the locations where coal- and gas-fired power plants are sited tend to have little or no impact on how much electricity those plants can produce so long as they have access to the fuel and water needed to operate.

Although wind and some other renewable energy resources suffer from locational constraints, they also have other attributes that increasingly put them in high demand. As mentioned above, one of the greatest advantages of most renewable energy strategies is that they help to meet present energy needs without measurably diminishing future supplies of energy resources. However, renewables presently generate only enough power to meet a small fraction of the nation's total electricity needs. The following are the U.S. Energy Information Administration (EIA) 2016 projections (in quadrillion Btu) of U.S. energy consumption from the nation's six largest sources of renewable electricity for 2017, in rank order:

Conventional hydropower	2.567
Wind energy	2.257
Wood biomass	2.015
Solar energy	0.833
Waste biomass	0.510
Geothermal energy	0.232

Source: U.S. ENERGY INFO. ADMIN., SHORT-TERM ENERGY OUTLOOK (2016)

For reasons highlighted in Chapter 8, very few new hydroelectric generating facilities have been added in the United States in the past decade and few are likely to come on line in the foreseeable future. By contrast, wind and solar energy technologies have proliferated at a blistering pace over the past several years, with rapid growth projected to continue for many years to come, as illustrated by Figure 1.2 below showing the EIA's 2016 U.S. growth projections for each major renewable energy source through 2040.

Figure 1.2. Renewable Energy Generation by Fuel Type

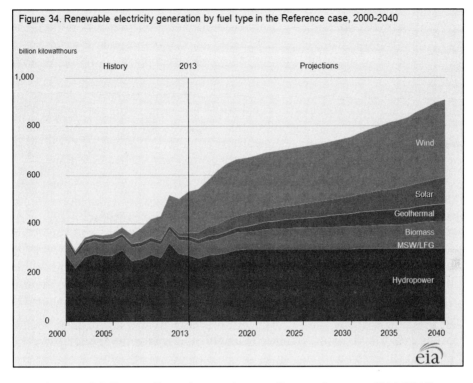

Source: U.S. ENERGY INFO. ADMIN., ANNUAL ENERGY OUTLOOK 2016 (2016)

b. Electricity Transmission

Once a power plant, wind farm, and other facility generates electric power, that power must travel to the homes and businesses where it is needed. Electricity *transmission* is the transportation of electric current from generating facilities to "load centers"—areas with high concentrations of electricity customers. Although electricity transmission is not an inherently renewable or nonrenewable energy activity, the emergence of renewable energy technologies is having profound impacts on electricity transmission siting and development activities in the United States.

When electric current travels across a power line from point A to point B, some of the current is inevitably lost. The electricity industry's use of alternating current (AC) rather than direct current (DC) is one way the industry helps to mitigate these electricity losses. The country's expansive transmission system also limits transmission-related losses by transporting enormous amounts of electric power at relatively high voltages every day. Less electric current is lost per mile when the current travels a higher voltage, so high-voltage lines are presently the most efficient means of transporting large quantities of power across long distances.

As illustrated on Figure 1.1 above, many electric generating facilities have transformers situated just outside them that increase the voltage of electric currents flowing out of the facility before moving it onto transmission lines. The electricity then flows at that higher voltage across the transmission system—a sort of interstate freeway system for electricity—until it reaches a substation near its ultimate destination. These substations are analogous to freeway exits for cars. At substations, different transformers reduce the voltage of electric current so it can safely and affordably travel relatively short distances to nearby customers.

Although discussions about electricity transmission sometimes refer to the *grid* as though it is a singular, interconnected transmission system, there are actually three separate power grids in the contiguous 48 states: the Western Interconnection, the Eastern Interconnection, and the Texas Interconnected System. A map showing the locations of these three grids is depicted in Figure 1.3 below. These massive interconnected grids allow utilities to more easily share generated electricity, which enables them to more inexpensively and reliably meet their customers' constantly-fluctuating demand for electric power.

Figure 1.3. United States Transmission Interconnections

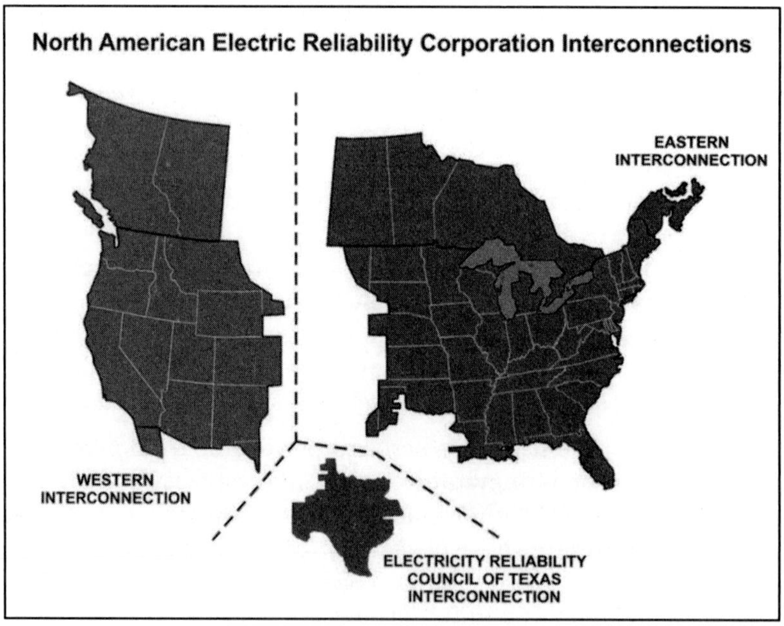

Source: U.S. Department of Energy

Through these interconnected grid systems, utilities and other electricity generators are repeatedly buying, selling, and delivering *wholesale* electric power every day that utilities ultimately resell to retail electricity customers. The Federal Energy Regulatory Commission ("FERC") serves as the primary regulator of this interstate transmission system and the wholesale power transactions associated with it. Among other things, FERC is empowered to regulate the rates and terms of most wholesale or "bulk" transmissions of electric power, pursuant to authority granted under the 1938 Federal Power Act. In addition to regulating much of the nation's transmission system, FERC also has primary regulatory jurisdiction over other aspects of the electricity industry that are interstate in nature or have nationwide impacts. For instance, FERC oversees the licensing of nuclear power facilities, which by their nature arguably present greater national-level risks than fossil fuel-fired plants. The agency likewise oversees most of the licensing of hydroelectric plants, which tend to operate on large rivers and affect multiple states.

Because the nation's legacy transmission system was primarily designed around centralized nuclear or fossil fuel-fired power plants, comparatively little transmission infrastructure exists in many remote areas of the country that are well suited for utility-scale wind or solar energy projects. This lack of transmission infrastructure to support new wind and solar energy development has emerged as a major impediment to renewable energy growth, as described more fully in Chapter 2. To address this problem, policymakers are increasingly reconsidering the nation's longstanding rules and procedures governing *transmission siting*—the process of determining where new interstate transmission lines will run and who will pay for them. Among other things, policymakers have attempted to increase FERC's authority over transmission siting to help overcome conflicts among states over the siting of new lines. Unfortunately, legal and political obstacles have complicated and slowed the progress of these reforms. Regardless of what solutions ultimately emerge, addressing these challenges will be critical to the long-term growth of domestic renewable energy.

c.   Electricity Distribution

As shown in Figure 1.1, after electric current passes out of the transmission system and through a second set of transformers that decreases its voltage, it flows into a *distribution system*—a localized, lower-voltage web of cables and wires designed to distribute electricity to customers. Utilities of various kinds facilitate the distribution and sale of this low-voltage power to retail customers. Customers' rapid adoption of renewable energy technologies is driving policy innovation in this area of the energy industry as well.

Most utility customers have a meter on their property that keeps track of how much electricity they consume each billing period. Typically, some of the total amount due appearing on a retail electricity bill is attributable to *fixed charges*—fees customers must pay regardless of how much power they consume during the billing period. In addition to these fixed charges, customers usually must pay *volumetric charges*—charges that vary depending on the total quantity of electricity the customer uses. Retail customer usage is generally measured in units called kilowatt hours (kWh). One kWh is enough electricity to keep ten 100-watt incandescent light bulbs glowing for a single hour.

The following simplified example helps to illustrate the basics of how electricity pricing is typically structured for ordinary residential customers. Suppose that Ariana owns a home and pays a monthly electricity bill to PowerCo. Suppose further that PowerCo charges all customers the following monthly charges, even if they consume no power during the month:

Monthly Service Charge	**$20.00**
Environmental Benefits Charge	**$5.00**
System Benefits Charge	**$10.00**

In addition to these fixed charges, suppose that PowerCo charges residential customers at a volumetric rate of **10 cents** for each kilowatt hour (kWh) of power they consume during the billing period. Based on these assumptions, if Ariana consumed 712 kilowatt hours of power during the period, her total bill would be:

$20.00 + $5.00 + $10.00 + ($0.10/kWh × 712 kWh)

= $35.00 + $71.20

= $106.20.

Electric utilities largely depend on revenues generated from the monthly billing process to recoup their investments in distribution and other infrastructure and to recover their operating costs. Until recently, most electric utilities have paid employees to physically visit each customer's building after every billing period and read the electricity meter on the building to determine how much power the customer had consumed during the period. By subtracting the number on its current meter reading (in kWh) from the previous month's reading, the utility could calculate the number of kWh consumed during the period and charge the customer based on that amount. Unfortunately, this antiquated measuring method provides no means for utilities to charge different rates for different times of the day or week. Consequently, utilities generally charge customers with these old-fashioned meters the same volumetric rate for all electricity consumed during the billing period, regardless of when the customers consume it.

It's worth noting that the structure and composition of utilities themselves vary significantly from place to place throughout the country. Roughly 75% of electricity customers in the United States receive their power from *investor-owned utilities* ("IOUs"). *See* JIM LAZAR ET AL., ELECTRICITY REGULATION IN THE US: A GUIDE (2011), http://www.rap online.org/wp-content/uploads/2016/05/rap-lazar-electricityregulationinthe us-guide-2011-03.pdf. IOUs are private companies and are usually subject to intensive state government oversight. The rest of the United States is served primarily by publicly-owned municipal electric utilities, utility districts, or cooperatives. For simplicity's sake, this casebook often refers collectively to these various electricity service providers as "utilities".

Some utilities are *vertically integrated*, meaning they are heavily involved in the generation, transmission and distribution of electricity. By contrast, many other electric utilities do not own large power plants or other electric generating facilities. Consequently, these utilities purchase most of their electricity supply on wholesale power markets, take delivery of it across transmission lines that they do not control, and then distribute to customers. As will be explored in greater detail in subsequent chapters, renewable energy technologies are beginning to greatly impact all of these types of electric utilities and the regulatory structures that govern them.

QUESTIONS

1.   Suppose that a wind turbine has a nameplate capacity of 3MW but that it produced only an average of 1.5MW of electricity during the previous year. What was the turbine's capacity factor for the year?

2.   Suppose that a rooftop solar array has a nameplate capacity of 10 kW but only had a capacity factor of 25% in the previous year. How much electricity, on average, did the solar array produce over the year?

3.   The southwestern United States gets considerably more sunshine than the northwestern United States. If a particular type of photovoltaic solar panel has been shown to have a capacity factor of about 30% in the southwest when optimally installed on rooftops, would you predict its capacity factor to be greater or less than 30% when installed in the northwest? Why?

4.   From a public policy perspective, what are some advantages of volumetric electricity pricing—pricing structures under which customers' electricity bills vary based on how much electricity they consume during the billing period? If a utility were to double its fixed fees but cut its volumetric (per-kWh) rate in half, how would those changes impact customers' incentives to conserve electricity or to invest in energy efficiency upgrades for buildings?

5.   Suppose that PowerCo, the utility in the example in Subsection 2.c. above, were to increase its volumetric rate to $0.20 per kWh rather than $0.10 per kWh but allow its fixed charges to remain as described in the example. If Ariana had consumed 500 kWh during the previous billing period, what would be the amount of her total electricity bill?

3.   LEGAL AND THEORETICAL BASES FOR UTILITY REGULATION

It is impossible to fully grasp the complex legal and policy issues facing utilities in this new renewable energy age without understanding how utilities reached their current condition. As power plants and electricity grids began popping up across America in the early 1900s, a few important policy principles soon emerged. First, nearly everyone agreed that it was generally in the country's best interest to ensure that nearly all homes and businesses had access to reasonably-priced and reliable supplies of electric power. Second, it quickly became evident certain characteristics of the new electricity industry made it inherently vulnerable to market failures and that this vulnerability would prevent the electricity industry from providing affordable, reliable, accessible power without strong government regulation.

The two principles just mentioned were the primary impetus for the development of modern electric utilities law—a system of unusually heavy regulation deemed necessary to prevent market costly failures in a crucially important industry. See Lazar, et al., *supra*. Indeed, the conventional utility regulatory model that has prevailed for the past century was borne out of necessity and effectively crafted to fit the distinct needs and characteristics of a critically important industry. The following subsections examine in more detail several legal and economic rationales for modern utility regulation that continue to impact policy debates today as renewable energy technologies disrupt the nation's electricity markets.

a.   Electric Utilities as "Clothed with a Public Interest"

Few industries are regulated more heavily than the electricity industry. In most states, laws restrict not only where an investor-owned utility may sell its power but also how much it charges, the basic terms of its agreements with customers, and even the utility's capital expenditures and operating budget. One justification for such strong regulation is that universal access to reliable, reasonably-priced electricity service is so critical to a modern economy's stability and growth that it's simply too risky to leave providers of the service to their own devices. This notion that heavy regulation is justifiable for industries that are "clothed with a public interest" is emphasized in the oft-cited U.S. Supreme Court case of *Munn v. Illinois*, which analyzed the constitutionality of state-level price regulations on grain storage services along the Chicago River. Portions of the case's majority opinion are excerpted below.

MUNN V. ILLINOIS
Supreme Court of the United States, 1876
94 U.S. 113

WAITE, C.J.

The question to be determined in this case is whether the general assembly of Illinois can, under the limitations upon the legislative power of the States imposed by the Constitution of the United States, fix by law the maximum of charges for the storage of grain in warehouses at Chicago and other places in the State having not less than one hundred thousand inhabitants, 'in which grain is stored in bulk, and in which the grain of different owners is mixed together, or in which grain is stored in such a manner that the identity of different lots or parcels cannot be accurately preserved.'

It is claimed that such a law is repugnant . . . [t]o that part of amendment 14 which ordains that no State shall 'deprive any person of life, liberty, or property, without due process of law, nor deny to any person within its jurisdiction the equal protection of the laws.'

. . . .

When one becomes a member of society, he necessarily parts with some rights or privileges which, as an individual not affected by his relations to others, he might retain. 'A body politic,' as aptly defined in the preamble of the Constitution of Massachusetts, 'is a social compact by which the whole people covenants with each citizen, and each citizen with the whole people, that all shall be governed by certain laws for the common good.' This does not confer power upon the whole people to control rights which are purely and exclusively private . . . but it does authorize the establishment of laws requiring each citizen to so conduct himself, and so use his own property, as not unnecessarily to injure another. This is the very essence of government, and has found expression in the maxim *sic utere tuo ut alienum non laedas*. From this source come the police powers. . . . Under these powers the government regulates the conduct of its citizens one towards another, and the manner in which each shall use his own property, when such regulation becomes necessary for the public good. In their exercise it has been customary in England from time immemorial, and in this country from its first colonization, to regulate ferries, common carriers, hackmen, bakers, millers, wharfingers, innkeepers, [etc.], and in so doing to fix a maximum of charge to be made for services rendered, accommodations furnished, and articles sold. To this day, statutes are to be found in many of the States [on] some or all these subjects; and we think it has never yet been successfully contended that such legislation came within any of the constitutional prohibitions against interference with private property. . . .

From this it is apparent that, down to the time of the adoption of the Fourteenth Amendment, it was not supposed that statutes regulating the use, or even the price of the use, of private property necessarily deprived an owner of his property without due process of law. Under some circumstances they may, but not under all. . . .

This brings us to inquire as to the principles upon which this power of regulation rests, in order that we may determine what is within and what [is] without its operative effect. Looking, then, to the common law, from whence came the right which the Constitution protects, we find that when private property is 'affected with a public interest, it ceases to be *juris privati* only.' This was said by Lord Chief Justice Hale more than two hundred years ago, in his treatise *De Portibus Maris*, 1 Harg. Law Tracts, 78, and has been accepted without objection as an essential element in the law of property ever since. Property does become clothed with a public interest when used in a manner to make it of public consequence, and affect the community at large. When, therefore, one devotes his property to a use in which the public has an interest, he, in effect, grants to the public an interest in that use, and must submit to be controlled by the public for the common good, to the extent of the interest he has thus created. He may withdraw his grant by discontinuing the use; but, so long as he maintains the use, he must submit to the control.

Thus, as to ferries, Lord Hale says, in his treatise *De Jure Maris*, 1 Harg. Law Tracts, 6, the king has 'a right of franchise or privilege, that no man may set up a common ferry for all passengers, without a prescription time out of mind, or a charter from the king. He may make a ferry for his own use or the use of his family, but not for the common use of all the king's subjects passing that way; because it doth in consequence tend to a common charge, and is become a thing if public interest and use, and every man for his passage pays a toll, which is a common charge, and every ferry ought to be under a public regulation, viz., that it give attendance at due times, keep a boat in due order, and take but reasonable toll; for if he fail in these he is finable.'

. . . .

And the same has been held as to warehouses and warehousemen. In *Aldnutt* v. *Inglis*, 12 East, 527, decided in 1810, it appeared that the London Dock Company had built warehouses in which wines were taken in store at such rates of charge as the company and the owners might agree upon. Afterwards the company obtained authority, under the general warehousing act, to receive wines from importers before the duties upon the importation were paid; and the question was, whether they could charge arbitrary rates for such storage, or must be content with a reasonable compensation. Upon this point Lord Ellenborough said (p. 537):

> 'There is no doubt that the general principle is favored, both in law and justice, that every man may fix what price he pleases upon his own property, or the use of it; but if for a particular purpose the public have a right to resort to his premises and make use of them, and he have a monopoly in them for that purpose, if he will take the benefit of that monopoly, he must, as an equivalent, perform the duty attached to it on reasonable terms. . . .[']

. . . .

But we need not go further. Enough has already been said to show that, when private property is devoted to a public use, it is subject to public regulation. It remains only to ascertain whether the warehouses of these plaintiffs in error, and the business which is carried on there, come within the operation of this principle.

For this purpose we accept as true the statements of fact contained in the elaborate brief of one of the counsel of the plaintiffs in error. From these it appears that 'the great producing region of the West and North-west sends its grain by water and rail to Chicago, where the greater part of it is shipped by vessel for transportation to the seaboard by the Great Lakes, and some of it is forwarded by railway to the Eastern ports. . . . Vessels, to some extent, are loaded in the Chicago harbor, and sailed through the St. Lawrence directly to Europe. . . . The quantity [of grain] received in Chicago has made it the greatest grain market in the world. This business has created a demand for means by which the immense quantity of grain can be handled or stored, and these have been found in grain warehouses, which are commonly called elevators, because the grain is elevated from the boat or car, by machinery operated by steam, into the bins prepared for its reception, and elevated from the bins, by a like process, into the vessel or car which is to carry it on. . . . In this way the largest traffic between the citizens of the country north and west of Chicago and the citizens of the country lying on the Atlantic coast north of Washington is in grain which passes through the elevators of Chicago. In this way the trade in grain is carried on by the inhabitants of seven or eight of the great States of the West with four or five of the States lying on the sea-shore, and forms the largest part of inter-state commerce in these States. The grain warehouses or elevators in Chicago are immense structures, holding from 300,000 to 1,000,000 bushels at one time, according to size. They are divided into bins of large capacity and great strength. . . . They are located with the river harbor on one side and the railway tracks on the other; and the grain is run through them from car to vessel, or boat to car, as may be demanded in the course of business. It has been found impossible to preserve each owner's grain separate, and this has given rise to a system of inspection and grading, by which the grain of different owners is mixed, and receipts issued for the number of bushels which are negotiable, and redeemable in like kind, upon demand. This mode of conducting the business was inaugurated more than twenty years ago, and has grown to immense proportions. The railways have found it impracticable to own such elevators, and public policy forbids the transaction of such business by the carrier; the ownership has, therefore, been by private individuals, who have embarked their capital and devoted their industry to such business as a private pursuit.'

In this connection it must also be borne in mind that, although in 1874 there were in Chicago fourteen warehouses adapted to this particular business, and owned by about thirty persons, nine business firms controlled them, and that the prices charged and received for storage were such 'as have been from year to year agreed upon and established by the different elevators or warehouses in the city of Chicago, and which rates have been annually published in one or more newspapers printed in said city, in the month of January in each year, as the established rates for the year then next ensuing such publication.' Thus it is apparent that all the elevating facilities through which these vast productions 'of seven or eight great States of the West' must pass on the way 'to four or five of the States on the seashore' may be a 'virtual' monopoly.

Under such circumstances it is difficult to see why, if the common carrier, or the miller, or the ferryman, or the innkeeper, or the wharfinger, or the baker, or the cartman, or the hackney-coachman, pursues a public employment and exercises 'a sort of public office,' these plaintiffs in error do not. They stand, to use again the language of their counsel, in the very 'gateway of commerce,' and take toll from all who pass. Their business most certainly 'tends to a common charge, and is become a thing of public interest and use.' Every bushel of grain for its passage 'pays a toll, which is a common charge,' and, therefore, according to Lord Hale, every such warehouseman 'ought to be under public regulation, viz., that he . . . take but reasonable toll.' Certainly, if any business can be clothed 'with a public interest, and cease to be *juris privati* only,' this has been. . . .

It is conceded that the business is one of recent origin, that its growth has been rapid, and that it is already of great importance. And it must also be conceded that it is a business in which the whole public has a direct and positive interest. It presents, therefore, a case for the application of a long-known and well-established principle in social science, and this statute simply extends the law so as to meet this new development of commercial progress. There is no attempt to compel these owners to grant the public an interest in their property, but to declare their obligations, if they use it in this particular manner.

It matters not in this case that these plaintiffs in error had built their warehouses and established their business before the regulations complained of were adopted. What they did was from the beginning subject to the power of the body politic to require them to conform to such regulations as might be established by the proper authorities for the common good. They entered upon their business and provided themselves with the means to carry it on subject to this condition. If they did not wish to submit themselves to such interference, they should not have clothed the public with an interest in their concerns. . . .

We conclude, therefore, that the statute in question is not repugnant to the Constitution of the United States, and that there is no error in the judgment. . . .

Judgment affirmed.

QUESTIONS

1.   According to the *Munn* court, what characteristics of the plaintiffs' business made it "clothed with the public interest" and thus subjectable to stringent price regulations?

2.   What relevant similarities exist between the grain storage facilities described in *Munn* and modern electric utilities?

3.   How do you think the fact that the plaintiffs in *Munn* faced relatively little market competition may have influenced the Court's analysis?

b.   Electric Utilities as Natural Monopolies

The fact that electric utilities' product—reliable, grid-supplied electric power—is crucial to the stability and health of modern economies makes their activities sufficiently "clothed with the public interest" to justify subjecting them to reasonable regulation. However, a conclusion that electric utilities may be regulated as a matter of law does not necessarily mean that they should be subject to as heavy a regulatory regime as currently governs most electric utilities. The most common policy arguments for stringent utility regulation are rooted in microeconomics principles. More specifically, most justifications for the intrusive regulatory structures governing electric utilities trace back to the fact that some components of electricity markets are prone to *natural monopoly* problems.

Natural monopolies are firms that can produce all the aggregate output demanded within their relevant market for a lower total cost than would be achievable if that output were produced by multiple smaller, competing firms. Utilities that distribute electricity to retail customers across a web of distribution lines often fit this definition. The unusually high costs of constructing and maintaining the networks of substations, power lines, and other infrastructure needed to reliably distribute power to hundreds or thousands of customers within a given city make it difficult for other companies to enter and effectively compete in areas where an incumbent firm is already supplying electricity service. Under such conditions, just one singular service provider—a *monopolist*—is likely to emerge in each geographic area. Shielded from competition because of the enormous cost barriers to entering their markets, these monopolists have a strong incentive to maximize their own profits by charging excessively high electricity prices, to the detriment of their customers and host communities.

Unregulated electricity service providers also have incentives to "cherry pick" which customers to serve, building distribution lines primarily in geographic areas with large numbers of well-heeled customers that live close to each other and are likely to pay their utility bills. Building dozens of miles of power lines to sell power at the same prices to sparse pockets of customers in remote rural areas is not nearly as profitable, so few utilities would voluntarily do that. In other words, electricity distributors who must charge the same basic prices to all retail customers likely would not provide electric service to all potential customers in a region unless regulations required it.

In microeconomics terms, the natural monopoly problem just described is a type of *market failure*—a situation in which unregulated free market competition produces inefficiency. Substantial market failures like those associated with unregulated electricity distribution markets arguably warrant government intervention in the form of regulations that address the market failures and promote more optimal policy outcomes.

Often, when a single firm captures too large a share of a market the prescribed policy solution is to break up the firm into multiple smaller ones. Federal antitrust laws authorize such breaking up of companies in certain contexts. However, that approach is often less advantageous when the monopolies involved are natural monopolies like those that would exist in unregulated electricity distribution markets. Policies that encouraged multiple competing firms to each build their own separate electricity distribution systems reaching every building in a town might theoretically help to promote price competition. However, such policies would also incentivize redundant and unnecessary development and squander valuable resources since often only a single network of distribution lines is needed.

Recognizing the unique vulnerability of the electricity distribution market to market failures, policymakers have long used highly intrusive regulatory structures to address these challenges. Their primary policy approach is commonly known as *cost of service regulation* and involves what amounts to an implicit agreement between electric utilities and their regulators. The next section introduces this policy approach, its origins, and how it functions in practice today.

4. UTILITIES' IMPLICIT "REGULATORY COMPACT"

Modern electric utility regulations are detailed and stringent rules aimed at incentivizing utilities to act in the best interest of their customers while still allowing utilities to recoup their costs and earn reasonable investment returns. Most of this regulatory structure resides and is enforced at the state government level, usually through state agencies called public utility commissions or public service commissions. Although the typical utility regulatory structure implemented through these agencies involves no actual written and signed agreement between utilities and their regulators, it does involve an implicit exchange of obligations and benefits and is thus sometimes colloquially referred to as a *regulatory compact*. In very general terms, this regulatory structure requires that regulators:

- protect electric utilities from competition by prohibiting any other utility from distributing electric power within their exclusive territories; and

- authorize utilities to impose charges and fees on their customers sufficient to allow the utilities to recoup their operational expenses and earn a reasonable rate of return on their capital investments.

To be eligible for these benefits, electric utilities generally must:

- provide service to all customers within their exclusive territories (utilities' so-called *duty to serve*); and

- charge reasonable prices as regulated by the state.

This basic regulatory model has done a decent job of addressing the market failures associated with natural monopolies in the electricity distribution for nearly a century. In a recent law review article, Professor Amy Stein further describes this "regulatory compact" idea:

> Entities that provide an essential public service, like electricity, can often capture certain efficiencies. For instance, it would be inefficient for there to be three sets of competing transmission lines that run alongside each other when one is all that is needed. Economists describe this situation as a natural monopoly, where one firm can "naturally" produce its goods at lower costs than others who are eventually priced out of the market.
>
> Capturing these efficiencies through one firm, however, creates a monopoly and a vulnerable end user, where the owner of

the one transmission line could charge extremely high prices to users of the line. Courts have struggled to find a regulatory balance between efficiency and consumer protection. To reap the benefits of efficiency while still protecting the public, jurisprudence developed that envisioned an implicit "regulatory compact" between the utility and the state, where utilities were granted an exclusive service area with regulated rates that provided more earnings stability than if they were in a nonregulated market. In exchange, the utilities accepted a universal "duty to serve" all customers within their service area (i.e., nondiscriminatory service), and consumers received protection from monopoly pricing. . . .

Amy Stein, *Distributed Reliability*, 87 U. COLO. L. REV. 887, 901 (2016).

Every aspect of the implicit regulatory compact between investor-owned utilities and their regulators traces its beginnings to an earlier era and plays an important role in promoting efficiency within modern electricity distribution markets. Among the most important aspects of the relationship are the basic duties the utilities owe to the regulators, both of which were outlined above. The following materials examine each of these duties in more detail.

a.   Duty to Serve

Utilities' duty to serve all potential customers within their service territories is a hallmark principle within utility law. As will be covered in Chapter 5, questions regarding the scope of utilities' duty to serve are increasingly arising today as rooftop solar energy and distributed energy storage technologies make it increasingly possible for homes and businesses to fulfill their own electricity needs without a connection to the grid. In the following excerpt, Professor Jim Rossi describes the genesis and evolution of the duty to serve and its critical role in electric utility regulation. Among other things, the excerpt highlights the famous English case of *Tripp v. Frank*, which many energy law scholars have cited as helping to provide a doctrinal foundation for utilities' modern-day duty to serve.

THE COMMON LAW "DUTY TO SERVE" AND PROTECTION OF CONSUMERS IN AN AGE OF COMPETITIVE RETAIL PUBLIC UTILITY RESTRUCTURING

Jim Rossi
51 VAND. L. REV. 1233, 1242–46, 1248–52 (1998)

Building on an ancient common law duty that applied to public utilities such as ferries, mills, and railroads, most state regulatory commissions in the twentieth century have imposed upon public utilities a "duty to serve"—an obligation to provide extraordinary levels of service to customers, especially small residential customers. The link between the public utility concept and the duty to serve has an extremely rich history in law. It has survived many different regulatory eras and institutional arrangements, garnering a variety of intellectual explanations. . . .

As applied today in most states, the public utility duty to serve entails several obligations, among them duties to interconnect and extend service if requested, to provide continuing reliable service, to provide advanced notice of service disconnection, and to continue service without full payment. Unlike other obligations that apply to private firms, even those representing or holding themselves out to serve the public, the duty to serve applicable to utilities requires the provision of service even where it is not profitable. . . .

A. Common Law Antecedents

The duty to serve can be traced to the English common law, which recognized that monopolies granted by the King entailed certain obligations. . . .

Medieval mills are perhaps the strongest analogy to the modern public utility. Without access to the services of a mill, the inhabitants of a medieval village or manor were left without flour for bread or malt for brewing. Yet the construction of a mill had to be financed by the lord, who needed an adequate incentive to invest capital in a facility large enough to provide access to everyone in the village or manor. Thus, in medieval times, the "mill-soke" obligation, enforced by injunction in the Manor Court, compelled all inhabitants of the medieval manor to grind all grain at the lord's mill. The feudal law of mills has been described by Professors Charles Haar and Daniel Fessler, the authors of a comprehensive modern study of the duty to serve, as arising from two primary factors: (1) access to a mill was a necessity for all local inhabitants, and (2) a relatively large investment was required to finance construction.

While mills were regulated primarily at the local level, the duty to serve was later extended to crown-answering services, such as ferries and markets. *Tripp v. Frank*, a ferry case decided in England in 1792, is illustrative. Tripp, the lessee of a common ferry that provided service across the River Humber, had claim to an exclusive right granted by the Crown to provide travel service between Barton (where the Lincoln road initially terminated) and Kingston, a major shipping point between York and London. Tripp's franchise was exclusive but others, such as Frank, had limited rights to water carriage on the Humber. In the case, it was conceded that Frank possessed a right to operate a market boat that departed from Barrow, two miles to the East of Barton, and that Frank also provided some service to Kingston. Tripp maintained, however, that Frank's right to provide this service was limited to high-demand times, particularly days during which a regional market was operating in Kingston.

When the Lincoln road was extended from Barton to Barrow, it became possible for a person traveling from York to quicken the journey by proceeding directly to Barrow. Not surprisingly, following the road's extension Frank saw it profitable to expand his service. Tripp filed a complaint, taking the position that the profits from Frank's expanded service were the rewards of Tripp's ferry. A jury in York returned a verdict for Tripp with a nominal award of one shilling, and Frank appealed. On appeal, in response to a question from the court, Tripp admitted that he had no obligation to provide service to any place other than Barton. Lord Chief Justice Kenyon, commenting on the implications of Tripp's obligation to provide service to Barton, observed:

> If certain persons wishing to go to Barton had applied to the defendant, and he had carried them at a little distance above or below the ferry, it would have been fraud on the plaintiff's right, and would be the ground of an action . . . . [However] it is absurd to say that no person shall be permitted to go any other place on the Humber than that to which the plaintiff chooses to carry them. It is now admitted that the ferryman cannot be compelled to carry passengers to any other place than Barton: then his right must be commensurate with his duty.

Tripp had rights under his franchise, but in order to establish competitive injury he would need to establish that travelers who presented themselves in Barrow did so with fraudulent intent.

Building on precedents such as *Tripp v. Frank*, the duty to serve was given a creative extension by American judges in the late nineteenth century. . . .

B.   *The Growth of the Modern Regulatory Compact*

Over the past century and a half or so, two discernable periods characterize American regulatory law. The first, stretching from approximately the 1870s until the end of the century, featured direct judicial intervention in regulation of public utility monopoly franchises. The second era, beginning at the turn of the twentieth century, was dominated by the establishment of new regulatory commissions, subject to direct judicial review. As the twentieth century progressed, the judicial doctrines regarding the duty to serve were eventually enshrined into statutes or administrative regulations—sometimes with modifications—or were adopted voluntarily by utilities in their tariffs. However, the duty to serve is richly steeped in the common law, and many of its direct judicial remnants continue to survive.

1.   Judicial Applications to Monopolistic Industries

The early American public utility cases on the duty to serve, building on the ferry and railroad common carrier cases, involved the refusal of telephone service. Telephone companies—the functional equivalent of telegraph companies, which were long-regarded as common carriers—almost always lost these cases. Like railroads, telephone companies were under a duty to provide access to all customers on an equal basis.

By the 1890s, the duty to serve had also been extended to gas companies. . . .

In similar manner, the duty to serve was extended to water suppliers.

Thus, by the beginning of the twentieth century, most courts recognized a public utility duty to serve, even with no statutory authorization. For example, the Indiana Supreme Court ordered a gas company to allow a prospective customer to interconnect with its gas lines, despite the utility's allegation that it lacked adequate supply to meet existing customers. Writing for the court, Justice Hadley wrote:

> The principle here announced is not new. It is as old as the common law itself. It has arisen in a multitude of cases affecting railroad, navigation, telegraph, telephone, water, gas, and other like companies, and has been many times discussed and decided by the courts; and no statute has ever been deemed necessary to aid the courts in holding that when a person or company has undertaken to supply a demand which is affected with a public interest, it must supply all alike who are like situated, and not discriminate in favor of nor against any.

. . . .

2.   The Growth of the Regulatory Commission

A centerpiece of early state regulation of utilities outside of courts was the utility franchise, a monopoly charter typically granted by local government. This was essentially a fictional contract, or "regulatory compact," that determined the respective rights and duties (sometimes referred to as "incumbent burdens") of the utility. After a number of years, this local system was abandoned for state-wide legislative approaches because of a perception of corruption. New York and Wisconsin were the first states to establish regulatory commissions, and their commissions soon became models for other states.

Most of the early statutes defining the jurisdiction of regulatory commissions were vague. A common approach was for a statute to require that telephonic, gas, or electric service be adequate and rates be reasonable. . . .

In the twentieth century, the public utility duty to serve evolved into two distinct obligations, which today appear in the regulations, statutes, and case law governing privately-owned public utilities: obligations regarding the extension of services and abandonment of service requirements. The extension duty requires public utilities to build facilities at least to a property line and to provide adequate pressure or power to transport service to the customer, even if the customer could not pay for the cost of extending service. Abandonment obligations include procedures governing service disconnection, and obligations to notify customers prior to shut-off and to continue with service provision even if a customer cannot pay in full.

QUESTIONS

1.   According to Professor Rossi, why are utilities obligated to provide electricity service to all customers within their service areas, even if extending service to some of those customers is unprofitable?

2.   In what sense was the ferryman in *Tripp v. Frank* case highlighted in Professor Rossi's article akin to an electric utility?

3.   How might utilities be tempted to "cut corners" in fulfilling their duties to serve? What aspects of utility regulation seek to deter that practice?

4.   If utilities' duty to serve were eliminated, which segments of the citizenry do you predict would be most impacted?

b.   Reasonable Pricing

In addition to serving all customers within their exclusive service territories, investor-owned utilities usually must obtain regulatory approval for the rates and fees they charge to retail customers. The basic rationale for utility rate regulation is that, without it, utilities would abuse their state-protected monopoly position by charging prices far in excess of their costs. Unfortunately, determining what constitutes a reasonable price for a product can be difficult when the product is a flow of electrons whose market value often varies depending on location and on the time of day and year. The fact that the producer of the flow of electrons is often a massive investor-owned utility with hundreds of millions of dollars in annual revenues and expenditures only further complicates attempts to determine a reasonable retail price. The full panoply of regulations typically associated with retail electricity rate setting is far too complex and detailed to fully explain in this book. Accordingly, the following is a general overview designed to acquaint readers with only the most basic principles and concepts that define this challenging area of utilities law.

Utility rate regulations seek to allow utilities to generate enough revenue to stay in business and provide reliable service without allowing them to generate excessively high profits. The basic model through which state regulators pursue this objective is known as *cost of service regulation*. Most of the legal and policy work associated with cost of service regulation occurs within *rate cases*—formal proceedings at which state regulators review a utility's expenditures and projections to determine or make adjustments to the rates the utility may charge. In most jurisdictions, rate cases do not automatically occur according to a regular schedule. Instead, utilities usually file petitions to initiate their own rate cases as a means of seeking increases to fees or rates. A rate case generally gives stakeholders, including the utility itself and its customers, opportunities to submit evidence, speak, and ask questions relevant to the utility's petition. The document that regulators ultimately release after a rate case that outlines the utility's approved conditions and pricing is called a *tariff*.

In most rate cases, a utility submits evidence in support of what it claims to be its *revenue requirement*—the total revenue the utility must earn to recoup its operating expenses and earn a reasonable return on its capital investment. A utility's *rate base*—the dollar amount of its aggregate investment in physical equipment and infrastructure—is a central component of its revenue requirement. The utility's *operating expenses*, which comprise its expenditures on employee salaries, fuel, and other non-capital items are the other main component. Expressed mathematically:

Revenue Requirement = (Rate Base × Rate of Return) + Operating Expenses

   or

$$R = B(r) + O$$

A simple numeric example helps to illustrate how regulators generally use this formula. Suppose that UtiliCo, a fictional investor-owned utility, has established within its current rate case a total rate base of $7 billion and annual operating expenses of $250 million. If regulators conclude that 10% is a reasonable rate of return on the rate base for this utility, UtiliCo's revenue requirement is:

($7 billion × 0.10) + $250 million =

$700 million + $250 million = $995 million.

Although actual rate cases involve a more complex formula and a series of calculations that account for depreciation, taxes, and other factors, the simplified formula above highlights the basic policy considerations and objectives that drive cost of service regulation. When cost of service regulation is functioning properly, investor-owned utilities are able to efficiently operate and remain in business but are precluded from abusing their monopoly position to generate excessive profits.

Once regulators determine a utility's revenue requirement, they can use this dollar figure to set a reasonable per-kWh retail price for the utility's electric power. To calculate that price, regulators first subtract from the revenue requirement all revenue the utility is expected to generate from fixed customer fees. Then, they divide the remaining balance by the number of kWhs of power the utility is expected to sell. For instance, suppose that UtiliCo's monthly fixed fees are expected to generate $195 million in total annual revenue. Suppose that the utility also charges the same rate to all of its customers all of the time and expects to sell 8 billion kWh of electricity per year. Based on these simplified numbers, UtiliCo's reasonable price for power is:

$$\frac{\text{(revenue requirement} - \text{expected fixed fee revenue)}}{\text{Expected \# of kWh sold}}$$

$$= \frac{(\$995 \text{ million} - \$195 \text{ million})}{8 \text{ billion kWh}}$$

$$= \frac{\$800 \text{ million}}{8 \text{ billion kWh}}$$

$$= \$0.10/\text{kWh}$$

As stated above, this simplified example and formula leave out much of the complexity that characterizes actual rate cases. However, they are sufficient to convey the general cost-based rate setting principles that predominate in these proceedings. A basic understanding of this formula is particularly important in the context of the growing policy debate over distributed renewable energy and energy storage, which is covered in detail in Chapters 5 and 7.

Some have argued that cost of service regulation incentivizes investor-owned utilities to build too much infrastructure and spend excessive amounts on their operations. According to a theory known as the *Averch-Johnson Effect*, overspending can be an appealing strategy under such rules because utilities can easily pass along extra costs to captive customers through rate increases and thereby drive up revenues and total profits. *See* Harvey Averch & Leland L. Johnson, *Behavior of the Firm Under Regulatory Constraint*, 52 AMER. ECON. REV. 1052 (1962). To limit overspending, regulators typically require investor-owned utilities to obtain approval for major capital expenditures and impose various other spending restrictions. Such strict regulation of even the utility's expenditures is generally justifiable for the reasons just described, but it only increases the already-heavy regulatory burden associated with cost of service regulation for electric utilities.

PRACTICE PROBLEMS

1.   Suppose that state regulators hearing an active rate case for PowerCo, an investor-owned utility within their state, determined that the following numbers described the utility's current state of affairs:

Rate Base:	$5 billion
Reasonable rate of return:	8%
Annual Operating Expenses:	$200 million
Annual revenue from fixed fees:	$100 million
Expected annual sales of power:	4 billion kWh

Assume that PowerCo charges the same rate for all of the power it sells. Based on these figures, what is PowerCo's revenue requirement? What should state regulators set as PowerCo's reasonable retail electricity price?

2.   Suppose now that PowerCo, the utility described in Problem 1, has received approval for a large new infrastructure upgrade that will increase its rate base by $1 billion. Suppose further that PowerCo has received approval for an increase of its rate of return to 10% and for a new fixed customer fee that will increase its annual fee revenue by $100 million.

Assuming all other figures from Problem 1 remain the same, what is PowerCo's new revenue requirement and what should state regulators set as PowerCo's reasonable retail electricity price under these revised assumptions?

c.   Protection   Against   Competition   Within   Exclusive   Territories

As described above, one benefit that regulated electric utilities typically enjoy under their implicit regulatory compact with regulators is protection from competition within their designated geographic service territories. In many jurisdictions, detailed maps delineate *service area* boundaries for electric utilities and firms are legally prohibited from distributed electric power outside their established service areas. Such regulations essentially amount to state-enforced protection against competition.

The following case involves a dispute between two electricity providers over how territory boundary lines are interpreted and enforced. Nintendo of America, Inc., the large electricity customer stuck in the middle of the dispute, was a large electricity customer whose property straddled the boundary line between the two utilities' exclusive service areas. Both utilities believed supplying power at Nintendo's site would be highly profitable and lucrative, so both aggressively tried to secure Nintendo's business. Ultimately, the Supreme Court of Washington was tasked with determining which of the two utilities was entitled to be Nintendo's electricity provider. Although the exclusive service area boundaries at issue in this case were contractually formed, the case illustrates the tension and controversy that can arise along borders between exclusive service areas.

TANNER ELEC. CO-OP. V. PUGET SOUND POWER & LIGHT CO.

Supreme Court of Washington, En Banc, 1996
911 P.2d 1301

MADSEN, J.

At issue in this case is whether the trial court erred in granting summary judgment on the question of whether a service area agreement between a public utility and a rural electric cooperative was breached. . . .

Tanner Electric Cooperative (Tanner) is a nonprofit rural electric cooperative which was formed in 1936 pursuant to the Rural Electrification Act. The basic purpose of the Act was to extend electric service to those rural areas of the country without central station service by providing government loans at low interest rates. Charles F. Phillips, Jr., *The Regulation of Public Utilities* 560 (1984). When Tanner began its operations it had thirty-two customers on thirteen miles of line. Tanner's headquarters are in North Bend, Washington. In addition to serving North Bend, Tanner serves the Ames Lake area and Anderson Island. Tanner's 1992 annual report stated that its business is "the transmission and distribution of electrical power to rural areas in King County and to Anderson Island at Pierce County". . . .

Tanner receives its electric power from Bonneville Power Administration (BPA) in accordance with a demand contract. This contract requires BPA to provide all of Tanner's power needs up to twenty-five megawatts. Puget Sound Power & Light Company (Puget) delivers BPA's power to Tanner pursuant to a 1966 general transfer agreement with BPA. Puget delivers the power to Tanner by "wheeling" it over Puget's transmission lines to a single breaker switch in Puget's North Bend substation (a point of delivery). . . . The Puget/BPA contract places a 2.6 megawatt limit on the power wheeled to Tanner.

On July 29, 1966, Tanner and Puget entered into a territorial service area agreement (hereafter referred to as the 1966 agreement). The 1966 agreement sets forth the boundaries of the respective service areas and also provides as follows:

1. Puget agrees to wheel BPA power to Tanner for use in Tanner's North Bend and Ames Lake service areas . . . for a period of twenty (20) years.

. . . .

4. Puget agrees that it shall not directly or indirectly distribute, wheel, transfer or sell electric energy within the limits of Tanner's service areas.

Ex. 2 at 2. Pursuant to RCW 54.48, which requires that agreements dividing service territories between public utilities and cooperatives be regulated by the Washington Utilities and Transportation Commission (WUTC or the Commission), the parties submitted the 1966 agreement to the WUTC for approval. Approval was granted in 1974, shortly after the enactment of RCW 54.48.

. . . .

In the spring of 1990, Nintendo of America, Inc. (Nintendo) purchased a 125-acre parcel of property in North Bend. Approximately eighty percent of the property that Nintendo purchased is within Tanner's service area, as set forth in the 1966 agreement, while the remaining twenty percent is within Puget's service area. Nintendo constructed a $50 million automated distribution facility on Tanner's side of the property. This facility is the only Nintendo distribution center in the United States. Once fully operational, the facility anticipated a daily production of some seventy trailer loads of Nintendo video games.

Elmer Sams, Tanner's manager, met with representatives of Nintendo several times in an effort to determine Nintendo's power needs and to solicit Nintendo's business. Nintendo's electrical contractor told Sams that Nintendo planned to build five buildings and a parking lot on the property over a six-year period. According to Sams, the contractor also projected that Nintendo's total electric load would be approximately twenty megawatts.

Sams recommended that Nintendo allow Tanner to install a primary service meter box along Northwest 8th Avenue, which borders part of the Nintendo site and divides the Tanner and Puget service areas. By making such an arrangement, the meter box could be tied into the underground cable that Tanner was planning to install at this location. . . . Sams gave Nintendo a proposed commercial rate schedule that was prepared solely for Nintendo. . . .

After several conversations with Sams, Nintendo officials grew concerned about Tanner's ability to serve the Nintendo facility. Of specific concern was that (1) Tanner's service crew consisted of four people who were responsible for the three service areas, which in some instances are separated by distances as great as sixty miles or are accessible only by ferry; (2) Tanner had less than a dozen employees, including office staff . . .

and (5) Tanner had never served a customer comparable to Nintendo. . . . Puget also told Nintendo that it would refuse to let Tanner tap Puget's Snoqualmie line near the Nintendo property, thus preventing Tanner from gaining a second point of delivery.

On July 19, 1990, Puget advised Tanner that it was terminating the 1966 agreement with the one-year notice required by that agreement. The termination date was September 27, 1991. Puget then suggested a possible purchase of Tanner, which Tanner rejected.

In September 1990, Puget told Tanner that it would be serving Nintendo's facility pursuant to Nintendo's request. Tanner told Nintendo that such an arrangement would violate section 4 of the 1966 agreement, quoted above. Despite this information, Nintendo accepted Puget's service on January 17, 1991, eight months before the 1966 agreement expired. Puget delivered power to a meter in a structure built by Nintendo on Puget's side of the service area boundary, located along Northwest 8th Avenue. From there, Nintendo, using its own lines, transported the electricity across the Puget-Tanner border to the Nintendo facility in Tanner's service area.

Shortly before this service began, Tanner filed a petition for a declaratory order with the WUTC, seeking a ruling that Puget had no statutory duty to serve Nintendo and that Puget had violated the 1966 agreement. The Commission concluded that Puget did not have a statutory obligation to serve Nintendo, but that no Commission law prohibited such service. The Commission found that it did not have jurisdiction to enforce or interpret the 1966 agreement.

On April 19, 1991, Tanner filed a complaint for injunctive relief and damages against Puget in King County Superior Court. Tanner sought an immediate cessation of Puget's service to Nintendo as well as an order requiring Puget to furnish whatever power Tanner needed to serve Nintendo. The trial court denied Tanner's requests, whereupon Tanner filed an amended complaint bringing claims for breach of contract, tortious interference, common law unfair competition, and violation of the Consumer Protection Act. Tanner's bases for these claims included Puget's service to Nintendo as well as Puget's failure to increase Tanner's wheeling demand limit or to allow Tanner a new point of delivery from which to serve Nintendo; Puget's failure to upgrade the transformer at the North Bend substation; and Puget's refusal to negotiate in good faith with Tanner and the BPA to finalize and implement a plan of service by which both Tanner and Puget would provide adequate service to all customers. Nintendo and the WUTC were granted leave to intervene in the action.

Tanner then moved for partial summary judgment on its breach of contract claim. The trial court granted Tanner's motion and concluded as follows:

While the Nintendo property straddles the boundary of the Puget/Tanner service areas and Puget delivers power to Nintendo at a point on the Nintendo property that is within [the] Puget service area, all of the Nintendo facility is located within the Tanner service areas. . . . The court has ruled that in construing this agreement, it is the point-of-use of power, not the point-of-delivery, that controls.

Clerk's Papers at 593. The trial court also held it undisputed that Tanner stood ready to deliver power to Nintendo in a sufficient quantity to meet Nintendo's needs. Puget's motion for reconsideration of the summary judgment ruling was denied.

The case was tried before a jury during February and March of 1993. . . . At the close of trial, and pursuant to the summary judgment ruling, the jury was instructed that Puget had breached the 1966 agreement. On March 4, 1993, the jury returned a verdict for Tanner on its three remaining theories of liability and awarded $2.5 million in damages. In addition, the court awarded $410,000 in attorney's fees under the Consumer Protection Act and $8,816.04 in costs. The final judgment totaled $2,918,816.04. Puget appealed, and this court accepted the motion to transfer the appeal. . . .

I

The first issue presented to us is the propriety of a summary judgment determination on Tanner's breach of contract claim. . . .

This case highlights the reasons for, and the importance of, the review process for administrative decisions. At issue here is not the alleged breach of a simple contract between two private parties, but the alleged breach of a service area agreement entered into by a public utility and a rural electric cooperative pursuant to statutory authority. Our review of the applicable statutes leads us to conclude that the WUTC has jurisdiction not only to approve or disapprove service area agreements but also to apply and interpret relevant statutes where a dispute arises pursuant to such an agreement and to issue appropriate orders. The following discussion shows why the WUTC's failure to fully exercise such authority rendered it necessary for this court to review the resulting issues.

When the disagreement initially arose between Tanner and Puget over service to Nintendo, Tanner appropriately sought intervention by the WUTC. In its petition to the WUTC filed in December of 1990, Tanner sought a ruling as to whether Puget had a statutory obligation to serve Nintendo upon request. Tanner also asked for an order declaring that Puget's service of Nintendo violated the 1966 agreement reached between Tanner and Puget and approved by the WUTC.

The 1966 agreement which Tanner sought to have interpreted by the WUTC sets forth the rights, responsibilities, and service boundaries of both Puget and Tanner. The 1966 service area agreement is authorized by RCW 54.48.030 . . . .

RCW 54.48 was adopted in 1969 to permit service area agreements between public utilities and cooperatives. Without this statutory validation, service area agreements would be invalid as violative of antitrust laws. . . . RCW 54.48.020 sets forth the purpose of this legislation and of the agreements it promotes:

> The legislature hereby declares that the duplication of the electric lines and service of public utilities and cooperatives is uneconomical, may create unnecessary hazards to the public safety, discourages investment in permanent underground facilities, and is unattractive, and thus is contrary to the public interest and further declares that it is in the public interest for public utilities and cooperatives to enter into agreements for the purpose of avoiding or eliminating such duplication.

RCW 54.48.030 specifies that the WUTC shall have the authority to approve these agreements and provides that compliance with such agreements is required by law. In addition to this specific grant of authority over service area agreements, RCW 80.01.040 grants the WUTC broad authority to regulate the practices of *public* utilities. (In return for their monopoly status, public utilities are regulated by the State through the WUTC[)]. . . .

In this case the WUTC issued its ruling on Tanner's petition in March of 1991. In that ruling it stated that Puget did not have a statutory obligation to serve Nintendo but that no Commission law prohibited such service. The WUTC also concluded that it had no jurisdiction to interpret or enforce the 1966 agreement or to determine the parties' rights thereunder. . . .

Tanner did, however, file a petition for injunctive relief in the King County Superior Court. When the superior court denied an injunction, Tanner filed the present action based on, among other claims, its allegation that Puget's service to Nintendo breached the service area agreement.

As noted earlier, the trial court granted summary judgment to Tanner on its breach of contract claim. To do so it ruled that the 1966 agreement between Tanner and Puget incorporated a point of use test for determining service disputes, and that Puget's service to Nintendo violated that test. . . .

The point of use test which the trial court applied is one of three tests used in the industry to resolve service area disputes. The point of use test dictates that only the utility authorized to serve within a territory may provide power to a facility within that territory. *Public Serv. Co. v. Public*

Utils. Comm'n, 765 P.2d 1015, 1019 (Colo. 1988). The point of service, or point of delivery, test focuses on the point at which electricity is delivered rather than on the point at which it is consumed. If a utility provides electricity to a customer within its territory, the sale is proper, even if the customer transports the power into the territory of another utility for the customer's use. . . .

Tanner argues that RCW 54.48 requires this court to read the point of use test into the 1966 agreement as a matter of law and thus uphold the trial court's finding of breach. Puget responds that the 1966 agreement preceded the adoption of RCW 54.48 and contends that only statutes in effect at the time a contract is made become a part of the agreement. . . .

RCW 54.48 does not mention what test should be applied in a dispute over service to a straddling customer. To conclude that the 1966 agreement incorporates a point of use test as a matter of law, therefore, it must be clear either that public policy requires such an interpretation or that the parties intended to incorporate the test into their agreement and the test is not contrary to law. . . .

While it is clear . . . that the point of use test has much to be said for it, especially in comparison to the point of delivery test, it is by no means apparent from them that the point of use test should apply in every service dispute between two electrical energy providers. . . .

Nor can we find that Puget's service to Nintendo in this case undermines the policies of RCW 54.48. . . .

In sum, it does not appear that either statutory law or public policy require us to insert a point of use test into the Puget/Tanner agreement.

Because we conclude that a point of use test is not required by RCW 54.48, we turn to the question of whether the parties intended that test to apply to boundary questions under the 1966 agreement. . . .

It is undisputed that the agreement contains no express reference to a point of use test or any other test. The 1966 agreement first sets out the boundaries of Tanner's service areas and then states as follows: "Puget agrees that it shall not directly or indirectly distribute, wheel, transfer or sell electric energy within the limits of Tanner's service area above described. . . ." Ex. 2 at 2. Tanner argues that this language clearly prohibits Puget from delivering power in its own territory if it is for use within Tanner's territory and reflects the parties' intent to apply a point of use test for straddling customers. . . .

We conclude . . . that the trial court erred in applying a point of use test to the 1966 agreement as a matter of law. Because issues of material fact exist as to what, if anything, the agreement contemplates in a straddling situation, we must reverse the grant of summary judgment for Tanner on this issue. . . .

The trial court also granted Tanner's motion for summary judgment on the basis that evidence of Tanner's inability to serve Nintendo was not material to Tanner's right to serve under the 1966 agreement. The section of the 1966 agreement at issue provides as follows:

> [I]n the event Tanner shall fail, refuse or be unable to serve any person within any of its said service areas and such person shall make application to Puget therefor, Puget shall have the right to serve any such applicant if and to the extent it may be required to furnish such service under the Public Service laws of the State of Washington. . . . If a party makes a bona fide offer to provide service under terms and conditions applicable generally to its other customer[s] of the same class and within the same area, it shall not be deemed to have failed, refused or been unable to provide service under this paragraph.

Ex. 2 at 3.

Puget argued vigorously before the trial court, as it does here, that Tanner's ability to provide adequate service to Nintendo was a factual issue that should have been decided by the jury. Both Puget and Nintendo discuss Nintendo's sophisticated power needs and Tanner's small-scale operations. They point to Tanner's four-member service crew, its single-source radial feed distribution system, Tanner's inadequate capacity and outdated equipment, its lack of an adequate plan of service for the Nintendo facility, and Tanner's lack of experience with any large industrial customer.

The trial court found these issues irrelevant given the wording of the 1966 agreement concerning a bona fide offer. . . .

We find it more than possible to read the "bona fide offer" provision of the contract as requiring a genuine offer of service to encompass terms and conditions offered to similar customers, and to render an offer made without such terms and conditions somewhat suspect. . . . Whether Tanner's offer of service to Nintendo, made without previous experience in serving such a large customer, was a true and actual offer is open to question. Given this uncertainty, the trial court erred in ruling that Tanner's ability to serve Nintendo was not a material factual issue that prevented it from granting Tanner's motion for summary judgment on its breach of contract claim.

We conclude that there is a factual question regarding whether the 1966 agreement allows consideration of the utilities' ability to serve similar customers when resolving a service dispute as well as whether the parties intended to incorporate a point of use test into the agreement. We therefore reverse the summary judgment order on Tanner's breach of contract claim.

———————

QUESTIONS

1.   What seems to be the difference between the point of use test and the point of service (or point of delivery) test described in the *Tanner* opinion? Which test do you think is preferable, and why?

2.   Another conceivable means of resolving these sorts of border conflicts would be for parties in the shoes of Tanner and Puget to competitively bid to supply power to Nintendo. What would be some advantages and disadvantages of this approach?

3.   Suppose you represented an investor-owned utility in a proceeding at which state regulators were revising the geographic boundaries of the utility's exclusive service territory. As part of the proceeding, the utility is permitted to submit its own proposed revisions to its service territory map. What specific characteristics of the geographic areas within or near its existing service territory would be relevant to the utility in the context of preparing its proposed revisions? Why?

4.   As mentioned in the *Tanner* opinion, state and federal antitrust laws specifically seek to prevent private firms from gaining excessive market power within a defined market, but state utility regulations often actively protect a firm's monopoly status. Do you think utilities' unique obligations under their implicit regulatory compact justify this opposite treatment? Why or why not?

5.   GRID LOAD MANAGEMENT

Many of the challenges associated with integrating renewables into the nation's existing electricity infrastructure relate to the task of balancing energy supply and demand on the electric grid. For decades, utilities and grid operators have worked around the clock ensure that there is always just enough power being fed onto the grid to meet the current electricity demand. When there is not enough power supplied to a grid system, disruptive interruptions in electricity service known as "brownouts" can result. On the other hand, if far too much of power is supplied onto the grid at any given time, the grid infrastructure can suffer extensive damage that can also interrupt electricity service. These practical realities associated with electric grids require utilities and grid operators to vigilantly monitor grid demand and adjust supplies of electricity in response to demand fluctuations.

Some fluctuations in electricity demand are fairly predictable. For example, in most regions, electricity use tends to peak in the late afternoon or early evening and then drops off precipitously in the late evening and early morning hours. The graph in Figure 1.4 below shows how the electricity demand in Great Britain on one day in January 2008 followed this typical pattern. At the peak on this date, which occurred at roughly 5:30PM, the load demand exceeded 57,000 MW. This level of demand is roughly 23,000 MW greater than at 4:30AM, which was the lowest point on the same day.

Figure 1.4. Electricity Demand in Great Britain on January 8, 2008

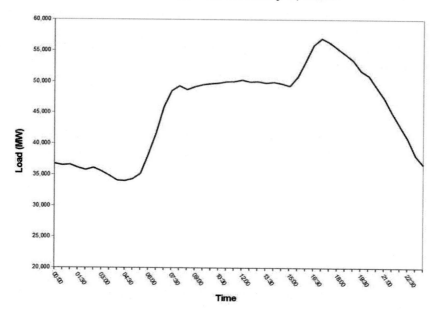

Source: Wikimedia Commons, available at
https://commons.wikimedia.org/wiki/File:Demand_graph.jpg

Original Data Source: *Electricity Transmission Operational Data*, NAT'L GRID

In response to the fluctuations in electricity demand on this date, grid operators in Great Britain likely "ramped down" some generating facilities during the early morning hours to avoid feeding too much excess power onto the grid. They also probably "ramped up" electricity production at some generating facilities in the late afternoon to meet the demand spike that occurred during that period. This process of constantly adjusting the amount of electricity fed onto the grid in response to demand shifts is no easy task since aggregate demand fluctuations are largely a product of weather conditions, human behavior, and other uncontrollable factors. The types of generating facilities involved can also greatly impact the ease or difficulty of this process because some facilities are far better than others at quickly increasing or decreasing electricity output.

The government-produced excerpt below provides a somewhat more detailed picture of how utilities and grid operators engage in grid load management—the never-ending task of balancing supply and demand on electric grids.

THE IMPORTANCE OF FLEXIBLE ELECTRICITY SUPPLY

National Renewable Energy Laboratory, U.S. Department of Energy
Solar Integration Series, Part 1 of 3 (May 2011)

Electricity demand is constantly changing, making variability and uncertainty inherent characteristics of electric systems. Control mechanisms have been developed to manage variability and uncertainty and maintain reliable operation. To understand the need for *flexibility* in the generation fleet, it is useful to examine the different grid operating timeframes, which can be divided into *regulation, load following,* and *unit commitment.* . . .

- *Regulation* typically ranges from several seconds to 5 minutes, and covers the variability that occurs between subsequent economic dispatches. Using automatic generation control (AGC), generation automatically responds to minute-by-minute load deviations in response to signals from grid operators. Changes in load during the regulation time are typically not predicted or scheduled in advance and must be met through generation that is on-line, grid-synchronized, and under automated control by the grid operator.

- *Load following* typically ranges from 5–15 minutes to a few hours. Generating units that have been previously committed, or can be started quickly, can provide this service, subject to operating constraints on the generator.

- *Unit commitment* typically covers several hours to several days. Unit commitment involves the starting and synchronizing of thermal generation so that it is available when needed to meet expected electricity demand.

Ramp rate is essentially the speed at which a generator can increase (ramp up) or decrease (ramp down) generation. Generating units have different characteristics, making some more suited to supplying certain needed functions.

Baseload units—typically large nuclear and coal-fired facilities—often supply the same amount of energy around the clock, although many coal units follow the diurnal load cycle, running at minimum generation levels at night and increasing during the day. These units have slow ramp rates and relatively high minimum generation levels, referred to as *turn-down capability.* They also can take a long time (days in some cases) to start back up once they have been cycled off. Large baseload units also tend to have lower operating costs relative to other fossil-fueled facilities.

Intermediate and *peaking units*, which are generally natural gas or oil-fired facilities, have faster ramp rates, relatively lower minimum generation levels, and can be shut down and started up relatively quickly—

however, they also have relatively higher operating costs. Intermediate and peaking units are most often used to provide load following generation service due to their ability to ramp up and down quickly. . . . In addition to intermediate and peaking units, there are many additional potential sources of flexibility, ranging from advanced thermal generators, institutional factors, demand response, fuel storage, and electricity storage. In general, the desired mix of flexibility is determined by the need to maintain reliability in the most economical way possible.

———————

QUESTIONS

1.   How does *regulation* differ from *load following* and *unit commitment*?

2.   What is the difference between a *baseload unit* and a *peaking unit*? If the per-kWh generating costs associated with both of these types of units were identical, which would a utility prefer? Why?

3.   Suppose it is June 15 and a week-long summer heat wave is expected to begin in UtiliCo's territory on June 17 and cause a major spike in the use of air conditioning systems throughout the region. Which of the three types of grid operating timeframes listed in Question 1 above would be most relevant for UtiliCo on June 15 as it tries to prepare for the coming heat wave?

4.   Suppose a utility found that it needed a way to more quickly increase and decrease its supply of power in response to short-term fluctuations in demand. All else equal, would adding a coal-fired power plant or adding a natural gas-fired power plant be more likely to help the utility address this issue? And what term would typically be used to describe your recommended new power plant—*baseload unit* or *intermediate/peaking plant*?

6.   UTILITY RESTRUCTURING AND DEREGULATION

Over the past few decades, regulatory and other changes have motivated many utilities to alter their organizational structures and to develop new ways of balancing electricity supply and demand on the grid. One of the most significant changes during this period has been a shift away from *vertically integrated utilities*—which engage in the generation, transmission, distribution, and marketing of electric power—toward greater specialization in just one or two of these functions. This shift has increased market competition in multiple areas of the electricity industry and has, in some cases, helped to fuel the growth of renewable energy.

One early catalyst for the nation's gradual movement away from vertically integrated utilities was Congress' enactment of the Public Utility Regulatory Policies Act of 1978, or PURPA. Among other things, PURPA requires utilities to purchase power from *qualifying facilities*—mostly smaller, independent electricity producers—at *avoided cost rates*. Avoided cost rates are prices that approximate what a utility's own costs would have been had it produced the power on its own. For the first time, PURPA opened the door for private companies—including renewable energy producers—to generate and sell power to utilities, which would then distribute and sell the purchased power to retail customers. Provisions in the Energy Policy Act of 1992 (EPAct) further expanded this opportunity for non-utility companies to participate in electricity generation markets. Among other things, provisions in the EPAct enabled many new types of electricity generators that did not meet PURPA's qualifying facilities requirements to begin generating and selling electric power to utilities. Additional federal regulatory changes and actions taken at the state level in the years following the EPAct have further chipped away at utilities' monopolies on electricity generation.

Most electric utilities today are still mostly vertically integrated, having exclusive rights over the generation, transmission, and distribution of electric power within their exclusive service areas. However, a slow and uneven trend toward the *deregulation* of generation markets has emerged over the past few decades. In states where electricity generation markets are deregulated, utilities do not own all accessible generating facilities within the market and non-utility entities are legally entitled to compete in markets for the sale of electricity.

In theory, the idea of deregulating electricity generation markets has some appeal because, as will be explored later in this Casebook, such markets are arguably less prone to the natural monopoly problem that serves as a primary rationale for traditional electricity regulation. However, many vertically integrated utilities themselves resist calls for deregulation because they fear new competition could destabilize their budgets and make it more difficult for them to recoup their investments in their own power plants—a situation commonly known as the *stranded costs* problem. A highly-publicized crisis and scandal in 2001 involving Enron Corporation and deregulated electricity markets in California also weakened support for deregulation in several states. Consequently, only a handful of states have deregulated electricity generation markets to date, and those deregulatory efforts have had varying degrees of success in those states. In the words of Professor Shi-Ling Hsu:

> The catchphrase "stranded costs" was born in the wake of widespread state efforts to deregulate electricity generation and liberalize energy markets. Liberalization means loss of monopoly power, and incumbent electricity generation firms in states trending towards deregulation complained loudly about the costs of power plants that had not yet been recouped from ratepayers. Estimates of the amount of money believed to be at stake in the mid-1990s, the height of deregulation speculation, ranged from $34 billion to $210 billion. . . .

The unusual characteristic of the electricity deregulation debate was that almost all of the parties, from integrated electric utilities, to consumer groups, to rural electric cooperatives, agreed: electricity deregulation could work, if done properly (their way). The disagreement was which path would be taken. Electric utilities spent $5.4 million in 1992 campaign contributions, which increased to $9.5 million in 1996. Interest groups self-reported a conservatively estimated total of $50 million in contributions. The end result is a mixed bag: fifteen states, plus Washington, D.C., either fully deregulated or actively regulated their electricity markets, and seven have suspended their deregulation plans, including California, which suffered the most humiliating failures of deregulation.

Shi-Ling Hsu, *Capital Rigidities, Latent Externalities*, 51 HOUS. L. REV. 719, 757–59 (2014).

Whether a state's utilities are vertically integrated or deregulated can greatly impact how the state approaches legal and policy issues related to renewable energy. Because of its influence on policymaking, the concept of deregulation resurfaces multiple times later in this Casebook.

As vertically integrated utilities have slowly given way to various forms of greater competition among electricity generators, *wholesale electricity* markets have also developed across much of the country. These markets sell power to electric power distributors at wholesale rates, who then distribute and resell it to customers at retail rates. Regional transmission organizations (RTOs) and independent system operators (ISOs) also emerged in some regions to help coordinate these wholesale transactions and the delivery of power from wholesale sellers to wholesale buyers across interstate transmission systems. Meanwhile, investor-owned utilities have increasingly opted to purchase power from others during periods of peak demand rather than constructing their own new generating facilities. The following two excerpts describe this evolution and some of its impacts on electricity markets.

THE ENVIRONMENTAL IMPACTS OF RESTRUCTURING: LOOKING BACK AND LOOKING FORWARD

Karen Palmer & Dallas Burtaw
1 ENVTL. & ENERGY L. & POL'Y J. 171, 173–77 (2005)

It is difficult to pinpoint when the restructuring of U.S. electricity markets began. Some have argued that a major milestone in the process of electricity restructuring was the passage of the Public Utilities Regulatory Policies Act of 1978, which included the requirement that regulated utilities purchase electricity from certain types of renewable generators and other so-called "qualifying facilities" at prices that were at or below the avoided cost of generating that electricity internally. The importance of the provision as a precursor to restructuring is that it offered the first significant departure from the legitimate monopoly franchise of electricity generation by regulated utilities. The practical implications of this provision varied across the states. For example, in states where the avoided cost of generation was set during periods of high fuel costs, a number of qualifying facilities were constructed and utilities began acquiring power from these independent generators in earnest. Contrary to prior fears about the loss of coordination associated with separating the ownership of generation from the ownership of utilities, the integration of purchased power into the mix of generation supplied by the vertically integrated utilities generally worked well. The success of this power purchasing activity, albeit sometimes at prices that turned out to be too high by market standards, demonstrated that separating generation from the power delivery system could work.

During the 1990s, the Energy Policy Act of 1992 was the major impetus for subsequent FERC orders requiring transmission-owning utilities regulated by FERC to provide open and nondiscriminatory access to their transmission lines to facilitate wholesale power transactions. Open transmission access is a necessary condition for competing generators to get their power to either wholesale or retail customers. FERC implemented this law in a series of three regulatory orders. Orders 888 and 889, issued in 1996, set forth the rules defining and governing open transmission access and the requirement for a centralized electronic bulletin board for sharing information about transmission availability and cost with potential customers. Order 2000, issued in 1999, built upon Order 888 by requiring utilities to actively consider participating in a Regional Transmission Organization (RTO), an independent entity that would operate the transmission grid and seek to prevent discrimination by the transmission owner against competing electricity generators. The structure and rules of any RTO (except the one in Texas, which is outside FERC jurisdiction) are subject to FERC approval and oversight.

Despite these FERC rulings, utilities in several states including those in the Southeast do not yet participate in an RTO, and wholesale competition in these areas is still more of an aspiration than a reality.

At the same time that FERC was paving the way for more effective wholesale competition, several states were actively seeking ways to provide real choice of electricity supplier to retail customers. The push for retail competition started in those states where prices were relatively high, including California, New York, and Massachusetts. Competition was seen as a means of lowering prices. In both California and Massachusetts, retail competition was enabled by legislation and took effect in 1998. In New York, retail competition was implemented through separate agreements between the state utility regulator and individual utilities. Pennsylvania started to allow competition in 1999, and it was phased in to include all classes of customers by January of 2001. Texas passed a law in 1999 that required retail competition to begin in 2002. In all of these states, except Pennsylvania and Texas, the restructuring legislation or regulation required a substantial fraction of electricity generation previously owned by integrated utilities to be sold to independent merchant generators. In Texas, only fifteen percent of existing capacity had to be sold.

During the debates over electricity restructuring, existing utilities showed an interest in being able to recover the sunk costs, commonly called "stranded costs," of past utility investments that might not be profitable in competitive markets. Utilities argued that because they had often made these investments at the behest of regulators and typically with their approval, it would be unfair for their shareholders to have to bear the costs due to a policy change. Compensating utilities for the vast majority of their stranded costs proved key to moving restructuring forward. In New Hampshire, one of the first restructuring laws was passed in 1996 and then stalled in court for several years because it allowed for only partial recovery of stranded costs. To facilitate stranded cost recovery, states typically imposed a nonbypassable charge on electricity distribution service that applied to all customers. Mechanisms for cost recovery were typically temporary and were eliminated once stranded costs were recovered. In many cases, these costs were actually recovered more quickly than initially anticipated due to a combination of high sales prices obtained for divested generating assets and higher than expected wholesale electricity prices.

During the transition period between price regulation and open competition, regulators set retail price caps or default service rates to protect customers from high prices and to provide a backup source of electricity should a competitive provider go out of business or decide to leave the market. The prices for these transition services were typically lower than the regulated electricity price prior to restructuring. In some cases this default service price proved too low to cover the wholesale market price of generation, which in many cases exceeded expectations due to higher fuel prices.

By the end of 2001, seventeen states plus the District of Columbia had passed laws or regulations introducing retail competition to their electricity markets and most were well on their way to implementing these changes. Missing from this set of seventeen states was California, one of the first states to introduce restructuring. After a summer of high prices and rolling blackouts in 2000 and widespread anticipation of more blackouts in the summer of 2001, the California Public Utility Commission of California declared an end to retail choice in September of 2001. . . . [M]any factors contributed to the problems experienced in 2000, but much of the blame has been laid at the door of electricity restructuring and the problems with specific design features of the California energy market.

The failure of the California market has helped stall enthusiasm for electricity restructuring in other states.

DISTRIBUTED RELIABILITY

Amy L. Stein
87 U. COLO. L. REV. 887, 902–06 (2016)

Implicit in [utilities'] duty to serve is a responsibility to provide the public with a reliable source of electricity. For decades, utilities have cooperated with one another to ensure that the bulk-power system is operated within tight voltage, frequency, and stability limits. For instance, utilities have established control areas to manage the grid, developed common operating standards, assisted one another with storm recovery, and undertaken other measures to keep power flowing to distribution facilities. This has helped the bulk-power system remain stable, so it can perform its transmission function and instantaneously balance electric supply with demand, while simultaneously protecting the generation and transmission equipment.

. . . .

For a hundred years, reliability of the electric grid was handled primarily "in house" by a vertically integrated utility. This utility controlled all three components of the electric grid: generation, transmission, and distribution facilities. The utility provided electricity for ratepayers within a state-defined service territory, owning the assets that provided these services and obtaining rate-based compensation for them. These utilities functioned under a regulated cost of service model where their investments in generation, transmission, and distribution facilities were judged by state public utility commissions (PUCs) for their prudence, with corresponding rate increases for qualifying investments. Utilities would make a determination about what assets were necessary for the grid based in part on reliability considerations, and their job was made easier by the centralized ownership and control of all the assets.

B. Post-Restructuring "Make and Buy" Utilities

Restructuring has forced many utilities to change from a "make" organizational model to a "make and buy" organizational model for energy resources, looking to external sources for significant amounts of both generation and reliability resources, while still relying on their internal firm structure for some of their electricity needs. In 1996, the Federal Energy Regulatory Commission (FERC) issued Order 888, requiring functional "unbundling" of the industry and requiring investor-owned utilities (IOUs) to separate their operation and access of their transmission assets from their generation assets. All investor-owned utilities have complied with FERC's unbundling requirements, and many states went even further in actually divesting *ownership* of their generation assets.

From 1997–2000, for instance, IOUs divested 22% of U.S. generation capacity. . . . Today, only a small fraction of the 3,000 utilities still perform all three functions—generation, transmission, and distribution.

Restructuring, and utilities' subsequent divestiture of their generation assets, has led nonintegrated utilities to become more reliant on external resources to satisfy their duty to serve. An example can be found in reliability resources used to balance for unforeseen differentials between supply and demand. A power system must operate within a narrow frequency range to avoid system collapse. "These balancing services are an important form of ancillary service for power systems, generally referred to as operating reserve[s]." The electric power grid must have minimum levels of operating reserves (readily available generating capacity and/or distributed resources) to ensure a reliable supply of electricity. Some of these operating reserves are provided by generation plants that perform double duty, functioning as both electricity and operating reserves. But some of these operating reserves are provided by peaker plants—small, single cycle natural gas plants, which can be quickly put into service for contingencies if another generator suddenly becomes unavailable or if demand for electricity is higher than usual. These peakers are inefficient reliability resources, often called upon for less than 10%, or a few hundred hours, of the year. Yet they have remained an important source of operating reserves. The Energy Information Administration indicated that 25% of all capacity added in 2013 was in the form of natural gas-fired peaker plants, with dozens of additional peaker units planned to be built between 2015 and 2023.

For years, utilities constructed their own peaker plants. But as the industry restructured, the utilities needed to look to a variety of external resources to satisfy their reliability needs. This came primarily in the form of outsourcing its peaker reliability resources to private "merchant" generators and maintaining control through contractual commitments. Today, most restructured utilities only own a portion of their peaker plants. For instance, of the twenty-four natural gas-fired peaker units within San Diego Gas & Electric's (SDG&E) service area, California's utility only owns three. In response to reliability concerns, SDG&E recently chose to enter into a power purchase agreement with an external merchant generator, NRG, for a 500 megawatt five-unit natural gas peaking plant in lieu of constructing one itself. Similarly, Southern California Edison owns only five peakers within its service area.

QUESTIONS

1.   Most of the increase in market competition in the electricity industry over the past three decades has been in electricity *generation* markets.

Meanwhile, electricity *distribution* largely continues to be subject to conventional cost of service regulation. Is this consistent with the natural monopoly theory materials covered earlier in this chapter? Why or why not?

2.   Private firms in countless industries have incurred stranded costs—investments in equipment or other capital expenditures they are never able to fully recoup from revenues. Do you think utilities should be deemed as having legally-protected rights to recover stranded costs, even though such costs are not ordinarily recoverable in purely competitive industries? Why or why not?

3.   According to the excerpts above, how do wholesale electricity markets and the transmission system potentially help to increase the reliability of retail electricity supplies? Why would some of those benefits be lost if all utilities were totally vertically integrated and unconnected to each other?

C. FACTORS DRIVING THE TRANSITION TO RENEWABLES

As already mentioned, renewable energy's rise over the past 15 years has been impressive by any measure. Many of the primary factors that have led to precipitous growth of the renewable energy industry in recent years are likely to continue to drive growth in the decades to come. This subsection focuses on three of these factors: (i) technological innovation; (ii) concerns about global warming; and (iii) policy innovation.

1. TECHNOLOGICAL INNOVATION

Dramatic improvements in renewable energy technologies have played an important role in recent years in helping renewable energy development to spread throughout the world. Above all, innovations that have made it possible to affordably convert the energy in wind currents and solar radiation to electric energy are reshaping electricity markets. Much of the planet's energy infrastructure—from transmission lines to light bulbs to household appliances—is already built to run on electricity. In contrast to nineteenth century windmills or skylights, which served only very limited functions, modern wind turbines and solar panels produce a type of energy so fungible and familiar to the developed world that its list of productive uses is endless.

The most influential renewable energy innovations over the past quarter century have involved wind and solar resources. Not surprisingly, the earliest wind turbines and solar energy systems were not even remotely cost-competitive with fossil fuels or nuclear energy. However, in recent decades, declines in the per-kWh costs of generating electricity from wind and solar have easily outpaced cost declines for electricity from coal, nuclear, or natural gas. Today, wind and solar are increasingly viewed as commercially viable or even superior alternatives to nonrenewable energy strategies.

Consider, for instance, the extraordinary price declines associated with solar PV systems, as shown in Figure 1.5 below. These prices fell from $76 per watt in 1977 to just $0.30 per watt in 2015 and have continued to fall even further since. As one reporter described it, "the cost of solar power has fallen to 1/150th of its level in the 1970s, while the total amount of solar has soared 115,000 fold." Tom Randall, *Wind and Solar Are Crushing Fossil Fuels*, BLOOMBERG (Apr. 16, 2016), http://www.bloomberg.com/news/articles/2016-04-06/wind-and-solar-are-crushing-fossil-fuels. Indeed, some of this rapid drop in prices is likely attributable to production economies of scale: as more solar panels are produced, the per-unit cost of producing them declines. "Swanson's Law", named after SunPower Corporation founder Richard Swanson, is one prominent stakeholder's observation about economies of scale in solar panel production. It suggests that, each time the total volume of solar PV cells being manufactured doubles, the per-unit manufacturing costs of those cells decreases by 20 percent. *See* Geoffrey Carr, *Sunny Uplands*, ECONOMIST (Nov. 21, 2012), http://www.economist.com/news/21566414-alternative-energy-will-no-longer-be-altern ative-sunny-uplands. This observation has seemingly proven true over much of the past quarter century.

Figure 1.5. The Declining Prices of Solar PV Cells

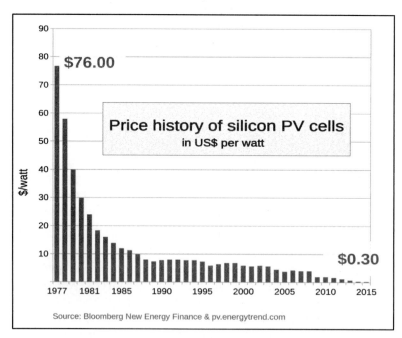

Source: Wikimedia Commons,
https://commons.wikimedia.org/wiki/File:Price_
history_of_silicon_PV_cells_since_1977.svg

The wind energy industry has likewise experienced extraordinary price declines over the past quarter century as wind turbines have grown ever larger and more efficient. From 1980 to 2013, the per-kWh cost of wind-generated energy—excluding federal tax incentives—decreased by more than 90%. *See* Dep't of Energy, *Wind Power in the United States: Recent Progress, Status Today, and Emerging Trends, in* WIND VISION: A NEW ERA FOR WIND POWER IN THE UNITED STATES (2015), http://www.energy.gov/sites/prod/files/wv_chapter2_wind_power_in_the_united_states.pdf. By 2016, onshore wind energy costs had dropped so far that in multiple markets new wind farms were more economical than new centralized power plants. Offshore wind energy technologies have the potential to bring even greater cost savings as those technologies mature in the coming years.

In addition to wind and solar energy, technological advancements associated with other forms of renewable energy also show great promise for the future. For example, researchers continue to pursue the possibility of hydrokinetic or wave energy technologies, which generate electricity from ocean waves. Airborne wind turbines could someday allow for wind energy deployment and generation even in areas that do not have strong near-the-ground wind resources. Even biogas from landfills, wastewater treatment, and livestock feeding operations is increasingly serving a renewable energy source. Collectively, these and other innovations could continue to drive renewable energy for many decades to come.

2. CONCERNS ABOUT GLOBAL WARMING

Fears about global warming and its negative consequences are also helping to drive the growth of renewable energy. Evidence continues to mount supporting the widely-held belief that humankind's fossil fuel extraction and consumption are causing gradual increases in the earth's atmospheric temperature. These increased temperatures appear to be already threatening some small island nations and increasing the severity of some major weather events. In the following excerpt, Professor Jeffrey Thaler describes climate change in more detail and a few of its numerous potential impacts on ecosystems and on modern society.

**FIDDLING AS THE WORLD FLOODS AND BURNS:
HOW CLIMATE CHANGE URGENTLY REQUIRES
A PARADIGM SHIFT IN THE PERMITTING
OF RENEWABLE ENERGY PROJECTS**

Jeffrey Thaler
42 ENVTL. L. 1101, 1107–18, 1120–23, 1124–28 (2012)

Greenhouse gases (GHGs) trap heat in the atmosphere. The primary GHG emitted by human activities is carbon dioxide (CO2), which in 2010 represented 84% of all human-sourced GHG emissions in the U.S. . . .

Beginning with the 1750 Industrial Revolution, atmospheric concentrations of GHGs have significantly increased with greater use of fossil fuels—which has in turn caused our world to warm and the climate to change. In fact, climate change may be the single greatest threat to human society and wildlife, as well as to the ecosystems upon which each depends for survival.

In 1992, the U.S. signed and ratified the United Nations Framework Convention on Climate Change (UNFCCC), the stated objective of which was:

> [To achieve] stabilization of greenhouse gas concentrations in the atmosphere at a level that would prevent dangerous anthropogenic interference with the climate system. Such a level should be achieved within a time-frame sufficient to allow ecosystems to adapt naturally to climate change, to ensure that food production is not threatened and to enable economic development to proceed in a sustainable manner.

In 2007, the Intergovernmental Panel on Climate Change (IPCC) concluded that it is "very likely"—at least 90% certain—that humans are responsible for most of the "unequivocal" increases in globally averaged temperatures of the previous fifty years. . . .

What are some of the growing economic, public health, and environmental costs to our country proximately caused by our daily burning of fossil fuels? The National Research Council (NRC) recently analyzed the "hidden" costs of energy production and use not reflected in market prices of coal, oil, and other energy sources, or in the prices of electricity and gasoline produced from them. For the year 2005 alone, the NRC estimated $120 billion of damages to the U.S. from fossil fuel energy production and use, reflecting primarily health damages from air pollution associated with electricity generation and motor vehicle transportation. Of that total, $62 billion was due to coal-fired electricity generation; $56 billion from ground transportation (oil-petroleum); and over $2.1 billion from electricity generation and heating with natural gas. . . . [A]dding infrastructure and ecosystem damages, insurance costs, air pollutant costs, and fossil-fueled national security costs . . . fossil [fuel] consumption costs Americans almost $300 billion each year—a "hidden" number likely to be larger in the future. . . .

[T]he NRC expects that each degree Celsius increase [in global average temperature] will produce double to quadruple the area burned by wildfires in the western United States, a 5%–15% reduction in crop yields, more destructive power from hurricanes, greater risk of very hot summers, and more changes in precipitation frequency and amounts. . . .

A 2011 IPCC Special Report predicted that:

It is virtually certain [99–100% probability] that increases in the frequency of warm daily temperature extremes and decreases in cold extremes will occur throughout the 21st century on a global scale. It is very likely [90–100% probability] that heat waves will increase in length, frequency, and/or intensity over most land areas. . . . It is very likely that average sea level rise will contribute to upward trends in extreme sea levels in extreme coastal high water levels.

. . . .

In 2011, the U.S. faced the most billion-dollar climate disasters ever, with fourteen distinct disasters alone costing at least $54 billion to our economy. In the first six months of 2012 in the U.S., there were more than 40,000 hot temperature records, horrendous wildfires, major droughts, oppressive heat waves, major flooding, and a powerful derecho wind storm, followed in August by Hurricane Isaac ($2 billion damages), and in October by Hurricane Sandy ($50 billion damages). . . .

Weather extremes also threaten our national security, which is premised on stability. In [2008]. . . . in the first ever U.S. government analysis of climate change security threats, the National Intelligence Council issued an assessment warning, in part, that climate change could threaten U.S. security by leading to political instability, mass movements of refugees, terrorism, and conflicts over water and other resources. . . .

Since 1980, sea levels have been rising three to four times faster than the global average between Cape Hatteras, North Carolina and Boston, Massachusetts. "[P]ast and future global warming more than doubles the estimated odds of 'century' or worse floods occurring within the next 18 years" for most coastal U.S. locations.

Although land-based glacier melts are not major contributors to sea level rise, they do impact peoples' food and water supplies. Virtually all of the world's glaciers, which store 75% of the world's freshwater, are receding in direct response to global warming, aggravating already severe water scarcity—both in the United States and abroad. While over 15% of the world's population currently relies on glacial melt and snow cover for drinking water and irrigation for agriculture, the IPCC projects a 60% volume loss in glaciers in various regions and widespread reductions in snow cover throughout the twenty-first century. Likewise, snowpack has been decreasing, and it is expected that snow cover duration will significantly decrease in eastern and western North America and Scandinavia by 2020 and globally by 2080.

Climate change thus increases food insecurity by reducing yields of grains, such as corn and wheat, through increased water scarcity and intensification of severe hot conditions, thereby causing corn price volatility to sharply increase. Globally, the number of people living in "severely stressed" river basins will increase "by one to two billion people in the 2050s. About two-thirds of global land area is expected to experience increased water stress."

. . . .

Extinctions from climate change also are expected to be significant and widespread. Between now and 2050, Conservation International estimates that one species will face extinction every twenty minutes; the current extinction rate is one thousand times faster than the average during Earth's history, in part because the climate is changing more than 100 times faster than the rate at which many species can adapt.

4.   *When Land Dries Out*

The warming trends toward the Earth's poles and higher latitudes are threatening people not just from melting ice and sea level rise, but also from the predicted thawing of 30%–50% of permafrost by 2050, and again as much or more of it by 2100. . . . Given the increasing average air temperatures in eastern Siberia, Alaska, and northwestern Canada, thawing of the Northern permafrost would release massive amounts of carbon dioxide (doubling current atmospheric levels) and methane into the atmosphere. . . .

Climate change also is exacerbating the geographic spread and intensity of insect infestations. . . . Over the past fifteen years the spruce bark beetle extended its range into Alaska, where it has killed about 40 million trees more "than any other insect in North America's recorded history." The drying and burning forests, and other increasingly dry landscapes, also are causing "flora and fauna [to move] to higher latitudes or to higher altitudes in the mountains."

The human and environmental costs from failing to promptly reduce dependence on carbon-dioxide emitting sources for electricity, heating, and transportation are dire and indisputable.

QUESTIONS

1.   How many different types of impacts are listed in the excerpt above as potential costs of global warming? What are some others that were not included in the excerpt?

2.   A large 2016 Pew Research Study found that less than half—just 48 percent—of United States adults believed that global climate change is caused by human activity. *See* Cary Funk & Brian Kennedy, *Public Views on Climate Change and Climate Scientists*, PEW RES. CTR. (Oct. 4, 2016), http://www.pew

internet.org/2016/10/04/public-views-on-climate-change-and-climate-scientists/. What might someone who does not believe in human-induced climate change argue in response to the excerpt above? What is your own position on this decisive and controversial question, and upon what specific evidence sources do you base your views?

3.   What are some factors that make it more difficult for policymakers to fully and accurately account for societal costs of global warming, like those highlighted in Thaler's article, when formulating energy policies?

———————

At the international level, the United Nations (UN) has sought for years to promote agreement among nations of the world on commitments to curb carbon dioxide (CO_2) emissions and thereby slow the pace of climate change. Among other things, the UN Framework Convention on Climate Change (UNFCCC) had held annual conferences for decades to evaluate progress toward addressing climate change and to promote international negotiations for legally binding agreements aimed at fighting the problem. Several major countries adopted the Kyoto Protocol in 1997—the first major legally binding UN agreement to cut CO_2 emissions—but Congress never ratified President Bill Clinton's signing of the treaty so the United States was never legally obligated to follow it. More recently, in December 2015, the United States and almost 200 other UNFCCC member nations negotiated the Paris climate accord—a much broader-reaching and more comprehensive agreement to slow climate change. Although 195 nations had signed the accord as of late 2017, the Trump Administration's plans to withdraw the United States from the agreement had cast significant uncertainty on its long-term stability.

Regardless of whether the United States withdraws from the Paris accord, concerns about climate change will continue to be a major driver of renewable energy growth for decades to come. Countless states, cities, and citizens throughout the country are strongly committed to curb their CO_2 emissions and are already taking aggressive steps toward their own carbon reduction goals, many of which involve greater reliance on renewable energy sources. The threat of global warming makes wind, solar, hydrokinetic, and geothermal energy sources especially appealing because generating electricity with them tends to require little or no combustion of carbon-based resources. By contrast, some other renewable energy sources, such as biomass, liquid biofuels, and biogas, must be burned to release their energy so increasing their use is a comparatively less effective means of combatting global warming.

Nuclear energy is not generally classified as renewable but has also gained increased favor recently as a means of combatting global warming because of its low greenhouse gas emissions. *See, e.g.*, Patrick McGeehan, *New York State Aiding Nuclear Plants with Millions in Subsidies*, N.Y.

TIMES A18 (Aug. 1, 2016). However, opponents of nuclear energy development often cite several other unique costs associated with nuclear power to argue that expanding it is not a justifiable means of slowing global warming. Among other things, nuclear energy brings with it the risk of catastrophic events akin to the 2011 disaster at Japan's Fukushima Daiichi nuclear energy facility, which required more than 100,000 nearby residents to indefinitely evacuate their homes. Moreover, as of 2017, the United States also had no active plans for where it would store the high-level radioactive waste generated at the nation's nuclear plants—a fact that further weakens arguments in favor of more nuclear energy.

In addition to nuclear power, there are multiple other energy strategies involving nonrenewable resources that can potentially reduce greenhouse gas emissions. For example, coal industry stakeholders often advocate for "clean coal" technologies, which retrofit coal-fired power plants to decrease their carbon dioxide emissions. Another potential means of reducing greenhouse gas emissions is to convert coal-fired power plants to run on natural gas—a cleaner-burning, plentiful, and less expensive fossil fuel due to advancements in hydraulic fracturing or *fracking* techniques. Unfortunately, the fracking technologies that have introduced an economical means of accessing vast stores of subsurface shale oil and gas are a double-edged sword to those concerned about global warming. On one hand, the newfound abundance of natural gas made accessible through fracking is accelerating the pace of decline of coal-fired electricity generation in the United States. On the other hand, the lower cost of natural gas makes it more difficult for wind energy and solar energy technologies to compete with gas-fired power.

Energy efficiency and conservation strategies can be an economical and highly effective means of combatting global warming as well. *See generally* EPA, ENERGY EFFICIENCY AS A LOW-COST RESOURCE FOR ACHIEVING CARBON EMISSIONS REDUCTIONS (2009), https://www.epa.gov/sites/production/files/2015-08/documents/ee_and_carbon.pdf. These strategies seek to help individuals and businesses to consume less energy while still enjoying essentially the same living standards and productivity levels. Even carbon capture and storage projects and initiatives focused on planting trees can help to reduce atmospheric carbon dioxide and its accompanying climate risks.

It's unlikely that any one strategy will single-handedly enable the nations of the world achieve their ambitious CO_2 reduction goals, but additional renewable energy development is certain to be part of that broad-based effort. Without question, the problem calls for a broad array of strategies on multiple fronts. The famous "stabilization wedge theory", developed by Princeton University Professors Rob Socolow and Stephen Pacala, effectively illustrates the magnitude of the world's climate change challenges and the need for a nearly "all of the above" approach to addressing it. Based on their assumptions, humankind would need to achieve at least seven of a list of 15 enumerated energy objectives or "wedges" to avoid doubling carbon dioxide emissions by 2055. *See* Rob Socolow & Stephen Pacala, *Stabilization Wedges: Solving the Climate Problem for the Next 50 Years with Current Technologies*, SCIENCE (Aug. 13, 2004), http://science.sciencemag.org/content/305/5686/968. As suggested above, their list of wedges includes many actions that do not involve renewable energy, such as increasing the energy efficiency of cars and buildings or replacing coal-fired power plants with plants that run on nuclear energy or natural gas. However, it is difficult to conceive of how the planet could reach the aggressive carbon dioxide emission reduction goals required under the model without dramatic increases in renewable energy generation.

3.   POLICY INNOVATION

A third important driver of renewable energy growth over the past quarter century has been an unprecedented period of ambitious policy innovation aimed at promoting renewables. This period of innovation arguably traces its earliest roots to the 1970s. Early in that decade Congress enacted the Geothermal Steam Act of 1970, which opened the door for the leasing of geothermal steam-related resources on public lands. Interest in renewable energy policy then expanded much further a few years later when the United States found itself under a crippling oil embargo from the Organization of Petroleum Exporting Countries (OPEC) after supporting Israel during the Yom Kippur War of 1973. These events sparked popular interest in promoting national energy security by reducing the nation's reliance on foreign energy sources. This popular sentiment ultimately engendered policies aimed at encouraging the development of home-grown energy resources, including renewables. In addition to PURPA (mentioned above), Congress enacted the Energy Tax Act of 1978, which included the nation's first federal major renewable energy subsidy in the form of a modest investment tax credit program. See Energy Tax Act of 1978, Pub. L. No. 95–618, 92 Stat. 3174 (1978). During this same period, state-level solar energy statutes and other forms of renewable energy legislation were also spreading throughout the country. President Jimmy Carter even had a solar energy system installed on the White House roof, reflecting the public's favorable and hopeful view of renewable energy technologies at the time.

However, by the early 1980s, the nation's exuberance for renewable energy and its possibilities had waned. The following decade represented a "dark ages" of sorts for renewable energy policy, with very few notable advancements. Wind energy development did take off in parts of California, but very minimal development spread outside of that state. The federal investment tax credit program was allowed to expire in 1986, only further dampening interest in renewable energy development.

With its enactment of the Energy Policy Act of 1992, Congress helped to revive some interest in renewables through the introduction of a production tax credit program for wind and solar energy. See I.R.C. § 45(a) (2006). These tax credits, which are discussed in much greater depth in subsequent chapters, eventually drove substantial new investment in wind energy and helped to lay a foundation for the much faster industry growth that eventually followed. By the mid-2000s, soaring energy prices and an increasing number of state-level renewable energy incentives were combining with federal policies to generate an unprecedented level of demand for wind and solar energy. State renewable portfolio standards and net metering policies—both of which are covered in detail later in this Casebook—were especially instrumental in helping to drive investment in renewables at that time and continue to help sustain this investment today.

D. RECURRING CONCEPTS IN RENEWABLE ENERGY LAW

A few overarching concepts recur throughout much of renewable energy law. Understanding these concepts and recognizing them as they arise can make it easier to draw connections among the diverse sets of issues arising in this emerging area of the law. The following materials introduce explain three of these concepts, which arise again at multiple points later in this Casebook.

1. EXTERNALITIES

Legal and policy conflicts within energy law often involve what economists call *externality problems*—another type of market failure that can warrant government regulation or other forms of intervention in private markets. The following excerpt provides a basic introduction to positive and negative externality problems and to some of the ways they can impact behaviors, markets, and policymaking decisions.

SOLAR, WIND AND LAND: CONFLICTS IN RENEWABLE ENERGY DEVELOPMENT
Troy A. Rule, pp. 3–8 (2014)

Positive Externality Problems

When the parties directly involved in renewable energy development ignore the external costs and benefits associated with their projects, market failures that economists describe as "externality problems" often result. Basic economics principles teach that some sort of government intervention—a new legal rule or policy program—is sometimes the best way to mitigate externality problems and thereby promote greater economic efficiency.

In recent years, policymakers around the world have made great strides in crafting programs to address the *positive* externality problems plaguing the renewable energy sector. Positive externality problems exist in this context because wind and solar energy development generate significant *benefits* that are distributed diffusely among the planet's billions of inhabitants, most of whom reside far away from the project site. Such benefits include reductions in the global consumption rate of fossil fuel energy sources and consequent reductions in harmful emissions, including carbon dioxide emissions that may contribute to global warming. Among countries that are net importers of fossil fuels, increasing the proportion of the national energy demand supplied through renewable resources can also promote economic growth, improve trade balances and advance greater economic stability.

Without some form of government intervention, rationally self-interested landowners and developers tend not to adequately account for external benefits in their decisions and thus engage in sub-optimally low levels of renewable energy development. Consider, for example, a rural landowner who leases thousands of acres of land to a developer for a commercial wind farm project. Such lease agreements typically give landowners an estimate of the monetary compensation they can expect to receive if the developer's project is completed. Through power purchase agreements or other means, developers can also approximate how much financial compensation they will earn in connection with a given project. By weighing the expected benefits that would accrue directly to them against their own budgetary or other costs, landowners and developers can make rational, self-interested decisions about their involvement in the wind farm.

However . . . renewable energy projects also generate numerous *other* benefits that accrue more generally to thousands or even billions of other people. In a completely free and open market, these ancillary benefits are not generally captured by project landowners or developers. Rational, self-interested landowners and developers are thus likely to place little or no value on these outside benefits and will instead weigh only their own potential benefits and costs when making development-related decisions. Because they rationally choose to ignore these external benefits, developers and landowners are likely to engage in sub-optimally low levels of renewable energy development without some form of government intervention. . . .

Governments across the world are well aware of this positive externality problem associated with renewable energy and have formulated a wide array of creative programs and policies aimed at countering it. Many of these programs seek to reduce the market cost of renewable energy development through direct subsidies, investment tax credits, special financing programs, streamlined permitting processes, and related means. . . .

In contrast, renewable portfolio standards, feed-in tariffs and some other incentive programs seek to correct or mitigate the positive externality problems associated with renewable energy by helping developers to internalize more of the external benefits of their developments. These programs, which directly or indirectly increase the market price of renewable energy. . . . Much of the recent growth in the global renewable energy sector can be attributed to these types of policies. . . .

Negative Externality Problems

Policymakers and academics devote comparatively less attention to many of the *negative* externality problems associated with renewable energy development. These problems arise when some of the costs associated with renewable energy projects are borne by individuals who do not directly participate in and have relatively less influence over development decisions.

The list of wind and solar energy development's potential costs to outsiders is expansive and continues to grow. Within the land use realm alone, this list includes aesthetic degradation, noise, ice throws, flicker effects, interference with electromagnetic signals, destruction of wildlife habitats and wetlands, bird and bat casualties, disruption of sacred burial grounds or historical sites, inner ear or sleeping problems, annoyance during the construction phase, interference with oil or mineral extraction, solar panel glare effects, exploitation of scarce water supplies, and heightened electrical, lightning, and fire risks. Theoretically, an excessive quantity of renewable energy development can result when project developers base their renewable energy development decisions solely on their own anticipated costs and ignore costs borne by others.

It is true that most of the costs of renewable energy development are borne by developers and by the landowners on whose property the development occurs. Developers typically incur the greatest costs associated with any given renewable energy project. They frequently invest large sums of money in project planning, buying or leasing real property, paying for adequate road and transmission infrastructure, purchasing expensive renewable energy systems, navigating the often-confusing government permitting scheme applicable to the project, and ultimately installing the systems. Landowners who lease or otherwise convey interests in their real property for such development can also incur significant costs associated with the presence of renewable energy devices and related infrastructure on their property. . . .

However, countless other parties, including those who own or use neighboring land, can also suffer significant costs associated with new wind or solar energy installations. These neighbors and other affected outsiders often have limited influence on where and how projects are built, and rational self-interested developers and landowners do not fully account for neighbors' costs when making development decisions. This classic *negative* externality problem can theoretically lead to an excessive amount of renewable energy generating capacity. . . .

More specifically, without government intervention, developers may install renewable energy facilities in unjustifiable locations simply because they do not bear all of the costs associated with doing so. Wind farms may hazardously encroach into migratory bird paths, solar energy projects may disrupt sacred Native American burial sites, or numerous other avoidable conflicts may result. Such conflicts are not only inefficient; they can also tarnish renewable energy's public image in ways that ultimately impede global progress toward energy sustainability.

When policymakers fail to anticipate and address the negative externalities associated with wind and solar energy development, outside parties who suffer injuries as a result become more likely to mobilize and oppose future projects—even worthwhile ones that pose minimal risks. And when laws governing renewable energy land use conflicts are unsettled and unclear, the resulting uncertainty can also slow the pace of development. Accordingly, any comprehensive set of policies for promoting renewable energy development must do more than merely correct positive externality problems by incentivizing more of it. It must also appropriately account for the external costs and conflicts that can arise from these projects.

QUESTIONS

1.   Which tends to result in excessive amounts of a particular activity: a *positive* externality problem or a *negative* externality problem? Why?

2.   According to the excerpt above, how can externality problems influence a given developer's decisions about her quantity of renewable energy development? Why do these impacts arguably matter from a public policy perspective?

3.   According to the excerpt above, how can laws and policies help to address the externality problems associated with renewable energy?

2. PUBLIC VS. PRIVATE

Another recurring theme throughout renewable energy law is controversy over whether certain assets and natural resources are better controlled by private parties or by governments.

One aspect of this tension between public and private control is akin to a tension that has always permeated natural resources and environmental law: where do private property rights end and public rights begin? Courts and policymakers have long struggled over this question as it relates to watercourses and even to the air we breathe. In the energy context, the public versus private debate reaches from the deep subsurface areas below the ground to the high-altitude airspace above it to the vast oceans of the earth. For example, should the federal government be empowered to place a moratorium on a wind energy project solely because an Air Force base situated 30 miles from the project site occasionally practices low-altitude maneuvers in the area? As highlighted briefly in Chapter 3, such objections have delayed or threatened numerous proposed wind energy projects over the past.

A second aspect of the public-versus-private dichotomy relates to whether certain industry activities are best left in the hands of private actors or whether they are more efficiently handled through governmental bodies. Consider, for instance, the debate over restructuring and deregulation in electric utilities law over the past 30 years. Stakeholders on both sides of this debate have been arguing for decades over the extent to which certain elements of the nation's electricity system should be open to free market competition. Other questions within this category include debates over whether governments should help to facilitate financing for private renewable energy projects or enterprises or whether private parties should be expected to attract financing entirely on their own. Even decisions about whether investor-owned utilities should be permitted to sell or lease rooftop solar to customer are ultimately "public versus private" debates. As the following chapters show, these debates emerge repeatedly within renewable energy law, adding to its rich complexity and challenging policymakers and courts to find workable solutions.

3. DISRUPTIVE INNOVATION VS. ENTRENCHED INDUSTRY STAKEHOLDERS

One other concept that appears in multiple contexts in renewable energy policy is the predictable resistance of well-established energy industry stakeholders to the rise of powerful new energy technologies. As renewable energy strategies have become increasingly cost-competitive with conventional energy sources, some of the energy industry's largest and most politically influential players have sought to preserve their longstanding business interests. Many traditional energy industry stakeholders have made enormous capital investments based on an assumption that relatively stable and predictable conditions would persist in their markets for decades into the future. The increasing growth and competitiveness of renewable energy in recent years casts doubt on those assumptions and can present a formidable long-term threat to these companies.

Tension between these incumbent stakeholders and the newcomers who are pushing disruptive innovations into energy markets is detectable throughout renewable energy law and throughout much of this Casebook. On the one side are countless companies that are aggressively seeking to harness wind, solar, energy storage, and other technologies in ways that could ultimately transform the nation's energy system. On the other side are numerous coal companies, oil and gas companies, nuclear energy interests, electric utilities, automobile manufacturers, and other entrenched stakeholders who understandably want to protect their long-held dominant market positions. Several sub-issues, principles, and theories surround this complex dynamic, including such concepts as stranded costs, fairness, exclusive territories, public choice theory, due process, and various others. Familiarity with these concepts and their general implications in the transition toward a more sustainable energy system is essential for modern energy lawyers.

The remaining chapters of this Casebook focus on specific types of renewable energy strategies and the primary legal and policy matters associated with each of them. Chapters 2 through 4 explore issues related to wind energy development—the nation's greatest source of new renewable energy capacity in recent decades. Chapters 5 and 6 focus on solar energy issues, covering everything from the environmental impacts of utility-scale solar projects to conflicts with utilities over growing numbers of rooftop solar panel installations. Chapter 7 examines the role of energy storage and smart grid technologies and the laws that govern them. Chapter 8 covers several other renewable energy strategies, including geothermal energy, ocean wave energy, and hydropower.

CHAPTER 2

WIND ENERGY POLICY

■ ■ ■

Over the past quarter century, wind energy development has been the single greatest contributor to renewable energy growth in the United States. As wind energy projects continue to proliferate across the country, lawyers are increasingly representing stakeholders on the wide range of issues arising from these projects. A general understanding of the wind energy development process and the unique legal and policy tensions associated with it is essential for attorneys who represent stakeholders in this growing industry.

Wind turbines generate electricity by converting the kinetic energy in wind—the natural movement of air through outdoor space—into electric current. As described in Chapter 1, humankind has been harnessing the power of wind and using it for centuries through windmills, sails, and other inventions. Prior to the industrial revolution, wind was among the world's most important energy sources. However, the wind energy industry is more relevant today than ever before, with individuals and businesses across the world rapidly embracing new wind power technologies and making productive use of wind at an unprecedented scale.

The U.S. wind energy industry has been expanding at breakneck pace for more than a decade. Wind energy accounted for only about 6% of all electricity generation in the United States as of 2017, but for several years its share of the nation's energy portfolio has risen faster than that of any other renewable energy source.[1] The rapid growth of wind energy is also likely to continue for decades to come. A 2015 U.S. Department of Energy report suggests the nation could derive as much as 20% of its electricity from wind power by 2030 and 35% by 2050.[2]

The next three chapters of this Casebook cover legal and policy issues associated with wind energy development. This chapter focuses on various policy strategies governments use to promote wind energy development and the debates surrounding many of these strategies. Chapter 3 explores several property, land use, and environmental law issues associated with wind energy development. Chapter 4 examines some of the typical legal

---

[1] *See* U.S. ENERGY INFO. ADMIN., SHORT TERM ENERGY OUTLOOK (2016).
[2] *See* U.S. DEP'T OF ENERGY, WIND VISION: A NEW ERA FOR WIND POWER IN THE UNITED STATES, at xxviii (2015).

work involved in wind energy development and some specific tasks lawyers often undertake to assist in the wind farm development process.

A. ADVANTAGES OF WIND AS AN ENERGY RESOURCE

Wind power's rapid growth over the past few decades is attributable in part to several distinct advantages of wind as a source of energy. From its renewable nature to its negligible greenhouse gas emissions to its minimal use of water, wind energy has multiple characteristics that make it a highly favorable energy source from a public policy perspective. The following materials highlight several of these desirable attributes of wind energy.

1. RENEWABLE-NESS

As described in Chapter 1, the renewable nature of wind resources is perhaps its single greatest virtue. The burning of fossil fuel resources depletes the planet's finite supplies of them, leaving less available for later use. By contrast, the energy in wind (which results primarily from uneven heat distribution across the planet's surface) derives largely from the sun and is nearly 100 percent renewable. Generating electricity from wind resources available today has no adverse impact on the quantity or quality of wind resources available tomorrow or even centuries into the future.

Although purely self-interested individuals might rationally care only about ensuring that the planet has plenty of energy resources during the duration of their own lifetimes, most people place at least some value on preserving resources for future generations. In the context of environmental policy, the ideal of *intergenerational equity* encompasses the goal of ensuring that present-day activities do not materially reduce the quantity or quality of the planet's resources available for future use. In the following excerpt, Professor Edith Brown Weiss discusses the concept of intergenerational equity and its policy implications. As you read the excerpt, consider how wind energy differs from fossil fuel-generated energy in its capacity to promote intergenerational equity.

IN FAIRNESS TO FUTURE GENERATIONS AND SUSTAINABLE DEVELOPMENT
Edith Brown Weiss
8 AM. U. INT'L. L. REV. 19, 19–22, 24–26 (1992)

Sustainable development is inherently an in*ter*generational question as well as an in*tra*generational question. Sustainable development relies on a commitment to equity with future generations. This ethical and philosophical commitment acts as a constraint on a natural inclination to take advantage of our temporary control over the earth's resources, and to use them only for our own benefit without careful regard for what we leave to our children and their descendants. This may seem a self-centered philosophy, but it is actually part of the logic that governs daily economic decisions about the use of our resources.

The recent and valid concern over environmental externalities focuses mainly on the costs that we and our contemporaries must bear when we pollute the air, water and soil by industrial expansion, deforestation and other aspects of economic development. Concern over these externalities is intended to ensure that the benefits from a contemplated action exceed its costs and that those who bear its costs are adequately compensated. But in practice the costs and benefits are assessed from the perspective of the present generation. The discount rate ensures that short-term benefits nearly always outweigh long-term costs.

For this reason, it is useful to address the issue of sustainability from a normative perspective. Sustainability requires that we look at the earth and its resources not only as an investment opportunity, but as a trust passed to us by our ancestors for our benefit, but also to be passed on to our descendants for their use.

This notion conveys both rights and responsibilities. Most importantly, it implies that future generations have rights too. These rights have meaning only if we, the living, respect them, and in this regard, transcend the differences among countries, religions, and cultures.

Fortunately, the notion that each generation holds the earth as a trustee or steward for its descendants strikes a deep chord with all cultures, religions and nationalities. Nearly all human traditions recognize that we, the living, are sojourners on earth and temporary stewards of our resources. The theory of intergenerational equity states that we, the human species, hold the natural environment of our planet in common with other species, other people, and with past, present and future generations. As members of the present generation, we are both trustees, responsible for the robustness and integrity of our planet, and beneficiaries, with the right to use and benefit from it for ourselves. . . .

The theory of intergenerational equity states that all generations have an equal place in relation to the natural system, and that there is no basis for preferring past, present or future generations in relation to the system. . . .

The corollary to the premise of equality is the concept of a partnership among generations. Edmund Burke observed that:

> As the ends of such a partnership cannot be obtained in many generations, it becomes a partnership, not only between those who are living but between those who are living, those who are dead, and those who are to be born.

The purpose of the partnership is to realize and protect the welfare and well-being of every generation in relation to the planet. The integrity of the planet requires proper care of the life support systems of the planet, the ecological processes and the environmental conditions necessary for a healthy human environment.

We must then ask how a generation determines the nature of its responsibilities and obligations with respect to the natural system. In answering this question it is useful to borrow from John Rawls who describes a condition of veiled ignorance in which every generation exists somewhere in the spectrum of time, but does not know in advance where it will be located. Future generations would want to inherit the Earth in as good a condition as did their ancestors and with at least comparable access to its resources. This requires that each generation leave the planet in no worse condition than it received it, and to provide succeeding generations equitable access to its resources and benefits.

Intergenerational equity may appear to conflict with the goal of achieving intragenerational equity, meaning equity among those who are living today. Certainly, we must urgently devote resources to helping all people meet their basic human needs for food, potable water, and shelter. In many instances, however, the actions needed to achieve intragenerational equity are consistent with those advancing intergenerational equity. People living today have an intergenerational right of equitable access to use and benefit from the planet's resources, which is derived from the underlying equality among all generations in relation to use of the natural system. . . .

Some argue that rights can only exist when there are identifiable interests to protect, and that future generations, therefore, cannot have rights. This view requires that we identify individuals who have interests to protect. Since we cannot know who the individuals will be until they are born, nor how many will exist, those future generations cannot, according to this argument, have rights. . . . However, the rights of future generations are not individual rights. Rather, they are generational rights in which the interests protected do not depend upon knowing the kinds of individuals that may exist or the numbers in any given future generation. . . .

The question of how to implement intergenerational rights and obligations can be approached at two levels: broad strategies and specific actions. . . .

The most important strategy is to give representation to the interests of future generations in decision-making processes, including the market. The decisions we make today will determine the initial welfare of future generations, but they are not effectively represented in our decision-making processes. Future generations might be willing to compensate present generations to prevent certain actions or to have us undertake others if they had a way of voicing their preferences. This representation has to take place in several forms: in administrative decision-making, judicial decision-making, and most importantly, in the marketplace. . . .

. . . [I]mplementing our responsibilities to future generations will be difficult. Our institutions, at the international, national and local levels are designed to handle relatively short-term problems of several years. They are, for the most part, not well-suited to addressing long-range problems—particularly when their effects may not be felt for a generation or more. Powerful political incentives encourage people in power to focus on short-term issues, to show tangible results. Similarly, private businesses are sometimes forced by the workings of the market to take a relatively short-term view. But our responsibilities to future generations demand that we take a long-term perspective. This requires adjustments in institutions, economic incentives, legal instruments, public consciousness and political will. Sustainable development requires that we begin this process.

QUESTIONS

1.   How does int*er*generational equity differ from int*ra*-generational equity? Think of at least one example of a situation in which these two ideals can run into conflict in the making of energy policy.

2.   What are some of the practical obstacles to achieving intergenerational equity mentioned in the excerpt? What are some specific policy strategies that could help to overcome some of these obstacles in the context of energy law?

3.   In what sense is the lack of intergenerational equity in the global energy industry an *externality* problem?

4.   Identify at least one potential policy change that would encourage private market participants in the energy industry to more fully account for the rights of future generations.

5.   Using the concept of intergenerational equity, construct an argument in favor of a new subsidy for wind energy development to be funded through increased taxes on fossil fuel resources.

2.   ENVIRONMENTAL BENEFITS

In addition to its status as a renewable energy source, wind power is also a comparatively environmentally-friendly means of generating electricity. Wind energy development can benefit the natural environment by reducing the need for more environmentally-damaging forms of electricity generation.

Obviously, wind energy generation itself can adversely impact natural environments. The mining of precious metals for wind turbine components, the energy-intensive turbine manufacturing process, and the transportation of turbines from manufacturing facilities to wind farm sites can all potentially create environmental harms. As explored in Chapter 3, the installation and operation of wind turbines on project sites and the transmission systems and other infrastructure necessary to support them can also impose a wide and substantial array of costs on wildlife, neighbors, and others.

However, when compared to most other major electricity generation strategies, wind energy's adverse environmental effects are relatively small. Wind power generates very few emissions of carbon dioxide or other greenhouse gases. Wind is a *cool renewable*, meaning that can generate renewable electricity without any combustion process—an environmental advantage that not even biomass or biofuels can claim. Moreover, unlike coal-fired power plants, wind energy generation does not create emissions of sulfur dioxide, which are known to contribute to acid rain and its attendant harms to agricultural land, forests, watercourses, and other environmental assets. Wind energy also differs from coal-fired power in that it doesn't generate nitrogen oxide emissions that can contribute to smog, higher rates of respiratory illness, and other impacts. Wind energy generation likewise produces no airborne emissions of mercury or numerous other toxic pollutants that are sometimes associated with coal-fired power and are known to increase risks of brain damage, birth defects, or various other diseases. On net, these numerous benefits make wind energy projects comparatively environmentally-friendly so long as developers site projects away from critical wildlife habitats or other sensitive geographic areas.

3. LOW MARGINAL COST OF GENERATION

One other advantage of wind farms over coal-fired power plants and most other thermal generation facilities is that, once wind turbines are manufactured, installed and connected to the grid, they can produce electricity for decades without any added fuel. A power plant that runs on coal, natural gas or nuclear energy requires a steady supply of fuel to continue to generate power. The costs of extracting, processing, transporting, and storing those fuel supplies add substantially to a thermal generation facility's per-kWh cost of power generation throughout the plant's useful life. By contrast, the per-kWh or *marginal cost* of electricity production at wind farms is minimal and typically comprises little more than some very modest operation and maintenance costs. So long as operators periodically replace and upgrade the nacelles, rotors and certain other wind turbine components as they age over time, established turbine sites can continue to supply low-marginal-cost power indefinitely into the future.

B. LIMITATIONS OF WIND AS AN ENERGY RESOURCE

Despite its many positive characteristics, wind energy is certainly not a perfect source of energy. Indeed, certain downsides of wind energy have limited its usefulness for centuries and prevented it from becoming a major energy source. Pre-industrial windmills and sails powered by wind energy suffered from at least three primary limitations, which these materials call (i) fungibility constraints, (ii) intermittency constraints, and (iii) geographic constraints. Although recent technological advancements have partially addressed some aspects of these limitations on wind energy, others continue to constrain wind energy growth.

First, early wind energy strategies such as windmills and sails suffered from energy *fungibility* constraints. Pre-industrial wind energy devices could only leverage the wind's kinetic energy to assist in certain specific and limited types of work such as the pumping of water, grinding of grain, or transportation of sailboats. As ingenious and useful as they were, these inventions and devices were incapable of converting wind energy into heat or artificial light or into a type of energy capable of performing countless other types of work.

One of the most significant benefits of modern wind turbine technologies is their capacity to overcome the energy fungibility limitations that limited the usefulness of early wind-powered devices. Modern wind turbines convert the wind's kinetic energy into electric current—a highly fungible energy form. Countless contemporary devices use electricity, from lamps to phones to computers. Wind turbines' increasing ability to efficiently convert the wind's energy into electric power and thereby overcome energy fungibility limitations has been a key contributor to steady growth in the wind energy industry over the past few decades.

Unfortunately, technological advancements have thus far been less successful at addressing the two other major limitations on the utility of wind as an energy source. The first of these other two constraints is the inherently *intermittent* nature of wind resources, meaning that natural wind resources are available to generate electricity only some of the time. Wind turbines can generate power only when the wind is blowing, and the wind doesn't always blow. Stakeholders and policymakers within the energy industry use the term *intermittency* to describe this inability to control when wind energy resources are available or how productive those resources are at any given moment.

The other major limitation on wind as an energy source is the reality that usable wind resources are available only in certain geographic locations and cannot easily be transported elsewhere. Wind energy development tends to be uneconomical in places that do not experience windy conditions near the ground on a relatively frequent basis. Large utility-scale wind turbines typically have *cut-in speeds* of about 10 miles per hour, meaning that they can generate electricity only when and where winds of at least that speed are blowing into their rotors. See *Glossary*, Wind Energy Found., http://windenergyfoundation.org/about-wind-energy/glossary/. Obviously, some parts of the country experience sufficiently strong surface winds far less frequently than others.

The latter two limitations on wind energy just described— intermittency constraints and geographic constraints—continue to significantly hinder the expansion of wind energy technologies across the globe. The following materials more thoroughly examine each of these two limitations and describe several technological and policy innovations aimed at addressing them.

1. INTERMITTENCY

As stated above, wind energy devices can generate electric power only under windy conditions and, in most geographic areas, the presence and strength of wind varies significantly from day to day and hour to hour. Even in onshore areas that developers consider to be prime locations for wind energy development, wind speeds on any given date and time are usually too high or too low to enable commercial wind turbines to be fully productive. Ideally, developers could overcome this intermittency problem by installing energy storage facilities near wind farms to act as giant batteries and store excess power for use when wind resources are not available. Unfortunately, such energy storage facilities are not yet available at a commercially reasonable cost in most markets so wind energy alone usually cannot serve as the sole energy source for an electricity grid system.

The intermittency of wind resources limits the ability of wind farms to reliably supply controllable quantities of electricity to utilities and their customers. Electric generating facilities that run on coal, natural gas, or nuclear energy generate *dispatchable* power, meaning that operators can generally ramp up electricity production at these facilities in response to short-term spikes in demand. By contrast, wind resources are *non-dispatchable*, meaning that an operator of a wind farm cannot add fuel and thereby trigger a temporary increase in the wind farm's electricity production in whenever demand suddenly increases. The maximum amount of electricity production on a wind farm at any given time is driven almost exclusively by the quantity and quality of wind resources available on the site at that moment. That quantity and quantity of wind resources are relatively unpredictable: it is difficult to accurately forecast how much electricity a given wind farm will generate on a certain day or even a few hours into the future.

In regions with lots of wind farms, the intermittency and unpredictability of wind resources further complicate grid operators' already-arduous task of managing load fluctuations on the electric grid. As described in Chapter 1, customers' demand for electricity varies across seasons of the year, changing even from hour to hour. To deal with this variability in demand, grid operators issue *dispatch orders* throughout the day to generating plants, requesting that they increase or reduce electricity production in response to temporary demand changes. Integrating wind energy facilities into a grid system adds an additional layer of complexity to this already-difficult balancing act because the amount of electricity a wind farm supplies to the grid throughout the day or year is generally based not on dispatch orders but on the whims of Mother Nature.

Figure 2.1 illustrates this point. The darker shaded area near the bottom of the graph depicts the quantity of wind energy generated in the state of Texas over a one-week period in late 2015. The lighter shaded area directly above it shows the amount of electricity generated from sources other than wind farms on those days. As shown on the graph, the quantity of wind power generated varied dramatically from day to day and even from hour to hour throughout each day. Grid operators thus had to dispatch non-wind electricity sources at ever-changing quantities throughout the period to ensure that there was enough grid-wide electricity production to meet load demand.

Figure 2.1. Texas Electricity Generation, Dec. 17–23, 2015

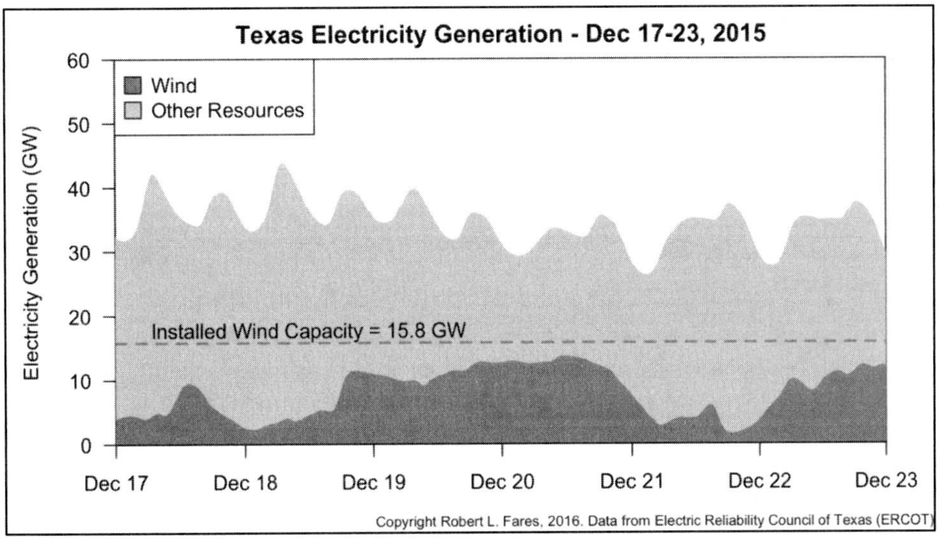

Source: Robert Fares, *Texas Sets New All-Time Wind Energy Record*, SCI. AM. (Jan. 14, 2016), https://blogs.scientificamerican.com/
plugged-in/texas-sets-new-all-time-wind-energy-record/

Not surprisingly, some geographic areas have more intermittent wind resources than others. The degree of intermittency of wind resources varies greatly from region to region and can also vary from location to location within a region. A wind farm site's geographic and topographical features tend to shape the degree of intermittency of its wind resources more than anything else. For example, wind resources tend to be less intermittent offshore, which is one significant advantage of offshore wind energy. In many regions wind resources are more productive at night, but in some other regions they are strongest during daylight hours.

The fact that wind resources are intermittent and controlled by Mother Nature also means that wind farms can sometimes generate *more* electricity than is presently needed. As described in Chapter 1, in much of the country aggregate electricity demand tends to be lowest during the late evening and early morning hours when most people are asleep. Grid systems connected to lots of wind farms can encounter unique difficulties during these times if it's windy outside but electricity demand on the grid is low. Unless utilities somehow increase their customers' appetite for electricity or reduce the quantity of power wind farms feed onto the grid during these periods, damaging grid "overload" problems can result.

Wind farms are more likely than fossil fuel-fired power plants to cause grid overload problems because of the extremely low marginal cost of producing wind energy. An operator of a coal- or gas-fired power plant incurs significant additional fuel costs each time it adds coal or gas to its boilers to ramp up electricity production. Such plant operators typically take these additional costs into account when determining how much electricity to generate at any given time. When short-term market prices for wholesale power (commonly known as *spot prices* in regions that have active wholesale electricity markets) are high because of a temporary spike in electricity demand, operators of power plants with excess generating capacity have incentives to add fuel and ramp up electricity production so they can sell more power at the elevated prices. When electricity supplies exceed the current demand, spot prices fall and thereby incentivize power plant operators to decrease electricity generation and conserve fuel supplies for some later time when prices have rebounded.

By contrast, the amount of electricity generated at a wind farm at any given time is often more a function of *weather* conditions than of *market* conditions. The up-front costs associated with wind energy generation— buying turbines, leasing a project site, and installing the turbines at the site—are significant, but once a wind farm is up and running the marginal cost of generating electricity at the site is nearly zero. The wind resources that fuel electricity production at wind farms are effectively inexhaustible and free of charge, so wind farms incur no significant incremental costs when they generate additional MWh of electricity. In fact, many wind farm operators earn tax credits for each additional unit of electricity they produce regardless of whether there is any market demand for that unit when it flows onto the grid. Consequently, even when spot prices for electricity are very low, wind farm operators often have incentives to keep generating power—a perverse incentive scenario that can contribute to grid overload challenges.

Although the intermittency of wind resources is unquestionably a major disadvantage of wind as an energy source, technological innovations are gradually emerging to address it. Governments and policymakers are also increasingly developing ways to manage wind's intermittency-related limitations so that utilities can integrate more wind resources into their energy mix without compromising the stability of grid systems. The following are brief descriptions of a few of these strategies.

a.   Combatting Intermittency Through Energy Storage

Increasing a grid system's energy storage capacity is one promising way of addressing challenges associated with the intermittency of wind energy resources. If an adequate amount of energy storage capacity were integrated into the electric grid, operators and customers could store excess wind-generated energy during periods of low electricity demand and then dispatch it later when the wind is not blowing or electricity demand spikes. Energy storage technologies are rapidly improving and could someday play a major role in overcoming wind energy's intermittency problems, but they also create their own unique policy challenges. Because of the great importance and scope of legal and policy issues related to energy storage, the topic it is covered separately in Chapter 7.

b.   Combatting Intermittency Through Imbalance Markets

Another means of addressing wind energy's intermittency-related constraints is to help a region's various power producers and utilities more easily buy and sell excess electricity among each other through interconnected grid systems. Many electric utilities have long engaged in some sharing of electricity across transmission systems to help balance loads. However, policymakers and industry stakeholders are increasingly developing systems and policies through which electricity generators, energy storage facilities, and utilities across large regions of the country can quickly and inexpensively purchase and sell electricity among each other based on changing daily conditions. Improving utilities' access to suppliers or demanders of electricity that are situated outside their own exclusive territories can help them more easily balance loads when intermittent renewable energy sources might otherwise cause electricity shortages or grid overloads.

A simple stylized example can help to illustrate how facilitating easier sharing of electricity across geographic regions could promote greater use of intermittent renewable energy resources. Suppose, for instance, that steady winds on a particular day are generating lots of electricity at wind farms of the Pacific Northwest—so much that the region has a large surplus of generated power. Meanwhile, suppose that on the same day thick cloud cover has reduced solar energy generation in portions of the desert Southwest, creating a temporary need in that region for additional electricity. Ideally, there would be a simple, low-cost way for electricity generators in the Northwest to sell and deliver their excess generated power to Southwest utilities to correct this temporary imbalance between electricity supply and demand.

By enabling diverse groups of utilities that collectively cover large geographic areas to buy and sell wholesale electric power in real time, innovative markets in some regions are already enabling intermittent renewable energy resources to play ever greater roles. *Energy imbalance markets* (EIMs) are nimble, partially-automated marketplaces for short-term, inter-utility transactions for the purchase and sale of wholesale electricity within an interconnected grid system. Electricity bought and sold through EIM transactions is swiftly dispatched to buyers via the grid's transmission infrastructure. As they become increasingly common, EIMs are helping more and more utilities to better balance the daily load fluctuations resulting from weather changes and other localized factors.

In the western United States, a recently-formed EIM is rapidly expanding and helping to facilitate the integration of intermittent renewables into the electricity grid. The California Independent System Operator (CAISO) launched the western EIM in 2014 and is its *market operator*, coordinating and facilitating transactions among the EIM's growing collection of member utilities spread across seven western states. Figure 2.2 shows the territorial boundaries of the many utilities participating or planning to participate in CAISO's western EIM. Pursuant to terms set forth in detailed contracts with each participating utility, electricity is bought and sold every 15 minutes and dispatched every five minutes through the EIM's sophisticated automated system. *See Market Processes and Products*, CAL. ISO, https://www.caiso.com/market/Pages/MarketProcesses.aspx.

Figure 2.2. Western Energy Imbalance Market

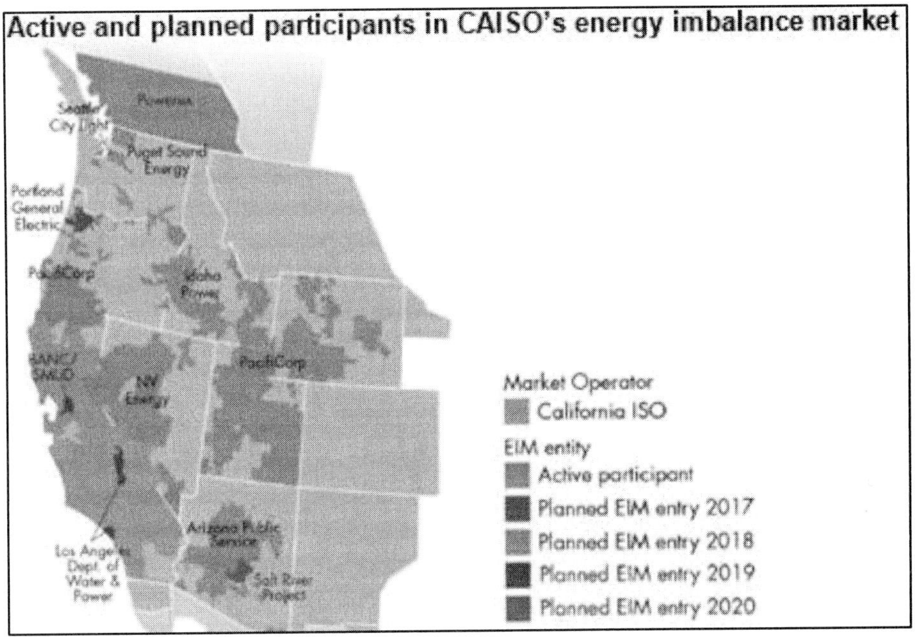

Source: US Energy Information Administration

EIMs are known simply as "balancing markets" in Europe and have been functioning throughout portions of that continent for several years. The following excerpt describes how Germany's balancing markets are facilitating the integration of wind energy and other intermittent energy sources in that country.

A TALE OF THREE MARKETS: COMPARING THE RENEWABLE ENERGY EXPERIENCES OF CALIFORNIA, TEXAS, AND GERMANY

Felix Mormann, Dan Reicher & Victor Hanna
35 STAN. ENVTL. L.J. 55, 87–90 (2016)

Critics of the large-scale build-out of solar and wind power in Germany and elsewhere often claim that the intermittent output profiles of these renewable resources jeopardize the stability and reliability of the electrical grid. . . . A look at Germany's . . . numbers casts serious doubt on such warnings.

From 2006 to 2013, Germany tripled the amount of electricity generated from solar and wind to a joint market share of 26%, while managing to *reduce* average annual outage times in its grid from an already impressive 22 minutes to just 15 minutes. California, too, actually managed to lower average annual outage times in its grid between 2006 and 2013 from over 100 minutes to under 90 minutes, while more than tripling the amount of electricity produced from solar PV and onshore wind to a joint market share of 8%. . . . Several recent studies confirm our observation that greater penetration of intermittent renewables may require greater grid management efforts but need not come at the expense of grid stability. . . .

Germany's impressive grid stability statistics should not be misconstrued as a sign that an electrical grid with a significant share of renewable energy is easy to operate. Indeed, Tennet TSO, Germany's second-largest grid operator, reports a near fivefold increase in its requests to plant operators to adjust their output to maintain grid stability from 209 requests in 2010 to 1,009 requests in 2013. Analysts have long acknowledged the need for fast-ramping, easy-to-dispatch power to keep the grid in balance when power production from solar, wind, and other non-dispatchable, intermittent renewable generation suddenly drops off. We here use the term "intermittency" to refer to output fluctuations both as the result of cloud coverage, wind lulls, or similar short-term meteorological conditions. . . .

. . . Germany has relied on its electricity markets to help balance the intermittent output of the country's growing fleet of solar and wind power generators. As the share of intermittent renewables continues to increase, Germany's balancing market has become ever more important, to the point where generators today can earn well over $15,000 for providing a single MW of fast-ramping balancing capacity for one hour in the weekly balancing market auctions. With the balancing market several orders of magnitude more lucrative than the wholesale electricity market, many have sought to enter or increase their presence, including Germany's incumbent utilities and, remarkably, some renewable energy entrepreneurs. Perhaps the most notable, Next Kraftwerke, has combined 570 MW of solar, wind, hydro, and biomass-powered cogeneration capacity to create a virtual power plant that bids, among others, over 170 MW of fast-ramping, partly instantaneous backup capacity into the German balancing market. In the same vein, incumbent utilities have begun to retrofit their coal-fired power plants to allow for faster ramping in response to load changes. Entrepreneurial innovation and greater competition among suppliers offer an explanation as to why the aggregate cost of Germany's grid management measures has gone down by 25% from 2009 to 2012—despite the dramatic increase in balancing interventions from grid operators. Germany's innovative and cost-effective grid management practices have helped maintain the country's high standards of grid stability—exceeding that of California or Texas—while integrating ever-higher shares of intermittent renewables.

NOTES & QUESTIONS

1. *EIM Expansion in the Western United States.* Early studies of the western EIM suggest that it is already producing substantial financial and environmental benefits in the western United States. In mid-2016, CAISO released a study suggesting that the western EIM had generated $23.6 million in benefits for the region in the second quarter of 2016 alone while facilitating the integration of ever-increasing quantities of renewable energy sources. Additional expansion of the western EIM to include major utilities in Arizona and the Pacific Northwest seems poised further increase these benefits in the coming years. *See* News Release, California ISO, *EIM Continues to Save Millions While Reducing Carbon Emissions* (July 28, 2016), http://www.caiso. com/Documents/EIMContinuesToSaveMillionsWhileReducingCarbonEmissions. pdf.

2. *Negative Electricity Prices?* Although an extremely low marginal cost of production is one of the most appealing attributes of wind energy, that characteristic can sometimes create unique challenges in wholesale power markets—especially in regions that rely heavily on nuclear power. Nuclear power plants can be valuable electricity generation sources, but they are also relatively expensive to shut off and start up again. Operators of nuclear plants typically avoid those expenses by keeping the plants running and generating some minimum amount of power around the clock, seven days a week. Historically, there was sufficient electricity demand on the grid to support this practice. Even when electricity demand hit its lowest point, nuclear plant operators were still able find someone to buy their minimum base load power for a positive price. However, the proliferation of wind farms in the region is beginning to change that because wind farms produce power at zero marginal cost and often earn valuable tax credits for reach kWh produced even when no one wants to buy it.

When the total quantity of electricity demanded in an interconnected grid system is so low that no buyers are willing to pay anything for an additional kWh of power, spot prices for electricity on wholesale markets can go negative. When this happens, some nuclear power plant operators essentially *pay* others to take their excess generated power off the grid to avoid the costs of temporarily shutting down production. *See, e.g.,* Julie Wernau, *Exelon Chief: Wind-Power Subsidies Could Threaten Nuclear Plants,* CHIC. TRIBUNE (Feb. 8, 2013), http://articles.chicagotribune.com/2013-02-08/business/ct-biz-0208-exelon-div--20130208_1_exelon-nuclear-plants-power-plants; Pilita Clark, *UK Power Prices Go Negative As Renewables Boom Distorts Market,* FINANCIAL TIMES (May 20, 2016), http://www.ft.com/cms/s/0/5164675e-1e7e-11e6-b286-cd dde55ca122.html#axzz4Da3wJgS9.

3. What policies have California regulators introduced to help address intermittency challenges associated with renewable energy generation in that state? What are some potential advantages and disadvantages of that approach?

4.   How are Germany's "balancing markets" driving innovations aimed at addressing intermittency challenges in that country?

5.   Which approach—California's or Germany's—do you think is most promising as a primary, long-term strategy for helping to smooth out electricity supplies, and why?

c.   Combatting Intermittency Through Curtailment Programs

Another policy strategy aimed at managing the adverse impacts of wind's intermittency is that of prohibiting or discouraging wind farms from feeding power onto the grid during periods when demand for that power is extremely low. *Curtailment* is a generating facility's intentional dispatch of a quantity of electricity that is *less* than the maximum amount it could readily produce. Grid operators issue *curtailment orders* when they anticipate that excessive supplies of power on the grid could otherwise cause congestion or overload problems.

Curtailment practices at power plants that run on coal, gas, or nuclear fuel are usually justifiable to both the plant and society because they conserve fuel for use at later periods of higher electricity demand. If these plants did not curtail electricity production during such times, they would waste money and scarce resources by using up valuable fuel even when the electricity it generates isn't needed. Accordingly, thermal generation facilities routinely and voluntarily comply with curtailment orders by temporarily decreasing their generation of electric power.

By contrast, curtailing production at a wind or solar energy facility is far less beneficial to facility owners or to society. Temporarily curbing production at a wind farm or solar generating facility affords no fuel cost savings and squanders an opportunity to generate energy from a clean, zero-marginal-cost resource. Assuming that wind or solar energy producers are not compensated for complying with curtailment orders, the adverse financial impacts of the curtailment are also generally greater for them than for thermal generation plants. A 2014 National Renewable Energy Laboratory study on curtailment practices aptly explains why curtailments are particularly damaging to the profitability of wind and solar energy projects:

> Dispatch below maximum output (curtailment) can be more of an issue for wind and solar generators than it is for fossil generation units because of differences in their cost structures. The economics of wind and solar generation depend on the ability to generate electricity whenever there is sufficient sunlight or wind to power their facilities. Because wind and solar generators have substantial capital costs but no fuel costs (i.e., minimal variable costs), maximizing output improves their ability to recover capital costs. In contrast, fossil generators have higher variable costs,

such as fuel costs. Avoiding these costs can, depending on the economics of a specific generator, to some degree reduce the financial impact of curtailment, especially if the generator's capital costs are included in a utility's rate base.

LORI BIRD ET AL., WIND AND SOLAR ENERGY CURTAILMENT: EXPERIENCE AND PRACTICES IN THE UNITED STATES 2 (2014), http://www.nrel.gov/docs/fy14osti/60983.pdf.

If wind energy curtailments reduce wind farms' revenues and impose broader societal costs, why do such practices exist? Sometimes, government officials impose curtailment orders on wind farms to protect wildlife or the general public from temporary hazards. For instance, as described later in this Chapter, some curtailment orders seek to prevent harms to bats or migratory birds during certain times when protected species are known or expected to be flying near a wind farm. However, the most common reason for a curtailment order at a wind farm is to limit grid congestion and prevent grid overloads. As the following case illustrates, uncompensated curtailment orders not only reduce the profitability of wind farms; they can also make it difficult for wind farm operators to fulfill their contractual obligations to supply power to utilities or other off-takers.

FPL ENERGY, LLC V. TXU PORTFOLIO MANAGEMENT CO., L.P.

Supreme Court of Texas, 2014
426 S.W.3d 59

GREEN, J.

In this contract interpretation case, TXU Portfolio Management Company, L.P. (TXUPM) contracted to receive electricity and renewable energy credits (RECs) from wind farms owned by FPL Energy, LLC. FPL failed to provide the required electricity and RECs. TXUPM sued FPL for breach of contract; FPL counterclaimed, arguing TXUPM failed to provide FPL with sufficient transmission capacity. The trial court. . . . issued a declaratory judgment that the contracts required TXUPM to provide transmission capacity. . . . Both parties appealed. The court of appeals reversed. . . .

. . . We affirm the court of appeals' holding that TXUPM owed no contractual duty to provide transmission capacity. . . . Accordingly, we reverse the court of appeals' judgment in part and remand to the court of appeals to determine damages.

I.   Factual and Procedural Background

In Texas, the electric industry consists of three main components: power generation, power transmission, and power distribution. Electric producers own and operate generating facilities. The Electric Reliability

Council of Texas, Inc. (ERCOT), with few exceptions, manages the transmission of electricity through an interconnected network—or grid—of transmission lines. Finally, retail electric providers distribute electricity directly to consumers.

In 1999, the Legislature created ambitious goals for renewable energy in Texas. . . . The Legislature charged the Public Utility Commission of Texas (PUC) with establishing minimum renewable energy production requirements for all Texas electric providers. . . . The Legislature also tasked the PUC with establishing a REC trading program. . . . A REC reflects one megawatt hour (MWh) "of renewable energy that is physically metered and verified in Texas." 16 Tex. Admin. Code § 25.173(c)(13). Electric producers thus simultaneously create both electricity from renewable sources and the corresponding RECs. . . .

TXU Electric, a retail electric provider (and a different entity than TXUPM), solicited proposals from renewable energy producers to meet the new renewable energy production requirements. In 2000, TXU Electric entered agreements with two wind farm subsidiaries of FPL: Pecos Wind I, L.P. and Pecos Wind II, L.P. Also in 2000, FPL acquired a third party's rights to a similar contract with TXU Electric for Indian Mesa Wind Farm, L.P. Under the contracts, FPL sells TXU Electric RECs and the renewable electric energy used to produce those credits. TXU Electric assigned the contracts to TXUPM. . . .

For approximately four years, FPL failed to produce the agreed upon electricity and RECs. TXUPM filed suit seeking damages for FPL's breach of the contracts. FPL counterclaimed, arguing that it could not meet its obligations because of congestion on the ERCOT grid. When the grid lacks capacity to transmit all energy produced in an area, ERCOT issues curtailment orders instructing certain facilities to cease production. FPL claims it received curtailment orders from ERCOT which, along with an unexpected lack of wind in the area, caused it to produce less energy than promised. FPL blamed the congestion and resulting curtailment orders on TXUPM, insisting that TXUPM bore responsibility to ensure transmission capacity for all energy FPL could produce.

Both parties filed motions for partial summary judgment. . . . [T]he court declared that the contracts unambiguously required TXUPM to provide all transmission services, including transmission capacity, to FPL.

. . . .

The court of appeals. . . . held that the contracts did not require TXUPM to provide the necessary transmission capacity. . . . We granted FPL's petition for review.

. . . .

We first consider whether the contracts require TXUPM to provide adequate transmission capacity to FPL. . . .

Section 2.03(a) of the contracts, entitled "Transmission," reads as follows:

> TXU Electric shall provide, by purchasing or arranging for, all services, including without limitation Transmission Services, Ancillary Services, any control area services, line losses except for line losses on [FPL's] side of the Delivery Point, and transaction fees, necessary to deliver Net Energy to TXU Electric's load from the Renewable Resource Facility throughout the Contract Term ("Required Transmission Services").

Section 1.02(a) of the contracts defines "Net Energy" as "the amount of electric energy in MWh produced by the Renewable Resource Facility *and delivered to the Connecting Entity*." (emphasis added). Under section 2.02, a Connecting Entity owns any "transmission or distribution system with which the Renewable Resource Facility is interconnected." The Connecting Entity serves as the "Delivery Point."

FPL urges a broad view of TXUPM's responsibility for transmission services. FPL contends that TXUPM's obligation to provide transmission services "without limitation" encompasses the capacity to deliver electricity from the Renewable Resource Facility (i.e. FPL) to the load (i.e. TXUPM's customer base). In support, FPL argues that Net Energy can refer only to a quantity and has no bearing on how and when delivery occurs. FPL further argues that the more specific language, "from the Renewable Resource Facility," should trump Net Energy, which is defined elsewhere in the contracts. *See Forbau v. Aetna Life Ins. Co.*, 876 S.W.2d 132, 133–34 (Tex. 1994) (stating the rule that, in contract interpretation, a more specific provision will control over a general statement). FPL points to congestion beyond the Delivery Point, explaining that as electricity is generated and delivered virtually simultaneously, it cannot stop and wait at the Delivery Point for congestion to clear. In a compelling visual, FPL suggests that the transmission towers might burn down if FPL generated and sent electricity without an available, guaranteed path to the consumer. FPL complains that TXUPM caused the grid congestion and thus prompted the resulting curtailment orders.[1]

---

[1]   The record shows that FPL earlier claimed that TXUPM: (1) prioritized its own fossil fuel-derived energy; (2) knowingly overstated to ERCOT its intention to transmit fossil fuel energy, resulting in curtailment orders for wind-produced energy; and (3) exercised its authority as a "Qualified Scheduling Entity," whose responsibility is to report anticipated electricity generation to ERCOT, to influence ERCOT's schedule for energy transmission on the grid. FPL's briefs, however, do not pursue these arguments. FPL petitioned this Court to review the meaning of the contracts as to TXUPM's obligations to provide transmission services, not TXUPM's alleged role in creating congestion. Thus, we will not consider these arguments. See Guitar Holding Co., L.P. v. Hudspeth Cnty. Underground Water Conservation Dist. No. 1, 263 S.W.3d 910, 918 (Tex. 2008) (holding issues waived if not presented in the petition for review or in the briefs).

TXUPM interprets the contracts as placing the risk of transmission system incapacity on FPL. TXUPM notes that the contracts identify "lack of transmission capacity" as an "Uncontrollable Force" outside the reasonable control of the parties. If capacity is beyond the control of the parties, TXUPM questions, how then can TXUPM bear responsibility for failure to provide capacity? Section 4.05 of the contracts reinforces this point by making clear that FPL must pay liquidated damages for failure to supply RECs even if the failure was the result of inadequate transmission capacity. Finally, TXUPM argues that the contracts' definition of Net Energy binds this Court; incorporating Net Energy, as defined, into section 2.03 means that TXUPM owes a duty to provide transmission services only after the Delivery Point. Under TXUPM's interpretation, if FPL could not deliver electricity because of congestion, FPL bore the risk and, thus, must bear the consequences. We agree with TXUPM's interpretation.

We begin by recognizing the apparent textual conflict. Read in isolation, section 2.03 contains language supportive of either a broad or narrow interpretation of TXUPM's transmission service responsibilities. "[F]rom the Renewable Resource Facility" implies that TXUPM would have to secure transmission capacity so FPL could deliver electricity. But the use of the term Net Energy, which exists only upon FPL's delivery to the Connecting Entity, suggests that TXUPM bears responsibility only if the grid possesses capacity for TXUPM to deliver any generated electricity.

We cannot interpret a contract to ignore clearly defined terms, *see Frost Nat'l Bank*, 165 S.W.3d at 313, and, thus, we must accord Net Energy its due meaning. The contracts assigned TXUPM responsibility only for transmission services required to deliver Net Energy, and Net Energy represents the amount of energy produced by FPL and delivered to the Connecting Entity. TXUPM's responsibility for transmissions services, then, begins once FPL-generated electricity reaches the Connecting Entity on the grid—the Delivery Point. The contracts' use of the phrase "from the Renewable Resource Facility" is simply a designation of where the energy originated. It does not alter the definition of Net Energy provided in section 1.02 or in other sections throughout the contracts.

The placement of section 2.03 in the context of all interconnection requirements reinforces this conclusion. Section 2.02 requires FPL to "make all arrangements . . . necessary to interconnect . . . with a transmission or distribution system," i.e. the Connecting Entity. . . . The contracts obligate FPL to secure interconnection with a Connecting Entity, or transmission service provider, which under the PUC rules cannot be TXUPM. . . . Reading sections 2.02 and 2.03 together, FPL must make all interconnection arrangements so that electricity can reach the Delivery Point, and TXUPM must ensure that facilities exist beyond the Delivery Point to allow for delivery to consumers. These provisions do not speak to the situation here, where both parties claim to meet their responsibilities but congestion on the grid inhibits energy generation and delivery.

Given these facts, then, we must consider which party is responsible for congestion beyond the Delivery Point. While FPL blames grid congestion on TXUPM, we believe the contracts recognize such congestion as beyond both parties' control. Section 6.02(a) of the contracts addresses "Uncontrollable Force," including "[e]vents or circumstances that are outside of a Party's reasonable control," which "may include . . . lack of transmission capacity or availability." The contracts mention transmission capacity only in this section. Congestion and curtailment issues, which affect transmission capacity and availability, must fall within this provision. Section 6.02(b) goes on to excuse a party from performance in the event of an Uncontrollable Force if certain criteria are met; there is no dispute that FPL did not meet those criteria.

Section 4.05, entitled "Effect of Outages and Uncontrollable Force," outlines the general rule that payment and other calculations in sections 4.01–.10 are not impacted by Uncontrollable Force. . . . In essence, the contracts allocate the risk of curtailment and congestion to FPL by clearly establishing that such events affect contract obligations only in certain instances not found here. We must respect and enforce this assignment of risk. See Gym-N-I Playgrounds, Inc. v. Snider, 220 S.W.3d 905, 912 (Tex. 2007) ("Freedom of contract allows parties to bargain for mutually agreeable terms and allocate risks as they see fit.").

To summarize, the contracts obligate FPL to interconnect with a Connecting Entity, which cannot be TXUPM. TXUPM bears responsibility for providing transmission services from the Delivery Point at the Connecting Entity. To the extent that lack of transmission capacity impairs electricity generation at the wind farms, the contracts provide that such lack of capacity is an Uncontrollable Force and FPL, therefore, bears the risk. . . .

Here, ERCOT issued curtailment orders, effectively constraining energy generation, rather than energy transmission. FPL was therefore prevented from generating electricity and meeting its contractual obligations. Although ERCOT made final curtailment decisions, that does not mean that neither party bore the risk in the event of congestion and curtailment.

We hold that the contracts did not require TXUPM to provide transmission capacity for FPL but rather allocated risk of inadequate transmission capacity to FPL. . . .

. . . [T]hus TXUPM did not breach the contracts.

NOTES & QUESTIONS

1. *Constraint Payments.* Most wind farm operators receive no compensation when grid operators or others compel them to temporarily reduce electricity production under curtailment orders. However, wind farms in some parts of the world do receive payments for curtailments. For example, wind energy producers in the United Kingdom have received payments from that country's system operator, National Grid, for curbing their electricity generation. These payments, known as *constraint payments* within the National Grid interconnection system, drew significant media attention in 2015 and 2016 when the payments reached unprecedented levels. *See, e.g.,* Jillian Ambrose, *Windfarms Paid Double the Market Price To Cut Power,* TELEGRAPH (Jan. 26, 2016), http://www.telegraph.co.uk/finance/newsbysector/utilities/12122543/Windfarms-paid-double-the-market-price-to-cut-power.html; Iain Ramage, *Highland Windfarm Operators Have Received £52million . . . For Switching Turbines Off,* PRESS & J. (May 5, 2016), https://www.pressandjournal.co.uk/fp/news/highlands/909874/undefined-headline-840/.

Some might wonder: why would any grid system operator pay energy producers to refrain from generating electricity? The answer to this question highlights the practical challenges associated with integrating intermittent renewable resources such as wind energy into existing grid systems. The United Kingdom's National Grid has sometimes made constraint payments to wind farms because of the structure of that country's load balancing market, the Balancing Mechanism (BM). During periods of excess electricity supply within the BM, power producers sometimes bid for rights to temporarily reduce the amount of electricity they supply to the grid to below previously-contracted levels. Thermal generating plants usually make *positive* bids for this privilege and pay National Grid for it because it allows them to conserve valuable fuel resources for later use.

In contrast, wind farm operators in the National Grid system conserve no fuel when they curtail generation, and curtailments force them to forfeit earning valuable renewable energy "certificates". Consequently, most wind farms within the system are only willing to temporarily shut turbines down and curtail their generation if they are paid to so. They make *negative* bids, offering to curb their electricity production only if they are compensated enough to make up for their loss of certificates. As offshore wind energy projects have proliferated off the coasts of Scotland in recent years, transmission line bottlenecks have made it increasingly difficult to deliver these projects' excess generated power to England, causing constraint payments in the region to steadily rise.

Recently, National Grid began addressing this issue by offering financial incentives to retail customers to shift their electricity use to times when there are excess electricity supplies. *See* Emily Godsen, *Balancing Demand 'Could Cost National Grid £2bn',* TELEGRAPH (June 27, 2016), http://www.telegraph.co.uk/business/2016/06/26/balancing-demand-could-cost-national-grid-2bn/.

Such demand-side approaches to addressing intermittency problems are explored in more detail in Chapter 7 and Subsection d. below.

2. *Wind Farm Curtailments to Protect Fish in Hydropower Facilities.* The Pacific Northwest is another region of the country where contentious disputes over wind farm curtailment orders have surfaced in the last decade. Historically, the Bonneville Power Administration (Bonneville) has sought to operate its several large hydropower facilities in the region in ways that mitigate harms to wild salmon species, as required under federal law. The rapid expansion of wind energy development in the Northwest has complicated those practices by increasing the use of transmission infrastructure in the region and thereby making it more difficult for Bonneville to release water hydroelectric through dams at certain times to avoid harms to fish populations. Language from a 2011 FERC order addressing this issue summarized it as follows:

> According to Bonneville, during high water periods (e.g., spring run-off during some years) Bonneville has two options: spill the excess water through the dam spillways, or run the excess water through the hydro facilities resulting in an over-generation of electricity. Because additional spill can result in an increase of total dissolved gas levels in the water, endangering salmon in potential violation of its Clean Water Act and Endangered Species Act obligations, Bonneville states that it must run the excess water through its hydro facilities, thereby increasing electricity production. Thus, Bonneville developed and implemented the Environmental Redispatch Policy to minimize spills by running excess water through its hydro facilities thereby increasing generation levels in Bonneville's Balancing Authority Area to amounts that exceed its load and export amounts. In order to ensure that its Balancing Authority Area does not face reliability problems associated with over-generation, Bonneville issues dispatch orders to curtail generation and substitutes energy from the hydro system to serve load.

> Under the Environmental Redispatch Policy, Bonneville initially redispatches thermal generators to the lowest generating level possible without threatening reliability. If Bonneville determines that additional generation relief is needed, it redispatches variable energy resources, such as wind, on a pro rata basis, and this redispatch may result in such generators being moved completely off-line. Bonneville will not pay negative prices during environmental redispatch because it has determined that paying negative prices: (1) could result in opportunities to distort the market; and (2) presents an unreasonable cost shift from those generators that can operate profitably during times of negative prices (e.g., the Petitioners) to Bonneville's fish and wildlife program and to Bonneville's power service ratepayers. In addition, Bonneville determined that payment of negative prices in order to assure the value of a wind generator's

Federal Production Tax Credits (PTCs) and/or Renewable Energy Credits (RECs) would impose an additional and unnecessary burden on Bonneville's fish and wildlife costs, as well as compromise Bonneville's cost recovery objectives and its need to maintain an economical power supply.

Iberdrola Renewables, Inc. PacifiCorp NextEra Energy Resources, LLC Invenergy Wind North America & LLC Horizon Wind Energy LLC v. Bonneville Power Administration, 137 FERC P 61185 (2011).

FERC ultimately ordered Bonneville to revise its Environmental Redispatch Policy to eliminate this practice. *See id.* However, there continues to be significant tension over curtailment orders between wind farm operators and existing hydropower projects in the Pacific Northwest. *See, e.g.*, Rob Chaney, *Snowpack Surplus Roils Northwest Power Market*, MISSOULIAN (Apr. 7, 2017), http://missoulian.com/news/state-and-regional/snowpack-surpl us-roils-northwest-power-market/article_577409a3-ed27-5ecc-8d03-4fee031b0 6b0.html.

3. *Expanding Transmission Infrastructure to Reduce Curtailments.* Within just a few years after *FPL Energy*, ERCOT managed to reduce curtailments within its interconnection to nearly zero by strategically adding new capacity to its transmission system. ERCOT identified "Competitive Renewable Energy Zones" where transmission was most needed and then gave priority to those zones when siting new transmission lines. This strategy appears to have yielded impressive results: curtailments dropped from 17% of all wind energy generation in 2009 to just 0.5% by 2014. *See* RYAN WISER ET AL., 2014 WIND TECHNOLOGIES MARKET REPORT 38 (2015), http://www.energy. gov/sites/prod/files/2015/08/f25/2014-Wind-Technologies-Market-Report-8.7. pdf.

4. How did ERCOT's curtailment orders impact FPL's ability to fulfill its obligations under its contracts with TXUPM to supply wind-generated power and renewable energy credits?

5. According to the court, which party bore the risk that ERCOT might issue curtailment orders that prevent FPL from meeting all its obligations to supply power—FPL or TXUPM?

6. According to FPL, how did TXUPM allegedly create excess congestion in the relevant area of the grid and thereby create the need for ERCOT's curtailment orders?

7. If you were representing a wind farm in a power purchase agreement, how might this case influence how you negotiated and drafted the provisions related to your client's contractual obligation to deliver some specified minimum quantity of power each contract period?

d. Combatting Intermittency Through Demand-Side Management

As mentioned above, one other set of strategies for dealing with the intermittency of wind resources is retail pricing schemes, which encourage retail electricity customers to shift some of their electricity consumption to times of the day or week when wind-generated power is abundant on the grid and load demand is relatively low. More and more utilities are integrating various forms of these *load-shifting* or *demand-side management* pricing schemes into their overall rate structures, and the intermittent nature of renewables is one factor driving this trend. Persuading customers to shift some of their electricity consumption to times when wind farms are generating excess supplies of power can help utilities flatten their load demand and thereby avoid building expensive new *peaker* plants or paying elevated wholesale prices for peak power. Because demand-side management—like energy storage—is an increasingly popular and important strategy for addressing the intermittency-related challenges of both wind energy and solar energy, coverage of this topic is separately addressed in more depth in Chapter 7.

2. LOCATIONAL CONSTRAINTS

In addition to being only intermittently available, wind resources also suffer from locational constraints that continue to limit their use as an energy source. Unlike fossil fuels, which companies routinely ship by rail or pipeline across great distances to centralized power plants, wind currents cannot be transported for use at a more convenient place and time. Wind turbines can convert the wind's kinetic energy into electric power only when and *where* the wind blows. These geographic limitations on the use of wind resources and the fact that wind resource quality varies dramatically from region to region and even from place to place within regions makes wind power one of the most location-constrained energy strategies.

Dramatic variability in the strength and frequency of wind currents across regions of the country has greatly impacted wind energy development patterns and the evolution of federal, state, and local wind energy policy. As highlighted earlier in this chapter, a wind turbine can generate electricity only when the wind at its hub height (i.e., the center of its rotor) is blowing at the turbine's cut-in speed or greater. Likewise, the amount of electricity that a given turbine generates over the course of a day or year depends heavily on the frequency and strength of winds at the turbine site. Consequently, wind resource quality is among the most important factors that developers must consider when deciding where to site wind energy projects.

Figure 2.3 depicts the differences in wind resource quality across regions of the United States. Areas shaded the darkest on the map have the strongest wind resources. It is evident from a quick glance at the map that much of the nation's strongest onshore wind resources are concentrated in the Midwestern states—from Texas in the south to the Dakotas and Minnesota in the north. Although it is less obvious on the map, localized portions of California and the Pacific Northwest also have excellent wind resources.

Figure 2.3. United States Wind Resources Map

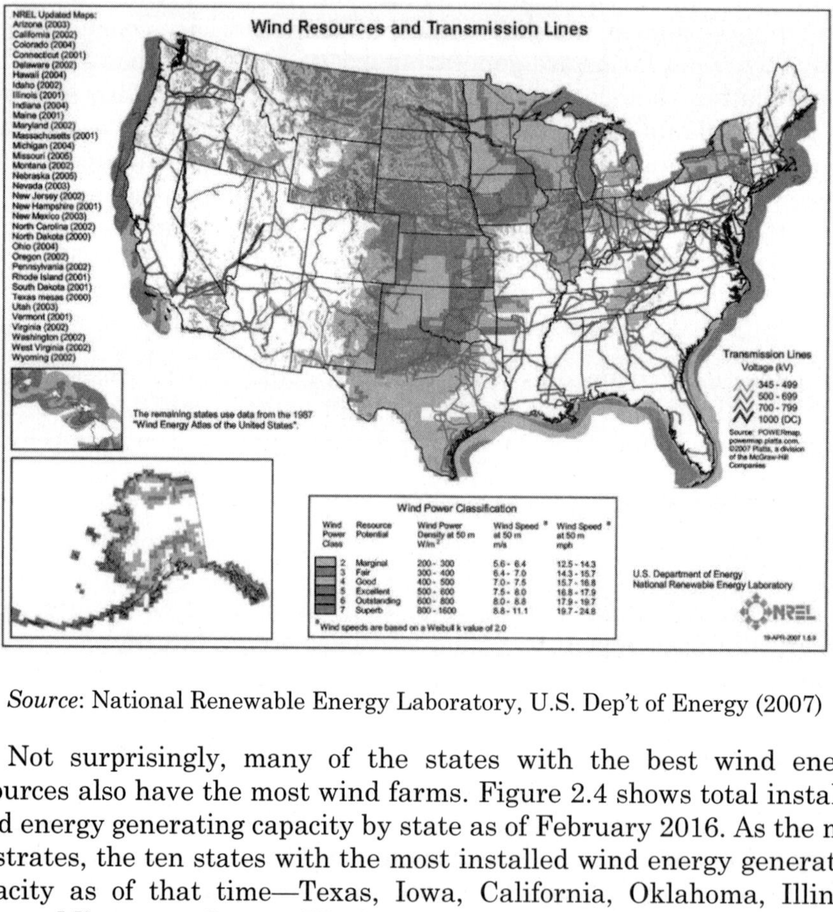

Source: National Renewable Energy Laboratory, U.S. Dep't of Energy (2007)

Not surprisingly, many of the states with the best wind energy resources also have the most wind farms. Figure 2.4 shows total installed wind energy generating capacity by state as of February 2016. As the map illustrates, the ten states with the most installed wind energy generating capacity as of that time—Texas, Iowa, California, Oklahoma, Illinois, Kansas, Minnesota, Oregon, Washington, and Colorado—all have excellent wind resources as well. On the other hand, some other states—such as South Dakota, Montana, Wisconsin, and Nebraska—have strong wind resources but comparatively few wind farms. This suggests that many of the nation's best wind resources remain untapped.

Figure 2.4. Map Showing Installed Wind Energy Generating Capacity by State

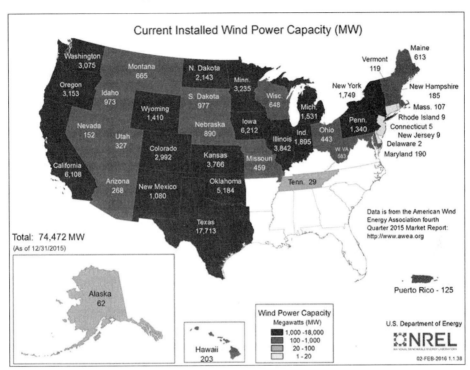

Source: National Renewable Energy Laboratory, U.S. Dep't of Energy (2016)

Why hasn't wind energy development been occurring as much in some Midwestern states that appear to have superior wind resources? One likely reason, which is covered in more detail later in this Chapter, is that state-level policies in these jurisdictions do not incentivize wind energy development as aggressively as those of other states. Another contributing factor is that many of these Midwestern states have relatively low populations and a comparatively low demand for additional supplies of electric power. Additional transmission infrastructure would thus be needed to transport wind-generated power from new wind farms in those low-population states to metropolitan areas in other states where utilities are willing to pay premium prices for renewable electricity.

a. Overcoming Locational Constraints Through Transmission

One potential means of addressing the geographic mismatch between the nation's largest cities and its windiest areas would be to greatly expand the country's interstate transmission systems with wind energy development in mind. As described in Chapter 1, the country's transmission infrastructure was originally designed to serve an electricity industry built around centralized thermal generation plants that were often conveniently located near the edge of urban centers. Consequently, relatively few high-voltage transmission lines run through the windy rural areas of the country's midsection where onshore wind resources are particularly strong.

i. *Jurisdictional Obstacles to Transmission Development*

Unfortunately, the antiquated regulatory structure governing interstate transmission development in the United States has become a major obstacle to the build-out of the nation's transmission infrastructure for wind energy. Building interstate transmission lines to connect windy rural areas with major population centers in other states requires hundreds of miles of easements and dozens of governmental permits. If government officials in a state through which a proposed interstate transmission line would run determine that construction of the line would not be in their state's best interest, should those officials have power to stop the interstate project? As beneficial as preserving state rights may be, giving each state government its own independent veto power over the siting of an interstate transmission line can make siting such infrastructure much more difficult. On the other hand, if states lacked veto authority over interstate transmission projects, what rules would govern disagreements among states about the siting of these important lines to ensure that one state is not treated unfairly?

States and the federal government have struggled to effectively coordinate interstate transmission line siting for nearly a century, and that struggle continues today as wind energy technologies increasingly call for expansions and upgrades to the country's aging electric transmission grids. In the excerpt that follows, Professor Alexandra Klass summarizes the history and basic shape of the nation's electricity transmission infrastructure and describes how it is complicating modern wind energy development.

THE ELECTRIC GRID AT A CROSSROADS: A REGIONAL APPROACH TO SITING TRANSMISSION LINES

Alexandra B. Klass
48 U.C. DAVIS L. REV. 1895, 1913–18, 1924–28 (2015)

By the late 1920s, the sixteen largest electric power private holding companies, which often owned a number of electric utilities in various jurisdictions, controlled more than 75% of all U.S. generation. States' [Public Utility Commissions ("PUCs")] began to regulate utility rates in exchange for grants to utilities of exclusive service territories. In this way, states, generally with the support of the utilities they regulated, created the rate-regulated, natural monopoly framework in electricity that continues to exist in most states today.

Also in the 1920s, utilities continued to seek economies of scale and worked together to integrate their systems by constructing interstate transmission lines and creating the start of the regional grids that exist today. When states attempted to regulate those interstate electricity sales, the Supreme Court held that such regulation violated the dormant Commerce Clause, creating a regulatory gap known as the "*Attleboro* gap" after the primary Supreme Court decision restricting state regulation. In 1935, Congress filled that gap by enacting the Federal Power Act ("FPA") granting FERC's predecessor, the Federal Power Commission ("FPC"), exclusive authority to regulate the transmission of electricity in interstate commerce and the wholesale sale of electricity in interstate commerce. The law left the regulation of retail electricity transactions to the states as well as the siting of interstate and intrastate transmission lines.

The FPC and FERC used their Congressional authority over wholesale electricity sales and transmission of electricity in interstate commerce to issue a series of orders to ensure reasonable rates and non-discrimination in wholesale electricity markets and transmission access. Congress provided additional authority to FERC to pursue these goals in the Public Utility Regulatory Policies Act of 1978 ("PURPA"), which allowed independent electricity producers with "qualifying" facilities access to the power grid and to make electricity sales. Then, in the Energy Policy Act of 1992, Congress authorized FERC to require utilities to provide access to transmission services on an open and non-discriminatory basis and to encourage transmission planning by RTOs, states, and utilities.

Today, [Regional Transmission Organizations ("RTOs")] and Independent System Operators ("ISOs") manage the grid and regional markets for wholesale power in many, but not all, states. In the regions where RTOs and ISOs have formed, those entities engage in regional grid planning, working with public utilities, states, and other grid participants. Despite the move to regional grid planning in parts of the country where RTOs exist, Congress has left the actual permitting, siting, and eminent domain authority for interstate transmission lines with the states, subject to a few exceptions detailed below. . . .

As noted above, although FERC has jurisdiction over wholesale power sales in interstate commerce and transmission of electricity in interstate commerce, states retain jurisdiction over retail electricity sales and the siting, approval, and grant of eminent domain authority for virtually all transmission lines, including interstate transmission lines. . . . As a result, a utility or other transmission operator that wishes to build an interstate transmission line must obtain siting permission and eminent domain authority from all of the states in the line's path, usually through the state PUCs, and follow each state's permitting process and standards. In some states, transmission operators must also obtain approval from counties and other local governmental entities before constructing a line. The transmission siting laws in each state vary, but generally require the transmission operator (whether a public utility or a private transmission company) to establish the "need" for the line, the effect of the line on reliability, alternatives to the proposed line, and the potential environmental impacts of the line. If successful, the transmission operator receives a "Certificate of Need" or a "Certificate of Public Convenience and Necessity."

In virtually all states, once a transmission operator receives its certificate, it can exercise the power of eminent domain if it fails to reach voluntary agreements with all landowners for the required easements. Generally, states define transmission lines as a "public use," which allows the use of eminent domain under both the Fifth Amendment to the U.S. Constitution as well as state constitution[s] with similar provisions that allow the taking of private property for a public use upon payment of just compensation. In a few states, public utility and/or private transmission operators can exercise eminent domain authority without first obtaining a certificate. Some states allow public utilities, but not private transmission operators, to exercise eminent domain authority under the theory that such privately built lines are not a "public use."

The problem with individual states determining whether there is a "need" for an interstate transmission line or whether the line is a public use is that a single state legislature, PUC, or court will necessarily focus on the need of the citizens of its own state. In most states, interstate transmission lines provide regional or national benefits that may overshadow any in-state benefits. This is particularly true for long-distance transmission lines designed to bring wind energy from one state to population centers several states away without any on-ramps or off-ramps in between. What is the benefit or public use to the states in between who will not see lower electricity rates, increased clean energy use in the state, or new markets for their own generation resources? While such states may see improved grid reliability because the new line will benefit the grid as a whole, that may be little consolation when weighed against the physical impacts to private lands, views, and natural resources caused by the line. . . .

As for augmenting the nation's supply of renewable electricity, new long-distance interstate electric transmission lines are a critical aspect of achieving that goal. Unlike competing sources of electricity such as coal, uranium, and natural gas, which can be transported to consumers via pipelines, rail, truck, or ship, large-scale renewable energy such as wind or solar energy can only be transported through transmission lines. As a result, expanding the electric transmission system is critical to increasing the nation's supply of renewable electricity because these sources of energy are generated in states like Kansas, North Dakota, South Dakota,

Montana, and rural parts of Texas, Illinois, Oregon, and Iowa, which are generally far from load centers.

The regulatory framework for transmission lines that gives states virtually exclusive siting and eminent domain authority for both interstate and intrastate transmission lines has significant implications for the future of the grid. A 2011 interdisciplinary study by MIT entitled *The Future of the Electric Grid* devotes an entire chapter to regulatory policy affecting transmission expansion, with particular focus on the issue of integrating large-scale renewable generation. It concludes that current siting procedures are often biased against approving interstate transmission projects and are a significant barrier to adequate and efficient transmission expansion. The report recommends better planning of regional transmission projects, better compilation of data on the U.S. bulk power system, the use of regional and interconnection cost allocation procedures to better share the cost of long-distance transmission, and enhanced federal siting authority for interstate transmission lines.

A 2013 report by the Bipartisan Policy Center entitled *Capitalizing on the Evolving Power Sector, Policies for a Modern and Reliable U.S. Electric Grid* also highlights the limitations of the state siting process for interstate transmission lines, particularly those high-voltage, long-distance lines necessary to transport renewable energy to load centers. According to the report:

> Siting new transmission lines is often a prolonged, expensive, and contentious undertaking. . . . In recent decades . . . the evolution of interstate and regional electricity markets has increasingly necessitated long-line, interstate transmission projects. Further, the extent of [variable energy resource] integration that will be required by existing state renewable portfolio requirements, and the reality that many renewable resources are located at a distance from load, will likely create a greater need for new long-line transmission in some regions.

> . . . Under the current siting regime, the developer of a multistate transmission line must obtain requisite approvals from state and local authorities along the full length of the line . . . . For their part, individual state authorities may be bound by state statutes to accept or reject the project on the basis of their in-state transmission needs, or the in-state benefits that the project offers. In these cases, states may not be empowered to consider the regional benefits of a proposed project. Thus, a project that transmits power generated in one state, passes through a second state, and serves load in a third state could have difficulty winning approval from regulators in the second state. In some states, regulators might even be required by law to reject a project that

does not serve load within the state's boundaries, even in cases where the project delivers broader benefits to the region at large that the state would share in over time.

Despite these regulatory hurdles, both public utilities and private or "merchant" transmission companies are attempting to build long-distance, interstate transmission lines to improve grid reliability and transport new sources of renewable energy to load centers. Recent efforts include:

- The Montana Alberta Tie Line, a 214-mile, 230-kV merchant line running between Lethbridge, Alberta and Great Falls, Montana to transport Montana wind energy.

- The Zephyr Transmission Project, owned by Duke-ATC, a proposed 950-mile 500-kV line from southeastern Wyoming to Las Vegas, Nevada designed to connect wind-rich areas of Wyoming to load centers in California and the southwestern United States and expected to be in service by 2020.

- The $6.8 billion Texas Competitive Renewable Energy Zone ("CREZ") project consisting of eight years of planning and new construction of 3,600 miles of high-voltage transmission lines across portions of central and West Texas to integrate 16,000 MW of wind energy into the Texas grid.

- The SunZia Southwest Transmission Project, two proposed bi-directional 500-kV lines in Arizona and New Mexico designed to spur development of renewable energy in those states and anticipated to be in service by 2020.

- Five separate DC high-voltage transmission projects by Clean Line Energy Partners, a merchant transmission company, each travelling between 200 and 900 miles designed to bring wind energy to population centers.

- The Multi-Value Projects ("MVPs") in the Midcontinent Independent System Operator ("MISO") region designed to enhance grid reliability and help the MISO states meet renewable portfolio standards by allowing more transmission of wind energy throughout the region, and imposing cost sharing among utilities within MISO.

- The Great Northern Transmission Line, a 500-kV line designed to run between Winnipeg, Manitoba and northeastern Minnesota to transport both hydropower and wind energy and proposed to be in service by 2020.

- The Northern Pass Transmission Line, a 187-mile power line to connect significant hydropower resources in Quebec to population centers in New England.

Both public utilities and private merchant lines are investing in new, large-scale transmission projects, many of which are DC rather than AC. Although the U.S. electric grid runs predominantly on AC, many of the proposed long-distance transmission lines for wind are DC because DC is more efficient and results in less line losses, even though it limits the number of "on ramps" and "off ramps" along the path of the line. Notably, the time, cost, and multi-state regulatory hurdles associated with such lines are significant and most of the projects listed above are still in the state permitting process.

NOTES

1.   *The Rise of RTOs.* The RTOs Professor Klass describes have played growing roles in U.S. electricity markets over the past few decades. As of 2016, there were 10 RTOs and ISOs operating in North America. A map depicting the territorial areas of these RTOs and ISOs appears in Figure 2.5. As the map shows, much of the Western United States, including areas where wind energy resources are plentiful, was not within an RTO or ISO.

Figure 2.5.   Regional Transmission Organizations (RTOs) and Independent System Operators (ISOs) in North America

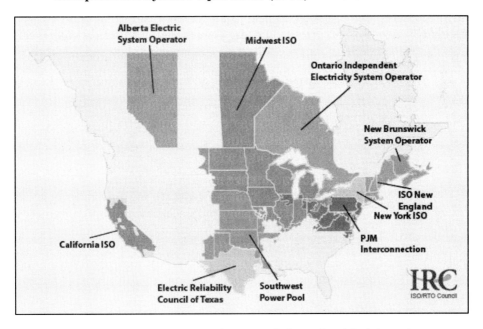

Source: ISO/RTO Council; U.S. Energy Information Administration

2.   *Overcoming Transmission-Related Limitations with Small Wind Turbines.* Installations of small wind turbines—often defined as turbines with generating capacities of less than 100kW—are one means of advancing wind energy development in windy areas that lack enough transmission grid access to support utility-scale wind projects. Because the electricity they generate is used on site, small turbines need not be installed near transmission lines. Although small wind turbine installations have rarely been a cost-justifiable option in the past, gradual improvements in production economies of scale and decreases in the soft costs associated with installations are beginning to make them more viable. *See, e.g.*, Stephen Lacey, *Distributed Wind Has Floundered for Years. Now Oil Companies Are Investing in It*, GREENTECH MEDIA (July 12, 2016), http://www.greentechmedia.com/articles/read/oil-companies-are-investing-in-distributed-wind.

ii.   *Efforts to Expand Federal Transmission Siting Authority*

One potential means of encouraging interstate transmission line development would be to strengthen the federal government's authority to oversee the siting and development process. In 2005, Congress enacted legislation that sought to do that in hopes of overcoming some of the gridlock that had arisen between states over where to site new lines. Among other things, the Energy Policy Act of 2005 (EPAct 2005) authorized the U.S. Secretary of Energy to designate "national interest transmission corridors"—geographic areas within which additional transmission capacity was particularly needed. Figure 2.6 is a map showing one of these national interest transmission corridor areas in the Southwest United States. Other provisions of EPAct 2005 also conferred new authority upon FERC to site new transmission lines within these corridors—even against states' objections in some cases.

Figure 2.6.   A National Interest Transmission Corridor in the Southwest United States

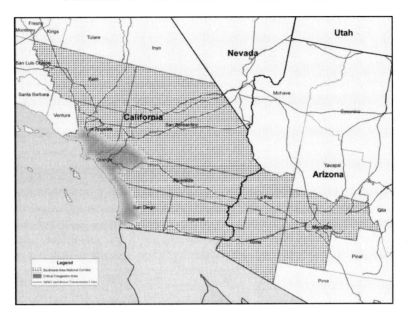

Source: U.S. Dep't of Energy (2007)

Unfortunately, the siting provisions of EPAct 2005 have encountered multiple legal challenges since their enactment that have limited their usefulness. The following are excerpts from the majority opinion in a Fourth Circuit case analyzing the federal transmission siting provisions of EPAct 2005 and ultimately holding that portions of them were unenforceable. Excerpts from a dissenting opinion in the case mirror some renewable energy advocates' frustration at the majority's holding.

PIEDMONT ENVIRONMENTAL COUNCIL V. FERC
United States Court of Appeals, Fourth Circuit, 2009
558 F.3d 304

MICHAEL, C.J.

Two state utilities commissions and two community interest organizations petition for review of several rulemaking decisions made by the Federal Energy Regulatory Commission (FERC or the Commission) in connection with FERC's implementation of the new § 216 of the Federal Power Act (FPA) and the National Environmental Policy Act (NEPA). Section 216 of the FPA, which was added in 2005, gives FERC jurisdiction in certain circumstances to issue permits for the construction or modification of electric transmission facilities in areas designated as national interest corridors by the Secretary of Energy. . . .

I.

The states have traditionally assumed all jurisdiction to approve or deny permits for the siting and construction of electric transmission facilities. As a result, the nation's transmission grid is an interconnected patchwork of state-authorized facilities. In recent times increasing concerns have been expressed about the capacity and reliability of the grid. Congress has reacted to these concerns by adding a new section (§ 216) to the FPA when it passed the Energy Policy Act of 2005, Pub. L. No. 109–58, 119 Stat. 594 (2005).

FPA § 216 authorizes the Secretary of Energy to designate areas with electric transmission constraints affecting consumers as national interest electric transmission corridors. 16 U.S.C. § 824p(a). Section 216 gives FERC the authority in national interest corridors to issue permits for the construction or modification of transmission facilities in certain instances, including the one at issue here: when a state entity with authority to approve the siting of facilities has "withheld approval for more than 1 year after the filing of an application" for a permit. *Id.* §§ 824p(b), 824p(b)(1)(C)(i).

FPA § 216(c)(2) directed FERC to issue rules specifying the form of, and the information to be contained in, an application for construction or modification of electric transmission facilities in a national interest corridor. *Id.* § 824p(c)(2). On June 26, 2006, FERC issued a notice of proposed rule-making, proposing regulations to fulfill this statutory requirement. . . .

In response to FERC's proposed rulemaking, petitioner Communities Against Regional Interconnect (CARI) and others submitted comments requesting that the Commission confirm that § 216(b)(1)(C)(i)'s phrase "withheld approval for more than 1 year" does not include a state's outright denial of a permit application within the one-year deadline. . . On November 16, 2006, FERC issued its final rule, which contained the Commission's substantive interpretation of § 216(b)(1)(C)(i)'s phrase "withheld approval for more than 1 year." . . . . FERC interpreted the phrase to include a state's *denial* of a permit within the one-year statutory time frame. . . .

In mid-December 2006 the four petitioners in this proceeding— Piedmont Environmental Council (Piedmont), the Public Service Commission of the State of New York (NYPSC), the Minnesota Public Utilities Commission (Minnesota PUC), and CARI—filed requests for rehearing on FERC's final rule. All argued to FERC that it had erred in holding that § 216(b)(1)(C)(i)'s phrase "withheld approval [of an application] for more than 1 year" includes a denial. . . . On May 17, 2007, FERC issued an order denying rehearing. . . . The Commission rejected the petitioners' arguments about the meaning of § 216(b)(1)(C)(i), saying that it "continue[d] to believe that a reasonable interpretation of the language of the legislation support[ed]" its earlier conclusion.

. . . .

Piedmont filed in this circuit a petition for review of FERC's final rule and its order denying rehearing.

. . . .

II.

Section 216(b)(1)(C)(i) of the FPA grants FERC the authority to issue permits for the construction or modification of electric transmission facilities in national interest corridors when a state commission has "withheld approval for more than 1 year after the filing of an application." 16 U.S.C. § 824p(b)(1)(C)(i). The petitioners challenge FERC's broad interpretation of this jurisdiction-granting provision.

A.

. . . [Our] review [of] FERC's construction of § 216(b) of the FPA . . . will be guided by *Chevron U.S.A. v. Natural Resources Defense Council*, 467 U.S. 837, 104 S.Ct. 2778, 81 L.Ed.2d 694 (1984). Under *Chevron* we first determine whether Congress has "directly spoken to the precise question at issue. If the intent of Congress is clear, that is the end of the matter." 467 U.S. at 842, 104 S.Ct. 2778. On the other hand, if we conclude that "the statute is silent or ambiguous with respect to the specific [question]," we then determine "whether the agency's answer is based on a permissible construction of the statute." *Id.* at 843, 104 S.Ct. 2778. In determining "[t]he plainness or ambiguity of statutory language," we refer "to the language itself, the specific context in which that language is used, and the broader context of the statute as a whole." *Robinson v. Shell Oil Co.*, 519 U.S. 337, 341, 117 S.Ct. 843, 136 L.Ed.2d 808 (1997).

B.

FERC interprets § 216(b)(1)(C)(i)'s phrase "withheld approval for more than 1 year after the filing of [a permit] application" to include a state's outright denial of an application within one year. We conclude that FERC's interpretation is contrary to the plain meaning of the statute. Simply put, the statute does not give FERC permitting authority when a state has affirmatively denied a permit application within the one-year deadline.

. . . .

We have analyzed the phrase "withheld approval for more than 1 year." Read by itself, the phrase does not include the outright denial of a permit application within the one-year deadline. We have also considered the phrase in the context of the entire statutory provision in which it appears. A reading of the entire provision reveals that Congress intended to act in a measured way and conferred authority on FERC only when a state commission is unable to act on a permit application in a national interest corridor, fails to act in a timely manner, or acts inappropriately by granting a permit with project-killing conditions. The broader context of § 216(b) thus confirms that the meaning of "withheld approval for more than 1 year" is plain: it means that action on a permit application has been held back continuously for more than one year. The continuous act of withholding approval does not include the final administrative act of denying a permit. Because Congress's intent is clear, our review under *Chevron* proceeds no further. For these reasons, we reverse FERC's interpretation of the phrase "withheld approval for more than 1 year."

. . . .

In conclusion, the petitions for review . . . are granted. . . . Here, we reverse FERC's interpretation. The phrase "withheld approval for more than 1 year"—under its plain meaning—does not give FERC jurisdiction under § 216(b)(1) when a state commission denies a permit application for the construction or modification of electric transmission facilities in a national interest corridor.

. . . .

The cases are remanded to FERC. . . .

TRAXLER, C.J., concurring in part and dissenting in part:

. . . [B]ecause I believe that FERC correctly interpreted "withheld approval [of a permit application] for more than 1 year" in 16 U.S.C.A. § 824p(b)(1)(C) to include the failure or refusal to grant a permit application for more than one year in cases in which the permit application was denied, I respectfully dissent from the contrary holding.

I.

A.

Before examining the specific statutory language in question, I pause briefly to discuss the circumstances that brought about the legislation. Most important among these circumstances is the shift, since the enactment of the Federal Power Act, in the way that electricity has been produced and delivered to consumers, from it being generated and consumed in the same general geographic area to it being transmitted great distances from the area in which it was generated.

> [U]nlike the local power networks of the past, electricity is now delivered over three major networks, or "grids," in the continental United States. . . . It is only in Hawaii and Alaska and on the "Texas Interconnect"—which covers most of that State—that electricity is distributed entirely within a single state. In the rest of the country, any electricity that enters the grid immediately becomes part of a vast pool of energy that is constantly moving in

interstate commerce. As a result, it is now possible for power companies to transmit electric energy over long distances at a low cost.

. . . A study issued in May 2002 by the Department of Energy noted . . . that construction of new transmission facilities has been unable to keep up with increasing demands for electricity, resulting in transmission bottlenecks that have increased consumer costs as well as the chances of blackouts. . . . The Study further determined and recommended:

> Rules and regulations that will improve procedures for the siting and permitting of transmission lines should be implemented immediately. The FERC should play a limited role focused on supporting state and regional efforts, but should also possess backstop authority to ensure that transmission facilities that eliminate national interest transmission bottlenecks are sited and constructed. The FERC should act if state and regional bodies are unsuccessful in siting and permitting national interest transmission lines.

Study at 58–59. In this regard, Senate Energy and Natural Resource Committee Chairman Domenici stated on the Senate floor concerning pending legislation that eventually would become the Energy Policy Act of 2005 ("EPAct 2005"), Pub. L. No. 109–58, 119 Stat. 594 (2005):

> To avoid future blackouts and provide our industry and consumers with the reliable electricity they need, we need to invest in critical transmission infrastructure; provide limited Federal siting authority of transmission lines to ensure the transmission of national interest lines, and avoid the most significant areas where we had gridlock; [and] streamline the permitting of siting for transmission lines to assure adequate transmission. . .

150 Cong. Rec. S3732 (daily ed. April 5, 2004) (statement of Sen. Domenici). It was in this context that Congress enacted EPAct 2005. . . .

. . . Applying the common meaning of the word "withhold" yields a straightforward rule that a state has "withheld approval for more than 1 year" when one year after approval has been sought, the state still has not granted it, regardless of the reason. See Funk & Wagnalls Standard Dictionary 936 (1980) (defining "withhold" in part as "[t]o keep back; decline to grant"). Indeed, this is the construction that FERC adopted.

Despite the apparent clarity of the words "withhold" and "approval," Petitioners maintain that even if a state has not granted approval more than a year after an application has been submitted, it has not "withheld approval for more than 1 year" if it has affirmatively denied the application. Petitioners argue that denying approval cannot constitute "withh[olding] approval" because a denial is a discrete event and it therefore makes no sense to speak of "denying approval for more than 1 year."

In my opinion, this argument is not sound. . . . Under the common meaning of the words "withhold" and "approval," approval is withheld, i.e., not granted, every day that no decision is issued granting approval, and it continues to be withheld on the day an application is denied (as well as every day that such a denial is not reconsidered). Thus, if a state denies an application, and then, ten months after submission of the application, reverses course and grants the application, it would certainly be the case that the state "withheld approval" for ten months before granting it. Similarly, if one year and one day after submission of an application a state has denied an application (and not reconsidered its decision), it has "withheld approval for more than 1 year." There is no other reasonable way to interpret those words. . . .

In sum, the reasons are numerous for concluding that § 824p(b)(1)(C)(i) plainly has the meaning that FERC adopted. Only FERC's interpretation gives Congress's words their common meaning, and only FERC's interpretation makes sense in the context in which the language is used and in the context of the statute as a whole. Indeed, as I have explained, that plain meaning is also the one indicated in the applicable legislative history. Finally, even assuming arguendo that the statute's meaning were not plain, I would conclude that FERC's interpretation was reasonable at the very least, and therefore entitled to deference under *Chevron*. I would therefore affirm FERC's interpretation.

QUESTIONS

1.   Which of the *Piedmont* parties' two opposing interpretations of "withhold approval for more than 1 year" do you believe more closely reflects the intent of Congress, and why?

2.   Why might stakeholders within the wind energy industry be discouraged by the majority's holding in the *Piedmont* case? How is the holding likely to impact wind energy development, and why?

3.   Suppose that you were serving as legal counsel to a United States senator who wanted to introduce a new bill in response to the *Piedmont* case. The senator wanted the bill's language to make clear that Congress was giving FERC transmission siting authority within national interest corridor areas in instances when a state denies approval of a transmission siting permit, not just when a state fails to take final action on a permit application for one year. Draft a revised version of the § 216(b)(1)(C)(i) phrase "withheld approval [of an application] for more than 1 year after the filing of an application" that would clearly communicate this rule.

iii. *Funding-Related Obstacles to Interstate Transmission Development*

One other major challenge in the effort to expand the nation's interstate transmission infrastructure is reaching agreement on who will pay for new transmission lines. Most new high-voltage interstate transmission lines benefit multiple stakeholders. Wind farm developers benefit from having additional transmission capacity available for new projects. Utilities can also benefit by gaining access to wind-generated electricity produced hundreds of miles away from their customers. Unfortunately, these benefits are often so contingent and diffused that it can be difficult to raise the funds necessary to build the lines. The federal government generally does not fund the construction of transmission lines through federal tax dollars in the way it funds interstate freeways, so securing the requisite funding for these lines is a comparatively arduous task. The following excerpt describes various strategies aimed at overcoming the challenges of interstate transmission funding and some shortcomings of these approaches.

SOLAR, WIND AND LAND: CONFLICTS IN RENEWABLE ENERGY DEVELOPMENT
Troy A. Rule, pp. 156–59 (2014)

Even if an interjurisdictional transmission line project has all necessary government approvals, it still may never materialize if stakeholders cannot agree on how to fund its construction. Extra high voltage transmission lines and supporting facilities are incredibly expensive. Estimations for one recent project in the United States put the cost of such lines at $1.7 million to $2.1 million per mile. As other commentators have noted, disputes over who could cover these costs can be "just as much of a barrier" to the development of an interstate transmission line project as disputes over siting of the line itself. It could cost up to $34 billion to expand transmission facilities enough to enable renewables to meet 33% of the annual electricity load in the western United States alone. An estimated 110 billion British pounds of investment would be needed to adequately upgrade the U.K.'s electricity infrastructure. Given the magnitude of these costs, it is no surprise that there is ongoing controversy about who should pick up this hefty tab.

A fundamental question frequently debated in disputes over transmission project funding is whether renewable energy developers should foot the bill or whether utilities should cover it. Laws in some jurisdictions have historically required energy developers to pay for the transmission infrastructure needed to serve their projects. For example, Australia has traditionally used a "developer pays" approach for transmission infrastructure, asking generators of electric power to finance the costs of connecting their generation facilities to the grid. This strategy is akin to the relatively common practice of requiring developers of new residential subdivisions on the outskirts of a town to pay much of the expense of building new public roads to connect the new subdivision to existing city streets. Theoretically, such requirements are reasonable and equitable because real estate developers can pass along much of these costs to homebuyers.

Although this "developer pays" model may be an effective way of financing transmission facilities for conventional power plants near urban areas, the model is more prone to inefficiency in the context of renewable energy development. Utility-scale wind and solar energy projects tend to be in relatively remote locations, so the costs of transmission expansions necessary to connect them to the grid tend to be greater than for connecting conventional power plants. Using a "developer pays" model to fund transmission expansions for renewable energy projects is thus more likely to lead to "free rider" problems in which developers strategically wait to build their own projects in a remote region until some other developer has built a nearby line. By waiting and being the second or third wind or solar energy project in a rural area, a patient renewable energy developer may be able to connect its own project into the newly-extended grid for a fraction of the cost it would have otherwise incurred. For obvious reasons, this sort of strategic waiting can inefficiently slow the pace of renewable energy development.

In contrast, some jurisdictions employ more of a "beneficiary pays" or "socialization" approach to fund new transmission lines. Under this approach, utilities generally finance most of the transmission improvements necessary to connect new renewable energy projects into the grid, even when such projects are not utility-owned. The utilities' customers—the beneficiaries—then ultimately pay for the infrastructure through their regular electricity bills. Laws applicable in the U.S. state of Texas have long used a version of this sort of funding regime.

Advocates of the "beneficiary pays" approach generally take the view that a well-functioning national electric grid is just as important as interstate freeway systems for automobiles or other interstate infrastructure projects that receive socialized funding and should thus be treated in the same way. Because this approach does not require renewable energy developers to directly fund transmission lines, even when their project is the first in a given area, it also evades the strategic waiting problems that can sometimes arise under "developer pays" regimes.

Unfortunately, "beneficiary pays" funding schemes can also be prone to controversy because it is not always clear who truly benefits from a new transmission line and should thus help to pay for it. Consider, for instance, a hypothetical transmission line project designed to increase interconnection between the windswept U.S. state of Montana and population centers in southern California. For purposes of determining who should pay for it under a "beneficiary pays" model, who would be the "beneficiaries" of this new line? Californians? Montanans? Someone else?

One cannot resolve the question of who "benefits" from a new transmission line by merely following the flow of the electric current itself. Given the complexity and interwoven nature of the United States' "Western Interconnection" grid system, it is impossible to route specific electrons generated on wind farms in Montana to particular California homes and businesses several hundred miles away. The reality is that much of the electricity generated at the wind farms would likely flow to electricity users in Montana or neighboring states rather than to California, but no one would argue that Montanans should solely pay for the transmission system on that ground. In fact, the additional transmission capacity provided by the new line could ease grid operations in multiple U.S. states in addition to Montana and California, thereby benefiting electricity users in those other states as well. Should these other states have to help finance the line, even though they are not directly involved in its planning or construction? A traditional "beneficiary pays" model does not squarely answer these sorts of inquiries.

"Beneficiary pays" funding models for interjurisdictional transmission can also be vulnerable to their own strategic behavior problems. For example, suppose that a law applying the model required all users of a large interconnected grid to collectively share the costs of new transmission lines regardless of their locations. Under such a law, some jurisdictions might be incentivized to advocate for new transmission development within their boundaries solely to get local economic boosts at the expense of others—the transmission equivalent of the infamous "bridge to nowhere." To quote an Australian official on this risk of socialization-based cost allocation schemes:

> [I]f transmission infrastructure building costs were to be recovered . . . from all end users, this could distort the operation of the market by encouraging generation connections in areas that are inefficient or more expensive than elsewhere."[3]

Attempting to address the incessant controversy surrounding cost allocation schemes for interstate transmission projects in the United States, FERC issued Order 1000 in 2011. This administrative order sets forth several vague "cost allocation principles" and requires that all new major transmission projects generally comply with them. For example, Order 1000 requires that cost allocations associated with any large

---

[3]   Anne Kallies, *The Impact of Electricity Market Design on Access to the Grid and Transmission Planning for Renewable Energy in Australia: Can Overseas Examples Provide Guidance?*, 2 RENEWABLE ENERGY L. & POL'Y REV. 147, 153–54 (2011).

transmission project be "roughly commensurate" with benefits received. Under the Order, FERC purportedly has authority to step in and determine a cost allocation method in situations when regions are unable to agree to such a method on their own.

Although FERC Order 1000 has the potential to reduce conflicts over cost allocation arrangements for interstate transmission projects, the magnitude of its long-term impact remains unclear. Order 1000's ambiguous cost allocation principles create significant uncertainty about how the Order is to be applied and enforced among the various public utilities and regional system operators that collectively oversee electric grid operations in the United States. Moreover, some of these regional operators view Order 1000 as an encroachment on their regulatory powers and have thus sought to use the judicial system to limit the Order's effects. As of late 2013, at least one federal appeals court had largely upheld Order 1000's cost allocation requirements. However, a claim challenging the Order in a different federal court was casting doubts about the Order's fate. It remains to be seen whether the Order will ultimately prove successful at reducing controversies in the United States over the funding of new interstate transmission lines.

As the importance of RTOs and ISOs expands, these organizations are also increasingly helping to overcome funding-related obstacles to interstate transmission development by facilitating cost-sharing for new lines to support wind energy. Although some states have filed claims challenging this funding approach, it has had some success. In the following case, Judge Richard Posner reviews a FERC approval of a request by two RTOs—MISO and PJM (both of which appear on the map in Figure 2.5)—to spread the cost of some new high-voltage lines among their several participating utilities. Notice how Judge Posner cites a general policy goal of promoting renewable power in support of the court's holding.

ILLINOIS COMMERCE COMMISSION V. FERC
United States Court of Appeals, Seventh Circuit, 2013
721 F.3d 764

POSNER, C.J.

Control of more than half the nation's electrical grid is divided among seven Regional Transmission Organizations [(RTOs)]. . . . These are voluntary associations of utilities that own electrical transmission lines interconnected to form a regional grid and that agree to delegate operational control of the grid to the association. . . . Power plants that do not own any part of the grid but generate electricity transmitted by it are also members of these associations, as are other electrical companies involved in one way or another with the regional grid.

The RTOs play a key role in the effort by the Federal Energy Regulatory Commission "to promote competition in those areas of the industry amenable to competition, such as the segment that generates electric power, while ensuring that the segment of the industry characterized by natural monopoly—namely, the transmission grid that conveys the generated electricity—cannot exert monopolistic influence over other areas. . . . [FERC] has encouraged the management of [RTOs] by 'Independent System Operators,' not-for-profit entities that operate transmission facilities in a nondiscriminatory manner." *Morgan Stanley Capital Group, Inc. v. Public Utility District No. 1*, 554 U.S. 527, 536–37, 128 S.Ct. 2733, 171 L.Ed.2d 607 (2008).

Two Regional Transmission Organizations are involved in this case— Midwest Independent Transmission System Operator, Inc. (MISO) and PJM Interconnection, LLC (PJM). . . . MISO operates in the Midwest and in the Great Plains states while PJM operates in the mid-Atlantic region but has midwestern enclaves in and surrounding Chicago and in southwestern Michigan.

Each RTO is responsible for planning and directing expansions and upgrades of its grid. It finances these activities by adding a fee to the price of wholesale electricity transmitted on the grid. 18 C.F.R. § 35.34(k)(1), (7). The Federal Power Act requires that the fee be "just and reasonable," 16 U.S.C. § 824d(a), and therefore at least roughly proportionate to the anticipated benefits to a utility of being able to use the grid. . . Thus "all approved rates [must] reflect to some degree the costs actually caused by the customer who must pay them." *K N Energy, Inc. v. FERC*, 968 F.2d 1295, 1300 (D.C. Cir. 1992). Courts "evaluate compliance [with this principle, which is called 'cost causation'] by comparing the costs assessed against a party to the burdens imposed or benefits drawn by that party." *Midwest ISO Transmission Owners v. FERC*, *supra*, 373 F.3d at 1368.

MISO began operating in 2002 and soon grew to have 130 members. . . . In 2010 it sought FERC's approval to impose a tariff on its members to fund the construction of new high-voltage power lines that it calls "multi-value projects" (MVPs), beginning with 16 pilot projects. The tariff is mainly intended to finance the construction of transmission lines for electricity generated by remote wind farms. Every state in MISO's region except Kentucky . . . encourages or even requires utilities to obtain a specified percentage of their electricity supply from renewable sources, mainly wind farms. Indiana, North Dakota, and South Dakota have aspirational goals; the rest have mandates. . . .

"The dirty secret of clean energy is that while generating it is getting easier, moving it to market is not. . . . Achieving [a 20% renewable energy quota] would require moving large amounts of power over long distances, from the windy, lightly populated plains in the middle of the country to the coasts where many people live . . . The grid's limitations are putting a damper on such projects already." Matthew L. Wald, "Wind Energy Bumps into Power Grid's Limits," *New York Times*, Aug. 27, 2008, p. A1. MISO aims to overcome these limitations.

To begin with, [MISO] has identified what it believes to be the best sites in its region for wind farms that will meet the region's demand for wind power. . . . Most are in the Great Plains, because electricity produced by wind farms there is cheaper despite the longer transmission distance; the wind flow is stronger and steadier and land is cheaper because population density is low (wind farms require significant amounts of land).

MISO has estimated that the cost of the transmission lines necessary both to bring electricity to its urban centers from the Great Plains and to integrate the existing wind farms elsewhere in its region with transmission lines from the Great Plains—transmission lines that the multi-value projects will create—will be more than offset by the lower cost of electricity produced by western wind farms. The new transmission lines will also increase the reliability of the electricity supply in the MISO region and thus reduce brownouts and outages, and also increase the efficiency with which electricity is distributed throughout the region.

The cost of the multi-value projects is to be allocated among utilities drawing power from MISO's grid in proportion to each utility's share of the region's total wholesale consumption of electricity. Before 2010, MISO allocated the cost of expanding or upgrading the transmission grid to the utilities nearest a proposed transmission line, on the theory that they would benefit the most from the new line. But wind farms in the Great Plains can generate far more power than that sparsely populated region needs. So MISO decided to allocate MVP costs among all utilities drawing power from the grid according to the amount of electrical energy used, thus placing most of those costs on urban centers, where demand for energy is greatest.

FERC approved (with a few exceptions, one discussed later in this opinion) MISO's rate design and pilot projects in two orders (for simplicity we'll pretend they're just one), precipitating the petitions for review that we have consolidated.

. . . .

MISO used to allocate the cost of an upgrade to its grid to the local area ("pricing zone") in which the upgrade was located. (There are 24 pricing zones in MISO.) But those were upgrades to low-voltage lines, which transmit power short distances and thus benefit only the local area served by the lines. MISO contends (and FERC agrees) that the multi-value projects, which involve high-voltage lines that transmit electricity over long distances, will benefit all members of MISO and so the projects' costs should be shared among all members.

The petitioners' objections fall into two groups. One consists of objections lodged by the Michigan utilities and their regulator (we'll call this set of objectors "Michigan"), the other of objections by other petitioners led by the Illinois Commerce Commission. We'll call these objectors "Illinois," though they include other state utilities and regulators; and we'll begin with their objections.

Illinois contends that the criteria for determining what projects are eligible to be treated as MVPs are too loose and as a result all MISO members will be forced to contribute to the cost of projects that benefit only a few. To qualify as an MVP a project must have an expected cost of at least $20 million, must consist of high-voltage transmission lines (at least 100kV), and must help MISO members meet state renewable energy requirements, fix reliability problems, or provide economic benefits in multiple pricing zones. None of these eligibility criteria ensures that every utility in MISO's vast region will benefit from every MVP project, let alone in exact proportion to its share of the MVP tariff. . . .

Bear in mind that every multi-value project is to be large, is to consist of high-voltage transmission (enabling power to be transmitted efficiently across pricing zones), and is to help utilities satisfy renewable energy requirements, improve reliability (which benefits the entire regional grid by reducing the likelihood of brownouts or outages, which could occur anywhere on it . . .), facilitate power flow to currently underserved areas in the MISO region, or attain several of these goals at once. . . .

Illinois also complains that MISO has failed to show that the multi-value projects as a whole will confer benefits greater than their costs, and it complains too about FERC's failure to determine the costs and benefits of the projects subregion by subregion and utility by utility. But Illinois's briefs offer no estimates of costs and benefits either, whether for the MISO region as a whole or for particular subregions or particular utilities. . . . MISO did estimate that there would be cost savings of some $297 million to $423 million annually because western wind power is cheaper than power from existing sources, and that these savings would be "spread almost evenly across all Midwest ISO Planning Regions." . . . . It also estimated that the projected high-voltage lines would reduce losses of electricity in transmission by $68 to $104 million, and save another $217 to $271 million by reducing "reserve margin losses." *Id.* That term refers to electricity generated in excess of demand and therefore (because it can't be stored) wasted. Fewer plants will have to be kept running in reserve to meet unexpected spikes in demand if by virtue of longer transmission lines electricity can be sent from elsewhere to meet those unexpected spikes. It's impossible to allocate these cost savings with any precision across MISO members.

The promotion of wind power by the MVP program deserves emphasis. Already wind power accounts for 3.5 percent of the nation's electricity . . . and it is expected to continue growing. . . . The use of wind power in lieu of power generated by burning fossil fuels reduces both the nation's dependence on foreign oil and emissions of carbon dioxide. And its cost is falling as technology improves. No one can know how fast wind power will grow. But the best guess is that it will grow fast and confer substantial benefits on the region served by MISO by replacing more expensive local wind power, and power plants that burn oil or coal, with western wind power. There is no reason to think these benefits will be denied to particular subregions of MISO. Other benefits of MVPs, such as increasing the reliability of the grid, also can't be calculated in advance, especially on a subregional basis, yet are real and will benefit utilities and consumers in all of MISO's subregions.

It's not enough for Illinois to point out that MISO's and FERC's attempt to match the costs and the benefits of the MVP program is crude; if crude is all that is possible, it will have to suffice. . . .

Illinois can't counter FERC without presenting evidence of imbalance of costs and benefits, which it hasn't done.

. . . .

Petitioners complain about MISO's decision to allocate all MVP costs to the utilities that buy electricity from its grid and none to the power plants that generate that electricity. . . . But the utilities benefit from cheaper power generated by efficiently sited wind farms whose development the multi-value projects will stimulate. . . .

An important consideration is that when wind farms are built in remote areas (which are the best places to site them), the costs of connecting them to the grid are very high, and by reducing those costs the multi-value projects, financed by the MVP tariff, facilitate siting wind farms at the best locations in MISO's region rather than at inefficient ones that are however closer to the existing grid and so would be preferred by the wind-farm developers if they had to pay for the connection.

. . . .

In summary, the challenged orders are affirmed. . . .

NOTES & QUESTIONS

1. The "cost causation" principle described in *Illinois Commerce Commission* seeks to ensure that the "costs assessed against a party" to fund

a major transmission line are proportionate "to the burdens imposed or benefits drawn by that party." Not all interstate infrastructure is funded in accordance with this principle. For example, the interstate freeway system for automobiles was funded primarily with federal government dollars. Why does that approach arguably not conform to the cost causation principle? What might be some practical difficulties of imposing the cost causation principle to fund interstate highways?

2.   According to Judge Posner, why does the recent growth of wind energy development in the Midwest United States arguably strengthen arguments for upholding the MVP tariffs challenged in the case?

3.   *Merchant Transmission Lines.* Recognizing that utilities and wind energy developers have been relatively ineffective at advancing interstate high-voltage transmission line development to accommodate wind energy projects, third-party companies are increasingly seeking to help. "Merchant" transmission lines are analogous to many toll roads: private companies build them and then collect fees from users to recoup construction costs and earn a profit. FERC policy changes in recent years have encouraged greater competition in interstate transmission development, including competition from merchant transmission line developers. See Christina Vitale, *How FERC Is Fueling New Merchant Transmission Projects*, Law360.com (Feb. 27, 2013), https://www.law360.com/articles/418080/how-ferc-is-fueling-new-merchant-transmission-projects. In response to these policy changes and to the high demand for additional interstate transmission capacity, investor-owned companies such as Clean Line Energy Partners are aggressively seeking to build new interstate lines along strategic routes in the country's midsection to facilitate greater wind energy development. Although various state and local regulatory hurdles have thus far limited their success, merchant transmission line developers could eventually play important roles in the buildout of interstate transmission infrastructure. See Herman K. Trabish, *Transmission: The unsung hero of the DOE grid reliability study*, UtilityDive.com (Sept. 5, 2017), http://www.utilitydive.com/news/transmission-the-unsung-hero-of-the-doe-grid-reliability-study/504120/.

iv. Transmission Development and Energy Sprawl

As useful as it might seem to massively expand the nation's interstate transmission infrastructure to accommodate more wind energy development, such an expansion would unquestionably have some undesirable spillover effects. Among them are increased costs from *energy sprawl*—adverse environmental, health, and safety impacts resulting from large-scale transmission and other energy development. Professor Sara Bronin elaborates in the excerpt below on how the growth of utility-scale wind and solar energy and the transmission infrastructure necessary to support it can contribute to energy sprawl and its attendant effects on communities and the environment.

CURBING ENERGY SPRAWL WITH MICROGRIDS
Sara C. Bronin
43 CONN. L. REV. 547, 552–54, 556 (2010)

Although the Nature Conservancy popularized the term "energy sprawl" in 2009, the phenomenon has an intuitive explanation. Simply put, energy sprawl refers to the land required to produce and move energy, measured in acres per total quantity of energy production. . . .

When Americans think of sprawl, they typically think of urban sprawl: the unplanned, and often unsightly, expansion of human development into previously undeveloped rural areas. Urban sprawl, as its name suggests, develops in roughly concentric circles around cities. In some cases, urban sprawl is contained within city limits. In other cases, it crosses urban growth boundaries, into other counties, or even into unincorporated areas. When urban sprawl warrants government attention, interested jurisdictions often include a city and a county government or neighboring city governments. At times, state legislatures weigh in to influence land use policies, but by and large regulating urban sprawl is a local government function.

Like urban sprawl, energy sprawl involves expansion into undeveloped areas. Energy sprawl, however, is linear, not concentric. Traditional energy infrastructure, which takes the form of generating facilities and distribution centers connected by transmission lines, looks like a web in maps. Another difference from urban sprawl is that energy sprawl does not necessarily follow existing settlement patterns. In fact, some of the largest energy generating facilities may be found in some of the most underpopulated places in the country. Builders of such facilities no doubt find it easier to locate in places far outside urban boundaries, where fewer people object and where natural resources like sunlight and wind are easier to capture. In such areas, only counties or states, or the Bureau of Land Management if federal land is involved, have jurisdiction over siting.

While extra-urban siting may be attractive for the problems it avoids, it has significant negative long-term impacts. In 2009, the Nature Conservancy's Energy Sprawl or Energy Efficiency report focused on one of these negative impacts: the reach, in purely spatial terms, of different methods of production. The environmental nonprofit estimated that at least 206,000 square kilometers—an area larger than the state of Nebraska—will be impacted by energy development over the next twenty years if Americans do not substantially increase energy efficiency. It predicted that energy will shift from fossil fuels to methods that may require greater amounts of land than fossil fuels require.

According to the calculations of the Nature Conservancy, among the least land-intensive methods of production are nuclear power, using about two square kilometers to produce a terawatt-hour annually and geothermal, using an average of seven and a half square kilometers to produce the same amount of energy. Biofuels and biomass, at around 350 and 550 square kilometers respectively, are among the most land-intensive. Somewhere in the middle are coal, at ten; solar thermal, at fifteen; natural gas, at nineteen; solar photovoltaic, at thirty-seven; petroleum at forty-five; hydropower at fifty-four; and wind at seventy-two square kilometers per annual terawatt-hour. The report estimates that the land use figures for geothermal, natural gas, and wind production can be divided into direct disturbance of land of about five percent and indirect disturbance, involving disruptions of larger ecosystems, habitats, and wildlife activity, for the remaining ninety-five percent.

To put this analysis in more concrete terms, take an example of one project using a somewhat land-intensive energy production method, wind farming. The largest wind farm in the world opened in October 2009, occupying almost 100,000 acres (or 405 square kilometers) in sparsely populated West Texas. The farm has 627 turbines, with each turbine taking up, on average, about 160 acres. It generates 781.5 megawatts . . . and powers 265,000 homes. For every megawatt generated, the farm uses about 128 acres of land. . . .

Beyond the 100,000 acres, large transmission lines must be built to get power to the 265,000 homes to be served by the wind farm. These lines take years to create, given the need to coordinate with private landowners, and are extremely expensive. Moreover, power lost in transmission is roughly ten percent. Accordingly, energy sprawl costs space, money, and energy itself.

Despite the many troubling effects of large, out-of-the-way developments, government continues to direct significant support to projects with many hundreds or thousands of end users. The Department of Energy has completed studies showing that the United States could obtain as much as twenty percent of its electricity from alternative energy sources such as wind power alone by 2030, much of it to be produced in large-scale facilities. As the government pushes for greater use of alternative energy, demand by large-scale alternative energy producers for land also grows. As one measure, the Bureau of Land Management has received four hundred applications for large solar and wind plants covering more than two million rural acres. The question now is not whether energy sprawl will occur, but to what extent it may be contained.

NOTES & QUESTIONS

1.   The geographic mismatch between the United States' major metropolitan centers and its remote regions with excellent onshore wind energy resources makes energy sprawl a particularly significant risk in the

context of wind energy. How, if at all, do you think the sprawling nature of wind energy development and its transmission infrastructure should affect policymaking aimed at incentivizing utility-scale wind power?

2.   Suppose that you are a landowner in a remote rural county with few significant employers and a stagnant local economy. Draft one paragraph arguing that lawmakers should give no weight to energy sprawl concerns when considering whether to enact government incentive programs to promote interstate transmission line projects supporting wind energy development.

3.   *Policy Approaches to Combatting Energy Sprawl.* Professor Uma Outka has persuasively argued that a better integration of land use law and energy policy could help renewable energy development to be far less sprawling and land-intensive. In Outka's words:

> It is becoming a common refrain that the land impact is a necessary "trade-off," a price we have to pay to shrink the carbon footprint. Yet in reflexively *assuming* a trade-off we risk hindering both causes, obscuring legitimate land use concerns and slowing renewable development. Even more troubling, we neglect the potential for reconciling the assumed conflict—a failing we cannot afford given the millions of acres at stake. . . [C]umulative land impacts should be a central consideration in the development and implementation of energy policy.

Uma Outka, *The Renewable Energy Footprint*, 30 STANFORD ENVT'L L.J. 241, 244 (2011). Professor Outka's article identifies five principles capable of furthering this integration and preventing unjustifiable renewable energy sprawl. Specifically, she argues that policymakers and developers should:

> . . . (1) avoid new infrastructure/new land impact; (2) reuse land that has already been developed or otherwise disturbed; (3) maximize land-efficient onsite and local energy potential; (4) identify early the least-harm sites for energy projects and strengthen mitigation measures for facilities we need; and (5) link transmission planning and renewable energy policy more closely.

Id. at 297. Although a diverse array of policies and strategies have emerged in recent years that incorporate one or more of these principles, limiting the land footprint of renewable energy projects continues to be a challenge for stakeholders across the country.

b. Accounting for Local Variations in Wind Resource Quality

The quality of wind resources not only varies across regions; it can also vary significantly across short distances within a region. Such highly localized spatial variation in resource quality is one characteristic that distinguishes wind energy from solar energy. On a clear day, solar resources are generally equally as strong everywhere within a given community at any given time. The same cannot be said of wind resources. The topographical features of the land—its elevation, the presence of hills or mountains, or the shape of a canyon or valley—can greatly impact wind resource quality at a particular spot. Indeed, a turbine's wind energy productivity potential at a specific site can be far better or worse than at other potential sites just a few hundred yards away. Accordingly, in places where there is substantial local variation in wind resources, the optimal siting of wind turbines is critical to a wind farm's success.

Developers carefully measure and consider spatial variations in wind resource quality when they *microsite* turbines within a larger wind farm site. To microsite turbines is to meticulously determine precise turbine site locations and layouts in hopes of maximize a project site's wind energy productivity. Developers often gather data for this micrositing process through wind measuring tools called *anemometers*, which they mount on mobile towers high above the ground and move from place to place across a project site over several weeks or months. The detailed location-specific wind resource data these anemometers generate inform where wind turbines are ultimately installed on a wind farm project and sometimes determines whether developers even continue pursuing wind energy development at a prospective project site.

The highly location-specific nature of wind resources impacts the legal and policy structures that govern wind energy development as well. For example, as will be explored in Chapter 4, most wind energy leases agreements have provisions that give the developer time to conduct detailed wind studies on the leased land before making any major financial commitments to the landowner. The spatial variation of wind resources also affects policymaking aimed at addressing wind turbine wake interference conflicts among neighbors—an issue examined in Chapter 3.

C. INCENTIVIZING WIND ENERGY

Despite wind energy's limitations, its numerous advantages make it one of the most promising long-term energy resources on the planet. Unfortunately, modern wind power—like many other renewable energy strategies—suffers from positive externality problems: many of the benefits of wind power accrue to parties other than those who build and operate wind farms. As suggested in Chapter 1, such positive externality problems tend to result in sub-optimally low levels of wind energy development under perfectly competitive market conditions—a market failure that potentially requires government intervention. Recognizing the broad public benefits associated with wind energy, governments in the United States have enacted a wide array of policies in recent decades aimed at promoting wind energy development. The following materials examine some of the most prominent of these policy approaches.

1. TAX CREDITS AND CASH GRANTS

The most straightforward way to correct a positive externality problem is to subsidize the externality-prone activity so that those who engage in the activity internalize its full benefits. In the United States, one prominent means of providing subsidies is through tax credits or deductions administered within the federal income tax system. An optimal subsidy, which economists call a *Pigouvian subsidy* after the famous economist Arthur C. Pigou, is one that allows recipients to internalize just enough of the external benefits of the subsidized activity to cause them to engage in it at the social optimal level. *See* Lily L. Batchelder et al., *Efficiency and Tax Incentives: The Case for Refundable Tax Credits*, 59 STAN. L. REV. 23, 44–45 (2006).

One type of subsidy that has been particularly influential in driving the growth of domestic wind energy over the past quarter century is the federal renewable energy *production tax credit* (PTC). Congress first created the PTC in the Energy Policy Act of 1992 as a way to encourage greater investment in renewable energy development. Since that time, Congress has extended, renewed, and modified the PTC several times, always with profound impacts on the domestic wind energy industry.

The PTC is a per-kWh tax credit for the generation and sale of qualifying electricity to unrelated persons during the taxable year. *See Renewable Energy Production Tax Credit*, DEP'T OF ENERGY, http://energy. gov/savings/renewable-electricity-production-tax-credit-ptc. Although the original amount of the credit in 1992 was $0.015 per kWh, statutory language requires the Internal Revenue Service (IRS) to annually adjust the credit amount based on inflation. As of 2016, the IRS inflation adjustment factor was 1.5556, so the amount of the credit was:

$0.015/kWh × 1.5556 = 2.3 cents per kWh.

Taxpayers who develop wind, geothermal, or closed-loop biomass energy projects can avail themselves of the PTC for the first ten years that the project is in operation. A credit equal to one half this amount is also available for certain other types of renewable energy.

A 2.3 cent-per-kWh credit may not sound like much at first blush, but it can greatly impact the potential profitability of a wind energy project. The availability of the PTC has enabled wind energy developers to negotiate with utilities and other off-takers to sell wind-generated electricity at prices that are much more competitive with nuclear or fossil fuel-driven power plants than they would otherwise be.

Congress most recently extended the PTC as part of the Consolidated Appropriations Act in December of 2015. This extension was different from several previous ones in that it did not merely extend the credit for one or two years but for a total of four years—from 2016 to 2019. The 2015 extension was also different in that, after the first extension year, the amount of the credit is scheduled to automatically decline by 20% per year (rounded to the nearest tenth of a cent) until it phases out completely in 2020. The size of credit available for any given wind farm is thus determined largely by the date that the taxpayer commences construction. A project for which construction was commenced in 2017 qualifies for 80% of the credit and a project commenced in 2019 qualifies for just 40% of the credit. Projects commenced after December 31, 2019, qualify for no credit (i.e., the credit drops from 40% to 0% after that date). This structure incentivizes wind energy developers to start projects as soon as possible to qualify for larger credits.

A simple numerical example may help to illustrate this idea and how the IRS calculates a taxpayer's PTC. Suppose that a developer is trying to decide whether to commence construction on a wind farm project in December of 2018 or in January of 2019. Suppose further that the IRS-determined inflation adjustment factors for those years are 1.60 and 1.65, respectively. If the developer were to commence construction in December of 2018, it would qualify for a credit equal to 60% of the full 2016 credit. Specifically, the credit would be:

$$\$0.015 \times 1.60 \times 0.60 = 1.4 \text{ cents per kWh.}$$

If, instead, the commencement of construction were delayed into early 2019, the amount of the credit would be just

$$\$0.015 \times 1.65 \times 0.40 = 1.0 \text{ cents per kWh.}$$

Given that just one utility-scale onshore wind turbine can generate millions of kWh of electricity per year, developers operating under these rules are strongly motivated to avoid excessive delays in beginning the construction process. Not surprisingly, disputes can also arise over precisely when construction is commenced. Congress has provided detailed guidelines for determining the date of *commencement of construction* for purposes of the PTC, but the statutory language still leaves some room for debate. The following excerpt from an IRS notice exemplifies how technical even the question of commencement of construction can become when large sums of tax credit money are on the line.

CLARIFICATION AND MODIFICATION OF NOTICE 2013–29 AND 2013–60

I.R.S. Notice 2014–46, 36 I.R.B. 520 (Aug. 9, 2014)

SECTION 1. PURPOSE

On January 2, 2013, the American Taxpayer Relief Act of 2012, Pub. L. No. 112–240, 126 Stat. 2313 (ATRA), modified the definition of certain qualified facilities under section 45(d) of the Internal Revenue Code (the

Code) by replacing the placed in service requirement with a beginning of construction requirement. . . .

Notice 2013–29 . . . provides two methods to determine when construction has begun on a qualified facility: (i) a "physical work" test and (ii) a five percent safe harbor. . . . This notice further clarifies Notices 2013–29 and 2013–60 regarding (i) how to satisfy the physical work test and (ii) the effect of various types of transfers with respect to a facility after construction has begun. In addition, this notice modifies the application of the five percent safe harbor.

. . .

SECTION 2. BACKGROUND

A taxpayer may establish the beginning of construction by beginning physical work of a significant nature as described in section 4 of Notice 2013–29 (Physical Work Test). Alternatively, a taxpayer may establish the beginning of construction by meeting the safe harbor provided in section 5 of Notice 2013–29 (Safe Harbor). A taxpayer can satisfy the Safe Harbor with respect to a facility by demonstrating, after the facility is placed in service, that five percent or more of the total cost of the facility was paid or incurred [before the applicable deadline]. . . . Both methods require that a taxpayer make continuous progress towards completion once construction has begun. . . .

After the publication of Notice 2013–60, the Treasury Department and the Service received requests for further clarification regarding how to satisfy the Physical Work Test. . . .

SECTION 3. PHYSICAL WORK TEST

The Physical Work Test requires that a taxpayer begin physical work of a significant nature (as defined in section 4.02 of Notice 2013–29) prior to January 1, 2014. This test focuses on the nature of the work performed, not the amount or cost. Notice 2013–29 describes several activities that constitute physical work of a significant nature. These activities are merely examples and not an exclusive list of the activities that will satisfy the Physical Work Test. For example, section 4.02 of Notice 2013–29 provides:

In the case of a facility for the production of electricity fro[m] a wind turbine, on-site physical work of a significant nature begins with the beginning of the excavation for the foundation, the setting of anchor bolts into the ground, or the pouring of the concrete pads of the foundation.

Section 4.05(1) of Notice 2013–29 provides: Physical work on a custom-designed transformer that steps up the voltage of electricity produced at the facility to the voltage needed for transmission is physical work of a significant nature with respect to the facility because power conditioning equipment is an integral part of the activity performed by the facility.

Section 4.05(2) of Notice 2013 29 provides: Roads that are integral to the facility are integral to the activity performed by the facility; these include onsite roads that are used for moving materials to be processed (for example, biomass) and roads for equipment to operate and maintain the qualified facility. Starting construction on these roads constitutes physical work of a significant nature with respect to the facility.

Beginning work on any one of the activities described above will constitute physical work of a significant nature.

Section 4.04(3) of Notice 2013–29 provides an example in which X, a developer of a 50 turbine wind farm, is found to satisfy the beginning of construction requirement in part based on the stated fact that, in 2013, for 10 of the 50 turbines, X excavates the site for the foundations of the wind turbines and pours concrete for the supporting pads. This example illustrates the "single project" concept set forth in section 4.04(2) of Notice 2013–29 and is not intended to indicate that there is a 20% threshold or minimum amount of work required to satisfy the Physical Work Test.

Assuming the work performed is of a significant nature, there is no fixed minimum amount of work or monetary or percentage threshold required to satisfy the Physical Work Test.

As provided in section 4.01 of Notice 2013–29 the Service will closely scrutinize a facility, and may determine that construction has not begun on a facility . . . if a taxpayer does not maintain a continuous program of construction. . . .

NOTES & QUESTIONS

1.   From an administrative cost perspective, which seems less burdensome: the Physical Work Test or the five percent Safe Harbor Test? What are some disadvantages of the Physical Work Test? Which test do you think is better from a public policy standpoint, and why?

2.   What would have to be true about the external benefits of additional wind energy generation for the 20% annual decrease of the PTC over four years and its eventual elimination to be optimal under Pigou's theory of externalities and subsidies? Would you guess that these decreasing tax credit amounts are consistent with Pigouvian subsidy theory? Why or why not?

3.   *The Trump EPA's Criticism of Federal Renewable Energy Tax Credits.* In late 2017, the Trump Administration's new EPA Chief, Scott Pruitt, expressed a desire for Congress to prematurely terminate the federal PTC and ITC. Some feared that the Trump Administration would seek to eliminate the credits early as part of its income tax overhaul plan. See Ari Natter, *EPA Chief Calls for Ending Wind Tax Credits to Help Coal Survive*, BLOOMBERG (Oct. 9,

2017), https://www.bloomberg.com/news/articles/2017-10-09/epa-chief-calls-for-ending-wind-tax-credits-to-help-coal-survive.

Although the PTC is the federal government's primary form of subsidy for wind energy, other federal subsidy programs for renewable energy do exist. In the following excerpt, Professor Felix Mormann contrasts the PTC with two other prominent federal subsidy programs: the *investment tax credit* (ITC) and the Section 1603 Cash Grant Program. As Professor Mormann explains, the ITC is not available for most utility-scale onshore wind farms, but the Section 1603 Cash Grant Program was instrumental in continuing the growth of wind energy development during the nation's deep 2008 recession.

BEYOND TAX CREDITS: SMARTER TAX POLICY FOR A CLEANER, MORE DEMOCRATIC ENERGY FUTURE

Felix Mormann
31 YALE J. ON REG. 303, 313–18, 335–36 (2014)

Federal tax credits seek to promote the deployment of renewable energy technologies by rewarding either the generation of electricity from renewables or the investment in equipment for renewable power generation. When the 2008–2009 recession stalled renewable energy deployment and threatened to put thousands of American workers in planning, manufacturing, construction, maintenance and other segments of the renewables industry out of work, Congress created the section 1603 cash grant as a temporary alternative to the federal tax credit regime.

1.   The Production Tax Credit

The Energy Policy Act of 1992 established production tax credits as the primary federal incentive for wind energy. Today, the federal tax code offers production tax credits to a range of renewable power generation technologies, including wind, biomass, geothermal, landfill gas, municipal solid waste, qualified hydropower as well as marine and hydrokinetic facilities. Eligible facilities receive tax credits in proportion to the quantity of electricity they produce.

. . . .

Production tax credits are available for a total of ten years as long as certain requirements are met. For instance, generated power must be sold to an unrelated party. In addition, renewable power generators are limited in their ability to combine production tax credits with other public policy incentives, such as grants, tax-exempt bonds, and other federal tax credits. Finally, the production of renewable electricity must be attributable to the taxpayer by virtue of and in proportion to its ownership interest in the renewable energy facility and its gross sales. Since its inception, the production tax credit has been subject to frequent, generally short-term extensions and occasional lapses. . . .

2.   The Investment Tax Credit

Investment tax credits for renewables were first established by the Energy Tax Act of 1978. Today the federal tax code provides investment tax credits for a variety of renewable energy technologies, including solar, combined heat and power, fuel cells, microturbines, geothermal, and small wind projects. In contrast to the production tax credit, the investment tax credit does not reward the actual generation of electricity from eligible renewable technologies but, rather, investment in the equipment required to generate renewable power. Solar, fuel cells, and small wind projects receive tax credits equal to thirty percent of the project's qualifying investment costs, whereas all other eligible technologies receive tax credits worth ten percent of their qualifying costs.

While the investment tax credit is realized in full the same year a project begins commercial operation, the credit vests linearly over a period of five years. As a result, any transfer of ownership before the end of this period leads to recapture of the unvested portion of the credit under the Internal Revenue Code. Thus, if a project owner sells her assets after two years, she will need to pay back sixty percent of the investment tax credit she received when the project was placed in service. After January 1, 2017 the investment tax credit will phase down to ten percent of qualifying costs for all eligible renewable energy technologies to anticipate and encourage the industry's continuous technology learning and cost improvements.

3.   The Section 1603 Cash Grant

The 2008–2009 recession presented a serious challenge for renewable energy project developers who were already struggling to raise capital for new projects. Many developers do not have tax bills that are high enough to reap the full and immediate benefits of tax credits for renewable energy. While renewable power plants do not incur the same fuel costs as their fossil fuel counterparts, they require greater up-front capital expenditures for planning, construction, and equipment. As a result, it typically takes ten or more years before a renewable power project has recovered these expenditures and begins to generate the necessary profits and tax liability to use its tax credits. In the case of a standalone wind project, for example, this lack of tax liabilities means that the developer may realize only one third of the value of her project's tax benefits. Except for the rare instance where a project developer happens to have enough tax liability from other sources to offset, the developer will need to bring in an outside investor with enough tax liability from other income. The outside investor's participation, commonly referred to as tax equity investment, enables the developer to monetize the project's tax credits in a timely fashion. Such tax equity investment effectively allows a renewable energy project to sell the tax credits that the project itself cannot presently monetize against its own income to the tax equity investor.

Historically, fewer than two dozen highly profitable and sophisticated entities—mostly large banks, insurance companies, and other financial firms—have been willing and able to support renewable energy projects through their tax equity investments. It was these financial firms that were hit particularly hard by the 2008–2009 financial crisis, leading many to pare back their tax equity investment activities or leave the tax equity market altogether, in some cases permanently. As a result, the number of tax equity investors dropped from twenty to eleven investors between 2007 and 2009, while the available tax equity volume for renewable energy investment shrank by over eighty percent from $6.1 billion in 2007 to $1.2 billion in 2009.

In response to these challenges, the American Recovery and Reinvestment Act of 2009 created the section 1603 cash grant to "temporarily fill the gap created by the diminished investor demand for tax credits" and to achieve the near-term goal of "creating and retaining jobs . . . as well as . . . expanding the use of clean and renewable energy and decreasing our dependency on non-renewable energy sources." The section 1603 cash grant gave eligible renewable energy developers the option to receive a cash grant from the Department of Treasury for up to thirty percent of their qualifying costs in lieu of their traditional production or investment tax credits. Following extension through the Tax Relief, Unemployment Insurance Reauthorization, and Job Creation Act of 2010, the section 1603 cash grant was available to qualifying projects that were placed in service or started construction from 2009 through 2011.

While the section 1603 cash grant has expired, its legacy lives on. The grant provides a powerful counterfactual against which to evaluate the efficacy and efficiency of federal tax credits for the promotion of renewable energy. . . .

The jury appears to be hung in its attempt to reach a verdict on the past success and future fate of tax credits for renewable energy. Support comes mostly from within the industry. Speaking for over 1200 member companies, the American Wind Energy Association praises the production tax credit as "an effective tool to keep electricity rates low and encourage development of proven renewable energy projects" adding that "it is crucial that it be extended." Representing roughly 1000 member companies, the Solar Energy Industries Association hails the investment tax credit as "the cornerstone of continued growth of solar energy in the United States" and "one of the most important federal policy mechanisms to support the deployment of solar energy in the United States."

Policy and financial analysts paint a less favorable picture of federal tax credit support for renewable energy. Analysts with Bloomberg New

Energy Finance find that a cash subsidy in lieu of tax credits "offers US taxpayers a better bang for their buck." Comparing the section 1603 cash grant to the production tax credit, researchers at Lawrence Berkeley National Laboratory reach a similar conclusion, highlighting the cash grant's greater value to project developers. Even the Congressional Research Service notes that "[s]ection 1603 grants may be a more economically efficient mechanism than tax credits for delivering benefits to the renewable energy sector." Similarly, the Bipartisan Policy Center finds that "while the tax-based incentive system has been enormously supportive for the renewable energy industry, it is also a sub-optimal tool and will likely be unsustainable as the industry matures."

. . . .

Empirical evidence and qualitative analysis illustrate the remarkable inefficiency of using federal tax credits to promote the deployment of renewable energy technologies. Unless a project developer has sufficient tax liability from other sources, she will not be able to reap the full value of her project's tax benefits. . . .

The tax expenditure literature has long recognized the broader challenges associated with government use of tax incentives to subsidize socially beneficial activities, especially by start-up companies and other revenue-challenged firms. Tax credits for renewable energy represent a particularly dramatic example of these challenges, for a variety of reasons. However one may feel about the tax system's general suitability for promoting climate change mitigation, technological innovation, and other non-tax policy goals through Pigouvian tax expenditures, a government subsidy becomes untenable based purely on efficiency grounds if only one to two thirds of its value actually goes to fund the targeted activity. Moreover, the ability of a small group of high-income entities to divert significant portions of the subsidy into their own pockets raises serious concerns over taxpayer equity. Lastly, the tax credit regime's inefficiencies translate to suboptimal deployment rates that, in turn, impede the timely decarbonization of America's energy economy, as required for effective climate change mitigation. . . .

Economists have long suggested that a price on greenhouse gas emissions, in the form of a carbon tax or cap-and-trade regime, is, in theory, the single most efficient policy to mitigate climate change and promote abatement technologies, such as solar, wind, and other low-carbon renewable energy technologies. A price on greenhouse gas emissions would require producers to internalize the cost of their emissions and thereby penalize pollution and encourage abatement. Over time, this direct, static effect would be complemented by an indirect, dynamic effect of encouraging refinement of existing and development of new abatement technologies. From an efficiency perspective, a tax on greenhouse gas emissions or a cap-

and-trade scheme would incur lower opportunity costs than direct subsidies for these technologies.

NOTES & QUESTIONS

1. From the federal government's perspective, which type of tax credit program is likely less expensive and less complicated to administer: ITCs or PTCs? Why?

2. Which type of tax credit program is more likely to ensure that a renewable energy project continues generating power even several years after the project is completed: ITCs or PTCs? Why?

3. Suppose that you are a policy advocate for a large stakeholder in the natural gas industry. Natural gas-fired power plants typically produce far less carbon dioxide emissions per kWh of generated power than do coal-fired power plants. Should natural gas-fired power plants qualify for tax credits comparable to the PTC or ITC? Why or why not?

4. What are some policy advantages of direct cash grant programs over tax credit programs? What are some disadvantages? Which would you favor for use in promoting wind energy, and why?

5. *Loan Guarantees.* Another potential form of federal subsidy for renewables is the providing of loan guarantees to private companies or developers to help finance renewable energy-related projects. For instance, under the 2009 American Recovery and Reinvestment Act's Title XVII-Section 1705 Program, the federal government guaranteed loans to private companies to help the companies secure financing for various renewable energy projects, including wind projects. Although the program was relatively short-lived, expiring in 2011, some advocates argue that it helped private lenders become more comfortable financing renewable energy projects. There appears to be some evidence to support this argument, including significant growth in private financing of utility-scale solar photovoltaic projects in the years following the 1705 Program's expiration. *See* U.S. DEP'T OF ENERGY LOAN PROGRAMS OFFICE, POWERING NEW MARKETS: UTILITY-SCALE PHOTOVOLTAIC SOLAR (2015), http://energy.gov/sites/prod/files/2015/02/f19/DOE_LPO_Utility-Scale_PV_Solar_Markets_February2015.pdf.

2. RENEWABLE PORTFOLIO STANDARD (RPS) POLICIES

In addition to the PTC and other federal-level incentives, multiple state government programs also seek to promote wind energy. Some states have enacted statutes providing special favored property tax, sales tax, or income tax treatment for wind projects. Some states also have laws that simplify siting approval processes to help promote wind energy projects and wind energy-oriented transmission development. However, the most influential state-level policies in promoting wind energy in recent years have been renewable portfolio standards (RPSs). RPSs require utilities to procure a specified minimum percentage or quantity of all of the electricity they sell from qualifying renewable energy sources. For example, as of 2017, Nevada's RPS generally requires utilities to source at least 25% of the electricity they sell from qualifying renewable energy resources by the year 2025. *See* NEV. REV. STAT. § 704.7801 et seq.

a. What Are RPS Policies and Renewable Energy Credits?

Although a majority of states have RPS policies of some kind, the details of those policies vary significantly from state to state. Figure 2.7 identifies those states with RPS policies as of 2015. Some states' RPS policies are merely goals, implying that there is no clear penalty for utilities if they fail to meet them. Many RPS policies also require that some proportion of the electricity used to meet RPS requirements come from specific types of renewable energy strategies—such as distributed energy, solar energy, or off-shore wind energy—or offer additional credit toward RPS requirements for utilities that use those strategies.

Figure 2.7. States with Renewable Portfolio Standard Policies

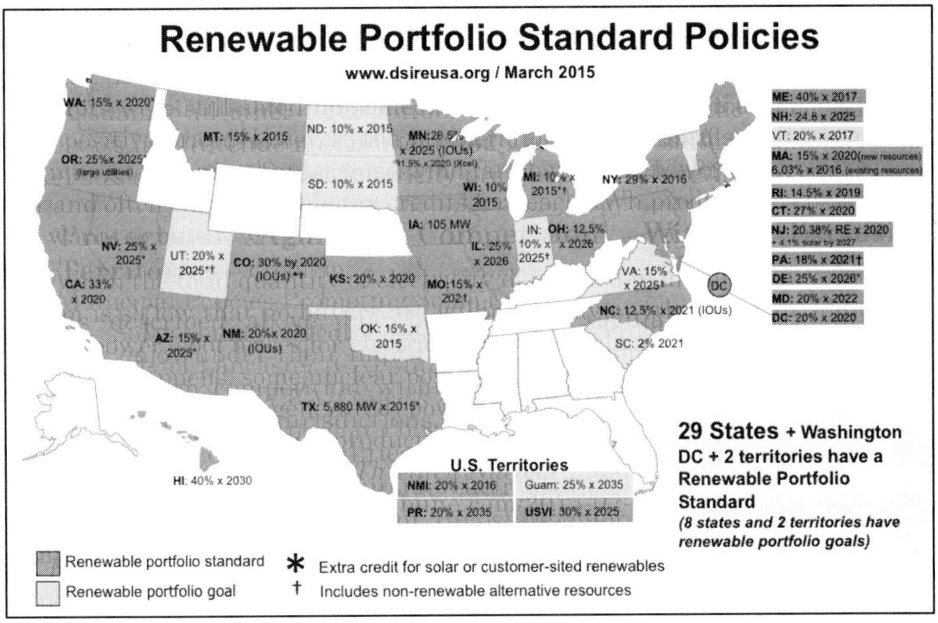

Source: www.dsireusa.org

Although RPSs do not directly subsidize renewable energy development, they do bolster demand for it by requiring utilities to purchase certain minimum quantities of renewable power. Moreover, most states with RPS policies allow parties who generate qualifying renewable energy to sell *renewable energy credits* (RECs) or certificates to others and the value of these RECs can act like a state-level subsidy of renewable energy. The excerpts from Missouri's Renewable Portfolio Standard below provide a better sense of the basic structure of RPS policies.

MISSOURI CLEAN ENERGY ACT (PROPOSITION C)
MO. REV. STAT. § 393.1020–1050 (2008)

§ 393.1020. Citation of law

Sections 393.1025 and 393.1030 shall be known as the "Renewable Energy Standard".

§ 393.1025. Definitions

As used in sections 393.1020 to 393.1030, the following terms mean:

(1) "Commission", the public service commission;

(2) "Department", the department of natural resources;

(3) "Electric utility", any electrical corporation as defined by section 386.020;

(4) "Renewable energy credit" or "REC", a tradeable certificate of proof that one megawatt-hour of electricity has been generated from renewable energy sources; and

(5) "Renewable energy resources", electric energy produced from wind, solar thermal sources, photovoltaic cells and panels, dedicated crops grown for energy production, cellulosic agricultural residues, plant residues, methane from landfills, from agricultural operations, or from wastewater treatment, thermal depolymerization or pyrolysis for converting waste material to energy, clean and untreated wood such as pallets, hydropower (not including pumped storage) that does not require a new diversion or impoundment of water and that has a nameplate rating of ten megawatts or less, fuel cells using hydrogen produced by one of the above-named renewable energy sources, and other sources of energy not including nuclear that become available after November 4, 2008, and are certified as renewable by rule by the department.

§ 393.1030. Electric utilities, portfolio requirements—tracking requirements—rulemaking authority—rebate offers—certification of electricity generated

1. The commission shall, in consultation with the department, prescribe by rule a portfolio requirement for all electric utilities to generate or purchase electricity generated from renewable energy resources. Such portfolio requirement shall provide that electricity from renewable energy

resources shall constitute the following portions of each electric utility's sales:

(1) No less than two percent for calendar years 2011 through 2013;

(2) No less than five percent for calendar years 2014 through 2017;

(3) No less than ten percent for calendar years 2018 through 2020; and

(4) No less than fifteen percent in each calendar year beginning in 2021.

At least two percent of each portfolio requirement shall be derived from solar energy. The portfolio requirements shall apply to all power sold to Missouri consumers whether such power is self-generated or purchased from another source in or outside of this state. A utility may comply with the standard in whole or in part by purchasing RECs. Each kilowatt-hour of eligible energy generated in Missouri shall count as 1.25 kilowatt-hours for purposes of compliance.

2. The commission, in consultation with the department and within one year of November 4, 2008, shall select a program for tracking and verifying the trading of renewable energy credits. An unused credit may exist for up to three years from the date of its creation. A credit may be used only once to comply with sections 393.1020 to 393.1030 and may not also be used to satisfy any similar nonfederal requirement... The commission, except where the department is specified, shall make whatever rules are necessary to enforce the renewable energy standard. Such rules shall include:

(1) A maximum average retail rate increase of one percent determined by estimating and comparing the electric utility's cost of compliance with least-cost renewable generation and the cost of continuing to generate or purchase electricity from entirely nonrenewable sources, taking into proper account future environmental regulatory risk including the risk of greenhouse gas regulation. . . . ;

(2) Penalties of at least twice the average market value of renewable energy credits for the compliance period for failure to meet the targets of subsection 1 of this section. An electric utility will be excused if it proves to the commission that failure was due to events beyond its reasonable control that could not have been reasonably mitigated, or that the maximum average retail rate increase has been reached. Penalties shall not be recovered from customers. Amounts forfeited under this section shall be remitted to the department to purchase renewable energy credits needed for compliance. Any excess forfeited revenues shall be used by the department's energy center solely for renewable energy and energy efficiency projects;

(3) Provisions for an annual report to be filed by each electric utility in a format sufficient to document its progress in meeting the targets;

(4) Provision for recovery outside the context of a regular rate case of prudently incurred costs and the pass-through of benefits to customers of any savings achieved by an electrical corporation in meeting the requirements of this section.

. . . .

4. The department shall, in consultation with the commission, establish by rule a certification process for electricity generated from renewable resources and used to fulfill the requirements of subsection 1 of this section. Certification criteria for renewable energy generation shall be determined by factors that include fuel type, technology, and the environmental impacts of the generating facility. Renewable energy facilities shall not cause undue adverse air, water, or land use impacts, including impacts associated with the gathering of generation feedstocks. If any amount of fossil fuel is used with renewable energy resources, only the portion of electrical output attributable to renewable energy resources shall be used to fulfill the portfolio requirements.

NOTES & QUESTIONS

1. Is it possible for a utility to comply with Missouri's RPS requirements without ever purchasing and selling any renewable power? Why or why not? Do you think that is problematic from a policy perspective? Why or why not?

2. What consequences await utilities that fail to comply with Missouri's RPS requirements? How does language within the statute ensure that the utility—and not its customer base—ultimately suffers the consequences for non-compliance?

3. What sorts of administrative costs are associated with Missouri's RPS program? How do you think these costs compare with those of other plausible state-level policy strategies for promoting renewable energy?

4. *RPS Carve-Outs.* The RPS policies in several states, including Missouri include *carve-out* provisions. Carve-out provisions require some minimum proportion of the renewable energy generation that utilities use to satisfy their RPS requirements come from a specific type of energy source. For example, investor-owned utilities and retail suppliers in Arizona must get 15% of the power they sell from renewable resource by the year 2025. In addition, however, 30% of the renewable power used to satisfy this RPS requirement (or 4.5% of all power sold) must specifically come from "distributed generation" sources. ARIZ. ADMIN. CODE § 14–2–1801 et seq. (2007).

5. *RPS Multipliers.* Several states have also included multiplier provisions within their RPS policies. These policies award extra credit toward

meeting RPS requirements for certain types of renewable energy strategies. For example, under Washington state's RPS statute, electricity from distributed generation count double toward a utility's RPS requirement. In other words, if a utility in that state purchased and sold 2MW of renewable energy generated with distributed sources during the past year, then the utility would get credit toward its RPS requirement in the amount of 4MW.

What is the multiplier under Missouri's RPS? How does it give special preference to solar energy generation within the state? Suppose that you represented a wind energy farm in a neighboring state that wanted to sell renewable power to Missouri utilities but was unable attract business because of Missouri's in-state RPS preference provision. What legal arguments might you make against the validity or constitutionality of this provision?

6. *RPS Cost Caps.* One other fairly common feature within state RPS policies is a *cost cap* provision. Cost caps are provisions designed to limit the amount by which electricity rates or utility costs may increase from efforts to comply with an RPS requirement. What is the size of the cost cap in the Missouri RPS statute? How does this cost cap provision help to ensure that compliant utilities in the state and their customers do not suffer major financial losses because of the RPS requirements? Why might including cost cap provisions be an important issue in some states' efforts to enact RPS statutes?

REC programs theoretically promote economic efficiency by harnessing market forces to incentivize additional renewable energy generation by those who can generate it at the lowest cost. However, in practice, REC programs have created several of their own unique legal and political controversies. The following excerpt provides basic information about RPSs and RECs and introduces some of the issues that have emerged within REC markets in recent years.

RENEWING ELECTRICITY COMPETITION

David Schraub
42 FLA. ST. U. L. REV. 937, 963–69 (2015)

Renewable Energy Credits are a joint product of generation and are separate from the actual kWh of energy produced. They are measured in energy units such as kWh and can be used to meet an electricity retailer's portfolio requirements in lieu of acquiring and selling at retail actual kWh generated from eligible renewable resources.

A Renewable Energy Credit typically represents a certain amount of clean energy placed onto the grid. Because RECs and actual produced energy are distinct entities, they may be unbundled and sold separately from one another. Once a REC is "used"—either to meet legal clean energy portfolio requirements or to offset dirty energy usage by end-use consumers—it is generally retired and cannot be reused.

Renewable Energy Credits are traded in two primary markets. The first is the "compliance" market. Many states require utilities to source a specified percentage of their energy from renewable providers, and the purchase of RECs is one way utilities can meet these statutory mandates. This marketplace is extensively regulated and has been the subject of significant discussion in the literature. However, RECs can also be bought and sold on the "voluntary" market. Even absent any legal requirement, some consumers may be willing to pay a premium for clean energy. While it is virtually impossible to discern whether the individual electrons that reach a particular consumer are "clean" or "dirty," RECs are a way of verifying that clean energy equivalent to the consumer's usage has been placed into the pool of electricity.

Unlike the compliance market, the voluntary market is subject to comparatively little regulation. . . .

A. Two REC Markets

1. The Compliance Market

Many states have imposed Renewable Portfolio Standards (RPS), which require state utilities to obtain a specified percentage of the electricity they sell from renewable sources. One way to meet these requirements, of course, is for the utility to invest in its own renewable generation facilities. Typically, though not always, states permit utilities to purchase RECs to meet these requirements in lieu of actually buying "clean" electricity themselves. This option may make sense if, for example, the utility's normal energy sources are insufficient to satisfy clean energy demand or the generators which can most efficiently produce renewable energy cannot cheaply transmit the actual wattage to consumers. Because these REC sales are made to satisfy state mandates, trading of this sort is known as the REC "compliance" market. . . .

RPS are creations of state law, and states have considerable latitude in determining the structure of REC trading, the types of energy sources which "qualify" as renewable and thus can create RECs, and other elements of the regulatory program. The preeminence of state authority over the field has led to two primary problems. First, states have naturally desired that RPS programs lead to enhanced renewable resources in the vicinity of the state itself—it does Georgia little good if its RPS subsidizes increased renewable generation in Iowa. State efforts to favor the purchase of locally produced clean energy (or RECs derived from such local sources) raise significant dormant commerce clause issues. Second, because states can and do have different definitions for what qualifies as a renewable resource, there are barriers to the interstate trade of RECs—a REC which may validly apply against RPS requirements in Utah may not do so in

Colorado. This raises commerce clause issues of its own; it has also prompted some commentators to press for a national RPS standard.

2.   The Voluntary Market

The compliance market derives its force from state-imposed legal requirements that give value to renewably generated electricity. Even where there is no legal duty to act, however, some consumers may wish to purchase green power on their own initiative. These "voluntary" purchases of green energy are a rapidly increasing proportion of renewable electricity sales.

One important area of distinction between the compliance and voluntary markets is the primary purchaser of the RECs. The compliance market is dominated by utilities, because RPS mandates are placed upon electricity retailers, not electricity consumers. Hence, utilities purchase RECs from renewable energy generators or brokers—either bundled or unbundled from the electric power itself. The consumers are not involved and, unless the utilities are permitted to pass their potentially higher costs onward, may not even be affected. Along this axis, compliance REC trading is not materially different from the electricity market norm.

In the voluntary market, by contrast, the consumers are usually the purchasers of the RECs. This places them in a relatively unique position of having the ability to interact and deal directly with power producers, or independent REC brokers, regardless of the regulated or deregulated structure of their state retail market. RECs are distinct in that they are an electricity "product" that is not tied to the flow of electrons and thus can be bought and sold outside the electricity grid system. REC sales thus bypass the natural monopoly and offer opportunities for buyers to interact with a multitude of potential sellers even where electricity markets are not otherwise open for competition.

Voluntary REC purchases come in three main varieties. In states with electricity competition, consumers often may simply choose to buy their electricity from companies that produce some or all of their electricity from renewable sources. Even in monopoly states, though, some states and utilities are offering "green pricing" plans, wherein the utility offers consumers the option to pay a premium for green power. Like in the compliance market, the utility then typically has a choice regarding whether it will directly source green energy or instead purchase an equivalent amount of RECs to cover the consumer's energy usage. Finally, there is an "unbundled" REC market where consumers can purchase just the RECs without acquiring any corresponding electricity voltage.

Because the voluntary market is decoupled from specific state mandates, regulation of RECs trading on the voluntary market is relatively minimal. In North Carolina, for instance, even the *definition* of a REC is restricted to those sold for purposes of complying with the state's RPS requirements. Indeed, the only regulation North Carolina has put forward with respect to voluntary REC sales is a requirement that a single REC not be "double-counted" for both voluntary and compliance purposes. [* * *]

At its broadest, a REC is a "green jewel box" which encompasses all positive environmental attributes of a given form of electricity production. But defining RECs broadly creates considerable ambiguity regarding what RECs actually represent and whether they actually transfer a property right to specific emissions reductions. It is of course very difficult to "dynamically score" the total environmental impact of any particular generation project. The more RECs are said to represent, the harder these claims are to verify and the further they begin to stray from a quantifiable good that represents a particular tradable attribute. Moreover, as the qualities of a "REC" grow more abstract and less amenable to standardization, their usefulness as a tradable instrument diminishes. As Michael Gillenwater puts it:

> Environmental markets that operate with a clearly defined commodity are more likely to have low transaction costs and produce public good benefits. Environmental commodities that lack clear definitions will have higher transaction costs. And when traded in separate markets, poorly defined commodities will more easily come into conflict and cause confusion among market participants.[149]

RECs can also be given a narrow scope to refer only to the fact that "(i) the underlying specific quantity of renewables-based electricity has been produced under the conditions specified by the standard information on the certificate and (ii) that the certificate has not yet been used for another application." "Used" must be interpreted broadly so as to not exploit consumer ignorance over renewable power transactions. The arrangement described in *SZ Enterprises LLC v. Iowa Utilities Board* provides a striking example. There, a solar energy company contracted with Dubuque, Iowa to construct a solar facility which would "provide the city with renewable energy." The city would purchase the entire output of the solar facility, but the solar company would retain ownership of the RECs (with the stated intention that they would sell them to other parties). The problem with this proposal is that once the RECs are sold, it is misleading to say that Dubuque is being provided with renewable energy. Though the RECs have not been "used" by Dubuque in a formal sense—they were apparently not retired or used to satisfy RPS requirements—by representing to the city and its citizens that it was providing them with renewable energy, Dubuque functionally used its renewable attributes, and the solar company should not have been allowed to reuse them for sale to other parties.

---

[149] Michael Gillenwater, *Redefining RECs (Part 2) Untangling certificates and emission markets*, 36 ENERGY POL'Y. 2120, 2121 (2008).

QUESTIONS

1. According to Schraub, what are some problems that have interfered with the effective functioning of interstate REC markets?

2. What does it mean for a REC to be *unbundled*? According to the excerpt, how can unbundling potentially facilitate the "double-counting" of RECs?

3. What is the difference between the compliance market and the voluntary market for RECs? Why might a consumer voluntarily choose to purchase a REC through a voluntary market?

4. Do you think states should be allowed to craft their RPS policies such that utilities can only use RECs arising from in state renewable energy generation to satisfy RPS goals? Why or why not?

b. Challenges to RPS Policies Under the Dormant Commerce Clause

As suggested in the excerpt above, RPS policies in many states have provisions that effectively favor in-state renewable energy over out-of-state renewable energy. On some occasions, these provisions have provoked constitutional challenges under the Dormant Commerce Clause doctrine. The Dormant Commerce Clause doctrine is rooted in the Commerce Clause of the United States Constitution, which empowers Congress "to regulate commerce . . . among the several states." U.S. CONST. art. I, § 8. The Dormant Commerce Clause doctrine basically prohibits states from enacting legislation that improperly burdens or discriminates against interstate commerce. In the following case, a court considers whether Colorado's RPS policies violate the doctrine.

ENERGY AND ENVIRONMENTAL LEGAL INSTITUTE V. EPEL

United States District Court, District of Colorado, 2014
43 F.Supp.3d 1171

MARTINEZ, J.

This action challenges the constitutionality of Colorado's Renewable Energy Standard statute, Colo. Rev. Stat. § 40–2–124. In this case's current posture, Plaintiffs seek a declaration that the provision requiring that Colorado utility companies obtain an increasing proportion of their electricity from renewable sources violates the Commerce Clause of the United States Constitution. . . .

Plaintiff Energy and Environment Legal Institute ("EELI") is a non-profit organization which describes itself as being dedicated to the advancement of rational, free-market solutions to land, energy, and environmental challenges in the United States. EELI also promotes coal energy, and believes that the impact human activities have had on the rise in global temperatures is an open question. Plaintiff Rod Lueck is a member of EELI who resides in Colorado. Defendants Joshua Epel, James Tarpey, and Pamela Patton are members of the Colorado Public Utilities Commission. The Intervenor-Defendants are various non-profit organizations devoted to preserving the environment or promoting renewable energy resources and industries. For purposes of this Order, the Court's reference to "Defendants" includes the named Defendants and the Intervenor-Defendants.

In 2004, Colorado voters passed Amendment 37, which was intended to promote the development and utilization of renewable energy resources. Amendment 37 was codified in 2005 as the Renewable Energy Standard statute (the "RES") at Colo. Rev. Stat. § 40–2–124. Although Plaintiffs originally challenged other aspects of the RES, at this point in the case, the only remaining claims assert that Colo. Rev. Stat. §§ 40–2–124(1)(c)(I),(V), (V.5) and 40–2–124(3),(4), and their implementing regulations . . . (together, the "Renewables Quota"), violate the Commerce Clause of the United States Constitution.

The Renewables Quota requires each retail utility to generate, or cause to be generated, renewable energy resources in specified minimum amounts. As originally formulated, the Renewables Quota required certain Colorado electric utilities to provide 10% of their retail electricity sales from renewable sources by 2015. Since the RES was adopted, the Colorado Legislature has amended the statute three times to increase the Renewables Quota and to add different kinds of electricity generation entities.

As it currently stands, the Renewables Quota includes three distinct requirements depending on the type and size of electric utility. By 2020, investor-owned utilities such as Xcel must obtain 30% of their retail electricity sales from renewable sources. . . .

The RES allows utilities to meet their Renewables Quota by either generating or buying renewable power directly, or by purchasing renewable energy credits. Colo. Rev. Stat. § 40–2–124(1)(d). The RES defines the types of energy that can be credited towards a utility's Renewables Quota, and includes certain types of both recycled energy and energy generated from renewable sources. . . . Recycled energy is energy captured from the heat from exhaust stacks or pipes that would otherwise be lost, and which does not combust additional fossil fuel. . . . The RES's definition of renewable energy resources includes solar, wind, geothermal, biomass, and hydroelectricity with certain restrictions. . . .

The RES and its implementing regulations also create a system of tradable renewable energy credits that may be used by a utility to fulfil its

Renewables Quota. . . . For a Colorado utility to use renewable energy (or renewable energy credits) towards its Renewables Quota, it must seek approval from Colorado's Public Utility Commission. . . . Certain utilities must also submit to the Public Utilities Commission a plan detailing how they intend to comply with the Renewables Quota, including estimates of the amount of renewable energy that will be generated by various sources. . . . An approved plan carries a rebuttable presumption that the utility is acting with prudence. . . .

III. ANALYSIS

"The Commerce Clause provides that 'Congress shall have Power . . . [t]o regulate Commerce with foreign Nations, and among the several States.'" *United Haulers Ass'n, Inc. v. Oneida-Herkimer Solid Waste Mgmt. Auth.*, 550 U.S. 330, 337, 127 S.Ct. 1786, 167 L.Ed.2d 655 (2007) (quoting U.S. Const. art. I, § 8, cl. 3). In addition to that express authority, courts have also interpreted the Commerce Clause to restrain state authority implicitly, which is referred to as the dormant Commerce Clause. *See id.* The "central rationale" of the dormant Commerce Clause "is to prohibit state or municipal laws whose object is local economic protectionism, laws that would excite those jealousies and retaliatory measures the Constitution was designed to prevent." *C & A Carbone, Inc. v. Town of Clarkstown*, 511 U.S. 383, 390, 114 S.Ct. 1677, 128 L.Ed.2d 399 (1994).

In this circuit, a state statute may violate the dormant Commerce Clause in three ways. First, a statute that clearly discriminates against interstate commerce in favor of intrastate commerce is virtually invalid *per se* and can survive only if the discrimination is demonstrably justified by a valid factor unrelated to economic protectionism. *KT & G Corp. v. Attorney Gen. of Okla.*, 535 F.3d 1114, 1143 (10th Cir. 2008). Second, a statute will be invalid *per se* if it has the practical effect of controlling commerce occurring entirely outside the boundaries of the state in question. *Id.* Finally, if the statute does not discriminate against interstate commerce, it will nevertheless be invalidated if it imposes a burden on interstate commerce which is not commensurate with the local benefits secured. *See Pike v. Bruce Church Inc.*, 397 U.S. 137, 142, 90 S.Ct. 844, 25 L.Ed.2d 174 (1970).

. . . .

B.   Discrimination Against Out-of-State Interests

"State laws discriminating against interstate commerce on their face are 'virtually *per se* invalid.'" *Fulton Corp. v. Faulkner*, 516 U.S. 325, 331, 116 S.Ct. 848, 133 L.Ed.2d 796 (1996) (quoting *Or. Waste Sys., Inc. v. Dep't of Envl. Quality of Or.*, 511 U.S. 93, 99, 114 S.Ct. 1345, 128 L.Ed.2d 13 (1994)). "In this context, 'discrimination' simply means differential treatment of in-state and out-of-state economic interests that benefits the former and burdens the latter." *United Haulers*, 550 U.S. at 338, 127 S.Ct. 1786 (quotation omitted).

Defendants move for summary judgment under this theory, arguing that the Renewables Quota does not discriminate against interstate commerce on its face, or in its purpose or effect. (ECF No. 186 at 19.) In response to this argument, Plaintiffs have made no attempt to identify specific facts showing that there is a genuine issue for trial. . . .

Thus, the Court finds that Plaintiffs have not met their burden of showing that any dispute of material fact exists as to whether the Renewables Quota discriminates against out-of-state interests. It therefore necessarily follows that the Court must grant Defendants' Motion for Summary Judgment as to this theory of establishing a dormant Commerce Clause violation.

C. Practical Effect of Extraterritorial Control

Both parties move for summary judgment under the theory that the RES violates the Commerce Clause by attempting to control wholly extraterritorial commerce. To determine whether a regulatory scheme violates the Commerce Clause under this theory, the Court must look beyond the plain language of the statute and evaluate its practical effect to discern whether it controls extraterritorial commerce. *KT & G Corp. v. Att'y Gen. of Okla.*, 535 F.3d 1114, 1143 (10th Cir. 2008). The legislative intent behind a statutory scheme is irrelevant. *Healy v. Beer Inst., Inc.*, 491 U.S. 324, 336, 109 S.Ct. 2491, 105 L.Ed.2d 275 (1989).

Courts have found that statutes which tie pricing decisions in one state to the prices charged for the same good in another state are invalid. . . .

Statutes that attempt to impose one state's policy decisions on other states are also invalid. For example, in *National Solid Wastes Management Association v. Meyer*, 63 F.3d 652, 653–54 (7th Cir. 1995), the court struck down a Wisconsin statute that conditioned imports of waste on the exporting jurisdiction's adoption of Wisconsin's recycling standards. Finally, statutes that regulate commercial transactions between two out-of-state entities also violate the Commerce Clause. . . . Despite the various ways this doctrine has manifested itself, "[i]n the modern era, the Supreme Court has rarely held that statutes violate the extraterritorality doctrine." *Rocky Mountain Farmers Union v. Corey*, 730 F.3d 1070, 1101 (9th Cir. 2013).

Plaintiffs argue that the Renewables Quota places a restriction on how out-of-state goods are manufactured in that it requires out-of-state electricity to be generated according to Colorado's terms. Plaintiffs contend that the Renewables Quota is a "mandate" which requires energy produced wholly out-of-state to comply with Colorado-approved methods for renewable energy. Plaintiffs argue that this mandate operates to project policy decisions made by voters in Colorado onto other states, such as Wyoming.

The Court disagrees. First, the Renewables Quota does not impact transactions between out-of-state business entities. If a Wyoming coal company generates electricity and sells it to a South Dakota business, the Colorado Renewables Quota does not impact that transaction in any way. The Renewables Quota only regulates Colorado energy generators and the companies that do business with *Colorado* energy generators. As Plaintiffs acknowledge, a state can regulate electricity generation occurring within its borders. Because the Renewables Quota does not affect commerce unless and until an out-of-state electricity generator freely chooses to do business with a Colorado utility, it does not impermissibly control wholly out-of-state commerce. . . .

Moreover, the Renewables Quota does not mandate that an out-of-state energy generator do business in any particular manner. Colorado energy companies are free to buy and sell electricity from any in-state or out-of-state generator. The RES does not limit these transactions, set minimum standards for out-of-state generators that wish to do business in Colorado, or attempt to control pricing of the electricity. Rather, the RES comes into play only with regard to whether energy purchased by a Colorado utility from an out-of-state electricity generator will count towards the Colorado utility's Renewables Quota. As such, the RES does not impose conditions on the importation of electricity into Colorado. . . .

The Court agrees with Plaintiffs that the RES may influence the way out-of-state electricity generators do business because the Renewables Quota provides Colorado utilities an incentive to purchase electricity that can be credited towards their Renewables Quota. However, the fact that this incentive structure may negatively impact the profits of out-of-state generators whose electricity cannot be used to fulfil the Quota does not make the Renewables Quota invalid. The dormant Commerce Clause neither protects the profits of any particular business, nor the right to do business in any particular manner. . . . Thus, the fact that the RES may economically harm companies—both in-state and out-of-state—that produce non-renewable energy does not mean that it violates the dormant Commerce Clause.

Moreover, the fact that the RES may provide an incentive for out-of-state companies to conduct their business in a manner that complies with Colorado's renewable energy standards also does not make the statute improper. . . . The dormant Commerce Clause does not prevent states from creating incentive structures to attract certain kinds of business. . . .

Plaintiffs also argue that the Renewables Quota violates the dormant Commerce Clause because it is inconsistent with other state statutes that promote renewable energy. For example, Plaintiffs point out that Utah's definition of a renewable energy fuel source includes a facility that derives its energy from methane gas from an abandoned coal mine. Other states that have a system similar to Colorado's RES permit credit for ocean thermal and wave generation electricity sources.

This contention by Plaintiffs fails, however, because the Commerce Clause has not been applied so broadly as to strike down any state regulation that differs from other states. The only cases in which the Supreme Court has held that the federal need for uniformity outweighs the state's ability to devise its own regulations involve areas like foreign trade and interstate transportation. . . . Plaintiffs have failed to demonstrate that there exists such a compelling need for uniformity in the market for renewable energy credits that having a system of different or even inconsistent state regulations is unworkable.

. . . .

In sum, out-of-state companies are free to generate electricity using whatever method they choose, can sell that electricity to whomever they choose—inside or outside of Colorado—and can do so at whatever price they choose. The RES does not control any aspect of a transaction between two out-of-state entities; it governs only whether electricity purchased by a Colorado utility counts towards that utility's Renewables Quota. As such, the Court finds that Plaintiffs have failed to show that there is any material fact in dispute as to whether the RES improperly regulates wholly out-of-state commerce.

D. *Pike* Test

Under *Pike v. Bruce Church, Inc.*, a state statute that does not directly regulate or discriminate against interstate commerce may nonetheless still be invalid if the "burden imposed on [interstate] commerce is clearly excessive in relation to the putative local benefits." 397 U.S. 137, 142, 90 S.Ct. 844, 25 L.Ed.2d 174 (1970). "[T]he extent of the burden that will be tolerated will of course depend on the nature of the local interest involved, and on whether it could be promoted as well with a lesser impact on interstate activities." *Id.* The party challenging the statute bears the burden of establishing a *Pike* violation. *See Dorrance v. McCarthy*, 957 F.2d 761, 763 (10th Cir. 1992).

The Tenth Circuit has held that, when considering the *Pike* balancing test, the Court must consider four factors: (1) the burden on interstate commerce; (2) the nature of the putative benefits conferred by the statute; (3) whether the burden is "clearly excessive in relation to" the local interests; and (4) whether the local interests can be promoted as well with a lesser impact on interstate commerce. *Blue Circle Cement, Inc. v. Bd. of Cty. Comm'rs*, 27 F.3d 1499, 1512 (10th Cir. 1994).

With regard to the burden on interstate commerce, Plaintiffs argue that the RES burdens interstate commerce due to a lack of uniformity in state laws. Plaintiffs point out that thirty states and the District of Columbia have mandatory renewable energy standards with various renewables requirements. The Supreme Court has held that a lack of uniformity amongst state laws can be a significant burden to interstate commerce, but those cases involve interstate travel such as railroads and trucking. *See Raymond Motor Transp., Inc. v. Rice*, 434 U.S. 429, 445, 98 S.Ct. 787, 54 L.Ed.2d 664 (1978) (striking down statute that limited length of tractor-trailers); *Bibb,* 359 U.S. at 526–27, 79 S.Ct. 962. The Renewables Quota does not make it more difficult for electricity to flow between states that are connected via the same grid. As such, these cases are readily distinguishable. Plaintiffs have failed to explain how the various renewables requirements imposed by the states ha[ve] limited interstate commerce in the electricity market.

Plaintiffs also contend that the RES burdens interstate commerce by impacting commerce beyond the borders of the state, specifically with regard to the reduction in the market for thermal coal and hydrocarbon electricity generation. While Plaintiffs have presented evidence showing that the Renewables Quota has caused an increased demand for renewable energy in Colorado, which correlates to a decrease in the market share for coal and hydro-carbon, Plaintiffs have failed to show that this shift in the market burdens interstate commerce. The critical inquiry is whether market shift caused by the Renewables Quota places a greater burden on interstate commerce than is placed on intrastate commerce. . . . There is no evidence in the record showing that the Renewables Quota causes greater harm to out-of-state coal and hydrocarbon electricity generators than is caused to in-state coal and hydrocarbon electricity generators. In fact, the record shows that demand for out-of-state coal has increased since the RES was enacted. As such, Plaintiffs have failed to show that the market shift away from coal and hydrocarbon electricity generation substantially burdens interstate commerce for purposes of the *Pike* test.

Finally, Plaintiffs contend that the Renewables Quota has burdened interstate commerce because it has reduced the size of the market, which alone is sufficient to meet the *Pike* burden. Though Plaintiffs cite *Exxon Corp.,* in support of their position, that case's holding in fact supports the conclusion that the Renewables Quota does not burden interstate commerce. In *Exxon,* the Supreme Court held that Maryland's statute barring all producers and refiners of petroleum products from operating any retail outlet within the state did not burden interstate commerce. 437 U.S. at 127, 98 S.Ct. 2207. Though the statute would cause some petroleum refiners to choose not to do business with Maryland, other refiners would step in to fill that spot in the market. *Id.* The Court held that "interstate commerce is not subjected to an impermissible burden simply because an otherwise valid regulation causes some business to shift from one interstate supplier to another." *Id.*

Like in *Exxon,* the Renewables Quota has caused a shift from electricity generated from non-renewable sources to electricity generated by renewable sources. However, this shift from one type of supplier to another has not resulted in a decrease in interstate electricity transmission between Colorado and elsewhere. In fact, the record shows that, since the RES was enacted, Colorado's demand for all kinds of electricity—both renewable and non-renewable—has increased. Prior to 2007, Colorado was a net exporter of electricity. By 2010, Colorado's electricity sales exceeded in-state production by 2,000 gigawatt-hours. Plaintiffs have shown only that there has been a shift in the source of electricity generation since the RES was enacted, not that there has been any reduction in the size of the Colorado electricity market or in the amount of electricity imported by Colorado. Thus, Plaintiffs have not shown that the RES has caused an overall decrease in Colorado's market for electricity—either for electricity produced in-state or out-of-state.

In sum, the Court finds that Plaintiffs have failed to show a genuine dispute of material fact as to whether the Renewables Quota or the RES in general burdens interstate commerce for purposes of the *Pike* test.

. . . .

Fifty-four percent of Colorado voters voted to approve renewable energy standards for the state in 2004. The Supreme Court has frequently admonished that courts should not "second-guess the empirical judgments of lawmakers concerning the utility of legislation." *CTS Corp. v. Dynamics Corp. of Am.,* 481 U.S. 69, 92, 107 S.Ct. 1637, 95 L.Ed.2d 67 (1987); *Ferguson v. Skrupa,* 372 U.S. 726, 729, 83 S.Ct. 1028, 10 L.Ed.2d 93 (1963) ("[I]t is up to legislatures, not courts, to decide on the wisdom and utility of legislation."). As Plaintiffs have failed to show that the RES burdens interstate commerce at all, much less that any such burden is clearly excessive in relation to the benefits conferred on the state by the RES, the Court finds that summary judgment i[s] also appropriate with regard to Plaintiffs' claim under the *Pike* test.

. . . .

The Clerk shall enter judgment in favor of Defendants on all claims.

NOTES

1. *An Unsettled Question.* Although the court in *Epel* declined to find any Dormant Commerce Clause violation in Colorado's RPS rules, not all courts have been as dismissive of Dormant Commerce Clause challenges to RPS requirements. In particular, RPS policies that give preference to

renewable energy generated in-state have encountered sufficient resistance. For example, Judge Richard Posner's dictum language in *Illinois Commerce Comm'n v. Federal Energy Regulatory Comm'n*, 721 F.3d 764 (2013), took a far less friendly position with regard to Michigan's RPS statute, which did not provide for any credit toward RPS goals for renewable power generated outside of that state. Posner strongly questioned the constitutionality of the statute, stating that "Michigan cannot, without violating the commerce clause of Article I of the Constitution, discriminate against out-of-state renewable energy." *Id.* at 776.

2. *Constitutional Challenges to In-State Preference Provisions.* Aside from general questions about the constitutionality of RPS statutes are queries regarding certain aspects of these policies. In particular, some scholars have questioned the constitutionality of provisions in many state RPS statutes that favor renewable energy generation occurring within the state over generation occurring out of state. For instance, Professor Steven Ferrey has drawn comparisons between RPS in-state preference provisions and "earlier discriminatory programs that states set up for giving preferences to in-state dairy and other interests" that were later held to be unconstitutional. Steven Ferrey, *Threading the Constitutional Needle with Care: The Commerce Clause Threat to the New Infrastructure of Renewable Power*, 7 TEX. J. OIL GAS & ENERGY L. 59 (2011–12). Despite these constitutionality questions, most state RPS policies include some form of in-state preference provision. *See* Harvey Reiter, *Removing Unconstitutional Barriers to Out-of-State and Foreign Competition from State Renewable Portfolio Standards: Why the Dormant Clause Provides Important Protection for Consumers and Environmentalists*, 36 ENERGY L.J. 45, 46 (2015) (noting that "in the vast majority of these states— 75%—the resources developed within the state are given various forms of preference over out-of-state resources.").

3.   LOCAL GOVERNMENT INCENTIVES FOR WIND ENERGY

In addition to federal and state governments, some local governments have also adopted ordinances aimed at promoting wind energy and other forms of renewable energy development. At the local level, support for wind energy development can vary dramatically from place to place. As will be explored in Chapter 3, a few localities have exhibited strong distaste for wind energy projects and enacted ordinances that effectively prohibit any utility-scale wind energy development within their boundaries. Hundreds of other municipal governments do not prohibit wind energy development but have adopted ordinances restricting turbine heights, locations, or noise, to help limit conflicts between wind energy and other land uses.[4]

---

[4]   The U.S. Department of Energy has posted a list with links to hundreds of local wind energy ordinances on its WINDExchange website at http://apps2.eere.energy.gov/wind/wind exchange/policy/ordinances.asp?page=1&field=default&order=asc&#links.

By contrast, some other municipal governments seem to view large wind energy projects as valuable sources of economic development or revitalization that they would love to attract into their jurisdictions. Rather than adopting prohibitions or strict limitations on wind energy development, many municipalities in this latter category have adopt ordinances specifically designed to lure developers into their cities and counties to develop wind farms. The following excerpts relate to a rural county in south-central Washington that adopted a somewhat unique strategy for attracting wind energy projects. Klickitat County, Washington, generated a programmatic Environmental Impact Statement (EIS) covering large areas of land within that county that it had believed could be well-suited for energy development. Based on the results of the programmatic EIS, county officials then delineated portions of those areas on an "energy overlay zone" map and adopted an ordinance designed to expedite and streamline the permitting process for energy development within these special energy overlay zones.

KLICKITAT COUNTY ENERGY OVERLAY ZONE
KLICKITAT CTY. CODE § 19.39:1–9 (2015)

19.39   Energy Overlay Zone

19.39:1 Purpose

A.   To provide areas suitable for the establishment of energy resource operations based on the availability of energy resources, existing infrastructure, and locations where energy projects can be sensitively sited and mitigated.

B.   To provide siting criteria for the utilization of wind and solar energy resources. Each energy resource project will be subjected to individualized review and the imposition of conditions based on site specific information which will be tailored to address project impacts in accordance with the siting criteria. The ultimate goal is to achieve a predictable but sensitive siting process which effectively and efficiently addresses project impacts.

19.39:2 Application

A.   The EOZ is an overlay over existing zones. Projects permitted through the EOZ shall comply with the standards of this chapter rather than the standards of the existing zone.

B.   The EOZ applies to the area demarcated on the zoning map. The area demarcated for wind and solar energy is the same. . . .

C.   Any applicant who has applied for a conditional use permit for an energy project authorized by this chapter, may, in the alternative, elect to be sited through the procedures in this chapter. The applicant need not reapply for a permit under this chapter. However, the County may require any supplementary information needed to complete review under this chapter and comply with its requirements.

D.   Energy systems listed in KCC 19.39:4, which can generate more than 25kw, or wind turbines greater than 120 feet in height, are subject to the requirements of this chapter.

E.   Energy systems that can generate no more than 25kw, solar panels attached to a building or providing energy primarily for on-site use, and wind turbines 120 feet in height or less are permitted outright by KCC 19.39:4, but are not subject to the additional requirements of this chapter.

* * *

19.39:3   Other Applicable Requirements

A.   Project applicants will need to comply with other applicable county requirements, such as . . . environmental review regulations, and building code requirements.

19.39:4   Principal Uses Permitted Outright

A.   Wind turbines

B.   Solar energy facilities

C.   Accessory buildings, uses, and structures needed for operation of the above permitted uses, including utilities and utility infrastructure needed for the principal use. For purposes of this chapter, accessory uses include the mining and utilization of on-site gravel for on-site use only, as necessary for the energy development, such as for the construction of internal roads.

D.   Temporary uses associated with investigatory work to determine the suitability of the site for energy development, such as meteorological towers. The placement of meteorological towers and other such equipment need not obtain a permit through this chapter. However, all other applicable code requirements apply.

19.39:5   Review Process for Energy Resource Operations

A.   Energy resource operations listed in Section 2.30:4 are permitted outright. . .

B.   All energy resource operations will be reviewed by the Klickitat County Planning Department and project conditions will be developed and imposed by the Klickitat County Planning Department. . .

2.30:6   Public Notice Requirements

A.   When an application is deemed complete, the County will post a notice of application on its website.

B.   The project applicant is responsible for holding at least one informal community meeting within the County to inform the public about the proposed energy facility. * * *

* * *

19.39:8 Development Standards

A.   Setbacks:

1.   Energy resource operations shall be sited a minimum of 200 feet away from existing residential structures. The location and density of residential uses in the vicinity may require increased setback requirements.

* * *

B.   Height Limits:

1.   Height limits are not set for wind turbines, transmission lines, wind data collecting devices such as anemometers, and towers required by the energy resource operation for air emissions. However, the county may place reasonable limitations on height (or impose other alternative mitigation) if necessary to mitigate impacts to existing uses or if necessary to address impacts to public safety.

2.   Building structures shall not exceed 65 feet unless additional height is necessary for the energy resource operation and impacts to existing uses can be mitigated to below a level of probable, adverse significance.

19.39:9 Use and Construction Standards:

A.   Project Conditions Tailored to Energy Resource Operation

1.   Permits shall incorporate project specific mitigation measures and conditions to mitigate . . . adverse project impacts. The conditions and mitigation measures shall be based on site specific studies provided by the applicant and other relevant environmental review.

2.   Conditions shall be designed to address each element of the environment . . . including but not limited to surface/groundwater; plants; habitat/wildlife (including avian impacts); cultural resources; health and safety; and traffic/ transportation.

LOCAL PLANNING FOR WIND POWER: USING PROGRAMMATIC ENVIRONMENTAL IMPACT REVIEW TO FACILITATE DEVELOPMENT

Keith H. Hirokawa & Andrew B. Wilson
33 ZONING & PLAN. L. REP. 1, 4–7 (2010)

Before 2004, Klickitat County, Washington was processing wind power facility applications without any internal guidance from its land use regulations or policies. In this area of uncertainty, wind power applications were subjected to a case-by-case, conditional use permit (CUP) review, under which consistency and uniformity became a challenge. Due to the often onerous burden of meeting CUP standards, the County perceived its regulations as a discouraging factor in bringing wind power to the region.

The County engaged in the planning process to encourage and simplify development of energy facilities. The process was led by the possibility that energy development could occur "where it will be less likely to have probable, significant, adverse environmental impacts that cannot be mitigated; where there is adequate infrastructure; where it is consistent with existing and planned land use; and where the development can take advantage of the County's energy resources." The County planners ultimately recommended adoption of an "Energy Overlay Zone" (EOZ) and prepared a non-project [Environmental Impact Statement] (EOZ EIS) under Washington's [State Environmental Policy Act] SEPA.

Under [an ordinance], which was adopted by the County, wind power projects were permitted outright in the overlay zone, subject to site plan review, critical areas and regulations and site-specific SEPA requirements. The overlay zone boundaries were drawn in consideration of wind resource areas identified. . . . It was intended that, although new developments would prepare site-specific environmental review, the analysis in the EOZ EIS (and the mitigation suggested therein) would satisfy the SEPA requirements for most of the impacts that are typical to wind energy development.

Although the Klickitat County EOZ EIS illustrates how to successfully use environmental review as an incentive for new and renewable energy development, it is arguable that the EOZ EIS did not maximize the benefits of the programmatic EIS process. . . .

. . . [T]he EOZ EIS vastly underestimated the volume of new energy development that would follow the adoption of the EOZ: for purposes of estimating cumulative impacts from wind power generation, Klickitat County's non-project EIS assumed that the energy market would support development of only four new wind power projects with a combined generating capacity of 1,000 MW in the twenty-year planning period between 2004 and 2024. However, as of mid-2008, there were seventeen operational and/or permitted wind projects, capable of approximately 2464 MW of generating capacity, and development of the resource has continued to grow since that time. The result was that, although new projects continued to seek out the expedited zoning status of the land use, many projects were forced to prepare EISs and were unable to fully benefit from the EOZ EIS.

A second shortcoming in the EOZ EIS concerned the goal of minimizing resource conflicts. As noted above, the EOZ EIS disclaimed any potential usefulness in analyzing the impacts of wind power development on most types of ground-disturbance impacts (including habitat disruption). The EOZ EIS was focused instead on analyzing and reconciling three factors in energy facility siting: the availability of resources for energy development; available infrastructure for transmission (including natural and built infrastructure); and locations of special habitats (such as migratory corridors). Unfortunately . . . the attention given to such impacts was undermined by the limited anticipation of energy development.

A third area of question in the EOZ EIS concerns the usefulness of mitigation analysis for project beneficiaries. The EOZ EIS was used to identify mitigation measures that could be applied to mitigate or even alleviate the more common environmental impacts. Of course, generalities in a programmatic EIS are typical, as the specificity of the discussion matches the generality of its analysis. For example, the EOZ EIS identifies cliffs and rims as locations less suitable for wind development due to the likelihood of avian impacts, where "raptor collision mortality would . . . likely be highest." The EOZ EIS suggested that "impacts to raptors could be reduced further by avoiding siting turbines directly at the crests and edges of hilltops where raptors use the uplift created by the cliff face." The EOZ EIS did not provide much analysis of mitigation for this impact based on the assumption that such "areas . . . will likely be excluded for geologic or flood hazard reasons." Nevertheless, several wind projects permitted under the EOZ proposed placement of turbines along ridge lines that were heavily used by raptors, and these areas were not excluded for geologic or flood hazard reasons. . . .

A.   Sending a Signal Through Increased Public Dialogue

The programmatic EIS provides an opportunity to energize the public behind wind power and engage the community in the identification of values that could drive wind siting policies. Of course, the programmatic approach to environmental analysis of wind energy development will not completely alleviate concerns about wind power in general or whether particular sites present appropriate opportunities for energy development. However, by providing a meaningful opportunity for public participation in a wind energy PEIS, local governments may be able to prevent significant controversy in project siting decisions.

This break from past practices is significant, as many developers of energy facilities have approached siting decisions without input from the public, particularly in jurisdictions where the siting decision is reviewed in an adversarial proceeding. In such situations, "considerable effort is expended to keep the project confidential for two reasons: competitors might learn of the proposed project and attempt to purchase the site; and local land values inevitably go up when a project is known to be looking for a site." In contrast, by prioritizing stakeholder involvement in the impact review and site selection, the PEIS process can help build consensus and community identity into wind energy development policies, by the recognition that the sites incentivized by the scheme have been pre-screened by the public during programmatic review.

B.   Realistic Wind Resource Assessment

Wind power sites need consistent winds to generate an economically viable amount of power. To determine site viability, studies are needed to determine reliable average wind speed predictions. . . . Wind speeds above Class 4 (15.7–16.7 mph at 164 feet) are generally preferred for utility-scale turbines.

When undertaken at a programmatic level, instead of by a proponent at a particular site, local governments may obtain a more realistic assessment of the resource. At a programmatic level, areas benefitting from suitable winds may be unsuitable for development due to access, resource, personal, or community conflicts.

. . . .

D.   Permitting Predictability and Expedited Review

Land use process is often targeted as the bane of efficient land use permitting. Regardless of the potential benefits enjoyed from land use procedures, process is also the source of permitting delay and increased development costs. Land use procedures are often blamed for providing "moving goalposts" or allowing for NIMBY interference with the siting of essential public facilities. In the meantime, land use procedures can expose local governments to potential liability for mistakes, misstatements and misunderstandings arising in particular applications.

Yet the land use process can be used effectively, particularly for projects from which the public will derive a substantial benefit. An effective programmatic environmental analysis can provide both transparency on the more controversial siting issues and an application review schedule on which developers may be entitled to rely. . . .

E.   Technology-Encouraging

. . . Addressing the adverse and beneficial impacts of wind power at a programmatic level has the potential to enlighten energy development policies, focus the public dialogue on particular projects, and raise the level of sophistication in permitting decisions. Wind planning will sharpen skills and technology related to assessing wind resources and natural resource conflicts.

QUESTIONS

1.   What type of signal did Klickitat County's EOZ ordinance send to wind energy developers that were contemplating whether to pursue wind energy projects in the county? How did it send that signal? Was it effective? Why or why not?

2.   What was the apparent impact of the Klickitat County EOZ ordinance on the pace of wind energy development within the county? Why do you think the ordinance had this effect?

3.   How did the Klickitat County EOZ ordinance seem to impact local citizens' opinions regarding wind energy development?

CHAPTER 3

WIND ENERGY: PROPERTY AND LAND USE ISSUES

■ ■ ■

For the first time in human history, wind energy resources have become a marketable asset throughout much of the world. Thanks to production economies of scale and recent improvements in wind energy technologies, in many locations it is now possible to convert the wind's kinetic energy into electric current at a per-kWh cost that is competitive with more traditional forms of electricity generation. In response to these changes and to the many policies described in Chapter 2, numerous developers across the United States today are actively siting and building utility-scale wind energy projects. In 2012 and again in 2015, wind energy development was the nation's leading contributor of new electricity generating capacity.[1]

In certain regions of the United States, an historic wind energy development boom has erupted in recent years. Developers in these regions are negotiating wind energy leases and easements with hundreds of landowners each year. Many of these landowners are farmers and ranchers that had previously viewed the wind blowing across their land as an annoying reality of rural life. Now, they increasingly view those wind conditions as a lucrative source of income.

This growing value of wind resources has brought new attention to several unsettled and complex legal questions. For instance, to what extent should courts and policymakers analogize to water law or other areas of natural resources law when legally defining "wind rights" and allocating those rights among landowners? Can landowners legally sever wind rights from their fee simple interest in land and convey those severed wind rights separately to others? And who should prevail when an upwind landowner's wind turbine creates a wake behind it that disrupts the wind flowing onto a downwind neighbor's property? This Chapter explores these and other emerging property law and land use law issues associated with the recent rise of wind energy technologies.

---

[1] *See Wind Energy Top Source for New Electricity in 2015*, AM. WIND ENERGY ASSOCIATION (Feb. 16, 2016), http://www.awea.org/MediaCenter/pressrelease.aspx?ItemNumber=8393.

A. WHAT ARE WIND RIGHTS?

Modern wind energy developers typically acquire the property rights necessary to develop wind farms by entering into wind energy lease or easement agreements with landowners. Despite their titles, these leases and easements are very different from the land leases and easements that landowners have used for centuries to facilitate various other types of private land use arrangements. For instance, an ordinary land lease typically gives the lessee rights to exclusively use and occupy the leased premises for the duration of the lease term. The lessor under such a land lease usually retains title to the land but has very limited rights to use or access it until the lease term expires. In contrast, lessors under wind energy leases can usually continue using most of the land covered under the lease. In that sense, wind energy leases are more akin to mineral rights leases or oil & gas leases than to land leases.

However, wind energy leases also differ from oil & gas or mineral leases because they do not entitle lessees to extract and remove any finite, tangible resources from the property. The specific rights and interests included within contractual definitions of *wind rights* or "wind development rights" focus more on what the lessee may build and do on the land than on what the lessee may extract and physically remove from it. Land leased for wind energy development generally has just as many energy resources associated with it on the first day of the lease term as it has on the day that the lease expires—a statement that does not hold true most under oil & gas or mineral rights leases.

Despite the unique nature of wind rights, most of the legal and contractual language appearing in wind energy leases and easements finds its origins in other, more settled areas of property and natural resources law. As most law students learn in their first-year Property Law course, a holder of fee simple title in land possesses a diverse collection of rights and privileges that professors and legal scholars often analogize to a "bundle of sticks" or interests. Within the United States, this bundle of interests generally includes rights to use and occupy the surface of land in accordance with applicable laws and rights to exclude others from physically entering upon the land without the owner's permission. Fee simple title often also includes broad rights to extract and keep any oil, gas, or minerals found directly below a parcel's surface—rights that have long held great importance within the context of energy law. Well-established common law doctrines additionally allow landowners to "sever" rights in subsurface petroleum and mineral resources and separately convey those rights to others, which helps to promote their efficient development and use. In recent years, lawyers and policymakers have attempted to apply many of these same legal concepts to wind rights, with varying degrees of success.

To some, the very notion of privately-held wind rights can be difficult to grasp given that wind currents themselves are ephemeral and intangible and are thus arguably incapable of being owned, bought or sold in a private marketplace. These distinct characteristics of wind resources have caused some to question whether the concept of private ownership of wind rights is viable at all. They even led New Zealand's Maori indigenous tribe to argue in 2012 that the Maori people collectively held interests in the wind resources above their ancestral lands—not the private owners of those lands. In the words of David Rankin, a spokesman for the group, "the wind was regarded as a deity in Maori society, and Maori do not consider the Crown to have the right to use it without Maori consent." Shelley Bridgeman, *Who Owns the Wind?*, N. ZEALAND HERALD (Sept. 13, 2012, 9:35 AM), http://m.nzherald.co.nz/lifestyle/news/article.cfm?c_id=6&object id=10833580. A cultural impact assessment for one proposed New Zealand wind farm further elaborated on the importance of wind in Maori culture:

> The wind has been used for recreation. The game with respect to wind is manu aute, kite flying. While this is something that can happen all year round, Maori kite flying has been the focus of Matariki. The Maori New Year was an opportunity to remember the past and celebrate the future by enjoying games like kite flying. . . . When Whatonga arrived in this new land he studied the skies and the winds and as he played with the manu aute he realised the power of the wind. . . . The wind is a source of power that has allowed tipuna to establish our people in this land.

RAWIRI SMITH, A CULTURAL IMPACT ASSESSMENT OF GENESIS ENERGY'S CASTLE HILL WIND FARM BEFORE THE AEE 18–19 (2011), http://www.gw. govt.nz/assets/Resource-Consents/Volume-4bSection-4-Cultural-Impact-and-Values-Effects-Assessments-3.-Ngati-Kahungunu-Ki-Wairarapa.pdf.

Based on these and similar arguments, the Maori people asserted that they would be injured if wind energy development were to proceed within New Zealand without their approval. Although the Maori people's claims ultimately failed, they highlighted the lingering legal uncertainty associated with wind rights ownership in modern times.

At least one provincial government in China has adopted regulations declaring that wind resources are owned by the government. In 2012, China's Heilongjiang Province passed a Regulation on Climate Resources Survey and Protection declaring that "climate resources"—including wind and solar energy resources—were "owned by the state." Jianlin Chena & Jiongzhe Cui, *Property Rights Arrangement in Emerging Natural Resources: A Case Study of China's Nationalization of Wind and Sunlight*, 27 COLUM. J. ASIAN L. 81, 90 (2013). This regulation, which authorizes large monetary fines against citizens who engage in wind or solar energy development without formal state permission, has proven deeply unpopular among the citizens of Heilongjiang. To quote one pair of scholars on the subject:

> This perceived assertion of state ownership over wind and sunlight was widely criticized by Chinese commentators. One popular jib is whether citizens must now pay to enjoy the breeze on a sunny afternoon, and another asks whether the state "owner" of wind and sunlight is liable for damages with respect to civil claims for injuries caused by wind and sunlight. . . . Echoing public sentiment, academics argue that wind and sunlight are resources that belong to the entire population and not the state and that the state is not permitted to impede or otherwise impose charges on the use of such resources by the people.

Id. at 84.

Although no laws declaring state ownership of wind resources over private land have been seriously considered in the United States, ambiguities regarding wind rights ownership remain. In an apparent effort to increase legal certainty about wind rights, multiple U.S. states have enacted laws in recent years aimed at clarifying the scope and delineation of property interests associated with wind resources. For example, the 2011 statute enacted in Wyoming expressly defines a "wind energy right" as "a property right in the development of wind powered energy generation." WYO. STAT. ANN. § 34–27–102 (2011). A Montana statute enacted that same year provides a similar sort of definition for wind rights. *See* MONT. CODE ANN. § 70–17–402(4) (2011).

Of course, even statutory provisions like those in Wyoming and Montana hardly begin resolve all the legal questions surrounding wind rights. For example, Wyoming's legislature has also imposed a special tax on wind-generated energy that some critics argue is based on a premise that the state itself holds something akin to a property interest in Wyoming's wind resources. *See* WYO. STAT. ANN. § 39–22–101 et seq. (2010); *see also* William Yardley, *Who Owns the Wind? We Do, Wyoming Says, and It's Taxing Those Who Use It*, L.A. TIMES (Aug. 14, 2016), http:// www.latimes.com/nation/la-na-sej-wyoming-wind-tax-snap-story.html. Such policy positions are arguably inconsistent with the state's own legislated definition of wind energy rights.

As explored below, the unique attributes of wind resources are also requiring courts and policymakers to clarify age-old property laws related to low-altitude airspace and to the practice of severing certain interests from a landowner's fee simple interest in land. The difficult balancing act underlying most of these policy debates is that of promoting efficient use of the nation's precious wind resources without unduly disrupting other areas of natural resources law.

1. WIND, AIRSPACE, AND THE *AD COELUM* RULE

Wind energy leasing practices in the United States rest upon the premise that holders of fee simple interests in a parcel of land possess all the property rights necessary for wind energy development on the land. Developers seeking to build wind farms on private land typically negotiate wind energy lease or easement agreements directly with private landowners. Under these agreements, developers agree to pay rents and royalties to landowners in exchange for rights to erect wind turbines and harvest wind energy resources flowing directly above the land's surface. Importantly, *land*owners are the lessors under these agreements and receive rents and royalties, even though the wind resources harvested on wind farms flow through the *airspace* situated high above the ground—not on the ground itself. This well-established approach of tying airspace-related property rights to interests in the land below is rooted in an old common law doctrine known as the *ad coelum* rule.

In most of the United States, the *ad coelum* rule has essentially governed the allocation of private property interests in subsurface coal, oil and gas for centuries by clarifying that owners of land possess rights not only to its surface but also to any resources found directly below it. In a similar fashion, the *ad coelum* rule allocates wind rights by providing that landowners hold rights in the low-altitude airspace situated directly above their parcels. Wind rights are not merely interests in the wind itself; they include limited interests in the land where the turbines are anchored and broad interests in the airspace above it. Onshore wind turbines have grown considerably taller in recent decades, with average heights of new utility-scale wind turbines now easily exceeding 350 feet and ascending high into the airspace above ground. Laws governing landowners' interests in and use of that airspace thus play an essential role in wind energy development.

As the excerpt below describes, the recent growth of wind and solar energy is increasing the value and relevance of airspace in much the same way that the oil and gas boom of the early nineteenth century raised the importance of property rights in resources below the ground.

AIRSPACE IN A GREEN ECONOMY
Troy A. Rule
59 UCLA L. REV. 270, 274–76, 278–90 (2011)

Airspace is among the most ubiquitous of all natural resources, present in every corner of the globe. Nonetheless, airspace is inherently scarce. Each cubic inch of it exclusively occupies a unique spatial position in the universe. The old adage "location, location, location" thus applies as much to the valuation of airspace as it does to the valuation of surface land: Ownership rights in a cube of remote, high-altitude airspace might be worth only pennies, even though rights in an equivalent volume of airspace above a city's downtown core might fetch millions of dollars. Airspace is distinct from "air"—the life-sustaining blend of mostly nitrogen and oxygen gases that circulates around the planet. Because air pollutants freely course throughout the world's air supply, air is sometimes characterized as a globally shared "commons." In contrast, much of the space through which air flows is not held in common but is separately owned or controlled.

Similarly, airspace is distinct from the countless invisible waves that pass through air. Vibrating objects transmit waves through the air to deliver music, spoken words, and other sounds to our ears. Modern electronic equipment can also transmit electromagnetic waves of varying frequencies through air, including waves capable of communicating information via devices such as cellular phones, radios, and wireless computer receivers. The radio spectrum itself is a highly regulated commons in the United States, subject to detailed policies from the Federal Communications Commission for allocating transmission rights at various frequencies among private and public parties. Nonetheless, all of these waves are distinct from the airspace through which they commonly pass.

On a similar theory, airspace is also fully distinguishable from the wind currents and solar rays that fuel renewable energy generation. On calm evenings, airspace can be largely devoid of wind and sunlight, whereas, on blustery days, airspace serves as the medium through which these resources travel. Because wind and solar radiation are practically inexhaustible, they arguably warrant no private property protection. In contrast, airspace—a finite, immovable resource—has justifiably enjoyed property protection for centuries. . . .

For much of recorded history, because most of the Earth's airspace was beyond the physical reach of humankind, few conflicts arose regarding its use. Out of practical necessity, the majority of the planet's airspace was merely a commons through which landowners enjoyed sunlight and views. It is true that laws in ancient Rome recognized that surface owners held rights in the airspace above their land. The English common law doctrine of ancient lights also indirectly limited some building heights to protect neighbors' access to sunlight. However, in early, agriculturally based societies, most landowners were primarily concerned with having rights to enough airspace to enable the growth of their crops.

As construction techniques gradually improved over the centuries, airspace became an increasingly valuable resource, and rules clarifying property interests in airspace naturally followed. Legal historians have traced the beginnings of modern airspace law as far back as to the 1300s, when Cino da Pistoia pronounced the maxim: *Cujus est solum, ejus est usque ad coelum*," or, "[To] whomsoever the soil belongs, he owns also to the sky." This doctrine, commonly known as the *ad coelum* rule, established simple private property rights in airspace based upon subadjacent parcel boundaries. The rule was subsequently cited in Edward Coke's influential commentaries in the seventeenth century and in William Blackstone's commentaries in the eighteenth century, cementing it as a fixture in English and American common law. By the early twentieth century, U.S. courts were applying the doctrine to find trespass for even minor intrusions into airspace above privately owned land. . . .

A clash between airplanes and farmers gave rise to what is perhaps the best known case clarifying the scope of landowners' airspace rights. The plaintiffs in *United States v. Causby* owned a chicken barn situated about 2200 feet from the end of a municipal airport runway. Commercial airplane flyovers had previously caused minimal problems for the Causbys' chicken farming operation, but that quickly changed when the U.S. military began leasing the airport in 1942. The heavy bombers and fighter planes that began roaring overhead repeatedly startled the plaintiffs' chickens into a panicked frenzy. Several chickens per day died from frantic collisions with the barn walls. Frustrated by the airplane flyovers and their effects on the farm, Mr. and Mrs. Causby sued to recover damages for what they claimed was the military's compensable Fifth Amendment taking of rights in the airspace above their land.

The U.S. Supreme Court ultimately decided the *Causby* case, upholding the lower court's ruling that Mr. and Mrs. Causby were entitled to compensation for the military's repeated flights over their land. The Court refrained from literally applying the *ad coelum* rule to reach its holding, noting that landowners' airspace rights did not extend indefinitely into the sky above their land. Instead, the Court cited federal legislation to declare that "navigable" airspace was a "public highway" for air travel and was not under the exclusive control of surface landowners. . . .

To quote from the opinion:

> The landowner owns at least as much of the space above the ground as he can occupy or use in connection with the land . . . The fact that he does not occupy it in a physical sense—by the erection of buildings and the like—is not material . . . We think that the landowner, as an incident to his ownership, has a claim to it and that invasions of it are in the same category as invasions of the surface.

Causby and related legislation clarified the scope of landowners' airspace rights to address conflicts that were arising from the introduction of modern flight. . . .

QUESTIONS

1.   Why might it be difficult to define and enforce private property interests in wind itself? How does basing allocations of wind rights on existing allocations of property interests in the airspace through which wind currents flow potentially address these challenges?

2.   Did *Causby* wholly reject the *ad coelum* rule or merely modify it? What specific limitations did the *Causby* court place on the rule? Do you think the limitations were justifiable given the advent of modern aviation? Why or why not?

3.   How do state statutes that expressly allocate wind rights among landowners based on *ad coelum* rule principles help to promote efficient levels of wind energy investment and development?

POLICY PROBLEM

In most areas of the United States, Federal Aviation Administration (FAA) regulations generally require that aircraft be operated more than 500 feet above the ground except during takeoffs and landings without special permission. *See* 14 C.F.R. § 91.119(c) (2010). In "congested" urban areas, aircraft generally must fly at least "1,000 feet above the highest obstacle within a horizontal radius of 2,000 feet of the aircraft." 14 C.F.R. § 91.119(b) (2010).

Suppose that a wind energy developer is seeking approval to install several 450-foot-tall turbines in a remote rural area of the United States. There are no airports within 20 miles of the project site. However, operators of small "crop duster" airplanes, having express authorization from the FAA, periodically apply insecticide on agricultural fields just a couple of miles away from the project site. The owners of those fields are now seeking to block your wind farm construction project on the rationale that it could interfere with their crop dusting activities.

1.   Suppose that you represent the wind energy developer in the hypothetical fact pattern set forth in the preceding paragraph. Craft a detailed set of legal and policy arguments for why you should be permitted to proceed with your project in spite of these farmers' objections.

2.   Suppose instead that you represent agricultural landowners nearby who periodically crop-dust their fields using small airplanes and fear that the proposed wind farm would interfere with their crop dusting activities. Craft a detailed set of legal and policy arguments for why FAA officials should possess authority to prohibit the wind farm's construction.

3.   Suppose that you are a government official charged with determining whether to allow the developer's wind farm project to proceed in the face of the neighbors' opposition. Which side do you believe has the strongest set of arguments in this conflict? Why?

Note: conflicts between wind energy development and aviation are highlighted again later in later portions of this chapter that describe ongoing tensions between wind farm developers and the United States Department of Defense.

2.   A SEVERABLE WIND ESTATE?

Wind energy leasing practices that treat wind rights much like mineral rights have inevitably given rise to another important legal question: may a landowner legally *sever* a parcel's wind rights and convey them to a separate party while retaining rights in the parcel's surface? Laws in most jurisdictions have long allowed landowners to sever and separately convey mineral rights associated with their land to other parties. In recent decades, some landowners have contemplated using analogous means to sever and reserve or separately convey wind rights. However, differences between mineral rights and wind rights complicate this relatively novel practice and call into question whether it should be permissible under the law.

The following two lower-court cases, which consider whether wind rights may be legally severed from surface rights, seem to produce a conflicting pair of holdings on this question. The first case examines this issue in the context of an eminent domain proceeding and ultimately holds that wind rights severance is allowable in that situation. The second case, from a different jurisdiction, analyzes the question in the context of a petition to partition a parcel of land and concludes that wind rights severance is not permissible in that instance.

Contra Costa Water District v. Vaquero Farms, Inc.

California Court of Appeal, First District, Division Two, 1997
58 Cal.App.4th 883

Ruvolo, A.J.

In this eminent domain proceeding, Contra Costa Water District (Water District) acquired approximately 3,500 acres of 6,000 acres owned by Vaquero Farms, Inc. (Vaquero) to be used by the Water District for the Los Vaqueros Reservoir Project (Reservoir Project). The issues on appeal involve the compensation awarded Vaquero for the taking of the property. Specifically, Vaquero contends: 1) the Water District must condemn its windpower rights, with a corresponding legal obligation to pay just compensation, even though the Water District chose to sever the property's windpower rights and reserve them to Vaquero. . . .

We conclude it was permissible for the Water District to sever and reserve to Vaquero its windpower rights. . . .

The Vaquero property is located approximately six miles north of the City of Livermore, and approximately six miles south of the City of Brentwood. . . . The 6,000 acres owned by Vaquero was and is primarily undeveloped. . . . The property has been used as a working cattle ranch for nearly 50 years. In 1984, large portions of the ranch (over 2,100 acres) were leased for windpower electrical production and about 260 wind turbines have been installed on the property.

The Water District filed its Complaint in Eminent Domain on June 14, 1993. By this action, the Water District sought to acquire four separate parcels of Vaquero's property, totaling approximately 3,500 acres, for the Reservoir Project. The Reservoir Project is a major public work including a reservoir, diversion facilities, pumping plants, and pipelines to convey water for storage and use. . . .

Each of Vaquero's four condemned parcels will be committed to a different use in connection with the Reservoir Project's implementation. . . .

Vaquero did not contest the right of the Water District to take its property. Instead, the focus of its answer to the complaint was the amount of "just compensation" to which appellant was entitled. . . .

. . . The only issues which proceeded to trial by jury involved the fair market value of the property taken, generally measured by the highest and best use for which it is geographically and economically adaptable . . . and an assessment of severance damages generally measured by the diminution in market value of the property remaining in the private property owner's possession . . . The ultimate issue of just compensation was a matter of widely-conflicting expert opinion. The Water District presented witnesses who valued the property and severance damages between $6.1 million and $7.7 million. Vaquero's witnesses placed the total value of the take at over $30 million.

The jury returned a verdict in the total sum of $14,428,327. This verdict was comprised of $13,428,327 representing the fair market value of the property taken and $1 million representing severance damages to the land remaining in Vaquero's ownership by reason of the taking. After Vaquero's motion for new trial was denied, this appeal followed.

SEVERANCE OF WINDPOWER RIGHTS

Vaquero advances the proposition that the Water District could not acquire the fee interest in its property while at the same time severing the windpower rights and windpower leasehold interests and reserving them to Vaquero. . . .

As noted, portions of the area being acquired and portions of Vaquero's remaining property are subject to leases with various companies engaged in the enterprise of generating and selling electricity derived from wind blowing across the property. At the time of trial, over 2,100 acres of the Vaquero property were subject to windpower leases, and approximately 260 wind turbines were built on that acreage between 1984 and 1986. . . .

The Water District's June 1993 resolution of necessity states that it is necessary to take Vaquero's fee interest but the Water District "does not, by the passage of this resolution of necessity, intend to acquire any of the windpower rights. . . ." Therefore, the Water District's complaint was limited to the acquisition of "[a]ll rights and incidents of the fee ownership interest vested in Vaquero Farms, . . . excepting and reserving to such defendants and their successors, and present and future assigns all rights for wind energy power conversion and the transmission of power generated by wind, including (1) the exclusive and perpetual right, . . . to develop, construct, install, maintain and operate windpower facilities, including but not limited to windmills, transmission lines and other facilities, necessary or advantageous for the purposes of generating or transmitting electric power from wind on the real property. . . ."

The severance included reserving to Vaquero the exclusive right "to develop, construct, install, maintain and operate windpower facilities," the exclusive right to sell electric power generated by windmills, and the exclusive right to sell or lease the windpower rights. Vaquero was granted continued access to the property through non-exclusive easements for "roadway, ingress and egress, and utility purposes. . . ."

By subsequent amendment to the complaint, the Water District acquired all the windpower rights in certain areas where it was determined Vaquero's use of these rights would be inconsistent with the Reservoir Project's proposed uses . . . As a result, Vaquero's windpower rights were ultimately reserved in areas generally remaining undeveloped open space after the transfer from private to public ownership.

Vaquero filed a general demurrer to the Water District's complaint alleging it failed to state a cause of action because the Water District was prohibited, as a matter of law, from condemning the fee interest and severing the windpower rights. In opposition to the demurrer, the Water District contended that it was legally permissible to acquire the land needed for the Reservoir Project without appropriating the windpower rights because California law authorizes the condemnor to sever rights it has determined are unnecessary for the public use. The court overruled Vaquero's demurrer, allowing the Water District to acquire the fee interest in the subject property while reserving and excepting the windpower rights to Vaquero.

The question before us may be stated as follows: When a public entity acquires property through eminent domain, are the windpower rights capable of segregation or are they so affixed to the underlying land that they must be acquired by the condemning authority? While the parties' dispute presents a question of first impression, its answer can be found by applying the reasoning of well-established California eminent domain law to this neoteric factual setting. . . .

A review of the case law reveals California eminent domain law authorizes the condemnor to select which right or combination of rights it needs to acquire from the full panoply of private ownership rights held within a fee simple estate. *See Federal Oil Co. v. City of Culver* (1960) 179 Cal.App.2d 93, 96–97, 3 Cal.Rptr. 519 [condemnation of lessee's surface rights without acquiring subsurface oil and gas rights]; *County Sanitation Dist. v. Watson Land Co.* (1993) 17 Cal.App.4th 1268, 1273, 22 Cal.Rptr.2d 117 [condemnation of permanent subterranean sewer easements and acquisition of temporary construction and occupational rights of way on the same properties]. . . . These cases remove any vestige of doubt that a condemnor cannot be required to take more severable rights in property than what it needs for the public use.

When closely examined, the gravamen of Vaquero's argument rests on the premise that windpower rights must be rooted to the fee interest because no case, to date, has recognized windpower rights as capable of segregation or severance. . . .

[W]indpower rights are "substantial rights" capable of being bought and sold in the marketplace, as evidenced by a 30-year lease which was entered into between Vaquero and a windpower developer, Altamont Energy Corporation, long before the Water District's condemnation action was initiated. The lease stands as irrefutable evidence that one may have a right to use windpower rights without owning any interest in the land. It memorializes Vaquero's agreement to convey the right to harness and develop windpower on its property until the year 2014 in exchange for monetary compensation, including a share of the gross annual revenue generated from the sale of electricity. Having itself derived economic benefit from the dissection of its property rights by separately leasing windpower rights to a third party, Vaquero's claim that these same rights are inextricably linked to the fee interest is unconvincing. Windpower rights clearly are "substantial" rights and thus may be condemned, or excluded from condemnation, despite their factual novelty under present law.

Vaquero complains that as a result of this partial take, its position has changed from fee owner with full and exclusive power over the use of the property to "an uncompensated lessor of land it does not own, with the theoretical right to develop wind production on someone else's property." According to Vaquero, this change of position prevents it from exercising even limited dominion as a lessor because "wind rights are dependent on control of the surface." Vaquero suggests to the court it can no longer give its windpower lessees authority to construct new windmills or relocate old windmills on land "it no longer owns."

These arguments are based on the erroneous premise that the Water District has acquired the sole right to occupy and use the entire surface of the land for public purposes to Vaquero's exclusion. As we have detailed earlier in this opinion, the record reflects otherwise. After the condemnation proceeding Vaquero will own all windpower rights in each of the affected parcels, together with an easement for ingress and egress and such other access rights as may be required for the maintenance and development of these windpower rights. Based on our request for supplemental briefing on the compatibility of the parties' joint use of the property, we are satisfied that private windpower generation is fully compatible with the Water District's public uses for the land being taken. The parcels involved are not physically encroached by the intended body of water and instead serendipitously must remain undeveloped to meet the environmental mitigation requirements of the Reservoir Project.

Vaquero's doubts that it could carry on windpower operations without ownership of the surface rights can be quelled by a simple comparison. It is well settled that subsurface minerals, gas and oil are distinct property rights which may be conveyed separately from the fee . . . We agree with the Water District's assertion that "[t]he right to generate electricity from windmills harnessing the wind, and the right to sell the power so generated, is no different, either in law or common sense, from the right to pump and sell subsurface oil, or subsurface natural gas by means of wells and pumps." The Water District persuasively points out, "[T]he argument that harvesting windpower somehow requires greater usage of the surface than harvesting oil and gas resources defies common sense to anyone who has seen a field of oil derricks."

Even without the assurances of the Water District, the law implies such surface rights of possession as are necessary and convenient to exercise the right to exploit the particular profit, estate or interest reserved . . . Therefore, Vaquero's musing about hypothetical conflicts that could arise in the future resulting from joint possession and use of the property is unavailing. It is not our policy to resolve abstract disputes. . . .

In conclusion, Vaquero's contention that the Water District cannot, as a matter of law, reserve windpower rights from a condemnation of property ignores the solidly-established tenet of California law that a condemnation of property for public use need not be unqualified, total, and unconditional. For this reason, the authorities relied upon by Vaquero, which all involve fee simple takings without reservations, have little bearing on the issues at hand. . . .

The judgment is affirmed.

ROMERO V. BERNELL

United States District Court, District of New Mexico, 2009
603 F.Supp.2d 1333

BLACK, DJ.

THIS MATTER is before the Court on a Petition to Partition . . . a section of land in Taos County. The Court having considered the briefs of counsel and having held oral argument . . . and performed additional research, finds the Petition for Partition should be Granted.

Discussion

Petitioners Martin E. Romero and Dennis C. Romero allege they are owners as tenants in common of Section 11, Township 27 North, Range 10 East, N.M.P.M., located approximately eight miles east of Tres Piedras, Taos County, New Mexico. Petitioners also own Section 12 which adjoins Section 11 on the west, and they also own Section 15 which is located to the southwest of Section 11. They seek to partition the land under NMSA 1978 § 42–5–1 (2007 Cum. Supp.). That provision provides:

> When any lands, tenements or hereditaments shall be owned in joint tenancy, tenancy in common or coparcenary, whether the right or title be derived by donation, grant, purchase, devise or descent, it shall be lawful for any one or more persons interested, whether they be in possession or not, to present to the district court their complaint in chancery, praying for a division and partition of such premises, according to the respective rights of the parties interested therein, and for a sale thereof, if it shall appear that partition cannot be made without great prejudice to the owners.

Respondent opposes the Petition for Partition on the ground that "the property cannot equitably be partitioned because the principal value of the property appears to be for a wind farm development." . . . . This is based on Respondent's underlying premise "that wind power rights, like mineral rights, are not capable of being partitioned."

. . . .

Partition is a remedy much favored by the law. *Sims v. Sims*, 122 N.M. 618, 930 P.2d 153, 164 (1996). This is because "[p]artition serves peace, promotes the enjoyment of property, and advances industry and enterprise." *Id.* Under New Mexico law, a cotenant is therefore entitled to a partition as a matter of right, not merely as a matter of grace, within the discretion of the court. . . . It can be denied only when the partition is against public policy, legal principles, equitable principles or is waived by an agreement of the parties.

Respondent's argument that he might be disadvantaged in the future if Petitioners develop a wind farm and if his share of the partitioned land is not invited to participate, is too speculative to contemplate. Initially, the Court rejects Respondents' premise that wind is analogous to minerals in situ. While New Mexico has no relevant statutory or case law on the subject, it does not appear minerals in the ground are the appropriate commodity to create a legal paradigm to analyze wind power. Minerals in place are considered real estate in New Mexico. *Bolack v. Underwood*, 340 F.2d 816 (10th Cir. 1965). When severed they become personal property. *Townsend v. State ex rel. State Highway Dept.*, 117 N.M. 302, 871 P.2d 958 (1994). Wind is never embedded in the real estate; rather, it is more like water or wild animals which traverse the surface and which do not belong to the fee owner until reduced to possession. Attorney Terry Hogwood made this comparison:

> Strictly speaking, the ownership of wind is a misnomer. Wind, in and of itself, does not appear to be susceptible of any ownership. It is not like oil and gas in place where there is a deposit of hydrocarbons which can be reduced to possession by one or more mineral owners of the tracts under which the hydrocarbon deposit resides. Wind itself is more akin to a wild animal or percolating waters which must first be reduced to possession before they have value. To reduce wind to "possession" appears to require that it be focused on driving the fins of a windmill which turn a generator and ultimately generates electricity. Then and only then can wind a) be reduced to possession and b) have value.

Terry E. Hogwood, *Against the Wind*, 26 Tex. Oil, Gas and Energy Resources Law Section 6 (Dec. 2001) (footnotes omitted). [* * *]

The right to "harvest" wind energy is, then, an inchoate interest in the land which does not become "vested" until reduced to "possession" by employing it for a useful purpose. Only after it is reduced to actual wind power can wind energy then be severed and/or quantified. *See, e.g., Contra Costa Water Dist. v. Vaquero Farms*, 58 Cal.App.4th 883, 68 Cal. Rptr.2d 272 (1997).

This analysis is consistent not only with logic but with New Mexico's legal treatment of the most analogous natural resource, water. It is long established in New Mexico that individual rights to water can be acquired only by appropriation and application of the water to beneficial use. *Hagerman Irr. Co. v. McMurry*, 16 N.M. 172, 113 P. 823 (N.M.Terr.1911); *Hydro Resources Corp. v. Gray*, 143 N.M. 142, 173 P.3d 749, 756 (2007). The only right obtainable in water is the right to appropriate so much as is actually used for some beneficial purpose. *Hydro Resources, supra; Walker v. United States*, 142 N.M. 45, 162 P.3d 882, 888–9 (2007). Once appropriated, the water right may become vested by continuous use or lost completely or partially through non-use. . . .

Respondents, then, have no legal objection to partition on the ground that the future "principal value of the Property appears to be for wind farm development."

. . . .

For the above stated reasons, Petitioners' Petition to Partition will be GRANTED. The parties may suggest the names of appropriate commissioners to go upon the premises and make partition of said land. . .

QUESTIONS

1.   How might the fact that the severance sought in the *Contra Costa Water District* case was in conjunction with a taking by eminent domain have colored the court's view of whether wind rights severance was permissible in that case? Why?

2.   What two types of resources does the *Romero* court conclude are most analogous to wind? Do you agree with this conclusion? Why or why not?

3.   If wind turbines had already been erected on the land at issue in *Romero*, how might that have impacted the court's analysis of the case based on the rules it set forth in the majority opinion? Do you think the installation of one or more wind turbines on land should be necessary for wind rights to become "choate" and cognizable under the law? Why or why not? What are some potential shortcomings of such a requirement?

As stated above, the *Contra Costa* and *Romero* courts reached conflicting holdings about the severability of wind rights from surface rights. Although major differences in the facts of these two cases might be partly to blame for their inconsistent conclusions, the cases still leave behind plenty of uncertainty on this issue. Accordingly, a handful of state legislatures have enacted statutory provisions addressing the wind rights severability question. Below are three examples of such state law provisions (from South Dakota, Montana, and Wyoming), all of which provide that wind rights are *not* a severable interest.

SEVERANCE OF WIND ENERGY RIGHTS LIMITED
S.D. CODIFIED LAWS § 43–13–19 (1996)

No interest in any resource located on a tract of land and associated with the production or potential production of energy from wind power on the tract of land may be severed from the surface estate . . . , except that such rights may be leased for a period not to exceed fifty years. Any such lease is void if no development of the potential to produce energy from wind power has occurred on the land within five years after the lease began. The payment of any such lease shall be on an annual basis.

SEVERANCE OF WIND ENERGY RIGHTS LIMITED
MONT. CODE ANN. § 70–17–404 (2011)

(1) A wind energy right in the wind resource located on and flowing over the real property, including without limitation a royalty, if applicable, associated with the production of wind energy may not be severed from the real property even though a wind easement may be created pursuant to this part.

(2) Nothing in this section may be construed to prohibit or limit the right of a seller of the real property to retain any payments associated with an existing wind option agreement or wind energy agreement.

DECLARATION OF WIND ENERGY RIGHTS
WYO. STAT. ANN. § 34–27–103 (2011)

(a) Wind energy rights shall be regarded as an interest in real property and appurtenant to the surface estate.

(b) Wind energy rights shall not be severed from the surface estate, except that wind energy may be developed pursuant to a wind energy agreement.

(c) A wind energy agreement is an interest in real property. A wind energy agreement or a notice or memorandum evidencing a wind energy agreement shall:

(i) Be recorded in the office of the county clerk where the land subject to the agreement is located; and

(ii) Shall include a description of the land subject to the agreement.

. . . .

(e) Wind energy becomes personalty at the point of conversion into electricity.

(f) Nothing in this act shall alter, amend, diminish or invalidate wind energy agreements or conveyances made or entered into prior to April 1, 2011 provided that a contract, lease, memorandum or other notice evidencing the acquisition, conveyance or reservation of the wind energy rights is recorded in accordance with subsection (c) of this section no later than July 1, 2011.

As of late 2017, no state legislature in the United States had enacted a statute expressly recognizing the severability of wind rights from surface rights. However, laws in many states are unclear on this question and there are legitimate reasons why some landowners might want to sever wind rights from surface rights. Moreover, as Part (f) of the Wyoming statutory provision above suggests, numerous landowners have already done so.

Landowners' motivations for severing wind rights from surface rights mirror those that typically lead landowners to sever their mineral rights from their surface rights. Given these potential benefits, why have state legislatures heretofore been unwilling to statutorily recognize wind rights severance? The following article excerpt ties together several of the concepts covered in this subsection of the Casebook and describes some potential adverse consequences of allowing landowners to sever their wind rights and convey them separately to others.

WIND RIGHTS UNDER PROPERTY LAW: ANSWERS STILL BLOWING IN THE WIND

Troy A. Rule
PROB. & PROP., Nov.–Dec. 2012, at 58–59.

. . . A question that has drawn significant legislative and academic attention in recent years is whether landowners should be permitted to sever a "wind estate" from their interest in a parcel of land. Such purported severances of wind estates have been occurring in some areas of the United States as means for landowners to reserve wind rights when conveying land to a buyer. In the estate planning context, severing a wind estate could also enable a parent to devise wind rights to one son or daughter who lives far away and to separately devise the surface rights to a different son or daughter who plans to remain on the family ranch or farm.

At least one court has held that wind rights can be severed from a surface estate in the same way that parties sever mineral rights. In *Contra Costa Water District v. Vaquero Farms, Inc.*, 58 Cal. App. 4th 883 (Ct. App. 1997), the California Court of Appeal considered whether a municipal water district could sever a property's wind rights from the fee estate and reserve such rights to a private landowner in a condemnation proceeding. Ultimately, the court concluded that "one may have a right to use windpower rights without owning any interest in the land." *Id.* at 893. Rejecting the notion that fee or surface ownership was inextricably connected to wind rights, the court embraced the water district's argument that "[t]he right to generate electricity from windmills harnessing the wind . . . is no different, either in law or common sense, from the right to pump and sell subsurface oil, or subsurface natural gas by means of wells and pumps," and that wind rights could thus similarly be severed from a surface estate. *Id.*

By contrast, the federal district court in *Romero v. Bernell*, (D.N.M. 2009), proved far less willing to accept the notion of a severed wind estate, at least not until turbines were operating on the land. The respondents in *Romero* were challenging a proposed partition of the land among tenants in common. Because no wind turbines had yet been installed on the subject property, the *Romero* court refused to recognize a wind estate in the parcel capable of confounding the equitable partition of the property. The court ruled instead that a "right to 'harvest' wind energy is . . . an inchoate interest in the land which does not become 'vested' until reduced to "possession' by employing it for a useful purpose." *Id.* at 1335.

Other than these conflicting holdings in *Contra Costa* and *Romero*, there is scant case law on the enforceability of provisions that purport to sever wind rights. As other scholars have noted, the "validity of such provisions is certain to be challenged" in the coming years. Ernest E. Smith & Becky H. Diffen, *Winds of Change: The Creation of Wind Law*, 5 TEX. J. OIL GAS & ENERGY L. 165, 176 (2009–10). Until these issues are resolved legislatively or in the courts, parties that seek to develop wind farms on land for which they hold only severed wind rights may have difficulty obtaining financing and title insurance for such projects.

In 2010, the Colorado state legislature considered a bill that, if enacted, would have allowed land-owners to legally sever wind rights from their surface estates. *See* H.R. 10–1158, 67th Gen. Assemb., 2d Reg. Sess. (Colo. 2010) (amending COLO. REV. STAT. § 38–32–102). The bill, however, was never enacted into law, in part because of concerns about the additional complications and legal questions that such a rule would have created. For example, as Prof. K.K. DuVivier observed, surface owners that have severed and transferred their wind rights are effectively "remove[d] from the . . . negotiating table" when a wind farm is developed on their properties. K. K. DuVivier, *Animal, Vegetable, Mineral—Wind? The Severed Wind Power Rights Conundrum*, 49 WASHBURN L.J. 69, 86 (2009). Their absence from negotiations can make it difficult for them to prevent excessive disruption of surface uses in the wind development process. Such non-involvement can also limit surface owners' ability to assist in resolving disputes between mineral rights holders and wind developers in cases in which the mineral rights have also been severed from the fee interest. *Id.* at 86.

Laws recognizing wind rights severance would likewise raise the question of whether the minerals estate or the wind estate for a given parcel is the "dominant" estate. If a wind rights holder wants to install a turbine at a specific location but a mineral rights holder wants to dig for minerals at the same spot, who wins? Although courts seem to have reached some agreement as to the priority relationship between mineral estates and surface estates, introducing a wind estate into the mix could create entirely new priority issues. . . .

In a move that exemplifies an emerging trend among western states, the Colorado legislature enacted legislation in 2012 that would *prohibit* wind rights severance—the exact opposite policy approach from that proposed in the legislature in 2010. Colorado's new statute provides that wind energy is an interest in real property appurtenant to the surface estate but cannot be severed from such estate—instead, owners of the real property can record wind energy agreements only in the nature of a lease, license, easement, or other agreement. COLO. REV. STAT. § 38–30.7–101 et seq. Colorado has joined a growing number of states that have recently enacted laws rejecting the notion of wind rights severance. *See* N.D. CENT. CODE § 17–04–04; S.D. CODIFIED LAWS § 43–13–19; WYO. STAT. ANN. § 34–27–103; MONT. CODE ANN. § 70–17–404; NEB. REV. STAT. § 76–3004. Many of these new state statutes contain clauses that acknowledge the validity of any conveyances of severed wind estates occurring before the statutes become effective. Such "grandfathered" wind estates could complicate title matters for their underlying parcels well into the future.

QUESTIONS

1.   What are some advantages of clarifying legal rules regarding to wind rights severance through statutes rather than through court decisions?

2.   Why do you think that the South Dakota state legislature included language in its wind rights statute that prohibits wind energy leases for terms exceeding 50 years?

3.   What is the difference between executing a wind energy lease or easement and severing a wind estate from the surface estate? Why do you think the former is allowed but the latter is not allowed under all state statutes that have addressed these issues?

4.   Suppose that a Wyoming landowner had severed the wind rights associated with her land in 2008 and then executed and delivered a deed conveying those rights to a neighbor later that year. Based on the Wyoming statutory provisions excerpted above, is her purported severance of those rights cognizable under Wyoming law? Why or why not? As a policy matter, do you think that the severance *should* be cognizable under the law? Why or why not?

B. WIND RIGHTS AND REGULATORY TAKINGS LAW

The possibility of a severable wind estate also raises the question of whether laws that prohibit any economically viable use of a severed wind estate might trigger a compensable regulatory taking. The Takings Clause prohibits governments from taking "private property . . . for public use, without just compensation." U.S. CONST. amend. V. The Takings Clause has long empowered governments to exercise eminent domain authority and unilaterally acquire private property so long as that property is needed for a public use and the private owners receive just compensation for their losses. However, courts have interpreted the Takings Clause to also provide that, if a law or regulation is so restrictive that it effectively destroys the economic value of certain property, it too can trigger a taking. These "regulatory takings" can likewise entitle citizens to just compensation even though they retain legal title to the affected property.

One of the primary means for a private citizen to establish a regulatory taking is through a showing that the law or regulation at issue precludes all "economically viable use" of the property involved. *Lucas v. South Carolina Coastal Council*, 505 U.S. 1003, 1004 (1992). Of course, because of laws that allow for the severance of mineral rights from surface rights, citizens sometimes hold no interest in the surface of land and possess only a mineral rights estate. At least one court has suggested that citizens in these situations might also have valid takings claims if a new regulation precludes all economically viable use of those severed rights. *See State ex rel. Shelly Materials, Inc., v. Clark Cnty. Bd. of Comm'rs*, 875 N.E.2d 59, 67 (Ohio 2007). The court in *Shelly Materials* expressly stated that "[a] mineral estate may be considered the relevant parcel for a compensable regulatory taking if the mineral estate was purchased separately from the other interests in the real property." *Id.* This begs the question: might similar constitutional protections exist for holders of severed wind rights?

Differences between mineral rights and wind rights and the uncertainty that looms over even mineral rights takings cases make it difficult to predict how courts might handle regulatory takings claims involving severed wind rights. One important difference is that wind rights holders are arguably more dependent than mineral rights holders on government approvals to engage in any exercise their rights. Wind energy development is subject to a wide array of government restrictions—many of which are explored in more detail in Chapter 4—that can severely constrain wind rights holders' ability to engage in wind energy development on any given parcel. In many instances, mineral rights holders must overcome fewer regulatory hurdles to exercise their interests.

On the other hand, courts have interpreted the Takings Clause to limit governments' regulatory power, holding that if regulations go "too far" in restricting the use of property, they can trigger a regulatory "taking" of that property and entitle private owners to just compensation. It is not entirely clear why severed wind rights would be treated any differently than severed mineral rights in applying that rule. Should a regulation that effectively prohibits any wind energy development on a large parcel of land trigger a compensable taking entitling a holder of severed wind rights to just compensation? Although the claimants in the following case did not hold severed wind rights, they did bring takings claims against a county based on a new ordinance prohibiting wind energy development. In this case, the court analyzed the claim under land use law's "doctrine of vested rights" and ultimately found no taking because the county had not yet granted any final permits to the claimants for construction of a wind farm. However, the *Zimmerman* court left open the possibility that, under certain circumstances, a prohibition on wind energy development could trigger a compensable regulatory takings claim.

ZIMMERMAN V. BOARD OF COUNTY COMMISSIONERS OF WABAUNSEE COUNTY

Supreme Court of Kansas, 2011
264 P.3d 989

NUSS, J.

This case involves a decision by the Board of County Commissioners of Wabaunsee County (Board) to amend its zoning regulations. Specifically, the Board permitted Small Wind Energy Conversion Systems (SWECS) but prohibited the placement of Commercial Wind Energy Conversion Systems (CWECS, *i.e.,* commercial wind farms) in the county. Plaintiffs are owners of land in the county. They were later joined by plaintiff intervenors (Intervenors), who are not landowners but owners of purported wind rights in the county.

The district court granted the Board's various dispositive motions. Plaintiffs and Intervenors appealed, and the Board cross-appealed. Pursuant to K.S.A. 20–3017, we transferred the case from the Court of Appeals.

In *Zimmerman v. Board of Wabaunsee County Comm'rs*, 289 Kan. 926, 218 P.3d 400 (2009) (*Zimmerman I*), we affirmed the district court's decision on several issues. . . .

Concurrent with the release of *Zimmerman I,* we ordered the parties to submit supplemental briefs on certain questions raised in the issues originally presented on appeal by both Plaintiffs and Intervenors. Those general issues, presently before us for review after the parties' supplemental oral arguments, focus on whether the district court erred in deciding as a matter of law that the Board did not violate the Takings Clause. . . .

Plaintiffs are owners of land in Wabaunsee County who have entered into written contracts for the development of commercial wind farms on their properties. Intervenors are not landowners but through various contracts are owners of purported wind rights concerning other properties in the county.

Defendant is the three-member Board of County Commissioners of Wabaunsee County. The county is roughly 30 miles long and 30 miles wide, containing approximately 800 square miles and 7,000 people. It is located in the Flint Hills of Kansas, which contain the vast majority of the remaining Tallgrass Prairie that once covered much of the central United States.

On October 28, 2002, the county zoning administrator told the Board that he had been contacted by a company desiring to build a wind farm in the county. At that time, the county had no zoning regulations relating specifically to wind farms. However, Article 2 of the county's zoning regulations captioned "Agricultural District Regulations," did generally provide:

> "The purpose of this [Agricultural] District is to provide for a full range of agricultural activities on land used for agricultural purposes, . . . and at the same time offer protection to land used for agricultural purposes from the depreciating effect of objectional, hazardous, incompatible and unsightly uses. The District is also intended to protect watersheds and water supplies; to protect forest and scenic areas; to conserve fish and wildlife habitat. . . ."

According to the Board, establishing wind farms first would have required the granting of conditional use permits to allow for the height of the wind turbine structures, *i.e.*, permission was not automatic but within the Board's discretion.

On November 12, 2002, the Board adopted a resolution placing a temporary moratorium on the acceptance of applications for conditional use permits for wind farm projects. The resolution provided, among other things, that during the moratorium the zoning administrator was to undertake a comprehensive review of both the current zoning regulations and wind farm projects, including the impact, if any, that such projects might have upon nearby properties. This moratorium, valid for 120 days upon publication, was later extended on at least five occasions.

The following month, December 2002, the county planning commission conducted its first public meeting to discuss amending zoning regulations regarding commercial wind farms.

According to Plaintiffs' briefs, in April 2003, 8 of the 12 Plaintiffs individually entered into "Amended and Restated Wind Farm Easement Agreement[s]" with J.W. Prairie Wind Power, L.L.C. for the purpose of providing for the development of CWECS on their respective properties. These include Plaintiffs Roger and Angelina Zimmerman, Harris and Virginia Zimmerman, Bill and Linda Unruh, and Robert and Janet Goss.

According to Plaintiffs' briefs, in June 2003, two more Plaintiffs, Kenneth and Colleen Anderson, individually entered into the same agreement with J.W. Prairie Wind Power for the purpose of providing for the development of CWECS on their property.

On July 24, 2003, the planning commission held a public hearing for discussion of the proposed zoning regulations, which included regulations of small and commercial wind farms. A month later, the Board ordered the planning commission to review and recommend updates to the 1974 Wabaunsee County Comprehensive Plan (Plan) because the Plan did not address changes that had occurred in the county in intervening years. After the Plan had been reviewed, the Board intended to consider the new proposed regulations regarding wind turbines.

On February 15, 2004, after input from the public, including a county-wide survey and focus groups, the planning commission formally recommended the adoption of the revised Comprehensive Plan 2004.

Eight days later, on February 23, the Board again voted to extend the wind farm moratorium, this time from March 31 to June 30, 2004, "to allow adequate time to complete a full study of the issues involved with wind energy conversion systems." The Board again directed—this time that prior to July 1—the county zoning administrator "shall not accept nor process applications for conditional use permits for wind energy conversion systems."

On March 1, 2004, the two Intervenors, A.B. Hudson and Larry French, were each the named "second party" in two separate documents entitled, "Corporation General Warranty Deed and Grant of Easement" signed by the first party, Workingman's Friend Oil, Inc. Among other things, the documents state they entitle Intervenors to:

> "[t]he exclusive and complete rights, titles, interest, and privileges in all the wind and air above and passing through the land, along with all related easements and covenants . . . and all right, title, and interest to develop or grant wind rights, wind easements, wind leases, . . . and [2] all rights to construct or cause to be constructed and operate through third party contracts, wind farms with related improvements. . . ."

. . . .

The next month, on April 26, 2004, the Board adopted the planning commission's recommended changes to the Plan and adopted the Comprehensive Plan 2004. . . .

The next month, on May 20, 2004, after the Board's adoption of the Comprehensive Plan, the planning commission held a public hearing to discuss proposed amendments to the zoning regulations regarding small and commercial wind farms. At its next meeting, the commission voted 8–

2 to recommend that the Board approve the proposed zoning amendments which would specifically allow CWECS as a conditional use, subject to certain conditions.

According to the briefs of the two Intervenors, on June 19, 2004, they entered into "Wind Option Agreements" with Zilkha Renewal Energy, LLC. . . .

On June 28, the Board . . . adopted the commission's recommendations regarding regulation of Small Wind Energy Conversion Systems (SWECS, *i.e.,* small wind farms). It rejected, however, the commission's recommendations regarding regulation of CWECS by absolutely prohibiting CWECS in the county.

The Board's decision was formally reflected in Resolution No. 04–18, passed 2 weeks later on July 12, 2004. The Resolution articulated the following basis for the Board's decision:

> "The basis of the amendments to the Zoning Regulation is that Commercial Wind Energy Conversion Systems would not be in the best interests of the general welfare of the County as a whole. They do not conform to the intent and purpose of the Zoning Regulations. In light of the historical, existing and anticipated land uses in the County, they would adversely affect the County as a whole. They would be incompatible with the rural, agricultural, and scenic character of the County. They would not conform to the Wabaunsee County Comprehensive Plan, including the goals and objectives that were identified by the citizens of the County and incorporated as part of the Plan. They would be detrimental to property values and opportunities for agricultural and nature based tourism. Each reason stands on its own. This motion is based upon what has been presented at public hearings, public meetings, letters and documents that have been produced, as well as experience and personal knowledge of the issues involved."

The Resolution also added the following definitions to Article 1–104 of the zoning regulations adopted in 1995:

> "207.   Wind Energy Conversion System (WECS). The combination of mechanical and structural elements used to produce electricity by converting the kinetic energy of wind to electrical energy. Wind Energy Conversion systems consist of the turbine apparatus and any buildings, roads, interconnect facilities, measurement devices, transmission lines, support structures and other related improvements necessary for the generation of electric power from wind.

"208.	*Commercial Wind Energy Conversion System*: A Wind Energy Conversion System exceeding 100 kilowatt or exceeding 120 feet in height above grade, or more than one Wind Energy Conversion System of any size proposed and/or constructed by the same person or group of persons on the same or adjoining parcels or as a unified or single generating system. (*Commercial Wind Energy Conversion Systems are specifically prohibited as a use in Wabaunsee County*.). . . .

. . . .

"210.	Small Wind Energy Conversion System. A wind energy conversion system consisting of wind turbine, a tower, and associated control or conversion electronics, which has a rated capacity of not more than 100 kilowatt, which is less than 120 feet in height and which is intended solely to reduce on-site consumption of purchased utility power." (Emphasis added.)

A new paragraph (30) also was added to Article 31–105. It reiterated that CWECS were prohibited in Wabaunsee County and certainly would not be permitted as a conditional use:

"30. Commercial Wind Energy Conversion Systems are *not a use that may be approved or permitted as a Conditional Use in Wabaunsee County* and are specifically prohibited." (Emphasis added.)

. . . .

Article 31–112 (Prohibited Uses) was also amended to include a new paragraph (5) concerning CWECS. It reiterated that such systems were prohibited in the county and any application for their use would not be considered:

"5.	No Commercial Wind Energy Conversion System, as defined in these Regulations, shall be placed in Wabaunsee County. No application for such a use shall be considered."

Plaintiffs sued the Board in district court, seeking a judicial declaration that the Board's action in passing Resolution No. 04–18 be null and void. Plaintiffs also sought damages under a number of different theories. . . .

Plaintiffs and Intervenors both contend the Board's decision to amend the zoning regulations constituted a compensable taking under the Fifth Amendment to the United States Constitution and that Judge Ireland erred in holding as a matter of law that no taking occurred. . .

We ordered the parties in their supplemental briefing to thoroughly analyze the particular nature of the rights allegedly taken—from landowners and from nonlandowners alike. In their initial brief, Plaintiffs only allege a taking of their lease rights with J.W. Prairie Wind Power,

LLC, to develop CWECS on their realty. In their supplemental brief, Plaintiffs also appear to allege a taking of a second interest: one "in the wind resources that flow across their properties."

Unlike Plaintiffs, Intervenors are not realty owners. Based upon their documents from Workingman's Friend Oil, Inc. ("deeds and grants of easements" which are in the record) and those from Zilkha Renewal Energy, LLC (which are not in the record but are denominated "wind option agreements"), they also appear to claim two interests were taken. First, through Workingman they claim severed wind estates, including the right to construct and operate commercial wind farms. Second, through Zilkha they claim contractual interests to utilize the wind rights, *i.e.,* in the commercial development of wind power.

The Board responds that Plaintiffs' and Intervenors' claim for alleged loss of "valuable contractual interests" fails because this court found no violation of the Contracts Clause in *Zimmerman I.* 289 Kan. at 969, 218 P.3d 400. Additionally, the Board contends that Intervenors only received an easement to use the land for a certain purpose—*i.e.,* to set up commercial wind farms—and that there is no such thing as a severable wind estate for takings analysis. . . .

We begin by acknowledging that the Takings Clause of the Fifth Amendment to the United States Constitution, which is applicable to the states through the Fourteenth Amendment, provides that private property shall not be "taken for public use, without just compensation." *Lingle v. Chevron, U.S.A., Inc.,* 544 U.S. 528, 125 S.Ct. 2074, 161 L.Ed.2d 876 (2005); *Estate of Kirkpatrick,* 289 Kan. at 558, 215 P.3d 561. The Fifth Amendment's guarantee "is designed to bar Government from forcing some people alone to bear public burdens which, in all fairness and justice, should be borne by the public as a whole." *Armstrong v. United States,* 364 U.S. 40, 49, 80 S.Ct. 1563, 4 L.Ed.2d 1554 (1960).

As the *Lingle* Court acknowledged, beginning with *Penn. Coal Co. v. Mahon,* 260 U.S. 393, 43 S.Ct. 158, 67 L.Ed. 322 (1922), the Supreme Court has

> "recognized that government regulation of private property may, in some instances, be so onerous that its effect is tantamount to a direct appropriation or ouster—and that such 'regulatory takings' may be compensable under the Fifth Amendment. In Justice Holmes' storied but cryptic formulation, 'while property may be regulated to a certain extent, if regulation goes too far it will be recognized as a taking.' 260 U.S. at 415 [43 S.Ct. 158]. The rub, of course, has been—and remains—how to discern how far is 'too far.' In answering that question, we must remain cognizant that 'government regulation—by definition—involves the adjustment of rights for the public good' [citation omitted] and that

'Government hardly could go on if to some extent values incident to property could not be diminished without paying for every such change in the general law,' *Mahon, supra,* at 413 [43 S.Ct. 158]." *Lingle,* 544 U.S. at 537–38, 125 S.Ct. 2074.

The United States Supreme Court has further observed that the "question of what constitutes a 'taking' for purposes of the Fifth Amendment has proved to be a problem of considerable difficulty." *Penn Central Transp. Co. v. New York City,* 438 U.S. 104, 123, 98 S.Ct. 2646, 57 L.Ed.2d 631 (1978). As a result, the Supreme Court was "unable to develop any 'set formula' for determining when 'justice and fairness' require that economic injuries caused by public action can be compensated by the government, rather than remain disproportionately concentrated on a few persons," with the result being "ad hoc, factual inquiries." *Frick v. City of Salina,* 290 Kan. 869, 886, 235 P.3d 1211 (2010) (citing *Penn Central,* 438 U.S. at 123–24, 98 S.Ct. 2646). . . .

We now turn to Plaintiffs' second contention. More specifically, they argue Judge Ireland further erred in granting judgment against them on their takings claims by declaring that the Board just "refused to expand the existing rights."

We begin our analysis by agreeing with the Board's assertion that there is no vested right in the continuity of zoning in a particular area so as to preclude subsequent amendment, *i.e.,* no right to have the existing zoning ordinance continue unchanged. *Houston v. Board of City Commissioners,* 218 Kan. 323, 543 P.2d 1010 (1975); *Colonial Investment Co., Inc. v. City of Leawood,* 7 Kan.App.2d 660, 646 P.2d 1149 (1982). However, under the vested rights doctrine, if a vested property right existed before the change in zoning, "the changed law cannot control without being subject to a successful takings claim." Laitos, *Law of Property Rights Protections: Limitations on Governmental Powers,* § 9.02[B][1] (2011 Supp.). *See* Delaney & Vaias, *Recognizing Vested Development Rights as Protected Property in Fifth Amendment Due Process and Takings Claims,* 49 WASH. U.J. URB. & CONTEMP. L., 27, 31 (1996) ("Only after landowners acquire vested rights under state law are they free to continue a project in the face of subsequent changes to land use regulations that would otherwise preclude continuing the project."). . . .

Accordingly, to prevail on a takings claim, a party seeking compensation must first establish that the property in question is one in which a vested interest exists, *i.e.,* a constitutionally cognizable property interest. *Landgraf v. USI Film Products,* 511 U.S. 244, 266, 114 S.Ct. 1483, 128 L.Ed.2d 229 (1994) ("The Fifth Amendment's Takings Clause prevents the Legislature [and other government actors] from depriving private persons of *vested* property rights except for a 'public use' and upon payment of 'just compensation.'"); *Goodwin,* 244 Kan. 28, Syl. ¶ 8, 766 P.2d 177 (where a party has no vested right in the use of land, restriction on that use by a city does not constitute a taking of property).

This court has held that "[a] vested right is a right so fixed that it is not dependent on any future act, contingency or decision to make it more secure." *Vaughn v. Nadel*, 228 Kan. 469, Syl. ¶ 3, 618 P.2d 778 (1980). Moreover,

> "[r]ights are vested when the right to enjoyment, present or prospective, has become the property of some particular person or persons as a present interest. [Citation omitted.] [On the other hand, a] '*mere expectancy of future benefit, or a contingent interest in property founded on anticipated continuance of existing laws, does not constitute a vested right.* [Citation omitted.]' " (Emphasis added.) *KPERS v. Reimer & Koger Assocs., Inc.*, 261 Kan. 17, 41, 927 P.2d 466 (1996).

The Board and *amicus curiae* Protect the Flint Hills, Inc. (Protect) present a multitude of arguments for why Plaintiffs and Intervenors have no vested property rights. We need address only one, for it is dispositive. More particularly, the Board essentially argues that whatever interests these parties purportedly possessed before the moratorium, those interests were conditioned upon the Board's discretionary issuance of a conditional use permit. Accordingly, interests such as developing, constructing, or operating CWECS were not vested rights. . . .

Because at all material times the Board's zoning regulations did not just provide that issuance of a CUP was purely discretionary but additionally the July 2004 regulation changes completely eliminated the possibility of a CUP issuance for CWECS in particular, we conclude no vested property right of any type has been taken from Plaintiffs or Intervenors by the Board. . . .

Because we have held there was no property for purposes of a takings claim, it is unnecessary to proceed with a full takings analysis. . . .

CONCLUSION

We affirm the district court's disposition of . . . the claim under the Takings Clause. . . .

NOTES

1.   *The Relevance of Receiving County Permits.* The court in *Zimmerman* largely skirted takings law analysis by holding that the plaintiffs held no vested property rights capable of being taken by the county ordinance because they had not yet received permits to install wind turbines on their property. Suppose one of the plaintiffs in the case *had* already received permits from the

county authorizing them to proceed with wind farm development when the ordinance was imposed. The reasoning in the majority opinion at least implies the case would have been analyzed differently under that set of facts.

2.   *Vested Rights in Minerals vs. Vested Rights in Wind.* The *Zimmerman* court focused in its analysis on the fact that none of the challengers in the case had received final approvals to build wind farms in the county. Based on this fact, the Court reasoned that the challengers lacked any "vested rights" capable of taken by government regulation. The court's reasoning arguably diverges from the rule set forth in *Shelly Materials* that severed mineral rights could be the "relevant parcel" for takings analysis regardless of whether the rights holder held all government approvals to exercise the rights.

3.   *The Possibility of Wind Rights Takings by the Military.* On several occasions, the United States Department of Defense (DoD) has worked with the Federal Aviation Administration (FAA) to block or severely restrict utility-scale wind energy projects that the DOD fears could interfere with military radar systems. In fact, the American Wind Energy Association has claimed that, in 2009 alone, almost 9,000 MW of proposed wind energy development was "abandoned or delayed because of radar concerns raised by the military and the [FAA]". Leora Broydo Vestel, *Wind Turbine Projects Run Into Resistance*, N.Y TIMES (Aug. 26, 2010), http://www.nytimes.com/2010/08/27/business/energy-environment/27radar.html?_r=0. Under what circumstances, if any, might these prohibitions on wind energy development trigger compensable takings? For a detailed analysis of this question, see generally Troy A. Rule, *Airspace and the Takings Clause*, 90 WASH. U. L. REV. 421 (2012).

C. WIND TURBINE WAKE INTERFERENCE

Like most valuable assets, wind rights are also capable of being damaged or devalued by the actions of others. Among other things, installing wind turbines or other tall structures on the land immediately upwind of an existing wind turbine can disrupt the flow of wind into the turbine and cause it to produce far less electric power. Wind turbines and other towering physical objects create a "wake" effect in the airspace immediately behind them—a swirling disturbance of the prevailing wind current that resembles the effect of a large boulder in a flowing river. The impact of these wakes can be substantial: one government study concluded that wake effects can reduce wind energy productivity by as much as 40 percent in the area situated immediately downwind of an operating wind turbine. *See* Nat'l Renewable Energy Laboratory, *Predicting Wind Power with Greater Accuracy* 9 (2014), https://str.llnl.gov/content/pages/april-2014/pdf/04.14.1.pdf.

In most jurisdictions, there are no clear rules to govern how wind energy resources are allocated and shared among neighbors so significant legal uncertainty often plagues conflicts over turbine wake interference. Should a wind turbine wake that causes measurable economic harm to a landowner situated downwind give rise to an actionable nuisance claim? Or should landowners be free to make productive use of the wind resources directly above their land without liability for adverse impacts on downwind neighbors' wind farms?

1. WHY DO WAKE INTERFERENCE LAWS MATTER?

Laws governing wind turbine wake conflicts have important policy implications because of their potential to impact turbine siting decisions. Among other things, an absence of clear legal rules to govern these conflicts can lead to inefficient wind turbine siting, especially when competing wind energy developers are micro-siting wind turbines on both sides of a common property line. Wind resources can be highly valuable, especially when located on lands with transmission access and other characteristics that make them prime wind energy development sites. Moreover, the quality of wind resources can vary a lot by location so installing turbines in the most productive locations is crucial to maximizing the productivity of the world's scarce wind energy resources. An optimal set of legal rules would clearly govern turbine wake interference conflicts without unduly restricting wind energy development or leading developers to install turbines in sub-optimal places to avoid conflicts with neighbors. The excerpt below describes the problem of wind turbine wake interference in more detail and highlights the policy approaches two other countries have used to address it.

WAKE EFFECTS, WIND RIGHTS, AND WIND TURBINES: WHY SCIENCE, CONSTITUTIONAL RIGHTS, AND PUBLIC POLICY ISSUES PLAY A CRUCIAL ROLE
Kimberly E. Diamond
40 WM. & MARY ENVTL. L. & POL'Y REV. 813, 816 (2016)

. . . A developer bases its turbine placement, including the layout modeling and location of each individual turbine, on the wind flow and wind speeds over different areas of the parcel. Complex terrain and different elevations on a particular parcel may impact wind speeds and turbulence for turbines sited on a particular location. Obstructions, such as trees, large silos, and other man-made buildings and structures, may cause a downwind turbine to be subjected to wind turbulence. Accordingly, having unanticipated obstructions placed too close to a turbine, particularly if such obstructions increase wind turbulence and diminish the wind speed of the wind flowing to such turbine, could cause the developer to lose revenue. If a number of turbines on a developer's property are impacted similarly, the developer could sustain significant financial losses that could ultimately render an entire project economically unfeasible. . . .

. . . The term "wind wake" is derived from the wakes moving ships leave behind them in the water. . . . Once wind flows through a turbine, the volume of air downwind from it has a reduced wind speed and increased turbulence compared to wind . . . that [an] obstruction has not impeded or redirected (such as a house, barn, tree, complex terrain including hills or mountains, or other obstacles such as another wind turbine). . . .

Scientists still are debating the length to which a wind turbine wake extends. However, the scientific community generally agrees that a wake from a utility-scale commercial wind turbine can extend a minimum distance of eight to ten times such turbine's rotor diameter. In fact, Texas Tech University's Wind Science and Engineering Center conducted a recent study using Doppler radar that shows turbine wakes persisting up to fifteen times the rotor diameter of the wake-generating turbine.

Siting a downwind turbine within the wake of an upwind turbine can have detrimental effects on the mechanical loads and operational capacity of the downwind turbine, as well as decrease the amount of energy the downwind turbine produces. . . . [T]he closer a downwind turbine is sited to an upwind turbine within the upwind turbine's wake, the greater the wake effect impact on such downwind turbine and the less power that downwind turbine will produce.

. . . .

Currently, in the United States, there is no Supreme Court ruling, national standard, federal guidelines, legislation, regulatory framework, or other measure that has established a federally protected property right to wind flowing over one's property, including non-interference with this wind flow by an immediately adjacent neighbor. However, other countries have ruled on this matter. For instance, in Norway, the Norwegian high court rejected a landowner's 2009 claim for compensatory damages due to an adjacent planned wind farm's violation of his property rights by "reduc[ing] [his] opportunity to exploit the wind across his property."[20] The plaintiff in this case argued that the blade tip of the proposed wind farm's nearest turbine would be located just over 12 feet from the property line between his property and the property on which the wind farm was to be located. The defendant wind company argued that having a right to install wind turbines on its property necessarily meant that it had an implied right to use the wind flowing across its property. The judges in this Norwegian case agreed with the defendant, holding that because wind is not subject to property rights, limiting the right to use of wind flowing across one's land is not applicable.

In contrast, in a recent case in Denmark . . . the Danish valuation authority ruled in favor of the plaintiff, a downwind landowner who

---

[20] Torgny Muller, *First Norwegian Ruling on the Question of Who Owns the Wind . . . Nobody Owns the Wind*, 33 NATURLIG ENERGI (2011) . . . available at http://www.sindal-lundsberg.com/ cms/from-my-desk/49-first-norwegian-ruling-on-the-question-of-who-owns-the-wind-nobody-owns-the-wind [https://perma.cc/U7EB-SCT4].

allegedly lost production revenues and experienced increased maintenance costs. [The Defendant's] nearest turbines were located only approximately 561 feet, or approximately 1.1 rotor diameters, away from plaintiff downwind landowner's existing turbines. . . . [T]he Danish valuation authority determined that the turbines from the repowering project "will result in an increased turbulence" for plaintiff's existing turbines. The Danish valuation authority upheld plaintiff downwind landowner's claim, awarding plaintiff compensatory damages in the amount of . . . approximately USD $140,765.26.

Notably, in a prior Denmark wind rights case . . . the Danish valuation authority held against a plaintiff who alleged potential damages with respect to its three installed turbines due to an adjacent neighbor's proposed installation of two wind turbines that would cause wake effects, reduce wind flow across plaintiff's land, and diminish expected power production from plaintiff's turbines.[27] In this. . . . [c]ase, the Danish valuation authority noted that the local municipality had previously announced its plans for both the plaintiff's land and its adjacent neighbor's land to be zoned for the siting of up to five turbines in total. Accordingly, such valuation authority determined that plaintiff had notice, was fully aware of the risks associated with plaintiff's parcel, and assumed the risk that its adjacent neighbor would likely install additional wind turbines on such neighbor's property. The Danish valuation authority ruled that plaintiff's acceptance of this risk precluded plaintiff from receiving what otherwise would have been compensable losses.

NOTES & QUESTIONS

1. What are the main differences among the approaches applied in the Norwegian and two Danish cases highlighted above? What was the apparent factual difference in the second Danish case that led the court find no liability for causing harmful wake effects? Do you think that factual difference should justify a finding of no liability? Why or why not?

2. What rule (or set of rules) would you recommend for addressing wind turbine wake interference conflicts? On what basis do you favor your proposed rule(s) over other possible rules?

3. *Similar Conflicts in the United States.* Although the examples in the excerpt above arose in other countries, wind turbine wake interference conflicts have arisen in the United States in recent years as well. *See, e.g.,* Lauren Donovan, *Two Energy Projects Competing for the Wind*, BISMARK TRIBUNE (Feb. 22, 2008), http://bismarcktribune.com/news/local/article_4bd1f

---

[27] Torgny Muller, *First Danish Ruling on Who Owns the Wind*, 33 NATURLIG ENERGI (2011) . . . available at http://www.sindal-lundsberg.com/cms/from-my-desk/51-first-danish-ruling-on-who-owns-the-wind [https://perma.cc/VKN9-45ZQ].

0d6-6616-512b-970f-b4301800f774.html (describing wind turbine wake interference conflicts in two counties in North Dakota); Charles C. Read & Daniel Lynch, *The Fight for Downstream Wind Flow*, LAW360 (May 25, 2011), http://www.law360.com/articles/247122/the-fight-for-downstream-wind-flow (describing a dispute between competing wind energy developers over potential wind turbine wake interference issues near Vansycle Ridge, Oregon).

4. *Merged Wakes and Project-to-Project Wake Interference.* Recent research suggests that turbine wake conflicts can arise not only between individual upwind turbines and downwind turbines. They can also arise on an aggregate scale between a whole wind farm and a separately owned wind farm situated downwind. A study published in 2014 on wake effects at offshore wind energy projects in Denmark found that a downwind wind farm's aggregate electricity productivity was significantly reduced when a new wind farm was erected about three kilometers (nearly 2 miles) directly upwind. According to the study, the wakes of multiple turbines in the upwind project merged to form a wide wake behind the entire project. *See* Nicolai Gayle Nygaard, *Wakes in Very Large Wind Farms and the Effect of Neighbouring Wind Farms*, 524 J. PHYS.: CONF. SER., 2014, at 1–10, http://iopscience.iop.org/article/10.1088/1742-6596/524/1/012162/pdf. These findings suggest that there could be similar sorts of aggregated wake impacts between onshore wind farms, which are often clustered together to take advantage of prime wind resources and transmission access. The potential for aggregate wake interference conflicts between wind farms raises multiple other legal issues that have yet to be addressed.

5. *Additional Reading on Turbine Wake Interference Issues.* Multiple other commentators have described and analyzed the legal issues associated with wind turbine wake interference conflicts in recent years. The following articles are a useful starting point for further exploration of this topic: Yael Lifshitz, *Winds of Change: Drawing on Water Law Doctrines to Establish Wind Law*, 23 N.Y.U. ENVTL. L.J. 434 (2015); Troy A. Rule, *A Downwind View of the Cathedral: Using Rule Four to Allocate Wind Rights*, 46 SAN DIEGO L. REV. 207 (2009).

2. WAKE INTERFERENCE-BASED SETBACK REQUIREMENTS

One way for governments to prevent most wind turbine wake interference conflicts is to impose turbine *setback* requirements on wind energy projects that space turbines far enough away from property boundary lines to prevent significant wake disturbances from reaching into neighbors' downwind property. The state of Minnesota has already embraced this approach to govern wind turbine wake conflicts in that state. Regulations adopted in Minnesota impose "wind access buffers" requiring developers to site wind turbines certain minimum distances away from parcels not under their control. The minimum distances for Minnesota's wind access buffer setbacks are based on industry knowledge about how far significant wake disturbances extend behind and to the side of operating wind turbines. These distances are tied to the diameter of the turbine's rotor, which exceeds 100 meters for many utility-scale wind turbines. For instance, a 5-rotor-diameter setback for a turbine with a 100-meter rotor diameter would be 500 meters—nearly one third of a mile. The specific language in Minnesota's wake setback rule provides:

> Wind turbine towers shall not be placed less than 5 rotor diameters (RD) from all boundaries of developer's site control area (wind and land rights) on the predominant wind axis (typically north-south axis) and 3 rotor diameters (RD) on the secondary wind axis (typically east-west axis), without the approval of the permitting authority. This setback applies to all parcels for which the permittee does not control land and wind rights, including all public lands.

Graphic depictions of these setback requirements are illustrated as rectangular boxes in Figure 1 below. Within these boxes on each parcel are five smaller, darker rectangles representing potential wind turbine sites staggered to minimize wake impacts. Although Minnesota's turbine wake setback requirements are effective at preventing wind turbine wake interference, they also preclude any wind energy development on much of the state's land that is particularly well-suited for such projects. For instance, all of land situated outside the large setback boxes in Figure 1 is unavailable for the siting of turbines. This effect of precluding development in vast areas of prime wind energy land is a clear disadvantage of Minnesota's setback-based approach to addressing turbine wake interference.

Figure 3.1. Minnesota's Wind Access
Buffer Setback Requirements

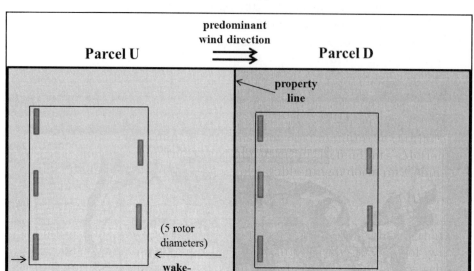

Source: TROY A. RULE, SOLAR, WIND AND LAND: CONFLICTS
IN RENEWABLE ENERGY DEVELOPMENT 59 (2014)

Minnesota's Public Utilities Commission administers and enforces the state's wake-based buffer requirements each time it considers applications for wind turbine siting permits under state law. In the following administrative ruling, a developer seeking a wind farm permit had requested a "variance" that, if granted, would have allowed the developer to build turbines closer to the property line than are ordinarily allowed under Minnesota's wake-based buffer requirements. As you read this ruling, pay particular attention to the developer's arguments in favor of the variance and to the Commission's reasons for denying it.

IN THE MATTER OF THE APPLICATION OF NEW ULM PUBLIC UTILITIES COMMISSION FOR A LARGE WIND ENERGY CONVERSION SYSTEM SITE PERMIT FOR THE NEW ULM WIND PROJECT IN NICOLLET COUNTY

Minnesota Public Utilities Commission
2010 WL 239236 (Minn. P.U.C. 2010)

On May 5, 2009, the New Ulm Public Utilities Commission (NUPUC, or the Applicant) filed with the Commission a large wind energy conversion system (LWECS) site permit application to construct and operate the 10.5 megawatt (MW) New Ulm wind project (Project) in Nicollet County.

On June 26, 2009, the Commission issued an Order accepting the application with conditions and finding that a certificate of need was not required for the Project. The Commission conditioned its acceptance on the requirement that the Applicant supplement the information filed by providing a clear project map. . . .

On July 10, 2009, the Office of Energy Security of the Minnesota Department of Commerce (the OES) solicited comments on issues that should be considered in developing the draft site permit for this project.

On July 30, 2009, the NUPUC supplemented its filing, responding to issues raised at the Commission meeting on June 11, 2009. In its submission, NUPUC also requested a variance from the Commission's general wind permit standards—specifically, the wind access buffer setbacks. This wind permit standard requires a wind access buffer setback of five rotor diameters from all boundaries of a developer's site control area (wind and land axis) on the predominant wind axis and three rotor diameters on the secondary wind axis.

. . . .

On December 15, 2009, the OES filed a letter again recommending that the Commission make a preliminary determination that the draft site permit be denied. The OES also asserted that the NUPUC had failed to provide sufficient justification for a waiver of the wind access buffer setback standard.

On December 21, 2009, the Commission met to consider the matter.

. . . .

In its July 30, 2009 submission to the Commission, NUPUC noted that the Commission's permitting process and particularly the buffer setback requirements are significantly different from the Nicollet County regulatory process under which the Project was commenced and leases negotiated. NUPUC requested a waiver of the Commission's Wind Permit Standards Order relating to the wind access buffer setback of five rotor diameters from all boundaries of a developer's site control area (wind and land axis) on the predominant wind axis and three rotor diameters on the secondary wind axis.

NUPUC asserted that a waiver of this requirement is justified in this instance. NUPUC argued that it has entered into long term leases on three parcels of land for this Project. Each parcel was selected because it contains prominent, high points better suited for the placement of wind energy conversion systems than the lower-lying surrounding lands. NUPUC further argued that given the economic realities of the wind energy conversion systems as well as the physics associated therewith, it is very unlikely that any of the parcels of land within the setback areas where the wind resources are not currently under the control of the NUPUC would ever be developed for such a wind use. . . .

In its November 24, 2009 letter to the Commission, the NUPUC concluded its argument by asserting that a waiver of the wind setback buffer requirements is warranted, arguing that the Project is environmentally sound, economically justified, and contains environmental benefits that outweigh the arguments put forth by its opponents.

The OES asserted that a waiver of the Commission's wind access buffer setbacks for this Project is not appropriate for four reasons: 1) a waiver based on the perceived interests of local property owners presents an unmanageable standard for the Commission; 2) a waiver of wind access buffer setbacks does not protect possible future wind development; 3) a waiver of wind buffer setbacks is not compatible with the state's interest in siting large wind energy conversion system[s] in a manner compatible with the statutory standards of environmental preservation, sustainable development and the efficient use of resources. MINN. STAT. § 216F.03; and 4) a waiver of the wind buffer setbacks could place the Commission in the position of determining whether the wind rights of all landowners are equal.

2.   Commission Action

The Commission concurs with the reasoning and analysis of the OES, and declines to grant the requested waiver of the Commission's wind access buffer setbacks, contained in the Wind Permit Standards Order, in this matter. The NUPUC's inability to obtain voluntary wind rights from affected landowners is not a sufficient basis on which the Commission may rely to grant the requested waiver. Further, a sufficient case has not been made to support such action.

The wind access buffer setback standards, as established in the Commission's 2008 Wind Permit Standards Order, are designed to protect wind rights and future development options of adjacent landowners who are not participating in the wind project under consideration. Despite the urging of numerous advocates to adopt a less conservative standard in the proceedings leading to the 2008 Order, the Commission declined to do so, thus maintaining the three rotor diameter by five rotor diameter setback previously established.

The Commission finds that the NUPUC has failed to show sufficient justification or support for its request for a waiver from the established setback standard. The NUPUC relies in large part on mere speculation and conjecture as to whether the parcels of land within the setback areas where the wind resources are not currently under the control of the NUPUC would ever be developed. The Commission declines to grant a waiver based only on the NUPUC's unsupported projections regarding future development, recognizing that to do so would involve a fundamentally unmanageable standard.

It is clear that technological advances in turbines and economic feasibility factors may change and further improve in the future. Maintenance of the established buffer setbacks will protect the wind rights and future development options of adjacent property owners. As evidenced here, several of the citizens filing public comments were not generally opposed to wind development on their property, but were rather opposed to having development forced upon them by the prospect of New Ulm exercising eminent domain proceedings.

Further, the Commission finds that the NUPUC's request for a waiver of the wind buffer setbacks is not consistent with the state's interest in siting large wind energy conversion systems in a manner compatible with the statutory standards in Minn. Stat. § 216F.03 of environmental preservation, sustainable development, and the efficient use of resources. Upholding the future wind rights of wind developers of all sizes and types provides certainty in their planning and ensures the orderly and sustainable development of wind resources. Finally, the Commission finds that no valid reason or rationale has been offered in the record in this proceeding to justify treating one person's wind rights differently from another's.

. . . .

This Order shall become effective immediately.

QUESTIONS

1.   Do you agree with the Minnesota Public Utilities Commission's assertion that denying NUPUC a waiver of the state's wind buffer setback requirements promotes the efficient use of resources in this particular case? Why or why not?

2.   How do the wind buffer setback requirements protect the "future development options of adjacent property owners", as stated in the Commission's ruling?

3.   How might the problem of wind turbine wake interference potentially be addressable through privately negotiated real property covenants and other contractual arrangements? Do you think that such an approach would be preferable to the Minnesota's setback-based approach? Why or why not?

D. OTHER LAND USE CONFLICTS INVOLVING WIND ENERGY

The impacts of utility-scale wind energy development on neighboring land uses obviously extend far beyond turbine wake effects. Wind farms have enormous footprints, sprawling out across vast stretches of land. Perched upon sky-scraping towers, modern wind turbine rotors are often as wide as football fields and conspicuously rotate at all hours of the day and night. Due to their massive size, utility-scale wind turbines can easily stick out like a sore thumb on the horizon and alter scenic vistas in remote rural regions. They can also disrupt communities that have long enjoyed relative peace and quiet and might even reduce the market value of some land. Given these risks and the relative novelty of wind farm development in much of the country, it is hardly surprising that proposed wind energy projects routinely encounter opposition from neighbors. Below are brief descriptions of some of the most commonly voiced concerns about the potential impacts of wind energy development on neighboring property.

1. WIND TURBINE NOISE

Neighbors who oppose nearby wind farm proposals often express concerns about potential wind turbine noise. When a wind turbine's giant rotor spins, it displaces air and thereby creates a whooshing sound. A turbine's gearbox and other parts also generate mechanical noise as the turbine rotates. The volume of this noise at any given turbine site is dependent upon a wide array of factors, ranging from the direction and speed of prevailing winds to the surrounding terrain to the turbine's size and design. In some instances, this noise is loud enough to materially interfere with other nearby land uses.

In land use regulations, noise is typically measured in an A-weighted decibel (dBA) scale. Although extended exposure to noises exceeding 85 dBA can result in hearing loss, long-term exposure to sounds of up to 75 dBA is unlikely to cause any loss of hearing. *See Noise-Induced Hearing Loss*, NAT'L INST. DEAFNESS & OTHER COMM. DISORDERS, https://www.nidcd.nih.gov/health/noise-induced-hearing-loss (last visited Sept. 14, 2016). According to a 2014 GE Global Research report, utility-scale wind turbines operating at top rotational speeds produce sounds of about 105 dBA—a level of noise is roughly equivalent to that of a backyard lawn mower. *See* Thomas Kellner, *How Loud is a Wind Turbine?*, GE REPORTS (Aug. 2, 2014), http://www.gereports.com/post/92442325225/how-loud-is-a-wind-turbine/. Although long exposure to this level of noise could potentially harm hearing, most utility-scale turbines are required to be sited at least 300 meters away from residential homes, and noise tends to dissipate with distance. From a distance of 300 meters, a utility-scale turbine's noise approximates just 45 dBA, or the hum of a household refrigerator. *See id.*

Small residential-scale wind turbines are generally sited far closer than utility-scale turbines to homes and businesses and are therefore potentially even more prone to create neighbor noise problems than their larger counterparts. Small turbines also have rotor blades that rotate much more rapidly than utility-scale turbines, which can make them disproportionately noisy given the relatively small amounts of power that they generate. At their top rotational speeds, small turbines have been reported as generating sounds as great as 57 dBA. *See* Brian F. Keane, *Let's Get Real on Turbine Noise*, HUFFINGTON POST (Oct. 8, 2010), http://www.huffingtonpost.com/brian-keane/lets-get-real-on-wind-tur_b_754584.html.

Aware of citizens' concerns about wind turbine noise, states and municipalities are increasingly adopting ordinances that establish maximum dBA levels for wind farms and small wind turbines. Under some such ordinances, maximum noise levels are measured from a wind energy project's boundary line. Under others, they are measured from the exterior of the nearest occupied building. Maximum allowable dBA levels in many jurisdictions also vary depending on the time of day, with the greatest restrictions typically imposed during nighttime hours when most nearby residents are trying to sleep.

Below is an example of a municipal ordinance provision restricting commercial wind turbine noise.

NOISE

Contra Costa County, California Ordinances § 88–3.612 (2011)

(a) Except as provided in subsection (b) of this section, a commercial [Wind Energy Conversion System (WECS)] may not generate or emit any noise at any time that exceeds a maximum level of sixty-five decibels (dBA), as measured at each line of the exterior project boundary.

(b) A land use permit issued for a commercial WECS may authorize a maximum noise level that exceeds the level specified in subsection (a) if the commercial WECS is adjacent to an already-existing or approved commercial WECS and upon a finding that existing legal offsite residences and general plan-designated residential areas will not be adversely affected.

(c) A residential WECS may not generate or emit any noise at any time that exceeds a maximum level of sixty decibels (dBA), as measured at each line of the parcel upon which the residential WECS is installed.

(d) The measurement of commercial or residential WECS noise levels may not be adjusted for, or averaged with, periods of non-operation of the WECS. A site-specific noise study may be required to confirm compliance with the applicable noise standard. If noise generated or emitted by a commercial or residential WECS exceeds the applicable standard, the WECS operator must take measures necessary to comply with the standard, which may include discontinued operation of one or more WECS.

Even when wind energy developers comply with applicable laws and permitting requirements aimed at preventing unreasonable turbine noise, opponents with noise-related concerns sometimes challenge governments' approaches to addressing the issue. Because wind energy development is relatively new in many jurisdictions, state agencies and municipalities are often still trying to determine how best to regulate it and their rules and procedures can be more vulnerable to attack. As illustrated in the following case, such legal challenges sometimes lead to expensive litigation and delays even for those wind energy developers who have dutifully secured all required permits for their projects.

FRIENDS OF MAINE'S MOUNTAINS V. BOARD OF ENVIRONMENTAL PROTECTION

Maine Supreme Judicial Court, 2013
61 A.3d 689

SILVER, J.

Friends of Maine's Mountains, Friends of Saddleback Mountain, and several individuals (collectively, Friends) appeal from a final order of the Board of Environmental Protection. The Board affirmed the Department of Environmental Protection's order approving the application of Saddleback Ridge Wind, LLC (Saddleback), for a permit to construct the Saddleback Ridge Wind Project.

Friends argues that the Board abused its discretion when determining which nighttime sound level limit to apply to the applications. . . . We vacate the Board's order related to nighttime sound requirements and remand for further proceedings.

I.   BACKGROUND AND PROCEDURE

On October 26, 2010, Saddleback filed with the Department applications pursuant to the Site Location of Development Law and the Natural Resource Protection Act, seeking a permit to build a wind energy development in the Towns of Carthage, Canton, and Dixfield. The applications described the development as a "12-turbine, 33 [megawatt] wind energy project and associated transmission line and substation." The applications included a noise impact study and a visual impact assessment, which the Department hired consultants to review as part of its application review. . . . The noise impact study assessed the effect of the noise from the project on the thirty-four residences located near the project.

Friends objected to the permit application, attaching exhibits including extensive scientific literature on the health effects of the noise emitted by wind turbines, and requested that the Department hold a public hearing. The Department reviewed the material, and the acting commissioner for the Department issued a letter denying the hearing request.

In response to the public interest in the project, the Department held a public meeting, pursuant to 38 M.R.S. § 345–A(5) (2012), in the Town of Dixfield. During the meeting, many individuals shared their concerns about the project. Apart from the meeting, the Department also received comments, articles, and petitions from individuals and organizations both for and against the project. . . .

In its final order, issued by the acting commissioner on October 6, 2011, the Department approved the application subject to certain conditions. Although only the Department has jurisdiction to grant wind energy applications . . . the Board conducts appellate review of the Department's expedited wind energy development decisions. . . . The Board is also tasked with responsibility for "major substantive rulemaking, decisions on selected permit applications . . . and recommending changes in the law to the Legislature." 38 M.R.S. § 341–B (2012) (stating the purpose of the Board).

Friends appealed the Department's order to the Board . . . The Board issued its final order on February 18, 2012 . . . affirming the Department's approval of the permit application.

Specifically, the Board affirmed the Department's decision to apply the nighttime sound level limit in effect at the time of the order, which was 45 dBA. . . .

While Saddleback's applications were pending before the Department, the Board, in its role as the body responsible for making rules and providing guidance to the Legislature, was studying the noise emitted by wind energy developments. A petition to amend the noise regulation at 2 C.M.R. 06–096 375–6 to –15 § 10 (2001) was filed with the Board on December 17, 2010, sixty days after Saddleback submitted its permit applications. The Board received comments and evidence regarding the amendment and held a hearing on July 7, 2011. On September 15, 2011—twenty-one days before the Department approved Saddleback's permit limiting the nighttime noise emission to 45 dBA—the Board provisionally adopted the amendment that, among other changes, lowered the nighttime sound limit for wind energy projects from 45 dBA to 42 dBA. *Compare* 2

C.M.R. 06–096 375–7 § 10(C)(1)(a)(v) (2001), *with* 2 C.M.R. 06–096 375–15 § 10(I)(2)(b) (2012). The Board submitted the rule to the Legislature for final adoption, pursuant to 5 M.R.S. § 8072 (2012). After legislative approval, the amendment went into effect on June 10, 2012.

As noted above, the Board's affirmance of the Department's decision to apply the 45 dBA limit to this project occurred on February 15, 2012, five months after the Board adopted the 42 dBA nighttime sound level limits, subject only to final legislative approval.

II. DISCUSSION

Friends asserts that the Board applied the incorrect nighttime sound level limit to Saddleback's permit applications . . . We review for an abuse of discretion the Board's decision regarding which sound level limit to apply. 5 M.R.S. § 11007(4)(C)(6) (2012). . . .

A.   Nighttime Sound Level Limits

The Board regulates the sound levels of wind projects to protect "the health and welfare of nearby neighbors." 2 C.M.R. 06–096 375–6 § 10(A) (2012). In order to fulfill this goal, the Board's rules provide it with the flexibility necessary to impose limits on proposed wind projects so that sound levels are adequately controlled. 2 C.M.R. 06–096 375–10 § 10(E) (2012). *See also Martha A. Powers Trust v. Bd. of Envtl. Prot.*, 2011 ME 40, ¶ 12, 15 A.3d 1273 (noting that the Board may alter sound level limits). The Department and then the Board are solely responsible for ensuring that wind energy developments do not present undue hazards to the health of Maine's people. While acting in its legislative capacity, the Board recognized that the 45 dBA limit did not adequately protect the health and welfare of a project's neighbors. Here, by applying the 45 dBA limit, the Board failed to meet its statutory obligation to protect the health and welfare of the project's neighbors. In so doing, it abused its discretion.

Saddleback's permit application shows that the project does meet the 45 dBA nighttime sound level limit, as required by the pre-amendment rules. *See* 2 C.M.R. 06–096 375–7 § 10(C)(1)(a)(v) (2001). The application does not show, however, that the project meets the amended nighttime sound level limit of 42 dBA. . . . Saddleback provided substantial evidence showing that the modeled sound level limit would meet the then-existing level of 45 dBA. It did not attempt to show that the project would meet the 42 dBA limit.

The Board does not commit an abuse of discretion simply by making discretionary judgments that we, as a reviewing court, disagree with. *Sager*, 2004 ME 40, ¶ 11, 845 A.2d 567. Here, however, the Board, in its legislative role, explicitly determined that 45 dBA does not protect nearby residents as a nighttime sound level limit for wind projects, but it does nonetheless continue to apply that sound level limit in its adjudicatory role.

As discussed above, in its legislative capacity, the Board adopted the reduced sound level limit in order to minimize the impact from wind projects on the health of nearby residents, noting "[t]he available data demonstrates that persons living near existing wind energy development with actual sound level measurements near the 45 dBA limit ... are experiencing adverse effects." The Board made this finding and took this action *before* Friends appealed the Department's decision to it.

Saddleback's noise impact study shows that the modeled nighttime sound level at the most significantly affected residence is 44 dBA, and it asserts that due to the use of conservative models, the monitored level is likely to be even lower. The Board appeared to rely on this model calibration in its decision to uphold the Department's approval of the permit application, stating:

> If the Board was convinced under specific facts that requiring lower sound levels in the modeling results was necessary in order to achieve adequate control of noise from a development the Board could do so under Chapter 375(10)(E). However, the Board finds that the Chapter 375 standards currently in effect should adequately control noise due to the reliability of the model and the facts and assumptions used by the applicant in its modeling.

In essence, the Board found that the residents would not be exposed to the effects of 45 dBA nighttime sound levels, but instead the noise would be somewhere below that limit. There is no indication, however, that the nighttime sound levels would be as low as 42 dBA.

Because the Board is responsible for regulating sound levels in order to minimize health impacts—and because when doing so it determined that the appropriate nighttime sound level limit to minimize health impacts is 42 dBA—the Board abused its discretion by approving Saddleback's permit applications. Although the project's models predict nighttime sound levels slightly below 45 dBA, the Board failed to give the nearby residents the acknowledged protection of the amended rules. We vacate the Board's order and remand for further review using the 42 dBA nighttime sound level limit as introduced in 2 C.M.R. 06–096 375–15 § 10(I)(2)(b)(2012).

. . . .

The entry is: Judgment vacated and remanded for further proceedings consistent with this opinion.

QUESTIONS

1. What is the difference between the permitted decibel level under the Contra Costa County ordinance above and the nighttime noise level cited in

the *Friends of Maine's Mountains* case? What do you think accounts for this difference?

2.   From a public policy perspective, would it be better to establish a single federal uniform standard for acceptable noise levels from wind farms and apply that single standard in every jurisdiction? Why or why not?

3.   Which party would you argue is better equipped to determine whether Saddleback's project sufficiently protected landowners from excessive noise: the Board or the court that reviewed the Board's decision? If you conclude that the Board is more qualified to make that determination, make an argument for why the court's holding in this case is still justifiable.

2. FLICKER EFFECTS

In addition to generating noise, spinning wind turbine rotors can also create bothersome "flicker" or "strobe" effects when sunlight shines through them during certain times of the day and year. These flicker effects occur when the sun is low in the sky and is casting dark shadows behind tall objects on the horizon. Under such conditions, a wind turbine's rotating blades can momentarily block direct sunlight and then allow it to pass through in a repeated, rhythmic pattern. If the turbine's shadows are being cast onto building windows, even those inside buildings can experience disruptive flashes of light and darkness—almost akin to someone repeatedly switching the lights on and off—for several minutes at a time. Some medical researchers have suggested that this strobe effect could even induce seizures for certain individuals with epilepsy. *See* Graham Harding et al., *Wind Turbines, Flicker, and Photosensitive Epilepsy: Characterizing the Flashing That May Precipitate Seizures and Optimizing Guidelines to Prevent Them*, 49 EPILEPSIA 1095 (2008). For obvious reasons, such flicker effects can likewise create safety hazards when rotating turbine blades cast shadows onto busy roadways.

Over the past few decades, engineers have developed sophisticated models that can predict the likely flicker impacts of wind turbines installed in any given place at any given time. These models have helped to mitigate the uncertainty associated with potential wind turbine flicker effects. Increasingly, developers and policymakers are relying upon these models to address potential flicker impacts before they arise. In some instances, developers micro-site turbines in different locations to avoid creating flicker problems. In other situations, governments require (as a condition to granting a turbine site permit) that an applicant agree to temporarily shut down the turbine during certain times of day on certain days of the year.

Below is an example of a municipal ordinance restricting flicker effects from small wind turbines. These provisions illustrate the potential role of flicker forecasting models in this regulatory area and the difficult balance that policymakers must strike between allowing wind energy development to proceed and protecting neighbors' safety and reasonable enjoyment of their land.

WIND ENERGY CONVERSION SYSTEMS: LOCATION
Mason City, Iowa Ordinances § 12–17–6.D (2015)

A dispersed wind energy system shall be located a minimum of five hundred (500) feet from the nearest inhabited residential structure, school, hospital or place of worship not on property owned or controlled by the owner/operator of the dispersed wind energy system. This setback can be reduced by up to fifty (50) percent, at the discretion of the Board upon a positive determination that:

1. A noise study, prepared by a qualified professional, demonstrates that except for intermittent episodes, the dispersed wind energy system shall not emit noise in excess of the limits established by City Code. . .

2. A shadow flicker model demonstrates that shadow flicker shall not fall on, or in, any existing residential structure. Shadow flicker expected to fall on a roadway or a portion of a residentially zoned parcel may be acceptable if the flicker does not exceed thirty (30) hours per year; and the flicker will fall more than one hundred (100) feet from an existing residence; or the traffic volumes are less than five hundred (500) vehicles on the roadway. The shadow flicker model shall:

    a. Map and describe within a 1,000-foot radius of the proposed dispersed wind energy system the topography, existing residences and location of their windows, locations of other structures, wind speeds and directions, existing vegetation and roadways. The model shall represent the most probable scenarios of wind constancy, sunshine constancy, and wind directions and speed;

    b. Calculate the locations of shadow flicker caused by the proposed project and the expected durations of the flicker at these locations, calculate the total number of hours per year of flicker at all locations;

    c. Identify problem areas where shadow flicker will interfere with existing or future residences and roadways and describe proposed mitigation measures, including, but not limited to, a change in siting of the wind energy conversion system, a change in the operation of the wind energy conversion system, or grading or landscaping mitigation measures. . .

QUESTIONS

1.   Suppose that a hypothetical wind energy developer unknowingly installed a wind turbine near the home of an epileptic individual. The turbine was installed properly and complied with all applicable turbine siting laws. One winter afternoon, shadow flicker effects triggered a seizure in the epileptic neighbor, causing the individual to fall and suffer a severe head injury. The individual filed a lawsuit against the wind farm owner, seeking (i) monetary damages for the injuries suffered during the epileptic seizure, and (ii) an injunction permanently prohibiting operation of the turbine that created the flicker effects.

   a.   Suppose that you represented the plaintiff, who was injured during the epileptic seizure triggered by the flicker effects. What specific legal claim(s) would you allege in your complaint? Trespass? Nuisance? Some other claim?

   b.   Suppose instead that you represented the owner of the wind farm named in the lawsuit. What arguments would you make in defense of your client? Do you think you would prevail? Why or why not?

   c.   A permanent injunction against operation of the wind turbine would prevent the turbine from generating a large quantity of clean, renewable electricity. What are some other possible arrangements capable of addressing the plaintiff's concerns about flicker effects without categorically precluding the turbine from producing power?

   d.   Would it be possible for this flicker effects scenario to arise on a law-abiding wind farm in Mason City, Iowa (the city whose ordinance provisions are excerpted above)? Why or why not?

3.   ICE THROWS

In regions where temperatures drop well below freezing, wind turbine ice throws can create yet another potential hazard. Particularly when the wind is calm and turbines are not moving, layers of snow and ice can accumulate on their enormous rotor blades. Much like icicles hanging from a rooftop, these icy layers can harden and grow as ice melts and refreezes over time. Then, when the wind picks up again and the turbine's blades begin to rotate, they can hurl large pieces of this ice hundreds of meters away, threatening the safety of humans, animals, and property below. *See, e.g.*, Murray Wardrop, *Wind Turbine Closed After Showering Homes With Blocks of Ice*, TELEGRAPH (Dec. 4, 2008), http://www.telegraph.co.uk/news/uknews/3547074/Wind-turbine-closed-after-showering-homes-with-blocks-of-ice.html; JOAKIM RENSTROM, MODELING OF ICE THROWS FROM WIND

TURBINES   (2015),   https://www.diva-portal.org/smash/get/diva2:805173/
FULLTEXT01.pdf.

A landowner whose wind turbine launches ice across the property line
could theoretically be liable for trespass. However, most wind turbine
siting regulations seek to prevent any such incidents in the first place. The
most straightforward means of preventing hazardous ice throws onto
neighboring land is to impose setback requirements during the turbine
siting process. To be effective, such setback requirements obviously must
preclude the siting of any turbines close enough away to the nearest
property line to potentially allow an ice throws to make it across the line.
Other requirements, such as sensors on turbines that detect ice buildup
and shut down turbines until the ice is cleared, can help to limit ice throw
hazards as well.

4. ELECTROMAGNETIC INTERFERENCE

Wind turbines can also interfere with the wide spectrum of invisible
electromagnetic signals that are constantly traversing much of the nation's
low altitude airspace, especially in urbanized areas. As attorney and wind
law expert Kathleen Law has explained:

> Wind   turbines,   like   all   structures,   can   interfere   with
> communication   or   radar   signals   when   these   signals   are
> interrupted   by   the   turbine   structure   or   the   rotor   plane. . . .
> Turbines   affect   microwave   bands   that   operate   over   a   wide
> frequency   range   (900mHz   to   40   GHz).   Systems   on   these
> frequencies . . .   provide, among other things, phone service, data
> interconnects   for   mainframe   computers   and   the   Internet,   and
> backhaul   for   cellular   and   personal   communication   devices.
> Therefore, in addition to affecting TV picture quality, interference
> may . . . hamper homeowners' ability to receive a full gamut of TV
> channels, disrupt their cell phone service, or affect GPS devices.

KATHLEEN K. LAW, A PRACTITIONER'S GUIDE TO REAL ESTATE AND WIND
ENERGY PROJECT DEVELOPMENT 156–58 (2015).

In many cases, wind turbines' impacts on electromagnetic signals
intended for devices on the ground are relatively minor and easy to address.
Most modern wind turbine blades are made primarily of nonmetallic
materials, making them less prone to reflecting signals and creating
interference. Switching to satellite-supported transmission can also often
to mitigate these conflicts because signals transmitted from satellites miles
above the ground traverse less of the low-altitude airspace where wind
turbines stand.

When a wind turbine does interfere with electromagnetic signals
intended for landowners on the ground, which of the two sides of the
conflict should prevail? And how far should laws require wind energy

developers to go to avoid electromagnetic interference conflicts with neighbors when siting wind turbines? Local governments have taken a wide range of approaches to this problem. Again, quoting Kathleen Law:

> [Some] municipalities simply require reasonable efforts to avoid signal interference, or impose a duty to mitigate any interference that does not occur, or both. Some even have wholesale prohibitions, using language like "shall not interfere." Failure to prevent or mitigate signal interference may force the wind facility to cease operations.

Id. at 160–61.

At least a few local governments have adopted what amounts to a first-in-time rule to address conflicts over electromagnetic interference. Under this approach, the law gives priority to the structure or device that first made use of the airspace in the area involved in the conflict., whether that is a wind turbine or some other edifice. The small wind turbine ordinance adopted in Madison County, Idaho, is one example of this approach. It provides:

> *Electromagnetic interference.* Small wind turbines can cause interference within microwave communication links, fixed broadcast equipment, retransmission facilities, reception antennas (including residential television), radios, satellite televisions, wireless phones or all other communication systems. This must be taken into consideration before installing a small wind turbine. Those who have prior installations of the communication facilities set forth in this subsection shall have prior rights. No turbine shall be installed in the proximity of these facilities.

MADISON CTY., IDAHO, CODE OF ORDINANCES § 109–122(p).

What could be some potential difficulties associated with using this type of first-in-time rule? Is it practical to prohibit small wind turbines from being installed within the proximity of smart phones or other wireless mobile devices? Finding an optimal balance between promoting wind energy and protecting the functioning of the nation's electromagnetic transmission infrastructure is likely to become more difficult as wind energy projects of all sizes continue to spread across the country.

In addition to interfering with electromagnetic signals aimed at the ground, wind turbines can also interfere with airplane and helicopter radar systems. A pilot flying through the sky relies on radar to identify potentially hazardous objects in its way. When an aircraft's radar system picks up a commercial wind turbine situated below, that detection can impair the system's ability to detect other potentially hazardous objects in the aircraft's immediate flight path. Upgraded radar systems are increasingly available that can adequately address this problem by removing wind turbines from detection, but those new technologies have yet to be adopted throughout much of the United States so radar interference remains a significant risk. In some instances, the FAA has sought to prevent the construction of wind energy projects in certain areas to preserve aviation safety. Understandably, such restrictions on development sometimes draw ire from wind energy developers and landowners, particularly when the FAA imposes them in areas that are far away from airports or runway flight paths.

E. NEIGHBOR OPPOSITION TO WIND FARMS

Concerns over wind turbine noise, flicker effects, ice throws, electromagnetic interference, and other potential impacts have compelled countless landowners to embrace an unyielding "Not In My Back Yard" (NIMBY) position when new wind farm projects are proposed nearby. Permit applications for new wind energy projects routinely draw opposition from neighbors and other stakeholders, and it is not uncommon for these objectors to allege several of the potential harms referenced above when challenging proposed wind farm projects. The most successful wind energy developers and their lawyers tend to be skilled at anticipating and proactively addressing such neighbors' concerns.

The case that follows describes one landowner's vigorous efforts to challenge a county ordinance amendment designed to simplify the county's approval process for wind farm projects. The plaintiff landowner cites a long list of potential injuries to her and her property—including many of those listed above—if the court permits the county's ordinance amendment to stand. In part because of the premature posture of the case, the plaintiff's arguments prove wholly unconvincing to the court.

MUSCARELLO V. WINNEBAGO COUNTY BOARD

United States Court of Appeals, Seventh Circuit, 2012
702 F.3d 909

POSNER, C.J.

The plaintiff owns three tracts of land zoned agricultural in Winnebago County, Illinois. Her suit attacks on a variety of grounds, both federal and state, a 2009 amendment to the County's zoning ordinance that makes it easier than it was before the amendment for an owner of such property to obtain permission to build a wind farm on it. She worries that a wind farm on land adjacent to property of hers would damage the property in a rather frightening variety of ways, including depriving the property "of the full extent of the kinetic energy of the wind and air as it enters" the property; subjecting it to "shadow flicker and reduction of light," "severe noise," "possible 'ice throw'" (from buildup of ice on spinning blades), and " 'blade throws' " (the blades of the windmill might fly off while spinning); interfering with radar, cell phone, GPS, television, and other wireless communications; creating an increased likelihood of lightning damage and stray voltage; increasing electromagnetic radiation; preventing crop dusting (presumably the concern is that crop-dusting aircraft might be endangered by the wind turbines); drying out her land; and killing raptors, thus compelling her to use more pesticides. Some of the feared harms—such as noise, ice throw, blade throw, shadow flicker (like a strobe light), and death of birds—are indeed potential side effects of wind farms. . . .

A reduction in wind speed downwind is an especially common effect of a wind turbine. . . . And that is the harm the plaintiff emphasizes—which is odd. For the only possible such harm that the wind farm could do to her would be to reduce the amount of wind energy otherwise available to her, and the only value of that energy would be to power a wind farm on her property—and she is opposed to wind farming.

Some of the harms to which wind farms are sometimes thought to give rise—interference with electronic communication, lightning damage, and electromagnetic radiation—are conjectural. . . . Even noise, an unquestioned by-product of wind farming, has no adverse effect on most *agricultural* activity; and the plaintiff does not live on any of the properties involved in this case. Moreover, there's nothing in the record about what agricultural activities are conducted on her properties, or indeed whether any are, and so there's no basis in the record for assessing harm present or prospective to her properties from the possibility that a wind farm may someday be built nearby.

The suit is against the County Board, the County Zoning Board of Appeals, and some County officials, and also against several affiliated companies that operate wind farms. . . .

The district court dismissed the suit, a blunderbuss of federal and state claims, on the ground that the complaint fails to state any claim on which the plaintiff would be entitled to relief. Fed.R.Civ.P. 12(b)(6). . . .

The same district judge had earlier dismissed a similar suit by the same plaintiff against officials of another Illinois county in which she owns property, and in *Muscarello v. Ogle County Board of Commissioners*, 610 F.3d 416 (7th Cir. 2010), we affirmed that dismissal. We reached none of her state law claims in that case, however, and anyway it involved a different amendment to a different county's zoning ordinance—an amendment that allowed wind farms only if authorized by special-use permits, just as Winnebago County's zoning ordinance did before the 2009 amendment challenged in this case. We held that the grant of a special-use permit for a wind farm to be built next to the plaintiff's property was not a taking. The wind farm had not yet been built, so no harm to her property had yet been done, although, the permit having been granted, the harms she anticipates from wind farming were more imminent than they are in this case.

Under the Winnebago County ordinance before it was amended in 2009, a property owner had to run an elaborate procedural gauntlet in order to obtain a special-use permit for a wind farm. . . . The 2009 amendment made wind farms a permitted use . . . and although a wind farm cannot be built before a zoning clearance and a building permit are obtained . . . a zoning clearance requires merely a demonstration of compliance with the zoning code . . . and obtaining a building permit presumably is routine. So the amendment made it easier to build a wind farm in the county, and that at bottom is the plaintiff's gripe, as she is a pertinacious foe of wind farms.

The ordinance was further amended in 2011, mainly to add provisions for environmental protection and increase the setback of wind turbines from property lines; that should have alleviated some of the plaintiff's concerns with wind farms, but apparently has not done so.

No one has yet applied for a zoning clearance or building permit for a wind farm in Winnebago County, and no wind farm has yet been built anywhere in the county. As a result, a pall of prematurity hangs over the case. But injury need be neither certain nor great to confer standing under Article III of the Constitution . . . If the plaintiff's allegations regarding the prospective dangers from an adjacent wind farm are true or even if they are just widely believed, and if she must wait until a wind farm is built adjacent to one of her properties to proceed at law, she may find it difficult to sell the properties now (even before a wind farm is constructed) at the price they would command were the zoning amendment invalidated.

In fact the complaint alleges that her properties have lost $500,000 in value because of the 2009 ordinance. The number is suspiciously round, and unexplained. But the complaint was dismissed without a hearing on jurisdiction; and given the surprising number of potential adverse environmental consequences of wind farms (even though the energy they produce is clean and also reduces consumption of fossil fuels and so contributes to U.S. independence from foreign oil supplies), it is not beyond reason that the prospect of having a windmill adjacent to one's property might cause the value of the property to decline. The plaintiff has submitted a map on which, she argues, is marked a wind farm that a company wants to build near one of her properties, and she adds that a wind company once approached her about buying a wind easement from her. The injuries she alleges are speculative but not so speculative as to deny her standing to sue.

Yet it is germane to the merits if not to jurisdiction that no property of the plaintiff's has yet been taken, or will be until and unless a wind farm is built near her property—and probably not even then. A taking within the meaning of the takings clause of the U.S. Constitution has to be an actual transfer of ownership or possession of property, or the enforcement of a regulation that renders the property essentially worthless to its owner. *Lucas v. South Carolina Coastal Council*, 505 U.S. 1003, 1015–16, 112 S.Ct. 2886, 120 L.Ed.2d 798 (1992); *Muscarello v. Ogle County Board of Commissioners, supra*, 610 F.3d at 421–22; *Gamble v. Eau Claire County*, 5 F.3d 285, 286 (7th Cir. 1993). The 2009 Winnebago ordinance does not transfer possession of any of the plaintiff's land or limit her use of it.

The Illinois takings clause, however, on which she also relies, is broader than the federal clause. Article I, section 15 of the state's constitution provides that "property shall not be taken or damaged for public use without just compensation." "Taken" is defined as under federal law, *Forest Preserve District v. West Suburban Bank*, 161 Ill.2d 448, 204 Ill.Dec. 269, 641 N.E.2d 493, 497 (1994), but "damaged" connotes merely "a direct physical disturbance" of the plaintiff's property that causes a loss of value. [*Citations omitted*]. But as no wind farm has yet been built, there has been no direct, or for that matter indirect, physical disturbance of the plaintiff's property.

She further contends, however, that by making it easier for her neighbors to build wind farms, the amended ordinance has deprived her of property without due process of law, in violation of the Fourteenth Amendment and the corresponding provision in the Illinois constitution. The word "property" in the due process clause is defined broadly, and includes for example liquor licenses and tenured employment contracts, rather than just real estate and other tangible property. . . . But all she's challenging is a change in the *procedure* by which the owner of adjacent property can get permission to build a wind farm. The harm caused her by a change in the procedural rights of other landowners—a change that imposes no restriction on her use of her land—is too remote to count as a deprivation of property. . . . At worst, it raises the spectre of some future deprivation; and the due process clause does not protect against spectres.

Her attack on the legality of the amended ordinance fails for a more fundamental reason. The wind farm ordinance is legislation. It applies throughout the county and thus to many different properties owned by different people having different interests. Some property owners want to be permitted to build wind farms—otherwise the ordinance would not have been amended to make it easier for them to obtain permission—and at least one does not. "Cities [and other state and local governments, including counties] may elect to make zoning decisions through the political process" rather than having to "use adjudicative procedures to make" such decisions. *River Park, Inc. v. City of Highland Park*, 23 F.3d 164, 166 (7th Cir. 1994). . . .

These are cases interpreting federal law, but we are given no reason to think that Illinois law is different. Adjudicative procedures would not be workable in a case like this. Evaluating the plaintiff's objections to the ordinance would require comprehensive knowledge not only of wind farms and their effects pro or con on the environment and on energy independence, but also of the most valuable potential uses of all rural land in the county. A judge could review the ordinance for rationality . . . , but that is an undemanding test, and the national interest in wind power as a clean source of electrical energy and as a contribution to energy independence is enough to establish the ordinance's rationality. (There is federal money to support wind farms; why shouldn't Winnebago County try to get a bit of it by making it easier to build wind farms in the county?) For a court to allow a hypothetical harm to one person's property from a yet to be built (or even permitted to be built) wind farm to upend a county-wide ordinance would be an absurd judicial intrusion into the public regulation of land uses.

Stepping down from the dizzying heights of constitutional law, we can restate the plaintiff's contention as simply that a wind farm adjacent to her property would be a nuisance. . . . That is a more sensible conceptualization of her claim than supposing as she does that she has a property right in her neighbors' use of their lands. Should any of them create a nuisance by building a wind farm, she can seek to abate the nuisance when the wind farm is built, or maybe a bit earlier, when a permit to build it is granted. The fact that the County Board has zoned agricultural property to allow wind farms would complicate her effort to establish that it was a nuisance, but not defeat it. The operation of the wind farm might turn out to cause a kind or amount of damage that the Board had not foreseen, and in that event the ordinance would not bar the suit. . . .

Sufficient unto the day is the evil thereof. For all one knows, no wind farm will ever be built close enough to any of the plaintiff's properties to do any harm, let alone harm sufficient to constitute a nuisance under the standard for determining nuisance, which involves a balancing of the costs and benefits of the land use claimed to have caused a nuisance. . . . Even a wind farm that was only a stone's throw from one of her properties might do no damage to it, given the use to which she puts her Winnebago County properties—of which we have not been informed.

. . . .

There is, in sum, no merit to the plaintiff's claim that the ordinance as amended in 2009 violates her constitutional rights. It is a modest legislative encouragement of wind farming and is within the constitutional authority, state as well as federal, of a local government. The judgment of dismissal is therefore

AFFIRMED.

NOTES & QUESTIONS

1.   What are ten specific adverse impacts the plaintiff in *Muscarello* asserted could result from the construction of a wind farm near her land?

2.   Why did the majority in *Muscarello* view the plaintiff's regulatory taking and nuisance claims as premature? If you represented the plaintiff, what arguments would you make in response to this view?

3.   *Triggering a Regulatory Taking by Allowing Wind Energy Development?* Subsection B above focused on whether the government could potentially trigger a compensable taking by prohibiting wind energy development on a citizen's land. The plaintiff in *Muscarello* makes a very different sort of Takings Clause argument, claiming that the government could trigger a regulatory taking of her wind rights by allowing upwind neighbors to build a wind farm and thereby reduce the potential energy productivity of wind currents flowing above her land. The far-fetched argument appeared to draw little sympathy from the court but further evidences the legal uncertainty surrounding the nature and scope of landowners' rights in wind resources.

4.   *A Pattern of Frivolous Claims?* The plaintiff in *Muscarello* tried again to challenge wind energy development in 2013 based on alleged adverse property value impacts. Ms. Muscarello's challenge proved unsuccessful once again, in part because she reportedly no longer held title to the property that she claimed would decrease in value if a wind farm were erected nearby. *See* David Ormsby, *Court Deflates 3rd Legal Challenge to Ogle County Wind Farm Ordinance*, CHIC. TRIBUNE (July 26, 2013), http://www.chicagotribune.com/suburbs/chi-ugc-article-court-deflates-3rd-legal-challenge-to-ogle-co-2013-07-26-story.html.

1.   COMMERCIAL WIND ENERGY AND NUISANCE LAW

Although the plaintiff's attempt in *Muscarello* to judicially challenge Winnebago County's wind energy ordinance amendment proved unsuccessful, Judge Posner suggested in the case's majority opinion that wind farms could potentially give rise to an actionable nuisance claim. Many of the potential impacts of wind farms described above involve some sort of "nontrespassory invasion of another's interest in the private use and enjoyment of land" and could thus plausibly create nuisance liability on that ground. RESTATEMENT OF TORTS (SECOND) § 821D (1979).

Nuisance claims are founded in part on the maxim *sic utere tuo ut alienum non laedas*, which requires that landowners use their land so as not to injure each other. However, mere evidence of interference with neighbors' use and enjoyment of land does not automatically establish an actionable nuisance. Even when the interference is intentional, it typically must be substantial and unreasonable to trigger nuisance liability. *See*

Hendricks v. Stalnaker, 380 S.E.2d 198, 200 (1989). Because its rules often require case-by-case analysis of such issues as the reasonableness of interference, nuisance law is notoriously unpredictable.

Under what circumstances should an ordinary wind farm operating in a usual way give rise to nuisance claims? Some potentially adverse impacts of wind energy development are more likely to create nuisance liability than others. Unfortunately, as is typical in nuisance law, resolving these claims often requires highly fact-specific inquiries so it is difficult to articulate many hard-and-fast rules for when wind farms are likely trigger nuisance liability. Nonetheless, wind energy developers who obtain all necessary permits for a new wind farm project and observe all government-imposed requirements surely reduce their risk of being held liable for nuisance. To quote one court on this point:

> The maxim, *"sic utere tuo ut alienum non laedas,"* is not a hard and fast rule, applied under all circumstances to the use of property by adjoining proprietors. If the business is lawful, and the facilities employed are not inherently noxious or dangerous but are operated by means of modern appliances in the usual and ordinary method, such business is not a nuisance per se. . . .

O'Day v. Shouvlin, 136 N.E. 289, 291 (Ohio 1922).

In the following case, the court adds credence to the notion that wind farms can trigger nuisance liability, overturning a lower court's dismissal of a landowner's claim seeking to enjoin the development of a proposed a wind farm on neighboring land based on a nuisance theory. As you read the excerpt from *NedPower* below, consider the factual distinctions between this case and *Muscarello* and whether you believe they justify the difference in outcomes.

BURCH V. NEDPOWER MOUNT STORM, LLC
West Virginia Supreme Court of Appeals, 2007
647 S.E.2d 879

MAYNARD, J.

The appellants appeal the April 7, 2006, order of the Circuit Court of Grant County that dismissed their nuisance claim in which they sought an injunction against the appellees, NedPower Mount Storm, LLC and Shell WindEnergy, Inc., to enjoin the appellees from constructing a wind power electric generating facility in close proximity to the appellants' property. For the reasons that follow, we reverse the circuit court and remand for proceedings consistent with this opinion.

I.

FACTS

By final order dated April 2, 2003, the Public Service Commission ("the PSC") granted NedPower Mount Storm LLC, an appellee herein, a certificate of convenience and necessity to construct and operate a wind power electric generating facility along the Allegheny Front in Grant County. NedPower has entered into a contract with appellee Shell WindEnergy, Inc., to sell the entire facility to Shell upon its completion. It is contemplated that the wind power facility will be located on a site approximately 14 miles long with an average width of one-half mile. The facility is to include up to 200 wind turbines. Each turbine is to be mounted on a steel tower approximately 15 feet in diameter and 210 to 450 feet in height, and have three blades of approximately 115 feet.

The appellants are seven homeowners who live from about one-half mile to two miles from the projected wind turbines. On November 23, 2005, the appellants filed a complaint in the Circuit Court of Grant County seeking to permanently enjoin NedPower and Shell WindEnergy, Inc., from constructing and operating the wind power facility on the basis that it would create a private nuisance. Specifically, the appellants asserted that they will be negatively impacted by noise from the wind turbines; the turbines will create a "flicker" or "strobe" effect when the sun is near the horizon; the turbines will pose a significant danger from broken blades, ice throws, and collapsing towers; and the wind power facility will cause a reduction in the appellants' property values.

The appellees subsequently filed a joint motion for judgment on the pleadings. . . .

By order of April 7, 2006, the circuit court granted the appellees' motion for judgment on the pleadings and dismissed the appellants' action with prejudice. The circuit court based its ruling on the following grounds: it has no jurisdiction to enjoin the construction of a project that was approved by the PSC; most of the assertions made by the appellants concern activities that constitute a public rather than a private nuisance; a prospective injunction is not a proper remedy in this case because the wind facility is not a nuisance *per se* and does not constitute an impending or imminent danger of certain effect; and the PSC's approval of the facility collaterally estops the appellants from challenging it in circuit court.

The appellants now appeal the circuit court's order. . . .

. . . .

Our reading of the appellants' complaint indicates that the appellants allege, as private nuisances, that the wind turbines will cause constant noise when the wind is blowing and an increase in noise as the wind velocity increases; the turbines will create an eyesore as a result of the turbines' "flicker" or "strobe" effect when the sun is near the horizon; and proximity of the appellants' property to the turbines will result in a diminution in the appellants' property values. We will now determine the legal effect of each of these allegations under our settled law of nuisance.

First, the appellants allege that the noise from the turbines will constitute a nuisance. This Court has held that "[n]oise alone may create a nuisance, depending on time, locality and degree." Syllabus Point 1, *Ritz v. Woman's Club of Charleston*, 114 W.Va. 675, 173 S.E. 564 (1934). We have further held that "[w]here an unusual and recurring noise is introduced in a residential district, and the noise prevents sleep or otherwise disturbs materially the rest and comfort of the residents, the noise may be inhibited by a court of equity." Syllabus Point 2, *Ritz, supra. See also Snyder v. Cabell*, 29 W.Va. 48, 1 S.E. 241 (1886) (affirming injunction against skating rink's operation where it was found that noise from the rink materially interfered with the comfort and enjoyment of nearby residents.). These holdings are grounded on a principle that is essential to a civil society which is that "every person . . . has the right not to be disturbed in his house; he has the right to rest and quiet and not to be materially disturbed in his rest and enjoyment of home by loud noises." *Snyder*, 29 W.Va. at 62, 1 S.E. at 251. Thus, we find that the appellants' allegation of noise is cognizable under our law as an abatable nuisance.

Second, the appellants allege that a "flicker" or "strobe" effect from the turbines will create an eyesore. Traditionally "courts of equity have hesitated to exercise authority in the abatement of nuisances where the subject matter is objected to by the complainants merely because it is offensive to the sight." *Parkersburg Builders Material Co. v. Barrack*, 118 W.Va. 608, 610, 191 S.E. 368, 369 (1937). This Court has explained in further detail that

> [e]quity should act only where there is presented a situation which is offensive to the view of average persons of the community. And, even where there is a situation which the average person would deem offensive to the sight, such fact alone will not justify interference by a court of equity. The surroundings must be considered. Unsightly things are not to be banned solely on that account. Many of them are necessary in carrying on the proper activities of organized society. But such things should be properly placed, and not so located as to be unduly offensive to neighbors or to the public.

Barrack, 118 W.Va. at 613, 191 S.E. at 371. When an unsightly activity is not properly placed, when it is unduly offensive to its neighbors, and when it is accompanied by other interferences to the use and enjoyment of another's property, this Court has shown a willingness to abate the activity as a nuisance. For example, in Syllabus Point 3 of *Mahoney v. Walter*, 157 W.Va. 882, 205 S.E.2d 692 (1974), it was held:

> The establishment of an automobile salvage yard with its incident noise, unsightliness, hazards from the presence of flammable materials, open vehicles, rodents and insects, and resultant depreciation of adjoining residential property values in an area which, though unrestricted and containing some commercial businesses, is primarily residential, together with the interference with the use, comfort and enjoyment of the surrounding properties caused by its operation, may be a nuisance and may be abated by a court of competent jurisdiction.

We hold, therefore, that while unsightliness alone rarely justifies interference by a circuit court applying equitable principles, an unsightly activity may be abated when it occurs in a residential area and is accompanied by other nuisances.

Third, the appellants allege that construction of the wind turbines will cause a reduction in their property values. With regard to the legal effect of mere diminution in the value of property, this Court has explained:

> Upon the question of reduction in value of the plaintiffs' properties, as the result of the establishment of the used car lot nearby, we find this statement in Wood on Nuisances, 3rd Edition, § 640: "Mere diminution of the value of the property, in consequence of the use to which adjoining premises are devoted, unaccompanied with other ill-results, is *damnum absque injuria*." Also in 66 C.J.S., Nuisances, § 19, P. 771, it is stated that: "However, a use of property which does not create a nuisance cannot be enjoined or a lawful structure abated merely because it renders neighboring property less valuable."

Martin, 141 W.Va. at 609–610, 93 S.E.2d at 843–844. However, the appellants in this case do not rely merely upon diminution of property values to support their nuisance claim, but also noise and unsightliness.

. . . .

. . . We hold, therefore, that an activity that diminishes the value of nearby property and also creates interferences to the use and enjoyment of the nearby property may be abated by a circuit court applying equitable principles. In addition, the landowners may seek compensation for any diminution in the value of their property caused by the nuisance.

Finally, the remedy sought by the appellants is an injunction against the construction and operation of the wind power facility.

It is a general rule that when the thing complained of is not a nuisance *per se,* but may or may not become so, according to circumstances, and the injury apprehended is eventual or contingent, equity will not interfere; the presumption being that a person entering into a legitimate business will conduct it in a proper way, so that it will not constitute a nuisance.

Syllabus Point 2, *Chambers v. Cramer*, 49 W.Va. 395, 38 S.E. 691 (1901). We have recognized that a lawful business or a business authorized to be conducted by the government cannot constitute a nuisance *per se*. . . . Further, according to Syllabus Point 6 of *Watson v. Fairmont & S. Ry. Co.*, 49 W.Va. 528, 39 S.E. 193 (1901),

> When a person or corporation is authorized by the legislature by an express statute to do an act, or by the council of a city or town to which the power to authorize it has been delegated by a legislative act, such person or corporation cannot be regarded as committing a nuisance in the execution of such act nor proceeded against merely upon the theory that it is a nuisance, either at law or in equity.

. . . Therefore, when we apply these holdings to the instant facts, we must conclude that, as a lawful business which has been granted a siting certificate by the PSC, the appellees' wind power facility cannot be considered a nuisance *per se*.

However, the fact that the appellees' electric generating facility does not constitute a nuisance *per se* a does not mean that it cannot be abated as a nuisance. It is also true that a business that is not a nuisance *per se* may still constitute a nuisance in light of the surrounding circumstances. In Syllabus Point 2 of *Mahoney*, *supra,* this Court held,

> As a general rule, a fair test as to whether a business or a particular use of a property in connection with the operation of the business constitutes a nuisance, is the reasonableness or unreasonableness of the operation or use in relation to the particular locality and under all the existing circumstances.

. . . Essentially, the proper test to determine whether a proposed activity should be enjoined on the basis that the activity will constitute a nuisance has been stated as follows: "To warrant the perpetuation of an injunction restraining, as a threatened nuisance, the erection of a building proposed to be used for legitimate purposes, the fact that it will be a nuisance if so used must be made clearly to appear, beyond all ground of fair questioning." Syllabus Point 3, *Chambers*, *supra*. . . .

. . . The appellants have alleged certain injury to the use and enjoyment of their properties as a result of constant loud noise from the wind turbines, the turbines' unsightliness, and reduction in the appellants' property values. If the appellants are able to adduce sufficient evidence to prove these allegations beyond all ground of fair questioning, abatement would be appropriate. Therefore, we find that the circuit court erred in ruling that the appellants failed to assert any facts of a private nuisance that would support a prospective injunction.

. . . .

In conclusion, having found no basis in law for the circuit court's ruling that dismissed on the pleadings the appellants' nuisance claim for an injunction, we reverse the April 7, 2006, order of the Circuit Court of Grant County, and we remand this case to the circuit court for proceedings consistent with this opinion.

Reversed and remanded.

———————

NOTES & QUESTIONS

1.   What specific differences in the facts of the *Muscarello* and *NedPower* cases do you think caused the two courts to differently analyze the plaintiffs' claims?

2.   Based on the *NedPower* opinion, under what sorts of circumstances might turbine flicker effects raise constitute an actionable private nuisance?

3.   In both the *Muscarello* and *NedPower* cases, no wind farm had been built yet near the plaintiffs' land. How does the necessarily *ex post* nature of nuisance claims arguably make them an unsatisfying means of governing potential conflicts between wind farms and neighboring land owners?

4.   *Other Wind Farm Nuisance Claims.* More than a decade after *NedPower*, neighbors of wind farms continue to bring common law nuisance claims based on noise and health concerns. For instance, in the Summer of 2017, a state superior court judge ordered the town of Falmouth, Massachusetts, to shut down two wind turbines it had installed and operated on municipal property on the basis that the turbines constituted a nuisance. See Adam Lucente, *Falmouth won't appeal order to shut down wind turbines*, CAPE COD TIMES (Jul. 10, 2017), http://www.capecodtimes.com/news/2017071 0/falmouth-wont-appeal-order-to-shut-down-wind-turbines. The Falmouth ruling appeared to embolden landowners in the nearby coastal town of Plymouth, Massachusetts, in their effort to fight against an existing wind farm in their community. See Ethan Gentner, *Falmouth ruling bolsters cause for neighbors of Plymouth turbines*, CAPE COD TIMES (Jul. 15, 2017), http://www. capecodtimes.com/news/20170715/falmouth-ruling-bolsters-cause-for-neighbors -of-plymouth-turbines.

2. NUISANCE CLAIMS BASED ON AESTHETIC IMPACTS

Not all nuisance claims against wind farms center on health impacts, noise, or related concerns. The plaintiff in the following case based its nuisance claim primarily on the potential visual impacts of having a wind turbine nearby. Concerns about aesthetic impacts are indeed among the most common objections that wind energy developers face. However, as the case excerpt below suggests, such claims rarely if ever succeed.

RANKIN V. FPL ENERGY, LLC
Texas Court of Appeal, Eastland, 2008
266 S.W.3d 506

STRANGE, J.

Several individuals and one corporation (Plaintiffs) filed suit against FPL Energy, LLC; FPL Energy Horse Hollow Wind, LP; FPL Energy Horse Hollow Wind, LP, LLC; FPL Energy Horse Hollow Wind GP, LLC; FPL Energy Callahan Wind Group, LLC; and FPL Energy Callahan, LP (FPL). Plaintiffs sought injunctive relief and asserted public and private nuisance claims relating to the construction and operation of the Horse Hollow Wind Farm in southwest Taylor County. FPL filed a motion for partial summary judgment directed at Plaintiffs' nuisance claims, and the trial court granted it in part dismissing Plaintiffs' claims to the extent they were based on the wind farm's visual impact. Plaintiffs' remaining private nuisance claim proceeded to trial. The jury found against Plaintiffs, and the trial court entered a take-nothing judgment. . .

Plaintiffs [as Issue One]. . . . contend that the trial court erred by granting FPL's motion for partial summary judgment. . . .

. . . .

2.   Texas Nuisance Law

Texas law defines "nuisance" as "a condition that substantially interferes with the use and enjoyment of land by causing unreasonable discomfort or annoyance to persons of ordinary sensibilities." *Schneider Nat'l Carriers, Inc. v. Bates*, 147 S.W.3d 264, 269 (Tex. 2004). Nuisance claims are frequently described as a "non-trespassory invasion of another's interest in the use and enjoyment of land." *See, e.g., GTE Mobilnet of S. Tex. Ltd. P'ship v. Pascouet,* 61 S.W.3d 599, 615 (Tex.App.-Houston [14th Dist.] 2001, pet. Denied). But despite this exclusionary description, in some instances an action can be both a trespass and a nuisance. *See, e.g., Allen v. Virginia Hill Water Supply Corp.,* 609 S.W.2d 633, 636 (Tex.Civ.App.-Tyler 1980, no writ) (continuing encroachment upon the land of an adjoining owner by either erecting or maintaining a building without any right to do so is a trespass and a private nuisance).

In practice, successful nuisance actions typically involve an invasion of a plaintiff's property by light, sound, odor, or foreign substance. For example, in *Pascouet,* floodlights that illuminated the plaintiffs' backyard all night and noisy air conditioners that interfered with normal conversation in the backyard, that could be heard indoors, and that interrupted plaintiffs' sleep constituted a nuisance. 61 S.W.3d at 616. In *Bates*, the court noted that foul odors, dust, noise, and bright lights could create a nuisance. 147 S.W.3d at 269. In *Lamesa Coop. Gin v. Peltier*, 342 S.W.2d 613 (Tex.Civ.App.-Eastland 1961, writ ref'd n.r.e.), a cotton gin's operations were a nuisance because of its loud noises and bright lights that could be seen and heard on plaintiff's property and because of the dust, lint, and cotton burrs that would be carried there.

Texas courts have not found a nuisance merely because of aesthetical-based complaints. In *Shamburger v. Scheurrer*, 198 S.W. 1069 (Tex.Civ.App.-Fort Worth 1917, no writ), the defendant began construction of a lumberyard in a residential neighborhood. Neighboring homeowners filed suit and contended that the lumberyard would be unsightly, unseemly, and have ugly buildings and structures. The court held that this did not constitute a nuisance, writing:

> The injury or annoyance which warrants relief against an alleged nuisance must be of a real and substantial character, and such as impairs the ordinary enjoyment, physically, of the property within its sphere; for if the injury or inconvenience be merely theoretical, or if it be slight or trivial, or fanciful, or one of mere delicacy or fastidiousness, there is no nuisance in a legal sense. Thus the law will not declare a thing a nuisance because it is unsightly or disfigured, because it is not in a proper or suitable condition, or because it is unpleasant to the eye and a violation of the rules of propriety and good taste, for the law does not cater to men's tastes or consult their convenience merely, but only guards and upholds their material rights, and shields them from unwarrantable invasion.

Id. at 1071–72. In *Dallas Land & Loan Co. v. Garrett*, 276 S.W. 471, 474 (Tex.Civ.App.-Dallas 1925, no writ), the court found that a garage being built for residents of an apartment complex was not a nuisance because "[m]atters that annoy by being disagreeable, unsightly, and undesirable are not nuisances simply because they may to some extent affect the value of property." In *Jones v. Highland Mem'l Park*, 242 S.W.2d 250, 253 (Tex.Civ.App.-San Antonio 1951, no writ), the court held that the construction of a cemetery on adjacent property did not constitute a nuisance, noting: "However cheerless or disagreeable the view of the cemetery in question may be to appellees, and no matter what unpleasant or melancholy thoughts the same may awaken, no reason is thereby shown why appellants should be restrained from making such use of their property."

3. Plaintiffs' Nuisance Claim

Plaintiffs advance several arguments why this caselaw does not preclude their private nuisance action. First, they argue that aesthetics may be considered as one of the *conditions* that creates a nuisance. Plaintiffs concede that, if their only complaint is subjectively not liking the wind turbines' appearance, no nuisance action exists. But, they contend that the jury was entitled to consider the wind farm's visual impact in connection with other testimony such as: the turbines' blinking lights, the shadow flicker affect they create early in the morning and late at night, and their operational noises to determine if it was a nuisance. Second, they note that nuisance law is dynamic and fact-specific; therefore, they contend that older case holdings should not be blindly followed without considering intervening societal changes. Third, nuisance claims should be viewed through the prism of a person of ordinary sensibilities and caselaw involving unreasonable plaintiffs asserting subjective complaints should be considered accordingly.

FPL responds that the trial court ruled correctly because no Texas court has ever recognized a nuisance claim based upon aesthetical complaints and notes that, in fact, numerous courts have specifically rejected the premises behind such a claim. *See, e.g., Dallas Land & Loan,* 276 S.W. at 474; *Shamburger,* 198 S.W. at 1071 ("the law will not declare a thing a nuisance because . . . it is unpleasant to the eye"). FPL argues that sound public policy supports such a rule because notions of beauty or unsightliness are necessarily subjective in nature and that giving someone an aesthetic veto over a neighbor's use of his land would be a recipe for legal chaos. Finally, FPL argues that the wind farm does not prevent any of the plaintiffs from using their property but at most involves an emotional reaction to the sight of the wind turbines and contends that an emotional reaction alone is insufficient to sustain a nuisance claim.

When FPL moved for summary judgment, Plaintiffs presented affidavits from the plaintiffs to establish that the wind farm was a nuisance. Plaintiffs' affidavits personalize individual objections to the wind farm's presence and to the use of wind turbines for generating electricity commercially. They also express a consistent theme: the presence of numerous 400-foot-tall wind turbines has permanently and significantly diminished the area's scenic beauty and, with it, the enjoyment of their property. Some Plaintiffs, such as Linda L. Brasher, took issue with the characterization of her complaint as just aesthetics. She acknowledged not liking the turbines' looks but contended that they had a larger impact than mere appearance. Brasher stated that she and her husband had purchased their land to build a home and to have a place "for strength, for rest, for hope, for joy, for security—for release." They had plans for building and operating a small bed and breakfast but cancelled those plans in response to the wind farm. Brasher characterized the presence of the wind farm as "the death of hope."

Plaintiffs' summary judgment evidence makes clear that, if the wind farm is a nuisance, it is because Plaintiffs' emotional response to the loss of their view due to the presence of numerous wind turbines substantially interferes with the use and enjoyment of their property. The question, then, is whether Plaintiffs' emotional response is sufficient to establish a cause of action. One Texas court has held that an emotional response to a defendant's lawful activity is insufficient. *Maranatha Temple, Inc. v. Enterprise Products Co.*, 893 S.W.2d 92 (Tex.App.-Houston [1st Dist.] 1994, writ den'd), involved a suit brought by a church against the owners and operators of companies involved in an underground hydrocarbon storage facility. The church's claims included a nuisance action. The trial court granted summary judgment against the church. *Id.* at 96. The question before the Houston First Court was whether a nuisance action could exist when the only claimed injury was an emotional reaction to the defendants' operations. The court found that a nuisance could occur in one of three ways: (1) by the encroachment of a physically damaging substance; (2) by the encroachment of a sensory damaging substance; and (3) by the emotional harm to a person from the deprivation of the enjoyment of his or her property, such as by fear, apprehension, offense, or loss of peace of mind. *Id.* at 99. The court noted that nuisance claims are subdivided into nuisance per se and nuisance in fact. *Id.* at 100. Because the operation of the storage facility—just like FPL's wind farm—was lawful, it could not constitute a nuisance per se. This last factor was critical. The court recognized that no case or other authority specifically gives a nuisance-in-fact cause of action based on fear, apprehension, or other emotional reaction resulting from the lawful operation of industry and affirmed the summary judgment. 893 S.W.2d at 100 & n. 6.

Plaintiffs do not contend that FPL's operations are unlawful but minimize this factor by arguing that even a lawful business can be considered a nuisance if it is abnormal and out of place in its surroundings. Plaintiffs are correct that several Texas courts have recited this general principle; but, in each of the cases cited by Plaintiffs, the nuisance resulted from an invasion of the plaintiff's property by flooding, flies, or odors. We cannot, therefore, agree with Plaintiffs that merely characterizing the wind farm as abnormal and out of place in its surroundings allows a nuisance claim based on an emotional reaction to the sight of FPL's wind turbines.

We do not minimize the impact of FPL's wind farm by characterizing it as an emotional reaction. Unobstructed sunsets, panoramic landscapes, and starlit skies have inspired countless artists and authors and have brought great pleasure to those fortunate enough to live in scenic rural settings. The loss of this view has undoubtedly impacted Plaintiffs. A landowner's view, however, is largely defined by what his neighbors are utilizing their property for. Texas caselaw recognizes few restrictions on the lawful use of property. If Plaintiffs have the right to bring a nuisance action because a neighbor's lawful activity substantially interferes with their view, they have, in effect, the right to zone the surrounding property. Conversely, we realize that Plaintiffs produced evidence that the wind farm will harm neighboring property values and that it has restricted the uses they can make of their property. FPL's development, therefore, could be characterized as a condemnation without the obligation to pay damages.

Texas caselaw has balanced these conflicting interests by limiting a nuisance action when the challenged activity is lawful to instances in which the activity results in some invasion of the plaintiff's property and by not allowing recovery for emotional reaction alone. Altering this balance by recognizing a new cause of action for aesthetical impact causing an emotional injury is beyond the purview of an intermediate appellate court. Alternatively, allowing Plaintiffs to include aesthetics as a condition in connection with other forms of interference is a distinction without a difference. Aesthetical impact either is or is not a substantial interference with the use and enjoyment of land. If a jury can consider aesthetics as a condition, then it can find nuisance because of aesthetics. Because Texas law does not provide a nuisance action for aesthetical impact, the trial court did not err by granting FPL's motion for partial summary judgment and by instructing the jury to exclude from its consideration the aesthetical impact of the wind farm.

. . . .

We affirm the judgment of the trial court. . . .

<hr>

QUESTIONS

1.   Why was the *FPL* court unwilling to recognize a valid nuisance claim based on the visual impacts of a wind farm?

2.   Why might a wise wind energy developer in Texas care about potential visual impacts of their projects, despite the holding in *FPL*?

3.   Can you think of any locations in the United States where the adverse visual impacts of a utility-scale wind farm are likely to outweigh the benefits of siting such a project in that place? Assuming that such locations exist, what legal and policy tools other than nuisance law exist to help prevent wind energy development in those places?

3. STATUTORY CLAIMS BASED ON AESTHETIC IMPACTS

Recognizing the limits of the common law of nuisance as a means of managing aesthetics-based conflicts over wind energy projects, some state governments have enacted statutory provisions specifically designed to help govern these disputes. The following case applies one such statute in the state of Maine.

CHAMPLAIN WIND, LLC v. BOARD OF ENVIRONMENTAL PROTECTION

Supreme Judicial Court of Maine, 2015
129 A.3d 279

SAUFLEY, C.J.

Champlain Wind, LLC, appeals from a decision of the Board of Environmental Protection in which the Board considered and balanced competing statutorily defined policies applicable to wind energy projects in Maine. The applicable statutes establish the dual policies of expediting wind energy development in defined geographic areas of Maine and at the same time providing enhanced protection for specific scenic resources. Champlain proposed the Bowers Wind Project to be situated within, but very near, the geographic border of the expedited permitting area. Within sight of the proposed wind turbines lie several scenic resources of state or national significance. On the record before us, we do not disturb the Board's balancing of the Legislature's policies, and we affirm the Board's denial of a permit for the Project.

I.   COMPETING LEGISLATIVE PRIORITIES

In 2004, the Maine Legislature enacted the Maine Wind Energy Act, and in 2008, it enacted additional statutes governing "Expedited Permitting of Grid-Scale Wind Energy Development." As subsequently amended, the Wind Energy Act has a stated purpose to "encourage the development, where appropriate, of wind energy production in the State." 35–A M.R.S. § 3402 (2014). To support and expedite permitting of wind energy projects, an "expedited permitting area" has been established to "reduce the potential for controversy regarding siting of grid-scale wind energy development by expediting development in places where it is most compatible with existing patterns of development and resource values when considered broadly at the landscape level." 35–A M.R.S. §§ 3402(2), 3451(3) (2014).

One of the primary goals of the wind energy statutes is to reduce and, where possible, eliminate costly opposition to wind projects based on the visual impact of the wind turbines. Recognizing that "wind turbines are potentially a highly visible feature of the landscape that will have an impact on views," *id.* § 3402(2)(c), the Board is prohibited by statute from denying a wind energy development permit on the sole basis that "generating facilities are a highly visible feature in the landscape." 35–A M.R.S. § 3452(3) (2014). Expedited wind energy developments are not required to meet the more stringent standard of "fitting . . . harmoniously into the existing natural environment," which is otherwise required by the environmental protection statute governing site location for development projects. 38 M.R.S. § 484(3) (2014); *see* 35–A M.R.S. § 3452(1) (2014).

Concurrently, to ensure that the statutes also protect certain scenic geographic areas, the Legislature has identified areas where the visual impact of prospective wind energy developments must be more closely scrutinized. Specifically, an expedited wind energy development must not "significantly compromise[ ] views from a scenic resource of state or national significance such that the development has an unreasonable adverse effect on the scenic character or existing uses related to scenic character of the scenic resource of state or national significance." 35–A M.R.S. § 3452(1). A "scenic resource of state or national significance" is defined to include national natural landmarks, certain historic places, national or state parks, great ponds, and other places of scenic significance. *See* 35–A M.R.S. § 3451(9) (2014).

Thus, the Legislature has attempted to improve the predictability of siting decisions by creating a more streamlined, lower-cost regulatory process for wind energy development in the expedited permitting area, while at the same time it has sought to protect particularly important scenic resources in Maine by requiring stricter scenic standards in specified geographic areas.

II. BOWERS WIND PROJECT

Both geographically and analytically, the Bowers Wind Project falls on the line between competing legislative purposes—expediting the development of wind power and protecting identified scenic resources. The Project would place sixteen wind turbines, with a combined generating capacity of forty-eight megawatts, just within the boundary of the expedited permitting area, making them visible from multiple scenic resources of state or national significance.

Champlain filed a consolidated application with the Department of Environmental Protection in October 2012 seeking permits to construct the Project in Carroll Plantation and Kossuth Township. *See* 35–A M.R.S. § 3451(4) (2014). Although the Project is proposed to be developed within the expedited permitting area, its turbines would be visible from nine great ponds, each of which is rated as outstanding or significant from a scenic perspective in the Maine Wildlands Lake Assessment and thus is classified as a scenic resource of state or national significance. *See id.* § 3451(9)(D)(2); Me. Dep't of Conservation, Land Use Regulation Comm'n, Maine Wildlands Lake Assessment, pt. V (Master List of Lakes) (June 1, 1987). Most of the area of the nine great ponds affected by the Project is excluded from the expedited permitting area.

The Department ultimately denied Champlain's application after evaluating data collected by both Champlain's and the Department's experts concerning the scenic impact that the Project would have on the affected great ponds, reviewing a user intercept survey, holding a public hearing, and conducting multiple site visits. The Department concluded that the Project did not satisfy the statutory scenic standard because the project "would have an unreasonable adverse effect on the scenic character and existing uses related to the scenic character" of the nine affected great ponds. With the exception of the scenic standard, the Department found that Champlain had met all of the permit criteria.

Champlain appealed from the Department's denial to the Board of Environmental Protection. *See* 38 M.R.S. § 341–D(4) (2014). The Board considered the evidence in the record, heard a presentation by the Department, and heard oral argument from the parties involved. Multiple parties submitted proposed supplemental evidence, but the Board did not admit any of that evidence into the administrative record because it found that the evidence was neither relevant nor material. *See id.;* 2 C.M.R. 06–096 002–12 § 24(D)(2) (2013).

In June 2014, the Board issued an order affirming the Department's denial of Champlain's permit application. Although the Board did not specifically find that the Project would have an unreasonable adverse effect on the scenic character or existing uses related to scenic character on any *one* of the affected great ponds, the Board concluded that "the proposed project would unreasonably adversely affect scenic character and existing uses related to scenic character." Champlain filed a timely petition for review of the Board's final agency action pursuant to 38 M.R.S. § 346(4) (2014), 5 M.R.S. § 11002 (2014), and M.R. Civ. P. 80C.

III. DISCUSSION

A.   The Dispute

Primarily, Champlain argues that the Board unlawfully aggregated the scenic impact of the Project on the nine affected great ponds in reaching its conclusion that the Project would have an unreasonable adverse scenic effect, contravening the plain language of the Wind Energy Act and related statutes. Champlain argues that because the Board did not find that the Project had an unreasonable adverse effect on the scenic character or existing uses related to scenic character of any one specific affected great pond alone, it could not have concluded that the project failed to satisfy the statutory standards. Champlain further argues that in aggregating the scenic impact, the Board applied the Act and related statutes arbitrarily because there are no standards to guide the exercise of the Board's discretion in evaluating aggregated scenic impacts.

The Board responds that it is authorized to consider the overall impact of the Project on the nine affected great ponds. Section 3452(3), it argues, authorizes the Board to take a "holistic approach" when considering the impact a proposed project may have on multiple scenic resources of state or national significance. Moreover, the Board argues that its decision to deny Champlain's permit application was not arbitrary; it simply applied the existing scenic standard to an unprecedented factual situation—a project that would simultaneously affect nine scenic resources of state or national significance, including many unusually interconnected great ponds, most of which were fully carved out of the expedited permitting area by the Legislature.

B.   The Role of the Board and the Standard of Review

As created by the Maine Legislature, the Board is uniquely situated to make decisions regarding competing legislatively established environmental policies. It has been entrusted with making "informed, independent and timely decisions" regarding those environmental policies. *See* 38 M.R.S. § 341–B (2014). Crucial to the matter before us, the very first paragraph of the Board's authorizing legislation establishes the Board's responsibility to "protect and enhance the public's right to use and enjoy the State's natural resources." 38 M.R.S. § 341–A(1) (2014).

Because the Board acted as the fact-finder and determined all legal issues de novo, we review the Board's decision—not the Department's decision—denying Champlain's application. *See* 38 M.R.S. § 341–D(4) ("The [B]oard is not bound by the commissioner's findings of fact or conclusions of law but may adopt, modify or reverse findings of fact or conclusions of law established by the commissioner."); *Passadumkeag Mountain Friends v. Bd. Of Envtl. Prot.*, 2014 ME 116, ¶¶ 8–10, 102 A.3d 1181 (holding in a wind energy case that the Board's decision, which was based on its independent analysis, was the decision on appeal, even though the Board did not supplement the administrative record in the course of its review); *see also Concerned Citizens to Save Roxbury v. Bd. Of Envtl. Prot.*, 2011 ME 39, ¶¶ 12–17, 15 A.3d 1263.

Our review of the Board's decision must therefore be "deferential and limited." *Passadumkeag*, 2014 ME 116, ¶ 12, 102 A.3d 1181 (quotation marks omitted). Although "statutory construction is a question of law, subject to de novo review," *FPL Energy Me. Hydro LLC v. Dep't of Envtl. Prot.*, 2007 ME 97, ¶ 11, 926 A.2d 1197 (alteration omitted) (quotation marks omitted), "[w]hen reviewing an agency's interpretation of a statute that it administers, we defer to the agency's construction unless the statute plainly compels a contrary result," *Passadumkeag*, 2014 ME 116, ¶ 12, 102 A.3d 1181. "We do not second-guess an agency on issues within its area of expertise; rather, we review only to ascertain whether its conclusions are unreasonable, unjust, or unlawful." *Town of Eagle Lake v. Comm'r, Dep't of Educ.*, 2003 ME 37, ¶ 8, 818 A.2d 1034 (quotation marks omitted).

C.   Interpretation of the Wind Energy Act and Related Statutes

The generating facilities and wind turbines that make up the Project are proposed to be sited within the expedited permitting area; however, most of the nine great ponds affected by the Project—all of which are rated as outstanding or significant from a scenic perspective—are fully excluded from the expedited permitting area. Thus, as previously noted, the Board was confronted with a project that falls directly between competing legislative priorities. It is from that perspective that we review the Board's application of the applicable statutes.

In reaching its determination that the Project would have an unreasonable adverse effect on the scenic character or existing uses related to scenic character of the nine affected great ponds, the Board considered (1) the "existing character of the surrounding area" and "significance of the potentially affected scenic resource," *see* 35–A M.R.S. § 3452(3)(A), (B); (2) the Legislature's intent in balancing the goal of encouraging and expediting wind power development with the goal of protecting Maine's scenic resources by limiting the geographic scope of the expedited permitting area; (3) the exclusion of most of the nine affected great ponds from the expedited permitting area; and (4) the unique interconnectedness of the affected great ponds, which would result in users being repeatedly confronted with views of the turbines from multiple scenic resources of state or national significance when traveling from one lake to another.

The statutes at issue neither prohibit nor explicitly allow or require the aggregated or "holistic" approach taken by the Board. They do, however, explicitly require the Board to consider the "significance of the potentially affected scenic resource of state or national significance" and the "expectations of the typical viewer." *Id.* § 3452(3)(A), (C). In this context of competing legislative priorities and unusually interconnected scenic resources, we cannot conclude that the Board acted unlawfully or arbitrarily in its determination that the visual impact of the Project would have an unreasonable adverse effect on the existing scenic character or existing uses related to the scenic character of the nine affected great ponds. *See Town of Eagle Lake*, 2003 ME 37, ¶ 8, 818 A.2d 1034.

Given the authority granted to the Board by the Legislature and the Board's superior position for addressing the unique characteristics of each project when considering the effect of wind energy development on Maine's scenic environment, we cannot conclude that the statutes compel a result contrary to that reached by the Board. Mindful of the unique circumstances before us, and of the legislatively defined interests at stake, we defer to the Board's interpretation of the Maine Wind Energy Act and the statutes governing expedited permitting for grid-scale wind energy projects. *See id.*

The entry is:

Judgment affirmed.

QUESTIONS

1.   How do Maine's wind turbine siting policies signal to wind energy developers which areas the state considers to be optimal or undesirable for wind energy development based on potential visual impacts? What are some advantages of this approach, compared that of relying solely on nuisance law to govern aesthetics-based conflicts over wind farms?

2.   Why do you think the court in *Champlain Wind* upheld denial of a wind farm permit based largely on potential visual impacts, while such aesthetics-based objections proved unsuccessful in the FPL case? Do you think that this distinction is justifiable? Why or why not?

3.   Suppose you were a private landowner in Maine who was opposed to having wind farms nearby. However, your land was not included within Maine's designated list of areas with important "scenic resources." Instead, your land was included within a state-designated "expedited permit" area for wind farm development. What specific arguments would you make against Maine's statutory system for governing visual impacts and wind turbine siting?

F. RESTRICTIONS ON SMALL WIND TURBINES

Although massive utility-scale wind farms account for the vast majority of the wind energy generated in the United States, a fraction of that generation is attributable to small, "distributed" renewable energy systems. While most new onshore utility-scale turbines have nameplate generating capacities in excess of 1 MW, small wind turbines are typically classified as those have generating capacities of 100kW or less. Many small wind turbines are intended to generate only enough electricity to meet a portion of the energy needs of a single home or business that still relies on the electric grid to supplement its power supply.

Wind turbines classified as "small turbines" come in a wide range of sizes and generating capacities. On one end of the spectrum, the Trinity wind turbine produced by Minnesota-based Skajaquoda is a tiny portable turbine that stands less than two feet high and has just 15 W of generating capacity—barely enough to power a single LED light bulb under optimally windy conditions. In contrast, PowerWorks' 100kW small wind turbines have 59-foot rotors and are capable of powering multiple homes. Small wind turbines in the 5kW to 10kW range are the most common. Turbines of that size, whose towers are usually at least 50 to 100 feet high, can greatly reduce a single home's reliance on grid-supplied electricity, particularly when installed in areas with excellent wind resources. They also qualify in many jurisdictions for net metering programs comparable to those for residential solar panels, which can enable turbine owners to earn valuable credit from their utilities for excess generated power.

The pace of small wind turbine installations has accelerated in the United States in recent years but not nearly as rapidly as that of rooftop solar installations. For multiple reasons, small wind energy has yet to become as economically viable as rooftop solar. One reason is that, in many of the nation's most heavily populated regions, average onshore wind speeds near the ground are simply not strong enough to generate significant amounts of power much of the time. By contrast, rooftop solar panels installed atop homes in many of the country's many sunny metropolitan areas can generate large quantities of electricity on most days of the year. Small wind turbines also must typically extend high above homes and other buildings to be fully productive and are thus more likely than solar panels to tarnish views or to fall onto people and other structures. Even the noise that small turbines generate when spinning can make them a less appealing distributed energy source than a quiet rooftop solar array.

Still, despite their shortcomings, small wind turbines are slowly appearing more and more across the country. Nearly 1,700 small wind turbines were installed in the United States in 2015, representing a total investment of nearly $21 million. *See* ALICE C. ORRELL & NIKOLAS F. FOSTER, 2015 DISTRIBUTED WIND MARKET REPORT (2016), http://energy. gov/sites/prod/files/2016/08/f33/2015-Distributed-Wind-Market-Report-08 162016_0.pdf. As the costs of small wind turbines continue to decline and technologies gradually improve, additional small wind turbine installations are likely to continue well into the future. Unfortunately, because they are often installed closer to buildings and neighbors, small turbines raise several legal and policy issues that are distinct from those arising from utility-scale wind farms. The following materials examine how governments are beginning to address them.

1.   LAND USE RESTRICTIONS ON SMALL WIND ENERGY

As already mentioned, one policy challenge facing small wind turbines is that their height and other characteristics make them very conspicuous in most urban and suburban settings. Accordingly, many local governments have ordinances that purposefully or incidentally restrict small turbine installations. Some advocates of small wind energy have argued that small wind turbines deserve special treatment under zoning and land use ordinances and that cities and counties should make an extra effort to accommodate them because of their positive environmental and other benefits. However, as the following case illustrates, neighbors of proposed small turbine installations are seldom persuaded by these arguments and usually want no leniency for small wind turbines under local land use restrictions.

HAMBY V. BOARD OF ZONING APPEALS OF AREA PLAN COM'N OF WARRICK COUNTY

Court of Appeals of Indiana, 2010
932 N.E.2d 1251

BROWN, J.

Timothy and Theresa Hamby, Greg and Cari Charness, Kevin and Kristina Coons, John Keil, Julia Pickens, Andres and Andrea Solis, Jack and Cindy Stierwalt, and Thomas and Jennifer Weber (collectively, "Homeowners") appeal the trial court's order in favor of the Board of Zoning Appeals of the Area Plan Commission of Warrick County (the "BZA") and the Board of Commissioners of Warrick County (the "Commissioners," and collectively with the BZA, the "County"). Homeowners raise one issue, which we revise and restate as whether the trial court erred in denying Homeowners' claim for declaratory relief. We affirm.

The relevant facts are not in dispute. David Johnson and Phyllis Stilwell (the "Applicants"), through their contractor Morton Energy, filed an application seeking a variance from the requirements as set forth in the Comprehensive Zoning Ordinance for Warrick County, Indiana "to allow an Improvement Location Permit to be issued for a wind turbine exceeding the maximum height requirement in an 'R–2' Multiple Family Zoning District. . . ." Appellants' Appendix at 47. The Applicants sought to erect the residential wind turbine "to use an alternative power source . . . to reduce their electric cost do [sic] to the increasing high utility bills, also reducing greenhouse gases." *Id.* The variance sought to allow an "additional 20 ft" which would "allow for the proper operation" of the turbine. *Id.* On September 24, 2008, the BZA held a hearing on the matter, and on October 22, 2008 it granted the variance.

On November 20, 2008, Homeowners filed a Verified Petition for Writ of Certiorari, Judicial Review and Declaratory Judgment containing two counts: Count I alleged that the variance granted by the BZA was "unsupported by substantial evidence; was arbitrary and capricious; and was in all other respects contrary to Indiana law;" and Count II alleged that "a free standing wind turbine is not a permitted use under the zoning ordinance in the R–2 district." *Id.* at 22–23.

. . . .

On November 17, 2009, the court issued an order on Counts I and II. . . . On Count I, Homeowners' *"verified petition for writ of certiorari and judicial review"* regarding the variance, the court concluded that the Applicants "did not present substantial evidence nor was there substantial evidence before the BZA to show that strict application" of the applicable zoning ordinance "will result in 'practical difficulties' in the use of the [Applicants'] property as residential real estate," and reversed the BZA's decision. *Id.* at 10.

On Count II, the court concluded as follows:

"Count II [claim for declaratory relief] seeks this court's determination as to whether under the zoning ordinance of Warrick County a free standing wind turbine tower is permitted as an accessory use in an R–2 district."

. . . .

The court concludes and declares that under the Comprehensive Zoning Article for Warrick County, a free standing wind turbine tower is permitted as an accessory use in an R–2 district upon the proper granting of a variance.

Id. at 10–11.

The sole issue is whether the trial court erred in denying Homeowners' claim for declaratory relief. To so decide, we are required to interpret provisions of the Comprehensive Zoning Ordinance for Warrick County, Indiana (the "Comprehensive Ordinance"). . . .

. . . Since there are no factual disputes in this case, our sole task in reviewing the trial court's decision is to determine whether the zoning regulations relied upon by Homeowners apply to prohibit the construction of a wind turbine in a R–2 district. *See City of Columbus Bd. of Zoning Appeals v. Big Blue*, 605 N.E.2d 188, 191 (Ind. Ct. App. 1992).

The Applicants' land was situated in a designated R–2 district. In the Comprehensive Ordinance, Article X, Section 1 states the "USE REGULATIONS" for R–2 districts as follows:

No building or structure, or part thereof, shall be erected, altered, or used, or land or water used, in whole or in part, for other than one or more of the following specified permitted uses:

(1) Any uses permitted in "R–1", "R–1A", "R–1B", "R–1C", "R–1D" districts subject to the USE REGULATIONS specified in said districts.

. . . .

(4) *Uses accessory to any of the above when located on the same lot and not involving the conduct of any business, trade, occupation or profession unless otherwise specified in this Article.*

Appellants' Appendix at 50 (emphasis added). Additionally, Article II, Section 2 of the Comprehensive Ordinance defines "ACCESSORY USE OR STRUCTURE" as "[t]he term applied to the BUILDING or USE which is incidental or subordinate to and *customary* in connection with the PRINCIPAL BUILDING or USE and which is located on the same lot with such PRINCIPAL BUILDING or USE." *Id.* at 49 (emphasis added).

Homeowners argue that the definition of accessory use or structure in the Comprehensive Ordinance is "without question clear and unambiguous," in requiring "that a valid accessory use be incidental or subordinate to and customary in connection with the principal building or use." Appellants' Brief at 6. Homeowners argue that "[t]he word 'custom' is defined as a 'habitual practice,'" and "[t]he term 'customary', which is derived from the word custom, is defined as 'of or established by custom; usual or habitual.'" *Id.* (citing *Webster Desk Dictionary of the English Language, Random House Dictionary Classic Edition Copyright 1983*). They further argue that "[e]ven if it could be shown that a free standing wind turbine is 'incidental or subordinate' a free standing wind turbine . . . could not by any reasonable interpretation be construed to be 'customary'." *Id.* at 7.

The County argues that. . . . "Homeowners' position[ ] that until wind turbines are 'customary' they are not permitted accessories, is a circular argument, for if a first wind turbine is never allowed to be constructed, it would be impossible for the device to become 'customary.'" *Id.* at 16. The County further states that "[b]y adopting Homeowners['] interpretation of the Ordinance, property owners could not install any wind turbine in an R–2 district and therefore [could not] benefit from the public policies enacted to spur the growth of alternative energy." *Id.* at 18.

Homeowners do not challenge the position that the installation of a residential wind turbine would be incidental or subordinate to the Applicants' residence. Rather, they say, the issue turns upon the phrase "customary in connection with," which is not defined in the Comprehensive Ordinance. "Undefined words in a statute or ordinance are given their plain, ordinary, and usual meaning." *600 Land, Inc.*, 889 N.E.2d at 309. . . . Additionally, "[z]oning regulations which inhibit the use of real property are in derogation of the common law and are strictly construed." *Discovery House, Inc. v. Metro. Bd. of Zoning Appeals of Marion County*, 701 N.E.2d 577, 579 (Ind. Ct. App. 1998), *reh'g denied, trans. denied*. "We will construe the ordinance to favor the free use of land and will not extend restrictions by implication." *Saurer v. Bd. of Zoning Appeals*, 629 N.E.2d 893, 898 (Ind. Ct. App. 1994).

We do not believe that the "customary in connection with" requirement for an accessory use structure should be construed so as to prevent the implementation of new technologies in residential districts. Indeed, if, as Homeowners contend, the definition requires that the intended use be demonstrated as a "habitual practice," this would preclude improvements in the standard of living since innovations in the production of energy and other technologies could not have been "established by custom; usual or habitual" at the time of the adoption of the Comprehensive Ordinance. Such a requirement would be contrary to public policy. We also note that Homeowners do not specify whether a "habitual practice" be confined to that by the Applicants' neighbors, to that within Warrick County more generally, or whether we should take a broader view. Moreover, Homeowners, as plaintiffs and appellants, have the burden of proof, and they do not include any evidence in the record to demonstrate that residential wind turbines are *uncommon* (or *not* customary) in Warrick County.

Also, although we acknowledge that homes have historically received electricity from a power company via a power plant, we recognize that state and federal governments have made it a priority to encourage the implementation of renewable energy technologies such as wind power. IND. CODE § 6–1.1–12–29, which was enacted in 1979, provides:

> The owner of real property . . . that is equipped with a wind power deviceis entitled to an annual property tax deduction. The amount of the deduction equals the remainder of (1) the assessed value of the real property . . . with the wind power device included, minus (2) the assessed value of the real property or mobile home without the wind power device.

IND. CODE § 6–1.1–12–29(b). Additionally, the federal government has incentivized residential renewable energy systems through a federal income tax credit equal to "30 percent of the qualified small wind energy property expenditures made by the taxpayer during such year. . . ." 26 U.S.C. § 25D(a)(4).

Because we construe a zoning ordinance to favor the free use of land and will not extend restrictions by implication, *see Saurer*, 629 N.E.2d at 898, and because the Comprehensive Ordinance under R–2 permits accessory use structures, we conclude that a residential wind turbine that meets all of the other requirements of the Comprehensive Ordinance is a permitted use in the R–2 zoning district. . . . Homeowners have not met their burden of proving that the trial court erred in denying their claim for declaratory relief.

For the foregoing reasons, we affirm the trial court's order.

Affirmed.

————————

QUESTIONS

1.   The small wind turbine proposed in *Hamby* violated the city's zoning height restrictions for land uses in "R–2" districts, so the landowners who wanted the turbine sought a variance from the local Board of Zoning Appeals— affirmative permission to violate the zoning rule. Why do you think that local zoning ordinances typically include a procedure for obtaining such variances? Do you think that a variance was warranted in this case? Why or why not?

2.   The *Hamby* court's analysis focused partly on the issue of whether small wind turbines were a "customary" accessory use in connection with residential homes. Why might requiring that an accessory land use be "customary" to be permissible prevent such a use from ever *becoming* customary?

3.   Should local government officials and courts be permitted to consider the environmental and other societal benefits of a proposed land use (such as a wind turbine or solar array) when determining whether to give that land use special treatment under zoning laws? Why or why not?

————————————

In an effort to prevent local land use laws from unduly constraining small wind energy, statutes in some states limit the extent to which local governments can restrict landowners' installations of small wind turbines on their properties. Such statutes highlight the sometimes-divergent interests of states and municipalities with respect to small wind energy installations. States often want to encourage small wind power within their boundaries, but some municipalities are more interested in ensuring that small wind turbines don't unduly disrupt neighbors or erode property values.

Because states generally possess greater land use regulatory authority than municipalities, they usually have the stronger hand in policy battles over small wind power. Most land use regulatory authority is viewed as falling within a state's "police power" reserved to the states under the Tenth Amendment to the U.S. Constitution. Recognizing that municipalities are often better equipped than state officials to make local land use regulatory decisions, states often delegate much of this regulatory authority to municipalities under state zoning enabling acts. However, state governments also impose limitations on the local exercise of this authority in certain contexts when they deem limitations on it to be in the state's interest. State-imposed constraints on the local regulation of small wind turbines are one example of this preemptive approach. Unfortunately, laws preempting local ordinances and limiting municipalities' regulatory power can sometimes generate tensions and animosity between municipalities and the state governments in which they reside. The following is a good example of a preempting statute enacted in California that seeks to protect small wind energy development from excessive local regulation. Although this specific statute was repealed in 2017, it remains a succinct illustration of how state preemption statutes can constrain local regulatory authority over distributed renewable energy.

ORDINANCES PROVIDING FOR INSTALLATION OF SMALL WIND ENERGY SYSTEMS; CONDITIONS; REMOVAL REQUIREMENTS

CAL. GOV'T CODE § 65896 (West 2010)
(repealed as of January 1, 2017)

(a) A county may adopt an ordinance that provides for the installation of small wind energy systems outside an urbanized area, but within the county's jurisdiction.

(b) The ordinance may impose conditions on the installation of small wind energy systems that include, but are not limited to, notice, tower height, setback, view protection, aesthetics, aviation, and design-safety requirements. However, the ordinance shall not require conditions on notice, tower height, setback, noise level, visual effects, turbine approval, tower drawings, and engineering analysis, or line drawings that are more restrictive than the following requirements and conditions:

(1) The parcel where the system is located shall be at least one acre in size and located outside an urbanized area.

(2) Tower heights of not more than 80 feet shall be allowed on parcels between one and five acres. Tower heights of not more than 100 feet shall be allowed on parcels above five acres. . .

(3) Minimum setbacks for the system tower shall be no farther from the property line than the system height, unless a greater setback is needed to comply with applicable fire setback requirements. . . .

(4) Decibel levels for the system shall not exceed the lesser of 60 decibels (dBA), or any existing maximum noise levels applied pursuant to the noise element of a general plan for the applicable zoning classification in a jurisdiction or applicable noise regulations, as measured at the nearest property line, except during short-term events, such as . . . severe windstorms.

(5) Notice of an application for installation of a small wind energy system shall be provided to property owners within 300 feet of the property on which the system is to be located. . . .

(6) The system shall not substantially obstruct views of adjacent property owners and shall be placed or constructed below any major ridgeline when visible from any scenic highway corridor . . . designated by a county in its general plan.

. . . .

(13) If a small wind energy system is proposed to be sited in an agricultural area that may have aircraft operating at low altitudes, the county shall take reasonable steps, concurrent with other notices

issued pursuant to this subdivision, to notify pest control aircraft pilots registered to operate in the county. . . .

(14) Tower structure lighting shall be prohibited unless otherwise required by another provision of law or pursuant to paragraph (13).

. . . .

(c) A county may impose, as a condition of approval, a requirement that a small wind energy system be removed if it remains inoperable for 12 consecutive months, and at that time the small wind energy system shall be subject to nuisance codes and code enforcement action.

NOTES & QUESTIONS

1. Why do you think it might be reasonable to require that small wind turbines be sited only on parcels at least one acre in size?

2. Why might a county wish to impose a requirement that a small wind turbine be removed if it has not been operable for at least 12 months?

3. Statutes like California Government Code § 65896 are an example of what Professor William Buzbee calls a "ceiling preemption" approach: they allow for local-level regulation, but only so long as it does not exceed the state's specified set of ceiling restrictions. *See* William W. Buzbee, *Interaction's Promise: Preemption Policy Shifts, Risk Regulation, and Experimentalism Lessons*, 57 EMORY L.J. 145, 145 (2007). Professor Buzbee has argued that such ceiling preemption approaches can produce inefficiency and undesirable policy outcomes in the context of environmental law by preventing localities from imposing stronger environmental protections based on their own local characteristics and preferences. *See id.* at 155–56. Do those same arguments seem applicable in the context of § 65896? Why or why not?

2. SMALL WIND TURBINES AS A NUISANCE

In places where land use restrictions do not limit small wind turbine installations, nuisance law can play a more prominent role in governing neighbor conflicts over small wind devices. Small wind turbine installations have provoked nuisance claims on several occasions because of their impacts on neighboring land uses. The following is a case involving a nuisance claim against a small wind turbine based primarily on the noise that a turbine produced while spinning. As you read this case, consider how local land use or zoning ordinance provisions could have potentially prevented this dispute from ever arising.

ROSE V. CHAIKIN

Superior Court of New Jersey, Chancery Division, Atlantic County, 1982
453 A.2d 1378

GIBSON, J.S.C.

This action seeks to enjoin the operation of a privately owned windmill. Plaintiffs occupy neighboring properties and allege that the unit constitutes both a private nuisance and a violation of local zoning laws. Defendants deny the allegations and have counterclaimed. Based on the evidence presented at trial, the following factual findings may be made.

All of the parties are residents and/or owners of single-family homes located in a contiguous residential neighborhood in Brigantine, New Jersey. On or about June 18, 1981 defendants, in an effort to save on electric bills and conserve energy, obtained a building permit for the construction of a windmill. Pursuant to that permit they erected a 60'-high tower on top of which was housed a windmill and motor. The unit is located ten feet from the property line of one of plaintiffs. Shortly after the windmill became operational it began to produce offensive noise levels, as a result of which plaintiffs experienced various forms of stress-related symptoms, together with a general inability to enjoy the peace of their homes.

Relief was initially sought through city council. Although certain orders were issued reducing the times when the windmill could operate, the problem continued more or less until an action was instituted in this court. Following an initial hearing here, there was a preliminary finding of a nuisance and a temporary restraining order was issued restricting the use of the machine except for a period of no more than two hours a day, that being the time claimed to be needed for maintenance purposes. By consent, those restraints were continued up through the time of trial and still continue.

Although the evidence was in sharp dispute concerning the impact of the noise levels existing when the windmill is operational, this court is satisfied that those levels are of such a nature that they would be offensive to people of normal sensibilities and, in fact, have unreasonably interfered with plaintiffs' use and enjoyment of their properties. Measurements at the site reveal that the sound levels produced by the windmill vary, depending on the location, but generally show a range of 56 to 61 decibels (dBA). In all instances those levels exceed the 50 dBA permissible under the controlling city ordinance. Ordinance 11–1981, § 906.6.3, City of Brigantine. Although there are other sources of sounds in the area, for the most part they are natural to the site. These background (or ambient) sounds include the ocean, the sounds of sea gulls, the wind and the distant sounds of occasional boat traffic in the adjacent inlet. An exception to these "natural" sounds is the heat pump owned by plaintiffs Joel and Isadora Rose, of which more will be said later.

The sounds of the windmill have been variously described. Generally, however, they most resemble those produced by a large motor upon which there is superimposed the action of blades cutting through the air. The sounds are distinguishable not just by the level of the noise produced (noise being defined as unwanted sound) but because they are unnatural to the scene and are more or less constant. Although a reduction in the wind speed to below eight m.p.h. will automatically shut down the unit, the prevailing winds at this site are generally above that. Given the proximity of the homes involved, the net result is a noise which is both difficult to ignore and almost impossible to escape.

The impact on plaintiffs is significant. Both the lay and expert testimony support the conclusion that, in varying degrees, all of them experienced tension and stress-related symptoms when the windmill was operational. Those symptoms included nervousness, dizziness, loss of sleep and fatigue. The sounds disturbed many of the activities associated with the normal enjoyment of one's home, including reading, eating, watching television and general relaxation.

Defendants counterclaim and seek to enjoin the operation of the Rose heat pump. Although the unrebutted testimony indicated that it, too, produced sound levels in excess of 50 dBA, the impact on defendants was relatively small. Complaints were limited to some disturbance of certain activities, such as causing a distraction during reading and dinner. There is no evidence that it unreasonably interferes with defendants' health and comfort. What disturbance does occur is limited not only in duration but in frequency. The unit is rarely used by the Roses, and when used is on for relatively short periods of time.

I.   *Private Nuisance*

The basic standards for determining what constitutes a private nuisance were set forth by our Supreme Court in *Sans v. Ramsey Golf & Country Club*, 29 N.J. 438, 149 A.2d 599 (1959). The court made clear that a case-by-case inquiry, balancing competing interests in property, is required.

> The essence of a private nuisance is an unreasonable interference with the use and enjoyment of land. The elements are myriad. . . . The utility of the defendant's conduct must be weighed against the *quantum* of harm to the plaintiff. The question is not simply whether a person is annoyed or disturbed, but whether the annoyance or disturbance arises from an unreasonable use of the neighbor's land. . . . [at 448–49, 149 A.2d 599]

Unreasonableness is judged

> "... 'not according to exceptionally refined, uncommon or luxurious habits of living, but according to the simple tastes and unaffected notions generally prevailing among plain people.'" 50 N.J. Super. 127, at page 134, 141 *A.*2d 335, citing *Stevens v. Rockport Granite Co.*, 216 Mass. 486, 104 N.E. 371 (Sup. Jud. Ct. 1914). [at 449, 149 A.2d 599]

Defendants resist plaintiffs' claim by advancing three basic arguments: first, that noise, standing alone, cannot constitute a private nuisance; second, that even if noise can amount to a nuisance, the noise from their windmill does not exceed the applicable threshold, and third, that in any event the circumstances of this case do not warrant the "extraordinary relief" of an injunction.

The first argument is without merit. New Jersey case law makes it clear that noise may, under the principles of unreasonable use, constitute an actionable private nuisance. *See, e.g., Benton v. Kernan*, 130 *N.J. Eq.* 193, 197–98, 21 *A.*2d 755 (E. & A. 1941); *Lieberman v. Saddle River Tp.*, 37 N.J. Super. 62, 67, 116 A.2d 809 (App. Div. 1955); *Malhame v. Demarest*, 162 N.J. Super. 248, 260–61, 392 A.2d 652 (Law Div. 1978); *Reilley v. Curley*, 75 N.J. Eq. 57, 59–60, 71 A. 700 (Ch. 1908). Noise is an actionable private nuisance if two elements are present: (1) injury to the health and comfort of ordinary people in the vicinity, and (2) unreasonableness of that injury under all the circumstances. *See Malhame v. Demarest, supra* 162 *N.J. Super.* at 261, 392 *A.2d* 652. The "circumstances" may be multiple and must be proven by "clear and convincing" evidence. *Benton, supra*, 130 N.J. Eq. at 198, 21 A.2d 755; *Lieberman, supra* 37 N.J. Super. at 68, 116 A.2d 809.

> Broadly stated, the noises which a court of equity normally enjoins are those which affect injuriously the health and comfort of ordinary people in the vicinity to an unreasonable extent.... *Thus, the character, volume, frequency, duration, time, and locality are relevant factors in determining whether the annoyance materially interferes with the ordinary comfort of human existence.* [*Lieberman v. Saddle River Tp.*, 37 N.J. Super. at 67, 116 A.2d 809; emphasis supplied]

To the factors listed in *Lieberman* may be added several others gleaned from New Jersey cases and cases in other jurisdictions applying a "reasonableness under the circumstances" test. For example, the availability of alternative means of achieving the defendant's objective has been found to be relevant. *See Sans, supra* 29 *N.J.* at 448, 149 *A.*2d 599 (change in location of golf tee feasible); *Malhame, supra* 162 N.J. Super. at 264–266, 392 A.2d 652 (plaintiffs failed to prove that alternative fire-siren system wouldn't just transfer nuisance elsewhere). So, also, might the social utility of defendant's conduct, judged in light of prevailing notions of progress and the demands of modern life, be relevant. *See Protokowicz v. Lesofski,* 69 *N.J. Super.* 436, 443, 174 A.2d 385 (Ch. Div. 1961) (in light of scientific progress, noise from Diesel engine cannot be considered nuisance *per se*). Whether a given use complies with controlling governmental regulations, while not dispositive on the question of private nuisance, *Monzolino v. Grossman,* 111 N.J.L. 325, 328, 168 A. 673 (E. & A. 1933), does impact on its reasonableness. *See, e.g., Desruisseau v. Isley,* 553 P.2d 1242, 1245–46 (Ariz. App. 1976); 58 Am. Jur. 2d, *Nuisances,* § 30 (1971).

An application of these factors to the present case supports the conclusion that defendants' windmill constitutes an actionable nuisance. As indicated, the noise produced is offensive because of its character, volume and duration. It is a sound which is not only distinctive, but one which is louder than others and is more or less constant. Its intrusive quality is heightened because of the locality. The neighborhood is quiet and residential. It is well separated, not only from commercial sounds, but from the heavier residential traffic as well. Plaintiffs specifically chose the area because of these qualities and the proximity to the ocean. Sounds which are natural to this area—the sea, the shore birds, the ocean breeze—are soothing and welcome. The noise of the windmill, which would be unwelcome in most neighborhoods, is particularly alien here.

The duration of the windmill noise is also significant. Since the prevailing winds keep the unit operating more or less constantly, the noise continues night and day. Interfering, as they do, with the normal quiet required for sleep, nighttime noises are considered particularly intrusive. *See Protokowitz v. Lesofski, supra* 69 *N.J. Super.* at 444, 174 A.2d 385; *Seligman v. Victor Talking Machine Co.,* 71 N.J. Eq. 697, 700, 63 A. 1093 (Ch. 1906). Since ambient sounds are normally reduced at night, an alien sound is even more offensive then. The sound levels are well documented and clearly exceed permissible limits under the zoning ordinance. Ordinance 11–1981. Independent of the ordinance, the evidence supports the conclusion that the noise is disturbing to persons of ordinary sensibilities. It can and does affect injuriously the health and comfort of ordinary people in the vicinity to an unreasonable extent. *Lieberman v. Saddle River Tp., supra* 37 N.J. Super. at 67, 116 A.2d 809.

When consideration is given to the social utility of the windmill and the availability of reasonable alternatives, the conclusion supporting an injunction is the same. Defendants' purpose in installing the windmill was to conserve energy and save on electric bills. Speaking to the latter goal first, clearly the court can take judicial notice that alternative devices are available which are significantly less intrusive. Evid. R. 9(1). As to its social utility, a more careful analysis is required. Defendants argue that the windmill furthers the national need to conserve energy by the use of an alternate renewable source of power. *See generally* Wind Energy Systems

Act of 1980, 42 U.S.C.A. §§ 9201–13, and Public Utility Regulatory Policies Act of 1978, 16 U.S.C.A. § 824a–3. The social utility of alternate energy sources cannot be denied; nor should the court ignore the proposition that scientific and social progress sometimes reasonably require a reduction in personal comfort. *Protokowitz v. Lesofski, supra* 69 N.J. Super. at 443, 174 A.2d 385; Annotation, "Nuisance—Operation of Air Conditioner," 79 A.L.R.3d 320, 328 (1977). On the other hand, the fact that a device represents a scientific advance and has social utility does not mean that it is permissible at any cost. Such factors must be weighed against the quantum of harm the device brings to others. *Sans v. Ramsey Golf & Country Club, supra*, 29 N.J. at 448–49, 149 A.2d 599.

In this case the activity in question substantially interferes with the health and comfort of plaintiffs. In addition to the negative effect on their health, their ability to enjoy the sanctity of their homes has been significantly reduced. The ability to look to one's home as a refuge from the noise and stress associated with the outside world is a right to be jealously guarded. Before that right can be eroded in the name of social progress, the benefit to society must be clear and the intrusion must be warranted under all of the circumstances. Here, the benefits are relatively small and the irritation is substantial. On balance, therefore, the social utility of this windmill is outweighed by the quantum of harm that it creates.

That is not to say that all windmills constitute a nuisance or even that this windmill cannot be modified in a way to justify a different conclusion. Every case must be examined on an individual basis. Given the circumstances here, however, the evidence clearly and convincingly establishes a nuisance and the imposition of an injunction is warranted. Although defendants assert defenses of estoppel, laches and unclean hands, these claims are without factual support and need not be treated further.

With respect to the counterclaim, defendants have failed to prove that plaintiffs' heat pump constitutes an actionable nuisance. While the noise of the pump may at times be as loud as that of the windmill, several factors distinguish it. The operation of the pump is limited in duration and frequency, as it is rarely used and then only for short periods; also, the sound is less alien. In addition, defendants' proofs have failed to clearly and convincingly prove that the pump "unreasonably affects their health and comfort." They complain only of minor disturbances and distractions, rather than nuisances. That is not to say that a heat pump can never be a nuisance, or even that, given more substantial evidence, this particular heat pump could not be deemed a nuisance. It is only to say that in this case, given these proofs, defendants did not meet their burden.

II. *Statutory Remedy*

10 *N.J.S.A.* 40:55D–18 of the Municipal Land Use Law entitles any "interested party" to secure an injunction against a zoning ordinance violation. Since Brigantine's Ordinance 11–1981 sets noise standards for windmills and is part of the city zoning ordinance, its violation is subject to restraint under the statute. Although plaintiffs did not specifically plead a cause of action under N.J.S.A. 40:55D–18, the proofs submitted at trial and in post-trial briefs fully addressed the subject. To the extent necessary, therefore, the case presents an appropriate occasion to conform pleadings to the proofs under *R.* 4:9–2. *See 68th St. Apts. v. Lauricella,* 142 *N.J. Super.* 546, 561, n. 3, 362 *A.*2d 78 (Law Div. 1976), *aff'd* 150 *N.J. Super.* 47, 374 *A.*2d 1222 (App. Div. 1977).

Defendants' violation of the zoning ordinance is uncontroverted. At all times the windmill operated in violation of the 50 dBA standard. Defendants' response is that the ordinance is arbitrary and unreasonable.

For the purposes of the Municipal Land Use Law an "interested party" is

> . . . in the case of a civil proceeding in any court . . . any person, whether residing within or without the municipality, whose right to use, acquire, or enjoy property is or may be affected by any action taken under this act, or whose rights to use, acquire, or enjoy property under this act, . . . have been denied, violated or infringed by an action or failure to act under this act. [N.J.S.A. 40:55D–4]

The city's failure to adequately halt the zoning violation by the windmill constitutes a "failure to act" under the Municipal Land Use Act. Therefore, to be deemed interested parties plaintiffs need only have shown that their property rights have been "denied, violated or infringed." Several factors suggest that the showing required is minimal. First, New Jersey's test for standing, particularly in zoning cases, is not a stringent one. *See Home Builders League of So. Jersey, Inc. v. Berlin Tp.,* 81 *N.J.* 127, 132–33, 405 *A.*2d 381 (1979) (citing 40:55D–4). Second, the legislative history of "interested party" indicates that a potential plaintiff must show merely that he has been denied the reciprocal benefits of a common zoning plan.

The current definition of "interested party" first appeared in N.J.S.A. 40:55–47.1 of the prior municipal land use statute. The Legislature intended that section to give individuals the same right to an injunction afforded municipalities under N.J.S.A. 40:55–47. *See* Assembly Bill 536 of 1969; *see also Alpine Borough v. Brewster,* 7 *N.J.* 42, 80 *A.*2d 297 (1951). Accordingly, an interested party, at most, must show the equivalent of what was traditionally described as "special damages," that is, damages "distinct from [those] suffered . . . in common with the community at large." *Morris v. Haledon,* 24 N.J. Super. 171, 179–80, 93 *A.*2d 781 (App. Div.

1952). *See also* Governor's Message re Assembly Bill 536, Dec. 1, 1969; *Alpine Borough v. Brewster, supra* 7 N.J. at 52, 80 A.2d 297; *Stokes v. Jenkins,* 107 N.J. Eq. 318, 321, 152 A. 383 (Ch. 1930).

Plaintiffs have clearly suffered special damages. Their proximity to the windmill denies them the equal benefit of enjoyment of their property, and causes them injury greater than that suffered by the general public. *See Stokes v. Jenkins, supra* at 322, 152 A. 383. Accordingly, plaintiffs are "interested parties" within the meaning of N.J.S.A. 40:55D–4 and are entitled to an injunction under N.J.S.A. 40:55D–18.

Defendants nevertheless contend that the windmill ordinance is arbitrary and unreasonable. That position is unpersuasive. Defendants argue that the ordinance violates equal protection guarantees by arbitrarily singling out windmills for noise control, and due process because it unreasonably limits windmill noise to 50 dBA while other ambient sounds often rise above that level. The ordinance, however, is a zoning regulation and was promulgated under the police power. Since it is "social" legislation it need be justified only by a showing that, in any state of facts, it reasonably advances a legitimate state purpose. *Dandridge v. Williams,* 397 U.S. 471, 485, 90 S.Ct. 1153, 1161, 25 L.Ed.2d 491 (1970). This same minimal standard satisfies the principle of substantive due process. *See Nebbia v. New York,* 291 *U.S.* 502, 54 *S.Ct.* 505, 78 *L.Ed.* 940 (1934); *Hutton Park Gardens v. West Orange,* 68 *N.J.* 543, 560–61, 350 *A.*2d 1 (1975). Thus, a showing that the ordinance reasonably advances a legitimate state purpose would defeat both claims.

Pursuant to a police power statute, the Brigantine ordinance legitimately protects public health and welfare by proscribing excessive noise. Limiting noise from windmills indisputably advances that legitimate purpose and does so in a reasonable way. The claim that "other ambient sounds" may exist above 50 dBA ignores the distinction between noise (unwanted sound) and natural ambient sounds. It is not unreasonable for Brigantine to classify a windmill's sound "noise" and thus limit it. Nor is it unreasonable for the city to attack the noise problem "one step at a time," beginning with windmills, "addressing itself to the phase of the problem which seems most acute to the legislative mind." *Williamson v. Lee Optical Co.,* 348 *U.S.* 483, 489, 75 *S.Ct.* 461, 465, 99 *L.Ed.* 563 (1955). Defendant's constitutional claims are thus without merit. It must also be remembered that this ordinance is entitled to a presumption of validity. That presumption "may be overcome by a clear showing that the local ordinance is arbitrary or unreasonable." *Quick Chek Food Stores v. Springfield Tp.,* 83 *N.J.* 438, 447, 416 *A.*2d 840 (1980). There has been no such showing here.

In conclusion, it is the view of this court that, for a variety of reasons, defendants' windmill constitutes an actionable nuisance. Under the same analysis plaintiffs' heat pump does not. An alternative basis for granting injunctive relief is defendants' violation of the municipal zoning ordinance. An order should be entered accordingly.

QUESTIONS

1.   Among other things, the *Rose* court considered the social utility of the windmill and the availability of reasonable alternatives in comparison to the quantum of harm that the windmill created for neighbors. Suppose that this same analytic approach were being applied to rooftop solar panels rather than the windmill at issue in *Rose*. Suppose further that the neighbors' primary objection to the solar panels was their aesthetic appearance. Do you think that the "social utility vs. quantum of harm" analysis applied in *Rose* would tip *more* or *less* in favor of allowing the rooftop solar panels? Why?

2.   Suppose that you represent the owner of a small wind turbine installed on a residential property that abutted a rail line, where passing trains routinely generated ambient noise levels in excess of 60 dba. A neighbor whose property also abuts the rail line has sued your client for nuisance, citing its noise levels of between 56 and 61 dba. Craft an argument, based upon the language and analysis in *Rose*, for why your client's small turbine should not amount to an actionable nuisance.

3.   On what basis did the court conclude that defendants' heat pump, which produced noise in excess over the 50 dba, is *not* an actionable nuisance but that their wind turbine producing comparable noise levels is an actionable nuisance? Do you agree with the court's disparate treatment of these two similar types of noise-making activities? Why or why not?

The following case, *Rassier v. Houim*, arose approximately 10 years after *Rose* and also involves a conflict between neighbors over a small wind energy device. Interestingly, in *Rassier* a split court held in favor of the defendant and found that the small wind turbine at issue did not give rise to an actionable nuisance claim. Consider how the timing of the turbine's installation and the plaintiff's moving onto the neighboring property affected the holding in this case.

RASSIER V. HOUIM

Supreme Court of North Dakota, 1992
488 N.W.2d 635

VANDE WALLE, J.

Janet Rassier appealed from a district court judgment dismissing her lawsuit which sought to abate a private nuisance created by the use of a wind generator in a residential area. We affirm.

Garry Houim erected a tower and installed a wind generator on his residential lot in north Mandan in 1986. In October 1988, Rassier and her family purchased the adjoining lot and moved a mobile home onto the lot. Two years later, in November 1990, she sued Houim, claiming that his wind generator was a private nuisance and that it was erected in violation of the restrictive covenants applicable to their residential development. After a bench trial, the district court dismissed Rassier's claims.

On appeal, Rassier contends that the court erred when it concluded that maintaining a wind generator did not constitute a private nuisance, and that Houim did not violate any restrictive covenants when he erected the generator and its tower.

In North Dakota, a nuisance is defined by statute. Section 42–01–02, NDCC, provides that:

"A private nuisance is one which affects a single individual or a determinate number of persons in the enjoyment of some private right not common to the public."

Section 42–01–01, NDCC, defines a nuisance, in part, as follows:

"A nuisance consists in unlawfully doing an act or omitting to perform a duty, which act or omission:

1.   Annoys, injures, or endangers the comfort, repose, health, or safety of others;

. . . .

4.   In any way renders other persons insecure in life or in the use of property."

We have said that the common-law nuisance concept does not apply in North Dakota. *Jerry Harmon Motors, Inc. v. Farmers Union Grain Terminal Ass'n.*, 337 N.W.2d 427 (N.D.1983) [common law does not apply when legislature has passed law on specific topic]; *see* NDCC § 1–02–01. Where, however, there is no conflict between the common law and a statute, common law remains relevant. *E.g., McLean County Comm'rs v. Peterson Excavating, Inc.*, 406 N.W.2d 674 (N.D. 1987). Accordingly, we have applied aspects of common-law nuisance, in particular, the "coming to the nuisance" doctrine. *Jerry Harmon Motors, supra.*

. . . .

In *Jerry Harmon Motors, supra*, we recognized the applicability of the coming-to-the-nuisance doctrine to a nuisance claim undersection 42–01–01, NDCC. We also indicated that the principle is one of the factors considered in determining whether a nuisance exists, *i.e.*, whether the defendant created a condition which unreasonably interfered with plaintiff's use of property. We noted that anyone who comes to a nuisance "has a heavy burden to establish liability." *Id.*

Other factors relevant to the reasonableness of a defendant's interference with the plaintiff's use of property include a balancing of the utility of defendant's conduct against the harm to the plaintiff, plaintiff's attempts to accommodate defendant's use before bringing the nuisance action, and plaintiff's lack of diligence in seeking relief. *Powell on Real Property, supra* at ¶¶ 704[2]–704[3], *see also* RESTATEMENT (SECOND) OF TORTS §§ 822, 826–30 (1977).

The trial court's conclusion that Houim's maintaining a wind generator was not a nuisance included the necessary finding that Houim did not unreasonably interfere with Rassier's use of her property. . . .

Rassier points to evidence supporting a finding of unreasonable interference, including the fact that the wind generator is located approximately 40 feet from her house and created noise measured by an environmental scientist from the North Dakota State Department of Health and Consolidated Laboratories, and a mechanical engineer who worked in the area of psychoacoustics, in the range from 50 to 69 decibels. Those North Dakota communities which have enacted noise ordinances prohibit noise exceeding 55 decibels in residential areas; Mandan has not enacted such an ordinance. Both witnesses indicated that noise at the measured levels could be irritating, stressful, and interfere with sleep. Rassier stated that her family's use of the yard was interfered with because the noise disrupted conversations. Rassier also indicated a concern with the safety of locating the generator and its tower near her house; she described one instance when she found a large ice chunk in her yard, an ice chunk she suspected was thrown from the wind generator.

Houim points to evidence that under these circumstances the wind generator does not unreasonably interfere with Rassier's use of her property. The wind generator was put up in 1986; Rassiers moved onto the adjoining lot in 1988. Rassier brought this action two years after her family moved into their house, after conflicts arose between Mr. Rassier and Houim. Several neighbors testified for Houim; no neighbor, other than Rassier, complained of noise from the wind generator. Houim offered to teach the Rassiers to turn the wind generator off when the noise bothered them, but they did not attempt this accommodation. Finally, Houim said that the tower supporting the generator was engineered for a larger model than his, and that safety features eliminated the danger of blades, or ice, being thrown from the wind generator.

After reviewing this evidence, we are not left with a definite and firm conviction that the trial court made a mistake in finding that Rassier had not proved a nuisance.

Rassier also argued that Houim erected the wind generator contrary to restrictive covenants applicable to their housing development. The evidence demonstrated that Houim, Rassier, and several other residents of the development had built on their lots without seeking approval from an architectural review board established under the covenants Rassier argued Houim had violated. The trial court concluded that Houim had not violated the covenants after finding that the developer and the residents of the subdivision had abandoned those provisions. *See Allen v. Minot Amusement Corp.,* 312 N.W.2d 698 (N.D. 1981) [right to enforce restriction or reservation may be lost by waiver or acquiesence]. The finding of the court is not clearly erroneous.

The judgment of the district court is affirmed.

ERICKSTAD, C.J., and JOHNSON, J., concur.

MESCHKE, J., concurring and dissenting.

. . . I believe that the trial court did not properly weigh the relevant factors, did not make necessary findings, and inappropriately applied "coming to the nuisance" as a controlling factor. Therefore, I respectfully dissent.

Excessive noise can annoy, disturb, and unreasonably interfere with other persons in the use and enjoyment of their homes. Consider some illustrative decisions. *Parker v. Reaves,* 505 So.2d 323 (Ala.1987) (Noise and odors of dogs that interfered with neighbors' enjoyment of their homes enjoined as private nuisance); *Anne Arundel County Fish & Game Conservation Ass'n v. Carlucci,* 83 Md. App. 121, 573 A.2d 847 (1990) (Trap and skeet shooting club required to implement noise abatement for adjoining homeowners in adjacent residential zone); *Wade v. Fuller,* 12 Utah 2d 299, 365 P.2d 802 (1961) (Noise from drive-in cafe enjoined as nuisance to nearby residences); *Kolstad v. Rankin,* 179 Ill. App. 3d 1022, 128 Ill. Dec. 768, 534 N.E.2d 1373 (1989) (Gunsmith's private firing range enjoined as nuisance to neighboring homes in rural agricultural area); *McQuade v. Tucson Tiller Apartments, Ltd.,* 25 Ariz. App. 312, 543 P.2d 150 (1975) (Music concerts at shopping center enjoined as private nuisance to adjacent apartment dwellers); *Rose v. Chaikin,* 187 N.J.Super. 210, 453 A.2d 1378 (1982) (Windmill that produced noise levels to 61 decibels enjoined as unreasonable interference with neighbors' use and enjoyment of their homes). Excessive noise is a classic breach of duty, and it is a private nuisance to a neighbor in a residential area.

There are good reasons for this. "The ability to look to one's home as a refuge from the noise and stress associated with the outside world is a right to be jealously guarded. Before that right can be eroded in the name of social progress, the benefit to society must be clear and the intrusion must be warranted under all of the circumstances." *Rose*, 453 A.2d at 1383. *See also* NDCC 12.1–31–01(2) (Crime of disorderly conduct includes annoyance by "unreasonable noise.") "The gravity of the harm from noises that disturb a person's sleep, for example, is ordinarily much greater when the noises occur at night than it is when the noises occur in the daytime." RESTATEMENT (SECOND) OF TORTS § 827 cmt. b, p. 125 (1979). *See also* 58 Am. Jur. 2d *Nuisances* § 136 (1989): "In general, all tangible intrusions, such as noise, . . . fall within the realm of nuisance, ..."

When Houim installed his wind generator, his lot and all other lots (including the adjacent vacant lot later purchased by Rassier) in Ventures First Addition were subdivided for residential purposes, zoned for residential use, and protected by recorded covenants "for residential purposes only." All uses for "commercial purposes" were prohibited.

The character of the locality at the time that the interfering activity is begun is one of the most important factors to be weighed. The Restatement explains:

> Even between socially desirable and valuable uses of land there is a degree of incompatibility that, in some cases, is so great that they cannot be carried on in the same locality. A slaughterhouse, for example, may be indispensable to the community, but it usually renders other land in its immediate vicinity unfit for residential use and enjoyment. This incompatibility between the various beneficial uses to which land may be put has, in nearly all communities, resulted in a segregation of certain uses in certain localities in order to avoid unnecessary conflict between those that are highly incompatible. Thus some localities come to be devoted primarily to residential purposes, others to industrial purposes, others to agricultural purposes and so on. Sound public policy demands that the land in each locality be used for purposes suited to the character of that locality and that persons desiring to make a particular use of land should make it in a suitable locality.

RESTATEMENT (SECOND) OF TORTS § 827 cmt. on Clause (d), p. 127. *See also* Annotation, *"Coming to Nuisance" As A Defense or Estoppel*, 42 ALR3d 344, 357 § 5 ("Location of Nuisance") (1972): "[T]he nature of the area where the nuisance is carried on-whether, for example, the area is primarily residential, industrial, or commercial-may affect the weight to be given to the defense that the complainant moved into the area after the defendant had done so." In this case, all the adjacent lots were intended for residential purposes at the time that Houim installed his wind turbine.

When a commercial nuisance comes to a residential area, application of the "coming-to-the-nuisance" factor to a residence built there later is inappropriate. The noise potential of Houim's wind turbine was unreasonable to an adjacent home and was thus incompatible with a residential neighborhood.

We have recognized the "coming-to-the-nuisance" factor in the context of an earlier agricultural industry (grain elevator) affecting an automobile dealership later located in an adjacent commercial district. *Jerry Harmon Motors, Inc. v. Farmers Union Grain Terminal Ass'n.*, 337 N.W.2d 427 (N.D. 1983). While that factor is no doubt important to protecting an agricultural industry in an agricultural state, it should not be applied to an inappropriate activity that interferes with the use of property planned, zoned, and dedicated to residential purposes.

Most courts hold that, in itself and without other significant factors, the "coming-to-the-nuisance" factor will not bar a plaintiff's nuisance claim. Powell explains:

> The rationale for the prevailing rule rejecting "coming to the nuisance" as a sufficient defense is that otherwise those who settled in an area would acquire complete control over the future of adjoining and nearby land, and the fluidity of land use-a basic aspect of the American economy-would be reduced.

5 Richard R. Powell & Patrick J. Rohan, *Powell on Real Property* ¶ 704[3], at 64–48 to 64–49 (1991). Here, residential development was planned, not unpredictable. Houim knew that the adjacent lot in this residential area was intended for a home. In my opinion, therefore, the trial court's conclusion, that "this action fails . . . because of the application of the principle of coming to a nuisance," was mistaken.

Houim's wind turbine on part of his lot was not well suited to this residential locale. On the other hand, Rassier's use of her property for a residence is well suited to the character of the locale. RESTATEMENT (SECOND) OF TORTS § 831. *See also* 58 Am. Jur. 2d *Nuisances* § 149. Because I would reverse and remand for necessary findings and for a decision properly weighing relevant factors with a correct view of the law of private nuisance, I respectfully dissent.

LEVINE, J., concurs.

QUESTIONS

1.   What factual differences between the *Rose* case and the *Rassier* seemed to be the most influential in leading the majority in *Rassier* to hold that the small wind turbine at issue in that case was not a nuisance? Do you

think that these factual differences with the *Rose* case justified a different holding? Why or why not?

2.   How did the two-year span between the time Rassier moved onto the neighboring property and the time Rassier brought the claim against Houim appear to influence the court's analysis?

3.   How did the fact that many landowners, including the plaintiff and defendant, had not complied with their residential development's restrictive covenants seem to impact the majority's willingness to apply restrictive covenants against Houim's wind turbine?

4.   In his dissenting opinion, Justice Herbert Meschke treats Houim's wind turbine as a commercial land use rather than as a residential use. How does this characterization as a commercial use affect Justice Meschke's analysis? Do you agree with this characterization? Why or why not?

Although nuisance law is most commonly applied *ex post* (i.e., after the fact) to restrict the operation of a disruptive land use after it has already begun, nuisance law can also prevent the siting of a potentially disruptive land use in the first place. This is illustrated in the following case in which a proposed small wind turbine installation falls victim to nuisance law even before the turbine is erected on the defendant's land.

SOWERS V. FOREST HILLS SUBDIVISION
Supreme Court of Nevada, 2013
294 P.3d 427

HARDESTY, J.

In this appeal, we address whether the district court properly concluded that, under the particular circumstances and surroundings of the case, a proposed residential wind turbine would constitute a nuisance warranting a permanent injunction against its construction. Below, respondents Forest Hills Subdivision, Ann Hall, and Karl Hall (collectively, the Halls) sought to permanently enjoin their neighbor, appellant Rick Sowers, from constructing a wind turbine on his residential property, asserting that the proposed turbine would constitute a nuisance. The district court agreed and granted the permanent injunction.

We conclude that, in this case, substantial evidence exists to support the district court's conclusion that the proposed wind turbine constitutes a nuisance. We also determine that the wind turbine at issue would create a nuisance in fact. In reaching our conclusion, we hold that the aesthetics of a wind turbine alone are not grounds for finding a nuisance. However, we conclude that a nuisance in fact may be found when the aesthetics are combined with other factors, such as noise, shadow flicker, and diminution in property value. In this case, the district court heard testimony about the aesthetics of the proposed wind turbine, the noise and shadow flicker it would create, and its potential to diminish surrounding property values. Based on this evidence, we conclude that substantial evidence supports the district court's finding that the proposed residential wind turbine would be a nuisance in fact. Thus, we affirm the order granting a permanent injunction prohibiting its construction.

FACTS AND PROCEDURAL HISTORY

Sowers informed residents of the Forest Hills Subdivision that he planned to construct a wind turbine on his residential property. After this announcement, Sowers' neighbors, the Halls, and the Forest Hills Subdivision filed a complaint in district court claiming that the proposed wind turbine posed a potential nuisance because it would generate constant noise and obstruct the views of neighboring properties. The Halls sought to permanently enjoin construction of the wind turbine and requested preliminary injunctive relief.

At the preliminary injunction hearing, the district court heard testimony that the subdivision was a very quiet area, and that the turbine would obstruct Mr. Hall's view and create noise and shadow flicker. Another resident, who was also a licensed realtor, testified that the proposed wind turbine would diminish property values in the neighborhood. A renewable energy specialist testified that the proposed wind turbine would likely generate the same level of noise as "the hum of a highway," and a contractor hired to construct the turbine testified that there was no way to mitigate the shadow flicker caused by the wind turbine.

The district court then conducted a site visit to the location of a comparable wind turbine. At this site visit, Sowers brought a decibel-reading machine that indicated that the noise from the wind turbine did not exceed 5 decibels from 100 feet away. A neighbor to that wind turbine testified that it produced some noise and shadow flicker, but that the turbine did not bother him. The district court also visited Sowers' home in Forest Hills, the proposed site for his wind turbine, but noted there was no way for Sowers to test the possible decibel level at that location.

Following the preliminary injunction hearing, the district court granted the permanent injunction. The district court heavily considered its visit to the site of the comparable turbine and its observation that it "was astonished by the size of the structure and the 'overwhelming impression of gigantism.'" The district court also considered that the Forest Hills Subdivision had panoramic views and was a very quiet neighborhood, and that the proposed wind turbine would likely lower property values in the area. Based on these findings and the site visits, the district court held that the proposed wind turbine constituted a nuisance because the turbine would substantially interfere with the neighboring residents' enjoyment and use of their property. As such, the district court ordered a permanent injunction enjoining construction of the wind turbine. Sowers now appeals.

DISCUSSION

On appeal, Sowers argues that the district court improperly concluded that the proposed wind turbine constituted a nuisance and improperly granted the permanent injunction. We disagree.

A nuisance is "[a]nything which is injurious to health, or indecent and offensive to the senses, or an obstruction to the free use of property, so as to interfere with the comfortable enjoyment of life or property." NRS 40.140(1)(a). There are several kinds of nuisances, two of which are pertinent to this discussion. A nuisance at law, also called a nuisance per se, is "a nuisance at all times and under any circumstances, regardless of location or surroundings." *See* 66 C.J.S. *Nuisances* § 4 (2013). A nuisance in fact, also called a nuisance per accidens, is "one which becomes a nuisance by reasons of circumstances and surroundings." *Id.*

We recognize that the Washoe County Development Code permits the construction of private wind turbines in residential areas if such turbines otherwise comply with the requirements of the Code. *See generally* Washoe County Code Ch. 326 (2010). We are also cognizant of this state's aggressive policy favoring renewable energy sources, such as wind turbines. *See* NRS 278.02077. We further acknowledge the testimony from the neighbor of the person owning the comparable wind turbine who said that the turbine did not bother him. Based on these considerations, we do not believe that wind turbines are severe interferences in all circumstances, and thus wind turbines are not nuisances at law.

However, even when a structure or act is not a nuisance per se, "[a] nuisance may arise from a lawful activity conducted in an unreasonable and improper manner." 66 C.J.S. *Nuisances* § 16 (2012) (footnote omitted). Thus, a wind turbine may "be or become a nuisance by reason of the improper or negligent manner in which it is conducted, or by reason of its locality, as where it is done or conducted in a place where it necessarily tends to the damage of another's property." *Id.* Accordingly, "a fair test as to whether a business or a particular use of a property in connection with the operation of the business constitutes a nuisance[ ] is the reasonableness or unreasonableness of the operation or use in relation to the particular locality and under all existing circumstances." *Burch v. Nedpower Mount Storm, LLC*, 220 W.Va. 443, 647 S.E.2d 879, 893 (2007) (internal quotations omitted).

"When deciding whether one's use of his or her property is a nuisance to his neighbors, it is necessary to balance the competing interests of the landowners, using a commonsense approach." 66 C.J.S. *Nuisances* § 13 (2012). Although we recognize that preserving a residential neighborhood's character is an important and substantial interest for subdivision homeowners, *see Zupancic v. Sierra Vista Recreation*, 97 Nev. 187, 194, 625 P.2d 1177, 1181 (1981), we have consistently held that a landowner does not have a right to light, air, or view. *See Probasco v. City of Reno*, 85 Nev. 563, 565, 459 P.2d 772, 774 (1969); *Boyd v. McDonald*, 81 Nev. 642, 651, 408 P.2d 717, 722 (1965). Thus, in resolving this issue on appeal, we must determine whether the proposed wind turbine is "so unreasonable and substantial as to amount to a nuisance and warrant an injunction" by balancing "the gravity of the harm to the plaintiff against the utility of the defendant's conduct, both to himself and to the community." *Cook v. Sullivan*, 149 N.H. 774, 829 A.2d 1059, 1066 (2003) (internal quotations omitted).

Substantial evidence supports the district court's conclusion that the proposed wind turbine is a nuisance in fact

The determination of whether an activity constitutes a nuisance is generally a question of fact. *Jezowski v. City of Reno*, 71 Nev. 233, 239, 286 P.2d 257, 260 (1955). This court will uphold the factual findings of the district court as long as these findings are not clearly erroneous and are supported by substantial evidence. *Kockos v. Bank of Nevada*, 90 Nev. 140, 143, 520 P.2d 1359, 1361 (1974).

To sustain a claim for private nuisance, an interference with one's use and enjoyment of land must be both substantial and unreasonable. *Lied v. County of Clark*, 94 Nev. 275, 278, 579 P.2d 171, 173 (1978). Interference is substantial " '[i]f normal persons living in the community would regard the [alleged nuisance] as definitively offensive, seriously annoying or intolerable.' " *Rattigan v. Wile*, 445 Mass. 850, 841 N.E.2d 680, 688 (2006) (quoting RESTATEMENT (SECOND) OF TORTS § 821F cmt. d (1979)). Interference is unreasonable when "the gravity of the harm outweighs the social value of the activity alleged to cause the harm." *Burch*, 647 S.E.2d at 887 (internal quotations omitted).

In the small body of national caselaw regarding wind turbines, noise and diminution of property values are the most universally considered factors in determining whether a private nuisance exists. Some states also consider the presence of shadow flicker in combination with noise and property value reduction.

Noise

In a case with similar facts from another jurisdiction, the Superior Court of New Jersey held that a residential wind turbine located in a quiet neighborhood constituted a nuisance solely on the basis of the constant loud noise that the turbine generated. *Rose v. Chaikin*, 187 N.J. Super. 210, 453 A.2d 1378, 1381–82 (N.J. Super. Ct. Ch. Div.1982). In *Rose,* the Superior Court found that the distinctive sound of the wind turbine produced a heightened level of intrusiveness because the neighborhood was quiet, separated from commercial and heavier residential noise, and the residents had specifically chosen to live in the area due to the peacefulness the community afforded. *Id.* We conclude that the citizens who were protected in *Rose* are analogous to the Halls and other Forest Hills residents, as the district court heard testimony of several persons living in the Forest Hills Subdivision that the subdivision was very quiet, and they were concerned that the level of noise from the wind turbine would change the character of the neighborhood they had sought to live in. Since a renewable energy expert testified that the noise created by the turbine would be similar to that of the hum on a nearby highway, there is some evidence that the quiet would most likely be gone. Based on this evidence, the district court could have determined that the proposed wind turbine constitutes a nuisance as a source of excessive noise.

Diminution to property value

Burch also allows for the consideration of potentially diminished property values where it is shown that a landowner's use and enjoyment of his or her property may be infringed. 647 S.E.2d at 892. Since the district court received testimony from subdivision residents that they feared an impact on the use and enjoyment of their property, it was fair for the district court to also take into account potential harm to property values. Thus, it was acceptable to include in its findings and conclusions the opinion of the real estate agent who testified that properties in proximity to wind turbines decreased in value.

Aesthetics and shadow flicker

. . . [A] district court may consider the aesthetics of the wind turbine only if factors other than unsightliness or obstruction of views are claimed. In *Burch*, the West Virginia court noted that shadow flicker was a kind of aesthetic concern that could be considered in conjunction with other factors. *Id.* at 898. It further anticipated how a commercial wind turbine facility abutting a neighborhood could constitute a private nuisance where constant shadow flicker was likely to ruin the enjoyment of residents. Here, Karl Hall testified that the wind turbine would create a shadow flicker on his property, and the contractor hired to construct the wind turbine testified that there is no way to mitigate shadow flicker. Thus, it was not clearly erroneous for the district court to consider shadow flicker.

Nor was it error for the district court to consider the size of the proposed wind turbine. Evidence was heard from a representative of the company who was supposed to construct the turbine indicating that the height of the proposed turbine exceeded 75 feet. The district court got to experience just how tall 75 feet is during its site visit to a comparable wind turbine. With this perspective, the site visit to Sowers' property revealed that his proposed turbine would be a significant imposition on the Halls' ability to use their property, as their land, which lays lower than Sowers' land, would now have a sizeable obstacle overshadowing it. Since evidence of other factors was presented, it was proper for the district court to add into its consideration the presence of shadow flicker and the size of the turbine and the impact on views.

As such, we conclude that this evidence concerning the noise, diminution in property value, shadow flicker, and aesthetics far outweighs any potential utility of the proposed wind turbine within the Forest Hills Subdivision. Accordingly, we conclude that the proposed wind turbine constitutes a nuisance in fact.

. . . .

While the district court expressed concern with the size of the proposed wind turbine, a review of the record reveals it did consider the anticipated noise level of the proposed wind turbine, the actual noise level of an existing wind turbine, the quietness of the Forest Hills Subdivision community, the effects of shadow flicker, and the diminution in value of surrounding properties that the wind turbine would cause. Since each of these findings is supported by evidence in the record, we conclude that the reasons for the injunction are readily apparent in the record and are sufficiently clear to permit meaningful appellate review.

Accordingly, we affirm the district court's order granting a permanent injunction.

NOTES & QUESTIONS

1.   The *Sowers* court held that, although a wind turbine's aesthetic impacts alone could not make it an actionable nuisance, those impacts combined with noise, flicker, property value reduction, and other effects could give rise to a nuisance claim. Do you believe this to be a defensible and justifiable rule? Why or why not? Should aesthetic impacts alone ever be sufficient to find an actionable nuisance against a small wind energy device?

2.   How tall was the proposed "small turbine" in *Sowers*? How do you think the size of the turbine affected the court's treatment of it?

3.   The landowner in *Sowers* sought to install a small wind turbine in a residential subdivision. How do you think the nature of that setting affected the court's disposition of the case? Do you think the outcome would have been different if the turbine were proposed in a remote rural area? Why or why not?

4.   *Wind Turbines and Property Values.* Not surprisingly, the evidence is mixed with regard to whether wind turbine installations harm property values and the extent of such harms. A 2013 Berkeley National Laboratory study involving more than 50,000 home sales near 67 different wind energy facilities throughout the United States found "no statistical evidence" of adverse impacts of wind turbines on property values. Ben Hoen, et al., *A Spatial Hedonic Analysis of the Effects of Wind Energy Facilities on*

Surrounding Property Values in the United States iii, Ernest Orlando Lawrence Berkeley National Laboratory, LBNL–6362E (2013). In contrast, a large 2014 London School of Economics study focused on utility-scale wind energy projects in England and Wales found price reductions of five to six percent in homes situated within 2 kilometers of and within sight of wind farms in that region.

3. UTILITY REGULATORS' RESTRICTIONS ON SMALL WIND

In addition to land use regulations and nuisance laws, public utility regulations can also restrict small wind energy development. State public service commissions or public utility commissions, which regulate various electric utility activities in most states, must sometimes provide approvals for installations of small wind turbines above a certain size. The largest turbines that still fall into the "small turbine" category produce significant amounts of electricity and are often net-metered, meaning that they feed excess electricity onto the grid that the utility must purchase at state-dictated prices. Accordingly, utility regulators in some states are empowered to deny permits for these turbines, even when they seemingly comply with state and local land use regulations. As shown in the following case, sometimes aesthetics-based objections from state utility regulators become the primary obstacle to small wind turbine installations in rural areas where few zoning ordinance restrictions apply.

IN RE HALNON
Supreme Court of Vermont, 2002
811 A.2d 161

ENTRY ORDER

Petitioner Tom Halnon appeals the Vermont Public Service Board's denial of his application requesting a certificate of public good (CPG) for a wind turbine net metering system pursuant to 30 V.S.A. § 219a. Halnon claims the Board abused its discretion by relying exclusively on observations made during its site visit, instead of evidence contained in the record, and that the Board's decision was contrary to the legislative intent and purpose underlying 30 V.S.A. § 219a. We find no abuse of discretion and therefore affirm the Board's order.

Halnon and his wife own sixty-two acres of land on North Branch Road in East Middlebury upon which Halnon seeks to erect and use a wind turbine. As a facility for electricity generation that employs a renewable energy source, a wind turbine constitutes a "net metering system," 30 V.S.A. § 219a(3)(E), requiring a CPG issued by the Board. *See* 30 V.S.A. § 248(a)(2). In accordance with CPG application requirements, Halnon sent notice to neighboring landowners, and other interested parties, informing them of his application. Various objections were made to Halnon's CPG application, the bulk of which focused on the project's perceived negative aesthetic impact.

Mr. and Mrs. Rimonneau are neighboring landowners and part-time residents of a parcel of land across North Branch Road from the Halnon property who are among those opposed to Halnon's application for aesthetic reasons. Their residence is located at a slightly higher elevation from the proposed project site and looks down into the portion of the four acre meadow where Halnon proposes to site the wind turbine. The proposed turbine has three 23-foot diameter blades installed on a 100-foot tall tubular tower approximately one foot in diameter; it will be directly in view of the Green Mountains from the Rimonneaus' residence. Approximately 450 feet separates the Rimonneau residence and the proposed turbine site. The area is predominantly wooded, comprised of mature poplar trees 30–75 feet in height. There are a small number of one- and two-story homes and hunting camps hidden in the woods but no other man-made structures in the area.

Hearings were held on Halnon's CPG application during which the Rimonneaus, among other parties, were granted intervention pursuant to Board Rule 2.209 . . . The bulk of the hearings focused on the issue of aesthetics, and proper application of the "*Quechee* test" utilized by the Board when reviewing issues of aesthetics under 30 V.S.A. § 248. The hearing officer held two site visits and several technical hearings and evaluated the proposed project under certain criteria detailed in 30 V.S.A. § 248. Applying the *Quechee* test the hearing officer's proposal for decision (PFD) determined that Halnon's CPG request should be denied "because the net metering system as proposed, would have an undue adverse effect on the aesthetics and scenic and natural beauty of the area in which it is proposed" in violation of 30 V.S.A. § 248(b)(5). The hearing officer found that there were alternative suitable sites for the proposed project and that Halnon had not availed himself of obvious and potentially effective mitigation steps which would lessen the aesthetic impacts of the project. Further, the hearing officer found the project would be offensive and shocking to the Rimonneaus and the average person in a similar situation. The PFD also invited the Board to reconsider this recommendation if Halnon could provide evidence that he has taken significant steps to minimize the negative effects that the project has on the Rimonneau's direct view.

Fundamentally at issue in this case was whether Halnon's proposed project survived scrutiny under the *Quechee* test. The parties in this matter offer differing interpretations regarding proper application of the *Quechee* test, alternately referring to both a two-part, and a three-part *Quechee* analysis. For purposes of clarification we restate the proper *Quechee* test for determining whether a project will have an undue adverse effect on the aesthetics or scenic and natural beauty of an area.

The two-part *Quechee* test was first outlined by the Environmental Board in a previous case and has since been followed by this Court. *See In re McShinsky*, 153 Vt. 586, 591, 572 A.2d 916, 919 (1990). Under this test a determination must first be made as to whether a project will have an adverse impact on aesthetics and the scenic and natural beauty of an area because it would not be in harmony with its surroundings. *Id.* at 591, 572 A.2d at 919. If the answer is in the affirmative the inquiry then advances to the second prong to determine if the adverse impact would be "undue." *Id.* Under the second prong an adverse impact is undue if any one of three questions is answered in the affirmative: 1) Does the project violate a clear, written community standard intended to preserve the aesthetics or scenic, natural beauty of the area? 2) Does the project offend the sensibilities of the average person? 3) Have the applicants failed to take generally available mitigating steps that a reasonable person would take to improve the harmony of the proposed project with its surroundings? *Id.* at 592, 572 A.2d at 920. An affirmative answer to any one of the three inquiries under the second prong of the *Quechee* test means the project would have an undue adverse impact. *Id.* at 593, 572 A.2d at 920.

The Board received comments on the hearing officer's PFD from all parties and intervenors, including the Rimonneaus, Halnon and the Department of Public Service. A duly noticed site visit, followed by oral argument, was held before the Board. Applying the second prong of the *Quechee* test analysis, the Board concluded Halnon has failed to present "any compelling reason why [he] could not use an alternative site," "has failed to take generally available mitigating steps which a reasonable person would take to improve the harmony of the proposed turbine with its surroundings," and further, that he had the "burden of proof in this case and has failed to demonstrate this mitigation would be unreasonable." Based on this conclusion and the conclusion that the turbine would offend the sensibilities of the average person faced with a situation similar to the Rimonneaus', the Board accepted the hearing officer's conclusion that the project failed the two-part *Quechee* test and would, therefore, have an undue adverse effect upon the aesthetic and scenic and natural beauty of the area.

Appellant argues on appeal that in reaching its decision the Board erred by improperly relying on information obtained through its site visit. Specifically, appellant cites portions of the Board's decision which reference the site visit, unsupported by any citation to the record:

> The Applicant has not fully addressed the feasibility of other possible alternative locations which we observed at the site visit.

From our site visit, it is apparent that there are some locations that could achieve approximately the same turbine height above surrounding terrain and vegetation with the same tower height as the proposed site.

Based upon our site visit to the area, we concur with the Hearing Officer's conclusion that the project in its presently proposed location will offend the sensibilities of the average person faced with a similar situation.

Appellant argues that these references demonstrate improper reliance on site visits as the exclusive basis for the Board's findings, in contravention of our case law mandating otherwise. *See In re Quechee Lakes Corp.*, 154 Vt. 543, 551, 580 A.2d 957, 962 (1990). Specifically, appellant claims that the Board's reliance on its own site visit observation improperly formed the basis for its finding that the project failed to pass muster under the second prong of the *Quechee* test regarding mitigation and whether the project offends the sensibilities of the average person in the Rimonneaus' position. . . .

     . . . .

We disagree with appellant that the Board relied exclusively on its own site visit as the basis for its conclusions. Rather, it is reasonable to conclude that the Board used its site visit observations merely to verify and affirm the hearing officer's conclusions. There is no evidence that the Board relied on its own site visit observations over and above, or to the exclusion of, other evidence before it. The Board's site visit observations constitute only a part of its total findings regarding the proposed project. There were more than 60 other findings made in support of the Board's final conclusion. Besides the site visit, the Board also heard testimony regarding the nature and scale of the turbine and the surrounding area and the project . . . There exists ample evidence in the record, in addition to the Board's findings gleaned from its site visit, to support the Board's ultimate conclusion.

Halnon further argues that the Board's denial of his application is contrary to the intent of 30 V.S.A. § 219a. Specifically, he cites legislative findings to demonstrate that with net metering, the Legislature intended to encourage investment in renewable energy resources, enhance diversification of Vermont's energy resources, and stimulate economic growth. 1997, No. 136 (Adj. Sess.), § 1. Appellant also finds further support for the above legislative intent in the net metering statute's mandate to the Board to "simplify the application and review process as appropriate." 30 V.S.A. § 219a(c)(3). Halnon claims that putting the burden of proof upon him to show that mitigation would be unreasonable, and denying his application for failure to meet that burden, constitutes an abuse of discretion in the context of a net metering application, and contravenes the intent of § 219a.

Again we find appellant's argument unpersuasive. The Board denied Halnon's application after carefully balancing all appropriate policy considerations and then succinctly detailing its reasons for denying the application. . . . Several alternative sites for the project that would effectively shield the project behind large pine trees, and thus, effectively screen the project from the Rimonneaus' view, and from visibility along North Branch Road, were identified by Halnon in discussions with the Rimonneaus or identified during site visits and subsequent testimony. Halnon, however, conducted no analysis of alternative sites, objecting to them on the basis that he would have to cut down trees near his house, that there would be increased costs of installation at the alternative sites, and that relocation would still leave the project visible to two houses, one a quarter mile away, the other two miles away. That implementing some of these mitigation measures would increase projects costs, cause power losses and may affect aesthetics on appellant's own property does not render the Board's conclusion that the turbine could be sited elsewhere an abuse of discretion.

Appellant also claims that the Board's abuse of discretion is further evidenced when its order in this case is contrasted with its order in *In re Blittersdorf*, CPG NM–11 (May 26, 2000). In that case the Board approved a CPG for a wind turbine in a neighborhood containing single family residences and inactive farms where the net metering system was "very visible from surrounding property and roads, with clear views of the turbine ranging from a few hundred feet in some directions up to one mile or more in other directions." *Id.* at 4–5. Appellant claims the Board's decision in the instant case is inconsistent with its decision in *Blittersdorf* and thereby thwarts the purpose of vesting statewide authority with the Board in order to effectuate uniform and fair statewide administration of public utility and electricity matters. Because of this, appellant claims the Board's decision was an abuse of discretion. We disagree. As the Board observed, the proposed wind turbine in *Blittersdorf* was not out of character with its less rural surroundings which included: residences, barns, silos, farm machinery, tall telephone poles and other large working structures. In addition, the neighbor opposing the *Blittersdorf* turbine was situated approximately 1300 feet from the turbine and possessed a panoramic view of the Adirondacks which would only be marginally affected by the wind turbine. By contrast, in the instant case, the area is predominantly rural and wooded, devoid of other large structures in the vicinity of the project and the Rimonneaus' home is situated only 450 feet from the proposed site. Their already limited view will be more severely affected by the presence of a turbine located directly in front of them. Given that the proposal in *Blittersdorf* and in the instant case were for wind turbines sited in significantly dissimilar environments, it was not abuse of discretion for the Board to find Halnon's proposed turbine offensive or shocking to the average person.

There is a strong presumption that orders issued by the Public Service Board are valid. *In re E. Georgia Cogeneration Ltd. P'ship*, 158 Vt. 525, 531, 614 A.2d 799, 803 (1992). In reviewing orders of the Board, this Court gives great deference to the particular expertise and informed judgment of the Board. *Id.* Operating under that standard, we are unpersuaded that the Board's order in this case warrants reversal.

QUESTIONS

1. Suppose that a state's Public Utilities Commission began conducting "aesthetic impact reviews" of every proposed rooftop solar installation throughout the state and began blocking rooftop solar installations that failed their review process, even when applicants held all requisite municipal land use approvals. Why might local land use regulators be better equipped than state utility regulators to conduct such aesthetic-based reviews of rooftop solar installations? Is state-level aesthetic regulation of small wind turbines like the turbine in *In re Halnon* any different in this regard? Why or why not? From a policy perspective, should state utility regulators even be conducting this type of review?

2. Where is the optimal line between state and local regulatory jurisdiction over view and aesthetic impacts from wind energy devices? Should that line be based on the height of the turbine, on its generating capacity, on whether it is for commercial or residential use, or on some other factor?

Having explored in this Chapter the general policy issues surrounding today's wind energy industry, this Casebook turns its focus in Chapter 4 to the primary legal concepts and rules governing modern wind energy development.

CHAPTER 4

WIND ENERGY DEVELOPMENT

▪ ▪ ▪

One of the greatest advantages of utility-scale wind energy development is that, once a wind farm is up and running, it can generate large quantities of clean electric power for decades without any added fuel. Unlike coal-fired, gas-fired, or even nuclear power plants, wind energy projects require no mining, extraction, refining, or transportation of energy sources to sustain their operations over time. Accordingly, most of the expense and work—including legal work—associated with wind energy relates to the initial siting, financing, and construction of wind energy projects.

Many of the legal issues and tasks associated with siting and building wind farms could arise in the development of almost any large-scale electric generating facility. For instance, lawyers often help wind energy developers to secure permits from energy regulators for projects and for the substations and transmission lines they require. Lawyers also often assist in the negotiating and drafting of agreements with utilities or other parties to govern long-term purchase and sale arrangements for the electric power a project is anticipated to generate.

Rather than covering generic issues that arise in most types of energy development, this chapter focuses primarily on environmental, real estate, finance, and permitting matters that are unique to the siting and development of utility-scale wind energy projects. Developers, landowners, lenders, investors, title insurance companies, construction contractors, and numerous other stakeholders routinely seek the assistance of legal counsel when confronting such matters. The most effective lawyers in these settings understand and account for the major differences between wind farms and other large energy facilities.

A. IDENTIFYING A PROJECT SITE

Although policy changes, technological advancements, and other factors have enabled wind energy to become increasingly competitive with other forms of electricity generation in recent years, not every corner of the United States is well suited for wind energy development. Identifying a suitable location is unquestionably one of the most important factors in the failure or success of a wind farm project. Seasoned wind energy developers are keenly aware of this fact and thoroughly research prospective wind farm sites before attempting to move the development process forward.

Obviously, high-quality wind resources are an essential characteristic of any potential wind farm site. Although most parts of the world experience windy conditions at least some of the time, only a fraction of the world's dry land is windy frequently enough to make it a viable site for a wind energy project. As Figure 4 in Chapter 2 illustrated, onshore wind energy resources are of below-average or marginal quality in most of the United States' high-population regions. Even in those regions of the country that appear on the map to have good wind resources, topographical and other features cause some parts of those regions to have far better wind resources than others. Because of this potential for dramatic differences in wind resource quality even within a single region or county, identifying project sites with excellent wind resources is a critical early step in the development process.

Of course, the mere fact that a potential wind farm site has first-rate wind resources does not guarantee its success. Numerous other factors can also impact whether a given a site is a viable location for a wind farm. For example, wind farm sites must have adequate access to the transmission grid to transport the project's generated power to customers. Usually, the electricity generated by a wind farm's turbines travels via a *collector system* of distribution lines from the turbines to one or more substations, where the power passes through transformers that ramp it up to a higher voltage and ultimately feed it into the transmission grid. As described in Chapter 2, the electric grid then acts like a freeway system, transporting the electricity at a high voltage across long distances to load centers—usually metropolitan areas with lots of homes and businesses in need of electric power. Unfortunately, the nation's transmission infrastructure was not designed with wind energy development in mind so many geographic areas with strong wind resources are situated too far away from high voltage transmission lines to be viable wind farm sites. Developers sometimes fund the construction of new substations and transmission lines traversing several miles to connect their wind energy projects into the grid, but often the costs of such new infrastructure are so high that they doom an otherwise promising project site.

To convince lenders and investors to help finance their projects, wind energy developers often must also secure up-front commitments from electric utilities or other parties to buy the project or its generated power when construction is completed. In some cases, a developer secures this commitment by executing an *asset purchase agreement* with a utility or other buyer that outlines terms and conditions for the purchase and sale of the entire wind farm project shortly after construction. In other instances, a developer opts to effectively retain ownership of the completed wind farm (often through a wholly-owned subsidiary), maintain and operate it, and sell its generated electricity for a profit. Under the latter type of arrangement, the developer and one or more *off-takers* usually execute a *power purchase agreement*—a highly sophisticated agreement governing the pricing, quantity and delivery of the project's power.

Even after identifying a potential project site with strong wind resources, adequate transmission access, and a willing purchaser or off-taker for the project or its generated power, wind energy developers still must evaluate a long list of other factors to determine whether the site is truly viable. For example, in mountainous areas, developers must ensure that construction of the project will be practically feasible—that the grading of roads won't be too steep or costly and that it will be possible to deliver and erect enormous towers and rotors to the specific locations where the turbines will be installed. Developers must likewise consider the regulatory climate within the state and county where the project site is situated and the likelihood of opposition from local stakeholders. For instance, have state and local governments having jurisdiction over the project site shown themselves to be accommodating of other wind energy development projects? Would a wind farm in the proposed location be visible to neighboring landowners who are likely oppose such a project on aesthetic grounds? Is the project site situated close to known Native American cultural sites or to land known to serve as habitat for a protected wildlife species? Or are there any military facilities or electromagnetic transmission stations nearby that might create conflicts with the project? Experienced wind energy developers evaluate these and many other potential obstacles before making major investments toward the development of a wind farm at any particular site.

B. WIND ENERGY LEASING

Once they are convinced that a specific site is well-suited for a new wind farm, developers begin talking with landowners in the area about the prospect of leasing their land. As described in Chapter 2, those landowners generally possess the property rights required for wind energy development on their land. The following materials provide an introductory look at several legal and practical issues that often arise in the drafting and negotiation of wind energy leases private landowners.

A developer's first task in the wind energy leasing process is to identify the holders of wind rights in the land where they hope to develop a project. Typically, the holder of a fee simple interest or the surface estate in a given parcel of land also possesses the wind rights associated with that parcel. Indeed, some states in recent years have even enacted statutes specifically declaring that wind rights are legitimate property interests appurtenant to the surface estate. *See, e.g.*, WYO. STAT. ANN. § 34–27–102 & 103 (2011); MONT. STAT. ANN. § 70–17–402(4) (2011). In the rural areas where wind energy development most commonly occurs, fee simple title is often vested in a single individual or in a married couple holding title jointly as husband and wife. Sometimes, a corporation or other business entity holds title. To avoid leasing land from someone that is not the true interest holder, wind energy developers typically rely on title insurance companies to provide them insurable information about the land's ownership before they commence lease negotiations.

1. LEASING AND THE WIND ESTATE

As highlighted in Chapter 3, landowners in some states have recorded documents that purport to sever a parcel's wind rights from its surface rights and to reserve those wind rights in a deed or separately convey them to a third party. Often, such instruments label the severed interests as a *wind estate* and use language akin to what lawyers have long used to sever a minerals estate from surface rights. In these rare instances where a landowner has severed the wind estate from the surface estate, a wind energy developer must negotiate with the wind estate holder rather than the surface rights owner. Because of the nature of the parties' respective rights, holders of severed wind estates are less likely to reside on the subject land and may have relatively infrequent contact with the surface owner. Although surface rights holders in these situations are more likely to live or have regular operations on the land, the have relatively limited power to influence wind energy leasing negotiations. For obvious reasons, this three-party dynamic can infuse additional complexity and difficulty into the leasing and development process.

Fortunately, only a small fraction of landowners have ever severed their wind estate from the surface estate, and this practice seems to be growing less common over time. Multiple state legislatures have even enacted statutes in recent years that expressly forbid severance of a wind estate from the surface estate. *See, e.g.*, COLO. REV. STAT. § 38–30.7–101–105 (West 2015); N.D. CENT. CODE § 17–04–04 (West 2007); S.D. CODIFIED LAWS § 43–13–19; WYO. STAT. ANN. § 34–27–103 (West 2011); MONT. CODE ANN. § 70–17–404 (West 2011); NEB. REV. STAT. § 76–3004 (West 2012). Lease negotiations involving holders of severed wind estates should therefore become increasingly rare in the coming decades. For more information about wind rights severance and its potential impacts on wind energy development, see K.K. DuVivier, *Animal, Vegetable, Mineral— Wind? The Severed Wind Power Rights Conundrum*, 49 WASHBURN L.J. 69 (2009); Troy A. Rule, *Wind Rights under Property Law: Answers Still Blowing in the Wind*, 26 PROB. & PROP., Nov.–Dec. 2012, at 56–59.

2. WHY LEASE?

Theoretically, a developer could acquire all the property rights required to develop a wind farm on a given parcel by simply purchasing the parcel and taking title under a recorded deed. However, wind energy developers that purchase *fee simple* title—the full bundle of rights that legally accompanies landownership—acquire far more rights and interests than are needed to develop a wind farm at the project site. Purchasing a fee simple interest in land for the sole purpose of developing a wind farm is akin to buying a banana split but only eating the banana and discarding the ice cream and toppings. It is usually far less expensive and more efficient for developers to secure only those property rights specifically needed for the wind farm project and to acquire them only for duration of project's lifespan. Most wind energy developers accomplish this through lease or easement agreements that are purposely tailored to transfer only those rights the project requires.

In some parts of the United States, developers primarily use lease agreements to secure wind energy development rights from landowners. In others, wind rights easement agreements are more common. Regardless of their titles, both types of agreements contain similar provisions that effectuate transfers of limited property rights in exchange for promises to pay rents and/or royalty payments. Parties have long used land leases to transfer temporary rights to exclusively possess real property. They have likewise long used easements to transfer limited access and use rights for specified durations of time. Wind energy leases and easements employ these flexible instruments to structure arrangements that allow for the development and operation of wind farms while allowing other compatible activities—such as ranching or farming—to continue at the project site.

Although *wind energy* leases share some similarities with *land* leases, they also bear several important differences. Conventional land leases usually give the lessee exclusive rights to occupy and use *all* of the leased premises throughout the lease term. By contrast, lessees under wind energy lease agreements acquire only *wind rights*—the small subset of land and airspace interests specifically required for wind energy development—and allow the landowner to retain all other interests. Accordingly, most wind energy leases allow the landowner to continue to graze animals, grow crops, have business operations, and even reside on most of the leased premises. This ability to tailor and govern the sharing of property interests between wind energy developers and landowners to suit both parties' needs makes wind energy leasing a crucially valuable part of wind energy development. By facilitating the transfer of only those interests that a wind farm project requires, wind energy leases also help developers to secure those interests at a much lower price.

PRACTICAL SKILLS EXERCISE: WIND ENERGY LEASING

Lease negotiations between wind energy developers and landowners usually involve large sums of money and a fair amount of complexity, so both parties to these negotiations often seek legal counsel to represent them in the leasing process. The following exercise offers an introductory glimpse at this process, using a simple fact pattern and sample lease agreement to introduce some of the most fundamental questions and considerations involved in wind energy leasing.

Suppose that WindWizard Development LLC, a hypothetical wind energy developer, is negotiating a wind energy lease with Sally Smith, a landowner in rural Kansas. Their hypothetical wind energy lease agreement below illustrates the general structure of wind energy leasing arrangements and highlights some of the primary issues parties address when negotiating wind lease transactions.[1] Before reading the lease agreement, skim the questions that follow immediately below it. The questions illuminate many basic wind leasing issues and emphasize how differences in the parties' approaches to resolving them can ultimately impact landowners and developers.

WIND ENERGY LEASE AGREEMENT

This Wind Energy Lease Agreement (this "Lease Agreement") is dated and effective as of March 15, 2018 (the "Effective Date"), between Sally Smith, an unmarried individual ("Owner"), and WindWizard Development, LLC, a Delaware limited liability company ("Lessee"):

1. Lease. For good and valuable consideration, the receipt of which is hereby acknowledged, Owner hereby leases to Lessee, and Lessee leases from Owner on the terms and conditions set forth below, that real property of Owner located in Windy County, Kansas, described on **Exhibit A** attached hereto (the "Property").

2. Permitted Use of the Property. The Property leased under this Lease Agreement shall be used and occupied by Lessee solely and exclusively for Wind Energy Development (as defined below), and Lessee shall have the exclusive right to use the Property for Wind Energy Development. For purposes of this Lease Agreement, "Wind Energy Development" means converting wind energy into electrical energy and collecting and transmitting the electrical energy so converted, together with any and all activities directly related thereto, including that of (a) determining the feasibility of wind energy generation on the Property, including studies of wind speed, wind direction and other meteorological data; (b) constructing, installing, using, replacing, relocating, and maintaining and operating, wind turbines, overhead and underground electric transmission lines, electric transformers, energy storage facilities, telecommunications equipment, roads, meteorological towers and wind measurement equipment, operation and maintenance buildings and yards, and related facilities and equipment (collectively, the "Windpower

[1] This simplified sample lease is for educational purposes only. It omits several important lease provisions and is therefore not suitable for use in actual wind energy leasing. Like many of the lease agreements that attorneys negotiate every day, this agreement is a conglomeration of language fragments and provisions from multiple existing wind energy leases and also contains some original drafted language tailored to its specific intended purpose.

Facilities") on the Property; and (c) undertaking any other activities, whether accomplished by Lessee or a third party authorized by Lessee to act on its behalf, that Lessee reasonably determines are necessary, useful or appropriate to accomplish any of the foregoing. Wind Energy Development shall include, without limitation, the following:

(i) Owner hereby grants unto Lessee an easement for unobstructed vehicular and pedestrian ingress to and egress from the Windpower Facilities, whether located on the Property, on adjacent property or elsewhere, over and across the Property by means of roads and lanes thereon if existing, or otherwise by such route or routes as Lessee may construct from time to time ("Access Easement"). The Access Easement shall run with the Property and shall inure to the benefit of and be binding upon Owner and Lessee and their respective transferees, successors, and assigns, and all persons claiming under them; and,

(ii) Owner hereby grants to Lessee an easement on, along, under and across the Property ("Transmission Easement") to erect, construct, reconstruct, replace, relocate, remove, maintain and use from time to time in connection with Windpower Facilities, whether located on the Property, on adjacent property or elsewhere: (a) lines of towers with such wires and cables as from time to time are suspended therefrom, and/or underground wires and cables, for the transmission of electrical energy and/or for communication purposes, and all necessary and proper foundations, footings and other appliances and fixtures for use thereof and (b) one or more substations or interconnection or switching facilities from which Lessee or others that generate energy may interconnect to a utility transmission system or the transmission system of another purchaser of electrical energy (said towers, wires, cables, substations, facilities and rights of way are herein collectively called the "Transmission Facilities"; and collectively, the Windpower Facilities and Transmission Facilities are referred to herein as the "Lessee Improvements.") The Transmission Easement shall run with the Property and shall inure to the benefit of and be binding upon Owner and Lessee and their respective transferees, successors, and assigns, and all persons claiming under them.

(iii) The term of the Access and Transmission Easements shall be the same as the term of this Lease Agreement unless sooner terminated by Lessee. The Access and Transmission Easements shall automatically terminate upon the expiration or termination of this Lease Agreement.

3. Term. The term of this Lease Agreement ("Lease Term") shall begin on the Effective Date hereof and shall end on the later of (a) five (5) years after the Effective Date or (b) twenty-five (25) years after the Commencement of Commercial Operations unless renewed or terminated as provided in this Lease Agreement. "Commencement of Commercial Operations" for purposes of this Lease Agreement shall mean the date, if

any, within five (5) years of the Effective Date hereof, on which the Lessee Improvements are constructed, tested, interconnected with the transmission provider's transmission and distribution system, staffed and operational as determined by Lessee and specified in a Notice of Commercial Operations delivered by Lessee to Owner. At the conclusion of the Lease Term, Lessee shall have a preferential right to lease the Property for Wind Energy Development for an additional term of up to twenty-five (25) years by providing written notice to Owner, at least 90 days and no more than one (1) calendar year prior to the expiration of the Lease Term. In the event Lessee provides such timely notice, Owner and Lessee shall enter into a new Wind Energy Lease Agreement evidencing the additional lease term. With respect to any additional lease term, Owner and Lessee shall execute in recordable form, and Lessee shall then record, a memorandum evidencing the additional lease term, satisfactory in form and substance to Owner and Lessee.

4. <u>Payments</u>. In consideration of the rights granted hereunder, Lessee shall pay Owner the following amounts:

4.1 <u>Initial Payment</u>. Upon execution of this Lease Agreement, Lessee shall pay to Owner an initial payment of Five Thousand and no/100 Dollars ($5,000.00).

4.2 <u>Annual Operating Payments</u>. From the Commencement of Commercial Operations until all Windpower Facilities are completely removed from the Property in accordance with <u>Section 12.2</u> ("<u>Removal Date</u>"), Lessee shall pay to Owner an annual operating payment (the "<u>Operating Payment</u>") which shall be the greater of (a) four (4) percent (4%) of Lessee's Gross Annual Revenues or (b) Five Thousand and no/100 Dollars ($5,000.00) for each megawatt ("<u>MW</u>") of installed capacity of wind turbines or other power generation facilities installed on the Property during or prior to such year. The amounts payable hereunder for a calendar year shall be prorated for each MW of installed capacity of Windpower Facilities for which the Operations Date or Removal Date occurs during such year, based on the number of days in such year following the Operations Date or prior to the Removal Date. The Operating Payments shall be paid annually and shall be due within thirty (30) days of the end of each calendar year. The Initial Payments and Operating Payments are collectively referred to herein as "<u>Rents</u>". In conjunction with each Operating Payment made to Owner, Lessee shall furnish to Owner a statement setting forth the amount of Gross Annual Revenues received by Lessee during the calendar year and calculation of the Operating Payment due Owner for such calendar year.

4.3 <u>Gross Annual Revenues</u>. For the purposes of this Lease Agreement, "<u>Gross Annual Revenues</u>" shall mean and include for the Lease Term all amounts actually received by Lessee from the sale of electricity generated on the Property, including the sale of credits for greenhouse gas reduction or the generation of renewable or alternative energy on the Property.

5. <u>Reclamation Bond</u>. At least thirty (30) days prior to the day that Lessee commences the construction of any Lessee Improvements on the Property (the "<u>Commencement of Construction</u>"), Lessee shall provide to Owner a letter of credit (issued in a form and by a financial institution reasonably acceptable to Owner), a cash deposit, a surety bond (from an issuer with a Best's Rating of not less than A), or other security reasonably acceptable to Owner (any of the foregoing hereinafter referred to as the "<u>Bond</u>") to cover Lessee's estimated removal and surface restoration costs as provided in <u>Section 12.2</u>. The initial amount of the Bond shall be the estimated cost of satisfying Lessee's removal and surface restoration obligations, as provided in <u>Section 12.2,</u> net of estimated salvage value, if any. The Bond shall remain in effect until Owner provides the issuer of the Bond written notice authorizing the expiration of the Bond based on Lessee's full compliance with its reclamation obligations under <u>Section 12.2</u>, as reasonably determined by Owner.

7. <u>Ownership of Lessee Improvements</u>. Owner shall have no ownership or other interest in the Lessee Improvements installed on the Property.

8. <u>Taxes</u>. Lessee shall be responsible for and pay all taxes, assessments, and any other fees or charges of any type, which may be levied against or assessed by reason of (i) Lessee's leasehold interest hereunder or Lessee's use of the Property, and (ii) the Lessee Improvements. Lessee shall not be responsible for the payment of any other taxes, assessments, or other fees or charges of any type associated with the Property.

9. <u>Grazing Activities and Crop Damage</u>. Lessee's use of the Property for Wind Energy Development, including, without limitation, its installation and operation of Lessee Improvements, shall not unreasonably disturb grazing or other permitted uses of the Property. Lessee shall pay Owner for any and all crop loss or destruction on the Property directly resulting from Lessee's activities on the Property within thirty (30) days of determination of the extent of any such damage. Lessee's Reclamation efforts as set forth in <u>Section 12.2</u> below shall include, without limitation, leveling, terracing, mulching and other work reasonably necessary to prevent soil erosion and to control noxious weeds and pests.

10. <u>Lessee's Representations, Warranties, and Covenants</u>. Lessee hereby represents, warrants, and covenants to Owner that:

10.1 <u>Care and Appearance</u>. Lessee shall at all times maintain the Lessee Improvements in a neat, clean and presentable condition. Lessee shall not use the Property for storage except for materials, construction equipment and vehicles directly associated with construction or maintenance of the Lessee Improvements on the Property or adjacent properties.

10.2   Fences and Gates. At Owner's request, Lessee shall repair or replace any fences, gates or cattle guards damaged or removed in connection with Lessee's activities on the Property. Fences removed from the Property, if replaced, shall be re-built by Lessee at its expense in mutually agreeable locations. Once completed, all replacement fences, gates and cattle guards shall be owned and maintained by Owner. To minimize the need for temporary fencing, Owner will cooperate with Lessee to avoid pasturing animals on or near the affected areas of the Property during Lessee's construction, maintenance or removal activities.

10.3   Requirements of Governmental Agencies. Lessee shall comply in all material respects with valid laws applicable to the Lessee Improvements. Lessee shall have the right, in its sole discretion and at its sole expense, to contest the validity or applicability to the Lessee Improvements of any law, ordinance, statute, order, regulation, property assessment or the like made by any governmental agency or entity. Lessee shall control any such contest and Owner shall cooperate with Lessee in every reasonable way in such contest, at no out of pocket expense to Owner.

10.4   Development Efforts. Upon Lessee's receipt of all necessary land use approvals, building permits, environmental impact reviews, and other governmental permits and approvals required for the financing, construction, installation, maintenance and operation of Lessee Improvements on the Property and other nearby properties, Lessee shall use commercially reasonable efforts to install all of the wind turbines on the Property as are so approved, using a reasonably diligent schedule for such installations.

11.   Owner's Representations, Warranties, and Covenants. Owner hereby represents, warrants, and covenants as follows:

11.1   Requirements of Governmental Agencies. Owner shall assist and fully cooperate with Lessee, at no out-of-pocket cost or expense to Owner, in complying with or obtaining any land use permits and approvals, building permits, environmental impact reviews or any other approvals required for the financing, construction, installation, replacement, relocation, maintenance, operation or removal of Lessee Improvements, including execution of applications for such approvals.

11.2   Exclusivity. Owner agrees that Lessee shall have the exclusive right to engage in Wind Energy Development on the Property.

11.3   No Interference; Multiple Use of the Property. Owner's activities and any grant of rights to the Property Owner makes to any person or entity subsequent to the Effective Date shall not unreasonably interfere with: Lessee's construction, installation, maintenance, or operation of the Lessee Improvements, whether located on the Property or adjacent properties; Lessee's access over the Property to such Lessee Improvements; or the undertaking of any other activities permitted by this Lease Agreement. Without limiting the generality of the foregoing, Owner shall not unreasonably interfere with the wind speed or wind direction over the Property, whether by placing wind turbines, planting trees, constructing buildings or other structures, or by engaging in any other activity on the Property that might cause a decrease in the output or efficiency of the Windpower Facilities. No transfer of mineral ownership, mineral rights, or the creation of any agency or representative relationship whatsoever, is intended or granted to Lessee by or through this Lease Agreement. This Lease Agreement is subject to any and all existing mineral leases, special use leases, temporary use permits, easements or other rights granted by Owner, which now cover some or all of the Property leased by Lessee for Wind Energy Development. For purposes of this Section, "minerals" means coal, oil, gas, or other minerals of any kind.

12. Default and Reclamation.

12.1 Events of Default. The following events shall be deemed to be events of default by Lessee under this Lease Agreement:

(a) Lessee shall fail to pay any amount payable under this Lease Agreement within thirty (30) days of when due; and

(b) Lessee shall fail to comply with any other term, provision or covenant of this Lease Agreement within sixty (60) days after notice from Owner to Lessee, specifying Lessee's failure to comply; provided, however, that if the nature of Lessee's obligation is of such a nature that it cannot reasonably be cured within such 60-day period, Lessee shall not be deemed to be in default so long as Lessee commences curing such failure within such 60-day period and diligently prosecutes the same to completion.

12.2 Reclamation. Upon the expiration or termination of this Lease Agreement, Lessee shall, within a period of 12 months (such period of removal, the "Removal Period") satisfactorily accomplish each of the following items (collectively, "Reclamation"):

(a) removal from the Property of all above-ground and below-ground Lessee Improvements to a depth of not less than two (2) feet below the surface grade, all in a manner which minimizes injury to the Property;

(b) restoration of the Property disturbed by Lessee to a condition reasonably similar to its original condition.

If Lessee fails to remove from the Property the Lessee Improvements, equipment, or any other personal property, within the Removal Period, Owner may do so, in which case Lessee shall reimburse Owner for all reasonable costs of removal and restoration incurred by Owner. Lessee agrees and acknowledges that in the event it fails to remove the Lessee

Improvements, equipment or any other personal property within the Removal Period, then Lessee shall forfeit ownership of the Lessee Improvements, equipment, or any other personal property and shall not be entitled to any portion of the proceeds Owner may realize from the sale of the Lessee Improvements, equipment, or any other personal property.

13. Miscellaneous.

13.1   Force Majeure. If performance of any obligation under this Lease Agreement is prevented or substantially restricted or interfered with by reason of an event of "Force Majeure" (defined below), the affected party, upon giving notice to the other party, shall be excused from such performance to the extent of and for the duration of such prevention, restriction or interference. The affected party shall use reasonable efforts to avoid or remove such causes of nonperformance and shall immediately continue performance hereunder whenever such causes are removed. "Force Majeure" means fire, earthquake, flood, or other casualty or accident; war, civil strife or other violence; any law, order, proclamation, regulation, ordinance, action, demand or requirement of any governmental agency or utility; or any other act or condition beyond the reasonable control of a party hereto.

13.2   Successors and Assigns. This Lease Agreement shall inure to the benefit of and be binding upon Owner and Lessee and their respective heirs, transferees, successors and assigns.

13.3   Memorandum of Lease. Owner and Lessee shall execute in recordable form, and Lessee shall then record a memorandum of this Lease Agreement satisfactory in form and substance to Lessee and Owner.

13.4   Confidentiality. Owner shall not disclose to others (except Owner's family, legal counsel, prospective mortgagees, assignees, and financial advisors who recognize and agree to preserve and maintain the confidentiality of such information) the terms of this agreement and information about Lessee's methods, power production, or availability of Windpower Facilities, or the material terms of this Lease Agreement unless the information is already in the public domain. Owner also agrees not to use such information for Owner's own benefit or permit its use by others for their benefit or to the detriment of Lessee.

13.5   Entire Agreement/Amendments. This agreement constitutes the entire agreement between Owner and Lessee respecting its subject matter and replaces and supersedes any prior agreements. Any agreement, understanding or representation respecting the subject matter of this agreement not expressly set forth in this agreement or a later writing signed by both parties, is null and void. This Lease Agreement shall not be modified or amended except in a writing signed by the parties or their successors in interest.

IN WITNESS WHEREOF, Owner and Lessee, acting through their duly authorized representatives, have executed this Lease Agreement on this day of March, 2018, with the intent that it be effective as of the Effective Date, and certify that they have read, understand and agree to the terms and conditions of this Lease Agreement.

"Owner"

Sally Smith, an unmarried individual

_____

"Lessee"

WINDWIZARD DEVELOPMENT, LLC,

A Delaware limited liability company

By: _____

Name: **Jane Johnson**

Its: **Manager**

EXHIBIT A

Legal Description of Owner's Property

The East Half of the Northwest quarter of the Northeast Quarter of Section 12, Township 40 North, Range 7 East, of the Fifth Principal Meridian, Windy County, Kansas.

_____

QUESTIONS

1.   If the Commencement of Commercial Operations under the lease above is August of 2020, on what date will the original Lease Term expire (assuming no renewals or extensions)?

2.   Suppose that, on April 20, 2018, an archeologist doing due diligence for WindWizard's wind energy project discovers and ancient burial ground on Sally's property. Based on this finding, WindWizard concludes that a wind energy project will not be feasible on Sally's land. What portion, if any, of the $5,000 payment that WindWizard paid to Sally on March 15 must Sally return to the company?

3.   Suppose instead that WindWizard wants to install large ground-mounted arrays of photovoltaic solar panels near the base of some of its turbines. According to the company, these panels will allow the project to continue generating electricity when the wind is not blowing and will thereby make it more profitable. Sally is concerned that the large solar arrays will take up too much of her wheat fields and further reduce her farm's overall wheat production. WindWizard insists it will compensate Sally for crop losses caused by the panels, but Sally still is opposed to them. Is Sally obligated under the Lease Agreement to allow WindWizard to install the solar panel arrays? Why or why not?

4.   Suppose instead that it is 2021, and WindWizard has just constructed a fairly large industrial building on Sally's property. The building, which has clean white aluminum siding and an aluminum roof, is situated along the area's main public road just a few hundred yards from Sally's house. Sally thinks the building is ugly and wants WindWizard to tear it down and restore her wheat field in the area. WindWizard, which had just accomplished its "Commencement of Commercial Operations" a few months earlier, insists it needs the building to house the wind farm's maintenance equipment and that the company chose the building site based on its road access and centralized location within the wind farm. Is WindWizard legally entitled under the Lease Agreement to keep the building as-is?

5.   Suppose instead that the Commencement of Commercial Operations was in October 1, 2020, and that WindWizard ultimately installed wind turbines with a total of 20 MW of electric generating capacity on Sally's land. WindWizard's Gross Annual Revenues (as defined in the lease) for the year 2022 were $2 million. What is the amount of the annual Operation Payment due to Sally for 2022? By what date is the payment due to Sally?

6.   What is the purpose of the Reclamation Bond required under Section 5 of the Lease?

7.   Assume again that Commencement of Commercial Operations was in October of 2020. In early 2021, Sally learned that the Windy County's tax assessor had reassessed the value of her property to be double that of the previous year so her property tax bill had also doubled. Furious at this discovery, Sally called the County Assessor, who told her the entire property tax increase was attributable to WindWizard's installation of valuable wind turbines on her land. Sally doesn't want to have to cover this new property tax increase. How much, if any, of the increase can Sally require WindWizard to pay?

8.   Suppose instead that, a few weeks after Sally executed the Lease Agreement, WindWizard informed her that an environmental consulting company would be coming onto the land in connection with its state-mandated environmental impact review for the project. Sally immediately protested and vehemently refused to allow the environmental consultants onto her land. She explained to WindWizard that she had paid hefty fines to the state Department of Health and Environment for improper pesticide spraying and disposal on her land after a surprise inspection a few years earlier and didn't want to something like that to happen again. Is she contractually obligated under the Lease Agreement to allow the consultants onto her land to do the inspections? Why or why not? Cite specific language in the Lease Agreement to support your conclusion.

9.   Suppose instead that it is June of 2023 and that WindWizard has not installed any turbines on Sally's leased property. When Sally expresses frustration that no power is being produced yet on the property, so she was not yet entitled to any annual rent payments, WindWizard encourages her to be patient a bit longer and promises the company will begin installing turbines

within a few weeks. Meanwhile, a competing wind energy developer, WindCo, has just offered a different wind energy lease to Sally for the same land. This new lease features a large $20,000 up-front signing bonus and rent payment terms that are far more favorable to her than those set forth in the WindWizard lease. Is Sally legally entitled to execute WindCo's new lease and tell WindWizard to vacate her property immediately? Why or why not? Cite specific language in the Lease Agreement to support your conclusion.

10. Shortly after executing the Lease Agreement with WindWizard, Sally is having breakfast at a local café when she runs into her neighbor, Tom. When Tom asks whether Sally is planning to sign a wind energy lease with WindWizard, Sally replies that she had already signed one. Tom then asks Sally what percentage of Gross Annual Revenues she was entitled to under her lease, and Sally replied "They're giving me four percent. Not too bad, if you ask me." Tom is angry at this news, saying he is about to sign his own lease with WindWizard, and that they are only offering him three percent. He immediately calls WindWizard and demands he also receive four percent of revenues. Under the terms of her WindWizard Lease Agreement, could Sally potentially be held liable to WindWizard for mentioning this information to Tom? Why or why not?

C. TITLE AND SURVEY REVIEW FOR WIND ENERGY PROJECTS

Although securing wind rights through leases or easements is unquestionably a crucial step in the wind energy development process, it does not guarantee that a developer has all the real property interests required to complete the project. For example, some of the land leased for a wind energy project may be burdened by negative covenants granted years ago that prohibit the construction of tall objects on the site. Some parcels within the leased project site may be subject to easements in favor of a pipeline company that plans to eventually install an underground pipeline in the area. Or, the supposed landowners who signed the wind energy lease may not have clear title to the land because of an inheritance dispute involving a distant relative. In any of these scenarios, third parties with interests or potential interests in the project site could threaten the project's success and ultimately inflict large financial losses on the developer and any project lenders or investors.

Fortunately, title insurance companies can often help to the mitigate title-related risks associated with wind energy development projects. Title insurance policies guarantee the validity and quality of title to specific real estate assets. If a title insurance company issues a policy covering a parcel of land and a third party later asserts a claim challenging the validity or scope of the policyholder's title, the insurer is contractually obligated to bear all reasonable and necessary costs of defending against the challenge. Moreover, if a court ultimately holds that the policyholder's rights in the insured parcel are less than what was guaranteed on the title insurance policy, the insurer must pay any damages resulting from the discrepancy. Title insurance policies are usually issued simultaneously to both wind energy developers and their lenders on the closing date of the developer's construction loan.

Lawyers are often instrumental in helping to identify and resolve title-related issues associated with large real estate development projects, including wind farm projects. Months before the anticipated closing date of the financing for a wind energy development project, wind energy developers and their lenders typically contact a title insurance company operating within the county and order preliminary title work covering the specific parcels involved. Acting on the request, the title insurer retrieves copies of all available documents recorded at the county recorder's office relating to those specific parcels. Based upon the insurer's review of these *supporting documents*, the title insurer then produces the *title commitment*—a non-binding document that describes in detail what the title insurer determines to be the legal status of title to the land. The title commitment identifies the vested owner(s) of the property, discloses any known defects or clouds on title, and lists all liens, easements, covenants, leases, and other encumbrances on title. Once the title insurer has prepared the title commitment, the commitment document itself and all supporting documents are delivered to the developer and lender for review.

In addition to ordering a title insurance commitment, wind energy developers and their lenders almost always engage a land surveyor to produce a land title *survey* of the project site. As a condition to closing the development loan, lenders ordinarily require that this survey conform to specific standards set forth by the American Land Title Association (ALTA) and the National Society of Professional Surveyors (NSPS). An ALTA/NSPS land title survey is a large map showing in meticulous detail the locations of the parcels involved and their boundaries, the locations of any buildings or other improvements on the land, the locations of any easement areas affecting the land, and numerous other specifics that can impact whether the proposed wind energy project at the site is legally and practically feasible. Per ALTA/NSPS requirements, the survey ties closely to the title insurance commitment and shows the specific locations of all easements and other recorded physical encumbrances on the land disclosed on the commitment.

Lawyers usually assist wind energy developers and their lenders in reviewing the title commitment and the survey, carefully examining both in search of encumbrances or other matters that might impede or create risks for the project. Although the principles and practices described in the following excerpt are relevant in almost any type of commercial real estate transaction, they are equally applicable in the title review process for wind energy financing and development.

A PRACTICAL GUIDE TO TITLE REVIEW (WITH FORM)

Shannon J. Skinner

Excerpted from PRAC. REAL EST. LAW., July 2005, at 35–43

Few real estate transactions are closed without a title insurance policy. In most real estate transactions, at least one party's satisfaction with the state of title is a key condition to the closing. Indeed, some transactions close only because of the insurer's agreement to provide coverage for a title problem that otherwise would cause the transaction to collapse. But the title insurance policy does not magically appear at closing. Much of a real estate lawyer's effort in closing the transaction is directed to reviewing the state of title, resolving issues with the title, determining which title risks are acceptable to the client, and deciding what types of affirmative coverage are appropriate for the client and the transaction. Thus, competent review of the preliminary title evidence and resulting policy is an essential skill for the real estate lawyer. . . .

TITLE EVIDENCE

The first step in reviewing title is to determine the type of title evidence under scrutiny. Preferred for most sophisticated real estate transactions is a preliminary commitment for title insurance prepared using the American Land Title Association ("ALTA") form. The preliminary commitment is not a report on the status of title but rather is a contract in which the insurer agrees to issue a policy subject to the conditions, exceptions, and exclusions shown in the commitment. Commitments are valid for a certain period of time (generally six months) and must be extended if necessary. They are organized in much the same fashion as title policies.

. . . .

SCHEDULE A MATTERS

The first matters to review in a preliminary commitment are those that will appear in Schedule A of the title policy. These are generally the first matters shown in the commitment and should be noted on the title review memorandum. These include:

- Date;
- Type of policy;
- Policy amount;
- Names;
- Quality of estate; and
- Legal description.

Date

The date of the commitment is important—how old is the information? Could a real estate tax payment have become delinquent since the commitment date? Has the commitment expired? Should it be updated?

Type of Policy

The commitment will also show the type of policy the insurer is committed to issue. Most sophisticated parties in real estate transactions require a policy issued on an ALTA form if available in the jurisdiction. The question usually focuses on which ALTA form to use.

. . . .

Policy Amount

The amount of the proposed policy and premium are also shown in the commitment. . . . The face amount of the policy is a limit on the amount that the insurer is obligated to pay (together with defense costs). In addition, damages are also capped by the value of the property (without the alleged defect) and the loan amount plus interest (for lender's policies), so the insured does not benefit from either over- or underinsuring its interest.

. . . .

Names

It is surprising how often the name of the proposed insured and the name of the vested title holder do not match the draft legal documents. For example, the purchaser's lawyer may learn that the party that signed the purchase and sale agreement is not fully vested in title (perhaps title is vested in a partnership or is jointly held with a spouse), which may raise questions about the enforceability of the agreement. The lender's lawyer may learn that the draft loan documents describe a borrower who is not in title (perhaps a name change or inter-entity transfer has occurred, or a partner never transferred title into the partnership). Resolving any discrepancies here is important. The answer may be as simple as adding a "who took title as" note to the vesting to describe name changes resulting from marriage or merger, or as difficult as requiring a deed to transfer title to the correct entity or re-underwriting a loan for the vested entity.

Quality of Estate

A quick glance at the type of estate is in order to be sure that the type of estate is as expected. Of course, fee simple estates are most common, but lesser estates, such as a vendee's interest in a land sale contract, a leasehold estate or an easement, will be shown here if applicable. More than one type of estate will also be shown if different parcels are vested differently.

Legal Description

The final important item in the Schedule A matters is the legal description. It may be presented in metes and bounds, platted lots, or sections. A critical part of reviewing the title is determining that the legal description is identical to that shown on the survey:

- In tracing a metes and bounds description around the survey back to the point of beginning, are there differences between the vested legal description (usually the one selected by the insurer from the last deed) and the on the ground measurements? How are these discrepancies explained?

. . . .

Easements

The legal description is also the place to show appurtenant easements that are being insured. By describing an easement estate in the Schedule A description of the "Land," e.g., "together with an easement for ingress and egress created by document recorded under no. xxxxx," the policy insures that the insured holds a valid easement (subject to the terms and conditions of the easement and any prior encumbrances on the easement, all of which will be shown in the Schedule B exceptions).

SCHEDULE B MATTERS

Schedule B of the title policy contains the general exceptions from coverage, the special exceptions, and the endorsements.

General Exceptions

The general exceptions are the standard off-record exceptions that apply to all properties rather than those recorded against the specific property. The first four general exceptions are fairly standard nationally and are:

- Exceptions for rights of parties in possession;
- Encroachments, boundary, and other matters that an accurate survey would disclose;
- Easements not shown by the public records; and
- Construction and worker's compensation liens.

The remaining general exceptions vary somewhat by jurisdiction . . . Whether some, none, or all of the general exceptions remain in the title policy depends on the type of policy requested.

Extended Policies

ALTA policies come in standard and extended forms. A policy becomes "extended" by removing some or all of the general exceptions. A lender's policy is almost always extended coverage and usually all of the general exceptions are removed from the lender's policy. . . .

Special Exceptions

The next Schedule B-I section contains the special exceptions affecting the particular property described in the commitment. This section contains:

- Easements;
- Covenants;
- Conditions;
- Restrictions;
- Encumbrances;
- Court actions;
- Taxes; and
- Matters relating to the parties (such as issues relating to partnership agreements, authority questions and marital status).

The title reviewer must examine each of the recorded documents corresponding to a special exception and briefly describe the exceptions in the title review memorandum. Each easement or other item that can be located on the survey must be so located. In general, the title reviewer should be looking for exceptions that may cause a problem for the client. . . . These include matters that:

- Interfere with the improvements (such as easements that run under buildings or mineral reservations that allow surface excavation);
- Interfere with the use of the property (such as covenants requiring residential use when the property is commercial); or
- Impose unusual costs on the owner (such as large governmental or owners' association assessments or mitigation covenants).

. . . .

Endorsements

Depending on the jurisdiction, endorsements may be available to expand or tailor coverage in the title policy. These endorsements may apply generally or be tailored to address an issue for the specific property. The available endorsements may number as few as a handful in states where the title insurance industry is heavily regulated or over 100 in states following the California model. In some states, special endorsements can be written if a form endorsement does not cover the issue. In others, substantive changes to endorsement forms must be approved by the state insurance commissioner.

. . . .

Some Common Endorsements

The following is a partial list of some endorsements to be considered, if available in the jurisdiction, for an extended coverage policy on a commercial property:

- *Comprehensive*—provides lender with assurances about the status of covenants, conditions, restrictions, and encroachments;

- *Easements*—provides insurance to lender, and sometimes owner, about the effect of the exercise of easement rights or encroachments onto easements;

- *Covenants, reverters*—provides owner and lender with assurances about the effects of violations of covenants or deed reverters;

- *Minerals*—insures owner and lender against damage to improvements resulting from the exercise of minerals reservation;

. . . .

- *Survey*—insures owner and lender that the land described on Schedule A of policy is same land as shown on a particular survey;

- *Contiguity*—insures owner and lender that certain parcels of land described in Schedule A are contiguous with one another. . .

- *Zoning and subdivision*—insure owner and lender about current zoning and permitted uses of property and status of legal description as not violating subdivision laws;

. . . .

Due Diligence Review

Obtaining a title insurance policy is not a guaranty that all matters addressed in the policy have in fact been resolved to all parties' satisfaction. It means that the insured and the insurer have agreed on a satisfactory contract of indemnity for the matters covered by the policy. This does not necessarily substitute for other due diligence, including examining zoning and other land use matters, physically inspecting the property, talking with neighboring landowners and so on. Obtaining extended coverage, even if available without a survey (as it sometimes is for lenders on a risk-underwritten basis) most certainly does not eliminate the need for careful review of a complete and current survey of the property.

THE POLICY

After all of the hard work in reviewing the title commitment and survey and resolving outstanding issues, the time following closing is not the time to rest on one's laurels. Mark the calendar to be sure that the policy is timely delivered. And, once delivered, carefully proofread the policy to be sure that it complies with the insured's instructions for policy issuance. Was the correct policy jacket attached? Were all requested endorsements included? Were all exceptions deleted that should have been and no new ones shown? If any corrections need to be made, promptly return the policy with instructions on the changes and calendar again the date by which the corrected policy should be returned. . .

CONCLUSION

The goal of the title review process is to examine the state of title as shown on the commitment, and, together with the client, decide on the appropriate coverages and acceptable exceptions to coverage. Title review is a critical part of the due diligence work necessary to help a lender or owner decide to acquire an interest in a particular piece of property. Lawyers and their paralegals are well suited to reviewing and resolving title issues and should view this process as a joint project in which the partners are the client, title officer, surveyor, and the other party and its counsel. Producing a clear written record of the title review in a memorandum form assists with this process. It is not unusual for each project to teach something new about title and title insurance issues; finding this education fun and challenging is what sets "dirt" lawyers apart.

PRACTICAL SKILLS EXERCISE: TITLE REVIEW FOR WIND ENERGY DEVELOPMENT

Suppose your client, WindWizard Development, LLC ("WindWizard"), is a wind energy developer that has negotiated with a landowner, Sally Smith, to lease her rural land and install wind turbines and related improvements on the land as part of a large wind energy project. On behalf of WindWizard, your law firm recently ordered a Commitment for Title Insurance from West-Central Title Insurance Company in connection with this wind energy project. The document below is a simplified, fictional Commitment for Title Insurance associated with Sally's land resembling the sort of title commitment a client might receive in such circumstances.[2]

---

[2]   Much of the language found in this simplified title insurance commitment was adapted (with changes) from various actual title insurance commitments, including a title insurance

A copy of the commitment is often also provided to a wind energy developer's proposed lender, who is considering whether to extend a large loan to the developer to help finance the project's construction. Suppose further you've ordered your client an ALTA/NSPS survey of the parcel—a large detailed map depicting the parcel, its boundaries, and various easements and other encumbrances—but the survey is not yet available for review. WindWizard has informed you that it hopes to close on its construction financing arrangement with BigBank by the end of the summer so that construction can begin in the early fall.

Before reading the sample title commitment below, skim through the questions that follow it. Reviewing this fictional title commitment and considering its accompanying provides a small sampling of the type of analysis involved in title and survey review, which is typically an integral part of the due diligence work real estate and finance lawyers do in connection with wind energy development projects.

---

commitment form produced by First American Title Insurance Company, a major title insurer. First American's complete 2006 form is available at http://www.firstam.com/assets/commercial/policy-jackets/alta-2006-commitment.pdf. This hypothetical document is intended for educational purposes only and is not suitable for practical use.

West-Central Title Insurance Company

123 Main St.

Anytown, KS 54321

COMMITMENT FOR TITLE INSURANCE

West-Central Title Company (the "Company"), for a valuable consideration, hereby commits to issue its policy or policies of title insurance, as identified in Schedule A, in favor of the Proposed Insured named in Schedule A, as owner or mortgagee of the estate or interest in the land described or referred to in Schedule A, upon payment of the all premiums and charges and compliance with the Requirements; all subject to the provisions of Schedules A and B and to the Conditions of this Commitment. This Commitment shall be effective only when the amount of the policy or policies committed for have been inserted in Schedule A by the Company. All liability and obligation under this Commitment shall cease and terminate six (6) months after the Effective Date or when the policy or policies committed for shall issue, whichever first occurs, provided that the failure to issue the policy or policies is not the fault of the Company.

IN WITNESS WHEREOF, West-Central Title Insurance Company has caused its duly authorized corporate officer to execute this Commitment on the date shown in Schedule A.

/s/ Jane Johnson

Jane Johnson
President

West-Central Title Insurance Company
COMMITMENT FOR TITLE INSURANCE
SCHEDULE A

1. Commitment Date: April 5, 2018

    Issue Date: _____

2. Policy (or Policies) to be issued:

    (a) ALTA LEASEHOLD OWNER'S POLICY — (6–17–06)

    Proposed Insured: **WindWizard Development, LLC, a Delaware limited liability company**

    (b) ALTA LOAN POLICY — (6–17–06)

    Proposed Insured: **BigBank Corporation, a New York Corporation**

    POLICY AMOUNT: _____

3. Fee simple interest in the land descried in this Commitment is owned, at the Commitment Date, by

    Sally Smith, an unmarried individual

4. The land referred to in this Commitment (the "Land) is described as follows:

    The East Half of the Northwest quarter of the Northeast Quarter of Section 12, Township 40 North, Range 7 East, of the Fifth Principal Meridian, Windy County, Kansas.

5. The Leasehold Owner's Policy to be issued will insure any and all leasehold estate interests in favor of WindWizard Development, LLC, conveyed under that Wind Energy Lease executed by Sally Smith and WindWizard Development, LLC, on April 2, 2018 (the "Leasehold"), a Memorandum of which was recorded under Recording No. 329402 on April 3, 2018, in the Windy County land title records (the "Public Records"). The ALTA Loan Policy to be issued will insure a mortgage interest in the Leasehold.

West-Central Title Insurance Company

COMMITMENT FOR TITLE INSURANCE

SCHEDULE B — SECTION I

REQUIREMENTS

Effective Date: April 5, 2018

The following requirements must be met:

(a) Pay the agreed amounts for the interest in the land and/or according to the mortgage to be insured.

(b) Pay us the premium, fees, and charges for the policy.

(c) Documents satisfactory to us creating the interest in the land and/or the mortgage to be insured must be signed, delivered and recorded. . . .

West-Central Title Insurance Company
COMMITMENT FOR TITLE INSURANCE
SCHEDULE B — SECTION II
REQUIREMENTS

Effective Date: April 5, 2018

Schedule B of this policy or policies to be issued will contain exceptions to the following matters unless the same are disposed to the satisfaction of the West-Central Title Company (the "Company"):

> Defects, liens, encumbrances, adverse claims, or other matters, if any, created or first appearing in the Public Records or attaching subsequent to the Effective Date hereof but prior to the date the proposed insured acquires, for value, of record the estate or interest or mortgage thereon covered by this Commitment.

STANDARD EXCEPTIONS:

1. Rights or claims of parties in possession not shown by the Public Records.

2. Easements or claims of easements, not shown by the Public Records.

3. Any encroachment, encumbrance, violation, or adverse circumstance affecting the Leasehold that would be disclosed by an accurate and complete land survey of the Land.

4. Any lien or right to a lien, for services, labor, or material heretofore or hereafter furnished, imposed by law and not shown by the Public Records.

5. Taxes or special assessments which are not shown as existing liens by the Public Records.

SPECIAL EXCEPTIONS:

1. **General taxes for the year 2018 and thereafter.**

2. **Mortgage made by Sally Smith, an individual, in favor of USA Bank, a Delaware corporation, dated October 3, 2011, and recorded under Recording No. 50218465 on October 5, 2011, in the Records of Windy County, Kansas, to secure a loan in the original amount of $225,000.**

3. **Water line easement granted to Public Water Supply District No. 15 by instrument recorded March 11, 1996, in Book 493, Page 223, Records of Windy County, Kansas.**

4. Electric line easement granted to Kansas Power and Light Company by instrument recorded July 11, 2004, under Recording No. 45935959, Records of Windy County, Kansas.

5. Oil & Gas Lease in favor of DeepOil Corporation evidenced by that Memorandum of Lease recorded April 30, 2010, under Recording No. 48635718, Records of Windy County, Kansas.

6. Pipeline easement granted to Midwest Pipeline Company, a Kansas corporation, by instrument recorded February, 2014, under Recording No. 54863257, Records of Windy County, Kansas.

7. Restrictive Covenant in favor of Conserve Kansas, a nonprofit corporation, recorded May 12, 2016, under Recording No. 61589524, Records of Windy County Kansas.

8. Right-of-way easement granted to AgriCorn, LLC, a Kansas limited liability company, recorded January 20, 2017, under Recording No. 63259724, Records of Windy County, Kansas.

--- END ---

QUESTIONS

1.   Do the terms of this commitment ever terminate? If so, when? Why do you think the document has a termination date?

2.   Is this a commitment for a "leasehold owner's" policy or for a "loan" policy of title insurance, or for both? What are some important differences between the real property interests these two policy types insure?

3.   There are two "proposed insured" parties under this policy—who are they? Most insurance policies (e.g., health insurance, fire insurance, etc.) allow only one insured party on a policy. Why do you think *multiple* parties can have coverage under the same title insurance policy?

4.   Who holds a "fee simple interest" in the property covered by the policy? Why does that differ from the names of the "proposed insured" parties? What does this suggest about the type of proposed transaction giving rise to title insurance commitment?

5.   Based on the information in the title insurance commitment, has WindWizard already entered into its wind energy lease with Sally Smith? If so, when did the party execute the lease?

6.   What type of title-related risk is the title insurance company declining to cover by including the Schedule B-II Standard Exception to coverage for "rights or claims of parties in possession not shown by the Public Records?" If that there were no title endorsements available to protect WindWizard against this risk, what additional due diligence activities would you recommend that the client engage in to ensure that this risk didn't threaten the project?

7.   Which of the Standard Exceptions in Schedule B-II should the title insurance company be willing to remove upon satisfactory review of an ALTA/NSPS land title survey of the Land? Why?

8.   Suppose that you represented BigBank Corporation, WindWizard's lead lender for the project. What are some risks to the project lenders because of the existence of a mortgage on Sally's property, as disclosed in Special Exception 2 on Schedule B-II? Describe the contractual terms of an agreement USA Bank (the mortgage holder) could execute and record against title that would mitigate this risk.

9.   Which Special Exceptions disclosed on Schedule B-II are likely to be identifiable on a complete ALTA/NSPS land title survey? How might identifying them on the survey map assist WindWizard and its lenders in evaluating whether they pose significant risks to the proposed wind energy project?

10.   Lawyers typically review all "supporting documents" for the Special Exceptions listed on Schedule B-II of the title commitment. These supporting

documents are full copies of the actual recorded easements, mortgages, covenants, and other instruments recorded against title. How might reviewing the supporting document accompanying Special Exception 7 above (the Restrictive Covenant) help WindWizard and its lawyers and lenders to evaluate the risk associated with that title exception?

NOTES

1.   *Consolidating Title Commitments.* Most utility-scale wind energy projects are far more complex than the simplified hypothetical project described above. Many such projects involve large acreages of land leased from several different landowners, so it is not uncommon for lawyers representing developers on these projects to review a dozen or more separate title insurance commitments covering particular portions of the project early in the development process. As the project financing closing approaches, title insurers often consolidate these numerous separate title commitments into a single document. Usually, just one owner's policy and one lender's policy are issued at the closing.

2.   *Multiple Phases and Multiple Lenders.* The total loan amounts sought in connection with utility-scale wind energy projects often reach well into the hundreds of millions of dollars, so stakeholders have developed practices to help them accomplish these enormous financings in more manageable sizes. One common strategy is to divide the large energy project into multiple phases and plan for separate financing closings for each different phase of the project. Lenders often prefer this approach because it enables them to see how well the borrower is performing and how well the project is coming along before agreeing to subsequent financing closings at each phase of the project.

Another common practice is for a group of lenders, rather than a single lender, to lend the total loan amount. For example, if the Phase I financing for a hypothetical wind energy project involves a requested loan amount of $200 million, one "lead" lender and that lender's council might be designated to represent the interests of a larger group of lenders in the financing negotiation. That lead lender might only actually lend $80 million of the total $200 million loan amount but still has a strong incentive to do thorough due diligence to ensure that the project is practically feasible and financially viable before giving final loan approval. The other lenders within the lender group, who participate in the financing by lending smaller amounts such as $30 million or $40 million, are often willing to rely on the lead lender's work and expertise to adequately protect their interests by ensuring that the project is feasible since the interests of all project lenders are closely aligned. This practice of involving multiple lenders in a single financing closing often benefits wind energy developers by limiting each lender's overall financial exposure and thereby enabling lenders to extend credit at a lower total cost.

3. *Extended Coverage Policies and Endorsements*. Wind energy developers and their lenders typically do not rely solely on basic title insurance coverage to insure against the title-related risks associated with major energy projects. Most obtain "extended coverage" title insurance policies, which protect policyholders from additional title risks by removing all or nearly all of the policy's "standard exceptions" to coverage and by providing some other additional protections. Title insurance companies are usually unwilling to issue these extended policies without first reviewing a certified ALTA/NSPS survey of the subject property, which is another reason that such surveys are typically an indispensable requirement for wind farm development loans.

As described in the excerpt above, developers and their lenders also ordinarily purchase "endorsements" to further supplement their title insurance coverage. Endorsements are provisions added to a title insurance policy that provide specific types of supplemental coverage. The ALTA has issued numerous boilerplate or "form" endorsements for title insurers to use that are available in most states. For example, developer and their lenders commonly obtain an ALTA "Contiguity—Multiple Parcels" Endorsement (Endorsement 19–06) in connection with energy projects involving multiple adjacent parcels. Among other things, this endorsement ensures the policy holder from any losses resulting because of a failure of all of the parcels in the project to be contiguous to each other. *See* FIRST AM. TITLE INS. CO., ENDORSEMENT GUIDE: A BRIEF OVERVIEW OF ALTA TITLE INSURANCE ENDORSEMENTS (2016), http://www.firstam.com/assets/commercial/endorse ment-guide/ncs-endorsement-guide.pdf.

In 2012, the ALTA released several new endorsements for wind energy projects that are specially tailored for use in connection with these projects. These new endorsements are even designed to vary based on whether the project's land is owned in fee simple, is leased under a wind energy lease, or is subject to a wind energy easement. These flexible new endorsements are already helping to simplify the title insurance process associated with wind energy projects. For more detailed information on title insurance issues for wind energy development and on these new energy-specific endorsements, see Kathleen Law, A PRACTITIONER'S GUIDE TO REAL ESTATE AND WIND ENERGY PROJECT DEVELOPMENT 75–92 (2015).

D. PERMITTING FOR WIND ENERGY DEVELOPMENT

Another critical task in the development of a utility-scale wind energy project is that of securing all required federal, state, and local government permits and other approvals. Commercial wind turbines are massive industrial devices. Their enormous rotors spin hundreds of feet above the ground. A typical wind farm consists of dozens or even hundreds of turbines dotting several square miles of land. Few types of rural land development are as conspicuous on the horizon as wind energy projects, and few have footprints spanning such vast areas. Given the potential impacts of wind farms on communities and ecosystems, it is hardly surprising that laws imposed at all major levels of government seek to regulate various aspects of wind energy development.

Many of the laws and regulations implicated in the permitting process for large wind farms are rooted in statutes that garner significant coverage in environmental law courses and casebooks. Environmental law is a distinct body of legal rules and concepts that is too voluminous and complex to cover thoroughly in this book. Rather than attempting to comprehensively cover these topics, the following materials provide a brief introduction to them and examples of how a few of them relate specifically to the development of wind farms.

1.   FEDERAL PERMITTING REQUIREMENTS

Developing a large wind energy project usually requires numerous permits and approvals from federal government agencies. For instance, under the Clean Water Act (CWA), developers of large-scale development projects such as wind farms often must submit a *Pre-Construction Notification* (PCN) to the Army Corps of Engineers (ACE) prior to the commencement of construction. The PCN must disclose a wide array of information about the project, including its potential impacts on wetlands, critical wildlife habitats, and cultural or historic resources. Ideally for developers, the ACE will respond to a PCN by issuing a *Nationwide Permit* (NWP) for the project. However, if the ACE determines that a project's potential impacts are too great for that streamlined approval approach, it can require the developer to go through a more time-consuming and individualized permit process.

Since most wind energy projects also disturb more than one acre of land, the CWA usually also requires that developers obtain a *National Pollutant Discharge Elimination System* (NPDES) permit prior to construction. Although many states now have authority to issue NPDES permits on their own, the authority associated with these permits originates at the federal level and the EPA still reviews NPDES permit applications and issues NPDES permits in a handful of jurisdictions. NPDES permit applicants usually must submit a *Notice of Intent* (NOI) containing information about the timing and location of construction of their proposed project and potential impacts on or near the project site. The NOI also generally includes a description of the developer's *Stormwater Pollution Prevention Plan* (SWPPP), which explains how the applicant intends to minimize stormwater drainage pollution during and after project construction.

Because most modern commercial wind turbines are upwards of 350 feet tall, wind farm developers also must formally notify the Federal Aviation Administration (FAA) long before commencing construction.

Under 14 C.F.R. § 77.9, citizens generally must submit a *Notice of Proposed Construction or Alteration* to the FAA at least 45 days before building or filing a construction permit to build any structure taller than 200 feet (or lower if the site is near an airport). The FAA then reviews the permit application to determine whether the proposed structure would pose a hazard to aviation. Developers who submit these notices hope to promptly receive a *Determination of No Hazard to Air Navigation* from the FAA effectively giving the green light for the wind farm project to proceed. If the developer instead receives a *Determination of Hazard to Air Navigation*, the project can face costly delays until the potential conflicts raised in the document are adequately resolved. If the conflict is solely with military radar systems, questions can arise over the appropriate limits on military authority to prevent wind energy development on private land. For more information on this topic, see generally Troy A. Rule, *Airspace and the Takings Clause*, 90 WASH. U. L. REV. 421 (2012).

a. NEPA Review of Projects on Public Lands

If a proposed wind farm sits at least partly on federal public lands, the developer likely must also secure approvals and development rights from the Bureau of Land Management (BLM) and work with that agency to complete the National Environmental Protection Act (NEPA) review process with the EPA and other federal agencies. This process requires the BLM (or whichever other federal agency controls the relevant land) to prepare an *Environmental Impact Statement* (EIS) thoroughly analyzing the potential impacts of the wind farm—a major "federal action"—on the natural environment. In some locations, a wind farm project might additionally require approvals from the U.S. Fish and Wildlife Service, U.S. Forest Service, Federal Communications Commission, Bonneville Power Administration, or other federal agencies. Identifying the various federal notices, licenses, permits, and approvals a proposed wind farm requires and successfully securing all of them is a critically important task for any large wind energy development project.

As the following case illustrates, paying ample attention to detail throughout the permitting process can be as crucial to ensuring a project's success as the work of obtaining the permits themselves. Notice the lengthy list of legal grounds on which the wind farm project's opponents challenged the developer's EIS and other aspects of the permitting process. Seasoned wind energy developers and lawyers recognize that defending these challenges can lead to significant additional costs and delays. Accordingly, they work diligently to anticipate potential issues and preemptively address them where possible. Such efforts seemed to have at least partially paid off in the case below.

PROTECT OUR COMMUNITIES FOUNDATION V. JEWELL

United States District Court, Southern District of California, 2014
2014 WL 1364453

SAMMARTINO, D.J.

In this action, Plaintiffs challenge the Bureau of Land Management's ("BLM") Record of Decision ("ROD") authorizing development of the Tule Wind Project, a utility-scale wind energy facility, on public lands in San Diego County. Plaintiffs maintain that BLM's approval of a right-of-way for Tule, a subsidiary of Iberdrola Renewables, Inc., to construct, operate, and maintain 62 wind turbines on 12,360 acres of federally-managed lands in the McCain Valley, approximately 70 miles east of the City of San Diego, violates the National Environmental Policy Act, 42 U.S.C. §§ 4321–4370h ("NEPA"); the Migratory Bird Treaty Act, 16 U.S.C. §§ 703–712 ("MBTA"); and the Bald and Golden Eagles Protection Act, 16 U.S.C. §§ 668–668d ("BGEPA").

Tule's original proposal for a wind energy facility contemplated up to 128 1.5 to 3.0 megawatt ("MW") wind turbine generators, producing up to 200 MW, on lands administered by BLM, the Ewiiaapaayp Indian Tribe, and the California State Lands Commission, as well as on private lands. To address concerns regarding the Project's environmental impacts, however, BLM approved only a scaled-down version of Tule's proposal, eliminating 33 turbines from BLM-administered lands, reducing the generating capacity of the Project to 186 MW, and requiring the undergrounding of certain transmission infrastructure.

BLM, together with the California Public Utility Commission ("CPUC"), prepared an Environmental Impact Statement ("EIS") for the Project, which aims to provide a comprehensive analysis of the Project's impacts on environmental, social, economic, biological, and cultural resources. . . .

LEGAL STANDARD

"Because the statutes under which [Plaintiffs] seek[ ] to challenge administrative action do not contain separate provisions for judicial review, [this Court's] review is governed by the [Administrative Procedure Act ("APA")]." *City of Sausalito v. O'Neill*, 386 F.3d 1186, 1205 (9th Cir. 2004). Under the APA, agency decisions must be upheld unless the Court finds that the decision or action is "arbitrary, capricious, an abuse of discretion, or otherwise not in accordance with law."

. . . .

ANALYSIS

1. NEPA

NEPA requires that an EIS be prepared for all "major Federal actions significantly affecting the quality of the human environment." 42 U.S.C. § 4332(2)(C). The EIS should "provide full and fair discussion of significant environmental impacts and . . . inform decisionmakers and the public of the reasonable alternatives which would avoid or minimize adverse impacts or enhance the quality of the human environment." 40 C.F.R. § 1502.1.

Judicial review of an agency's EIS under NEPA is limited to a "rule of reason that asks whether an EIS contains a reasonably thorough discussion of the significant aspects of the probable environmental consequences." *City of Sausalito*, 386 F.3d 1186, 1206–07 (quoting *Idaho Conservation League v. Mumma*, 956 F.2d 1508, 1519 (9th Cir. 1992)). "The key question is whether the EIS's form, content, and preparation foster both informed decisionmaking and informed public participation." *Id.* (quotation omitted).

The Court may not substitute its judgment for that of the agency however. . . . NEPA does not contain substantive environmental standards, nor does the statute mandate that agencies achieve particular substantive environmental results. . . . Rather, this Court's role is to ensure that the agency "has taken a 'hard look' at a decision's environmental consequences." *City of Sausalito*, 386 F.3d at 1207.

In this action, Plaintiffs contend that BLM violated NEPA by (1) failing to articulate a legitimate public purpose and an actual need for the Tule Wind Project, (2) prematurely dismissing the "distributed generation" alternative without in-depth analysis or discussion, (3) failing to take a "hard look" at the Project's environmental impacts, and (4) improperly deferring specification and analysis of mitigation measures. The Court considers each of Plaintiffs' arguments in turn.

A. *Did BLM Fail to Articulate an Adequate Purpose and Need for the Project?*

NEPA's implementing regulations state than an agency must "briefly specify the underlying purpose and need to which the agency is responding in proposing the alternatives including the proposed action." 40 C.F.R. § 1502.13.

. . . .

Here, the Final EIS sets forth BLM's purpose and need for the proposed action:

Taking into account the BLM's multiple use mandate, the purpose and need for the proposed action is to respond to a [Federal Land

Policy and Management Act ("FLPMA")] right-of-way application submitted by Tule Wind, LLC to construct, operate, maintain, and decommission a wind energy-generating facility and associated infrastructure on public lands managed by the BLM in compliance with FLPMA, BLM right-of-way regulations, and other applicable Federal laws and policies.

. . . .

Thus, BLM's purpose and need, as articulated in the Final EIS, is "grounded in both the [agency's] duty to act on . . . [right-of-way] applications and federal objectives promoting renewable energy." (Fed. Def. Cross Mot. for Summ. J. 11, ECF No. 31.).

. . . .

Here, Plaintiffs' argument that BLM's statement of purpose merely parrots Tule's private objectives is simply unsupported by the record. In the Final EIS, BLM sets forth a statement of purpose and need . . . that reflects the influence not only of Tule's goals, but also of statutory, executive, and administrative directives regarding the promotion of renewable energy on federal lands.

. . . .

B. Did BLM Improperly Dismiss the Distributed Generation Alternative?

. . . . Here, BLM considered a variety of different alternatives, ultimately selecting seven of them for in-depth study and analysis. . . .

Ultimately, BLM selected the "Reduction in Turbines" alternative, which calls for the removal of 63 turbines from the proposed Project, including 33 turbines planned for BLM-administered lands, most of them near the western side of the Project site. BLM determined that removing the selected wind turbines would substantially reduce adverse impacts to golden eagles and other rare and special-status birds.

Plaintiffs take issue with the EIS because BLM refused to conduct an in-depth analysis of their preferred alternative, which relies on distributed energy generation. Under this alternative, the Tule Wind Project would not be built, and instead BLM would rely on widespread development of solar photovoltaic systems, or "rooftop solar," on residential and commercial structures in San Diego County, as well as development of other small-scale renewable energy sources, such as hydrogen fuel cells and biofuels.

As explained in Section C of the EIS, BLM determined that the distributed generation alternative did not merit in-depth study because it fails to fulfill several Project objectives and is infeasible from a regulatory, technical, and commercial perspective. To begin with, BLM found that the alternative is infeasible because applicable California regulations do not provide sufficient incentives for development of rooftop solar. (AR 412.) Although California recently introduced a system of tradable renewable energy credits, BLM found that the market for such credits "has yet to be defined and is not yet active." (*Id.*) Next, BLM determined that the alternative remains highly speculative because installation of at least 100,000 new rooftop solar energy systems would be required in order to generate the amount of electricity anticipated from the Project, an unprecedented increase over current installation rates. (*Id.*) Third, BLM found that rooftop solar projects implemented on the scale contemplated by Plaintiffs would create "rapid localized voltage drops" as a consequence of "intermittent performance." (AR 413.) This development would require "extensive upgrading to local substations," the environmental impacts of which BLM could not evaluate with certainty. (*Id.*)

Finally . . . BLM concluded that the distributed generation alternative does not further the policies set forth in the statutory, executive, and administrative directives invoked in the statement of purpose and need. BLM determined that the referenced policies require evaluation of *utility-scale* renewable energy development, rather than distributed generation, as well as siting and management of renewable energy projects *on public lands*, rather than on private structures.

. . . .

Plaintiffs also maintain that distributed energy generation is not only commercially feasible, but actually more cost-effective than utility-scale wind energy. According to Plaintiffs, distributed energy projects " 'can get built quickly and without the need for expensive new transmission lines' " and also reduce cost by "minimizing the vulnerability of the electrical grid to fires and other natural disasters." (Mot. for Summ. J. 13, ECF No. 18 (citing AR 20660–20663).)

Lastly, Plaintiffs maintain that distributed generation would contribute to state and federal renewable energy resource goals, while imposing far less drastic environmental impacts than utility-scale wind. Plaintiffs argue that the statutory, executive, and administrative directives invoked by BLM do not justify the agency's narrow focus on utility-scale development; indeed, Plaintiffs suggest that there is "nothing about [those provisions] that is mandatory." (*Id.* at 11.)

The Court agrees with Tule and Federal Defendants that BLM provided more than sufficient discussion and analysis of the distributed generation alternative to satisfy NEPA.

. . . .

. . . The EIS acknowledges that distributed generation projects would contribute to renewable energy sourcing goals . . . but the Project's objectives are far more specific and demanding than these broad aims.

Distributed generation would fall short with respect to these objectives, such as providing renewable energy to meet California's renewable portfolio standard target of 33% renewable sources by 2020, as well as fulfilling BLM's obligation to seek to approve 10,000 MW of renewable energy projects on public lands by 2015. . . . Accordingly, BLM's discussion of Project alternatives complied with NEPA and was not "arbitrary [or] capricious." 5 U.S.C. § 706(2)(A).

C. Did BLM Fail to Take a "Hard Look" at the Project's Environmental Impacts?

"Under NEPA, an EIS must contain a 'reasonably thorough' discussion of an action's environmental consequences." [*National Parks & Conservation Ass'n v. Bureau of Land Management*], 606 F.3d at 1072. "An EIS must 'provide full and fair discussion of significant environmental impacts.' " *Id.* (quoting 40 C.F.R. § 1502.1). The Court's review is "limited to whether an EIS took a 'hard look' at the environmental impacts of a proposed action." *Id.* The Court must make a " 'pragmatic judgment whether the EIS's form, content, and preparation foster both informed decision-making and informed public participation.' " *Id.*

Plaintiffs maintain that BLM failed to take a hard look at several of the Tule Wind Project's environmental consequences, including (1) noise impacts, (2) electric and magnetic field ("EMF") pollution, (3) impacts on avian species, and (4) impacts on climate change. The Court discusses each issue in turn.

(1) Noise Impacts

(a) Audible Noise Impacts

Section D.8.3 of the EIS identifies several adverse noise impacts resulting from construction and operation of the Project: (1) "[c]onstruction noise would substantially disturb sensitive receptors and violate local rules, standards, and/or ordinances;" (2) "[c]onstruction activity would temporarily cause groundborne vibration;" (3) "[p]ermanent noise levels would increase due to corona noise from operations of the transmission lines and noise from other project components;" and (4) "[r]outine inspection and maintenance activities would increase ambient noise levels." (AR 1599.)

As the EIS makes clear, BLM adopted a cautious and conservative approach to measuring turbine noise. . . . BLM modeled a worst-case scenario, utilizing noise levels associated with the noisiest turbine model, multiplied to reflect the maximum number of proposed turbines. Accordingly, the EIS acknowledges that "wind turbine project-related noise levels range from 36 dBA to 54 dBA" and that "[w]ithout mitigation and assuming all turbines utilized a maximum noise emission of 111 dBA (109 dBA plus 2 dBA for uncertainty), the project would exceed maximum allowable nighttime noise limits ... at five property boundaries and daytime noise limits ... at three properties." (AR 1618.) The EIS concludes that "[b]ecause the noise generated by wind turbines would exceed the allowable noise level limits at several identified receptors, the impact would be adverse under NEPA." (*Id.*)

In light of these projections, the EIS outlines a site-specific noise mitigation plan. . . . The noise mitigation plan is designed to ensure that "noise from turbines will not adversely impact surrounding residences" and that the "operation of the turbines will comply with [applicable local noise ordinances]." (AR 1619.) The mitigation plan calls for measures to diminish noise from turbine operations, including "revising the turbine layout, [curtailing] nighttime use of selected turbines, [utilizing] an alternate turbine manufacturer (or combination of manufacturers), implementation of noise reduction technology," and other unspecified methods. (AR 1619–20.)

Despite BLM's extensive discussion of noise impacts, Plaintiffs insist that the EIS is deficient because BLM failed to model turbine noise using larger, more powerful 3.0 MW turbines. The Court agrees with Tule and Federal Defendants, however, that BLM's careful analysis of the Project's audible noise impacts was more than sufficient to satisfy NEPA. BLM relied on its expertise in reaching the conclusion that the more powerful 3.0 MW turbines were unsuitable for modeling the Project's noise impacts—the agency found that larger turbines require greater setback distances and produce lower noise emissions, thereby underestimating overall noise levels. . . .

(b)   Inaudible Infrasound and Low Frequency Noise ("ILFN") Impacts

i.   BLM's Analysis of Potential ILFN Impacts

In addition to audible noise, the EIS also addresses the impacts of infrasound and low frequency noise ("ILFN"). "Low frequency sound is generally sound at frequencies between 20 and 200 Hz," while "infrasound commonly refers to sound at frequencies below 20 Hz." (AR 3424.) "Sound is perceived and recognized [both] by its loudness (pressure) and pitch (frequency)," but the "human ear does not respond equally to all frequencies." (*Id.*) Thus, the human ear can most easily recognize sounds in the "middle of the audible spectrum," between 1000 to 4000 Hz, but perception is attenuated at the extremes of the spectrum. (*Id.*) For this reason, ILFN is typically inaudible, *i.e.*, outside the range of perception at ordinary pressure levels.

. . . .

. . . After canvassing the available literature, BLM concluded that inaudible ILFN is not expected to have adverse health effects. Rather, BLM determined that exposure to ILFN has been shown to be harmful only at "very high [pressure] levels," exceeding the "internationally recognized threshold for perception of infrasound."

. . . .

. . . In sum, BLM carefully evaluated the available scientific evidence regarding the health impacts of ILFN emissions, rejected Plaintiffs' concerns, and reached a permissible conclusion.

. . . .

(2) *Electric and Magnetic Field ("EMF") Pollution*

(a) EMF Emissions Measurement and Monitoring

Section D.10.8 of the EIS assesses the potential health impacts of electric and magnetic fields ("EMFs"). The EIS explains that EMFs need not be considered for "determination of environmental impact because there is no agreement among scientists that EMFs create a health risk and because there are no defined or adopted . . . NEPA standards for defining health risks from EMFs." (AR 1845–46.) Nonetheless, the EIS goes on to provide substantial information regarding EMFs "for the benefit of the public and decision makers." (*Id.*)

To begin with, the EIS distinguishes between electric fields and magnetic fields—electric fields are "typically not of concern because [they] are effectively shielded by materials such as trees, walls, and structures," whereas magnetic fields are "not easily shielded by objects or materials." (*Id.*) Consequently, the EIS focuses its discussion primarily on magnetic fields.

The EIS explains that there is "little or no evidence" to support a relationship between magnetic fields and health effects. (AR 1848, 1851–53 (relying on scientific studies and reports by national and international authorities, such as the World Health Organization, the U.S. Environmental Protection Agency, and the Health Council of the Netherlands).)

. . . .

Contrary to Plaintiffs' account . . . BLM did not "shunt aside" Plaintiffs' concerns regarding EMF impacts with mere "conclusory statements," nor was BLM's analysis of EMF impacts "uninformed." *Found. for N. Am. Wild Sheep v. U.S. Dep't of Agric.*, 681 F.2d 1172, 1179, 1180 (9th Cir.1982). Rather, BLM presented a thorough overview of the scientific literature regarding the impacts of EMFs on human health and then relied on its own interpretation of the evidence, ultimately concluding that there is no scientific consensus regarding the health impacts of EMF exposure. In sum, BLM did not rely on the absence of evidence or information, but rather on its own expert assessment of the available science. *Cf. Wild Sheep*, 681 F.2d at 1180.

. . . .

(3) Impacts on Avian Species

(a) Noise Impacts on Birds

Section D.2 of the EIS addresses Project impacts on biological resources, including avian species. [T]he EIS lists 11 significant biological resource impacts, including "direct or indirect loss of . . . sensitive wildlife" and "potential loss of nesting birds" as a result of construction activities, as well as possible "electrocution of, and/or collisions by . . . sensitive bird and bat species" as a result of wind turbine operations. (AR 560.)

The EIS also discusses the impact of construction noise and human presence on birds in the Project area, specifically analyzing the impacts on golden eagles, California condors, and other special-status raptors, as well as southwestern willow flycatchers and other special-status songbirds. (AR 602–08.) The EIS acknowledges that "increased human presence and noise has the potential to cause the loss of nesting birds . . . ." (AR 608.)

Accordingly, the EIS also sets forth several mitigation measures . . . including the establishment of buffer zones between Project activity and known or potential nesting sites based on an assessment of anticipated "noise level[s] and quality." (*Id.*)

In the Responses to Comments section, BLM further explains that the Avian and Bat Protection Plan ("ABPP") developed by Tule "incorporate[s] measures to protect bird species from noise associated with project construction and operations." (AR 3766.) The ABPP indicates that noise impacts to birds are likely to be low and will be avoided or mitigated by specific measures taken during the design, construction, and operation of the Project, such as "minimization of surface disturbance, seasonal restrictions on ground disturbance, burial of collector lines, and trash abatement programs." (AR 13475.)

Plaintiffs contend, however, that the EIS fails to take a "hard look" at the impacts of noise on birds in the Project area. According to Plaintiffs, the Final EIS is deficient because (1) it focuses exclusively on construction, rather than operational, noise; (2) it discusses only nesting and fledgling birds, ignoring birds at other stages of life and neglecting to discuss bird reproductive and foraging success; and (3) it relies on conclusory statements about potential impacts, rather than site-specific data and analysis. . . .

Plaintiffs' argument that the EIS entirely ignores the impacts of operational noise from wind turbines is misleading, however. The EIS discusses both construction and operational noise, and the ABPP, which is incorporated by reference into the EIS, explicitly concedes that operational noise may impact birds and sets forth concrete measures to mitigate this risk.

. . . .

. . . BLM did not merely "shunt[ ] aside" Plaintiffs' concerns, *Wild Sheep*, 681 F.2d at 1179, but rather provided a full and fair discussion of the problem, basing its analysis on geographic considerations and an assessment of existing data.

(b) Nocturnal Bird Mortality

Plaintiffs also argue that BLM "entirely failed to conduct any nighttime bird surveys in the Project area, thus leaving the public and decisionmakers alike to speculate about the Project's impacts to burrowing owls, long-eared owls, and other nocturnal bird species." (Mot. for Summ. J. 25, ECF No. 18.) . . . .

Federal Defendants and Tule emphasize that the EIS determined that night-migrating birds, even "when flying over or along a ridge that results in them flying at a lower elevation, are at an elevation ranging from 702 to 2,523 feet," whereas the "proposed turbines of the Tule Wind Project . . . [will be] 492 feet tall." (AR 528–29.) Moreover, Federal Defendants and Tule point out that the nocturnal birds that Plaintiffs are concerned with, *e.g.,* long-eared owls and burrowing owls, have not been located within the Project area at all and are not believed to reside there.

Here, BLM's conclusion that the Project is unlikely to have significant impacts on night-migrating birds is supported by the available evidence. . . .

(4) Climate Change

. . . The EIS states that greenhouse gas ("GHG") emissions from the Tule Wind Project, including both operational emissions and amortized annual construction emissions, would amount to 646 metric tons of carbon dioxide equivalent per year. . . . BLM also suggested that the project might "potentially [decrease] overall emissions attributable to electrical generation in California." (AR 2454.).

. . . .

. . . BLM's choice of methodology in evaluating climate change impacts is grounded in legitimate concerns and is therefore entitled to respect from the Court. . . .

D. Did BLM Improperly Defer Specification and Analysis of Mitigation Measures?

NEPA requires that an EIS "discuss measures to mitigate adverse environmental requirements." [*City of Carmel-by-the-Sea v. U.S. Dept. of Transportation*], 123 F.3d at 1154. "Mitigation must 'be discussed in sufficient detail to ensure that environmental consequences have been fairly evaluated.' " *Id.*

Plaintiffs contend that the EIS "improperly defers formulation of multiple important mitigation plans," including a habitat restoration plan, an avian protection plan, and a site-specific noise mitigation plan, "until after completion of environmental review." . . .

Federal Defendants maintain, however, that the EIS fleshes out the proposed mitigation measures in far more detail than is required by NEPA. Federal Defendants emphasize that mitigation efforts must be flexible and contingent in order to address "on-the-ground conditions[ ]" . . . .

Here, the Court agrees with Federal Defendants that the EIS provides a reasonably thorough and complete discussion of mitigation measures.

. . . .

In short, Plaintiffs' claim that proposed mitigation measures were entirely undeveloped is not supported by the record. . . .

2. MBTA and BGEPA

The MBTA provides that, unless otherwise permitted, "it shall be unlawful at any time, by any means or in any manner, to pursue, hunt, take, capture [or] kill . . . any migratory bird . . . nest, or egg of any such bird" unless permitted by the Secretary of the Interior. 16 U.S.C. § 703(a). " 'Take' means to pursue, hunt, shoot, wound, kill, trap, capture, or collect." 50 C.F.R. § 10.12. The MBTA is a criminal statute enforced by the [Fish & Wildlife Service (FWS)]. *See* 16 U.S.C. §§ 706, 707(a), (d). Although the MBTA does not create a private right of action, Plaintiffs may bring suit under the APA for violations of the MBTA.

The BGEPA prohibits the taking, possession, sale, or transport of bald and golden eagles, except pursuant to Federal regulations. 16 U.S.C. § 668(a); 50 C.F.R. Part 22. Under the BGEPA, FWS issues permits to take, possess, and transport bald and golden eagles for a variety of purposes provided such permits are compatible with the preservation of the bald eagle or the golden eagle. 16 U.S.C. § 668a; 50 C.F.R. §§ 22.21–22.29. In September 2009, FWS published a final rule establishing, among other revisions to Part 22, a new regulation, 50 C.F.R. § 22.26, that provides for permits to take eagles where the taking is associated with, but not the purpose of, otherwise lawful activities, *i.e.*, incidental take. . . .

Plaintiffs argue that BLM was required to obtain a permit under the MBTA because the Project will inevitably cause bird fatalities, either through collision with wind turbines or transmission lines, or through habitat modification and destruction. . . . Similarly, Plaintiffs claim that BLM was required to seek a permit for incidental take under the BGEPA because the Project will inevitably kill or disturb golden eagles.

. . . .

Although the Court is deeply troubled by the Project's potential to injure golden eagles and other rare and special-status birds, the Court nonetheless agrees with Tule and Federal Defendants that BLM was not required to obtain permits under the MBTA or the BGEPA prior to granting Tule's right-of-way application. Federal agencies are not required to obtain a permit before acting in a regulatory capacity to authorize activity, such as development of a wind-energy facility, that may incidentally harm protected birds. . . . Indeed, the governing interpretation of the MBTA in the Ninth Circuit is quite narrow and holds that the statute does not even prohibit incidental take of protected birds from otherwise lawful activity. . . .

Similarly, BLM is not required to seek a BGEPA permit—BLM's approval of Tule's right-of-way application does not, by itself, harm or molest golden eagles. Tule has also satisfied its obligations under the BGEPA by developing the ABPP in consultation with BLM and FWS. FWS has determined that Tule should seek, as an initial matter, to avoid impacts to eagles from the Project through phased implementation, monitoring, and adaptive management. (AR 5904 ("[FWS] believes that the ABPP for the Tule Wind Energy Project is appropriate in its adaptive management approach to avoid and minimize take of migratory birds, bats and eagles within the Phase I project area.").) Accordingly, BLM's decision to grant Tule's right of way application, prior to obtaining MBTA or BGEPA permits, was not "arbitrary, capricious" or without observance of procedure required by law. 5 U.S.C. §§ 706(2)(A), (D).

CONCLUSION

For the reasons stated above, the Court **DENIES** Plaintiffs' motion for summary judgment and **GRANTS** Tule's and Federal Defendants' cross motions for summary judgment.

NOTES & QUESTIONS

1. *Still Fighting Years Later.* The Tule Wind Energy Project, in part because of its location in and near an important golden eagle habitat area in Southern California, encountered several years of legal opposition that slowed its development. When the U.S. District Court released its decision in *Protect Our Communities Foundation*, over two years had transpired since the BLM had issued its December 2011 Record of Decision approving the project. As of Spring 2017, Phase I of the project was not yet completed and the BLM and developer had just prevailed in another U.S. District Court case challenging the project based on its potential wildlife impacts and other concerns. *See* Rob Nicolewski, *Tule Wind Project Expansion Clears Legal Hurdle*, SAN DIEGO UNION TRIBUNE (Mar. 8, 2017), http://www.sandiegouniontribune.com/business/energy-green/sd-fi-tule-wind-20170308-story.html.

2. *Wading Through Acronyms.* As evidenced in *Protect Our Communities Foundation*, federal environmental law is notoriously peppered with acronyms and terms that are largely unfamiliar to those who do not routinely operate within this sphere. An obvious advantage of this heavy use of acronyms is that it keeps written and oral communication from becoming too bogged down with lengthy names and titles. Unfortunately, these special terms and acronyms can also be an obstacle for lawyers who are inexperienced or primarily practice in other substantive areas. Gaining sufficient familiarity with the jargon and acronyms of environmental law is thus an important rite of passage for attorneys seeking to handle legal matters within that field. To quote one scholar, "Environmental law's acronyms are legion. Mastery of these acronyms is a de facto credential for any practitioner claiming to be an environmental lawyer." Richard J. Lazarus, *Meeting the Demands of Integration in the Evolution of Environmental Law: Reforming Environmental Criminal Law*, 83 GEO. L.J. 2407, 2431–32 (1995).

3. The court in *Protect Our Communities Foundation* determined that the developer's EIS had sufficiently considered and properly dismissed "distributed generation"—in the form of rooftop solar installations—as a potential alternative to the Tule wind energy project. What specific distinctions between rooftop solar and the wind energy project did the court cite in support of its conclusion that it was reasonable for the BLM to conclude that rooftop solar was not a viable alternative? What other rationales did the court give for dismissing the alternative of distributed generation? Do you agree with the court's disposition of this issue? Why or why not?

4. What specifically did the "hard look" doctrine require the BLM to do in connection with its EIS for the Tule wind energy project? What are some specific aspects of the BLM's EIS that the *Protect Our Communities Foundation* court cited as evidence that the agency took a sufficiently "hard look" in this instance?

5. Would you suspect that NEPA's "hard look" requirement leads to *longer* EIS statements or *shorter* ones? Why?

6. Why might it arguably be difficult for appellate court judges to effectively determine whether the "hard look" standard is met in any given case? Who do you think is better equipped to make that determination: the BLM or courts?

7. The plaintiffs in *Protect Our Communities Foundation* claimed that the BLM failed to take a sufficiently hard look at the proposed Tule wind energy project's climate change-related impacts. The case also mentions that the EIS estimated the project would generate roughly 646 metric tons of annual CO_2 emissions. If you represented the BLM, how would you approach the question of whether these projected CO_2 emissions were justifiable as a matter of public policy? What other information would be relevant to that determination?

8.   One could argue that the BGEPA effectively allows citizens to receive a license to kill a protected bird species under certain circumstances, even though such a killing would otherwise trigger criminal liability under federal law. One of the primary concerns of the plaintiffs in *Protect Our Communities Foundation* was that the project site was within what the group considered to be important golden eagle breeding territory and was highly likely to kill multiple golden eagles in the area. Suppose you were a policy advocate for the wind energy industry and Congress was considering eliminating the BGEPA's "incidental take" rules for protected bird species. Craft a detailed set of arguments in defense of this statute as it relates to wind power.

b.   Wind Farms and the Endangered Species Act

Majestic eagles and raptors are not the only animals to create additional permitting challenges for wind energy developers. Because wind energy projects affect vast areas of land and are often sited in relatively remote locations, they have generated controversies involving dozens of other wild animal species. *See* TROY A. RULE, SOLAR, WIND AND LAND: CONFLICTS IN RENEWABLE ENERGY DEVELOPMENT 74 (2014) (noting that renewable energy developers "have encountered opposition based on their projects' potential effects on wild birds, bats, bears, tortoises, lizards, rats, roads, foxes, porpoises, and even bighorn sheep"). Understandably, challenges based on a wind farm's potential impacts on species listed as "threatened" or "endangered" under provisions of the Endangered Species Act (ESA) can severely delay or even thwart development plans.

Of course, it is nearly impossible to completely avoid killing any animals when developing and operating massive industrial projects, including wind farms. Policymakers thus attempt to craft laws and regulations promoting an optimal balance between promoting development and protecting wildlife. Congress' effort to promote this balance is evident in both the ESA and BGEPA. Much like the BGEPA provisions described in *Protect Our Communities Foundation*, the ESA has provisions authorizing the issuance of permits to citizens that allow those citizens to incidentally "take" or kill protected animal species under certain specified conditions. Without these provisions, significantly less wind energy development would be possible in the United States.

For reasons described in *Animal Welfare Institute* below, wind farms have proven to be particularly hazardous for some species of bats. Accordingly, when a developer proposes a new wind farm in a known habitat for a protected bat species, wildlife conservation groups often challenge the proposal or engage in other activities aimed at ensuring the developer takes reasonable steps to mitigate the project's adverse impacts on the protected animals. Although bats typically do not garner as much public admiration and affection as bald eagles or many other winged creatures, they do play a crucial role in the nation's agricultural industry and in protecting the natural environment. In particular, bats gobble up billions of insects each year that would otherwise harm crops and require greater use of pesticides. One 2011 study estimated the economic value of these benefits at roughly $3.7 billion per year. *See* Justin G. Boyles et al., *Economic Importance of Bats in Agriculture*, 332 SCIENCE 41 (2001). *Animal Welfare Institute* initially arose when an animal rights group brought a claim alleging that its proposed wind farm would kill bats in violation of the Endangered Species Act.

ANIMAL WELFARE INSTITUTE V. BEECH RIDGE ENERGY, LLC

United States District Court, District of Maryland, 2009
675 F.Supp.2d 540

TITUS, D.J.

This is a case about bats, wind turbines, and two federal polic[i]es, one favoring protection of endangered species and the other encouraging development of renewable energy resources. It began on June 10, 2009, when Plaintiffs Animal Welfare Institute ("AWI"), Mountain Communities for Responsible Energy ("MCRE"), and David G. Cowan (collectively, "Plaintiffs") brought an action seeking declaratory and injunctive relief against Defendants Beech Ridge Energy LLC ("Beech Ridge Energy") and Invenergy Wind LLC ("Invenergy") (collectively, "Defendants"). Plaintiffs allege that Defendants' construction and future operation of the Beech Ridge wind energy project ("Beech Ridge Project"), located in Greenbrier County, West Virginia, will "take" endangered Indiana bats, in violation of § 9 of the Endangered Species Act ("ESA"), 16 U.S.C. § 1538(a)(1)(B).

One month after this action was initiated, Defendants filed an answer and brought a counterclaim for costs. The next day, Plaintiffs filed a motion for a preliminary injunction and Defendants thereafter filed an opposition. . . . Defendants agreed to continue construction on only 40 of the 124 planned turbines, pending a disposition of the merits. . . .

I.   The Endangered Species Act

Congress enacted the ESA in 1973 in response to growing concern over the extinction of animal and plant species. *See Gibbs v. Babbitt*, 214 F.3d 483, 487 (4th Cir. 2000). The text of the Act as well as its legislative history unequivocally demonstrate that Congress intended that protection of endangered species be afforded the highest level of importance. Congress concluded that threatened and endangered species "are of esthetic, ecological, educational, historical, recreational, and scientific value to the Nation and its people." 16 U.S.C. § 1531(a)(3). Accordingly, Congress passed the ESA "to provide a means whereby the ecosystems upon which endangered species and threatened species depend may be conserved, to provide a program for the conservation of such endangered species and threatened species, and to take such steps as may be appropriate to achieve the purposes of [certain enumerated] treaties and conventions" signed by the United States. 16 U.S.C. § 1531(b).

Not long after the passage of the Act, the Supreme Court in *Tennessee Valley Authority v. Hill* proclaimed that the ESA represented "the most comprehensive legislation for the preservation of endangered species ever enacted by any nation." 437 U.S. 153, 180, 98 S.Ct. 2279, 57 L.Ed.2d 117 (1978). . . . Chief Justice Burger, writing for the majority, observed that "examination of the language, history, and structure of the legislation under review here indicates beyond doubt that Congress intended endangered species to be afforded the highest of priorities," *id.* at 174, 98 S.Ct. 2279, and that Congress' purpose "was to halt and reverse the trend toward species extinction, whatever the cost," *id.* at 184, 98 S.Ct. 2279. . . .

Section 9 of the ESA, the cornerstone of the Act, makes it unlawful for any person to "take any [endangered] species within the United States." 16 U.S.C. § 1538(a)(1)(B). The ESA defines the term "take" as "to harass, harm, pursue, hunt, shoot, wound, kill, trap, capture, or collect, or to attempt to engage in any such conduct." 16 U.S.C. § 1532(19).

The U.S. Fish and Wildlife Service ("FWS" or the "Service") has passed regulations implementing the ESA that further refine what activities constitute an impermissible "take." The regulations define the term "harass" as:

> an intentional or negligent act or omission which creates the likelihood of injury to wildlife by annoying it to such an extent as to significantly disrupt normal behavioral patterns which include, but are not limited to, breeding, feeding, or sheltering.

50 C.F.R. § 17.3. The regulations also define the term "harm" as:

> an act which actually kills or injures wildlife. Such act may include significant habitat modification or degradation where it actually kills or injures wildlife by significantly impairing essential behavioral patterns, including breeding, feeding or sheltering.

Id. In 1981, the FWS added to its definition of the term "harm" the "word 'actually' before the words 'kills or injures' . . . to clarify that a standard of actual, adverse effects applies to section 9 takings." 46 Fed. Reg. 54,748, 54,750 (Nov. 4, 1981). . . .

Anyone who knowingly "takes" an endangered species in violation of § 9 is subject to significant civil and criminal penalties. . . . In order to provide a safe harbor from these penalties, Congress amended the ESA in 1982 to establish an incidental take permit ("ITP") process that allows a person or other entity to obtain a permit to lawfully take an endangered species, without fear of incurring civil and criminal penalties, "if such taking is incidental to, and not the purpose of, the carrying out of an otherwise lawful activity." § 1539(a)(1)(B). Congress established this process to reduce conflicts between species threatened with extinction and economic development activities, and to encourage "creative partnerships" between public and private sectors. . . .

A person may seek an ITP from the FWS by filing an application that includes a Habitat Conservation Plan ("HCP"). . . . A HCP is designed to minimize and mitigate harmful effects of the proposed activity on endangered species. Applicants must include in a HCP a description of the impacts that will likely result from the taking, proposed steps to minimize and mitigate such impacts, and alternatives considered by the applicant including reasons why these alternatives are not being pursued. . . . If an ITP is issued, the FWS will monitor a project for compliance with the terms and conditions of a HCP, as well as the effects of the permitted action and the effectiveness of the conservation program. . . .

Congress also provided under Section 11 of the ESA that "any person" may bring a citizen suit in federal district court to enjoin anyone who is alleged to be in violation of the ESA or its implementing regulations. 16 U.S.C. § 1540(g). Congress included this provision to encourage private citizens to force compliance with the Act for the benefit of the public interest. . . .

The ESA's plain language, citizen-suit provision, legislative history, and implementing regulations, as well as case law interpreting the Act, require that this Court carefully scrutinize any activity that allegedly may take endangered species where no ITP has been obtained.

II. The Indiana Bat

The FWS originally designated the Indiana bat (*Myotis sodalis*) as in danger of extinction in 1967 under the Endangered Species Preservation Act of 1966, the predecessor to the ESA. . . . The species has been listed as endangered since that time. . . .

The current range of the Indiana bat includes approximately twenty states in the mid-western and eastern United States, including West Virginia. . . .

The Indiana bat population has declined since it was listed as an endangered species in 1967, and was estimated by the FWS in 2007 at approximately 468,184. . . . However, research suggests that the West Virginia population of hibernating Indiana bats has increased since 1990, with an estimated current population of about 17,000. . . .

The Indiana bat is an insectivorous, migratory bat whose behavior varies depending on the season. In the fall, Indiana bats migrate to caves, called hibernacula. The bats engage in a "swarming" behavior in the vicinity of the hibernacula, which culminates in mating. Indiana bats ordinarily engage in swarming within five miles of hibernacula, but may also engage in swarming beyond the five mile radius. During swarming, the bats forage for insects in order to replenish their fat supplies. . . .

In April and May, Indiana bats emerge from hibernation. After engaging in "staging," typically within five miles of the hibernacula, they fly to summer roosting and foraging habitat. In the summer, female Indiana bats form maternity colonies in roost trees, where they give birth to "pups," and raise their young. Studies suggest that reproductive female Indiana bats give birth to one pup each year. . . .

Like other bats, Indiana bats navigate by using echolocation. . . . Specifically, bats emit ultrasonic calls and determine from the echo the objects that are within their environment. *See, e.g.*, DONALD R. GRIFFIN, ECHOES OF BATS AND MEN 84–95 (Anchor Books 1959). Call sequences are typically composed of multiple pulses. *Id.* at 85–87.

The FWS published the original recovery plan for the Indiana bat in 1983 and a draft revised plan in 1999. In April 2007, the FWS published the current Draft Recovery Plan. . . . The current plan provides substantial background information regarding the behavior of the Indiana bat and the many threats that endanger the species. The plan also sets forth a recovery program designed to protect the Indiana bat and ultimately remove it from the Federal List of Endangered and Threatened Wildlife.

III. Wind Turbines and Bat Mortality

Research shows, and the parties agree, that wind energy facilities cause bat mortality and injuries through both turbine collisions and barotrauma. . . . Barotrauma is damage caused to enclosed air-containing cavities (e.g., the lungs, eardrums, etc.) as a result of a rapid change in external pressure, usually from high to low. The majority of bat mortalities from wind energy facilities has occurred during fall dispersal and migration, but bat mortalities have also occurred in the spring and summer. At the Mountaineer wind energy facility in West Virginia, which is located approximately 75 miles from the Beech Ridge Project, a post-construction mortality study resulted in an estimated annual mortality rate of 47.53 bats per turbine.

The construction of wind energy projects may also kill, injure, or disrupt bat behavior. For example, the cutting of trees may kill or injure roosting bats and destroy potential roosting sites. *See, e.g.*, BHE Envtl., Inc., Chiropteran Risk Assessment 31–32 (June 19, 2006) (Pls.' Ex. 126); *House v. U.S. Forest Serv.*, 974 F.Supp. 1022, 1032 (E.D. Ky. 1997) (finding that the cutting of trees will destroy Indiana bat roosting habitat).

IV. The Beech Ridge Project

Defendant Invenergy is the fifth largest wind developer in the United States, with an aggregate wind-energy generating capacity of nearly 2,000 megawatts. Beech Ridge Energy, a wholly-owned subsidiary of Defendant

Invenergy, intends to construct and operate 122 wind turbines along 23 miles of Appalachian mountain ridgelines, in Greenbrier County, West Virginia. . . . The first phase of the project currently consists of 67 turbines and the second phase consists of 55 turbines.

The footprint for the transmission line will be approximately 100 acres and the footprint for the wind turbines will be approximately 300 acres. . . .

The Beech Ridge Project will cost over $300 million to build and will produce 186 megawatts of electricity, equivalent to the amount of electricity consumed by approximately 50,000 West Virginia households in a typical year. The project is projected to operate for a minimum of twenty years. . . . Sixty-seven turbines, the number of turbines in the first phase of the project, are required to produce this amount of electricity.

V. The Beech Ridge Project Development History and Environmental Studies

In 2005, David Groberg, Vice President of Business Development for Invenergy and the lead developer of the Beech Ridge Project, hired BHE Environmental, Inc. ("BHE") as environmental consultant to the Beech Ridge Project. . . . Russ Rommé, then Director of the Natural Resources Group at BHE, became the BHE project manager and was responsible for, among other things, assessing potential risks to bat species at the Beech Ridge Project site and consulting with state and federal regulatory agencies.

In July 2005, Rommé contacted Frank Pendleton, an employee at the FWS Field Office in Elkins, West Virginia ("FWS West Virginia Field Office"). Rommé then wrote an e-mail to Pendleton to "create a record of our phone conversation," in which Pendleton told Rommé that BHE's proposal to conduct a preconstruction bat presence survey consisting of fifteen mist-net sites "was a reasonable level of effort" but with the specific caution that the proposed mist-netting survey would *only* reflect the presence of bats in the area during the *summer*. Pendleton also stated that Thomas Chapman, Field Supervisor at the FWS West Virginia Field Office, would have the lead on any further discussions with the FWS regarding the Beech Ridge Project.

From July 22–26, 2005, BHE conducted a mist-net survey at fifteen sites near proposed turbine locations. The summer survey consisted of sixty-two net nights . . . and was conducted during full moon or near full moon conditions. At the time, the FWS recommended a minimum of three net nights per site, a minimum of two net locations at each site, and a minimum of two nights of netting. U.S. Fish and Wildlife Serv., Agency Draft, Indiana Bat (*Myotis sodalis*) Revised Recovery Plan 52–53 (Mar. 1999).

During the July survey, BHE captured a total of seventy-eight bats, representing six species. . . . BHE captured no Indiana bats in the mist nets.

On November 1, 2005, Beech Ridge Energy applied to the West Virginia Public Service Commission ("WV PSC" or the "Commission") for a siting certificate to construct a wind-powered generating facility at the Beech Ridge Project site. . . . Shortly thereafter, BHE provided the FWS and the West Virginia Department of Natural Resources ("WV DNR") a draft Chiropteran Risk Assessment.

Based on post-construction mortality studies conducted at the Mountaineer wind energy facility, the draft Chiropteran Risk Assessment estimated that the Beech Ridge Project will cause approximately 6,746 annual bat deaths as the result of turbine collisions. BHE Envtl., Inc. *Chiropteran Risk Assessment*, 22 (Nov. 9, 2005). The draft Chiropteran Risk Assessment also raised the possibility that Indiana bats are present at the Project site and that they may be injured or killed by the turbines once they are in operation:

> The proposed Beech Ridge site presents potential concerns in that it is proximate to Indiana bat hibernacula, sites where Indiana bats have been identified in the summer, and caves used in winter and summer by Virginia big-eared bats. Proximity of these species occurrences increases the likelihood the species will be present in the project area and have potential to collide with turbine blades during spring, summer, or fall. . . .

> With Indiana bat hibernacula in Greenbrier County, and in other nearby counties[,] it is likely male Indiana bats are present in the county during summer, but are as of yet undetected. Considering known proximate locations of summer and winter occurrences of Indiana bats, it is reasonable to presume individuals of this species move through Greenbrier County in spring and fall. It is unlikely female and juvenile Indiana bats will occupy the project area during summer. Thermal conditions in the project are less than ideal, and may be entirely unsuitable for use by females and young.

Id. at 22, 25 (internal citations omitted).

On November 10, 2005, BHE and Invenergy participated in a conference call with Barbara Douglas, from the FWS, and Craig Stihler, from the WV DNR. The meeting minutes indicate that after a preliminary review of the mist-net report, the regulators believed that BHE properly conducted the *summer* mist-net survey and that the clearing of land is unlikely to adversely affect Indiana bat *maternity colonies*.

However, the meeting minutes also reveal that the regulators believed that potential impact on "migrating and swarming Ibats [Indiana bats] will still need to be addressed," *id.*, and that they remained concerned about the risks posed by the Beech Ridge Project to Indiana bats.

. . . .

From March 2–7, 2006, BHE conducted a cave survey, examining data on 140 caves and visiting 24 caves within five miles of the Beech Ridge Project. Of these 24 caves, 12 were not surveyed by BHE because of flooding or blocked entrances. BHE did not identify any Indiana bats in the 12 caves that it actually surveyed.

. . . .

XI. Presence of Indiana Bats at the Beech Ridge Project Site

When confronting the issue of whether Indiana bats are present at the Beech Ridge Project site, the parties analyzed a variety of factors, including: (i) the existence of hibernacula in the vicinity of the turbines; (ii) the physical characteristics of the Beech Ridge Project site; (iii) the mist-net data collected during the pre-construction surveys; and (iv) the acoustic data recorded by Libby.

A. Hibernacula

Plaintiffs argue that the existence of Indiana bat hibernacula near the Beech Ridge Project site increases the likelihood that the bats are present. However, Defendants contend that because the hibernacula are located more than five miles from the nearest turbines, Indiana bats are unlikely to be encountered at the site.

. . . .

The fact that there are no caves within five miles of the project site known to currently contain Indiana bats makes it less likely that Indiana bats are present at the site in large numbers during fall swarming and spring staging than if there were hibernacula within this area. However, the absence of hibernacula within five miles does not eliminate the possibility that Indiana bats are present at the site. For example, Indiana bats have been found more than five miles from hibernacula during fall swarming. *See, e.g.*, U.S. Fish and Wildlife Serv., Indiana Bat (*Myotis sodalis*) Draft Recovery Plan: First Revision 41 (Apr. 2007) (noting that Indiana bats have been found 9 miles and 19 miles from caves during fall swarming).

Moreover, the five mile distance has no bearing on the question of the presence of Indiana bats during *migration*. Indiana bats have been observed to travel hundreds of miles from their hibernacula during migration.

. . . .

Putting aside serious questions raised about the adequacy of the techniques employed, BHE's failure to capture any Indiana bats during its July 2005 and June 2006 mist-net surveys would only support an argument that it is less likely that Indiana bats are present in large numbers at the Beech Ridge Project site *during the summer*. However, even if credited, the BHE mist-net survey results do not establish that Indiana bats are absent from the site at other times of the year. Mist nets often fail to capture bats, especially rare species like the Indiana bat.

. . . .

Considering all of the evidence in the record, the Court concludes by a preponderance of the evidence that there is a virtual certainty that Indiana bats are present at the Beech Ridge Project site during the spring, summer, and fall. (Indiana bats are not likely to be present during winter, when the bats are hibernating.)

. . . .

Based on the evidence of nearby hibernacula, the physical characteristics of the project site, the acoustic data, and the behavioral traits of Indiana bats, the Court concludes by a preponderance of the evidence that Indiana bats are present at the Beech Ridge Project site during the spring, summer, and fall.

XII. Likelihood of a Take of Indiana Bats at the Beech Ridge Project Site

It is uncontroverted that wind turbines kill bats, and do so in large numbers. Defendants contend, however, that Indiana bats somehow will escape the fate of thousands of their less endangered peers at the Beech Ridge Project site.

. . . .

Defendants also point out that no Indiana bat has been confirmed dead at any wind power project in the country, which they contend supports a conclusion that Indiana bats, unlike other bat species, are somehow able to avoid harm caused by wind turbines.

However, other *Myotis* species have been reported killed at wind power projects.

. . . .

Based on the evidence in the record, the Court therefore concludes, by a preponderance of the evidence, that, like death and taxes, there is a virtual certainty that Indiana bats will be harmed, wounded, or killed imminently by the Beech Ridge Project, in violation of § 9 of the ESA, during the spring, summer, and fall.

XIII. Effectiveness of Discretionary Post-Construction Adaptive Management Techniques

Defendants point to adaptive management after completion of construction as the appropriate way to address any perceived threat to Indiana bats. Even if adaptive management is ultimately the best way to reduce the risk of death and injury to Indiana bats posed by the Beech Ridge Project, Defendants are not currently *required* to implement *any* minimization or mitigation techniques.

. . . .

Because entirely discretionary adaptive management will not eliminate the risk to Indiana bats, the Court has no choice but to award injunctive relief.

. . . .

This Court has concluded that the only avenue available to Defendants to resolve the self-imposed plight in which they now find themselves is to do belatedly that which they should have done long ago: apply for an ITP. The Court does express the concern that any extraordinary delays by the FWS in the processing of a permit application would frustrate Congress' intent to encourage responsible wind turbine development. Assuming that Defendants now proceed to file an application for an ITP, the Court urges the FWS to act with reasonable promptness, but with necessary thoroughness, in acting upon that application.

The development of wind energy can and should be encouraged, but wind turbines must be good neighbors. Accordingly, the Court will, albeit reluctantly, grant injunctive relief as discussed above.

NOTES & QUESTIONS

1.   What did the *Animal Welfare Institute* court expect the developer to do soon after the issuance of this opinion? What could the developer have done at an earlies stage of the wind farm's development to avoid the delays and expense associated with this litigation?

2.   The *Animal Welfare Institute* opinion quotes a declaration by Justice Burger in *Tennessee Valley Authority v. Hill* that Congress intended for the ESA "to halt and reverse the trend toward species extinction, whatever the cost." If regulators and courts were to interpret this statement literally when applying ESA provisions, would you expect there to be more or less wind energy development in the United States? Why?

3.   Suppose you were serving as legal counsel to a wind energy developer and animal conservation groups had quoted the language in Question 2 above when challenging your proposed wind farm that was anticipated to kill

between zero and 10 endangered bats per year over project's 20 years of operation. How would you respond?

4.   What specific reasons did the court cite to support its determination that BHE's initial bat impact studies were flawed and insufficient? What does this suggest about the importance of conducting complete and thorough environmental and wildlife impact studies up front when engaged in the permitting process for large renewable energy projects?

5.   *Wind Energy's Wildlife Impacts in Perspective.* When opponents of wind farms portray them as hazards to birds and other animals, some wind energy advocates respond by noting that many other common energy strategies are far more harmful to wildlife populations. For example, a 2013 study concluded that between 140,000 and 328,000 birds died at wind farms each year in the continental United States. By comparison, researchers have estimated that roughly 7.9 million birds die each year from activities related to coal energy and that transmission lines kill between 12 and 64 million birds per year. See Alan Neuhauser, *Pecking Order: Energy's Toll on Birds*, U.S. NEWS & WORLD REPORT (Aug. 22, 2014), https://www.usnews.com/news/blogs/data-mine/2014/08/22/pecking-order-energys-toll-on-birds.

2.   STATE-LEVEL PERMITTING AND THE PREEMPTION DEBATE

In addition to complying with federal permitting requirements, wind energy developers must complete a second layer of licensing and permitting processes at the state government level. These additional requirements vary significantly from state to state, making it difficult to make general statements about they operate across the country. Legislatures in some states, such as Wisconsin, have enacted statutes that appear to reserve nearly all regulatory power over the siting of wind farms for the state government and prohibit municipalities from imposing their own localized restrictions. In many other states, localities continue to exercise broad siting authority over wind farms. For a state-by-state analysis of state-level wind energy siting and permitting regulation, see generally National Wind Coordinating Committee, PERMITTING OF WIND ENERGY FACILITIES (2002) available at https://www.nationalwind.org/wp-content/uploads/assets/publications/permitting2002.pdf.

As wind energy development has spread throughout the country, multiple disputes have arisen over the allocation of regulatory authority between states and local governments. Most state governments delegate a significant amount of land use regulatory authority to municipalities under state zoning enabling acts and other legislation. Because localities derive most of their regulatory authority from the state government, states ordinarily have broad power to preempt local land use restrictions that they don't like. However, the mere fact that a state possesses legal authority to preempt a local law does not necessarily mean that doing so is defensible as a matter of public policy. The *Bayshore Regional Sewerage Authority* case below highlights this ongoing preemption debate. The case involves a dispute between a New Jersey state agency and a municipality regarding the proper division of regulatory authority over wind energy siting. It also provides a glimpse into the multi-faceted and often confusing array of regulatory hurdles that wind energy developers face at the state and local level.

BAYSHORE REG'L SEWERAGE AUTHORITY V. BOROUGH OF UNION BEACH

Superior Court of New Jersey, Appellate Division, 2014
2014 WL 2971460

PER CURIAM.

This appeal continues the on-going dispute related to the Bayshore Regional Sewerage Authority's (BRSA) efforts to construct a wind turbine at its Borough of Union Beach (Union Beach) water treatment plant. Union Beach appeals from a June 23, 2010 Law Division judgment in this declaratory judgment action, restraining enforcement of Union Beach Ordinance 2009–150 (the ordinance), adopted on January 2, 2010, which is designed to regulate the construction of wind energy projects. The Law Division judge concluded enforcement of the ordinance against BRSA's permitted project was preempted by N.J.S.A. 40:55D–66.12(c) of the Municipal Land Use Law, N.J.S.A.40:55D–1 to –163 (MLUL). Union Beach argues the judge erred in interpreting the statute as preempting BRSA's project. We disagree and affirm.

We recite the factual background as taken from a prior unpublished opinion in a related action . . . involving the project:

> BRSA is a regional sewerage authority created by the Townships of Hazlet and Holmdel and . . . Union Beach. . . . The treatment plant . . . is capable of treating 16,000,000 gallons of wastewater each day. BRSA uses electricity for fuel to operate onsite pumps and large pumping stations throughout the eight communities BRSA serves at a cost of $1,000,000 annually.

> To reduce its electricity costs, BRSA decided to install a wind turbine. It applied for and obtained a permit from the New Jersey Department of Environmental Protection (NJDEP) to construct the wind turbine on its property, which is located in the Coastal Management Zone controlled by the Coastal Area Facility Review Act (CAFRA), N.J.S.A. 13:19–1 to –45. BRSA also applied for and received a low interest loan to fund the project from the New Jersey Environmental Infrastructure Trust and a grant from the federal American Recovery and Reinvestment Act of 2009.

Throughout the permit process, BRSA kept the local community apprised of the project. In addition to the public notice and hearings required for the CAFRA permit, BRSA appeared before the Union Beach Planning Board (the Planning Board) and the municipal governing body to inform local officials of its plan to construct two wind turbines on its property. On November 13, 2009, the municipal governing body notified BRSA that a subcommittee had been appointed to meet with the Executive Director of BRSA [and] to negotiate a Community Benefit to "reasonably compensate [Union Beach] and the Community as host to the renewable energy project[.]" BRSA also obtained all building permits, including a zoning permit, from [Union Beach] to construct the wind turbine. On October 16, 2009, NJDEP authorized BRSA to advertise for bids for the project.

The CAFRA permit issued on October 1, 2009, and modified on October 28, 2009, authorized construction of a wind turbine. The permit provides that BRSA may erect a 1.5 megawatt, 262-foot high wind turbine (380 feet from the base to rotor tip) on a 1700 square foot pile cap foundation and all associated electrical infrastructure. The modified permit imposes certain conditions to protect migratory birds. These conditions include the prohibition of guide wires to anchor the turbine and a limitation on the lights installed on the tower to no more than the lights required by the Federal Aviation Administration. The permit is conditioned on compliance with certain conditions, including application for and receipt of federal or other state or local government approvals when such permits or approvals are necessary. No work may commence until all other required permits or approvals are in place.

. . . .

Union Beach's ordinance, ultimately codified in §§ 13–2.5 and 13–10.15 of Section XIII of the Union Beach "Land Use and Development Regulations," seeks to regulate the construction of certain wind energy systems located within the municipality. Relevant here, the ordinance provides: (1) no system shall exceed 120 feet in height; (2) the setback of any system from a property line must equal its total height and must be measured from the tips of its blades to the property line; (3) the minimum required lot areas for small systems is 20,000 feet; and (4) noise produced by a system shall not exceed fifty decibels, which "may be exceeded during short term events such as utility outages and/or severe storms." As applied the ordinance would prohibit construction of BRSA's proposed project because it exceeds the ordinance's height restriction and cannot meet the setback requirement because the turbine would abut its property line with the turbine blades extending and rotating over [adjacent] property.

The MLUL was amended to add N.J.S.A. 40:55D–66.12, which specifically established limits on municipal regulation of the installation and operation of small wind energy systems. Further, the Office on Clean Energy in the New Jersey Board of Public Utilities drafted model ordinance provisions, addressing small wind energy systems, in accordance with proposals from the statewide Wind Working Group for New Jersey, and the NJDEP proposed amendments to and new rules for Chapter 7 of the Administrative Code regulating coastal permit programs. The statute reflects a clear legislative preference to thwart "unreasonable limits or hindrances" imposed by local efforts to impede development of small wind energy projects. N.J.S.A. 40:55D–66.12(a) provides:

> Ordinances adopted by municipalities to regulate the installation and operation of small wind energy systems shall not unreasonably limit such installations or unreasonably hinder the performance of such installations. An application for development or appeal involving a small wind energy system shall comply with the appropriate notice and hearing provisions otherwise required for the application or appeal pursuant to the "[MLUL.]"

Subsection (b) of the statute identifies proscribed "[u]nreasonable limits or hindrances to performance of . . . small wind energy system[s]" and includes provisions guiding a municipality as to acceptable regulatory provisions. Finally, subsection (c), which triggers the preemption controversy at hand, provides:

> [i]f the Commissioner of Environmental Protection has issued a permit for the development of a small wind energy system under [CAFRA], prior to the effective date [Jan. 16, 2010] of [this statute], provisions of subsection b. of this section shall not apply to an application for development for that small wind energy system if the provisions of that subsection would otherwise prohibit approval of the application or require the approval to impose restrictions or limitations on the small wind energy system, including but not limited to restrictions or limitations on tower height or system height, the setback of the system from property boundaries, and noise levels.

[N.J.S.A. 40:55D–66.12(c).]

The conflict is whether the trial judge correctly discerned the import of subsection (c), when she found it preempts application of Union Beach's ordinance to BRSA's project, because it was already approved by NJDEP and CAFRA as evinced by permits issued prior to the ordinance's adoption. Union Beach argues the adoption of the statute cannot affect the valid preexisting local ordinance.

"Preemption is a judicially created principle based on the proposition that a municipality, which is an agent of the State, cannot act contrary to the State." *Overlook Terrace Mgmt. Corp. v. Rent Control Bd. of W. New York*, 71 N.J. 451, 461 (1976). An ordinance would be invalid "if it permits what a statute expressly forbids or forbids what a statute expressly authorizes." *Summer v. Teaneck*, 53 N.J. 548, 554 (1969).

Application of the doctrine "in any given circumstance 'turns upon the intention of the Legislature.'" *C.I.C. Corp. v. Twp. of E. Brunswick*, 266 N.J. Super. 1, 7 (App.Div.1993) (quoting *Mack Paramus Co. v. Borough of Paramus*, 103 N.J. 564, 573 (1986)), *aff'd*, 135 N.J. 121 (1994).

. . . .

In this matter, we consider this narrow question: whether N.J.S.A. 40:55D–66.12(c) preempts application of Union Beach's ordinance to BRSA's small wind energy system because the project had been previously approved by the NJDEP. The applicability of the doctrine of preemption is a legal issue, as is the interpretation of N.J.S.A. 40:55D–66.12(c).

. . . .

In adopting N.J.S.A. 40:55D–66.12, the Legislature desired to stave off parochial aversion to small wind energy systems using zoning ordinances to limit or preclude their construction or operation. N.J.S.A. 40:55D–66.12(a). By prohibiting attempts to unreasonably limit the installation or hinder the operation of small wind energy systems, the Legislature signaled its preference for the development of such projects. Subsection (b) imposes conditions on local limitations, listing acceptable and unacceptable standards. On close review of subsection (c), we note it applies only to projects approved by NJDEP that were subject to CAFRA, with approvals issued prior to the enactment of the statute. It is undisputed BRSA's project qualifies under this provision because the NJDEP granted permits for the project on October 1, 2009.

. . . .

Our interpretation of the statute—that is, municipal regulations, even if within the range of reasonableness as identified in subsection (b), cannot be used to thwart construction of an already existing CAFRA-permitted small wind system—harmonizes the language and overall intent of N.J.S.A. 40:55D–66.12. *Fiore, supra*, 140 N.J. at 466. Further, the scant legislative history accompanying N.J.S.A. 40:55D–66.12(c) supports this view, stating: "The amended bill exempts from its provisions an applicant for the development of a small wind energy system from the restrictions set forth in the bill, such as those concerning height, setbacks and noise, if the applicant has already been issued a permit under [CAFRA]." *Assembly Hous. and Local Gov't Comm., Statement to A. 3740* (January 4, 2010). This description of intent eliminates all doubt subsection (c) was designed to curb the exercise of municipal authority, which cannot be imposed on an already state permitted project.

If subsection (c) were read to remove the limitations on municipal regulation of small wind energy systems established in subsections (a) and (b), as Union Beach suggests, the result would be to lessen the restrictions on municipalities seeking to restrict the local use of turbines. Such a reading is inimical to the policy objective readily apparent by the statute's language. *See H.K. v. Div. of Med. Assistance and Health Servs.*, 379 *N.J. Super.* 321, 328 (App. Div.) ("We will not construe a statute or regulation in a manner that produces an absurd result or that renders a part of it meaningless."), *certif. denied*, 185 N.J. 393 (2005).

Our interpretation also meshes with the overall purpose of the MLUL, designed to "guide the appropriate use or development of all lands in this State, in a manner which will promote the public health, safety, morals, and general welfare[,]" N.J.S.A. 40:55D–2(a), including the need to "promote utilization of renewable energy resources[,]" N.J.S.A. 40:55D–2(n).

We conclude the Legislature in adopting N.J.S.A. 40:55D–66.12(c) specifically preempted application of a municipal ordinance reasonably regulating wind energy systems, if the ordinance would prohibit installation of wind turbines because of violations of its height and setback requirements, when such systems were previously approved and granted permits by the NJDEP under CAFRA. BRSA's project meets the statutory requirements. Accordingly Union Beach's ordinance may not be applied to thwart the construction and operation of this project. . . .

. . . While the statutory scheme in this recently developing area is not deep, we determine it is found throughout provisions of the MLUL, comprehensively assuring implementation of the Legislature's policy to prevent unnecessary obstacles to the development of this renewable source of energy, such as those posed by a local attempt to regulate a project that had been approved.

. . . .

Affirmed.

QUESTIONS

1. The citizens of Union Beach are likely to bear most of the direct impacts of any local wind energy installations, and the community's adopted ordinances suggest a majority of these citizens would prefer to severely limit local wind energy development. Nonetheless, the court in *Bayshore Regional Sewerage Authority* effectively disregarded local preferences by ruling that the Borough's local ordinance restrictions were preempted by New Jersey state law. From a policy standpoint, what do you perceive to be the primary advantages and disadvantages of this preemption approach? Should courts

give more deference to local governments and local voters on such matters? Why or why not?

2.   Land use lawyers sometimes use the term *LULU* (an acronym for "Locally Undesirable Land Use") to describe a development project that would provide a net positive value to broader society but draws ire and resistance from host communities and neighbors who would bear many of the project's costs. Positive externality problems (a concept highlighted in Chapter 1) often explain the divergence of support for such projects. Describe in one paragraph the positive externality problem associated with wind energy development that helps to explain why Union Beach sought to *prevent* the wind energy project at issue in *Bayshore Regional Sewerage Authority* while the state of New Jersey strongly *supported* it.

3.   Suppose you are a wind energy developer hoping to develop wind farms in the state of New Jersey. Are you pleased about the holding in *Bayshore Regional Sewerage Authority* or disappointed? Why?

3.   THE LOCAL PERMITTING PROCESS

At the local government level, wind energy developers and their lawyers must typically navigate yet one additional regulatory structure when siting and developing new wind farm projects. Municipal ordinances—which add to an already-lengthy list of federal and state permitting requirements—often require developers to secure a numerous local permits and approvals. For instance, developers typically must obtain multiple approvals from local planning and zoning authorities. They must likewise secure a building permit from the local building department, which ensures that the proposed turbines, maintenance buildings, and other project structures are well-engineered and structurally sound. They often must also obtain local permits to transport oversized turbine blades and other turbine parts on city or county roads. When aggregated together with federal and state, permitting requirements, the panoply of regulations and compliance obligations developers face can potentially place heavy burdens on them that deter or slow the pace of wind energy development.

Land use controls in most municipalities have provisions that provide some flexibility to accommodate very large industrial projects, and those provisions can make it somewhat easier to site wind farms. For example, many county ordinances allow utility-scale wind energy projects within agricultural or industrial zoned districts upon approval through a *conditional use* permitting process. Conditional use permitting enables local governments to place specific conditions upon the approval of certain types of development projects, helping them to limit such projects' adverse impacts on neighbors and the broader community.

However, zoning ordinance provisions on the books in many localities also unintentionally discourage wind energy development in various ways. When traditional zoning ordinances adopted decades earlier fail to account for the unique characteristics of wind farms, such ordinances can create unnecessary uncertainty and headaches for developers. Recognizing this problem, a growing number of municipalities have amended their zoning ordinances in recent years to better account for the distinctive characteristics of wind farms.

a.   Zoning to Promote Wind Energy

Adopting ordinance provisions that are designed to more easily accommodate wind farms is a relatively inexpensive way for a municipality to encourage or attract local wind energy development. However, some opponents of wind energy view municipal ordinances aimed at accommodating wind energy projects as unjustly favoring one specific type of development over others or as inadequately protecting the interests of neighboring landowners. In the following case, opponents challenge a recently-enacted county zoning ordinance that specifically allows wind energy development by right in certain zoning districts. Like other cases in this Casebook, *Plaxton* also illustrates one municipality's struggle to strike an optimal balance between attracting renewable energy development and ensuring that an adequate regulatory structure is in place to prevent wind farms from causing unjustifiable local harms.

PLAXTON V. LYCOMING COUNTY ZONING HEARING BD.
Commonwealth Court of Pennsylvania, 2009
986 A.2d 199

SIMPSON, J.

In this land use appeal, Arthur and Elke Plaxton (Objectors), representing themselves, ask whether the Lycoming County Zoning Hearing Board (ZHB) erred in denying their substantive validity challenge to certain amendments to the Lycoming County Zoning Ordinance (zoning ordinance), which permit, by right, wind energy facilities in certain zoning districts in the County. Objectors assert the ordinance amendments are invalid because they: do not promote the public health, safety and welfare; improperly intrude on a judicial function; are arbitrary and unreasonable; and, fail to satisfy the constitutional and statutory mandate that zoning laws promote and protect the preservation of the natural, scenic and historic values of the environment. Because we discern no error in the ZHB's denial of Objectors' substantive validity challenge, we affirm.

I.   Background

In January 2005, Laurel Hill Wind Energy, LLC (Laurel Hill) requested a special exception under the then-existing County zoning ordinance. Through its special exception request, Laurel Hill sought to construct and operate a wind energy project along the Laurel Ridge in Jackson and McIntyre Townships, Lycoming County, on land primarily within the County's Resource Protection (RP) Zoning District. Specifically, Laurel Hill proposed to construct a 70.5 megawatt wind-powered electric-generating, transmitting and interconnecting facility that would consist of approximately 47 (later reduced to 35) individual wind turbines located along Laurel Hill Ridge; an approximate two-mile long, 34.5 kilovolt, overhead transmission line; and, a switch yard and substation. The project would occupy an area of approximately 706 leased acres in Jackson and McIntyre Townships.

The zoning ordinance in effect at the time permitted, by special exception, a "public service use." Prior to the commencement of hearings on Laurel Hill's special exception request, the County Zoning Administrator determined Laurel Hill's proposed project fell within the "public service use" classification. A landowner whose property was adjacent to Laurel Hill's proposed project appealed the Zoning Administrator's determination.

After hearings, the ZHB affirmed the Zoning Administrator's determination. On further appeal, the Court of Common Pleas of Lycoming County (trial court) upheld this determination. The neighboring landowner then filed an appeal to this Court, but subsequently discontinued that appeal.

Numerous hearings then ensued before the ZHB on Laurel Hill's special exception request. After these hearings, the ZHB issued an opinion denying Laurel Hill's special exception request on the grounds: the proposal was inconsistent with the purpose of the RP District and the County's Comprehensive Plan; the proposal would create substantial, adverse impacts not typically generated by a public service use; and, Laurel Hill did not show it could adequately mitigate these adverse impacts. Laurel Hill appealed the ZHB's decision to the trial court.

In May 2007, the trial court issued an opinion and order affirming the ZHB's decision. The trial court determined the objectors to the special exception application proved to a very high probability that Laurel Hill's proposed wind energy project would generate adverse impacts not normally generated by a "public service use," and these impacts would pose a threat to the health, safety and welfare of the community as well as the wildlife community. Laurel Hill filed a timely appeal to this Court, but it subsequently discontinued its appeal.

II. Validity Challenge

On November 15, 2007, the Lycoming County Commissioners enacted amendments to the zoning ordinance. Among other things, these amendments allow, by right, the use of wind energy facilities in the County's RP, Agricultural and Countryside Zoning Districts. Wind energy facilities are not permitted in the County's other zoning districts.

In February 2008, Laurel Hill filed an application for a zoning permit to begin construction of its proposed wind energy facility. After a review of Laurel Hill's application, including various clarifications requested and provided, the zoning officer issued the zoning permit, with conditions, on May 9, 2008.

Approximately a month later, Objectors filed a substantive validity challenge to the zoning ordinance amendments.

. . . .

A hearing ensued before the ZHB. At hearing, Objector Arthur Plaxton represented himself. . . .

. . . Plaxton primarily argued the ordinance amendments were invalid based on the prior trial court decision that upheld the ZHB's denial of Laurel Hill's special exception request on the grounds the proposed project would have a detrimental impact on the health, safety and welfare of the community. Plaxton asserted this prior decision concluded that Laurel Hill's proposed wind energy facility was detrimental to the public health, safety and welfare and, as a result, the ZHB was required to conclude the ordinance amendments, which permit such facilities by right, were invalid.

Ultimately, the ZHB issued an opinion in which it determined Objectors did not satisfy their burden of proof on their substantive validity challenge. Objectors appealed to the trial court.

Without taking additional evidence, the trial court affirmed the ZHB's decision. This appeal by Objectors followed.

On appeal, Objectors argue the ordinance amendments are invalid because they: do not promote the public health, safety and welfare; improperly intrude on a judicial function; are arbitrary and unreasonable; and[ ] fail to satisfy the constitutional and statutory mandate that zoning laws promote and protect the preservation of the natural, scenic and historic values of the environment.

I.   Police Powers/Applicability of Collateral Estoppel

Objectors first argue the zoning ordinance amendments violate the Pennsylvania Constitution and several statutes. . . .

In particular, Objectors contend several Pennsylvania statutes and cases require zoning ordinances promote the public health, safety and welfare. They assert Laurel Hill's wind energy project for which a zoning permit was granted after the passage of the ordinance amendments had, prior to the amendments, been denied a special exception. Objectors note the trial court previously upheld the denial of the special exception on the ground the objectors in those proceedings proved the project was generally detrimental to the public health, safety and welfare. Objectors argue that when a zoning ordinance enables a project that was judicially determined to be contrary to the public health, safety and welfare, the ordinance is not promoting the public welfare.

Objectors also maintain the trial court here erred in determining that the prior trial court decision, which denied Laurel Hill's special exception request and which determined Laurel Hill's proposal was detrimental to the public welfare, was inapplicable here. . . . Applying collateral estoppel here, Objectors assert, the prior trial court determination that Laurel Hill's project was detrimental to the public health, safety and welfare should bar a contrary determination here that the zoning ordinance amendments, which permit such projects by right, is consistent with the public health, safety and welfare. For the reasons set forth below, we reject Objectors' assertions.

. . . .

In *Woll v. Monaghan Township,* 948 A.2d 933 (Pa. Cmwlth. 2008), *appeal denied,* 600 Pa. 767, 967 A.2d 962 (2009), this Court further explained:

> It is well settled law in Pennsylvania that a municipality may enact zoning ordinances reasonably restricting the property right to protect and promote the public health, safety and welfare under its police power. A zoning ordinance is presumed to be valid. Therefore, one challenging the zoning ordinance has the heavy burden of establishing its invalidity. Where the validity of the zoning ordinance is debatable, the legislative judgment of the governing body must control.

Id. at 938 (citations and footnote omitted). Before a reviewing tribunal may declare a zoning ordinance unconstitutional, the challenging party must clearly establish the provisions of the ordinance are arbitrary and unreasonable. *Adams Outdoor Adver., LP v. Zoning Hearing Bd. of Smithfield Twp.,* 909 A.2d 469 (Pa. Cmwlth. 2006), *appeal denied,* 592 Pa. 768, 923 A.2d 1175 (2007). A legislative enactment can be declared void only when it violates the fundamental law clearly, palpably, plainly and in such a manner as to leave no doubt or hesitation in the mind of the court. *Id.* . . . .

In rejecting Objectors' substantive validity challenge here, the ZHB made the following pertinent findings:

. . . .

12. The [zoning] [o]rdinance defines wind energy as a natural resource and provides "wind energy facilities are permissible to harvest wind as a natural resource."

13. The [zoning] [o]rdinance requires a permit [a]pplicant to submit a general site plan, in accordance with Section 10240 of

the [zoning] [o]rdinance, which must be complete prior to issuance by the [z]oning [a]dministrator of the [c]ertificate of [o]ccupancy. Specific information is required with the general site plan as set forth at [zoning] [o]rdinance Section 3230C.1(2)(a).

14. In addition, information specifications, including a community and environmental impact analysis by consultants mutually agreed upon by the [a]pplicant and the County, are required. [Zoning] [o]rdinance Section 3230C.1(3).

15. Supplemental controls address a wide range of issues including: tower safety; operations; setbacks; avoidance of designated natural or wild areas; protection against signal interference; requirements for liability insurance; host municipality agreements; decommissioning and restoration of site; a requirement that the [a]pplicant sign a standard agreement with the Pennsylvania Game Commission; and[,] an outline of the permitting process.

16. The [zoning] [o]rdinance specifically provides "as a use permitted by right, the wind energy facility is determined consistent with the adopted Lycoming County Comprehensive Plan Phases I and II."

. . . .

20. As noted above, the [zoning] [o]rdinance provides for the [a]pplicant's submission of detailed information including not only a site plan but also hydrologic and geologic analysis, land use impacts, transportation impacts, wildlife impacts, and community impacts, among other things. . . .

. . . .

23. The [ZHB] specifically finds that on the face of the [zoning] [o]rdinance itself, the provisions for wind energy facilities:

    a) Are not fatally inconsistent with the [z]oning [o]rdinance as a whole;

    b) Are not irrational deviations from the overall [z]oning [p]lan;

    c) Are not an unlawful confiscation of real property rights or an impermissible interference with real property rights;

    d) And, do adequately consider environmental factors, including the environmental rights of the citizens of the Commonwealth.

24. The [ZHB] finds that the [z]oning [o]rdinance provisions at issue are, in fact, a rational addition to the [z]oning [p]lan in

Lycoming County and are not unfairly discriminatory to County citizens and landowners.

ZHB Op., Findings of Fact (F.F.) Nos. 10–24.

No error is apparent in the ZHB's determinations. More particularly, before the ZHB, Objectors presented *no* evidence to carry their heavy burden of establishing the ordinance amendments are arbitrary and unreasonable and bears no substantial relationship to promoting the public health, safety and welfare. . . .

Moreover, as noted by the ZHB, the ordinance amendments changed the prior zoning ordinance to allow, by right, wind energy facilities in certain zoning districts. . . . The obvious purpose of the ordinance amendments is to permit the harvesting of wind as a natural resource in order to convert it to energy as a source of power to provide electricity to the public.

In addition, as stated by the ZHB, the detailed amendments require a comprehensive application review process by the Zoning Administrator, which includes, among other things: a community and environmental impact analysis; hydrologic and geologic analyses; a land use impact analysis; a transportation impact analysis; tower safety requirements; setback requirements; and, a decommissioning process. . . . Clearly, these provisions are aimed at mitigating the potential effects on the public of the construction and operation of wind energy facilities.

In light of the foregoing, we believe the ordinance amendments are valid because they promote public health, safety or welfare and the provisions are substantially related to the purpose the amendments seek to serve. More specifically, the goal of the ordinance amendments, to harvest wind as a natural resource and to convert it to energy as a source of power to provide electricity to the public, promotes public health, safety or welfare, and the provisions of the amendments are substantially related to this purpose. Objectors did not meet their heavy burden of proving a lack of any rational relationship to a legitimate governmental purpose.

Nevertheless, Objectors strenuously and repeatedly assert that, based on the prior trial court determination that Laurel Hill's project was detrimental to the public health, safety and welfare, the doctrine of collateral estoppel bars a contrary determination here that the ordinance amendments, which permit such projects by right, is consistent with the public health, safety and welfare. We disagree.

Collateral estoppel, or issue preclusion, is designed to prevent relitigation of questions of law or issues of fact, which have already been litigated in a court of competent jurisdiction. *McGill v. Southwark Realty Co.*, 828 A.2d 430 (Pa. Cmwlth. 2003). Collateral estoppel is based on the policy that "a losing litigant deserves no rematch after a defeat fairly suffered, in adversarial proceedings, on an issue identical in substance to the one he subsequently seeks to raise." *Id.* at 434 (citation omitted).

. . . .

Upon review, we agree with the ZHB that the doctrine of collateral estoppel is inapplicable here. More specifically, the issue decided in the prior action involving Laurel Hill's special exception request is not identical to the issue presented in Objectors' validity challenge. To that end, the issue presented in Laurel Hill's special exception request was whether the objectors showed a high probability that Laurel Hill's proposed wind energy facility would generate adverse impacts not normally generated by a "public service use" and whether these impacts posed a substantial threat to the health and safety of the community. On the other hand, the issue presented in Objectors' validity challenge was whether Objectors could clearly establish the ordinance amendments were arbitrary and unreasonable or that it had no substantial relationship to promoting the public health, safety and welfare. Because these issues are clearly not identical, no error is apparent in the ZHB's determination that the doctrines of res jud[icata] and collateral estoppel are inapplicable here.

. . . .

IV. Consistency with Purpose of RP District

Objectors next argue the ZHB erred in overlooking the fact that the use of wind energy facilities is inconsistent with the zoning ordinance's stated purpose for the RP District.

. . . .

. . . [W]e perceive no inconsistency between the amendments which permit wind energy facilities by right and the purpose of the RP District. To that end, the zoning ordinance provides that the purpose of the RP zone is to:

> [P]rotect the most important and sensitive natural areas as designated in the County Comprehensive Plan, which contribute greatly to the quality of life in Lycoming County. Protection of timber and other forest resources, wildlife habitat, special plant communities, scenic resources, and other natural areas is the primary objective. *Continued harvesting of resources such as timber and game is an important activity of this district and can be beneficial to the resource if conducted properly.*

. . . .

Section 2310(A) of the zoning ordinance.

Despite their assertions that a wind energy facility use is inconsistent with the purpose of the RP District, Objectors offered no evidence before the fact-finder to demonstrate any alleged inconsistency.

. . . .

For the foregoing reasons, we affirm.

QUESTIONS

1.   The Objectors in *Plaxton* argued, among other things, that the fact that the County had already rejected developer's wind farm proposal should have precluded the County from later approving the same proposal. Do you agree? Why or why not? What are the specific legal doctrines cited by the Objectors in support of those arguments?

2.   It is doubtful that any landowners in Lycoming County were entitled to develop natural gas-fired power plants as a "matter of right" within any zoning district within the jurisdiction. However, such facilities arguably resemble wind farms in that they use a natural resource to produce significant amounts of electric power. Do you think the County's ordinance provisions providing for special treatment wind energy development unjustly favor it over other types of energy development? Why or why not?

3.   What rule did the *Plaxton* court cite regarding the amount of deference owed to local legislative bodies in disputes over local ordinances? How, if at all, do you think the rule affected the outcome of the case?

b.   Waiving Zoning Restrictions to Accommodate Wind Farms

As noted above, the distinct characteristics of wind farms—whose massive turbines reach high into the sky and often stretch for miles across rural landscapes—sometimes create unanticipated complications under local land use laws. The ordinance provisions described in *Tioga Preservation Group* below exemplify this problem. As written, the provisions seemed to require the wind energy developer in the case to preserve natural "screening" and install fences in certain locations to mitigate its proposed wind farm's aesthetic impacts on a nearby neighborhood. Because of the wind farm's height and size, these screening and fencing requirements would have substantially increased development costs, so the local planning commission essentially waived them. A local conservation group then challenged the waivers and the project developer's receipt of a local land use permit. When reading *Tioga Preservation Group*, notice how a unique attribute of wind energy development—the height of the turbines—and the lack of an ordinance provision accounting for it unintentionally made a wind energy project vulnerable to legal challenge.

TIOGA PRES. GROUP V. TIOGA CTY. PLANNING COMM'N
Commonwealth Court of Pennsylvania, 2009
970 A.2d 1200

FRIEDMAN, S.J.

Tioga Preservation Group, Dr. Stephen Ollock and Patricia Ollock (collectively, Tioga Preservation) appeal from the August 8, 2008, order of the Court of Common Pleas of Tioga County (trial court), which denied Tioga Preservation's appeal and upheld the decision of the Tioga County Planning Commission (Commission) approving the waiver/modification request filed by AES Armenia Mountain Wind, LLC (AES) and granting preliminary conditional approval of AES's land use application. We affirm.

On September 24, 2007, AES filed a Land Development Application (Application) with the Commission seeking preliminary approval for construction of a wind farm (the Project) on properties located in eastern Tioga County and in Bradford County. The Project was to consist of up to one hundred and twenty-four wind turbines, two substations, transmission lines, private access roads and an operations and maintenance building. AES also sought a modification or waiver of the "screening" requirement found in Article VII, section 709.06 of the Tioga County Subdivision and Land Use Ordinance (Ordinance), which requires that natural screening or fencing be provided where an industrial development abuts residential property or other incompatible uses. AES explained that, because of the turbines' height, it would not be feasible to completely screen the wind turbines from view. However, AES indicated that it intended to leave as much of the natural vegetation in place around the Project as would be practical, and, when combined with the setbacks for the wind turbines, this would help shield the homes near the Project from views of the wind turbine towers. AES further stated that, in accordance with the Ordinance, it would include screen plantings around the low-lying structures, and it would fence the substations in accordance with utility safety standards.

The Commission held a series of public meetings to consider the Application and waiver request. As indicated in the Application, AES had executed option agreements to lease over 4,000 acres in Tioga County and had recorded memoranda confirming those options with the office of the Recorder of Deeds of Tioga County. AES submitted an example of a recorded memorandum agreement, a list of all the properties under agreement in Tioga County, a representative copy of the "Option Agreement for Wind Energy Lease" (Option Agreement) and a copy of the lease agreement that would go into effect if AES exercised its option. In addition, AES submitted three volumes of technical and environmental data to support the Application.

At a December 12, 2007, public meeting, Tioga Preservation objected to the Application by letter directed to Jim Weaver, Director of the

Commission. Notwithstanding Tioga Preservation's objection, the Commission granted preliminary conditional approval by voice vote at that hearing. By letter dated December 18, 2007, the Commission memorialized its approval of the Application subject to AES's satisfaction of all of the conditions set forth by the Commission, including a requirement that AES obtain all of the required permits from various state and federal agencies before a building permit would be issued. AES accepted the conditions by letter dated January 14, 2008.

On January 17, 2008, Tioga Preservation filed a land use appeal with the trial court, arguing that the Commission abused its discretion or committed an error of law in granting AES preliminary approval of the Project. After considering the parties' arguments and the certified record from the Commission, the trial court rejected all of Tioga Preservation's assertions of error and upheld the Commission's decision. Tioga Preservation now appeals to this court.

Tioga Preservation first argues that, because AES holds only an option to lease the subject properties in the future, it does not have the required ownership interest in the properties to make it a proper "applicant" pursuant to section 107 of the Pennsylvania Municipalities Planning Code (MPC), and, therefore, the Commission erred in considering the Application. Although Tioga Preservation is correct that AES's future interest in leasing the subject properties does not, by itself, confer "landowner" status under the MPC, we agree with AES that, through the Option Agreement, the subject property owners confer upon AES the necessary property interest to make it an "applicant" under the MPC.

Section 107 of the MPC defines "applicant" as a "landowner or developer, as hereinafter defined, who has filed an application for development including his heirs, successors and assigns." 53 P.S. § 10107. A "landowner" is defined as "the legal or beneficial owner or owners of land including the holder of an option or contract to purchase (whether or not such option or contract is subject to any condition), a lessee if he is authorized under the lease to exercise the rights of the landowner, or other person having a proprietary interest in land." *Id.* The MPC does not define "proprietary" or "proprietary interest," but Black's Law Dictionary defines "proprietary" as "[o]f, relating to, or holding as property" and "proprietary interest" as "[t]he interest held by a property owner together with all appurtenant rights." Black's Law Dictionary 829, 1256 (8th ed. 2004).

In this case, section 8 of the Option Agreement provides:

Effect of Option Agreement; Interest in Real Property. The parties intend that the Option Agreement **create a valid and present interest in the Property** in favor of AES. Therefore, **this Option shall be deemed an interest in and encumbrance upon the Property which shall run with the land and shall**

be binding upon the Property and Owner and its successors and assigns and shall inure to the benefit of AES and its successors and assigns. Owner covenants and agrees that during the Option Period, **Owner shall not convey the Property or any interest therein or permit any lien or encumbrance to attach to the Property unless the transferee or lien holder, as the case may be, shall agree, in writing, to be bound by this Option Agreement**. Owner shall also protect and defend AES's interest in the Property and its rights and benefits under this Option Agreement.

(R.R. at 713a) (*emphasis added*). A "present interest" is a "property interest in which the privilege of **possession or enjoyment is present** and **not merely future. . . .**" BLACK'S LAW DICTIONARY 829 (8th ed. 2004) (emphasis added). Moreover, section 6 of the Option Agreement grants AES an **exclusive easement** during the option period, allowing AES to enter the property to perform various studies to determine the suitability of the property for the Project. It is clear from the terms of the Option Agreement that the owners of the subject properties have granted AES an interest beyond that of a "proposed leaseholder" and have conferred upon AES a proprietary interest in the subject properties. Accordingly, we conclude that AES was a proper applicant under section 107 of the MPC and that the Commission did not err in considering the Application.

. . . .

Finally, Tioga Preservation asserts that the Commission erred in granting AES a waiver from the Ordinance's screening requirements for the wind turbines because AES offered no information that would permit the Commission to evaluate AES's inability to fully comply with the Ordinance's requirements. Again, we disagree.

Pursuant to [local law], a governing body or planning agency may administer waivers or modifications from the literal compliance of its ordinance where literal enforcement will exact undue hardship. Article VII, Section 704 and Article IX, Section 902 of the Ordinance both authorize the Commission to grant a modification or waiver where the literal enforcement of the Ordinance's requirements are unreasonable or will result in undue hardship, or where the Commission concludes that the land development plan is an innovative design that advances the purpose of the Ordinance. Moreover, we have held that a waiver is proper where an additional requirement would offer little or no additional benefit and where literal enforcement would frustrate the effect of improvements. *Monroe Meadows Housing Partnership, LP v. Municipal Council*, 926 A.2d 548 (Pa. Cmwlth. 2007); *Ruf v. Buckingham Township*, 765 A.2d 1166 (Pa. Cmwlth. 2001).

In its Application, AES asserts that it would not be feasible to screen the wind turbines with natural screening, i.e., trees or shrubs, or fences, due to the turbines height of more than 200 feet. AES also explained that the setbacks for the wind turbines will allow for significant natural screening to help shield residences in the immediate vicinity of the turbines from views of the turbines. Moreover, the Application clearly indicates that one of the reasons for selecting this location for the Project was that the wind on the mountain is unobstructed and, therefore, quite strong. Denying the waiver and requiring AES to construct 200-foot-high fences around the turbines would unquestionably frustrate the effect of the wind turbines, and the Project as a whole, as it would obstruct the needed wind flow. In addition, it would be unreasonable to require AES to construct such fencing where it would provide little or no additional benefit to the community. Thus, the Commission did not err in granting AES's request for a waiver from the Ordinance's screening requirements.

Accordingly, we affirm.

QUESTIONS

1.   In the case above, Tioga Preservation unsuccessfully argued that the developer lacked an ownership interest in the project site and that therefore the local planning commission should never have reviewed the developer's wind farm permit application. Fortunately for the developer, the court concluded that rights granted under the Option Agreement were sufficient to enable the developer to apply for the permit. Suppose the court had reached the opposite holding and determined that a fee simple ownership interest was required to be a valid permit applicant under municipal law. How might such a rule change the structure of agreements between developers and landowners in connection with wind energy projects? What would be some of the primary disadvantages and costs of such a rule?

2.   What are some of the dangers of having provisions allowing local officials to waive or modify local land use restrictions like officials did to benefit the developer on *Tioga Preservation Group*? Should wind energy projects be entitled to such waivers because of their distinct characteristics? Why or why not?

3.   Suppose you are legal counsel for a group of landowners who own land near the site of the proposed wind farm site at issue in *Tioga Preservation Group*. What specific policy arguments would you make against the county's decision to waive screening requirements for the wind farm?

4.   Suppose you are legal counsel to the developer in *Tioga Preservation Group*. Why is it arguably more justifiable to waive screening requirements for a wind farm project than for other types of industrial land uses, such as factories or coal-fired power plants?

E. OFFSHORE WIND ENERGY DEVELOPMENT

Some of the most promising potential sources of wind-powered electricity are found just a few miles off of the nation's coastlines. As one commentator aptly explained, offshore wind energy has several uniquely desirable characteristics as a renewable energy source:

> The advantages of offshore wind over onshore wind are substantial. First, the winds offshore are typically stronger and less intermittent than onshore winds. . . .

> Second, more predictable offshore wind conditions reduce wind shear, which causes the wear and tear of turbine components. The reduction in wind shear that offshore wind farms offer can extend the life of wind turbines from an estimated twenty to twenty-five years (typical for onshore turbines) to an estimated fifty years for offshore wind turbines.

> Third, offshore wind farms can be built near population centers . . . As "more than half of the U.S. population" resides on the east and west coasts, this proximity to population centers is immensely important for the United States.

> Fourth, wind turbines that are situated far enough offshore are unlikely to provoke complaints regarding aesthetic concerns.

Bradford Alexander Hillman, *Stuck in Limbo: Can Offshore Wind Ever Break Free in New England Amid a Maze of Regulatory and Political Challenges?*, 18 VT. J. ENVTL. L. 308, 314–15 (2016).

Developing a wind energy project offshore certainly involves some additional engineering and construction challenges that are non-existent in the development of wind farms onshore. However, developers in Europe have made significant strides over the past several years to more effectively and affordably address those challenges in the siting and construction of offshore wind projects. Thanks in part to these new innovations, the potential profitability of offshore wind has never been greater. In the United States, the opportunity for significant offshore wind energy development in the coming decades is perhaps greatest along Northern portions of the Eastern seaboard. This region has several large population centers, relatively high electricity prices, and more coastal areas with physical characteristics amenable to offshore wind energy development.

Unfortunately, the United States' complex and risky regulatory environment for offshore wind energy has caused the nation to lag far behind several European countries in the development of offshore wind resources. Controversies surrounding the Cape Wind project—an offshore wind energy project proposed for an area within Nantucket Sound off the Massachusetts coast—perhaps best showcase the impacts of these regulatory obstacles. Since 2001, Cape Wind's developers have spent more than 15 years and millions of dollars on permitting and related costs in an attempt to develop the nations' first offshore wind farm. As of 2017, they still had not obtained all the permits required to begin construction.

The article excerpt below describes some of the primary hurdles to offshore wind energy developments in the Eastern United States and highlights how these hurdles have impacted the Cape Wind project. It also describes how innovative regulatory structures in Rhode Island helped to facilitate siting and construction of the Deepwater Wind project in that state—the nation's first operating offshore wind energy project. The excerpt ultimately suggests that policymakers in the United States could still do much to improve upon the regulatory structure that governs offshore wind energy.

The *Hopper* case, which follows immediately after the article excerpt, showcases just a few of the many types of challenges the Cape Wind Energy Project developers have faced in their effort to develop that project. When reading these excerpts, consider how the unique characteristics of offshore wind energy and regulators' relative inexperience in permitting them have added uncertainty and additional obstacles to the project approval process.

THE COST OF CONTENTIOUSNESS: A STATUS REPORT ON OFFSHORE WIND IN THE EASTERN UNITED STATES

Lawrence Susskind & Ryan Cook
33 VA. ENVTL. L.J. 204, 208–10, 215–20, 224 & 228–30 (2015)

Offshore wind energy is an untapped resource in the United States. The National Renewable Energy Laboratory ("NREL") estimates that America's offshore wind energy potential exceeds 4,000 gigawatts ("GW") nearly four times the total capacity of the nation's electric power system. The Atlantic coast accounts for over 1,300 GW of this potential. The U.S. Department of Energy has established installation targets of 10 GW installed by 2020 at a market price of $0.10/kWh and 54 GW installed by 2030 at a price of $0.07/kWh.

In the past decade, terrestrial wind energy has made a major contribution to the American renewable energy sector. From 2000–2013, over 58 GW of wind energy capacity was added to the domestic electric grid. This amounts to eighty-two percent of renewable energy capacity built in that time period, and fourteen percent of all added energy capacity. Despite the strong growth of the United States' wind sector, all commercial American wind energy projects have, thus far, been located onshore.

Globally, the story is different. Europe boasts seventy-four offshore projects as of the end of 2014, the first of which was developed in Denmark in 1991. Of the 129 GW of installed wind energy in Europe, 8 GW are located offshore. The national leaders in offshore wind development are the United Kingdom (4,494 MW) and Denmark (1,271 MW). Over the last five years, China has also become a player in the offshore wind sector, having developed 390 MW of capacity. Japan is now attempting to enter the market as well.

The United States has lagged behind in the development of offshore wind projects, though it has not been for lack of interest.

. . . .

The combination of politics, economics, and technological development creates a number of barriers for offshore wind projects, all of which contribute to the projected high costs of the technology. For an American offshore wind energy industry to be cost-competitive without strong government subsidies, a number of improvements are necessary. . . .

Jurisdiction over coastal waters in the United States is split between state and federal governments. Up to three miles offshore, coastal leasing powers belong to the relevant state. Beyond this threshold, the federal government has leasing authority, though states retain oversight of transmission infrastructure located both in state waters and on land that must be built to connect projects to the existing electric grid. As will be discussed below, states have also been assertive to varying degrees in engaging with and influencing federal land use decisions beyond three miles offshore. These factors combine to produce a fragmented landscape of jurisdictional control over siting decisions in which the ease of developing an offshore wind project will vary strongly depending on the governments involved. States with well-thought out regulations will offer a more attractive arena for developers than those that have not paid specific attention to offshore wind development. For a cohesive offshore wind energy sector to emerge off of the Atlantic coast, the fourteen east coast states and the federal government must improve and collaborate on policy and regulatory oversight.

These policies and regulations are still evolving and have done so rapidly in the last decade. . . . Until quite recently, there were no regulatory procedures in place to deal specifically with proposed offshore wind energy projects.

State and federal governments did not develop regulatory mechanisms for siting and permitting offshore wind until after developers had begun to propose specific projects. This meant that the early proposals faced a large amount of regulatory uncertainty as there were no defined processes for them to follow in securing necessary approvals, and government action came largely in response to the proposals of individual developers.

. . . .

To residents of Massachusetts, controversy over offshore wind projects is nothing new. Cape Wind—proposed in 2001 by Energy Management, Inc.—has been the subject of newspaper headlines for over a decade and has cast a shadow over the offshore wind sector both regionally and nationally.

. . . .

Cape Wind is sited in a pocket of federal waters between Cape Cod, Martha's Vineyard, and Nantucket Island—three of New England's premier vacation destinations. The prime location has solicited a strong negative reaction in some local circles. Complaints include concerns about environmental effects such as visual blight and damage to fisheries, negative impacts on tourism, and interference with tribal activity. Several notable residents—including Senator Ted Kennedy, his nephew and environmental activist Robert Kennedy Jr., and Walter Cronkite—have also objected to the site, claiming that it would spoil the area's natural beauty. Project supporters have dismissed this opposition as a minority view held by a number of wealthy individuals living in proximity to the proposed site.

. . . .

Part of the reason that opponents have been so effective in delaying the construction of the Cape Wind project is the lack of consistency that the federal regulatory review system has offered. For example, when the project was first proposed, there was no federal regulatory process for leasing offshore lands for wind energy projects. Energy Management Inc., along with other early potential developers, first applied for project approval to the U.S. Army Corps of Engineers ("USACE"), which has general authority over the construction of new structures in offshore waters.

Recognizing the possibilities for offshore renewable energy development, the 2005 Energy Policy Act authorized the Department of the Interior ("DOI") to create a process to lease federal offshore lands for wind energy and other emerging energy projects. This process was akin to the way that offshore oil and gas leases were already being treated. Currently, DOI manages this authority through the Bureau of Ocean Energy Management ("BOEM").

While the creation of a new federal process to deal specifically with offshore energy projects was certainly a positive step for government regulation, it did put Cape Wind and other early projects in a difficult position. As a guinea pig for offshore wind leasing and permitting, Energy Management Inc. was forced to abandon the progress it had made towards securing permits and approvals through the USACE and repeat much of the work with DOI.

Beyond dealing with the changing of the federal guard, Cape Wind has also had to negotiate a complicated array of overlapping federal, state, and regional jurisdictions. While Energy Management, Inc. has enjoyed consistent state-level support from the Massachusetts government, it initially had difficulty receiving approval for an on-shore transmission connection from the Cape Cod Commission, the regional planning agency, and it was only able to move forward after obtaining a controversial "super-permit" from the Massachusetts State Energy Facilities Siting Board which overruled the objections of the commission and provided all necessary state and local approvals. Cape Wind has also obtained multiple other necessary permissions from state and federal agencies, many over bitter opposition. One particularly dramatic challenge came from two area Wampanoag tribes, which objected that the proposed project interfered with the tribes' cultural practices and would violate their historic burial grounds. The tribes attempted to have Nantucket Sound registered in the National Register of Historic Places, which would block the development of the project. This controversy culminated in a high-profile announcement from former DOI Secretary Ken Salazar that the Obama Administration would support the Cape Wind project despite the Wampanoag's concerns.

While the large number of approvals required from different agencies and levels of government would present a difficulty for Cape Wind in their own right, local opponents have proven effective at using this complex structure to cause costly delays in the project's development. With each approval that Energy Management, Inc. obtained, project opponents were afforded a fresh opportunity to contest the project. Project supporters decried the frequency with which opponents issued legal challenges as a "stall tactic." One federal judge, in dismissing a 2014 appeal, wrote, "There comes a point at which the right to litigate can become a vexatious abuse of the democratic process. For that reason, I have dealt with this matter as expeditiously as possible". Cape Wind's developers estimate that they have spent over seventy million dollars fighting regulatory and legal battles associated with the project.

. . . .

Cape Wind's prolonged development process is a cautionary tale that demonstrates the need for a fair, predictable, and efficient manner of structuring offshore wind siting and permitting. Major infrastructure projects such as a large offshore wind development must be thoroughly vetted and undergo a rigorous public approval process to ensure that they are well-sited and are truly in the best interest of the public. However, developers should also have the benefit of a well-defined, transparent, and consistent approval process, and they should not be forced to fight the same battle on multiple fronts. The proposed Cape Wind project has operated in the absence of such a process, which has strongly contributed to the project's long wait for approval and, potentially, its ultimate failure.

. . . .

C. *Deepwater Wind—A Dark Horse from the Ocean State*

While projects in Massachusetts . . . have struggled due to fragmented regulatory powers and inconsistent political support, another New England state has provided a more positive example of the impact that well-managed regulation can have on offshore wind development.

In April 2008, the state of Rhode Island issued [a Request for Proposal] seeking a developer to pursue an offshore wind project in state waters. The state government had previously conducted a survey of potential sites and—based on the combination of wind levels, sea depths, and competing commercial uses—identified a site within state waters south of Block Island as a potentially advantageous location for offshore wind production.

The RFP was won by Deepwater Wind. . . . Since winning the RFP, Deepwater Wind has pursued the construction of a five-turbine, 30 MW wind project south of Block Island.

Like Cape Cod and the surrounding islands, Block Island is a popular vacation and recreation destination, albeit on a smaller scale. However, while location was a liability for Cape Wind, for Deepwater Wind the Block Island location was a positive. The town of New Shoreham (which is coterminous with Block Island) is the only Rhode Island town not connected to the mainland electric grid. Instead, the island's electricity is provided by diesel fuel that is shipped from the mainland by boat. This reliance on diesel has made electricity costs on the island both very high and very volatile, approaching 40 cents/kWh as of early 2012, compared to a statewide average of just over 12 cents/kWh. Because the proposed project would include the construction of a transmission line connecting Block Island to both the offshore wind farm and the mainland grid, the town of New Shoreham believes that the Block Island project will reduce its electricity costs by thirty percent.

While Deepwater Wind's Block Island proposal has not been without its share of difficulties, the intensity of the conflict has been nowhere near that of the political firestorm that enveloped Cape Wind. In a public hearing held on Block Island in May 2013, the number of local residents speaking out in favor of the project outnumbered opponents two-to-one, and the New Shoreham city council supported the project by a vote of three to two. As with Cape Wind, courts have consistently ruled against complaints brought by local opponents, and in January 2015 the Rhode Island State Supreme Court threw out the final legal challenge to the pilot project. . . .

Much of the credit for the public support the project has received must go to the state of Rhode Island, which identified a site where offshore wind development would be seen as a positive rather than a negative and provided consistent state support to the project. Deepwater Wind's ability to work with stakeholder groups has also been a contributing factor, as demonstrated by the developer's commitment to avoid construction in early spring, when the endangered Right Whale migrates through the region. Finally, the location of the project in state waters has advantages, as the decidedly pro-development Rhode Island state government has led the permitting process.

PUBLIC EMPLOYEES FOR ENVT'L RESPONSIBILITY V. HOPPER

United States Court of Appeals, District of Columbia, 2016
827 F.3d 1077

RANDOLPH, SENIOR CIRCUIT JUDGE:

The Cape Wind Energy Project is a proposal to generate electricity from windmills off the coast of Massachusetts. It calls for the "construction, operation and maintenance . . . of 130 wind turbine generators" in the Horseshoe Shoal region of Nantucket Sound. The turbines have an estimated life-span of twenty years, and during that time they are expected to generate up to three-quarters of the electricity needs for Cape Cod and the surrounding islands. The project's "underlying purpose" is to help the region achieve Massachusetts's renewable energy requirements, which "mandate that a certain amount of electricity come from renewable energy sources, such as wind." *See* MASS. GEN. LAWS ch. 25A, § 11F.

Offshore energy providers like Cape Wind must comply with a slew of federal statutes designed to protect the environment, promote public safety, and preserve historic and archeological resources on the outer continental shelf. They must also go through "several regulatory and administrative procedures" to satisfy regulations promulgated under these statutes. . . .

Cape Wind first sought government approval for its project in 2001 when it filed a permit application with the United States Army Corps of Engineers, the federal agency then regulating outer continental shelf wind energy projects. . . . Four years later, the Energy Policy Act of 2005 . . . amended the Outer Continental Shelf Lands Act . . . and transferred primary regulatory authority over offshore renewable energy projects to the Bureau of Ocean Energy Management, an agency within the Department of the Interior. . . . Since then, this Bureau has promulgated regulations governing the development of "renewable" energy production on the outer continental shelf. *See* 30 C.F.R. § 585.100 et seq. ("Renewable Energy and Alternate Uses of Existing Facilities on the Outer Continental Shelf"). The regulations require the Bureau both to collect information about projects and to "consult with relevant [f]ederal agencies," including *inter alia* the United States Coast Guard and the Fish and Wildlife Service. *Id.* § 585.203; *see id.* § 585.600. . . .

Plaintiffs are the Alliance to Protect Nantucket Sound, Public Employees for Environmental Responsibility, and others. They claim that the government violated half a dozen federal statutes in allowing Cape Wind's project to move through the regulatory approval process. . . . The Bureau allegedly violated the National Environmental Policy Act (NEPA), 42 U.S.C. § 4332(2)(C), the Shelf Lands Act, 43 U.S.C. § 1337(p), the National Historic Preservation Act, 54 U.S.C. § 306108, and the Migratory Bird Treaty Act, 16 U.S.C. § 703(a). The Bureau and the United States Coast Guard allegedly violated the Coast Guard and Maritime Transportation Act. . . . The Fish and Wildlife Service allegedly violated the Endangered Species Act, 16 U.S.C. § 1538.

On March 14, 2014, the district court rejected most of these claims and granted partial summary judgment to the government agencies. . . . On November 18, 2014, the court rejected plaintiffs' remaining claims, granted summary judgment, and dismissed the case. We "review *de novo* the district court's grant[s] of summary judgment," and "apply the arbitrary and capricious standard of the Administrative Procedure Act, 5 U.S.C. [§ 706]" to determine whether the government complied with federal law. *WildEarth Guardians v. Jewell*, 738 F.3d 298, 308 (D.C. Cir. 2013). . . .

I

Plaintiffs challenge the Bureau's decision to issue the lease for Cape Wind's project without first obtaining "sufficient site-specific data on seafloor and subsurface hazards" in Nantucket Sound. They argue that the Bureau violated [NEPA] by relying on inadequate "geophysical and geotechnical" surveys. We agree.

Under NEPA, an agency must "consider every significant aspect of the environmental impact of a proposed action." *Balt. Gas & Elec. Co. v. NRDC*, 462 U.S. 87, 97, 103 S.Ct. 2246, 76 L.Ed.2d 437 (1983); *see* 42 U.S.C. § 4332(2). The agency must then "inform the public that it has indeed considered environmental concerns in its decisionmaking process." 462 U.S. at 97, 103 S.Ct. 2246. In other words, agencies must "take a 'hard look' at [the] environmental consequences" of their actions, and "provide for broad dissemination of relevant environmental information." *Robertson v. Methow Valley Citizens Council*, 490 U.S. 332, 350 . . . (1989). . . . This "hard look" requirement applies to the "authorization or permitting of private actions" like the Cape Wind Project. *Sierra Club v. U.S. Army Corps of Engineers*, 803 F.3d 31, 36–37 (D.C. Cir. 2015).

The principal way the government informs the public of its decisionmaking process is by publishing environmental impact statements. *See* 42 U.S.C. § 4332(2)(C). Agencies must "prepare and make publicly available" these statements for all "major [f]ederal actions significantly affecting the quality of the human environment. . . ." *Sierra Club*, 803 F.3d at 37. Among other things, impact statements must describe a proposed "action's anticipated direct and indirect environmental effects." 803 F.3d at 37.

In 2004, the Army Corps of Engineers issued a draft impact statement for the Cape Wind project. After the Bureau assumed authority, it reviewed the Corps's draft statement, "identified information requirements and/or issue areas that [were] incomplete," and announced that it would issue its own impact statement. . . . The Bureau published draft and final impact statements in 2008 and 2009, respectively. . . .

Plaintiffs argue that the Bureau's 2009 impact statement is arbitrary and capricious because it does not adequately assess the seafloor and subsurface hazards of the Sound. They claim that the statement relies on inadequate geological surveys, which according to the Bureau's internal guidance, help determine whether "the seafloor [is] able to support large structures," and whether "important archaeological and prehistoric features [can] be protected." In support, plaintiffs refer to a series of internal Bureau emails describing "the dearth of geophysical data over the entire area" of the proposed wind farm. For example, in December 2006, Richard Clingan, the Bureau geologist overseeing the impact statement's geophysical data section, emailed a list of concerns to the Bureau's "Cape Wind Project Manager," Rodney Cluck, including that "[t]here is no indication that [Cape Wind] ha[s] adequate data to address" various geological hazards, and that Cape Wind's surveys "don't seem to conform (even loosely) to the 'Guidance Notes on Site Investigations for Offshore Renewable Energy Projects'. . . ." . . . In June 2007, Clingan repeated his "geophysical data concerns," and Rodney Cluck forwarded to the Bureau's "NEPA Coordinator" Clingan's conclusion that Cape Wind "has not acquired sufficient geophysical data and information to adequately delineate in detail geologic hazards and conditions in the vicinity (1000m radius) of even one proposed turbine location. . . ."

The Bureau downplays the significance of its geologist's concerns, attributing them to "a robust internal debate," and claiming that there was at least sufficient data "to support [the Bureau's] *initial* decision . . . to offer a lease," if not to justify final construction of the windmills. Defendants Br. at 41–42. The Bureau also disputes whether Clingan actually harbored such serious concerns, noting that his email "acknowledge[s] that the data . . . constitute[s] 'an informative reconnaissance-level survey of the project area. . . .' " Defendants Br. at 40.

We do not think the Bureau has "fulfilled its duty to take a 'hard look' at the geological and geophysical environment" in Nantucket Sound. Defendants Br. at 40. NEPA requires federal agencies to prepare impact statements for all "major [f]ederal actions significantly affecting the quality of the human environment." *Sierra Club*, 803 F.3d at 37. The Bureau does not contest that issuing a renewable energy lease constitutes a major federal action. . . . Therefore, the question is whether the Bureau "consider[ed] every significant aspect of the environmental impact" of the project, including the subsurface environment. *Balt. Gas*, 462 U.S. at 97,

103 S.Ct. 2246. The Bureau distinguishes between the "*initial* decision" to issue a lease and the consequences of that decision. Cape Wind also points out that the impact statement required "additional geophysical . . . surveys" once the project was authorized, and claims these surveys were completed in 2012. But there is no evidence the Bureau relied on any additional surveys in its impact statement, and NEPA does not allow agencies to slice and dice proposals in this way. Agencies must take a "hard look" at the environmental effects of a major federal action "*and consequences* of that action." *Robertson*, 490 U.S. at 352, 109 S.Ct. 1835 (italics added). The impact statement must therefore look beyond the decision to offer a lease and consider the predictable consequences of that decision. By relying solely on data so roundly criticized by its "own experts," the Bureau failed to fulfill this duty. . . . Without adequate geological surveys, the Bureau cannot "ensure that the seafloor [will be] able to support" wind turbines.

The Bureau therefore violated NEPA, but that does not necessarily mean that the project must be halted or that Cape Wind must redo the regulatory approval process. . . . To decide whether "the project should be halted pending completion of an [impact statement]," we must perform a "particularized analysis of the violations that have occurred," "the possibilities for relief," and "any countervailing considerations of public interest," including "the social and economic costs of delay. . . ." *NRDC v. U.S. Nuclear Regulatory Comm'n*, 606 F.2d 1261, 1272 (D.C. Cir. 1979). . . . Delaying construction or requiring Cape Wind to redo the regulatory approval process could be quite costly. The project has slogged through state and federal courts and agencies for more than a decade. . . . Meanwhile, Massachusetts's renewable energy requirements continue to increase. *See* MASS. GEN. LAWS ch. 25A, § 11F. Allowing the project to move forward could help meet these requirements. On the other hand, it would be imprudent to allow Cape Wind to begin construction before it can "ensure that the seafloor [is] able to support" its facilities. Cape Wind has "no prior experience developing/operating offshore wind farms," and the construction site "lie[s] in the frontier areas of the [outer continental shelf,] where *detailed* geological, geophysical, and geotechnical data and information is generally lacking." Therefore, we will vacate the impact statement and require the Bureau to supplement it with adequate geological surveys before Cape Wind may begin construction. We will not, however, vacate Cape Wind's lease or other regulatory approvals based on this NEPA violation.

. . . .

II

Plaintiffs next argue that Coast Guard and the Bureau violated the Maritime Transportation Act by failing to include adequate terms and conditions in Cape Wind's Renewable Energy Lease. . . . Before issuing a lease, the Bureau must consult with relevant federal agencies and "respond to findings of those agencies. . . ." *Id.* § 585.203. One such agency is the Coast Guard, which has the authority and responsibility under § 414 of the Maritime Transportation Act to "specify the reasonable terms and conditions the [Coast Guard] determines to be necessary to provide for navigational safety with respect to the proposed lease" and to "each alternative to the proposed lease . . . considered by the [Bureau]." 120 Stat. 516, 540, § 414(a). The Bureau must then incorporate the Coast Guard's terms into any lease it issues. *See id.* § 414(b). Plaintiffs claim that the Coast Guard and the Bureau violated § 414 by including terms that do not sufficiently "ensure navigational safety," and by failing to include terms "for each alternative" to the proposed lease. Alliance Br. at 10, 19. We do not think either claim requires the Coast Guard to reissue its terms.

The Coast Guard released its terms and conditions for the Cape Wind Project on August 2, 2007. The terms required Cape Wind to satisfy several immediate conditions, such as devising a turbine "marking scheme" to aid in navigation through the wind farm, some ongoing reporting obligations, like filing monthly "construction status" reports, and some future research requirements, including examining whether the turbines "would interfere in any way with marine communications or navigation systems. . . ." According to the Coast Guard, its terms would sufficiently "provide for navigational safety" in Nantucket Sound.

Plaintiffs argue that the Coast Guard's terms requiring ongoing reporting and research violate § 414. They say that § 414 requires the Coast Guard to "assure navigational safety *before* the [p]roject is approved," and that these forward-looking terms mean that the Coast Guard will be able to do so "*only after* various analyses . . . are completed." Alliance Br. at 9, 11. The district court disagreed. . . .

We agree with the court that the Coast Guard's terms comply with § 414, but for different reasons. Section 414 requires the Coast Guard to "specify the reasonable terms and conditions *the [Coast Guard] determines* to be necessary to provide for navigational safety" in Nantucket Sound. 120 Stat. 516, 540, § 414(a) (italics added). The Coast Guard stated that its terms met this requirement, and we are hesitant to second guess that determination "given the Coast Guard's expertise" in "maritime safety. . . ." *Collins v. Nat'l Transp. Safety Bd.*, 351 F.3d 1246, 1253 (D.C. Cir. 2003). . . . In short, the Coast Guard believed that its terms would provide for navigational safety, and the fact that some of those terms are forward-looking is not enough to disregard this expert judgment.

. . . .

III

Plaintiffs' final contention is that the Fish and Wildlife Service violated the Endangered Species Act. *See* 16 U.S.C. § 1538. Under the Act and its regulations, agencies must determine whether approved actions "may affect," 50 C.F.R. § 402.14(a), any "endangered [or threatened] species of . . . wildlife," and if so, must consult with the Service. . . . The Service must then provide the agency with a written statement "explaining how the proposed action will affect th[ose] species" and recommending "reasonable and prudent" measures to minimize any harm. *Bennett v. Spear*, 520 U.S. 154, 158, 117 S.Ct. 1154, 137 L.Ed.2d 281 (1997); *see* 16 U.S.C. § 1536(b); 50 C.F.R. § 402.14(g)-(i). The Service must include its recommendations in what is known as an "incidental take statement," 520 U.S. at 158, 117 S.Ct. 1154, and must base them on the "best scientific and commercial data available," 50 C.F.R. § 402.14(g)(8). *See* 16 U.S.C. § 1536(a)(2), (c)(1). Plaintiffs argue that the Service's incidental take statement for the Cape Wind Project is arbitrary and capricious because it is not based on the best available scientific data, and because it excludes a particular mitigation measure.

The Bureau began consultations with the Service in November 2005 to determine whether the project could harm any endangered or threatened species. On October 31, 2008, the Service estimated that although Cape Wind's activities would not "jeopardize the continued existence" of any listed species, 50 C.F.R. § 402.14(g)(4), the turbines would nonetheless kill 80–100 endangered roseate terns and ten threatened piping plovers over the life of the project. . . . The Service therefore issued a draft incidental take statement recommending measures to minimize harm to roseate terns and piping plovers in Nantucket Sound. One recommendation was to temporarily turn off the windmills during poor visibility periods to "reduce the risk of collision" by birds flying through the wind farm—a process ironically called "feathering" the turbines. Cape Wind and the Bureau objected to this recommendation because they were concerned it would shut down the turbines for too long. The Service heeded these concerns. On November 21, 2008, it published a final version of its incidental take statement that did not recommend feathering. The Service explained that it had excluded the measure because the Bureau and Cape Wind had "determined" that feathering would "modif[y] the scope of the project in a manner that is adverse to the project's stated purpose and need," "have a deleterious [e]ffect on anticipated revenues, financing, and power purchasing agreements," and ultimately have a steep enough "economic cost" to make the measure "not feasible."

In June 2010, Plaintiffs challenged the incidental take statement on the grounds that the Service had "improperly delegat[ed] to Cape Wind and to the [Bureau]" its duty to independently evaluate and recommend mitigation measures. *Pub. Emps.*, 25 F.Supp.3d at 107. The district court initially agreed, explaining that the Endangered Species Act requires the Service to "make an independent determination" whether feathering "was a reasonable and prudent measure. . . ." *Id.* at 130. The court therefore remanded the case. . . .

. . . In July 2014, the Service filed a letter with the district court claiming that it had complied with the remand order and had made an "independent evaluation of the initially proposed feathering [measure]. . . ." The Service explained that after consulting with its "in-house economist," it had "conclude[d] that the draft feathering [measure] should not be included" in the incidental take statement. . . .

Plaintiffs argued that because the Service considered its economist's 2014 analysis, the Service was required to considered plaintiffs' submissions as well. Plaintiffs also challenged the merits of the Service's decision to exclude feathering. . . .

. . . The Service decided to exclude feathering based on "[t]he expert opinion of [its] in-house economist," which he communicated to the Service on May 28, 2014. That he reviewed information available in 2008 is beside the point. He analyzed the information in 2014. He did so "in response" to the court's 2014 remand order. The Service concedes that his opinion "reflected an *additional* analysis of the decision" to exclude feathering, Defendants Br. at 63, and that the Service then relied upon this opinion "[i]n particular" to "find that the draft feathering [measure] would not be reasonable." By doing so, the Service reopened the record and was required to consider plaintiffs' submissions.

We therefore hold that the Service's decision to disregard plaintiffs' submissions was arbitrary and capricious, and we vacate the incidental take statement. . . .

IV

We reverse the district court's judgment that the Bureau's environmental impact statement complied with NEPA and that the Service's incidental take statement complied with the Endangered Species Act, and we vacate both statements. *See* 5 U.S.C. § 706(2). We affirm the district court's judgment dismissing plaintiffs' remaining claims, and remand the case for proceedings consistent with this opinion.

So ordered.

NOTES & QUESTIONS

1.   *Success at Block Island.* In late 2016, the five turbines comprising Deepwater Wind's Block Island pilot project became operational, giving the project the distinction of being the nation's first commercial offshore wind

farm. This achievement is remarkable in part because its developers first began pursuing the project more than seven years after permitting work began for Cape Wind. See Tatiana Schlossberg, *America's First Offshore Wind Farm Spins to Life*, N.Y. TIMES A15 (Dec. 15, 2016).

2. What seem to be the primary differences between the regulatory structure for offshore wind energy in Massachusetts and the structure applicable in Rhode Island? How did those differences help to facilitate the successful siting and development of Deepwater Wind's Block Island project?

3. What are some differences related the project sites themselves that were likely factors in enabling the successful development of the Block Island project while the Cape Wind project languished?

4. Based on the readings above, do you think the permitting process for offshore wind energy development in the United States will become *more* burdensome and expensive as more projects are built over time, or *less* burdensome and expensive? Why?

5. In the *Hopper* case, which six federal statutory laws did the plaintiffs allege were violated in connection with government permitting for the Cape Wind Energy Project? How might the fact that few or no wind energy projects had ever been permitted in the United States have disadvantaged Cape Wind's developers in their effort to secure all requisite permits for the project?

6. Are the claims in *Hopper* focused on deficiencies in the developer's actions, or are they focused primarily on the actions of government entities involved in the Cape Wind permitting process? What does this case suggest about the ability of relevant government agencies to effectively site these projects?

7. *Reason for Optimism*. Although the United States has unquestionably lagged behind much of the developed world in harnessing offshore wind energy technologies, there are reasons to believe that this pattern is changing. In its early days, the Trump administration proved surprisingly open to offshore wind energy. For example, in March of 2017, the Department of Interior auctioned off a large offshore wind energy site to a private developer for $9 million and announced plans to auction off significantly more areas in the months to follow. Not surprisingly, some state governments have even more aggressively embraced offshore wind energy development and are making plans to dramatically increase it within their own jurisdictions. For example, under the leadership of Governor Andrew Cuomo, the New York announced a goal in early 2017 of developing 2.4 GW of offshore windpower in that state by 2030—an amount of generating capacity sufficient to power roughly 1.25 million homes. *See* Press Release, N.Y. Governor Andrew M. Cuomo's Office, *Governor Cuomo Announces Approval of Largest Offshore Wind Project in the Nation* (Jan. 25, 2017), https://www.governor.ny.gov/news/governor-cuomo-announces-approval-largest-offshore-wind-project-nation. These and other recent policy signals suggest that offshore wind energy development work could increase substantially in the coming years.

CHAPTER 5

SOLAR ENERGY POLICY

■ ■ ■

A. INTRODUCTION

Throughout human history, the sun has been the most important of all energy sources. From sunrise to sunset, the earth's inhabitants rely on the sun daily as their primary source of the light and heat necessary to work, grow food, and otherwise sustain life. Even the energy stored in the coal, petroleum, wind, and flowing water that meet most of the world's electricity demands originates from the sun.[1] In recent years, however, humankind's capacity to use sunlight as an energy source has advanced into an entirely new realm with modern technologies that allow for the affordable conversion of solar radiation into electricity. Today's solar energy technologies and markets are driving fundamental changes in many aspects of the energy industry, and attorneys have important roles to play in this transition. The following two chapters of this Casebook focus on various legal and policy issues that are emerging as solar energy technologies spread across the globe.

The modern-looking solar panels that increasingly cover rooftops around the world trace their origins to the pioneering research of the French physicist Edmund Becquerel. Becquerel first discovered and wrote about what he called the photovoltaic (PV) effect in 1839. Becquerel observed that when photons strike semiconducting materials such as silicon, they transfer much of their energy into electrons in the atoms that make up those materials. See *History of Solar Energy, Solar Power, and Solar Panels*, Verengo Solar, http://www.verengosolar.com/blog/history-of-solar-energy-solar-power-and-solar-panels (last visited Sept. 16, 2017). The atoms respond to this influx of energy by releasing their newly-energized electrons, thereby generating electric current. In 1954, roughly 115 years after Becquerel's discovery of the PV effect, scientists at Bell Laboratories in New Jersey applied it to create the first silicon PV cell

---

[1]   Only a few major energy resources originate from sources other than the sun. Nuclear energy is perhaps the most significant: nuclear power plants generate electricity by harnessing energy released from nuclear fission or fusion. Wave energy and geothermal energy are two other noteworthy energy sources not derived from solely solar resources. Although winds are the main driver of ocean waves, much of the kinetic energy found in ocean tides results from the gravitational pull between the sun and the moon. And geothermal energy originates from the radioactive decay of minerals found in the earth's core. Of course, the sun itself technically generates its energy through the fusion of hydrogen atoms into helium—a type of nuclear energy.

capable of converting sunlight into electric power. Bell Laboratories' work was an important milestone in the progression of solar energy technologies, but its simple PV cell was of limited value because it was only about six percent efficient: it could convert just six percent of the energy in the sunlight striking it into usable electric energy. Fortunately, the efficiency and affordability of solar PV cells have since dramatically improved. Today, numerous companies across the globe are mass-producing large panels of solar cells with efficiency ratings approaching 20 percent.

As improvements in solar PV cell designs have gradually increased their efficiency, demand for them has grown and the scope and scale of solar PV manufacturing have increased. This increase in production volume has also had positive impacts, enabling the industry to achieve economies of scale led to steady declines in solar panel manufacturing costs and prices. As was shown in Figure 1.5 in Chapter 1, from 1977 to 2015 the per-watt market price of silicon PV cells fell from $76.00 per watt to just $0.30 per watt. As of early 2017, those price precipitous declines were continuing and spot prices for solar PV cells had fallen further to roughly $0.20 per watt. To see information on current spot market prices, visit http://pv.energytrend.com/pricequotes.html.

Despite decades of improvements in solar PV efficiencies and steady price declines, until recently it was still considerably more expensive to generate electricity from sunlight than to generating it from coal or other conventional energy sources. Today, however, solar PV prices have fallen so far that solar energy has reached or is approaching *grid parity* in much of the country. From the perspective of a retail electricity customer who is considering a purchase of rooftop solar panels, grid parity is the point at which "the levelized cost of solar falls below gross electricity bill savings in the first year of a solar PV system's life." Cory Honeyman, *U.S. Residential Solar Economic Outlook 2016–2020: Grid Parity, Rate Design and Net Metering Risk*, GREENTECH MEDIA, https://www.greentechmedia.com/research/report/us-residential-solar-economic-outlook-2016-2020 (last visited Sept. 16, 2017). According to the report, as of 2016 residential solar had already achieved grid parity in 20 U.S. states and 22 more states were expected to achieve grid party for residential solar by 2020. *See id.*

As solar power has grown more cost-competitive with conventional energy sources, the pace of solar energy development has accelerated. Figure 5.2 illustrates the rapid increase in annual solar PV installations in the United States from 2000 to 2016. According to the Solar Energy Industries Association, total solar PV development (measured in MW of new generating capacity) in the United States increased by 97 percent in 2016 alone. For more details on the remarkable growth of the nation's solar industry in that year, visit http://www.seia.org/research-resources/solar-market-insight-report-2016-year-review.

Figure 5.1. Solar Energy Growth in the United States

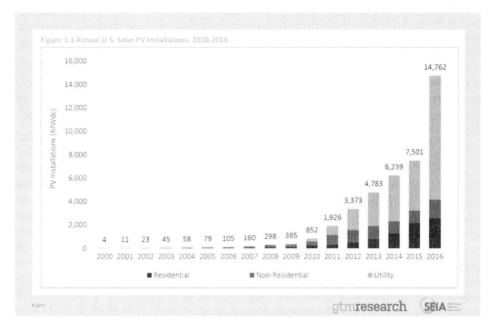

Source: Solar Energy Industries Association

As illustrated above, most of the nation's solar energy growth in recent years has come in the form of *utility-scale* solar energy projects. Utility-scale solar farms are very large projects typically sited in rural or outlying areas. Project operators typically transmit and distribute the electric power generated on these solar farms to utilities and other off-takers situated many miles away. The two primary types of utility-scale solar farms are *concentrating solar power (CSP) projects* and *ground-mounted PV projects*, both of which are described in considerable detail in Chapter 6.

Over the past couple of decades, *residential-scale* solar energy development has also rapidly increased in the United States. Most residential solar energy projects consist of relatively small PV solar panel arrays installed onto the rooftops of single-family homes under lease or financed purchase arrangements with private solar energy companies. Homeowners with solar panels typically use most of the electricity their panels generate to power their own homes. Of course, they also still rely on their local utility to supply electricity via the grid at night and during other times when the panels don't generate enough power to fully meet the household's electricity needs. During other times when the panels generate more power than needed onsite, the excess generated electricity typically flows onto the electric grid so neighbors can use it. Most states have *net metering programs* that give customers with solar panels valuable credit for this excess power they send onto the grid. The specific structures and terms of net metering programs vary across the country and are increasingly topics of heated public debate. Detailed coverage of net metering programs and of the ongoing policy discussion over how to best structure these programs follows later in this chapter.

Some solar energy development projects are larger than residential-scale rooftop solar arrays and smaller than utility-scale solar farms. For example, consider the fairly large rooftop solar PV installations appearing on a growing number of Wal-Mart or Target stores. See Adam Johnston, *Target Hits Bullseye As Top 2016 US Corporate Solar Installer*, CleanTechnica.com (Oct. 23, 2016), https://cleantechnica.com/2016/10/23/target-hits-bulls-eye-top-2016-us-corporate-solar-installer/. For simplicity's sake, Figure 5.1 agglomerates these other solar energy strategies into a single category labeled *non-residential* solar energy. This category encompasses at least two noteworthy types of solar energy development. The first is *commercial-scale* solar, which refers to installations of PV solar panel arrays onto the rooftops of commercial or government buildings or other non-residential structures. Commercial-scale solar is generally viewed as distinct from utility-scale solar because a majority of the power generated in commercial-scale solar arrays is used onsite under a net metering arrangement. The second notable type of non-residential solar energy strategy is *community solar*, which generally involves medium-sized solar PV installations governed under a shared ownership or use structure. A diverse and growing set of community-scale solar energy projects and programs have emerged throughout the country in recent years. Chapter 6 of this Casebook features a more comprehensive examination of these and other categories of solar energy development.

B. ADVANTAGES AND LIMITATIONS OF SOLAR ENERGY

Whether it takes the form of small rooftop PV arrays or massive CSP projects, solar energy development is among the most promising and rapidly-growing areas of the modern energy industry. Several attributes of solar resources make them particularly well suited to help fulfill the world's energy needs, and innovation and other factors are enabling solar to serve that rule more now than ever before. The following materials describe some of solar energy's greatest strengths as an energy resource.

1. POLICY ADVANTAGES OF SOLAR ENERGY

Solar electricity generation produces minimal greenhouse gases or other costly airborne emissions.

One obvious advantage of solar energy technologies is they generate electricity without burning fossil fuels or other carbon-based materials. The only greenhouse gas emissions associated with solar electricity generation result from the manufacture, transportation, installation, maintenance, and disposal of solar energy generating equipment itself. Accordingly, solar PV generates far fewer greenhouse gas emissions per unit of energy than does coal, oil, or natural gas. It also generates far fewer airborne emissions of sulfur dioxide, nitrous oxide, mercury and numerous other harmful gases or substances.

Solar resources are highly renewable.

Solar energy is also an appealing energy strategy because solar radiation is among the most renewable of all energy resources. One of the greatest drawbacks of fossil fuel energy resources is their finite nature: consuming them today leaves fewer resources available for consumption tomorrow. Comparable resource depletion costs are nonexistent in the context of solar energy. Indeed, humankind could increase the world's installed solar energy generating capacity by an hundred-fold and make full use of that capacity every day without causing any reduction in the quantity of solar resources available to future generations.

Developable solar energy resources are widely geographically available.

Yet another upside of solar resources is they are available in large quantities across most of the globe. Certainly, some geographic areas have stronger solar energy resources than others. Figure 5.2 illustrates this variation in solar resource quality across regions in the United States. The darkest areas on the map are in the Southwest, whose solar energy resources have greater energy production potential than many other regions of the country.

Figure 5.2. Photovoltaic Solar Resource Map

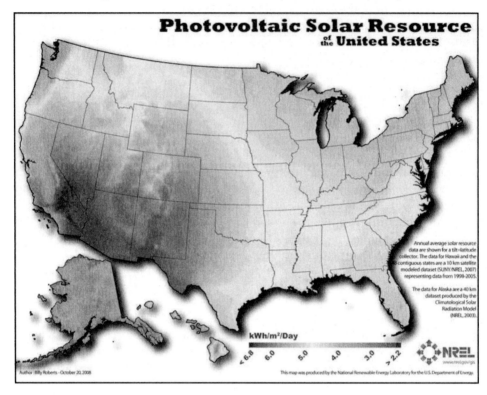

However, PV solar panels can and do still generate significant amounts of electricity in comparatively less sunny regions of the United States such as New England and the upper Midwest. Due to improved technologies and declining solar PV prices, cost-justifiable solar energy development is possible in a proportion of the country than is much larger than the proportion that is adequately suited for other major renewable energy strategies. Figure 5.3 supports this fact, showing that East Coast states such as New Jersey, Massachusetts, and North Carolina are among the top solar energy-producing states in the country.

Figure 5.3. Cumulative Installed Solar Generating Capacity (MW) (2015)

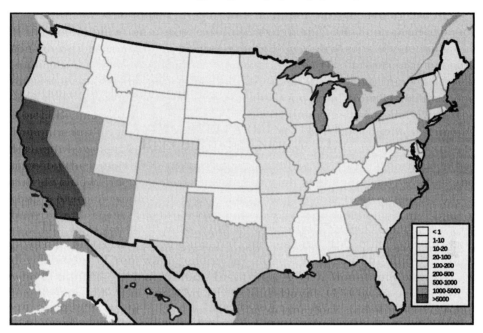

Source: Wikimedia Commons (data from Solar Energy Industries Association)

In many regions, the availability of solar resources peaks during seasons and times when there is relatively high electricity demand.

In much of the country, another advantage of solar in comparison to wind energy is that sunlight tends to be more abundant during seasons and times when demand for electricity is high. Solar panels obviously do not to produce electricity at 2:00AM when it is dark outside, but that is generally of little concern because most households and businesses aren't using much electricity at that hour anyway so utilities can easily meet their customers' low electricity demand using other sources. By contrast, solar panels are usually highly productive during afternoon hours and in the summer months—periods when electricity demand tends to be relatively high in many regions of the United States.

To be clear, the correlation between peak solar energy productivity and peak electricity demand is not perfect. Solar energy production tends to peak at around noon when the sun is at its highest point in the sky, but in many regions the aggregate demand for grid-supplied electricity typically peaks a few hours later. Fortunately, time-based electricity pricing models (covered later in this Chapter) and various temporary energy storage strategies (discussed in Chapter 7) are increasingly helping to close this time gap. Such strategies and technologies will become increasingly important in the coming decades as the nation's reliance on solar energy continues to expand.

It is possible to affordably convert sunlight into electricity at nearly any scale.

One other advantage of solar resources is they can generate electric power without fuel nearly anywhere the sun is shining. This unique capability of solar power is evident in the expanding number of portable solar energy devices on retail shelves. These innovative devices range from handheld solar-powered lanterns to foldable solar panels paired with lithium battery systems that can collectively provide power for weeks or months without any grid connection. These portable solar power technologies aren't just for camping: charitable organizations are increasingly harnessing them to bring limited electric power access to some of the millions of households around the world that still lack grid-supplied electricity service.

2.   POLICY DISADVANTAGES SOLAR ENERGY

Of course, despite its numerous advantages, sunlight also has several major limitations as an energy resource. To varying degrees, each of these limitations continues to constrain solar energy growth. The following are brief descriptions of some of the main drawbacks of solar radiation as a source of energy.

The availability of solar resources is intermittent and somewhat unpredictable.

Like wind resources, solar resources are available only intermittently—a condition that has historically limited their usefulness as an energy source. Most solar PV arrays and solar farms are what energy industry stakeholders call *non-dispatchable* generating sources. Grid operators cannot ramp up the electricity generation of solar farms or rooftop PV arrays at will in response to changes in grid demand because their productivity level varies depending on their sunlight access. Solar energy systems and devices do not produce power during night hours when the sun is down, and they usually produce less power during winter months and on overcast or cloudy days. This intermittency problem has historically limited the usefulness of sunlight as an energy source.

On the bright side, the intermittency characteristics of solar energy are often less problematic than those of onshore wind energy. As stated above, one reason for this is solar resources are the most available during daylight hours when the demand for electricity also tends to be higher. By contrast, the availability of wind resources is less tied to the time of day and is less predictable. In fact, in Texas and some other regions wind resources tend to be stronger on average at night, when most utility customers asleep and the electricity demand tends to be lower. Still, solar radiation is unquestionably an intermittent resource, and engineers and policymakers are continuously searching for ways to address this intermittency problem.

As will be highlighted later in this Chapter, policies promoting innovation in wholesale and retail electricity pricing models can do much to mitigate the adverse impacts of the intermittency of solar energy. Policy strategies that accelerate the development and adoption of energy storage technologies could also play important roles in overcoming the intermittency-related limitations of solar power. Chapter 7 features a more in-depth discussion of those strategies.

Utility-scale solar energy projects occupy large footprints of land.

Utility-scale solar projects are somewhat disadvantageous in that they sprawl out across large areas of land and usually preclude any other significant uses of the land's surface. Although many wind farm sites stretch across more total square mileage than the typical solar farm, landowners can usually continue to farm or ranch the land below and around wind turbines so the actual land disturbance associated with wind farms is low in comparison to that of solar energy projects. Thermal generating facilities such as nuclear or natural gas-fired power plants obviously occupy even less land per unit of produced power, thereby leaving more land available for other valuable uses.

A few research studies have sought to quantify differences in land coverage for major energy sources, and utility-scale solar energy generally performs poorly in those studies. For example, according one 2015 study, the "land intensity of energy generation" (measured in square kilometers per TWh of electricity generated per year) for the average solar resource in the United States was 7.58. By comparison, wind energy's land intensity measure was only 1.37 and nuclear energy's measure (based on data associated with California's San Onofre Generating Station) was just 0.017. *See* Jesse Jenkins, *How Much Land Does Solar, Wind and Nuclear Energy Require?*, ENERGY COLLECTIVE (June 25, 2015), http://www.the energycollective.com/jessejenkins/2242632/how-much-land-does-solar-wind-and-nuclear-energy-require. Based on these figures, utility-scale PV solar projects are roughly five and a half times more land-intensive than utility-scale wind projects and are a whopping 445 times more land-intensive than nuclear power. Of course, solar energy farm impacts often extend well beyond project borders and onto neighbors, host communities, and local ecosystems as well. Chapter 6 explores several major environmental and neighbor-related issues associated with large solar energy projects.

Solar energy systems require unshaded access to sunlight.

Although rooftop solar installations in urban and suburban settings are far less land-intensive than utility-scale solar projects, they are also more likely to raise shading conflicts among neighbors. One risk associated with solar energy is that southern neighbors[2] will grow tall trees or add additional stories to buildings next door that shade solar panels, making them less productive. This shading risk tends to be the greatest for *distributed solar energy* installations—relatively small solar panel arrays on building rooftops and in other developed areas that generate electricity primarily for onsite use. As will be described in significant detail in Chapter 6, courts and policymakers over the years have developed a diverse set of *solar access laws* to help address this risk of shading between neighbors.

Rooftop solar arrays can disrupt the look and feel of neighborhoods.

In addition to creating potential shading conflicts, rooftop solar installations can also attract neighbor opposition based on aesthetic concerns. These concerns are sometimes manifest in local ordinances prohibiting or greatly restricting rooftop solar. In other instances, they are evident in language found in private Covenants, Conditions and Restrictions (CC&Rs) that forbids solar installations in certain neighborhoods or subjects them to onerous architectural review procedures. Restricting rooftop solar installations is unquestionably warranted in some circumstances, such as in historic districts where a solar array might detract from the historic look and feel of a community. However, in many jurisdictions it is not totally clear under existing laws how far a municipality or homeowners association may go in restricting rooftop solar in more ordinary settings. Chapter 6 offers a more thorough examination of those issues as well.

The costs of solar energy still exceed those of fossil fuel-fired generation in much of the country.

Perhaps the greatest drawback of solar energy is that, despite the extraordinary declines of solar PV prices over the past few decades, solar energy remains more expensive than natural gas-fired electricity in many regions of the United States. This cost differential is partly due to relatively recent advancements in oil and gas extraction techniques, including hydraulic fracturing, which have substantially reduced domestic natural gas prices. Regardless, the costs associated with solar energy must continue to decline for it to assume a major role in meeting the nation's energy needs.

Scientific innovation and economies of scale are gradually helping to reduce the *hard costs* associated with solar energy development—the costs of the solar panels or other equipment itself—and this trend is likely to continue as solar energy becomes more prevalent. Meanwhile, a wide range

---

[2]   This Casebook assumes that readers are in the Northern Hemisphere, where trees and structures located to the south of any given location can potentially cast shadows onto the site. Solar energy users in the Southern Hemisphere (i.e., south of the Equator), must consider the risk of shading from trees or structures situated on neighboring property to the north. Some limited shading from neighbors to the east and west is possible in both hemispheres.

of governmental and private efforts are helping to reduce the *soft costs* associated with solar energy development—the permitting, interconnection, and other transactional and administrative costs involved in adding to the nation's solar generating capacity. These efforts to reduce the soft costs of solar energy development implicate numerous legal and policy issues, discussions of which are interspersed throughout the next two Chapters.

Substantial externality problems affect the pace of solar energy development.

One overarching challenge of solar energy and many other renewable energy strategies is that various externality problems will prevent it from growing optimally without significant government intervention. As discussed in Chapter 1, externality problems arise when actors do not bear or receive the full costs or benefits of an activity. Negative and positive externality problems in various forms hinder the advancement of the solar energy industry and generate inefficiency and social welfare losses. It can be difficult for stakeholders and government officials to craft and adopt policies capable of optimally addressing these problems.

The basic *positive* externality problem associated with solar energy is simple: individuals and businesses that invest time and resources into solar energy-related endeavors often cannot capture many of the benefits of those investments. For example, consider a hypothetical landowner whose electric utility relies primarily on coal-fired generating plants to supply it electric power. If the landowner purchases a solar panel array for her rooftop, her utility will burn less coal and thus emit fewer greenhouse gases and other harmful emissions. However, most rationally self-interested individuals and businesses do not directly capture those emissions-related benefits and would therefore not give them much weight when deciding whether to "go solar" or determining the size of their rooftop solar array. When aggregated across the entire market, such positive externality problems lead to sub-optimally low levels of solar energy investment and development.

This same basic challenge can alternatively be framed as a *negative* externality problem: fossil fuel-fired electricity generation creates significant environmental and other costs that those who produce and use electricity do not fully bear. For instance, a utility's projected per-unit cost of generating additional electricity with a new gas-fired power plant may be significantly lower than that of generating with a new utility-scale solar energy project. However, the gas-fired plant would deplete massive quantities of a finite natural gas resource and would emit environmentally-harmful greenhouse gases and other emissions throughout its life cycle. Unfortunately, a utility focused solely on providing electricity to its customers at the lowest achievable retail price does not factor in those external costs when deciding whether to build a natural gas-fired plant or a solar energy project. Absent some form of government intervention, this negative externality problem can cause utilities to excessively support fossil fuel-generated power and consequently underinvest in solar energy.

Such positive and negative externality problems are among the most common justifications for government policies and programs aimed at promoting solar energy. Later portions of this chapter describe many of these policies, beginning with federal policies and then highlighting those at the state and local levels of government in the United States.

Distributed solar energy companies pose a competitive threat to electric utilities.

One further obstacle the solar energy industry faces is the reality that distributed solar energy technologies create long-term uncertainty and instability for electric utilities. Each kWh of electricity generated on a residential utility customer's rooftop is one additional kWh the utility does not get supply and sell. In that sense, distributed solar energy technologies have the potential to seriously disrupt retail electricity markets and cut deeply into utilities' (historically 100%) market share. Rooftop solar installations and net metering programs are already eroding utilities' revenues in some states and could eventually undermine the effectiveness of longstanding utility regulatory models. Accordingly, although many electric utilities are happy to promote and investing in utility-scale solar energy projects (which are more akin to traditional power plants), they tend to be less supportive of policies that encourage distributed solar energy. The complex questions surrounding this ongoing tension between utilities and the rooftop solar energy industry are explored in considerable detail later in this chapter.

C. FEDERAL POLICIES PROMOTING SOLAR ENERGY

Aware of the distinct advantages and disadvantages of solar energy, policymakers today are developing new ways to harness its strengths and address its weaknesses as they work to integrate more of it into the nation's energy mix. A diverse collection of laws, regulations, and programs spanning all major levels of government seeks to further this goal. The following materials examine several of the federal government's approaches to encouraging the adoption of solar energy technologies in the United States.

1. FEDERAL INVESTMENT TAX CREDITS

At the federal government level, the most impactful government incentive policy to date for promoting solar energy has been the federal investment tax credit (ITC) program. Although the *production* tax credit

(PTC) for utility-scale wind energy development highlighted in Chapter 2 does not apply to solar energy projects, the ITC does. The ITC is a tax credit that qualifying taxpayers can use to reduce their federal income tax liability. Unlike the PTC, which is based on the amount of electricity a project generates, the amount of a taxpayer's ITC is a percentage of the total qualifying energy investment the taxpayer makes. The ITC is available not only for solar energy investments—as of 2017 it was also available for investments in certain other types of renewable projects such as geothermal and small wind energy. Developers of utility-scale wind energy projects can alternatively elect to claim the ITC in lieu of the PTC on their projects. However, as set forth in the statutory excerpts below, the credit phase out schedule for the ITC is different for utility-scale wind projects than it is for solar energy projects.

The ITC's structure makes it well-suited for residential landowners buying rooftop solar panel installations but can complicate the structuring of equity financing for large solar energy projects. To quote Professor Tracey Roberts:

> The investment tax credit ("ITC") was first made available in 1962 with the goal of stimulating the economy and bolstering the competitiveness of domestic companies in international trade. The current version of the ITC, developed under the Energy Policy Act of 2005, provides a credit against tax liability based on the total project cost for qualifying projects, which include solar energy projects. . . . Unlike the PTC, the ITC may be layered with government-sponsored low interest loan programs and other subsidies to finance renewable and energy projects. . . . The ITC is realized the first year after the facility is placed in service, but the project owner is the only party eligible to use the credit. A tax equity investor must retain his interest in the project for at least five years for the full amount of the credits to vest; if the project is sold before all the credits have vested, the credits are disgorged. The ITC has expired periodically and Congress has reinstated and modified it a number of times. The ITC has been most recently extended under the Consolidated Appropriations Act, 2016. A number of solar technologies will continue to receive the thirty percent ITC through December 31, 2019, after which the credit is reduced in phases to ten percent.

Tracey M. Roberts, *Picking Winners and Losers: A Structural Examination of Subsidies to the Energy Industry*, 41 COLUM. J. ENVTL. L. 63, 98–100 (2016).

Lawyers representing developers of solar energy projects obviously must understand the basic features and limitations of the tax credit programs applicable to their client's projects. Even if they are providing representation on just one aspect of a solar energy project, such as real estate or environmental permitting, being familiar with the ITC and how it functions helps attorneys to avoid pitfalls that could harm the clients' interests. The following are excerpts from the Internal Revenue Code describing the ITC and some of its limitations. Read the excerpts carefully, then apply these provisions to respond to Questions 1 and 2 that follow.

26 U.S.C.A. § 48 (2016)

(a) Energy credit.

(1) In general.—For purposes of section 46, except as provided in paragraphs (1)(B), (2)(B), (3)(B), and (4)(B) of subsection (c), the energy credit for any taxable year is the energy percentage of the basis of each energy property placed in service during such taxable year.

(2) Energy percentage.

(A) In general.—Except as provided in paragraph (6), the energy percentage is—

(i) 30 percent in the case of—

(I) qualified fuel cell property,

(II) energy property described in paragraph (3)(A)(i) but only with respect to property the construction of which begins before January 1, 2022,

(III) energy property described in paragraph (3)(A)(ii), and

(IV) qualified small wind energy property, and

(ii) in the case of any energy property to which clause (i) does not apply, 10 percent.

. . . .

(3) Energy property.—For purposes of this subpart, the term "energy property" means any property—

(A) which is—

(i) equipment which uses solar energy to generate electricity, to heat or cool (or provide hot water for use in) a structure, or to provide solar process heat, excepting property used to generate energy for the purposes of heating a swimming pool. . . .

. . . .

(5) Election to treat qualified facilities as energy property.

(A) In general.—In the case of any qualified property which is part of a qualified investment credit facility—

(i)   such property shall be treated as energy property for purposes of this section, and

(ii)   the energy percentage with respect to such property shall be 30 percent.

(B)   Denial of production credit.—No credit shall be allowed under section 45 for any taxable year with respect to any qualified investment credit facility.

(C)   Qualified investment credit facility.—For purposes of this paragraph, the term "qualified investment credit facility" means any facility—

(i)   which is a qualified facility (within the meaning of section 45). . . .

. . . .

(iii)   with respect to which—

(I)   no credit has been allowed under section 45[3], and

(II)   the taxpayer makes an irrevocable election to have this paragraph apply.

. . . .

(E)   Phaseout of credit for wind facilities.—In the case of any facility using wind to produce electricity, the amount of the credit determined under this section (determined after the application of paragraphs (1) and (2) and without regard to this subparagraph) shall be reduced by—

(i)   in the case of any facility the construction of which begins after December 31, 2016, and before January 1, 2018, 20 percent,

(ii)   in the case of any facility the construction of which begins after December 31, 2017, and before January 1, 2019, 40 percent, and

(iii)   in the case of any facility the construction of which begins after December 31, 2018, and before January 1, 2020, 60 percent.

(6)   Phaseout for solar energy property.—

(A)   In general.—Subject to subparagraph (B), in the case of any energy property described in paragraph (3)(A)(i) the construction

---

[3]   Author's note: 26 U.S.C.A. § 45 is the Internal Revenue Code section that establishes and governs eligibility for Production Tax Credits (which area available for utility-scale wind energy projects). 26 U.S.C.A. § 45(a)(5)(C)(iii) effectively allows developers to opt to claim investment tax credits for a utility-scale wind energy project in lieu of claiming production tax credits on the project.

of which begins before January 1, 2022, the energy percentage determined under paragraph (2) shall be equal to—

 (i) in the case of any property the construction of which begins after December 31, 2019, and before January 1, 2021, 26 percent, and

 (ii) in the case of any property the construction of which begins after December 31, 2020, and before January 1, 2022, 22 percent.

(B) Placed in service deadline.—In the case of any property energy property described in paragraph (3)(A)(i) the construction of which begins before January 1, 2022, and which is not placed in service before January 1, 2024, the energy percentage determined under paragraph (2) shall be equal to 10 percent.

NOTES & QUESTIONS

 1. Suppose it is 2018 and your client, Big Wind LLC, intends to construct a large new wind energy farm within the year. If the client were to commence construction in 2018 and irrevocably elect not to claim any PTCs on the project, what percentage ITC would the project qualify for?

 2. Suppose it is March of 2021 and your client, Big Solar LLC, intends to construct a new utility-scale solar energy project. Big Solar anticipates it will complete the project by early 2023. Assuming Big Solar stays on that schedule, what percentage ITC would it qualify for?

 a. Suppose further that Big Solar plans to sell off the solar farm to a different party in 2024. Identify and explain any potential adverse consequences of executing such a plan.

 b. Suppose that, due to unforeseen delays, Big Solar's project is ultimately not finished until late 2024. What percentage credit will the project qualify for, and why?

 3. *Leveraging Private Investment.* A common argument in favor of renewable energy tax credits is that the credits will trigger greater private investment and create new jobs. Solar energy industry advocates highlighted these benefits in 2016 after Congress extended the ITC for several additional years. Among other things, the Solar Energy Industry Association estimated that the 2015 ITC extension would lead to an additional $40 billion in private investment in solar energy projects and create 180,000 additional jobs that would not have been created without the extension. *See Fact Sheet: Impacts of Solar Investment Tax Credit Extension*, Solar Energy Indus. Ass'n, http://www. seia.org/research-resources/impacts-solar-investment-tax-credit-extension (last visited Sept. 16, 2017).

2. FEDERAL RESEARCH GRANTS

Tax credits have been fairly effective at accelerating the adoption of solar energy technologies in the private marketplace. However, tax credit programs are generally not effective at incentivizing basic solar energy research at public universities and other nonprofit institutions—another important aspect of solar energy policy. Much of the knowledge borne out of such institutional research is what economists call a *public good*, meaning that it is largely *non-excludable* (individuals cannot be effectively excluded) and *non-rivalrous* (use by one does not diminish availability for others). For example, once a municipality integrates new policy strategy into a local solar energy ordinance, other cities can easily access those strategies and adopt them too without having to pay for them. Likewise, one city's use of such a policy strategy generally does not diminish its capacity for use by countless others. This non-rivalrous nature of new knowledge gained through institutional research favors policy strategies that ensure that such knowledge is made widely available.

Public goods such as knowledge gained through institutional research tend to be underfunded in private markets because entities producing them cannot easily capture all of their benefits. For several decades, the federal government has funded a wide array of research grant programs and initiatives, helping to incentivize more optimal levels of institutional research in countless areas ranging from computer science to medicine. Recognizing the potential social value of advancements in solar energy and other renewable energy technologies, federal officials have similarly funded an unprecedented amount of research in those areas in recent years.

Using federal grant programs to fund institutional research, including solar energy research, can be an effective means of overcoming to public goods-related underfunding problems. The availability of grant funding frees researchers from having to attempt to capture the value of their research in a private marketplace. Because they are bankrolled with government dollars, most grant-funded research publications are also generally available to the public at little or no cost.

a. The Sunshot Initiative

Over the past couple of decades, multiple federal grant programs have funded research aimed at advancing solar energy technologies and the solar energy industry. The SunShot Initiative has been among the most influential federal grant programs under the U.S. Department of Energy (DOE) focused on solar energy policy. The Initiative has funded numerous public and private research projects aimed at finding ways to reduce the per-unit costs of solar energy development. The Initiative's webpage describes it as "a national effort to support solar energy adoption by making solar energy affordable for all Americans through research and development efforts." It awards monetary grants for "research, development, demonstration, and deployment projects by private companies, universities, state and local governments, nonprofit organizations, and national laboratories to drive down the cost of solar electricity." *See About the SunShot Initiative*, https://energy.gov/eere/ sunshot/about-sunshot-initiative (last visited Sept. 16, 2017).

When the DOE first launched the SunShot Initiative in 2011, it declared a goal of reducing the levelized costs of solar-generated electricity to certain ambitious targets by the year 2020. By late 2016, the initiative had already achieved its cost target for utility-scale PV projects and was quickly approaching its other targets ahead of schedule so the DOE revised its cost targets for the year 2030 to make them even more aggressive. Those new targets and the DOE's progress in pursuit of them are illustrated in the DOE's graphic representation in Figure 5.4. As of mid-2017, the initiative had provided grant funding for more than 300 different research or development projects aimed at reducing the costs of solar energy. The funded projects cover numerous areas, including strategies for reducing *soft costs*—various administrative, permitting and other costs of solar energy development other than the costs of physical equipment and space.

Figure 5.4. U.S. Department of Energy's SunShot Initiative

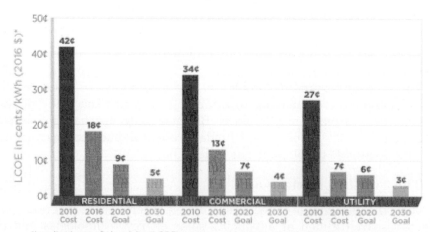

3. LOAN GUARANTEE PROGRAMS

The ITC and DOE's SunShot initiative are just two examples from a long list of federal government programs that promote solar energy. Federal loan guarantee programs have been another impactful solar energy policy tool for helping to kick-start the nation's utility-scale solar energy industry. As recently as 2009, there was not a single PV solar energy project in the United States with more than 100 MW of generating capacity, and developers also showed relatively little interest in pursuing CSP projects. *See* Mark A. McCall, *5 Big Wins in Clean Energy from the Loan Programs Office*, DEP'T ENERGY (Feb. 17, 2016), https://energy.gov/articles/5-big-wins-clean-energy-loan-programs-office. However, new loan guarantee provisions enacted in the American Recovery and Reinvestment Act (ARRA) of 2009 helped to change that, catalyzing unprecedented period growth in utility-scale solar development.

ARRA's primary purpose was to stimulate a national economy still struggling to recover from the Great Recession. With PV solar cell costs falling and CSP technologies rapidly improving, there was growing interest in 2009 in the development of utility-scale solar projects. Unfortunately, developing these projects required large sums of money, and finance markets had not yet fully rebounded from the mortgage meltdown crisis. At the time, few lenders operating within that challenging lending environment were willing to affordably finance utility-scale solar projects because such projects and their technologies were still perceived as unproven and high-risk. ARRA's Section 1705 Loan Guarantee Program helped to address these financing obstacles by furnishing a way for qualified developers to have their project development loans "guaranteed" by the federal government. In layman's terms, these loan guarantees effectively meant that, if a solar project developer was ever unable to make its loan payments, the government would step in and make the payments on the developer's behalf.

The Section 1705 Loan Guarantee Program, which came in the form of amendments to an existing loan guarantee program under Title XVII of the Energy Policy Act (EPAct) of 2005, was also available for wind energy, geothermal, and energy storage projects. However, Section 1705's positive impact on the utility-scale solar energy industry was arguably its greatest achievement. Under the Program, the federal government issued guarantees for five utility-scale PV projects and five CSP projects before the Program expired in 2011. The proven success of those guaranteed projects persuaded stakeholders in private finance markets of the viability of utility-scale solar development and ultimately enabled dozens of developers to secure private project financing without loan guarantees in the years that followed. According to the DOE, at least 28 more utility-scale solar PV projects were financed without loan guarantees from 2011 to 2016 alone. *See id.*

Although most of the loan guarantees issued under the Section 1705 Loan Guarantee Program have been successful, the failure of one company that received a federal loan guarantee drew enormous amounts of negative media attention. The private solar manufacturer Solyndra applied under the Program for a $535 million loan guarantee to help finance construction of a large manufacturing plant. After receiving the loan guarantee and securing its financing, the company's business failed and it filed for bankruptcy protection in 2011, leaving the federal government on the hook for Solyndra's massive loan. In the years following the bankruptcy, investigations revealed that Solyndra executives had made misrepresentations to the government when trying to secure the loan guarantee. Investigations also revealed that government officials had insufficiently vetted the Solyndra proposal before granting the guarantee. *See* Kellan Howell & Stephen Dinan, *Solyndra Misled Government to Get $535M Solar Project Loan: Report*, WASH. TIMES (Aug. 25, 2015), http:// www.washingtontimes.com/news/2015/aug/26/solyndra-misled-government-get-535-million-solar-p/.

For several years after Solyndra's failure, countless politicians and pundits cited the incident as supposed evidence that renewable energy incentive programs were corrupt and unjustifiable. However, the Section 1705 Loan Guarantee Program seems to have ultimately been relatively successful in spite of Solyndra's failed guarantee. As of late 2016, most of the loan guarantee recipients under Section 1705 were still timely repaying their debts and the federal government was been collecting hundreds of millions of dollars in interest payments from those transactions. In fact, interest payments received under the Program well exceeded losses, suggesting that the program was turning a profit for federal taxpayers. *See* Stephen Edelstein, *Solyndra Who? The Energy Department's Loan Program Is Now Profitable*, CHRISTIAN SCI. MONITOR (Oct. 17, 2016), http:// www.csmonitor.com/Business/In-Gear/2016/1017/Solyndra-who-The-Energy-Department-s-loan-program-is-now-profitable.

When the Section 1705 Loan Guarantee Program stopped issuing new guarantees in September 2011, developers reverted to using a less generous loan program that was already in existence years before ARRA's enactment. Section 1703 of Title XVII of the EPAct contains loan guarantee provisions comparable to those of Section 1705 and, as of late 2017, the Section 1703 Loan Guarantee Program remained operational with no expiration date in sight. There was one major difference between the Section 1705 program and the Section 1703 program: under Section 1703, borrowers must pay the "credit subsidy cost" associated with their loans— the government's cost of assuming the default risks of the loan. Borrowers whose loans were guaranteed under Section 1705 did not bear those costs because ARRA specifically appropriated funds to cover them. Increasingly, lenders have become more comfortable with the risks of solar energy development, enabling developers to more easily secure private project financing without the need of a federal loan guarantee. Still, Section 1703 continues to provide an additional potential tool to help developers of large solar energy projects secure project financing.

4. BONUS DEPRECIATION FOR COMMERCIAL SOLAR

As stated above, an addition to three programs just highlighted there are numerous other federal programs that promote renewable energy. Among these are certain federal tax code provisions enacted under the Protect Americans from Tax Hikes Act of 2015 (PATH). PATH's provisions allow commercial purchasers of solar energy systems and other qualifying capital equipment to claim valuable tax depreciation deductions on accelerated schedules through 2019. Until the end of 2017, companies were permitted to depreciate half (50%) of the depreciable *basis* or cost of such equipment in the year they placed them into service—a much larger percentage than is ordinarily permitted under the tax code. PATH provided that the amount of this so-called *bonus depreciation* would drop to 40% in 2018 and 30% in 2019. The tax depreciation and cost recovery benefits available under PATH have served as yet another means of encouraging additional solar energy investment.

Obviously, businesses pay federal income taxes and most companies would prefer to pay fewer taxes. A primary way for companies to reduce their tax liability is to claim various tax deductions and credits under provisions of the Internal Revenue Code (IRC). One important class of deductions for many companies is *depreciation deductions*. The IRC's basic deduction provisions allow businesses to gradually deduct the capitalized costs of qualifying tangible business property over some specified number of years. Claiming these deductions reduces a company's *taxable income*—the income measure the IRS ultimately uses to compute the company's tax bill.

Ordinarily, under a method known as the Modified Accelerated Cost Recovery System (MACRS), a business must *depreciate* (i.e., deduct from taxable income) the cost of a newly-purchased solar PV system over a five-year period, deducting no more than 20% of the system's cost in each of those years. However, most companies would prefer to deduct a larger percentage of the system's cost up front and thereby reduce their tax bills sooner. Through 2019, PATH's bonus depreciation provisions make investments in rooftop solar energy systems more financially appealing to businesses by doing just that.

A simple numerical example helps to illustrate how PATH's accelerated depreciation provisions encourage private investment in solar energy. Suppose that, in the year 2020, a small business purchases a $100,000 rooftop solar array for the roof of its headquarters building.

Assuming the array is installed and placed into service in that year, the array will likely qualify for a 26% ITC under the IRC § 48 provisions excerpted earlier in this chapter. Under provisions found elsewhere in the IRC, the *depreciable tax basis* of a rooftop solar system is reduced by half of any claimed ITC, which would be 13% of the total cost in this example (resulting in a depreciable basis of $87,000). Assuming the laws as of 2017 remain the same such that no bonus depreciation is available for such purchases in 2020, the company will qualify only for depreciation of 20% of the depreciable basis in that taxable year. More specifically, the company would be able to deduct ($87,000 × 0.20) = $17,400 from its taxable income in 2020 under the IRC's cost recovery provisions.

Now suppose that the company had placed the solar array into service in *2017* instead of 2020. Since the percentage amount of the ITC remains at 30% through 2019, the company would have qualified for the full 30% ITC that year. As stated in the previous example, the IRC first requires taxpayers to reduce the depreciable basis of new renewable energy equipment by half of any claimed ITC. In this case, that would mean a reduction of 15% of the $100,000 cost (i.e., $15,000), reducing the basis to $85,000. However, in 2017 the company would have also qualified for 50% "bonus depreciation" since PATH's bonus depreciation provisions apply through 2019. The company could first deduct 50% of the depreciable basis of the array, or ($85,000 × 0.50) = $42,500. In that same taxable year, the company could still *also* deduct an additional 20% from that further-reduced basis according to the MACRS five-year schedule, or ($42,500 × 0.20) = $8,500. In total, the company would thus get to deduct ($42,500 + $8,500) = $51,000 from its taxable income in 2017 alone.

A comparison of the 2020 example to the 2017 highlights the benefit of PATH's bonus depreciation provisions. A company purchasing a $100,000 solar energy system in 2017 would get to claim a $51,000 tax deduction in that year. By contrast, it would qualify for only a $17,400 deduction if it made the purchase in 2020—a difference of $33,600. If the company's effective tax rate were 25%, this difference would result in ($33,600 × 0.25) = $8,400 less tax liability under the 2017 tax provisions than under the 2020 provisions. Although PATH's bonus depreciation allowance provisions have not been "game changers" for the renewable energy industry, they have provided one additional incentive for businesses to move forward with investments in solar energy systems.

5. THE PUBLIC UTILITY REGULATORY POLICIES ACT OF 1978 (PURPA)

In recent years, the Public Utility Regulatory Policies Act of 1978 (PURPA) has become yet another increasingly important driver of solar energy growth. PURPA is a decades-old federal statute requiring electric utilities to contract to purchase wholesale electricity at *avoided cost* rates from qualifying small renewable energy facilities (QFs). A utility's avoided cost is generally price the utility would have to pay at any given place and time if the utility were purchasing the power in the wholesale electricity market rather than from some specific producer. Renewable energy projects with no more than 80MW of generating capacity generally qualify as QFs under PURPA's provisions and are thus eligible to compel utilities to buy their generated power at avoided cost prices.

Unforeseen policy developments have unexpectedly elevated the relevance of PURPA for solar energy developers in recent years. From the early 2000s until the mid-2010s, state renewable portfolio standards (RPS), which are discussed later in this chapter in the materials on state policies, provided adequate motivation for utilities in most states to execute long-term power purchase agreements (PPAs) to buy power from smaller renewable energy projects. However, as more and more states have reached and exceeded their existing RPS goals, some utilities become less motivated to purchase additional renewable power. In this changing market, some developers of commercial-scale solar energy projects are increasingly relying upon PURPA's provisions to compel utilities to buy their projects' generated power. Due largely to falling PV module prices, as of 2017 developers in a growing number of states could earn sizable profits by building solar PV projects fitting PURPA's size requirements and sell the projects' power at avoided cost rates.

Many investor-owned utilities would prefer not to buy power from QFs such as commercial-scale solar projects, even at avoided cost rates. Instead, most would prefer to build their own renewable energy projects or to execute long-term PPAs with owners of larger utility-scale generating facilities. Investor-owned utilities that build their own renewable energy projects are generally able to recoup their capital investments in those projects and a reasonable rate of return on those investments through approved increases in their retail electricity rates. Utilities also tend to view larger utility-scale generating facilities as creating less uncertainty, fewer financial risks, and fewer operational challenges than smaller-scale renewable energy systems.

Provisions in PURPA allow FERC to waive a utility's obligation to purchase power from a QF, but only under certain narrow conditions. Specifically, FERC can waive this obligation only if the relevant wholesale electricity market is so open and competitive that the QF should have no difficulty selling the power at avoided cost rates to one or more other utilities. As of 2017, disputes over this waiver authority were becoming more common as PURPA-driven solar energy development spreads across the nation. Some utilities had even begun asking FERC to reinterpret PURPA as growing numbers of renewable energy developers seek to rely on the statute's provisions to compel utilities to purchase their projects' power at avoided cost rates. The importance of PURPA will likely continue to increase as renewable energy technologies grow more and more cost-competitive with conventional energy sources in the coming decades. *See* Robert F. Shapiro, *PURPA and Solar*, NORTON ROSE FULBRIGHT (Apr. 2017), https://www.chadbourne.com/purpa-and-solar-project-finance-april-2017.

6. SOLAR LEASING ON FEDERAL PUBLIC LANDS

One other category of federal laws and regulations associated with solar energy are those specifically governing the development of utility-scale solar energy projects on federal public lands. The United States has millions of acres of federal public lands with excellent solar energy resources. Some of these lands are managed by the U.S. Forest Service, Fish and Wildlife Service, or National Park System. However, the Bureau of Land Management (BLM) manages the greatest proportion of the nation's federal lands—roughly 250 million acres in all. *See* Quoctrung Bui & Margot Sanger-Katz, *Why the Government Owns So Much Land in the West*, N.Y. TIMES (Jan. 5, 2016), https://www.nytimes.com/2016/01/06/upshot/why-the-government-owns-so-much-land-in-the-west.html?_r=0.

The BLM is an agency within the U.S. Department of the Interior whose purpose and mission is to "to sustain the health, diversity, and productivity of the public lands for the use and enjoyment of present and future generations." *BLM Facts*, BUREAU LAND MGMT., https://www.blm.gov/nhp/facts/ (last visited Sept. 16, 2017). As authorized and directed under the Federal Land Policy and Leasing Act (FLPLA) and Mineral Leasing Act (MLA), the BLM oversees the leasing of BLM lands for renewable energy development. Renewable energy developers interested in siting projects on specific areas of BLM land must apply to the BLM for lease rights. Developers typically pay rents and fees in exchange for those rights, and the BLM has broad discretion to restrict where and how developers site and construct renewable energy projects under BLM leases.

The BLM has garnered mixed reviews on its solar energy leasing duties over the past couple of decades. On the one hand, the agency has facilitated an unprecedentedly high volume of solar energy development on BLM land in recent years. Until 2008, there were hardly any utility-scale solar energy projects on BLM lands. Then, in 2009, BLM solar leasing activity rapidly accelerated. From 2009 to 2016, the agency approved a total of 60 new utility-scale renewable energy projects on BLM lands capable of generating enough electricity to power 5.1 million homes. Most of those approved projects—36 out of 60—were doe solar energy development. *See* Press Release, Bureau of Land Mgmt., U.S. Dep't of Interior, *Department of the Interior Finalizes Rule Providing a Foundation for the Future of BLM's Renewable Energy Program* (Nov. 10, 2016), https://www.blm.gov/node/7653.

On the other hand, the BLM has also severely constrained future solar energy development on BLM lands by limiting which lands in Western states are potentially eligible for profitable solar energy development. A prime example of this was the BLM's 2016 release of its Desert Renewable Energy Conservation Plan (DRECP). The DRECP was the culmination of nearly eight years of research efforts aimed at identifying which BLM lands in California were best suited for renewable energy development. Out of roughly 10.8 million acres of potentially developable BLM land, the agency ultimately designated just 388,000 acres as eligible for the DRECP's streamlined permitting process and financial incentives. Although some environmentalist groups lauded the DRECP, some solar energy industry advocates suggested that it unjustifiably stifled utility-scale solar development on public lands within the state. *See Why Solar Developers Aren't Happy With the Desert Renewable Energy Plan*, FORTUNE (Sept. 14, 2016), http://fortune.com/2016/09/15/desert-renewable-energy-plan/.

7. POLICIES PROMOTING SOLAR ENERGY IN INDIAN COUNTRY

A handful of federal programs seek to specifically promote solar energy projects and other types of renewable energy development on Indian trust lands. According to the DOE, roughly 5 percent of the nation's developable renewable energy resources reside on Indian trust lands, even though those lands comprise less than 2 percent of the country's total land area. Unfortunately, several factors have made it difficult for tribes to attract solar energy development on trust lands. For instance, many otherwise desirable sites are not situated close enough to existing transmission lines to make renewable energy development viable there. It can also be more difficult for tribes and members of tribes to use tax credits such as the ITC because they generally do not pay federal tax on income derived from trust lands.

The Indian Tribal Energy Development and Self-Determination Act of 2005, which Congress enacted as Title V of the EPAct of 2005, sought to address some of these impediments and thereby increase renewable energy development in Indian country. Unfortunately, the statute has had only limited success. The following excerpts describe some of the unique obstacles under federal law that tribes have faced in their efforts to develop solar energy projects on trust lands.

COMMUNITY SOLAR: WATT'S IN IT FOR INDIAN COUNTRY?

Racheal White Hawk

40 ENVIRONS 1, 5–6, 8–9, 15–17 (2016)

The United States holds approximately fifty-six million acres of land in trust on behalf of Indian tribes and individuals. This land has the potential for 17.6 billion kilowatt-hours ("kWh") per year of solar energy production, or 4.5 times the total national energy generation in 2004. Currently, 83 of the 326 reservations in the U.S. have the solar resources needed for economically viable concentrated solar power generation.

. . . .

Overall, Indian lands hold great potential for solar energy development. Numerous reservations have the degree of solar radiation necessary for optimal concentrated solar energy development. Community-scale solar power, however, has even *more* potential on Indian lands because such systems are less location-dependent than concentrated systems and can be very cost-effective for many remote Indian lands throughout the United States.

. . . .

. . . However, there are significant obstacles to community-scale solar energy implementation in Indian country. Tribes face significant funding issues, cultural barriers may sometimes prevent solar project development, current technology for energy storage remains inadequate or too expensive, and tribal jurisdictional authority over solar projects is not always clear.

. . . .

. . . Currently, the most successful federal investments for solar energy are those for community-scale projects, such as installing solar panels on a casino and reducing energy costs for tribal governments. That community-scale projects are the most successful federal projects is evidenced by the fact that there are currently only two tribal utility-scale solar projects in the U.S., both of which are operated by the same tribe. Utility-scale projects on Indian lands generally require an energy purchaser. There are many tribes that possess phenomenal solar resources, but that have no external purchaser. For example, although the Jemez Pueblo in New Mexico received a DOE grant and planned to create a utility grid of solar PV panels to deliver energy, the Pueblo ultimately was forced to decline the award because it could not find a buyer for its excess solar energy.

. . . .

Overlapping and uncertain regulatory jurisdiction also impede the development of small solar energy projects on Indian lands. Overlap and uncertainty can result from conflicts between neighboring tribes. However, conflicts often arise over state and tribal authority to regulate and tax activities that take place on Indian lands as well. Renewable energy production may result in sales, property, and corporate income taxes that can create uncertainty as to whether the state, tribe, or both have the authority to regulate and tax the energy production. . . .

One federal law in particular, the Indian Long-Term Leasing Act ("ILTLA"), has been a major impediment to land development in Indian country. Under the ILTLA, leases of Indian lands require the approval of the Secretary. Leases for solar energy projects are typically approved under the ILTLA. Requiring Secretarial approval for leases significantly lengthens the leasing process, which expands the development timeline. ILTLA might apply to permanent improvements on Indian lands as well, including houses and other structures, which could limit an individual's ability to enter into a lease to install a rooftop solar panel on his or her home. ILTLA also limits the ability of tribes to enter into leases with solar developers to implement community-scale solar projects because of the need for Secretarial approval. However, in 2012, President Obama signed into law the Helping Expedite and Advance Responsible Tribal Homeownership Act ("HEARTH Act"), amending the ILTLA to expedite leasing on tribal lands. The HEARTH Act allows tribes to approve their own leases as long as the tribe's regulations have been approved by the Secretary.

Provisions in NEPA are also relevant to certain types of community-scale solar energy development in Indian country. Federal actions in Indian country are subject to NEPA. Secretarial approval of a lease in Indian country constitutes such federal action. Leases and similar uses of trust land generally require the approval of the Secretary. Therefore, surface leases of Indian trust land may require compliance with NEPA. Because NEPA violations may be raised by tribal members and any non-Indian with standing, a tribe's failure to properly follow NEPA procedures under a lease approved by the Secretary could lead to costly litigation, which would prevent projects from moving forward in a timely, cost-efficient manner.

Additionally, for community-scale projects, a right-of-way may also be needed to connect the solar power generated from the project to an energy substation. Such a right-of-way would fall under the 1948 General Rights-of-Way Act governing rights-of-way on Indian lands. Although the BIA recently updated regulations to streamline the process of obtaining grants of rights-of-way on Indian land, the process could still delay the implementation of a community-scale solar project.

NOTES & QUESTIONS

1.   The graphic in Figure 5.4 suggests that the SunShot Initiative has been quite successful thus far in furthering its objectives. Suppose you represented a client advocating for the elimination of the SunShot initiative. Craft at least two specific arguments rebutting the assertion that, based on Figure 5.4, the SunShot initiative has been highly successful and deserves continued funding.

2.   According to the materials above, why have private lenders grown increasingly willing in recent years to finance utility-scale solar energy projects without requiring that borrowers secure loan guarantees through the federal government? What does this shift in lender requirements suggest about the success or failure of ARRA's Section 1705 Loan Guarantee Program? Why?

3.   Suppose that, in the year 2018, the retail grocer MarketCo purchased a $500,000 PV solar array and had it installed on MarketCo's distribution warehouse. The array was fully operational by October of 2018 and was supplying more than 80% of the warehouse's electricity needs. When MarketCo filed its 2018 corporate taxes, the company successfully claimed the applicable Investment Tax Credit (ITC). It also claimed all allowed tax depreciation associated with the purchase of the solar array. Using the hypothetical examples above as a guide, answer the following questions related to MarketCo.

a.   What was the dollar amount of MarketCo's ITC?

b.   What was the depreciable basis of the MarketCo's solar array, *before* the company claimed any depreciation deductions?

c.   What was the total amount of MarketCo's allowable depreciation deduction for the solar array for 2018 (i.e., the sum of its bonus depreciation and MACRS depreciation)?

4.   Based on the materials above, describe in one paragraph in your own words how utilities' successful compliance with RPS requirements in recent years has made PURPA's provisions increasingly important to the success of solar energy development.

5.   Suppose you served as legal counsel for a utility that was lobbying Congress to amend PURPA's provisions such that utilities were no longer statutorily required to purchase power from QFs within their territories at avoided cost rates. Craft a one-paragraph statement making at least three distinct arguments in favor of the amendment.

6.   Based on the materials above, identify at least three unique obstacles to solar energy development on Indian trust lands. Briefly describe and defend a potential legislative solution to each of the three obstacles you identify.

7.   *State Solar Tax Credits and Rebates.* In addition to the federal tax credits highlighted above, many states also offer tax credits and rebates to incentivize investments in solar energy. Numerous states and utilities throughout offer rebates of various kinds to private utility customers who

purchase or install distributed solar PV systems, solar water heaters, or solar swimming pool heating. A frequently-updated database describing this long list of potential rebates is available at the DOE's website at https://energy.gov/ savings. Major distributed solar energy companies also typically assist customers in identifying and taking advantage of these rebates and state tax credit programs.

8. FEDERAL ANTITRUST LAWS AFFECTING SOLAR ENERGY

As utilities struggle to adapt to the emergence of distributed energy technologies in the coming years, federal antitrust laws may become increasingly relevant to the evolution of solar energy policy as well. As described in the materials on state-level policies below, utilities are increasingly seeking policy reforms aimed at protecting their monopolies on electricity markets against the rooftop solar industry—an increasingly viable competitive threat. Some of the policy reforms utility companies have sought drive rooftop solar energy companies out of those markets in ways that could arguably implicate antitrust laws. This raises a difficult question: is it even possible for a regulated electric utility to violate antitrust laws by protecting itself against competition from a disruptive innovator?

When the Arizona utility SRP imposed large new monthly charges on retail customers with solar panels in late 2014, rooftop solar industry stakeholders pressed this issue by raising antitrust arguments as part of their challenge of the new charges. The following excerpt from a 2015 case describes these arguments, which may be a harbinger of more to come as distributed energy technologies continue to strain utilities' longstanding centralized generation model in the coming decades.

SOLARCITY CORPORATION V. SALT RIVER PROJECT AGRICULTURAL IMPROVEMENT

United States District Court, District of Arizona, 2015
2015 WL 6503439

RAYES, D.J.

In December 2014, the Salt River Project ("SRP") announced a new rate structure for sale of retail electricity, which included additional fees for consumers who obtain part of their electricity from rooftop solar energy systems. Solar energy companies, environmentalists, and other interest groups opposed the rate change, arguing the new fee would dissuade consumers from installing solar energy systems. SRP approved the new rates in February 2015. Plaintiff SolarCity Corporation brings this action challenging the new rate structure under federal and state antitrust laws.

Before the Court are Defendant Salt River Project Agricultural Improvement and Power District's (the "District") motion to dismiss, and Defendant Salt River Valley Water Users' Association's (the "Association") motion to dismiss. The District has also filed a request for judicial notice. The Court held oral argument on October 14, 2015. For the reasons stated below, the District's motion to dismiss is granted in part, the Association's motion to dismiss is granted, and the District's motion for judicial notice is granted in part.

BACKGROUND

I. The Parties

SolarCity is the country's "largest installer of distributed solar energy systems." (Doc. 39, ¶ 15.) It sells and leases solar energy systems to residential and commercial customers "who then use the systems to generate electricity and thereby displace a portion of their electricity purchases from an electric utility." (*Id.*, ¶ 16.) Prior to the rate change, SolarCity "averaged almost 400 installations per month in SRP's service area." (*Id.*, ¶ 17.)

SRP is a power-and-water utility comprised of two separate entities: the District and the Association (collectively referred to as "SRP"). "The Association is a private, for-profit corporation that files reports with the state listing its Board members as 'directors' of the corporation." (*Id.*, ¶ 26.) It was formed in 1903 by private Salt River Valley landowners in order to "enter into contracts with the federal government for the irrigation of their land." (*Id.*, ¶ 27.) It continues to operate as a private corporation for the benefit of private landowners.

The District was created in 1937 "for the purpose of refinancing the Association's debts by issuing interest-free bonds, thereby saving the private landowners very large sums of money each year." (*Id.*, ¶ 28.) The District is responsible for power and water storage work, and the Association manages "water delivery as an agent of the District." (*Id.*) The revenues generated from the District's sale of electricity subsidize the Association's "money-losing water operations, by [$100 million] per year." (*Id.*, ¶ 35(b).) The District "cannot impose ad valorem property taxes or sales taxes, enact any laws governing the conduct of citizens, or administer [other] such normal functions of government[.]" (*Id.*, ¶ 40.) The Arizona Corporation Commission ("ACC"), Arizona's public utility regulatory authority "has no rate-setting or review authority over the District or its retail operations." (*Id.*, ¶ 42.)

II. Industry Allegations

SRP operates in the Phoenix-metro area. It provides electricity to residential and commercial customers. . . .

SolarCity participates in this market, which it defines as "the provision of electric power to end-use residential, governmental, and businesses consumers[.]" (*Id.*, ¶¶ 48–49.) It alleges it "directly competes with SRP because it offers equipment and services that provide electricity—specifically solar-generated electricity—to customers." (*Id.*, ¶ 50.) When customers purchase SolarCity's equipment and services, it reduces the amount of electricity they must purchase from SRP.

SolarCity alleges "SRP has monopoly power in the retail market within the geographic market, currently providing more than 95% of the electricity used by retail customers in SRP territory." (*Id.*, ¶ 53.) This is evidenced by SRP's ability to "extract supra-competitive profits from its electrical operations and use them to fund its money-losing water operations," as well as the high-barriers to entry in the market. (*Id.*, ¶¶ 54–55.) Moreover, "[w]hether SRP customers self-generate power . . . or not, all or virtually all of them still need to purchase both retail electric power and grid access from SRP to have access to power at times that alternative sources of power . . . cannot meet the customers' needs." (*Id.*, ¶ 63.)

III. The Dispute

For several years, SRP provided incentives for customers to install distributed solar systems. In 2011, however, "distributed solar increased in popularity and efficiency [and] SRP began to recognize that distributed solar could become a competitive threat in the longer term." (*Id.*, ¶ 78.) In response, "SRP developed its 'Community Solar' program, where customers purchase solar-generated electricity." (*Id.*, ¶ 79.). . . .

In December 2013, SRP lowered pricing for the Community Solar program, and shortly thereafter, "eliminated incentives to install distributed solar." (*Id.*, ¶¶ 82, 85.) One year later, in December 2014, "SRP announced its intent to adopt new [Standard Electric Price Plans ("SEPPs")] to apply new service terms and rates to its customers." (*Id.*, ¶ 89.) Around the same time, SRP held several hearings and disclosed information relating to the SEPPs. SolarCity participated in this process and voiced its opposition to the SEPPs.

On February 26, 2015, the District's Board of Directors approved the SEPPs. The SEPPs retain the normal rate structure for customers that purchase all of their electricity from SRP. These customers are charged a specific rate per kilowatt usage along with a fixed monthly service charge. But for customers that purchase electricity from SRP and also generate their own electricity, the SEPPs impose a nearly 65% rate increase from the previous rate structure. This increase appears as several additional charges applicable only to self-generating customers, as well as "reduced bill credits for the power that distributed solar customers send *back* into SRP's grid for SRP to re-sell to other customers." (*Id.*, ¶ 108(c) (emphasis in original).)

On March 2, 2015, SolarCity filed this action seeking damages and injunctive relief under federal and state antitrust laws. On May 20, 2015, SolarCity filed an amended complaint alleging nine counts: (1) Monopoly Maintenance in violation of § 2 of the Sherman Act; (2) Attempted Monopolization in violation of § 2 of the Sherman Act; (3) Unreasonable Restraint of Trade in violation of § 1 of the Sherman Act, (4) Exclusive Dealing in violation of § 3 of the Clayton Act; (5) Monopoly Maintenance in violation of the Arizona Uniform State Antitrust Act ("AUSAA"); (6) Attempted Monopolization in violation of AUSAA; (7) Unreasonable Restraint of Trade in violation of AUSAA; (8) Intentional Interference with Prospective Economic Advantage; and (9) Intentional Interference with Contract. The District and the Association both move to dismiss all counts.

. . . .

A. Allegations Against the Association

The Association argues SolarCity fails to directly implicate it in any wrongful conduct. It claims it has nothing to do with setting electricity rates and that the District enacted the SEPPs on its own. The Court agrees.

. . . .

B. Antitrust Claims Alleged Against the District

The District raises two threshold arguments: (1) SolarCity fails to properly allege a relevant market, and (2) SolarCity fails to allege antitrust injury. The District also argues SolarCity fails to adequately allege several elements of its antitrust claims. The Court will address the threshold issues first.

1.   Threshold Issues

a.   Relevant Market

. . . Each claim requires SolarCity to allege "that the defendant has market power within a 'relevant market.'" *Newcal Indus., Inc. v. Ikon Office Solution*, 513 F.3d 1038, 1044 (9th Cir. 2008). "Without a definition of [the relevant] market there is no way to measure [the company's] ability to lessen or destroy competition." *Walker Process Equip., Inc. v. Food Mach. & Chem. Corp.*, 382 U.S. 172, 177 (1965).

"[T]he [relevant] market must encompass the product at issue as well as all economic substitutes for the product." *Newcal Indus.*, 513 F.3d at 1045. "The outer boundaries of a product market are determined by the reasonable interchangeability of use or the cross-elasticity of demand between the product itself and substitutes for it." *Brown Shoe Co. v. United States*, 370 U.S. 294, 325 (1962). Interchangeability and cross-elasticity of demand refer to "the availability of products that are similar in character or use to the product in question and the degree to which buyers are willing to substitute those similar products for the product." *F.T.C. v. Swedish Match*, 131 F. Supp. 2d 151, 157 (D.D.C. 2000). . . .

SolarCity alleges "the relevant product market is the provision of electric power to end-use residential, governmental, and businesses consumers. . . . In this market, power may be provided by various sources, such as through outright sale of power, or by the lease or sale of distributed systems. . . ." (Doc. 39, ¶ 49.) It alleges that its rooftop solar energy systems provide customers the ability to "generate their own electricity on their own property," which "reduces the amount of electricity that customers need to buy from SRP [and] allows customers to save money, and conserve natural resources." (*Id.*, ¶ 3.) In addition, distributed solar systems and SRP's Community Solar plan are close substitutes. (*Id.*, ¶ 57.)

SolarCity's relevant market, though narrowly defined, is not facially unsustainable. The product market is the provision of electricity to residential and commercial customers, which includes public utilities and distributed solar systems. The geographic market extends to the outer boundaries of SRP's service area, at which point consumers must purchase electricity from another regional source. Because distributed solar systems produce electricity at a cheaper rate than from public utilities, customers increasingly made the switch to self-generate, reducing the amount of electricity they had to purchase from the District. Outside of distributed solar and public utility electricity, there are no other economically feasible electricity sources for consumers.

. . . .

The fact that customers who purchase SolarCity's product still have to purchase electricity from the District does not undermine the interchangeability of the two products. Customers can either purchase electricity from the District, or they can purchase SolarCity's product (or other distributed solar products) and generate some of their own electricity, which reduces their need to purchase the District's product. The extent to which the product is entirely interchangeable is lessened, but either way, the customer is receiving electricity. . . .

SolarCity's alleged relevant market is defined narrowly because electricity customers allegedly have only two economically feasible choices for obtaining electricity in the area, either from the District or from solar power. Prior to the District's implementation of the SEPPs, SolarCity was installing a large number of distributed solar systems in the District's territory. (Doc. 39, ¶ 17.) Distributed solar systems were reducing the amount of electricity the District sold, thereby depriving it of business. *See Newcal Indus.*, 513 F.3d at 1045. When SRP imposed an extra fee for customers with self-generating systems, customers switched back to purchasing all of their electricity from SRP. This dynamic illustrates that SolarCity and the District have the actual ability to deprive each other of significant business in the relevant market. *See Newcal Indus.*, 513 F.3d at 1045 (quoting *Thurman*, 875 F.2d at 1374).

b.   Antitrust Injury

In order to have standing to bring its claims, SolarCity must demonstrate antitrust injury. . . .

"Antitrust injury is defined not merely as injury caused by an antitrust violation, but more restrictively as 'injury of the type the antitrust laws were intended to prevent and that flows from that which makes defendants' acts unlawful.'" *Glen Holly*, 343 F.3d at 1007–08 (quoting *Brunswick Corp. v. Pueblo Bowl-O-Mat, Inc.*, 429 U.S. 477, 489 (1977)). In addition, "'the injured party [must] be a participant in the same market as the alleged malefactors.'" *Id.* at 1008. . . .

SolarCity plausibly alleges that it is a competitor of the District. It claims that it "offers equipment and services that provide electricity— specifically solar-generated electricity—to customers. By using SolarCity's equipment and services, customers reduce the amount of power that consumers purchase from SRP." (Doc. 39, ¶ 50.) It alleges it has the ability to deprive SRP of business. SolarCity further claims that "SRP fully recognizes that SolarCity and other distributed solar providers are competitors," given that at least one SRP employee has referred to SolarCity as "the enemy." (*Id.*, ¶ 51.) In addition, "a trade group with which SRP corresponded during the SEPPs' approval process—has published a report noting that distributed solar is one of many 'disruptive technologies . . . *that may compete with utility-provided services*' and that '[a]s the cost curve for these technologies improves, they could directly threaten the centralized utility model.'" (*Id.* (emphasis in original)). . . .

. . . .

The District . . . argues that SolarCity fails to allege harm to competition. But SolarCity alleges the SEPPs "have the purpose and effect of eliminating future distributed solar installations" and that the "only practicable way to escape the charges is to forgo installing distributed solar systems or to radically reduce peak usage," which is impracticable. (Doc. 39, ¶¶ 107, 109.) SolarCity further alleges the SEPPs make it "impossible for commercial, municipal, and educational customers to obtain any viable return on a new distributed solar investment," and that the "clear purpose of the SEPPs is not to recoup reasonable grid-related costs from distributed solar customers, but to prevent competition from SolarCity (and other providers of distributed solar) by punishing customers who deal with such competitors[.]" (*Id.*, ¶¶ 111, 113.) It asserts it has lost substantial business because the SEPPs have "made rooftop solar profoundly uneconomical." (*Id.*, ¶ 123.) These allegations sufficiently allege harm to competition in the retail electricity market. SolarCity has adequately alleged antitrust injury.

2. Antitrust Claims

. . . .

c. Monopoly Claims

. . . The District does not dispute allegations that it has monopoly power in the relevant market. Instead, it argues SolarCity fails to adequately plead any anticompetitive conduct because there are no allegations of below-cost pricing or an antitrust duty to deal. These arguments mischaracterize SolarCity's theory and are unpersuasive.

"Section 2 of the Sherman Act makes it unlawful for a person to monopolize or attempt to monopolize 'any part of the trade or commerce among the several States.' " *Aerotec Intern., Inc. v. Honeywell Intern., Inc.*, 4 F. Supp. 3d 1123, 1136 (D. Ariz. 2014) (quoting 15 U.S.C. § 2). "The possession of monopoly power alone is not an antitrust violation. It must be accompanied by an element of anticompetitive conduct." *Id.* at 1136–37. An antitrust plaintiff must demonstrate both the monopoly power of the defendant in the relevant market, and " 'the willful acquisition or maintenance of that power as distinguished from growth or development as a consequence of a superior product, business acumen, or historic accident.' " *Verizon Commc'ns Inc. v. Law Offices of Curtis v. Trinko, LLP*, 540 U.S. 398, 407 (2004). . . .

. . . .

. . . [SolarCity] alleges the District is a monopolist and imposed the SEPPs to exclude SolarCity from a market that was previously supporting such competition: "SRP has reversed a long-time course of conduct that had generated customer goodwill, benefitted SRP in the short-[term] and medium-term . . . for the sake of excluding longer-term competition by preventing customers in its service area from installing distributed solar from competitors like SolarCity." (Doc. 39, ¶ 119(c).) SolarCity claims the SEPPs limit the choices of consumers because they will decide against purchasing SolarCity's products. These allegations plausibly allege anticompetitive conduct by an alleged monopolist.

. . . .

Accordingly, SolarCity has plausibly alleged that (1) the District has monopoly power, (2) it made a decision to change the market, (3) this decision was motivated by a desire to restrict competition, and (4) the decision has the effect of limiting competition.

. . . .

D. The District's Defenses

The District raises several defenses to SolarCity's claims, many of which rest on its status as a political subdivision of the state. Each will be addressed in turn.

1.   Local Government Antitrust Act

The Local Government Antitrust Act ("LGAA") provides that "[n]o damages, interest on damages, costs, or attorney's fees may be recovered under section 4 . . . of the Clayton Act . . . from any local government[.]" 15 U.S.C. § 35(a). "Local government" is defined in relevant part as "a school district, sanitary district, or any other special function governmental unit established by State law in one or more States[.]" *Id.* § 34(1). . . .

The District argues it falls under the protection of the LGAA because it is a special function governmental unit established under A.R.S. § 48–2301. As a matter of law, the District is a political subdivision of the state created by state law and the state constitution. *See* A.R.S. § 48–2302; *see also* Ariz. Const. art. 13, § 7. SolarCity's allegations do not undermine the District's status. Consequently, the LGAA shields the District from SolarCity's antitrust damages claims.

. . . .

4.   State Action Doctrine

The District argues it is immune from antitrust liability under the state action doctrine, which "exempts qualifying state and local government regulation from federal antitrust, even if the regulation at issue compels an otherwise clear violation of the federal antitrust laws." *Cost Mgmt. Servs., Inc. v. Wash. Nat. Gas Co.*, 99 F.3d 937, 943 (9th Cir. 1996) (internal quotation marks and citation omitted). "A state law or regulatory scheme cannot be the basis for antitrust immunity unless, first the State has articulated a clear and affirmative policy to allow the anticompetitive conduct, and second, the State provides active supervision of anticompetitive conduct undertaken by private actors." *F.T.C. v. Ticor Title Ins. Co.*, 504 U.S. 621, 631 (1992).

The question of whether Arizona has articulated a clear policy permitting anticompetitive conduct in the retail electricity market and "the question of whether a state has 'actively supervised' a state regulatory policy [are] a factual one[s] which [are] inappropriately resolved in the context of a motion to dismiss." *Cost Mgmt. Servs.*, 99 F.3d at 942–43. SolarCity alleges that Arizona has a policy permitting competition in the relevant market and that the District operates without supervision. (Doc. 39, ¶¶ 42, 65.) This is all that is necessary at this stage.

. . . .

CONCLUSION

. . . Counts three and four, as well as SolarCity's claims for damages under federal and state antitrust laws, are dismissed.

IT IS ORDERED that

1.   The District's motion to dismiss is **GRANTED IN PART**.

2.   The Association's motion to dismiss is **GRANTED**.

3.   The District's request for judicial notice is **GRANTED IN PART**.

NOTES & QUESTIONS

1.   *Saved from Antitrust Liability by Governmental Status?* The *SolarCity* court dismissed some, but not all, of the antitrust claims lodged against SRP. The court's primary justification for dismissing some of the claims was a statutory rule that protects governmental units against antitrust claims. SRP's unique character as a political subdivision of the state of Arizona seemed to be a critical factor in the court's analysis. It is less certain whether a court would recognize such a defense in the case of an investor-owned utility engaged in the same behavior, given that most IOUs are not political subdivisions of the states in which they operate. The court also concluded that the *state action doctrine* might not fully immunize SRP and that additional facts would be needed to make that determination. As distributed solar energy and energy storage become more affordable and competitive with grid-supplied electricity and utilities seek to defend themselves against this new competition in their markets, these issues are likely to become even more relevant in the coming years.

2.   The *SolarCity* case is relatively unusual in that it involves a private corporation's antitrust claims against a natural monopoly. Do you think that utilities like SRP should be subject to antitrust laws? Why or why not?

3.   On what basis did the court conclude that SolarCity was a producer within the same relevant market as SRP? Do you agree with this determination? Why or why not?

4.   Why do you think at least one SRP employee has described the solar energy industry as "the enemy"? What do you think this statement suggests about whether utilities like SRP should be subject to antitrust laws?

5.   A primary objective of antitrust laws is to prevent sub-optimally high monopoly pricing, which harms consumers and breeds inefficiency. Suppose you were an advocate for low-income utility customers in SRP territory. Would you be more likely to favor SolarCity or SRP in this litigation? Why? What do your answers suggest about relevant differences between this antitrust dispute and more typical antitrust suits?

6.   In addition to the several federal policies and initiatives described in this Chapter, federal agencies have introduced numerous other programs over the past couple of decades that have helped to promote the adoption of solar energy technologies in various ways. A few examples of these other programs include the HUD Green Retrofit Grant program, the USDA Rural Energy Assistance Program (REAP) grant program, and the FHA PowerSaver Loan and Grant programs. The Obama administration likewise introduced the National Community Solar Partnership in 2015—a collaborative initiative

involving multiple federal agencies in programming aimed primarily at increasingly the deployment of solar energy technologies among low- to moderate-income households. Some of these smaller programs have already expired. Others still exist but have had only modest impacts on the solar energy industry.

Suppose you are a hired policy advocate for solar energy and your opponents are arguing that it would be preferable to rely upon just one or two federal level policies to promote solar energy instead of a lengthy list of diverse programs and initiatives like that described above. Craft a detailed argument for why having several different types of solar energy incentive programs is preferable to having just one or two pro-solar federal policies and focusing on those.

7.   *Anticompetitive Behavior in International Solar Equipment Markets.* A very different type of anticompetitive conduct has generated legal issues in international markets for solar panels. In the mid-2010s, controversy arose when the United States International Trade Commission (the "Trade Commission") issued an official determination that Chinese producers of solar PV products had sold certain products within U.S. markets at below cost. The practice of selling products or services at below cost is known as "dumping." Dumping practices potentially violate federal trade laws because it can drive competitors out of a market and thereby increase the dumping producer's market power and accompanying ability to generate excessive profits. In 2015, the United States Court of International Trade affirmed the Trade Commission's determination that the Chinese solar PV producers had violated federal antidumping laws. *See Changzhou Trina Solar Energy Co. Ltd. v. U.S. Intern. Trade Com'n*, 100 F.Supp.3d 1314 (2015). Although the issue of dumping of Chinese solar PV equipment on U.S. markets occupied less attention in the years following the *Changzhou* dispute, the influence of Chinese solar policies on global solar equipment prices remains very high, because the country has become the world's primary solar PV equipment producer. For instance, when the Chinese government weakened its domestic incentives for solar PV installations in late 2016, the Chinese demand for solar PV products plummeted, causing global prices for solar PV equipment to fall dramatically as well. *See* Keith Bradsher, *When Solar Panels Became Job Killers*, N.Y. TIMES (Apr. 9, 2017), https://www.nytimes.com/2017/04/08/business/china-trade-solar-panels.html?mcubz=1. Unfortunately, not all solar energy industry stakeholders are excited when solar panel prices drop. Domestic solar manufacturers have increasingly been unable to compete and many have encountered solvency problems because of falling market prices. As of late 2017, there was widespread speculation that the Trump Administration would impose hefty tariffs and price floors on solar panels imports to protect and encourage domestic solar panel manufacturing. Solar installers were fearful that these tariffs and price floors, if imposed, would greatly increase the domestic prices of solar energy generating systems and lead to massive layoffs in their industry. *See* Josh Siegal, *Thriving solar industry braces for Trump's decision on tariffs*, WASHINGTON EXAMINER (September 21, 2017),

http://www.washingtonexaminer.com/thriving-solar-industry-braces-for-trumps-decision-on-tariffs/article/2634976.

D. STATE POLICIES AFFECTING SOLAR ENERGY

Although federal laws govern several aspects of solar energy development, the legal and regulatory apparatus with the greatest capacity to impact the emerging solar energy industry resides at the state government level. The following materials describe several state policies that are particularly important for solar energy and highlight some of the ongoing debates surrounding them.

1. STATE RENEWABLE PORTFOLIO STANDARDS

Like the federal investment tax credit, state *renewable portfolio standards* (RPSs) have been fairly effective at driving solar energy growth across much of the United States. RPSs, which Chapter 2 explored in significant detail in the context of wind energy development, compel utilities to source some minimum percentage of their power from qualifying renewable energy sources, including solar power. By requiring utilities to buy renewable power, RPS policies have generated new demand for it and thereby incentivized great investment in solar energy and other forms of renewable energy development.

As of 2017, more than 40 states had adopted some type of RPS policy. Some RPS policies, such as those adopted in Hawaii and California, are very aggressive. For instance, Hawaii's RPS requires its utilities sell only renewable electricity by the year 2045, and California's RPS mandates that at least 50 percent of the electricity sold by its utilities come from qualified renewables by the year 2030. By contrast, other states have merely adopted soft voluntary RPS targets that have done comparatively little to drive renewable energy development. For example, Indiana's "Clean Energy Portfolio Goal" encourages utilities only to aim to have 10 percent of the electricity they sell come from "clean" energy sources by the year 2025. Many utilities in states with less-aggressive RPS policies have been well ahead of schedule in meeting the standards.

As of 2017, RPSs in more than 20 states contained provisions that specifically promoted solar energy or distributed energy beyond other renewable energy strategies. Figure 5.5 identifies those states whose RPS policies as of 2015 included special provisions related to distributed or solar energy. As shown on the map, these special provisions have taken a variety of different forms. The most common are RPS *carve-out provisions* imposing specific additional standards on utilities to source some minimum percentage of their power from solar energy or distributed energy. More than half of all state RPS standards feature some type of solar or distributed generation carve-out requirement. *See* Richard L. Revesz &

Burcin Unel, *Managing the Future of the Electricity Grid: Distributed Generation and Net Metering*, 41 HARV. ENVTL. L. REV. 43, 58 (2017). Unlike ordinary RPS requirements, which mandate only that utilities source a certain percentage of their electricity from any of a lengthy list of qualifying renewable energy resources, carve-out provisions specifically require utilities to meet some proportion of the percentage through solar energy or distributed energy sources.

Figure 5.5. States with Special Solar or Distributed Energy RPS Provisions

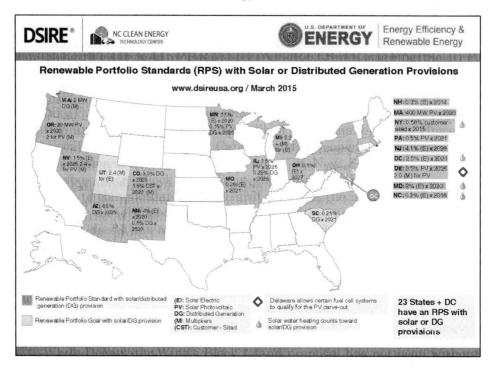

Source: U.S. Dep't of Energy

The following is an excerpt from the Arizona Administrative Code setting forth Arizona's RPS. Arizona has a carve-out provision requiring that at least 4.5% of a utility's electricity sold in the state be sourced from "distributed renewable energy resources" by the year 2025. As shown in the excerpts below, that term is defined to encompass a wide range of qualifying energy resources. However, the code language describing qualifying types of rooftop solar energy is especially significant given the state's excellent solar resources.

RENEWABLE ENERGY STANDARD AND TARIFF
ARIZ. ADMIN. CODE §§ 14–2–1802 & 1805 (2007)

§ 1802.

A. "Eligible Renewable Energy Resources" are applications of the following defined technologies that displace Conventional Energy Resources that would otherwise be used to provide electricity to an Affected Utility's Arizona customers:

. . . .

10. "Solar Electricity Resources" use sunlight to produce electricity by either photovoltaic devices or solar thermal electric resources.

. . . .

B. "Distributed Renewable Energy Resources" are applications of the following defined technologies that are located at a customer's premises and that displace Conventional Energy Resources that would otherwise be used to provide electricity to Arizona customers:

1. . . . "Solar Electricity Resources," as . . . defined in subsection[ ] . . . (A)(10).

2. "Biomass Thermal Systems" and "Biogas Thermal Systems". . . . For purposes of this definition "Biomass Thermal Systems" and "Biogas Thermal Systems" do not include biomass and wood stoves, furnaces, and fireplaces.

3. "Commercial Solar Pool Heaters" are devices that use solar energy to heat commercial or municipal swimming pools.

4. "Geothermal Space Heating and Process Heating Systems" are systems that use heat from within the earth's surface for space heating or for process heating.

5. "Renewable Combined Heat and Power System" is a Distributed Generation system, fueled by an Eligible Renewable Energy Resource, that produces both electricity and useful renewable process heat. Both the electricity and renewable process heat may be used to meet the Distributed Renewable Energy Requirement.

6. "Solar Daylighting" is the non-residential application of a device specifically designed to capture and redirect the visible portion of the solar beam, while controlling the infrared portion, for use in illuminating interior building spaces in lieu of artificial lighting.

7. "Solar Heating, Ventilation, and Air Conditioning" ("HVAC") is the combination of Solar Space Cooling and Solar Space Heating as part of one system.

8. "Solar Industrial Process Heating and Cooling" is the use of solar thermal energy for industrial or commercial manufacturing or processing applications.

9. "Solar Space Cooling" is a technology that uses solar thermal energy absent the generation of electricity to drive a refrigeration machine that provides for space cooling in a building.

10. "Solar Space Heating" is a method whereby a mechanical system is used to collect solar energy to provide space heating for buildings.

11. "Solar Water Heater" is a device that uses solar energy rather than electricity or fossil fuel to heat water for residential, commercial, or industrial purposes.

12. "Wind Generator of 1 MW or Less" is a mechanical device, with an output of 1 MW or less, that is driven by wind to produce electricity.

§ 1805.

A. In order to improve system reliability, each Affected Utility shall be required to satisfy a Distributed Renewable Energy Requirement by obtaining Renewable Energy Credits from Distributed Renewable Energy Resources.

B. An Affected Utility's Distributed Renewable Energy Requirement shall be calculated each calendar year by applying the following applicable annual percentage to the Affected Utility's Annual Renewable Energy Requirement:

The annual increase in the annual percentage for each Affected Utility will be pro rated for the first year based on when the Affected Utility's funding mechanism is approved.

2007	5%
2008	10%
2009	15%
2010	20%
2011	25%
After 2011	30% . . .

C. An Affected Utility may use Renewable Energy Credits acquired in any year to meet its Distributed Renewable Energy Requirement. Once a Renewable Energy Credit is used by any Affected Utility to satisfy these requirements, the credit is retired.

D. An Affected Utility shall meet one-half of its annual Distributed Renewable Energy Requirement from residential applications and the remaining one-half from non-residential, non-utility applications.

QUESTIONS

1.   As of late 2017, Arizona's RPS requirement was for 15% renewables by the year 2025. As described in § 1805 above, the state's distributed energy carve-out provisions require utilities to use qualifying distributed renewables to satisfy at least 30% of the general 15% RPS requirement. Based on those two facts, use a simple calculation to explain why Arizona utilities must source at least 4.5% of their overall sold power from distributed renewable energy sources.

2.   Suppose that, in the year 2025, an Arizona investor-owned utility were to source (i) 2% of its total sold electricity from rooftop solar panels and other residential distributed energy systems, (ii) 3% from commercial rooftop solar arrays and other non-residential, non-utility distributed energy systems, and (iii) 11% from utility-scale solar energy and wind energy projects. Would this utility be in full compliance with the state's RPS requirements? Why or why not?

3.   Suppose several customers of an Arizona investor-owned utility have purchased and installed solar water heating systems for their backyard swimming pools. The utility would like to count these systems toward meeting its RPS distributed energy requirements. Craft (i) an argument interpreting the Arizona Administrative Code to provide that these systems **do** qualify toward the § 1805 Distributed Renewable Energy Requirement and (ii) an argument interpreting the Arizona Administrative Code to provide that they **do not** qualify toward the requirement. Which statutory interpretation argument do you think is stronger, and why?

4.   In late 2016, at least one member of Arizona's chief utility regulatory body, the Arizona Corporation Commission, advocated for eliminating the state's carve-out requirement for distributed generation. *See* Robert Walton, *Arizona Regulator Proposes Doubling Renewables Standard To 30% By 2030*, UTILITY DIVE (Aug. 24, 2016), http://www.utilitydive.com/news/arizona-regulator-proposes-doubling-renewables-standard-to-30-by-2030/425026/. Which stakeholders would be most likely to favor this change: Arizona utilities or Arizona rooftop solar installers? Why?

2.   NET METERING AND ELECTRICITY RATE DESIGN

Second only to RPS policies, the state-level policies that have most positively impacted the growth of distributed solar energy in recent years have been *net metering* programs. Net metering programs make distributed solar energy more financially rewarding by crediting retail customers with rooftop solar energy systems for their excess generated power. When a customer's solar panels generate more electricity than the customer currently needs, the extra power typically flows onto the grid. Under retail-rate net metering programs, customers get one-for-one credit for each kWh of excess solar-generated power that the utility receives via the grid. Utilities then typically sell the excess electricity to the customer's neighbors at the applicable retail price. Customers use the credit to offset charges for grid-supplied electricity they use at night or during other times when their solar panels aren't generating enough power to fully meet their demand. Without net metering or equivalent programs, customers with solar panels get no compensation or credit for the power they feed onto the grid so it can take a much longer time for them to fully recoup the cost of a new rooftop PV system.

As of late 2017, 42 states had mandatory net metering rules, meaning that regulated utilities in those states were legally required to credit customers for excess power their distributed energy systems generate and supply to the grid. 41 of those states are highlighted in dark gray in Figure 5.6 below. The other state, Nevada, re-embraced rooftop solar net metering under a modified set of rules in the summer of 2017.

Figure 5.6. Solar Net Metering Programs, By State (2016)

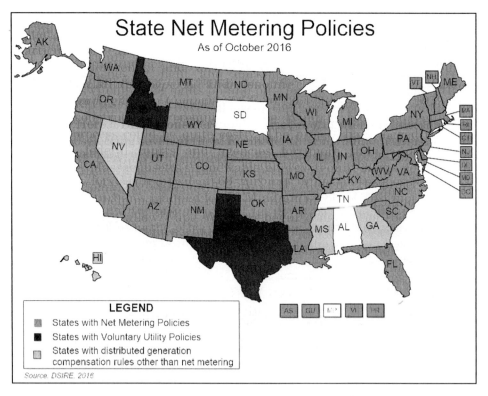

Source: National Conference of State Legislatures

a.   The Utility "Death Spiral" Narrative

Initially, the impacts of solar net metering programs on utilities' budgets and operations were minimal because relatively few customers had solar panels. However, as the market penetration of rooftop solar PV technologies has increased over time, several utilities across the country have expressed concerns about the potential financial and practical effects of these programs. The three excerpts below describe utilities' primary concerns about net metering and provide multiple perspectives on the ongoing debate over the extent to which net metering programs should continue as the nation's distributed solar energy market continues to expand. While reading the excerpts, consider how the unique regulatory structure governing electric utilities constrains their ability to respond to the impacts of distributed solar energy technologies on retail electricity markets.

SOLAR ENERGY, UTILITIES, AND FAIRNESS
Troy A. Rule
6 SAN DIEGO J. CLIMATE & ENERGY L. 115, 118–21 (2015)

As exciting as the rapid rise of distributed solar energy has been for companies within that industry, some utilities seem to take a less enthusiastic view of these changes. As rooftop solar development becomes more commonplace, it is likely to dampen demand for grid-supplied power and thereby cut into utilities' profits. Concerned about these and other impacts, a growing number of utilities have begun actively seeking to weaken or eliminate net metering programs within their territories.

1.   A Utility Death Spiral

From the perspective of regulated utilities, net metering and distributed energy technologies can represent a growing threat to the comfortable business model under which they have operated for decades. Utilities' concerns about the potential long-term consequences of net metering are often encapsulated in what has come to be known as the "death spiral" scenario. When only a tiny fraction of a utility's customers have solar panels, most utilities can absorb these customers' impacts on their finances and day-to-day operations. But as its quantity of solar-using, net-metered customers grows, a utility sells less and less power and its revenue stream begins to shrink. To compensate for this drop in revenue, utilities typically must petition to increase the per-unit price of the electricity they sell. Unfortunately, these rate increases only make the relative price of distributed solar energy seem more attractive to utility customers. Additional customers are thus enticed to get solar panels of their own, causing utilities to suffer even further revenue declines.

As solar arrays appear on more and more rooftops within a given area, a utility's daily task of balancing load supply and demand on the electricity grid also becomes more difficult. In addition to ramping centralized power plants up or down in response to shifts in load demand, utilities operating in territories with large numbers of rooftop solar installations have to also predict and respond to changes in the amount of power that these systems supply into the grid. Balancing loads in a grid with thousands of rooftop solar energy systems requires estimating how productive all of these customer-controlled systems will be at any given moment—a chore that can be particularly difficult on partly cloudy days when the amount and intensity of sunlight in a region is constantly in flux. Further rate increases are often the only feasible way for utilities to fund the expensive grid upgrades needed to address the new load management challenges associated with distributed solar power. Of course, rate increases aimed at covering these additional costs only motivate more customers to invest in their own solar arrays.

This vicious cycle of declining utility revenues, rising electricity rates, and shrinking demand for grid-supplied power could theoretically spiral on and on until nearly every customer has rooftop solar panels or some other distributed energy system. At that point, electric utilities would devolve into mere suppliers of high-priced, temporary backup electricity. Retail rates for that backup power would have to be astronomically high for utilities to recoup their costs under such a model, so small-scale distributed energy storage or generators could likely become viable alternatives to reliance on utilities. Insolvent and devoid of customers, conventional utilities caught in such a world would quickly fade into extinction.

2.   Proposals to Slow or Stop the Spiral

Although the death spiral scenario just described is not likely to wipe out most utilities anytime soon, net metering programs and the growing rooftop solar energy industry are already whittling away at investor-owned utilities' profits and complicating utilities' operations in some jurisdictions. Even in regions where solar panel installations are still relatively uncommon, utilities seem to increasingly view net metering and distributed solar energy as credible threats to their stability over the long term. . . .

DOES DISRUPTIVE COMPETITION MEAN A DEATH SPIRAL FOR ELECTRIC UTILITIES?

Elisabeth Graffy & Steven Kihm
35 ENERGY L.J. 1, 2–3, 9–11, 14–16 & 23–27 (2014)

A surge in rooftop solar systems in the United States is driving heated debate about the future shape of the electric power sector, especially the status of electric utilities. Are legacy utilities, which have served public interests for more than a century, becoming obsolete? If so, with what implications for the industry and for society? If not, what role will they have in the emerging sector? With market and regulatory conventions in substantial flux, the fundamental question is whether changes underway will lead to a more resilient, sustainable energy system or simply destabilize the present one.

The characterization of renewable energy innovations, such as rooftop solar, as a "mortal threat" or "radical threat" to utilities and utilities themselves as in a "death spiral" reflects an awareness that unconventional risks have emerged. However, most analyses fail to explain how this has occurred, what it signifies more broadly, and what—if anything—utilities might do to thrive in the new environment. This potentially increases risks both to utilities themselves and to society, which depends upon the availability of safe, secure, accessible, and abundant energy. . . .

. . . .

. . . Disruptive competition facing electric utilities involves the entry of new ideas and actors in [several] sectors, calling into question basic assumptions in ways that can fundamentally transform market structure.

This synergistic wave, not technology alone, is what utilities experience as a threat and risk to their established business model. The surge in distributed solar PV installations is best understood as the leading edge of this wave, which should be expected to bring more new ideas, actors, and technological breakthroughs. Utilities are not, by definition, unable to ride that wave, but doing so requires some dramatic strategic shifts to which they are not accustomed. Conventional strategies for managing competition fail to suffice, and failure to adapt in a proactive and timely manner can produce dire results for affected firms. . . .

. . . Electric utilities, as quasi-public institutions, share characteristics with, and can learn lessons from, both private and public sector experiments but face some unique considerations. . . .

. . . .

III. THE SIGNIFICANCE OF DISRUPTIVE COMPETITION FOR REGULATED MONOPOLIES

Even though expansion of renewable energy is overall deemed positive and, indeed, a striking policy success as well as a potential pathway for business opportunities and economic growth, the scope and pace of change have begun to exceed the capacity of electric utilities to adapt, both technologically and financially. Increasing the share of renewables in the supply portfolio brings the technical challenge of incorporating the inherent spatial and temporal variability of those resources into systems that were designed around the unique characteristics of fossil fuel feedstocks like coal and natural gas. Moreover, the utility business model, in which financial viability is based on economies of scale and long-term cost recovery of investments in physical infrastructure, makes utilities reluctant to abandon infrastructure with decades of remaining useful life. This reluctance is reinforced by existing regulatory controls, creating a tension between the past and the future that is unlikely to be resolved by perpetuating traditional practices.

The origin of utilities as centralized, regulated monopolies corresponded to societal needs and goals at the time, not to some absolute definition of how things should or must be. . . .

. . . .

IV. THINKING STRATEGICALLY AND OPPORTUNISTICALLY UNDER DISRUPTIVE COMPETITION

Electric utilities are no strangers to competition, but disruptive competition poses a set of challenges not commonly seen and, therefore, not accommodated in standard operating procedure. The best way to understand how this state of affairs could exist and why new strategies are required is illustrated by the historical and legal context of utilities. . . .

Electric utilities connected by regional, centralized transmission systems emerged in the early 1900s as a governance innovation that could best meet the public policy goal of providing low cost, reliable power to communities nationwide. The then-emerging energy production and transmission systems lent themselves to physical centralization of generation, highly controlled transmission, and concentrated ownership by natural monopolies and associated market and policy systems. These systems co-evolved, first at municipal and then state and regional scales, to support the stability of that system, using regulation to enhance efficiency and access to capital while protecting against the potential for market exploitation and corruption. For the most part, citizens throughout the United States have benefitted from this model and utilities have generally thrived.

. . . .

In recent decades, elevated attention has come to focus on the vulnerabilities of a complex and aging grid, the availability and sustainability of fossil-fuel-based generation, the security of centralized infrastructure to attack, and the resilience of utility systems to extreme storms. These concerns prompted incremental innovation in the sector along several simultaneous tracks, including promoting aggressive conservation and efficiency programs, upgrading to a so-called "smart" grid, exploring decentralized energy options, and instituting a range of policies aimed at accelerating adoption of renewable energy. None of these aimed to fundamentally challenge the underlying utility model as much as to refine and adapt it. Whereas even solar leasing was initially designed to fit within the utility distribution network, hostility by utilities to this arrangement appears to be stimulating a ripple of innovations aimed at accelerating the potential for off-grid systems. . . .

Regulation is not designed to forestall or prohibit disruptive competition from entering a market even where firms hold monopoly status but rather to foster sectoral stability under certain conditions. The regulated monopoly model can, somewhat counter-intuitively, make utilities perversely more vulnerable to disruptive competition precisely because such challenges are, by definition, relatively rare and adaptation requires a departure from standard operating procedures that are deeply ingrained and, while helpful for continuity, contrary to supporting rapid change.

Herein lies the vulnerability of regulated utilities. The model is designed to maintain institutional stability in order to uphold social welfare objectives (in the historical case of energy, for example, to ensure low cost, reliable service), not to uphold the welfare of utilities themselves. Historical precedent clearly shows that when emerging conditions create a critical tension between upholding social welfare objectives and upholding continuity of a utility for its own sake, courts will decisively favor social welfare objectives and markets play no favorites. Indeed, neither regulators nor courts can ultimately protect regulated utilities from all competition, even when—perhaps especially when—the character of that competition challenges the viability of their fundamental business model.

. . . .

VI. MANAGING DISRUPTIVE COMPETITION WITH REGULATORY PROTECTION: *MARKET STREET RAILWAY*

The case of Market Street Railway, a streetcar utility in San Francisco, illustrates that utilities which encounter disruptive competition face critical decision points. Furthermore, decisions made at such times focused on cost recovery alone can lead to a position of extreme and unbalanced risk from which it is difficult or impossible to recover. By the 1920s, Market Street had been a viable, innovating enterprise for many decades. However, at a critical decision point, it was unwilling or unable to adapt to its new competitive environment and tried to rely reactively and almost entirely on regulators for defensive insulation against risks instead of on repositioning itself in a proactive way for resilience.

The utility rationally viewed involvement by regulators as a natural first step, but it failed to recognize that it had slid from the stable regulatory zone to the disruptive competition zone in which its own innovative initiative-taking would need to play a larger role. . . .

The disruptive competitive threat at that point was not so much the automobile but rather the intra-city bus, which cost less to purchase, could carry more passengers, and could alter its route with ease—all desirable characteristics in growing cities. Streetcar ridership in the United States peaked in 1920 and then declined as buses and automobiles gained dominance as preferred modes of transportation.

The bus era peaked in 1948, and bus ridership declined as the automobile became the primary mode of transportation in the United States. . . However, unlike streetcars and despite a decline from dominance, a strong and steady bus presence has remained in the transportation portfolio of most cities, albeit under new ownership and regulatory structures.

Market Street Railway operated in San Francisco until the mid-1940s. As a traction utility, the Railroad Commission of California set its rates (fares). Market Street was beset with competition on all sides. Not only was it losing riders to the aforementioned buses but to other streetcar companies, including one operated by the City of San Francisco.

Under a five-cent fare, Market Street found that it was operating at a loss; it could not recover its accounting-based costs. In a competitive market, firms must lower their prices to meet those offered by the competition, find a way to differentiate themselves from the other providers without dropping their prices, or focus on a particular segment of the market where they have a competitive advantage. Market Street took none of those actions, instead continuing to offer the same service that it always had and simply asking regulators for a fare increase to seven cents, which was approved.

The higher fare did not increase Market Street's revenues nor restore it to profitability. The new revenue gained from the higher fare that customers paid was offset by the revenue lost due to customer defections to other transportation options. In essence, Market Street's rate calculations were based on accounting arithmetic, not on market conditions. In addition, the Commission determined that "service had constantly deteriorated and was worse under the seven-cent fare than under the former five-cent rate. . . .

Seeing that the seven-cent fare provided no financial benefit to Market Street, the Railroad Commission reversed its decision and reduced the fare to six cents, prompting a judicial appeal by the utility. In 1945, that appeal made its way to the U.S. Supreme Court. Market Street relied on the high Court's decision a year earlier in the landmark *Hope* case to support its contention that the regulator's approved rate was unreasonably low. It argued that any rate that resulted in a negative return clearly failed to meet the *Hope* standards for a "fair" return-one that instills confidence in the utility's investors, among other considerations.

Both parties and the Court agreed that a six-cent fare would prevent the utility from earning a return that would satisfy investors, thereby restricting its access to capital. The problem was that in the competitive environment in which Market Street operated, if it continued to offer the same service it always had while competitors did just as well or better, no fare increase would allow it to recover the full amount of its historical investment, let alone earn a profit. Indeed, even while arguing for a higher rate to recover its accounting-based costs, Market Street admitted that it did not expect the new rate to make it whole . . . contending that the potential loss in revenue from a rate reduction constituted a taking under the Fourteenth Amendment of the U.S. Constitution.

The Court made it clear that conflating a fair return and a takings argument, based on the *Hope* standard and the Fourteenth Amendment, respectively, reflected a fundamental misunderstanding of the law and that, furthermore, neither offers the protection the utility sought. If market values decline in response to successful competition, utilities simply cannot look to their regulators to undo the impact of fundamental changes in market forces. Utilities have no constitutional protection from the economic damage caused by competitors. . . .

Given Market Street's circumstances, Justice Jackson's majority opinion dismissed the common interpretation of the *Hope* standard as inapplicable. He explained that it applies only when the utility has monopoly power, not when it is besieged by disruptive competition that it is failing to navigate. . . .

This story has significant implications for electric utilities facing increasing and especially disruptive competition. . . . That Market Street responded to disruptive competition by simply requesting rate increases from its regulator reveals denial that their economic woes were due to fundamentally changed circumstances that required new organizational strategy, not just regulatory intervention. Market Street, while fully understanding the existence of threats to its viability, showed no real signs of innovation or adaptation in this regard, but rather continued a reliance on conventional cost-accounting-based utility ratemaking practices to the bitter end.

If utility-proposed solutions rely overly on regulatory recovery of accounting-based costs in lieu of strategic innovation and repositioning to accommodate the risks posed by the emergence of disruptive competition, then utilities may be headed in the same direction as streetcar companies as competition heats up.

GETTING DISTRIBUTED GENERATION RIGHT: A RESPONSE TO "DOES DISRUPTIVE COMPETITION MEAN A DEATH SPIRAL FOR ELECTRIC UTILITIES?"

David Raskin
35 ENERGY L.J. 263, 264–67 & 271–73 (2014)

The May 2014 edition of the *Energy Law Journal* includes an article entitled *Does Disruptive Competition Mean a Death Spiral for Electric Utilities? Death Spiral* envisions a utopian (for customers) and dystopian (for utilities) near future in which electricity from the utility grid is widely displaced by distributed energy sources that supply electricity at prices below utility service from the electric grid. . . .

. . . .

The authors argue the utility industry should embrace this future ("ride the wave") by abandoning opposition to regulatory policies adopted to advance the distributed alternative. Instead, the industry should be "adaptive" and "proactive" by restructuring its offerings to create value for consumers within the context of this new industry paradigm in lieu of the industry's historical practice of focusing on "cost recovery."

Death Spiral argues, specifically, that the pursuit of "cost recovery" in regulatory proceedings, such as recent utility proposals to include fixed cost components in retail rate designs as a response to net metering, represents an unsustainable alternative strategy to forward-looking "value creation."

. . . .

The authors also contend that the utility industry cannot rely on asserted legal rights to recover investments in the grid that are stranded by competition, because the law does not afford a right to recover such investments when customers voluntarily choose to take advantage of more attractive offerings in the marketplace. They believe legal rights will ultimately give way to "social welfare objectives" that they claim have been historically favored over the rights of troubled industries. . . .

Death Spiral's legal argument against stranded cost recovery is based primarily on the authors' interpretation of the Supreme Court's 1945 decision in *Market Street Railway Co. v. Railroad Commission of State of California (Market Street)*, in which the Court held that the Fourteenth Amendment to the Constitution did not offer rate protection for a failed street railway business that was unable to attract sufficient customers to recover its costs at any rate level. Based on that decision, the authors conclude that, whereas cases such as *Federal Power Commission v. Hope Natural Gas Co. (Hope)* provide assurance that regulators will set utility rates high enough to recover costs and earn a return on investment when the public needs utility service, it affords no such protection when the demand for such service evaporates.

. . . .

. . . I do not share the authors' dire predictions for the electric utility industry and consider their proposed prescriptions to be unrealistic and unhelpful. *Death Spiral* exaggerates the threat from distributed generation by disregarding the critical role that subsidies play in making distributed generation attractive and failing to acknowledge other shortcomings that may (or may not) be overcome over time. The authors also misunderstand the essential role the utility industry will play for decades, even if, and long after, their predictions about the growth of distributed generation come true, and the laws that recognize this role.

Articles similar to *Death Spiral* have appeared in growing numbers recently, especially as the utility industry's opposition to "net metering," the driver of most distributed generation growth, has become more pronounced. . . .

Death Spiral does not address the *cost* of distributed generation or attempt to show that it is, or how it will soon become, a realistic substitute for utility service. The sellers of distributed generation, as I will show, understand that their business model fails without substantial government subsidies. . . .

. . . .

. . . The point of the current regulatory debate, which *Death Spiral* claims is the product of an inordinate utility focus on cost recovery, is that distributed generators want the consistency and reliability provided by the utility grid *without paying for it* in order to make their product appear more attractive and drive consumer demand. This strategy can work only for so long as distributed generation remains a minor niche alternative. The cost shifting effects of subsidized distributed energy will soon be noticeable, and this will threaten the current system of subsidies (especially net metering) that is driving distributed generation growth.

It is also unlikely that consumers will rapidly abandon utility service *en masse*, even if and when a realistic alternative exists. New technology will emerge, it will enter production in small numbers, it will be tried by new adopters, and then, assuming the public is sufficiently attracted, it will be produced in larger numbers and sold. This is a long-term process, during which most of the public will continue to rely on service from the grid for some or all of their demand. Many Americans, including some of the most economically vulnerable, will be unable to take advantage of distributed alternatives. A transition to distributed generation will therefore be protracted and will raise difficult issues over the appropriate sharing of the cost of the still-essential utility grid.

Finally, the authors neglect the potential for technological advancements that make electric service from the utility grid more efficient and desirable. No reason exists to believe that technological and economic improvements will occur solely in the sphere of distributed generation and storage. . . . Electric service from the utility-owned grid may ultimately emerge as the winner in the fierce competition that *Death Spiral* envisions.

. . . .

The economic effects of using net metering are not very different from the system of subsidies that Germany adopted under its *Energiewende* program. Thus, Germany's experience offers a laboratory for assessing the impacts of net metering and other clean energy subsidies. For over a decade, Germany has subsidized solar PV energy with feed-in tariffs sometimes equal to or in excess of the full retail rate and has provided distributed renewable energy priority access to the electric grid. The impact on German electric consumers has been horrendous. Residential electric rates in Germany have doubled and now average approximately $0.40 per kWh (in comparison with the United States average of approximately $0.125).

The German subsidies and grid priority have, as is intended, hurt the economics of central station generation that is needed to provide base load energy and balance the system, causing some experts to worry that the grid is reaching a point of instability. Germany had hoped that the rate impacts of *Energiewende* would be contained and that pro-renewable policies would reduce CO_2 emissions. But after falling initially, CO_2 emissions in Germany are rising due to the expanding use of coal and lignite generation. One of the architects of this policy, Sigmar Gabriel, who is currently Germany's Minister of Energy and Environment, has raised alarms about the potential adverse impacts of *Energiewende* as currently implemented, stating that it threatens serious economic harm. . . .

Concerns about Germany's renewables policy could fade with technological improvements, but they are serious and reinforce my point. Distributed generation technology is not sufficiently mature to replace service from the grid and the economics are now unfavorable. Until this situation changes, policies such as net metering that induce an over-investment in non-competitive, variable sources of distributed energy are harmful to electric consumers, do not necessarily produce CO_2 reductions, and could threaten the security of the electric grid.

. . . .

Supporters of these uniquely large subsidies argue the adverse effects are outweighed by the need for aggressive policies to reduce the use of fossil fuels and thereby address climate change. That is the basic argument behind Germany's *Energiewende*. Thus, the argument goes, overpaying for distributed generation at this time is justified if it stimulates investment in the development of this technology, lowering its cost over time, and ultimately creating an environmentally superior alternative to utility service. I have a number of problems with this argument, even accepting that climate change warrants a strong policy response.

First, this argument ignores the fact that net metering and other subsidies to distributed generation discriminate against central station generation alternatives that emit no carbon dioxide. This artificially suppresses investment in these clean alternatives and inhibits their development and use. These central station alternatives include wind energy, central station solar, hydroelectric energy, and nuclear energy, none of which are able to sell their energy output at multiples of the wholesale market price for energy. Therefore, they are at a competitive disadvantage relative to net metered energy. Clearly, this disadvantage in the market limits their ability to attract capital for growth and innovation. . . .

Second, because the carbon-free central station alternatives described are currently more efficient than behind-the-meter distributed solar energy, advocates of net metering and other subsidies to distributed generation are increasing the overall cost of reducing CO_2 emissions, making it less likely that aggressive CO_2 reduction targets will be met. It is logical to assume that the aggregate investment that this or any country is willing to make to address climate change is limited, even if addressing it is a high priority. Therefore, the more costly the policies used to achieve a level of substitution for fossil energy the less substitution will occur, and the less likely that aggressive CO_2 reduction targets will be achieved.

Third, if one wishes to argue that the higher cost of electricity resulting from the widespread use of subsidies like net metering is justified, one should be willing to admit in public forums that the subsidy exists, so that the public (including those who choose not to or cannot install rooftop solar panels) can decide whether the economic penalty hidden in their electric bills is worthwhile. . . . In fact, the industry is trying to reduce or eliminate particularly aggressive subsidies that threaten to harm the majority of consumers (including low income consumers who do not have the option of installing solar panels on their rooftops) and other clean energy technologies.

NOTES & QUESTIONS

1.   According to Graffy and Kihm, what is the disruptive innovation that is now threatening utilities' longstanding business and regulatory models? Why is this innovation having such profound impacts?

2.   According to Graffy and Kihm, what are some factors that make it more difficult for utilities to respond to a new disruptive innovation in their market?

3.   What do you think Graffy and Kihm meant when they wrote that the existing utility regulatory "model is designed to maintain institutional stability in order to uphold social welfare objectives (in the historical case of energy, for example, to ensure low cost, reliable service), not to uphold the welfare of utilities themselves"? If this statement is true, what does it imply about how utility regulators should approach disputes between the rooftop solar energy industry and utilities?

4.   In what specific ways is the Market Street Railway's situation in the 1940s analogous to that of electric utilities today?

5.   What does the Graffy and Kihm excerpt suggest about how electric utilities should respond to the growth of rooftop solar energy in their territories?

6.   In no more than three sentences, summarize Raskin's arguments in the excerpt above responding to Graffy and Kihm. Do you find Raskin's arguments more persuasive than those of Graffy and Kihm? Why or why not?

7.   One common objection to net metering programs is that they disproportionately harm low-income residential utility customers who are unable to afford rooftop solar PV systems. Suppose you represented the rooftop solar energy industry. Craft an argument outlining at least three reasons why this argument does not justify eliminating solar net metering.

8.   *Feed-in Tariffs.* The Raskin excerpt above makes a reference to Germany's controversial *feed-in tariff* (FIT). FITs resemble net metering programs in that both compensate or credit customers with solar energy systems for the excess power that their systems generate and feed onto the grid. However, many FITs often go even further, requiring utilities to purchase customers' excess generated power at prices well exceed the retail electricity rate. As Raskin suggests, FITs can promote rapid increases in renewable energy development, but they also tend to drive up retail electricity rates and threaten the solvency of utility companies.

Relatively few U.S. utilities use FITs for distributed solar energy today. However, a growing number of utilities are beginning to use fixed-amount credits or tariffs to compensate customers for electricity their distributed solar arrays feed onto the grid. These new credits and tariffs resemble FITs in that they are for fixed amounts, but they differ in that they are usually *lower* than retail electricity rates and are supposedly based on regulators' estimations about the electricity's value. The materials in the next subsection contain more information on these fixed credits and tariffs.

b.   Net Metering Reform

The distributed solar energy industry's recent exponential growth has captured the attention of utilities and policymakers across the nation. As distributed solar has become increasingly cost-competitive with grid-supplied power, utilities have grown increasingly wary about this potential market threat and some have advocated for policy changes to better protect them. In 2016 alone, 47 states took some type of policy action related to distributed solar energy or community solar. *See The Fight to Put a Value on Rooftop Solar Power*, CLIMATE NEXUS, http://climatenexus.org/climate-issues/energy/the-net-metering-fight/ (last updated Apr. 20, 2017). One of the most straightforward ways many state policymakers have responded to distributed solar energy growth is through various reforms limiting or weakening net metering programs. The following are descriptions of some of the types of net metering reforms that have emerged in recent years.

Capping Participation in Net Metering

One simple means of limiting utilities' revenue losses from net metering is to cap the size or scope of net metering programs. Over the past decade or so, utilities and regulators in states throughout the country have capped net metering programs in a wide variety of ways. For detailed information on net metering caps found in jurisdictions across the country, visit *State Net Metering Policies*, NAT'L CONF. STATE LEGISLATURES (Nov. 3, 2016), http://www.ncsl.org/research/energy/net-metering-policy-overview-and-state-legislative-updates.aspx.

Many states use *aggregate capacity limits* to cap net metering programs. Under this approach, regulators cap the total aggregate generating capacity of distributed energy systems that a regulated utility must allow to participate in net metering within its service territory. Some states express these caps as a total number of MWs of generating capacity. For instance, as of 2017, a New Hampshire statute capped that state's total net metered distributed generation capacity at 100 MW. Other states, such as California, express caps as a percentage of a utility's aggregate peak customer demand. As of 2017, once certain California utilities met a five percent net metering cap of that variety, customers interconnecting new distributed solar PV systems to the grid faced additional charges and received less credit for their excess power. *See, e.g.*, Rob Nikolewski, *San Diego About to Hit Net Metering Cap*, SAN DIEGO UNION-TRIBUNE (July 17, 2016), http://www.sandiegouniontribune.com/sdut-solar-metering-cap-20 16jun17-story.html. Regardless of the cap's structure, distributed solar energy industry advocates typically oppose proposals for new net metering caps and utilities usually favor them.

Reducing Net Metering Credits

Another common means of reforming net metering programs is to reduce the size of the credit customers receive for feeding excess power onto the grid. A *full retail net metering* program credits customers in an amount equal to their retail electricity rate. For example, if a customer's residential retail rate were 10 cents per kWh, the utility would give the customer at 10 cent credit for each kWh of excess generated electricity her rooftop solar array feeds onto the grid. Although most early versions of net metering programs provided full retail net metering, state regulators are increasingly revisiting those policies and decreasing the amount of the credits.

Utilities' primary argument for reducing the size of net metering credits is that full retail net metering programs force utilities to overcompensate net metered customers for their excess power. A utility that routinely purchases electricity from natural gas-fired power plants for four cents per kWh is not likely to be enthused about having to pay 10 cents per kWh to thousands of scattered residential customers for small, unpredictable amounts of electricity supplied at irregular times throughout the day. As explained earlier in this chapter, the prospect of increasing retail electricity rates to cover any revenue losses resulting from net metering programs is also not an appealing option to most utilities. Such rate increases would only fuel the so-called "death spiral" by making rooftop solar even more cost-competitive with grid-supplied power. Most utilities would prefer instead to reduce net metering credits, which would have an opposite effect and actually diminish customers' financial benefits of having rooftop solar panels.

Utilities, customers, and rooftop solar companies all have much at stake when regulators calculate and adjust net metering credits, so such proceedings are often contentious. There are countless possible approaches to reducing the credits, and each group of stakeholders tends to have its own strong opinions about which approach to use. Many utilities have advocated crediting customers only at avoided cost or wholesale rates— prices that approximate what the utility would pay if it purchased the power from more conventional sources. In response, rooftop solar advocates often emphasize various unique societal and other benefits of distributed solar power and argue that the amount of net metering credits should fully account for those benefits, even if some of them do not accrue to utilities themselves.

Policymakers in some states have sought to replace retail net metering with *value-of-solar tariff* (VOST) programs. Under a VOST program, government officials first estimate the true "value" of a kWh of distributed solar energy within their jurisdiction. Utilities then use that pre-determined per-kWh "value" instead of the retail rate when crediting customers for excess power fed onto the grid. Austin Energy, a publicly-owned Texas utility, is sometimes credited with pioneering this approach. Austin Energy's VOST considers more than just the avoided cost of a kWh of power; it accounts for such benefits as compliance with environmental laws and avoided transmission and distribution costs. *See, e.g.*, Annie Lappe, *Austin Energy's Value of Solar Tariff: Could It Work Anywhere Else?*, GREENTECH MEDIA (Mar. 8, 2013), https://www.greentechmedia. com/articles/read/austin-energys-value-of-solar-tariff-could-it-work-any where-else.

Unfortunately, the VOST approach is not immune to controversy because opposing stakeholders still tend to have widely divergent opinions about how to value a kWh of distributed solar power. For instance, one 2015 study reviewed various recent analyses of the value of distributed solar. The study found that eight out of 11 analyses of the value of solar determined that it was worth *more* than the retail rate at the time and place of the study. All three of the analyses that determined otherwise had been commissioned by utilities. *See* LINDSAY HALLOCK & ROB SARGENT, SHINING REWARDS: THE VALUE OF ROOFTOP SOLAR POWER FOR CONSUMERS AND SOCIETY (2015), http://www.environmentamerica.org/sites/environment/files/reports/EA_shiningrewards_print.pdf.

State government efforts to valuate distributed solar energy have likewise produced vastly different results. Minnesota regulators calculated the value of solar in that state to be well above the retail rate, which deterred utilities from adopting it for years. *See* Mike Taylor, *The Minnesota Solar Experiment: Value of Solar—Part II*, RENEWABLE ENERGY WORLD (Dec. 16, 2016), http://www.renewableenergyworld.com/articles/2016/12/the-minnesota-solar-experiment-value-of-solar-part-iii.html. By contrast, in late 2016, Arizona regulators voted in favor of a "Resource Comparison Proxy" model that valued distributed power as less than the retail rate for that state's largest utility, with an expectation that the valuation would continue to decline for several years into the future. *See* Herman K. Trabish, *The Lurking Surprise for Solar in Arizona's Recent Ruling to End Net Metering*, UTILITY DIVE (Jan. 26, 2017), http://www.utilitydive.com/news/the-lurking-surprise-for-solar-in-arizonas-recent-ruling-to-end-net-meteri/433555/.

One explanation for the continued controversy surrounding VOST approaches is the true value of a kWh of distributed solar power depends greatly on the location, time of day, and numerous other factors. Fortunately, policymakers are beginning to tackle this problem by developing valuation models sophisticated enough to account for these and other important factors. The New York Public Service Commission has led the way in this ambitious effort, approving an innovative "Value of Distributed Energy Resources" formula in 2017 as part of its broader "Reforming the Energy Vison (REV) process. The formula is based upon a "value stack" comprised of multiple factors that seek to account for the location, time, and environmental value of power when determining how much to compensating retail customers for feeding it onto the grid. *See* Christian Roselund, *New York Approves Formula for Valuing Distributed Solar*, PV MAG. (Mar. 9, 2017), https://pv-magazine-usa.com/2017/03/09/new-york-approves-formula-for-valuing-distributed-solar/.

Other Net Metering Reforms

In addition to the main categories of net metering reforms just described, utilities have sought a wide range of other changes to net metering policies aimed at limiting the scope or impact of these programs. The case excerpt below highlights two types of net metering reforms that fit into this category.

The first approach, which regulators have adopted in several states, imposes *system capacity limits*—limits on the sizes of distributed energy systems that are eligible for net metering. Some states limit sizes based simply on a system's generating capacity. For example, utility customers in Massachusetts can participate in net metering only with distributed energy systems having generating capacities of up to 10 kW. The Wisconsin utility in the case below advocates a similar rule that would grant eligibility only to those customers with renewable energy systems having generating capacities of 20kW or less. Other states structure the limit differently, basing it instead on a generating system's size relative to its owner's on-site electricity demand. For instance, most Arizona utility customers can participate in net metering only with distributed energy systems whose generating capacities are no more than 125% of their own "total connected load."

The *Renew Wisconsin* case below also considers a renewable energy advocacy group's request for a change to the *netting period* utilities use to compensate customers for unused net metering credits. Most utilities with net metering programs periodically terminate any credits customers have accumulated but never used to offset their use of grid-supplied power. Some utilities pay cash to customers at the retail rate for these unused credits when wiping them out. Other utilities compensate customers based on a wholesale rate or some other rate that is less than the retail rate. Still other utilities simply wipe out the credits and pay customers nothing at all. Depending on the rate at which customers are credited and compensated, the frequency of this netting and payment can have sizable financial impacts on utilities and their net metered customers. As you read *Renew Wisconsin*, think carefully about why the renewable energy advocacy group wanted the utility to conduct the netting and credits process less frequently in this instance.

RENEW WISCONSIN V. PUBLIC SERVICE COMMISSION OF WISCONSIN

Wisconsin Court of Appeals, 2016
370 Wis.2d 787
(Unpublished Disposition)

PER CURIAM.

Public Service Commission of Wisconsin (the Commission) and Wisconsin Public Service Corporation (WPSC) each appeal the circuit court's order remanding the Commission's Final Decision for further consideration. This dispute arises from (1) WPSC's application to reduce the capacity limit for customer-owned energy generation systems (which we will call generation systems) eligible for the Pg–4 tariff rate from 100 kW to 20 kW, and (2) [Renew Wisconsin's (RENEW's)] proposal to change the energy netting period for Pg–4 customers from monthly to annually. The Commission granted WPSC's application to reduce the capacity limit and denied RENEW's proposal to change the netting period.

RENEW petitioned for judicial review of the Commission's Final Decision. The circuit court remanded to the Commission for further consideration. On appeal, the Commission argues that we should reverse the circuit court's order and affirm its Final Decision because that decision is "reasonable, articulates a rational[ ] basis for the conclusions made[,] and is based on substantial evidence in the record." WPSC also argues that we should affirm the Commission's Final Decision because it is supported by substantial evidence.

RENEW argues that we should affirm the circuit court order remanding to the Commission for further consideration because the Commission's decision "lacks sufficient explanation to be reviewable" and "is not supported by substantial evidence that generating systems larger than 20 kilowatts or annual netting cause the utility to under-collect fixed costs or provide a cross-subsidy." RENEW also argues that the Commission's decision is arbitrary and capricious because "it treats customer-generators served by [WPSC] differently than customer generators served by other large investor-owned utilities in Wisconsin" and because it targets generating systems larger than 20 kW as receiving a cross-subsidy while ignoring the half of customers who also receive the cross-subsidy because they buy less than the average amount of electricity. For the reasons set forth below, we agree with the Commission and reject RENEW's arguments. Therefore, we reverse the circuit court's order and affirm the Commission's Final Decision.

BACKGROUND

We briefly summarize the undisputed facts and relate additional pertinent facts in the discussion.

The Commission is an independent state agency charged with jurisdiction to supervise and regulate every public utility in Wisconsin. *See* WIS. STAT. § 196.02(1) (2013–14). WPSC is a public utility in Wisconsin that provides electricity and natural gas service to customers in Wisconsin. RENEW is a not-for-profit organization that represents approximately "115 renewable energy companies doing business in Wisconsin as well as approximately 300 individuals who are electric ratepayers in Wisconsin."

WPSC offers a net energy billing program (Pg–4 tariff) that allows customers with renewable resource generation to offset their monthly electric consumption, also known as net metering, and, at times, "push" or sell excess electricity back to the WPSC system. Under the Pg–4 tariff, self-generating customers receive a credit at the applicable retail rate for self-generated electricity up to the customer's monthly usage, and a credit at the lower "wholesale" rate for self-generated electricity in excess of the customer's monthly usage. In other words, if a customer uses more electricity than she generates during the course of the month, the customer pays WPSC at the applicable retail rate for the "net" amount (total used minus total self-generated). If the customer generates more electricity than she uses during the month, her net amount purchased from WPSC is zero and she also sells the excess amount (total self-generated minus total used) to WPSC at the lower wholesale rate. The period over which this net energy use is calculated is called the netting period.

WPSC's Pg–4 tariff is limited to customers with generation systems under a certain capacity limit. Prior to 2011, that capacity limit was 20 kW. In 2011, the Commission increased that capacity limit to 100 kW.

In March 2013, WPSC filed an application with the Commission to adjust its electric rates, which included a request to reduce the generation system capacity limit allowed under the Pg–4 tariff to "20 kW or less." Public hearings were held in September and November 2013 to receive comments and testimony.

RENEW intervened in the proceedings and, pertinent to this appeal, proposed that the Commission: (1) "[m]aintain the current 100 kW size cap"; and (2) "require that WPSC use an annual, as opposed to monthly, netting period."

In December 2013, the Commission issued a Final Decision in which it reduced the capacity limit allowed under the Pg–4 tariff from 100 kW to 20 kW and maintained the current monthly netting period.

In January 2014, RENEW filed a petition for judicial review of the Commission's Final Decision as to both the capacity limit and the netting period. RENEW argued in its petition that the Commission's decision is arbitrary because it lacks a sufficient explanation and lacks a factual basis in the record, contrary to WIS. STAT. § 227.57(6).

The circuit court accepted RENEW's arguments. Accordingly, the court remanded to the Commission for further fact-finding and to establish a sufficient record on the capacity limit and the netting period.

DISCUSSION

As already stated, the Commission argues that we should reverse the circuit court's order and affirm the Commission's Final Decision because that decision is "reasonable, articulates a rational[ ] basis for the conclusions made[,] and is based on substantial evidence in the record." WPSC also argues that we should affirm the Commission's Final Decision because it is supported by substantial evidence. RENEW argues that we should affirm the circuit court order remanding to the Commission for further consideration because the Commission's decision "lacks sufficient explanation to be reviewable" and "is not supported by substantial evidence that generating systems larger than 20 kilowatts or annual netting cause the utility to under-collect fixed costs or provide a cross-subsidy." RENEW also argues that the Commission's decision is arbitrary and capricious because "it treats customer-generators served by [WPSC] differently than customer generators served by other large investor-owned utilities in Wisconsin" and because it targets generating systems larger than 20 kW as receiving a cross-subsidy while ignoring the half of customers who also receive the cross-subsidy because they buy less than the average amount of electricity. As we proceed to explain, we reject RENEW's arguments, reverse the circuit court's order, and affirm the Commission's Final Decision.

. . . .

B.   Sufficient Explanation

RENEW concedes that the legislature granted the Commission discretion in setting electricity rates and tariffs. However, RENEW argues that the Commission's decision to reduce the generation capacity limit allowed under the Pg–4 tariff and to maintain the monthly netting period "lacks sufficient explanation to be reviewable." As we will explain, we reject RENEW's argument because the Commission's Final Decision provides sufficient and rational explanation.

"[A]dministrative agencies are to be given broad power within their respective jurisdictions and this court is hesitant to interfere with administrative determinations." *Transport Oil, Inc. v. Cummings*, 54 Wis.2d 256, 265, 195 N.W.2d 649 (1972). "In order for this balance between the administrative and judicial branches of government to be effective, however, it is essential that the agency exercise the power the legislature has given it." *Id.* "Such power requires a clear articulation of the reasons for a particular determination." *Id.* However, "a detailed or explicit explanation of the [agency's] reasoning is not necessary." *Oneida Seven Generations Corp. v. City of Green Bay*, 2015 WI 50, ¶ 49, 362 Wis.2d 290,

865 N.W.2d 162. "The decision need only contain enough information for the reviewing court to discern the basis of the [agency's] decision." *Id.*

Although the Commission's explanation could benefit from greater specificity, we conclude that it contains enough information for this court to discern the basis of the Commission's decision. The Commission decided that it is "reasonable to modify the Pg–4 tariff so as to reduce the capacity limit from 100 kW to 20 kW per customer premises," and that it is "reasonable to retain WPSC's existing monthly netting structure for the Pg–4 tariff." The Commission based its decision on its finding that "interest in customer-owned distributed generation will continue to increase" and that "the focus should be on getting the right policies in place before this becomes a more significant cost issue."

As to its decision to reduce the capacity limit, the Commission explained that "given the fixed-cost recovery issues raised by the utility, the identified uncertainties, and the potential for unreasonable cross-subsidies, the Commission believes that a conservative approach is warranted with respect to the Pg–4 tariff." The Commission found "it reasonable to reduce the capacity limit for WPSC's Pg–4 Net Energy Billing service from 100 kW to 20 kW." The Commission explained that "[l]owering the capacity limit of the Pg–4 tariff will limit the risk of possible cross-subsidization by non-participating customers."

As to its decision to maintain the monthly netting period, the Commission found that there is "merit in the concerns raised by WPSC regarding possible fixed cost recovery issues associated with net metering, and possible cross-subsidization by non-participating customers [customers not eligible for the Pg–4 tariff]." The Commission found that "there is insufficient evidentiary support in the record to support modifying the netting structure of WPSC" as proposed by RENEW and, therefore, concluded that it is "reasonable to retain the existing monthly netting structure for WPSC's Pg–4 Net Energy Billing Service."

In other words, the Commission decided to act conservatively with respect to WPSC's ability to recover fixed costs from net-metering customers and to limit subsidization by customers who do not participate in net-metering (cross-subsidization), and to focus on "getting the right policies in place before this becomes a more significant cost issue." The Commission believed it could curb the magnitude of any potential cross-subsidization by limiting the availability of the Pg–4 tariff to small-generators and by maintaining the current monthly netting period. In sum, we conclude that the Commission's Final Decision provides a sufficient and rational explanation.

C.   *Substantial Evidence Supporting the Commission's Factual Finding*

RENEW argues that there is a lack of substantial evidence in the record to support the Commission's factual finding. We begin by examining the substantial evidence in the record supporting the Commission's finding that there are fixed-cost recovery issues and a potential for unreasonable cross-subsidization by non-generating customers. We then reject RENEW's arguments to the contrary.

. . . .

WPSC presented evidence that its estimated "fixed costs" to service residential customers is $52.18, and the Commission estimated that the fixed cost of service is $41.24. Given either amount, however, even with the increase authorized in the Commission's Final Decision, WPSC is only permitted to recover $10.40 per residential customer per month as a fixed charge under the approved rate structure. This means that WPSC must recover the bulk of its fixed costs through the variable energy charge to customers (retail rate). In other words, a portion of the fixed costs is built into the retail rate of $0.11143 per kWh, which is greater than the estimated variable cost of $0.0338 per kWh (WPSC's estimate), or $0.0415 per kWh (Commission's estimate). This rate structure, in effect, creates a "subsidy" from customers who purchase a lot of electricity to customers who purchase less electricity.

Because the Pg–4 tariff allows customers to offset their electricity use at the retail rate up to their monthly use, these customers are able to offset not only their variable cost but also the fixed cost that is built into the retail rate. Thus, for the same reason—that customers who purchase a lot of electricity subsidize customers who purchase less electricity—it can be reasonably concluded that non-generating customers "subsidize" self-generating customers who "purchase" less electricity from WSPC because they are able to offset their electricity use. Indeed, the record shows at least one self-generating customer who not only offset his entire electricity use—all of his variable costs plus the fixed costs built into the retail rate—but also generated so much excess electricity as to offset much of the fixed charge, resulting in a monthly bill of fifty-three cents. Thus, we conclude that the record includes substantial evidence to support the Commission's finding that there are fixed-cost recovery issues and a potential for cross-subsidization by non-generating customers that the Commission could believe is unfair.

RENEW makes three arguments to the contrary, which we reject as follows.

First, RENEW argues that the actual costs of providing service to "any particular customer—or to any subset of customers, like those that self-generate some of their electricity—is not in the record." RENEW further argues that "to the extent there is any evidence specific to costs caused by customers who self-generate some of their electricity, that evidence actually shows that such customers *cost less to serve* than a typical customer because they reduce peak demands, reduce transmission, provide a fuel hedge, and decrease system losses." While we recognize that there is evidence in the record showing the existence of benefits, albeit non-quantified, conferred upon society by generating systems, these benefits merely provide an alternative view that the Commission could have adopted. That is, this limited evidence could have led the Commission to conclude that there is less of an issue of cross-subsidization because the benefits offset, to some extent, any potential subsidy. . . . Here, in finding that there are issues of cross-subsidization and fixed cost recovery, the Commission decided to accept the view unfavorable to RENEW.

Second, RENEW argues that the substantial evidence standard requires "some actual data and some attempt to actually quantify" the cross-subsidy. Assuming without deciding that that is the standard, we disagree with RENEW's contention that there is no significant evidence of actual data or quantification of the cross-subsidy here. One example of quantified data is from a policy analyst employed by the Commission who estimated possible "losses" of between $93,000 and $117,000 per year in fixed-cost recovery . . . a reasonable view from the evidence in the record is that customers entitled to the Pg–4 tariff cause some difficulty in fixed-cost recovery for WPSC.

. . . .

CONCLUSION

For the reasons set forth above, we conclude that the Commission's decision is sufficiently explained, supported by substantial evidence, and rational. Therefore, we reverse the circuit court's order and affirm the Commission's Final Decision.

Order reversed.

_____

QUESTIONS

1.   Why do you think distributed solar energy industry advocates tend to oppose net metering cap policies while utilities favor them? Suppose you represent a retail electricity customer advocacy group. What factors would you consider in determining whether your group should support or oppose a proposal for a new net metering cap in your jurisdiction?

2.   How does capping net metering participation as described in the materials above help to prevent the utility "death spiral" scenario? What are some potential policy disadvantages or practical challenges associated with capping net metering participation?

3.   Based on the materials above, why is it often difficult to accurately measure the monetary value of a unit of solar-generated electricity? How do the views of utilities and third-party private rooftop solar installers differ

regarding the optimal methodologies for calculating the value of distributed solar power? How might technological advancements help to overcome those difficulties?

4.   In the *Renew Wisconsin* case, why do you think the renewable energy advocacy group wanted the utility to more frequently net its customers' credits? Hint: the reason has to do with the difference between how retail and wholesale rates are applied in the netting and payment process.

5.   What is the alleged "cross-subsidy" described in the *Renew Wisconsin* case? In other words, who is allegedly subsidizing whom? According to WPSC, how does tightening the eligibility requirements for net metering potentially help to limit the size of this purported cross-subsidy?

6.   How does the *Renew Wisconsin* court's willingness to defer to the Commission's determinations impact the disposition of the case? Based on your answer, do you think there should be limits on the extent to which utilities may contributed financial support to the election campaigns of state public utility commissioners or those who appoint them? Why or why not? The issue of utility funding of commissioner campaigns is explored in greater detail later in this chapter.

c.   Retail Rate Design Reform

In addition to seeking net metering reforms, numerous utilities have also sought state regulators' approval to reform the structures of their retail electricity rate designs in ways that would slow the growth of rooftop solar energy. Seeking changes to retail rate structures has become an increasingly popular way for utilities to respond to distributed solar energy growth in their service areas. The following paragraphs highlight the main types of proposed changes to retail rate designs that have emerged in this context.

Imposing Special Fees on Customers with Solar Panels

Perhaps the most straightforward way for utilities to increase revenues from net metered customers with solar panels is to single these customers out and charge them special fees. Some of the earliest retail rate reform efforts related to distributed solar energy tried this approach, with minimal success. Arizona Public Service Co. (APS), Arizona's largest investor-owned utility, campaigned to impose special monthly fees on solar-using residential customers in 2013. APS initially sought regulatory approval to impose special monthly fees on solar users in the range of $50 to $100 per month. After a heated debate that drew widespread attention in the media, regulators ultimately approved a much smaller monthly fee on solar owners that amounted to only about $5 per month. *See* David Wichner, *Regulators Approve Fee on APS Solar Customers*, ARIZ. DAILY STAR (Nov. 15, 2013), http://tucson.com/business/local/regulators-approve-fee-on-aps-solar-customers/article_a45718d0-db56-53df-bd02-2b27b79d06

3e.html. In the years following the APS solar fees decision, few other have utilities succeeded in securing regulatory approval for special fees on residential solar users.

Increasing Monthly Fixed Fees on All Retail Customers

Perhaps recognizing that widespread support for solar energy would make it difficult to get regulatory approvals to single out solar-using customers and impose special fees on them, many utilities have sought more rate structure reforms aimed at increasing revenue from solar users. In the mid-2010s, dozens of utilities sought to do that by increasing the proportion of retail customers' electricity bills that is fixed and payable regardless of how much electricity the customer uses over the billing period.

Rather than citing distributed solar energy growth as their reason for these proposed rate design changes, utilities advocating for higher fixed retail fees often emphasized a desire to better align retail rate structures with the utility's cost structure. Many of the costs utilities routinely face— debt payments for power plants and power lines, employee salaries and benefits, etc.—are relatively fixed because utilities must pay them each month regardless of how much power they sell. Increasing fixed cost alignment usually involves increasing the fixed fees that appear on retail electricity bills and correspondingly decreasing the per-kilowatt-hour rates customers pay. Such changes cause customers' ratio of fixed to variable charges to be more closely aligned with utilities' ratio of fixed to variable costs of providing electricity service.

A simple numeric example helps to illustrate the concept of fixed cost alignment in electricity rate design. Suppose that fixed capital costs account for 70 percent of the revenue requirement of the hypothetical utility PowerCo and that PowerCo's variable costs of producing and delivering electricity accounted for the other 30 percent of the requirement. Suppose further that Anaya, a residential PowerCo customer, consumes an average of 900 kWhs per billing period and has historically paid electricity bills to PowerCo averaging $100 per month for electricity service. The $100 billed to Anaya consisted of a $10-per-month fixed service fee (charged to all customers) and $90 in volumetric rate charges based on PowerCo's flat rate of $0.10 per kilowatt hour (kWh). Expressed mathematically, she paid:

Fixed service fee		$10.00
Volumetric charges	(900 kWh × $0.10/kWh)	$90.00
TOTAL BILL		$100.00

Based on these figures, PowerCo's rate structure could theoretically achieve pure fixed cost alignment if the utility increased its fixed monthly service fee from $10 to $70, thereby aligning the proportion of its *costs* that were fixed (i.e., 70%) with the proportion of Anaya's monthly *bill* that was fixed. To prevent Anaya's total electricity bill from increasing because of this change, PowerCo would need to correspondingly reduce the volumetric rate Anaya paid so the total amount collected on that portion of her bill was only $30. Decreasing PowerCo's volumetric rate from $0.10 per kWh to $0.033 per kWh would produce that result. Assuming Anaya's electricity consumption habits did not change as a result of these reforms, Anaya's new average bill under this revised rate structure with perfect fixed cost alignment would be:

Fixed monthly service fee		$70.00
Volumetric charges	900 kWh × $0.033/kWh	$30.00
TOTAL BILL		$100.00

For customers like Anaya who have no rooftop solar panels, the rate structure changes just described would arguably have no major financial impact: Anaya pays $100 per month for 900 kWh of power regardless of whether her fixed monthly fee is $10 or $70. However, for customers with rooftop solar panels, the impact of large increases in fixed monthly fees is often far more pronounced.

To illustrate this difference, suppose that Anaya's neighbor, Bianca, also used 900kWh of power per month but that she also had a net-metered solar PV array on her rooftop that generated an average of 800 kWh of electricity each month. Bianca thus typically only purchased 100 kWh of power each month from PowerCo. Assuming PowerCo imposed a $10 fixed fee and used $0.10/kWh volumetric rate, Bianca's monthly bill would be:

Fixed monthly service fee		$10.00
Volumetric charges	100 kWh × $0.10/kWh	$10.00
TOTAL BILL		$20.00

However, if PowerCo were to increase its monthly service fee on all customers from $10 to $70 and correspondingly reduce its volumetric rate from $0.10/kWh to $0.033/kWh as suggested in the earlier example, Bianca's monthly bill would more dramatically increase. Specifically, it would be:

Fixed monthly service fee		$70.00
Volumetric charges	100 kWh × $0.033/kWh	$3.33
TOTAL BILL		$73.33

As this simple example shows, increasing the fixed proportion of retail customers' power bills may not have a major impact on non-solar-using customers, but it can have enormous consequences for customers with solar panels. In this example, Anaya's bill stayed the same under both plans but Bianca's increased from $20 per month to $73.33 per month—a 367% increase. Increasing fixed fees thus bears striking similarity to the special monthly fees described above: it increases utility revenues from residential solar users and makes rooftop solar panels far less economically justifiable for retail customers.

One other disadvantage of fixed fee increases is that the commensurately lower volumetric rates associated with them reduce the marginal retail price of electricity, incentivizing customers to increase electricity consumption. When customers pay less for each additional unit of electricity they use (e.g., $0.033 per kWh versus $0.10 per kWh in the fact pattern above), basic microeconomics principles suggests they will use more power. Energy efficiency and conservation practices are often among the lowest-cost ways of reducing electricity-related greenhouse gas emissions, and rate design changes that incentivize customers to use more power deter those practices. *See* ENVTL. PROTECTION AGENCY, ENERGY EFFICIENCY AS A LOW-COST RESOURCE FOR ACHIEVING CARBON EMISSIONS REDUCTIONS (Sept. 2009), https://www.epa.gov/sites/production/files/2015-08/documents/ee_and_carbon.pdf.

By 2017, fewer utilities were seeking fixed fee increases and many had moved on to other strategies for responding to distributed solar energy growth. However, a few utilities continued to call for increased fixed fees, suggesting the policy debates over rationales for such increases were likely to linger for years to come.

Imposing Mandatory Demand Charges

Yet another proposed retail rate design reform that has drawn increased attention in recent years is that of imposing monthly *demand charges* on residential retail customers. A demand charge is an additional retail charge that is calculated based on a customer's own peak electricity consumption over the billing period. For instance, a demand charge might be based on the highest number of kWh a customer consumes within any 15-minute stretch of time during the previous month. A higher peak usage amount results in a higher demand charge on the customer's electricity bill.

Many electric utilities have imposed demand charges on industrial or commercial customers for decades, and those charges often comprise a large proportion of their overall bill. Imposing demand charges on big industrial customers is often justifiable because the peak electricity use of just one such customer can impact grid operations and require special attention and infrastructure investments. For instance, some factories consume enormous amounts of electricity when operating at full capacity but consume very little power at other times. Utilities must build enough power lines and other infrastructural equipment to meet those factories' peak electricity needs, and demand charges help to ensure that the factories cover the costs of that extra infrastructure and attention. However, some utilities have recently proposed imposing major demand charges on residential customers. Justifying demand charges on small residential electricity users is much more difficult than justifying them for enormous industrial customers. A single residential customer is incapable of using enough power to materially impact grid load balancing activities or require lots of extra infrastructure to accommodate periods of peak usage.

Despite its deficiencies, the idea of residential demand charges has appeared multiple times in recent years. In particular, the large Arizona utility Arizona Public Service Co. (APS) filed a rate request in 2016 seeking to impose demand charges on nearly all of its residential customers. To partially offset this new charge, APS proposed to lower its retail per-kWh electricity rate. Solar energy advocates opposed these changes, which would have reduced the benefits of having net-metered rooftop solar panels by increasing the fixed portion of customers' utility bills and giving them less credit for the excess electricity they send back onto the grid. *See* Ryan Randazzo, *APS Seeks $11 Monthly Rate Hike, Demand Charges*, AZ CENTRAL (June 6, 2016), http://www.azcentral.com/story/money/business/energy/2016/06/01/aps-seeks-11-monthly-rate-hike-demand-charges/8524 1962/. APS ultimately withdrew its mandatory demand charge proposal as part of a settlement agreement with the rooftop solar industry stakeholders. See Press Release, *APS, diverse group reach consensus rate review agreement*, Ariz. Pub. Service Co. (Mar. 1, 2017), https://www.aps.com/en/ourcompany/news/latestnews/Pages/aps-diverse-group-reach-consensus-rate-review-agreement.aspx. Oklahoma Gas & Electric also proposed a mandatory residential demand charge in 2016 but regulators ultimately rejected it. *See* Paul Monies, *OG&E Customers Will Be Due Refund in Rate Case Vote*, NEWS OK (Mar. 21, 2017), http://newsok.com/article/5542416.

Although the APS and OG&E demand charge proposals were particularly aggressive, many other utilities have proposed demand charges in various forms in response to the growth of distributed solar energy in their markets. In 2015, more than a dozen utilities had proposed imposing demand charges on residential solar energy users. *See* BENJAMIN INSKEEP ET AL., THE 50 STATES OF SOLAR: 2015 POLICY REVIEW, Q4 QUARTERLY REPORT 32 (2016), https://nccleantech.ncsu.edu/wp-content/uploads/50sosQ4-FINAL.pdf.

A simple numeric example helps to illustrate how demand charges can increase the fixed proportion of a retail electricity customer's bill and discourage customers from getting rooftop solar panels. Returning to hypothetical fact pattern set forth above involving Anaya, Bianca and PowerCo: suppose that PowerCo opted to impose a new mandatory demand charge instead of a higher fixed fee. Specifically, the utility got regulatory approval to charge just $0.033 per kWh for electric power but to also collect a new demand charge of $6.00 per kW based on each customer's peak demand during the billing period. Assume further that Anaya's peak demand during the period—which she reached one late afternoon while simultaneously running her dishwasher, washing machine, and air conditioner in her home—was 10 kW. Meanwhile, Bianca's peak demand was only 5 kW despite her simultaneous use of the same appliances because her solar panels offset some of her electricity use during that time. Based on these assumptions, the amount due on Anaya's utility bill would be exactly the same as under the two other possible rate designs described earlier. Specifically, it would be:

> fixed charge + volumetric charge + demand charge
>
> = $10.00 + ($0.033/kWh × 900kWh) + ($6.00/kW × 10kW)
>
> = $10.00 + $30.00 + $60.00
>
> = $100.00

By contrast, the amount due on Bianca's bill (which was just $20.00 without the demand change since her solar panels generated 800 kWh of power during the month) would go up dramatically. PowerCo would calculate it as follows:

> fixed charge + volumetric charge + demand charge
>
> = $10.00 + ($0.033/kWh × 100kWh) + ($6.00/kW × 5 kW)
>
> = $10.00 + $10.00 + $30.00
>
> = $50.00

As these calculations show, the introduction of demand charges can sharply and disproportionately increase the monthly utility bills of customers like Bianca who have rooftop solar energy systems. Accordingly, introducing such charges unquestionably reduces customers' incentives to purchase distributed solar energy systems. Time will tell whether the idea of imposing mandatory residential demand charges ultimately fades away or whether it gains additional traction as utilities continue searching for ways to respond to distributed solar energy growth.

Time-Based Pricing

In lieu of the possible rate design reforms described above, a few utilities have begun using time-based pricing to help address the rise of rooftop solar power. One major disadvantages of distributed solar energy growth is that it can complicate grid load balancing operations. During the mid-day, when rooftop solar panels are the most productive, the aggregate load demand drops off in regions with lots of rooftop solar panels because many customers are generating their own power and thus need less power from the utility. However, as the sun sets in the early evening, those thousands of rooftop panels stop generating power and the load demand for grid-supplied electricity rapidly increases. Utilities must therefore scramble to ramp up production at centralized electricity plants quickly enough to meet this spike in demand.

Industry insiders often depict this challenge with some version of the infamous "duck curve" diagram shown in Figure 5.7. The top line in the diagram reflects the overall demand for electricity (including solar and non-solar) over the course of a day, which typically peaks in the early evening when individuals get home, cook dinner, watch television, and use various other appliances in their air-conditioned homes. The bottom line in the diagram shows how aggregate electricity production from distributed solar energy systems changes throughout the day. The middle line shows how daytime rooftop solar energy production reduces the demand for grid-supplied electricity during those hours but then requires that the utility swiftly ramp up non-solar energy production once the sun goes down to meet peak demand in the early evening. As the market penetration of rooftop solar increases, the demand for grid-supplied electricity declines further and further, causing the "duck" in the diagram to get progressively fatter and further exacerbating these operational challenges for utilities.

Figure 5.7. The "Duck Curve" Problem

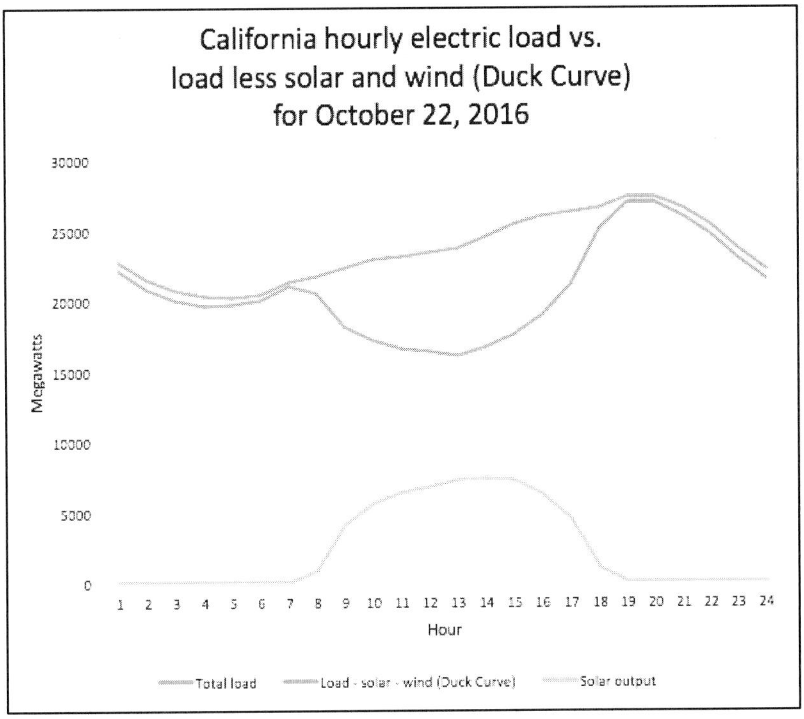

Source: Wikimedia Commons

Time-based electricity pricing can help to "shave" peak loads and flatten the demand line for electricity power across the day and year, making it easier to balance loads throughout the day and reducing the need to build additional fossil fuel-fired "peaker" plants to supply power during peak periods. As described in detail in Chapter 7 of this Casebook, time-based electricity pricing takes many forms. Many utilities have offered programs allowing retail customers to voluntarily opt in to time-based pricing structures for years. However, the proliferation of rooftop solar and the growing adoption of smart meters capable of facilitating time-based pricing appear to be driving unprecedented levels of interest in this more advanced pricing approach.

In 2016 and 2017, several major electric utilities rolled out new voluntary time-of-use (TOU) electricity rate plans for residential customers. Customers who enroll in these plans pay a per-kWh rate for electricity during the utility's times of peak aggregate electricity demand much higher than the ordinary flat volumetric rate. In exchange for accepting those higher peak-period rates, customers enjoy rates during off-peak times that are far lower than the flat volumetric rate. Customers enrolled in TOU plans can often save money each month by shifting some of their more discretionary electricity use to off-peak times. Utilities are also increasingly open to offering TOU rates because they can help to mitigate the "duck curve" problems resulting from distributed solar energy growth. Some studies suggest many customers who have solar panels may also benefit from TOU pricing because solar energy production is more "on peak" than "off peak" in many markets.

A few utilities across the country, such as Arizona's TEP and APS, have gone one step further and made TOU rates the default rate for new customers. *See, e.g.*, Julia Pyper, *Arizona Public Service, Solar Industry Reach Critical Settlement in Contentious Rate Case*, Greentech Media (Mar. 1, 2017), https://www.greentechmedia.com/articles/read/Arizona-Public-Service-Solar-Industry-Reach-Critical-Settlement-in-Content; David Wichner, *TEP's New Rate Plans Could Cost More If Customers Fail to Alter Usage*, ARIZ. DAILY STAR (Mar. 25, 2017), http://tucson.com/business/tucson/tep-s-new-rate-plans-could-cost-more-if-customers/article_0bc95c8 4-e76d-51b8-ae19-565c023d477f.html. Unlike large fixed fees, demand charges, or special fees on customers with solar panels, time-based electricity price structures may be a "win-win" approach to electricity rate design reform in some regions of the country. Time-based pricing in its various forms may help some electric utilities to integrate increasing quantities of distributed solar generating capacity into their grid systems without unduly harming their revenues or operations.

The following article critiques the idea of mandatory residential demand charges and contrasts it with proposals for greater use of TOU retail electricity rates. When reading the article, consider whether you agree with its author's arguments in favor of TOU rates over demand charges.

RESIDENTIAL DEMAND CHARGES: BAD CHOICE

Charles Cicchetti
154 PUB. UTIL. FORT. 34, 35–37 (2016)

An increasing number of utilities propose to add demand charges to rooftop solar customers' tariffs. Other jurisdictions are considering applying demand charges to all residential customers.

. . . [A]ny residential demand charges would sharply reduce the economic incentive for all customers to purchase energy efficient appliances and devices for the home.

Demand charges would significantly increase the amount rooftop solar customers pay.

. . . .

The first conceptual flaw and problem with demand charges for rooftop solar customers is that the utilities propose a demand charge based on a customer's total household consumption. This unreasonably ignores the amount of peak period energy and related capacity that rooftop solar customers purchase from the utility.

In effect, the utilities' proposed demand charge forces rooftop solar customers to pay for both capacity they no longer use and for capacity the utility no longer must provide to rooftop solar customers for an extended number of years, likely forever.

Regulators should reject the proposed residential demand charges for rooftop solar because such charges do not recognize the difference between a rooftop solar customer's maximum household consumption, which includes the electricity the customer self-generates, and the same customer's maximum purchase from the utility, particularly during peak demand periods.

A second problem with requiring demand charges for rooftop solar customers can be readily understood with an example based on an assumed monthly electricity bill. Current tariffs roll the cost of capacity into the basic energy charge.

For example, suppose a customer consumes a thousand kilowatt-hours each month, and pays ten cents per kilowatt-hour to the utility, for a monthly electricity bill of a hundred dollars. Potential rooftop solar customers under prevailing residential tariffs compare the all-in solar costs per kilowatt-hour that they produce to a utility average rolled-in price of ten cents per kilowatt-hour, which represents average energy and capacity costs bundled together.

Continuing the example, suppose the utility imposes an eight dollar per kilowatt demand charge on rooftop solar customers. And, for simplicity, assume the customer in question is an average residential user, who has maximum peak consumption of eight kilowatts.

This would result in a new tariff for rooftop solar customers that collected sixty-four dollars per month in demand charges. The remainder of the customer's one hundred dollars per month, or thirty-six dollars per month, would be collected in an energy charge.

The new energy price would decrease from 10 cents per kilowatt-hour to 3.6 cents per kilowatt-hour.

The customer would already be paying for the rooftop solar system she uses to self-generate, and she would pay the additional sixty-four dollars per month in demand charges. . . .

It is inconceivable the rooftop solar customer could ever come close to saving enough on her remaining utility purchases to make any significant dent in the sixty-four dollars per month hole she would find herself in, after paying both a demand charge to the utility for capacity she no longer needs, and also for the rooftop solar system she added to her home.

This makes the decision to go solar very uneconomic for prospective new solar customers. If demand charges were required retroactively, her investment in rooftop solar made under prior tariffs would become under-water.

Incentives to add rooftop solar would be sharply diminished. Potential rooftop solar customers would compare the reduced utility energy price of 3.6 cents per kilowatt-hour, not the previous 10 cents per kilowatt-hour, to her expected all-in solar costs.

Quite obviously, there would be fewer rooftop solar installations if the utility energy prices were reduced to 3.6 cents per kilowatt-hour. . . .

The household's economic incentives for installing rooftop solar would virtually disappear. This would happen just as the installed cost of solar panels is decreasing, and their performance is on the upswing.

A third reason for rejecting utility proposals to introduce demand charges is that there is a better tariff reform that regulators should consider. This alternative is Time-of-Use tariffs, where the residential customer would pay higher than average energy prices during peak periods of utility system demand, likely during daylight hours on weekdays in the summer.

The customer would also pay less than peak prices for electricity during intermediate hours and days when system demand was less. And even less during off-peak periods with relatively low system demand. . .

Time-of-Use tariffs would be based on the utilities' marginal or avoided costs that reflect how utility engineers and competitive wholesale markets actually and conceptually dispatch electricity generation. Peak demand periods, both hourly and days of the week, have higher utility marginal costs because as utility load or customers' demand increases, electric companies or the wholesale market dispatch increasingly more expensive-to-operate generation.

Time-of-Use pricing would signal varying electricity marginal costs to consumers, in either real-time or by relying on objectively-determined projections of electricity prices for different time periods.

Under Time-of-Use pricing, the ten cents per kilowatt-hour average residential energy price might, for example, become twenty cents per kilowatt-hour during peak hours and days. Of -peak prices might become five cents per kilowatt-hour. There could be interim period prices of nine cents per kilowatt-hour.

Time-of-Use tariffs introduce incentives for rooftop solar that are dramatically different than either rolled-in residential tariffs or tariffs that add demand charges. Much of the electricity that rooftop solar produces would come during peak and interim periods. Therefore, potential rooftop solar customers would compare their expected all-in rooftop solar self-generation costs mostly to the utility's peak and, perhaps to a lesser extent, interim prices.

Time-of-Use tariffs would increase the expected savings for potential rooftop solar customers because at the times rooftop solar would typically be generating electricity, the customer would save twenty cents per kilowatt-hour, not the ten cents per kilowatt-hour under the previous rolled-in residential tariffs.

More importantly, the incentives are very different than the much reduced incentive for self-generation based on the 3.6 cents per kilowatt-hour energy component for the demand charge tariff. The potential rooftop solar residential customers would also pay less for the electricity they purchase from the utility during of -peak nights and weekends when their rooftop solar facilities were not producing electricity. These prices would likely be less than the pre-existing average or rolled-in price of ten cents per kilowatt-hour.

. . . .

Regulators should not be misled by pitches that utility companies are making to fix the rooftop solar problem by requiring customers to pay demand charges. . . . The new demand charge tariffs quash competition from a burgeoning rooftop solar industry.

The conclusion that Time-of-Use tariffs are the preferred fit for rooftop solar customers stands on its own. It increases in strength when regulators consider other rooftop solar benefits, including environmental and climate change advantages, local jobs, and economic security.

6. THE "GRANDFATHERING" DEBATE

One other issue that sometimes rears its head when policymakers reform net metering or retail electricity rate structures is whether and to what extent customers who invested in distributed energy systems under the pre-reform policies should be entitled to continue operating under those original rules. Utilities and utility regulators sometimes seek to retroactively apply new net metering or rate design policies in ways that make it far more difficult for customers who purchased solar panels under prior policies to recoup their investments. The customers in these situations naturally feel entitled to continue receiving the benefits that were available when they bought their solar panels. Usually, policymakers ultimately resolve these debates in favor of customers by including provisions that given them *grandfathering* rights—privileges to continue under the old policies throughout the useful life of their solar arrays. Nonetheless, this issue continues to arise from time to time and utilities sometimes resist granting grandfathering rights.

It is easy to understand why grandfathering rights are important to customers who already have rooftop solar panels when regulators reform net metering programs or retail rate structures. As of 2017, a typical residential rooftop solar array cost upwards of $20,000 and full retail net metering benefits were often crucial to making such expenditures a worthwhile investment. Imagine a customer who had purchased solar panels long before her utility communicated plans to alter its net metering program. If her utility suddenly began crediting her for excess power based on wholesale rates rather than much-higher retail rates, her monthly electricity bills would skyrocket and it would unexpectedly take her several additional years to fully recoup her investment.

On the other hand, awarding grandfathering rights to existing net metered customers can be costly and burdensome for utilities, so some utilities have tried to avoid doing it. In 2015, state regulators authorized the investor-owned utility NV Energy to retroactively apply sweeping policy changes to thousands of net metered customers in ways that dramatically undermined those customers' rooftop solar investments. *See* Jacques Leslie, *Nevada's Solar Bait-and-Switch*, N.Y. TIMES: OPINION (Feb. 1, 2016), https://www.nytimes.com/2016/02/01/opinion/nevadas-solar-bait-and-switch.html?mcubz=1. Roughly nine months later, after enduring a vigorous public outcry against the retroactivity of the changes, Nevada regulators reversed their decision and restored grandfathering rights to the utility's existing net metered customers. *See* Julia Pyper, *Nevada Regulators Restore Net Metering for Existing Solar Customers*, GREENTECH MEDIA (Sept. 16, 2016), https://www.greentechmedia.com/

articles/read/nevada-regulators-restore-net-metering-for-existing-solar-customers. Arizona's Salt River Project similarly reversed its initial position against grandfathering in 2015 in the face of strong public resistance. *See* Ryan Randazzo, *SRP Board OKs Rate Hike, New Fees For Solar Customers*, AZ CENTRAL (Feb. 26, 2015), http://www.azcentral.com/story/money/business/2015/02/26/srp-board-oks-rate-hike-new-fees-solar-customers/24086473/.

Although proposed amendments to a 2016 Senate bill that sought to prohibit retroactive changes to net metering never became law, there appears to be a trend in favor of protecting grandfathering rights of existing solar energy users. *See* Danielle Ola, *US Senate Scraps Retroactive Net Metering Protection Provision*, PV TECH (Apr. 26, 2016), https://www.pv-tech.org/news/us-senate-passes-new-energy-act-scraps-retroactive-net-metering-protection. Still, some difficult questions related to the grandfathering of net metering privileges remain. For instance, controversies occasionally still arise over how long existing net metered customers should enjoy grandfathering privileges. Stakeholders on each side of the debate unsurprisingly tend to have divergent opinions over whether customers should be grandfathered for 10 years, 20 years, or longer. The legal principles governing *pre-existing nonconforming land uses* and *amortization periods* under land use and zoning laws might ultimately be a valuable source of guidance to courts and policymakers grappling with these issues.

NOTES & QUESTIONS

1.   Public utility commissioners often play important roles in the types of controversial policy discussions highlighted above. In such policy debates, whose interests do you think these commissioners should seek to advance the most: those of retail customers, utilities, or rooftop solar energy companies? Why?

2.   What are some types of retail customers who might be adversely impacted if electric utilities moved to mandatory TOU pricing? What policy solutions would you advocate for addressing the unintended impacts of a transition to time-based pricing models on certain customers?

3.   Is solar energy more likely to be a plentiful source of "near peak" power in the Southwest United States or in the Northeast? Why? What differences would you anticipate in the severity of the "duck curve" problems associated with solar energy and in the effectiveness of TOU pricing in addressing those problems between these two regions?

4.   Summarize, in one sentence each, the three arguments Charles Cicchetti sets forth in favor of time-of-use rates over mandatory residential

demand charges. Which of these three arguments do you think is the weakest, and which do you think is the strongest? Why?

5.   Suppose you represent a utility that is seeking to impose new mandatory demand charges on all residential customers. Craft a detailed two-paragraph responding to Charles Cicchetti's arguments above in favor of time-of-use rates and against demand charges.

6.   *Stranded costs*, which David Raskin referenced in his article earlier in this chapter, are capital infrastructure expenditures that utilities are unable to recover through their revenues because of market or policy changes. In advocating for various rate design and net metering changes, some utilities have cited concerns about having significant stranded costs if distributed solar growth prevents them from fully recouping their investments in centralized power plants or other facilities. *See, e.g.*, Scott Hempling, *From Streetcars to Solar Panels: Stranded Cost Policy in the United States*, 3 ENERGY REG. Q. (2015), http://www.energyregulationquarterly.ca/articles/from-streetcars-to-solar-panels-stranded-cost-policy-in-the-united-states#sthash.PogQPtQu.dpb. Suppose you were a hired advocate for the rooftop solar industry. Craft an argument in favor of grandfathering rights for existing net metering customers that draws a comparison to utilities' own stranded cost concerns.

7.   *Using Energy Storage Devices to Avoid Demand Charges.* As distributed energy storage technologies (which are covered in detail in Chapter 7) become more affordable, some utilities are growing concerned that commercial and industrial retail customers will use energy storage devices to flatten out their own demand and thereby avoid large demand charges. As described above, many utilities have imposed mandatory demand charges on large industrial and commercial electricity customers for decades. In some cases, these charges account for more than half of the amount due on a commercial customer's electricity bill. Distributed energy storage systems can potentially enable commercial customers to greatly reduce their own peak demand during each billing period and thus pay much lower power bills for using the same amount of energy. Ironically, these technologies might ultimately compel some utilities to seek to replace demand charges with more volumetric pricing schemes in the coming years. See Dennis Warnsted, *Storage Puts Utilities In A Big Bind On Demand Charges*, THE ENERGY COLLECTIVE (Sept. 25, 2017), http://www.theenergycollective.com/djwamsted/2413367/storage-puts-utilities-big-bind-demand-charges.

7.   STATE LAWS DISTINGUISHING INDEPENDENT SOLAR ENERGY PRODUCERS FROM REGULATED UTILITIES

As distributed solar energy has become an increasingly viable alternative to grid-supplied electricity, some utilities have sought to have rooftop solar companies regulated as utilities. As explained in Chapter 1, state public utility commissions heavily regulate most investor-owned utilities, which distribute and sell much of the nation's electric power.

These utility commissions intrusively regulate nearly every aspect of an electric utility's operations, including its capital expenditures, the geographic boundaries of its market, and even the retail pricing of its products. Ordinary businesses, including rooftop solar companies, are subject to far less regulation. The proliferation of distributed solar energy technologies across the country in recent years has blurred the lines between regulated investor-owned utilities and ordinary corporations and engendered new debates about how to more clearly delineate those lines in this new age of rooftop solar energy. The following materials explore a few of the complex issues that are arising in this context.

a.   Are Distributed Solar Companies "Utilities"?

As mentioned in the Cicchetti excerpt above, one benefit utilities have long enjoyed under their implicit regulatory compact with state governments is protection from competition within their service territories. Most investor-owned utilities have exclusive rights to distribute and sell electric power within specified geographic territories, and that protection against competition has long been a critically important aspect of utility regulation. Unfortunately, to investor-owned utilities, it can feel like the state has shirked its duty to protect them from competition when thousands of customers within their exclusive service territories are purchasing or leasing rooftop solar PV systems and relying primarily on the power those systems generate meet their electricity needs. In response to this trend, some utilities have asked state utilities commissions to regulate solar energy companies as though they were utilities. Rooftop solar advocates tend to rebut these arguments by citing the many salient differences between rooftop solar companies and electric utilities. To date, very few courts or policymakers have opted to treat solar companies as utilities or fully subject them to the same regulatory structure. However, as illustrated in *SZ Enterprises* below, policymakers and courts continue to struggle with how to characterize rooftop solar businesses in light of their unique characteristics and their growing impact on electricity markets.

SZ ENTERPRISES, LLC v. IOWA UTILITIES BD.

Supreme Court of Iowa, 2014
850 N.W.2d 441

APPEL, J.

In this case, we consider whether SZ Enterprises, LLC, d/b/a Eagle Point Solar (Eagle Point) may enter into a long term financing agreement related to the construction of a solar energy system on the property of the city of Dubuque under which the city would purchase from Eagle Point, on a per kilowatt hour (kWh) basis, all of the electricity generated by the system. Prior to proceeding with the project, Eagle Point sought a declaratory ruling from the Iowa Utilities Board (the IUB) that under the proposed agreement (1) Eagle Point would not be a "public utility" under Iowa Code section 476.1 (2011), and (2) Eagle Point would not be an "electric utility" under Iowa Code section 476.22. If Eagle Point was a public utility or an electric utility under these Code provisions, it would be prohibited from serving customers, such as the city, who were located within the exclusive service territory of another electric utility, Interstate Power and Light Company (Interstate Power). *See* Iowa Code § 476.25(3).

The IUB concluded that . . . Eagle Point would be a public utility and thus was prohibited from selling the electricity to the city under the proposed arrangement. Because of its ruling on the public utilities question, the IUB found it unnecessary to address the question of whether a party who was not a public utility could nevertheless be an electric utility under the statute.

Eagle Point brought a petition for judicial review. *See id.* § 17A.19(1). The district court reversed. According to the district court, Eagle Point's provision of electric power through a "behind the meter" solar facility was not the type of activity which required a conclusion that Eagle Point was a public utility. The district court further found that although it was conceivable under some circumstances that an entity that was not a public utility could nevertheless be an electric utility under the applicable statutory provisions, Eagle Point's proposed arrangement with the city did not make it an electric utility for purposes of the statutes. The IUB and intervenors MidAmerican Energy Company, Interstate Power, and Iowa Association of Electric Cooperatives, appealed. Eagle Point filed a cross-appeal challenging the reasoning, but not the result, of the district court's electric utility holding.

For the reasons expressed below, we affirm the decision of the district court.

I.   Factual Background and Proceedings.

A.   Introduction. Eagle Point is in the business of providing design, installation, maintenance, monitoring, operational, and financing assistance services in connection with photovoltaic solar electric (PV) generation systems. The city of Dubuque desires to develop renewable energy for the use of the city.

Eagle Point proposed to enter into a business relationship known as a third-party power purchase agreement (PPA) with the city that would provide the city with renewable energy. Under the PPA, Eagle Point would own, install, operate, and maintain an on-site PV generation system at a city-owned building to supply a portion of the building's electric needs. The city would purchase the full electric output of Eagle Point's solar power generation facility on a per kWh basis, which escalated at a rate of three percent annually. The payments by the city would not only provide consideration for the electricity provided by the project, but would also finance the cost of acquiring the generation system, monetize offsetting renewable energy incentives related to the system, and cover Eagle Point's costs of operating and maintaining the system. Eagle Point would also own any renewable energy credits associated with the generation system but would credit to the city one third of any revenues received from the sale of those credits. At the conclusion of the agreement, Eagle Point would transfer all ownership rights of the PV generation system to the city.

The PV generation system constructed by Eagle Point would be on the customer side of the electric meter provided by the city's electric utility, Interstate Power. This means that electricity generated by the system would not pass through Interstate Power's electric meter. Due to size limitations, Eagle Point's PV generation system would not be able to generate enough electricity to power the entire building. The city would remain connected to the electric grid and continue to purchase electric power from Interstate Power to meet its remaining needs at the premises.

B.   Proceedings Before the IUB. Eagle Point filed a petition for a declaratory ruling. . . . from the IUB that it was not a public utility under Iowa Code section 476.1 and was not an electric utility under Iowa Code section 476.22. If Eagle Point was not a public utility or an electric utility under these Code provisions, its proposed relationship with the city would not run afoul of Iowa's statutory scheme that provides for exclusive service territories for Iowa's electric utilities. *See id.* § 476.25(3). On the other hand, if Eagle Point were operating as a public utility and an electric utility under these Code provisions, its proposed arrangement with the city would be an unlawful incursion into the exclusive service territory of Interstate Power. *See id.*

The IUB held that under the proposed arrangement, Eagle Point would be acting as a public utility under Iowa Code section 476.1. . . .

. . . .

The IUB placed strong emphasis on the fact that unlike the usual arrangement in an ordinary facilities lease, Eagle Point was selling electricity on a per kWh basis. Further, the IUB observed that Eagle Point's promotional materials indicated that it would offer its services to other members of the public and would not limit its activities to the city. While recognizing that there was not always a bright line regarding what activities constitute the activities of a public utility, the IUB concluded that Eagle Point would cross the line if it were allowed to proceed.

. . . .

. . . Traditionally, electricity has been provided in the United States by large enterprises that made heavy capital investments to provide power over transmission lines to customers. . . . Over time, the utilities providing electric service came to be highly regulated in order to advance the public interest and to limit the effects of monopoly or near monopoly power on consumers. . . .

In recent decades, however, the traditional approach has been challenged by several developments. First, there has been an increased belief in deregulation and competitive marketplaces generally. . . . Deregulation in the airline, natural gas, telephone, trucking, and railroad industries has been largely accomplished, and although deregulation of public utilities providing energy has not proceeded in a similar fashion, support for the regulated monopoly approach has been questioned more recently than in the past decades. . . .

In addition, the desire to promote alternate energy sources seen as more environmentally friendly has contributed to the search for alternate models of energy delivery. The federal government has promoted investment in alternate energy facilities by providing powerful tax incentives, including a thirty-percent investment tax credit in certain types of "energy property" and accelerated tax depreciation deductions for alternate energy projects. . . .

Finally, in the field of PV generation, technological advances have made it increasingly feasible to install generation capacity at the source of consumption without use of centralized power generation and extended transmission lines. . . . The sheer number of such solar energy facilities has thus grown rapidly in recent years. . . .

As detailed in a recent technical report published by the United States Department of Energy, however, there are significant barriers to the installation of on-site solar energy facilities. . . . Most prominently, the initial capital costs remain quite high, often in the millions of dollars or more. . . . Additionally, some potential PV investors are weary of unpredictable fluctuations in electricity prices and are concerned about their ability to provide maintenance and upkeep for facilities driven by unfamiliar technology. . . .

In order to overcome these barriers, proponents of alternate energy facilities have developed a method of financing construction of solar facilities called third-party power purchase agreements, or PPAs. . . . Under the PPA model, the developer builds and owns the PV generation system, which is constructed on the customer's site. . . . The developer-owner then sells the electric power to the consumer at a preestablished fixed rate, thereby providing the customer with a hedge against price increases from the traditional electric utility serving the location. . . . PPAs thus minimize the up-front cost barrier . . . and greatly stabilize, if not reduce, costs for the consumer thereafter. . . . Moreover, the developer-owner, who maintains the system, is an expert with PV technology. . . . Thus, under a PPA, the developer-owner absorbs the high initial costs, retains the responsibility of maintenance of the system, and is compensated based on electricity actually produced by the system.

A fundamental legal question, however, is whether PPAs may coexist with traditional public utilities within the existing state regulatory environment. A threshold question is often whether the developer-owner in a third-party PPA is a public utility or electric supplier subject to state regulation. This definitional question often turns on whether the developer-owner in a third-party PPA is regarded as furnishing or supplying electricity "to the public."

The consequences of this threshold determination are critical to the viability of third-party PPAs. In states where public utilities have exclusive service areas, a finding that a PPA is a public utility generally means that a PPA violates the exclusive territory provisions of state law and is thus unlawful. *See, e.g.*, IOWA CODE §§ 476.1, .22, .25(3). In states where public utilities do not have exclusive service areas, the consequence is that PPAs may be subject to substantial regulation as a public utility, including requirements to submit tariffs and to provide service to all who desire it.

B. State Caselaw on What Constitutes a "Public Utility" Providing Services "to the Public." The notion that private entities may be so affected by the public interests that public duties arise from their activities has ancient common law origins. For example, at common law, mills provided essential services to medieval inhabitants and gave rise to a common law duty to serve. *See* Jim Rossi, *The Common Law "Duty to Serve" and Protection of Consumers in an Age of Competitive Retail Public Utility Restructuring,* 51 VAND. L. REV. 1233, 1244–45 (1998). Medieval subsistence farmers without access to the mill went hungry and, as a result, duties to serve were imposed. *See id.* The common law duty to serve was later extended to ferries, markets, and other essential enterprises. *Id.* at 1245.

The common law tradition has influenced some state courts when construing statutes defining public utilities or service to the public. One line of authority relies on the notion that in order to be a public utility serving the public generally, the entity must directly or indirectly hold itself out as providing service to all comers. . . .

On the other hand, a different line of authority has developed a more flexible notion of what amounts to a public utility. These cases use a functional approach and concentrate on the nature of the underlying service and whether there is a sufficient public need for regulation. . . .

. . . .

3. *States resolving the issue through legislative action.* A number of states have resolved the status of third-party PPAs by enacting legislation

explicitly addressing the issue. For example, in California, Public Utilities Code section 218 specifically exempts from regulation

> a corporation or person employing cogeneration technology or producing power from other than a conventional power source for the generation of electricity solely for. . . .[t]he use of or sale to not more than two other corporations or persons solely for use on the real property on which the electricity is generated.

CAL. PUB. UTIL. CODE § 218(b)(2) (West 2004). California has been a leader in the development of third-party PPAs, including significant government-owned projects, like the Moscone Center in San Francisco. . . .

New Jersey has also legislated in this area. Under its public utility statutes, a "basic generation service provider" is an electric generation service provided "to any customer that has not chosen an alternative electric power supplier." N.J. Stat. Ann. § 48:3–51 (West Supp.2014). "Electric generation service" is the "provision of retail electric energy and capacity which is generated *off-site from the location at which the consumption of such electric energy and capacity is metered for retail billing purposes." Id.* (emphasis added).

Similarly, Colorado Revised Statute section 40–1–103 provides that

> [t]he supply of electricity . . . from solar generating equipment located on the site of the consumer's property, which is owned or operated by an entity other than the consumer, [is not a public utility provided that the supply generated is] no more than one hundred twenty percent of the average annual consumption of the electricity [from that site].

COLO. REV. STAT. § 40–1–103(2)(c) (2013).

. . . .

. . . [t]he IUB notes that the regulatory regime under chapter 476 would be compromised if Eagle Point were found not to be a public utility. It argues that if Eagle Point were allowed to proceed with its third-party PPA, it could "cherry pick" large commercial customers, thus upsetting the settled expectations of Interstate Power, which has been granted exclusive territory as part of the regulation of electric power by the IUB. The IUB notes that the purpose of the granting of exclusive territory is to establish the basis for the creation of a stable electric grid and to ensure that all customers, large and small, receive reliable electric power at an affordable price. Further, Interstate Power, as the exclusive provider of electric power in the territory, which includes the city, has made investment decisions based upon its status as a regulated monopoly. . . .

. . . .

In our view, in this case, the balance of factors point away from a finding that the third-party PPA for a behind-the-meter solar generation facility is sufficiently "clothed with the public interest" to trigger regulation.

. . . .

For all the above reasons, the decision of the district court is affirmed.

QUESTIONS

1.   Identify (i) at least three specific characteristics of Eagle Point or its proposed business arrangement with the city of Dubuque that substantially resemble those of a conventional electric utility, and (ii) at least three specific characteristics of Eagle Point or its business arrangement with the city of Dubuque that make it substantially *different* from a conventional electric utility.

2.   What are at least two primary "barriers" to commercial-scale solar energy development referenced in *SZ Enterprises,* and how does Eagle Point's "PPA model", as described in the case, help customers to overcome those barriers?

3.   If Iowa's state legislature had enacted statutory provisions comparable to the California, New Jersey, and Colorado provisions cited in the *SZ Enterprises* opinion, would that have prevented this litigation? Why or why not?

4.   IUB argued in *SZ Enterprises* that not classifying solar energy companies such as Eagle Point as public utilities would allow such companies to " 'cherry pick' large commercial customers", thereby harming establishing established public utilities. What does this mean? How might a solar company's "cherry picking" of large commercial customers harm the existing public utility within that territory?

5.   Describe as specifically as possible the *SZ Enterprise* court's standard for determining whether a solar energy company was a public utility under Iowa law. Do you agree with this standard? Why or why not?

b. Should Utilities Be Permitted to Compete Directly in Private Rooftop Solar Markets?

The dividing line between electric utilities and distributed solar energy companies has also blurred recent years as some utilities have sought to compete directly against private companies in rooftop solar markets. When a regulated utility begins selling distributed solar energy products and services that closely resemble those available through private companies, the utility has ventured into a private competitive marketplace where utilities were arguably never intended to go. As more and more utilities attempt to compete within distributed solar markets in the coming years, courts and policymakers will face complex questions about the appropriate legal limits on these activities.

Throughout the United States, thousands of privately-owned businesses routinely engage in the sale, installation, and leasing of distributed solar energy systems. These businesses, ranging from the smallest mom-and-pop installers to massive publicly traded companies such as Vivint Solar, compete daily against each other on price, quality, and customer service in an active, competitive marketplace. That competition has proven highly effective at helping to rapidly drive down prices and promote innovation in a growing industry. Of course, that highly competitive marketplace contrasts sharply with the heavily regulated monopoly markets in which electric utilities have long operated. The following excerpt highlights important differences between these two markets and argues for clearer rules that prevent regulated utilities from directly competing with private rooftop solar companies.

UNNATURAL MONOPOLIES: WHY UTILITIES DON'T BELONG IN ROOFTOP SOLAR MARKETS

Troy A. Rule
52 IDAHO L. REV. 401, 401–405 (2016)

Distributed solar energy development has increased exponentially in the United States over the past decade. Much of this development has come in the form of photovoltaic ("PV") solar panel installations on the rooftops of homes and small businesses. A combination of government incentive programs and falling PV prices has made these rooftop solar energy systems an increasingly attractive investment for electric utility customers throughout the country.

Although most rooftop solar energy companies surely welcome this coming-of-age of their industry, many electric utilities understandably take a less favorable view of it. Utility customers with rooftop solar panels tend to purchase far less electricity from their utilities than customers who have no solar panels. Consequently, the recent growth of distributed solar energy is beginning to adversely impact utilities' revenues. . . .

Interestingly, a small number of utilities have recently begun experimenting with an entirely new, "if you can't beat 'em, join 'em" sort of response to the rapid rise of distributed solar. This type of strategy is manifest in a handful of . . . projects that would essentially allow utilities to directly compete as producers in private rooftop solar markets. Perhaps most notable among these projects is the one announced in 2014 by the investor-owned utility Arizona Public Service Co. ("APS"), which services more than one million customers in Arizona. Under its plan, APS will lease rooftop space from 1,500 residential households in exchange for a $30 per month credit on those households' electricity bills. APS will then contract with private companies to install solar PV systems on all 1,500 rooftops. APS will own all of the solar panels involved in the project and the electricity the panels generate, which will flow directly onto the grid. Importantly, the $30 bill credit APS is offering to customers under its plan exceeds the average monthly net utility bill savings APS customers can presently get by purchasing or leasing rooftop solar panels in the private market and thereby buying less power from the utility. In other words, the APS plan will undercut pricing in the competitive private rooftop solar energy market within its territory, giving customers little economic reason to go solar through any entity other than APS.

Shortly after APS released its proposed rooftop solar plan, Tucson Electric Power ("TEP")—a different investor-owned utility that also operates in Arizona—proposed a very similar sort of project. Under TEP's proposed plan, residential customers would lease their rooftop space to the utility in exchange for the right to lock in a fixed price for grid-delivered electric power for 25 years. Like APS, TEP anticipates hiring local contractors to install solar PV systems on the rooftops of the homes of customers who enroll but TEP would own the systems and all of the power they generate. Comparable utility proposals have recently been floated in other states as well.

. . . Policies allowing electric utilities to enter into established, competitive markets are unprecedented and raise significant policy concerns. The impropriety of welcoming utilities into the rooftop solar energy market is most easily illuminated through the basic microeconomics framework that has long served as the primary theoretical basis for utility regulation itself.

A. Natural Monopoly Theory

The basic characteristics of electricity distribution make it inherently prone to a condition that economists describe as the "natural monopoly" problem. A natural monopoly is a firm that can produce all of the output demanded in its relevant market for a lower aggregate cost than is achievable by a group of smaller, competitive firms. This capability clearly exists for utilities in retail electricity distribution markets. The large up-front expenditures associated with building out an extensive infrastructure system capable of distributing electric power to customers throughout a region make it very difficult for firms to enter such markets and effectively compete with incumbent utilities. In the absence of government intervention, such utilities would thus be largely free to act like monopolies, charging excessively high prices and raking in large profits without serious risk of a loss of market share.

In recognition of this market failure, a heavy regulatory structure has long sought to prevent inefficient behavior by natural monopolies within the electricity distribution industry. Such regulations generally prohibit utilities from charging excessive prices and ensure that utilities provide service to all qualified customers within their service areas. In exchange for these obligations, state regulators protect utilities from certain types of competition and allow them to earn a reasonable return on their infrastructure investments. Although it is far from perfect, this regulatory approach has been fairly effective at promoting reliable, low-cost electric power distribution for a very long time.

B. Rooftop Solar Markets are Not Prone to Natural Monopoly Problems

Unfortunately, the current utility regulatory system is poorly suited for use in competitive markets such as the market for rooftop solar energy installations. Unlike markets for grid-supplied electricity, the market for rooftop solar energy installations is not prone to the natural monopoly problem. Entering the rooftop solar market as a producer does not require exceptionally large up-front investments. Low barriers to entry allow multiple retail solar panel sellers and installers to efficiently compete on price, quality and service. Likewise, it is not a waste of resources for multiple smaller, competing rooftop solar businesses to co-exist in the same geographic area. Accordingly, healthy market competition already exists in the rooftop solar industry, helping to promote continued innovation, quality products, and reasonable profit margins. Like the existing markets for rooftop shingles or rooftop gutters, the market for rooftop solar PV can function very efficiently without the sort of heavy government intervention that electricity distribution markets require.

These fundamental differences between electricity distribution markets and the rooftop solar markets greatly affect how policymakers should approach project proposals like those of APS and TEP described above. Since rooftop solar markets are not prone to natural monopoly problems, utilities operating within regulatory regimes designed to address natural monopoly problems have no place in these markets. Allowing elements of a heavy regulatory structure designed to govern natural monopolies to creep into such private competitive markets is akin to administering a powerful prescription drug to a patient who is not sick: no real benefits are likely to result, yet it has the potential to cause costly and harmful side effects.

To permit regulated utilities to compete as producers in rooftop solar markets through projects like those proposed by APS and TEP would essentially stack the deck in such utilities' favor. Regulated utilities often have access to lower-cost capital, large customer bases, and market risk protections that simply are not available to non-utility rooftop solar installation firms. Lacking equivalent advantages, many companies are likely to pull out of rooftop solar markets where utilities are permitted to directly compete. As they do, an industry that once thrived under healthy competition will gradually degenerate into one unnecessarily burdened with inefficiencies and stifled innovation.

C. Avoiding an "Unnatural Monopoly" Problem in the Rooftop Solar Industry

The present struggle between electric utilities and the rooftop solar energy industry is not the first time that a regulated utility has sought to protect its monopoly against disruptive innovation. Some have used the term "unnatural monopoly" to describe such instances when a regulated utility is permitted to enter an industry that is not prone to natural monopoly problems. Policies that perpetuate such unnatural monopoly problems tend to be highly inefficient and are rarely cost-justified.

For example, an analogous sort of unnatural monopoly problem existed toward the end of AT&T's control of telecommunication markets in the 1980s and 90s. Understandably, AT&T would have liked to respond to technological advancements that were transforming the landline telephone industry through new ventures enabled the company to compete directly in the emerging markets that threatened its monopoly position. However, Congress and regulators eventually erected various barriers between AT&T and those emerging technology markets to help prevent AT&T from abusing its incumbent utility status to gain an anticompetitive advantage in those new industries.

A similar sort of policy response is needed today in the context of rooftop solar energy. Policymakers would never permit a regulated electric utility to begin selling rooftop shingles or rooftop gutters in the private marketplace. For similar reasons, entities that enjoy the advantages of being regulated electric utilities should not be permitted to compete directly in the market for rooftop solar installations. Electric utilities and their subsidiaries should be required to forfeit all regulatory protections and become fully privatized before competing as producers in these markets. This principle should apply even to subtle forms of market entry like those exemplified by the recent APS and TEP project proposals. Policies that consciously guard against unnatural monopoly problems through these and other means will promote greater economic efficiency as innovation continues to transform electricity markets in the coming years.

————————

NOTES & QUESTIONS

1.   Why do you think utilities such as APS and TEP are increasingly interested in helping residential customers to get rooftop solar panels through the utilities rather than through private companies?

2.   The article above argues strongly against allowing regulated utilities to engage in the business of selling or leasing rooftop solar energy systems to their retail customers. Suppose you represented a utility interested in offering a program like the APS program described in the article. Craft an argument highlighting at least three specific reasons why the law arguably *should* allow regulated utilities to compete in rooftop solar markets.

3.   *Solar Pricing "Rider" Programs: An Alternative Way of Competing Against Rooftop Solar?* Utilities have also retained customers who were contemplating a rooftop solar installation by offering them subscription-based programs that allow them to essentially adopt solar panels that the utility has installed elsewhere. NV Energy proposed a *solar pricing rider* program in 2017 that reflected this approach. Under NV Energy's program, customers would voluntarily purchase "blocks" of solar-generated electricity from the utility's centralized solar PV project for a premium of roughly $2 extra per 100kWh block per month.

NV Energy framed its proposed program as a valuable alternative for renters and others who have strong interests in supporting solar energy but are not yet ready make long-term commitments to lease or acquire their own rooftop solar arrays. However, many third party rooftop solar companies seem less enthused about such programs because they can also potentially dampen the demand for distributed solar installations. *See* Krysti Shallenberger, *NV Energy Proposes Residential Green Rider Program As Rooftop Solar Alternative*, UTILITY DIVE (Mar. 14, 2017), http://www.utilitydive.com/news/nv-energy-proposes-residential-green-rider-program-as-rooftop-solar-alterna/437987/.

c.   Should Utilities Be Treated Differently than Ordinary Corporations Under Campaign Finance Laws?

As distributed energy technologies raise the stakes of electric utility rate cases and similar public utility commission (PUC) proceedings, the distinction between utilities and ordinary corporations is also gaining relevance within campaign finance law. Public utility commission PUC decisions on numerous policies—from the characteristics of net metering programs to the structuring of retail rates—have borne greater significance than they do in this age of rooftop solar, duck curves and distributed storage. Recognizing how important PUC decisions have become to their success, investor-owned electric utilities in some states have begun contributing generously to the election campaigns of PUC commissioner candidates and candidates for other influential state government positions in recent years.

Whether investor-owned regulated utilities have rights to donate generously to state PUC commissioner campaigns depends in part on whether such utilities are distinguishable from ordinary corporations under modern election law. In its famous decision in *Citizens United v.*

Federal Election Commission, 558 U.S. 310 (2010), the U.S. Supreme Court held that private corporations' status as "citizens" constitutionally entitles them to anonymously and almost limitlessly contribute to political campaigns. If courts interpret *Citizens United* to apply equally to regulated utilities, then utilities may be able to do the same—even when contributing to the election campaign of a commissioner to serve on the very PUC that heavily regulates them. Assuming that the controversial *Citizen United* holding continues to stand in the coming years, regulated utilities facing the threatening impacts of distributed energy growth in their territories are likely to be increasingly tempted to seek to influence the composition of state PUCs through indirect campaign contributions. The following excerpt explores this issue and describes some possible means of addressing it.

BUYING POWER: UTILITY DARK MONEY AND THE BATTLE OVER ROOFTOP SOLAR

Troy A. Rule

5 LSU J. ENERGY L. & RESOURCES 1, 1–2, 4–18 (2017)

. . . As the popularity of rooftop solar energy increases, legal uncertainty regarding the extent to which utilities can indirectly fund their own regulators' election campaigns is becoming a growing problem, particularly in jurisdictions where these regulators are popularly elected.

Public choice theorists have long identified state Public Utility Commissions (PUCs) as being susceptible to "regulatory capture," a condition arising when private parties exert undue influence over their own regulators to the detriment of the general public. PUCs are vulnerable to capture problems largely because of the tremendous impact that PUC decisions can have on a utility's bottom line. PUCs often exercise significant control over utilities' expenditures, pricing, and rates of return on capital investments. Given what is at stake in their interactions with PUCs, utilities are understandably tempted to try and curry commissioners' favor in hopes of furthering their own interests, above those of their customers or those of the state in which they operate.

However, new market pressures and newly loosened campaign finance laws have recently elevated regulatory capture risks at some PUCs to a new level. In states where PUC commissioners are elected rather than appointed, some utilities seem to believe they have a legal license to effectively purchase seats on the very state commissions that heavily regulate their activities. Further, there is growing evidence that this sort of pernicious activity is already beginning to occur and is hampering the nation's transition toward a cleaner, more sustainable electricity system. . . .

. . . .

The emergence of rooftop solar energy creates an unprecedented challenge for electric utilities, which are not generally accustomed to facing market competition. State PUCs have vigorously protected most electric utilities from competition for more than half a century by actively preventing rival utilities from distributing retail electricity within clearly drawn exclusive service territories. Having historically relied upon state utility regulators to shield them from competition, utilities today are understandably now looking to these same regulators to help them protect their interests and incumbent monopoly position against the rooftop solar industry—a totally new type of competitor.

Over the past few years, utilities have petitioned state utility regulators for a wide range of policy and rate reforms that would slow the growth of distributed solar energy. Utilities in some states have sought PUC approval to dramatically raise the "fixed" portion of retail customers' utility bills, thereby increasing the total monthly charges paid by customers owning solar panels. In other states, utilities have secured PUC approvals to modify net metering programs in ways that make rooftop solar far less cost-competitive with grid-supplied power. . . . However, despite utilities' increasingly vigorous resistance, the rooftop solar industry continues to expand and become an ever more popular and attractive option for utility customers throughout much of the country.

II. UTILITIES' GROWING INCENTIVES AND ABILITY TO INFLUENCE PUCs

The growing popularity of rooftop solar energy is amplifying the importance of PUCs—the primary regulators of electric utilities at the state level. In an era where utility customers in some regions are installing rooftop solar arrays in droves, PUCs' decisions on issues such as solar energy fees, demand charges, and net metering reforms are having greater consequences on electric utilities' bottom lines. As these decisions are made, utilities' incentives to impact the composition of these PUCs are increasing as well.

A. Citizens United *and its Potential Implications for Utilities*

Recent developments in campaign finance law have potentially introduced a powerful new way for investor-owned utilities to leverage their substantial financial resources to influence who serves on state PUCs. Chief among these developments was the U.S. Supreme Court's landmark holding in *Citizens United v. Federal Election Commission* in 2010. *Citizens United* and other related cases effectively allow corporations to contribute unlimited amounts of money to non-profit political entities known as 501(c)(4) organizations, which can use those funds to indirectly bankroll elections. Corporations typically are not required to publicly disclose the amount of these so-called "dark money" contributions or that they contributed any money at all.

Although the *Citizens United* decision and its progeny have drawn substantial criticism within the legal academy and among the general public, the basic holding in the case remains the law. The 5–4 majority in *Citizens United* based its holding largely on the notion that corporations hold First Amendment free speech rights substantially equivalent to those of individual citizens. Accordingly, corporations are equally entitled to express their political views through undisclosed contributions to qualified nonprofit political action groups.

Importantly, however, neither *Citizens United* nor any subsequent, major appellate case has involved a set of facts in which the maker of dark money campaign contributions was also a heavily regulated utility. Thus the question still looms whether the five-justice majority in *Citizens United* intended for the lax corporate campaign finance rules it validated to fully extend to investor-owned electric utilities whose expenses, prices, and returns on capital investments are largely dictated by the state. It seems doubtful that the Court contemplated creating such a wide and problematic loophole for utilities; yet, recent activities suggest that some utilities may already be availing themselves of these lax corporate finance rules, helping shield their monopolies from an escalating tide of rooftop solar energy installations.

B. *A Case Study: Bright Sunshine and Dark Money in Arizona*

The potentially hazardous impacts of *Citizens United* on state utility regulation are perhaps most visible in Arizona, where a heated battle between electric utilities and the rooftop solar energy industry has been brewing for years. Arizona has characteristics that make it particularly vulnerable to utility regulatory capture in this era of affordable rooftop solar energy and permissive dark money laws. For example, the state has excellent solar energy resources. . . . However, Arizona is also one of about a dozen states that elect, rather than appoint, its utility regulators. All five seats on the Arizona state agency regulating electric utilities—the Arizona Corporation Commission (ACC)—are filled through popular elections. In states such as Arizona, where commissioners are elected rather than appointed, utilities can more easily use indirect "dark money" campaign contributions to impact the outcome of commissioner elections.

Historically, elections for seats on the ACC have been relatively quiet and uneventful affairs involving only modest levels of campaign expenditures. However, that changed in 2014, when two of the five commission seats came up for grabs. The 2014 ACC election cycle seemed especially important to Arizona's largest utility, Arizona Public Service Co. (APS)—an investor-owned utility with more than one million in-state customers. The pace of rooftop solar installations had been rapidly increasing in Arizona. In response to this growth, APS had recently become the first major utility in the country to earn regulators' approval to single out customers with solar panels and charge them an extra monthly fee. But the new fee was small and based on the nature of the negotiations that led to the fee, it was evident that APS wanted it to be much higher. It was clear to all stakeholders that the composition of the ACC over the coming years would have a tremendous impact on how soon the utility could obtain approval to increase its new solar fees.

With so much at stake in the 2014 ACC elections, APS, or its parent company, Pinnacle West, appear to have availed itself of the loose "dark money" campaign finance rules resulting under *Citizens United* to have a material impact on the election outcome. Specifically, it is widely suggested in the media—and neither APS nor Pinnacle West has denied—that the utility or its affiliates funneled millions of dollars into third-party groups that waged an aggressive campaign to promote the election of two particular candidates to the ACC. Tom Forese and Doug Little, a pair of candidates who ran for the ACC together and benefited from substantial dark money support that APS or Pinnacle West [would] not deny contributing, ultimately prevailed in what was a relatively close election.

The practical consequences of APS's apparent purchase of seats on the ACC began to emerge less than five months after the 2014 election. In April of 2015, APS submitted a proposal to the ACC to more than quadruple the size of the utility's new fees on rooftop solar energy users. In a surprisingly bold decision, a 3–2 majority on the newly-composed commission—including Forese and Little—voted a few months later to allow the ACC to address this fee increase request outside the context of a formal rate case.

To many outside observers, it seemed that by early 2015, APS had lawfully succeeded in capturing the government body charged with regulating its activities. The term "regulatory capture," which appears frequently within the public choice and legal academic literature, describes such instances when a regulated private party exerts heavy influence over its regulators and thereby advances its own interests above the broader policy objectives that the regulators were entrusted to protect. . . .

III. PRESERVING PUCS' INTEGRITY IN THE DARK MONEY ERA

As distributed solar energy becomes a more viable alternative to grid-supplied power, utility dark money controversies like that in Arizona are likely to grow more common. Particularly in states where public utility commissioners are elected rather than appointed, utilities' perceived license to use dark money contributions to impact who regulates them is deeply troubling. In the wake of *Citizens United*, what can be done to limit utilities' influence on PUC elections in these states?

A. The Recusal Approach

One strategy for combating utility regulatory capture issues, akin to the apparent situation in Arizona, is to demand that sitting PUC commissioners known to have received heavy financial support from a particular entity during their election bids recuse themselves from PUC matters that involve that entity or its affiliates. Moreover, the U.S. Supreme Court's holding in the 2009 case of *Caperton v. A.T. Massey Coal Co., Inc.* arguably requires such recusal when an entity's support of a PUC commission candidate was so substantial that it likely impacted the outcome of the election.

Caperton involved a large coal company that had recently been ordered in state court to pay a $50 million judgment for fraudulently canceling a coal mining agreement. Rather than simply paying the judgment, the company, Massey Coal, appealed the decision to the West Virginia Supreme Court of Appeals—a court whose justices are popularly elected. While waiting for the higher court to hear the case, Massey Coal's Chief Executive Officer, Don Blankenship, then contributed $3 million through a non-profit corporation to the election campaign of a particular candidate—Brent Benjamin—to fill a vacancy on that same court. Blankenship's $3 million contribution exceeded all other funds raised or spent by Benjamin or his campaign committee and ultimately helped Benjamin to win the election and take a seat on the court. When Massey Coal's appeal eventually came before the court, Caperton requested that Justice Benjamin recuse himself from hearing it. Caperton justified his request by arguing that Blankenship's sizable contributions to Justice Benjamin's campaign created too great a risk of bias in favor of Massey Coal.

In a 5–4 decision, the U.S. Supreme Court held that Justice Benjamin was indeed legally obligated to recuse himself from hearing the *Caperton* case. Writing for the majority, Justice Kennedy stated:

> [T]here is a serious risk of actual bias—based on objective and reasonable perceptions—when a person with a personal stake in a particular case had a significant and disproportionate influence in placing the judge on the case by raising funds or directing the judge's election campaign when the case was pending or imminent.

The majority opinion in *Caperton* also explains how decisions regarding whether recusal is required in these situations. According to the court, such inquiries must center on the "contribution's relative size in comparison to the total amount of money contributed to the campaign, the total amount spent in the election, and the apparent effect such contribution had on the outcome of the election."[41] In Blankenship's case, his "significant and disproportionate influence" on the outcome of Justice Benjamin's election," "coupled with the temporal relationship between the

---

[41] *Id.*

election and the pending case," caused the "probability of actual bias" to rise to "an unconstitutional level."[42]

1.   Recent Calls for Commissioner Recusals in Arizona

The facts in *Caperton* bear a striking resemblance to those alleged in connection with Arizona's 2014 ACC elections. The $3.2 million that APS, or Pinnacle West, purportedly contributed to 501(c)(4) groups supporting the joint campaigns of Tom Forese and Doug Little easily exceeded all other expenditures by all candidates in the 2014 ACC elections; thus, it quite possibly had a material effect on the election outcome. Further, the ACC's website states that commissioners act in a judicial capacity when hearing rate cases, suggesting that Forese and Little were acting in a capacity that was legally equivalent or at least similar to that of Justice Blankenship in *Caperton*. Moreover, the fact that APS submitted a request to more than quadruple its monthly fees on retail customers with rooftop solar energy systems just a few months after Forese and Little took their new seats on the ACC shows a temporal relationship not unlike that in *Caperton*.

Given the strong similarities between the facts in *Caperton* and those surrounding the APS dark money controversy in Arizona, it is hardly surprising that there have already been calls for Commissioners Forese and Little to recuse themselves from APS-related matters before the PUC. In particular, two former ACC commissioners filed a formal request in September of 2015 for Commissioners Forese and Little to recuse themselves from the ACC's consideration of APS's request to quadruple its fees on rooftop solar users. Tellingly, less than one week after the former commissioners filed their request, APS voluntarily withdrew its fee-quadrupling proposal. This quick APS response suggests that the mere threat of recusals based on *Caperton* are already helping to temper regulatory capture issues at the ACC and could eventually serve a similar function in other jurisdictions.

2.   The Limits of Recusal-Based Strategies for Policing Utility Regulatory Capture

Although the threat of recusal demands is one plausible means of policing against utilities' use of dark money contributions to influence PUC elections, it also suffers from some serious limitations. Perhaps chief among these limitations is the fact that the most important evidence needed to succeed in such recusal demands is arguably shielded from disclosure. To win a court order based on *Caperton* requiring a commissioner's recusal from a particular entity's PUC matter, the person seeking the order must provide evidence that the entity made sizable contributions favoring that commissioner's candidacy. Yet, obtaining evidence of these contributions is difficult in an era where most

---

[42]   Caperton v. A.T. Massey Coal, Co., 556 U.S. 868, 886–87 (2009).

corporations can legally make large donations through dark money channels without disclosing their identities.

. . . .

A second disadvantage of relying on *Caperton*-based calls for recusal to limit regulatory capture at PUCs is that it is a purely *ex post* solution to the problem. Because one can make such recusal demands only after a commissioner has already won election and is sitting on a PUC, this recusal approach can weaken a PUC's capacity to effectively regulate. Some state PUCs have as few as three members, so the absence of even one commissioner can substantially hinder a PUC's ability to govern on a particular utility's matters for years at a time.

. . . .

B.   *A Broader Approach: Distinguishing Utilities from Other Corporations under* Citizens United

Given the shortcomings of recusal-based approaches to limiting utility regulatory capture, is there any other means of addressing these risks? A more comprehensive means of addressing them would be through a major appellate court decision that distinguished heavily regulated utilities from ordinary corporations under *Citizens United* and established that utilities had comparatively narrower rights to contribute to political campaigns.

Suppose, for example, that a state enacted legislation prohibiting regulated utilities and their affiliates from directly or indirectly contributing more than $2,500 per election cycle to campaigns for public utility commission seats and required full disclosure of any such contributions. If an investor-owned electric utility challenged such a law, it is uncertain as to how the U.S. Supreme Court would rule on the issue. Given the significant unpopularity and backlash associated with the *Citizens United* holding, the Court may be willing to carve out investor-owned utilities from the case's permissible campaign finance rules.

At first glance, it seems that any such restrictions on corporate contributions to campaigns would be unconstitutional under *Citizens United*. After all, investor-owned utilities like APS are typically private corporate entities and are not all that different from Microsoft, Amazon, or any other corporation. Moreover, the *Citizens United* line of cases essentially establishes that corporations have First Amendment rights to secretly make limitless contributions to 501(c)(4) organizations that support particular candidates.

However, investor-owned utilities arguably have distinctive attributes that make them materially different from ordinary corporations and thus deserving of a less permissive set of campaign finance rules. Unlike Microsoft or Amazon, many investor-owned electric utilities enjoy state protected monopolies and, in exchange, have impliedly consented to having their expenditures, pricing, and rate of return effectively dictated by a government agency. Surely, this special type of corporation, which is effectively an arm of the state and has always been uniquely prone to regulatory capture problems, is deserving of separate treatment under campaign finance laws.

Language from Justice Antonin Scalia's concurring opinion in *Citizens United* supports the notion that the majority in that case did not contemplate having its loose campaign finance principles apply to heavily regulated utilities, even when those utilities are investor-owned corporations. A known originalist, Justice Scalia reasoned in his concurring opinion that the Founders did not originally extend broad campaign finance privileges to corporations because corporations during that era were fundamentally different from those operating today. Justice Scalia reasoned that "[m]ost of the Founders' resentment towards corporations was directed at the state-granted monopoly privileges that individually chartered corporations enjoyed. Modern corporations do not have such privileges, and would probably have been favored [for broad speech rights] by most of our enterprising Founders."

Scalia's observations certainly ring true as to most modern corporations; however, they definitely do not apply to electric utilities, which do have "state-granted monopoly privileges." In fact, Justice Scalia's originalist rationale for distinguishing modern free-market corporations from early state-chartered ones arguably supports applying separate, more stringent campaign finance rules to investor-owned utilities, instead of conflating them with the Amazons and Microsofts of the world.

Language appearing later in Justice Scalia's concurring opinion in *Citizens United* further bolsters the argument that the majority in that case did not intend for regulated utilities to enjoy the same loose treatment under campaign finance laws as ordinary corporations. Scalia emphatically stated, ". . . to exclude or impede corporate speech is to muzzle the principal agents of the modern free economy." This statement reveals again Scalia's presumption in *Citizens United* that the "corporate speech" at issue was speech by a prototypical corporation—one that is generally free to make its own reasonable decisions about expenditures, pricing, and where it does business. Those sorts of entities are agents of the "modern free economy" and tend to operate in at least somewhat competitive markets.

In contrast, regulated electric utilities, which operate solely within exclusive, government-dictated territories and pursuant to heavy legal constraints on their expenditures, pricing and other activities, are not "agents of the modern free economy" at all. Excluding or impeding their speech through reasonable campaign finance rules thus arguably has no troublesome "muzzling" effect akin to what Justice Scalia described. Instead, it prevents utilities from leveraging their government-provided advantages and incumbent monopoly status to drown out the voices of other less-privileged stakeholders, to capture their own regulators, and to stifle innovation.

A relevant case before the U.S. Supreme Court would be the most straightforward way to establish that utilities are materially distinguishable from ordinary corporations under *Citizens United* and subject to more stringent campaign finance rules. But how would such a case ever make it to the highest court? One way would be for a state legislature to enact a bill that, like the hypothetical previously described, that restricts regulated utilities' campaign contributions and requires them to publicly disclose all such activities. Unfortunately, utilities' heavy influence within many state legislatures might also create obstacles to the passage of such a bill.

NOTES & QUESTIONS

1.   According to the excerpt above, why are questions about the status of regulated electric utilities as "citizens" potentially important in determining the scope of utilities' rights to avail themselves of the relaxed campaign finance limitations established under *Citizens United*?

2.   According to the excerpt above, what is regulatory capture, and why are PUCs arguably particularly vulnerable to it? How has the proliferation of distributed energy technologies potentially increased the risk of regulatory capture within some PUCs?

3.   Describe at least three differences or similarities between investor-owned electric utilities and ordinary corporations you believe are relevant to determining whether such utilities should enjoy full "citizen" status under *Citizens United*.

4.   Suppose that a private rooftop solar company operating in Arizona was fearful that, unless it took swift action, the state's utility commission would soon consist solely of commissioners who had received large indirect campaign donations from certain electric utilities in the state and were thus prone to favor their policy positions. If the private solar company were to make its own indirect contributions to commissioner candidates who favored its positions, do you think such contributions would be permissible under *Citizens United*? Should the company be allowed to make such contributions even if courts determine that the utility is prohibited from making them? Why or why not?

5.   *The Disclosure Barrier.* The excerpt above mentions that one potential obstacle to seeking utility commissioner recusals under *Caperton* is the need for evidence showing that a utility or its affiliates truly made the "dark money" contributions in question. As of mid-2017, this obstacle continued to impede efforts to formally address concerns about potential utility

dark money donations in Arizona. ACC Commissioner Bob Burns filed subpoenas in August 2016 against APS and Pinnacle West demanding disclosure of their "marketing and advertising expenditures, charitable donations, lobbying expenses, contributions to 501(c)(3) and (c)(4) nonprofits and political contributions" made between 2011 and 2014. APS responded by suing Burns for allegedly "harassing" the utility. In March 2017, the ACC then voted to fire Burns' lawyer, making it difficult for him to defend himself against APS or to seek enforcement of the subpoenas. In August 2017, Burns sought the reversal of a major APS rate increase based on allegations that the ACC's vote for the rate hike was unconstitutional due to potential bias from some Commissioners whose election campaigns had supposedly benefited from large utility dark money contributions. *See* Ryan Randazzo, *Utility regulator wants APS' $95M annual rate hike reversed*, THE ARIZONA REPUBLIC (Aug. 23, 2017), http://www.azcentral.com/story/money/business/energy/2017/08/23/arizona-corporation-commissioner-robert-burns-wants-aps-rate-hike-reversed/594366 001/.

POLICY PROBLEM

As of 2017, Arizona was one of only 13 states in the nation that elected their state utility commissioners. In the other 37 states, the governor or legislature appoints individuals to these positions. *See Background and Organization*, ARIZ. CORP. COMMISSION, http://www.azcc.gov/Divisions/ Administration/about.asp (last visited June 15, 2017). Changing Arizona's system to provide that commissioners were appointed rather than elected would require an amendment to the state constitution—a difficult obstacle to overcome given the sizable consequences of such a change and the complex web of stakeholders involved.

The following questions provide opportunities to consider how some stakeholders might view a proposed state constitutional amendment providing that Arizona's five utility commissioners no longer be popularly elected and that the state governor have power to appoint them instead.

1.   Suppose you are the general counsel for a large investor-owned electric utility in Arizona. What factors do you think would be most relevant to the utility's determination of whether to favor or oppose the proposed amendment described above? Based solely on the facts provided, would you favor the proposed amendment? Why or why not?

2.   Suppose you are legal counsel to a group representing the policy interests of residential electric utility customers in Arizona. What factors do you think would be most relevant to your client's determination of whether to favor or oppose the proposed amendment described above? Based solely on the facts provided, would *you* favor the proposed amendment? Why or why not?

3.   Suppose instead that you represent the Arizona state governor's office. Would *you* favor the proposed amendment described above? Why or why

not? Based on your position, craft at least three specific arguments for or against the amendment.

4.   Suppose you represented a policy advocacy group for the distributed solar energy industry in Arizona. Would *you* favor the proposed amendment described above? Why or why not? Based on your position, draft at least three specific arguments for or against the amendment.

E. MUNICIPAL POLICIES PROMOTING SOLAR ENERGY

In addition to the extensive solar energy-related policymaking that has occurred at the federal and state government levels, countless municipalities have also adopted ordinances aimed at promoting solar energy development. Although some ordinances (which are covered in Chapter 6) relate to land use restrictions and project permitting, many others seek simply to increase the number of solar energy installations and projects within a municipality's boundaries. The following materials describe some of these pro-solar local policies.

1. SOLAR MANDATE ORDINANCES & MITIGATION PROGRAMS

Local governments often have very limited financial resources, so most of them are unable to offer significant subsidies, tax credits, or other financial incentives to encourage solar energy development. However, most localities do wield significant authority over land use development in their communities. Accordingly, some localities have tried a very different approach to promoting solar energy: adopting ordinances that *require* real estate developers to install or fund some minimum amount of new solar generating capacity as a condition to approving their commercial or residential development projects. Municipalities that have adopted some version of this of policy include Sebastopol (CA), Lancaster (CA), Santa Monica (CA), San Francisco (CA), Boulder County (CO), Pitkin County (CO), and Blaine County (ID). *See* Troy A. Rule, *Solar Mandates for Real Estate Development: A Guide and Model Ordinance* (2013), *available at* https://papers.ssrn.com/sol3/papers.cfm?abstract_id=2530115. Lancaster's citizens had such a favorable experience with that city's original 2014 solar mandate ordinance that the city adopted amendments significantly strengthening its solar mandate requirements in 2017. Below are provisions from the City of Lancaster Municipal Code and Pitkin County Code establishing versions of solar mandate requirements in those cities.

CITY OF LANCASTER (CA) MUNICIPAL CODE § 17.08.305
(2017)

§ 17.08.305—Implementation of solar energy systems.

A. **Purpose and intent**. It is the purpose and intent of this section to provide standards and procedures for builders of new homes to install solar energy systems in an effort to achieve greater usage of alternative energy.

B. **Applicability**. These specific standards are applicable for all new single-family homes with a building permit issuance date on or after January 1, 2014.

C. **Provision of solar energy systems**.

    1. A builder shall provide solar energy systems for new detached single family homes in accordance with the energy generation requirements as listed in Section 17.08.060 of the Lancaster Municipal Code. It is intended that no individual installed system shall produce less than 2 watts per square foot of each home built by the builder. For example a 2,000 square foot home would require builder to install a 4 kW system. A builder may also adjust the amount of solar installed after demonstrating to the building official that the zero net energy requirements can be met with the installation of a smaller system.

    2. Installation of solar energy systems is required for all new single family detached homes within a production subdivision. A builder may also meet the solar requirement by paying a solar mitigation fee based on the square footage of the living space of each home that is built.

    3. Builders shall demonstrate through building plan check their intention to meet the solar zero net energy requirement.

    4. Builders shall build solar energy systems on model homes, reflective of the products that will be offered to homebuyers.

    5. If a tract is built in phases, the solar energy generation requirement shall be fulfilled for each phase, or release of homes.

    6. Solar energy systems shall meet the development standards and guidelines as described in the Lancaster Zoning Code.

    . . . .

D. **Alternative methods of compliance**. If site-specific situations make it impractical for a builder to meet the requirements of this section, the builder may propose an alternative method of compliance with the intent of this section. An alternative method of compliance shall be approved where the building official finds that the proposed alternative is satisfactory and complies with the intent of the provisions of this section.

(Ord. No. 989, § 1, 4–9–2013; Ord. No. 1020, §§ 2, 3, 2–14–2017)

PITKIN COUNTY (CO) CODE § 11.32
(2011)

"Residential Renewable Energy Mitigation Program"

. . . .

Section 106 Residential Renewable Energy Mitigation Program (RREMP) for houses 5,000 square feet and more. A new residence 5,000 sq ft or more in area (as defined by the building code), or a residence receiving an addition which brings the area of the residence to 5,000 sq ft or more, is required to offset a portion of its fossil fuel energy consumption through the use of on-site renewable energy or through a fee payment to REMP. . . .

Section 106.2. The on-site renewable energy requirement can be met by the installation of a two kilowatt solar photovoltaic or equivalent renewable energy system. This requirement can alternatively be satisfied off-site by payment of a REMP fee as follows. The fee for buildings over 4,999 sq. ft. shall equal the floor area as defined by the building code. For example:

5,000 sq. ft.	$5,000
8,255 sq. ft.	$8,255

2.   OTHER LOCAL PRO-SOLAR POLICIES

Relatively few municipalities presently embrace the approach of Lancaster or Pitkin County and require citizens to install solar energy systems or to help fund offsite installations as a condition to doing other forms of real estate development. However, municipalities are promoting solar energy development in numerous other ways.

Cities' most common way of increasing solar energy development within their boundaries is to do it themselves. Countless municipalities throughout the country have installed PV on the rooftops of city buildings or other city facilities. For example, the city of Palm Desert, CA, has installed PV at its city hall site, on top of bus shelters, on affordable housing projects, and on other municipal buildings. *See Solar Program*, CITY PALM DESERT, http://www.cityofpalmdesert.org/our-city/energy-/ solar-program (last visited June 21, 2017).

Numerous other cities have sought to promote solar energy development by crafting and adopting expedited solar permitting procedures. Provisions the California legislature enacted as part of Assembly Bill 2188 in 2015 amended that state's Solar Rights Act to require that California municipalities adopt streamlined permitting processes for distributed solar energy systems. Several California cities have already complied with the statute by adopting new expedited solar permitting ordinances. *See, e.g.*, SAN CLEMENTE MUNICIPAL CODE § 15.04.080 (2015). Outside of California, numerous other cities from Milwaukee to Salt Lake City have adopted their own expedited solar permitting ordinances.

Cities and counties that have their own municipal electric utility and don't depend on an investor-owned utility for electricity service have some potentially significant advantages in efforts to drive solar energy policy at the municipal level. Among other things, municipal utilities tend to be more attuned to local preferences and more subject to local political control than large investor-owned utilities—factors that have enabled municipal utilities in several progressive communities to take aggressive action in promoting solar. Some municipal utilities offer rebates to customers who install solar panels. Others offer low-interest loans to customers to help fund the cost of certain energy-related home improvements, including rooftop solar installations. Still other municipal utilities, such as Wisconsin's River Falls Municipal Utilities, encourage distributed solar by offering to purchase rooftop solar-generated power from customers at rates well above the utility's retail electricity rate. *See* SOLAR FOUND., THE ROLE OF MUNICIPAL UTILITIES IN DRIVING SOLAR DEPLOYMENT (2014), http://www.thesolarfoundation.org/the-role-of-municipal-utilities-in-driving-solar-development/.

In part because of what they perceive as greater ability to affect innovative policy through municipal utilities than with investor-owned utilities, some cities currently residing in the service territories of investor-owned private utilities have sought in recent years to *municipalize* their electricity distribution systems. Unfortunately, municipalization of existing electric utility assets is rarely an easy task. The incumbent investor-owned utility involved is typically not very enthusiastic about the prospect of shrinking its exclusive territory and losing many of its customers. Moreover, it can be difficult for a municipality to come up with the funding to purchase all of the distribution lines and other assets required to separate and begin providing electricity service on its own. Still, the growing influence of disruptive innovations such as solar energy and distributed energy storage seems likely to drive more attempts to municipalize electric utilities over the next century.

NOTES & QUESTIONS

1.   How does Lancaster's solar mandate ordinance differ in its approach from that of Pitkin County? Which ordinance applies to a broader proportion

of the real estate development occurring within each jurisdiction? Why is Pitkin County's ordinance arguably better tailored for its jurisdiction given that county's unique characteristics (where luxury homes, ski lodges, and condominiums are the norm)?

2.   Suppose you are a citizen in Lancaster, CA, who already owns a home. Does Lancaster's adoption of the ordinance provisions excerpted above require *you* to do anything different? Whom does the ordinance affect the most? How do you think the ordinance is likely to affect the cost of building *new* homes in the city? Based solely on your responses to the previous questions, would you be inclined support the ordinance? Why or why not?

3.   Suppose that a real estate developer is building a subdivision in Lancaster, CA, that would feature 10 brand-new 3500-square-foot homes. Under the city's ordinance provisions, how much rooftop solar PV would the developer likely be required to install in connection with this subdivision? If for some reason installing that many solar panels within the subdivision seems impracticable, what alternative options might the developer have to comply with the ordinance?

4.   Suppose your client is building a new 6,500 square foot vacation home for her family in Pitkin County, Colorado, that will have a large roof capable holding a large solar PV array. Suppose further that, after all applicable tax credits and rebates, it would cost her $7,000 to purchase and install a small two-kilowatt PV solar energy system on her rooftop. What are the two main ways she could comply with the county's Residential Renewable Energy Mitigation Program requirements in connection with her new home? Which compliance option would you recommend that she take, and why?

5.   Many cities that have adopted solar mandate ordinances are relatively geographically isolated or are high-end luxury communities that may be less interested than most in attracting additional residential development. Why might a suburban city surrounded on all sides by similar cities that competes with them for new development be potentially less interested in adopting a solar mandate ordinance?

6.   *Boulder's Long Municipalization Effort.* One of the most highly-publicized efforts to municipalize electric utility service involves the city of Boulder, Colorado. As of 2017, the city was still working after five years to part ways with its investor-owned utility, Xcel Energy, and municipalize its electricity distribution system. *See* Alex Burness, *Boulder to Consider Settlement Offers From Xcel In 7-Year Municipal Utility Saga*, DAILY CAMERA (Mar. 31, 2017), http://www.dailycamera.com/news/boulder/ci_30892858/boulder-xcel-reach-potential-settlement-citys-municipal-utility.

F. SOLAR ENERGY AS A TOOL FOR HUMANITARIAN AID

One other set of notable solar energy policy issues relates to solar energy's unique potential to supply electricity to individuals and communities that lack access to an electric grid system. As mentioned earlier in this chapter, solar PV technologies are deployable on the smallest of scales, which makes them particularly useful in efforts to improve quality of life in underdeveloped nations and areas where grid-supplied electricity is unlikely to be available at any time in the near future. Law and policy innovation could play a valuable role in accelerating the deployment of small-scale solar energy technologies for this purpose to those who need them the most.

The first excerpt below describes the grossly inadequate electricity service available to one American community—the Navajo nation—and highlights the potential for small-scale solar energy to address this problem. The second excerpt contains portions of a model "lighting" law. Legal scholars in the United States developed this model law in hopes of encouraging greater deployment of small-scale solar technologies to improve the quality of life of those residing in undeveloped countries and regions throughout the world.

18,000 AMERICANS WITHOUT ELECTRICITY: ILLUMINATING AND SOLVING THE NAVAJO ENERGY CRISIS

David Tarasi et al.

22 COLO. J. INT'L ENVTL. L. & POL'Y 263, 265–70 (2011)

The Navajo Nation is a Native American reservation located in northeastern Arizona, southeastern Utah, and northwestern New Mexico. The Nation is divided into five agencies, with eighteen to thirty-one chapters in each agency. It covers a land area of over 26,000 square miles, making it larger than each of the ten smallest U.S. states, with a total population of approximately 180,462 people.

Despite being located in the United States, the Navajo Nation suffers from extreme poverty. According to the 2000 census, 42.9 percent of residents of the Navajo Nation lived below the poverty level, meaning they had an income of less than $8,350 per year. The proportion of impoverished people was more than four times the average poverty level in the United States. In addition, 21.4 percent of Navajo families lacked plumbing, and 62.6 percent lacked basic telephone service.

B. Electricity Issues on the Navajo Nation

In addition to extreme poverty, many Navajo households do not have access to electricity. Although the census does not collect data on household electrification, it is conservatively estimated that around 18,000 of the 48,000 households on the Navajo Nation lack electricity. This poses a number of significant problems for those families without electricity, including lack of access to adequate lighting, heating, and refrigeration. Alternatives to grid-tied electricity, like kerosene for lighting, diesel generation for electricity, and wood stoves for home heating, are often expensive, dangerous, unhealthy, and insufficient. There are many reasons for the lack of access to electricity on the Navajo Nation, including geographic isolation, high poverty levels, and legal and political pressures.

1.   Geographic Issues

One of the main causes for the lack of access to electricity in the Navajo Nation is the geographic isolation of many chapters, and of individual households within each chapter. The Navajo Nation is slightly larger than West Virginia, but it has one-tenth the population spread across the same area. This means that most of its communities are located a significant distance from each other, requiring long power distribution lines to bridge these gaps. In addition to the distance between Navajo communities, individual households are often located relatively far apart from each other. Even if a community has access to electricity, only some households may have electricity, while others just down the road are out of reach of the current power distribution lines.

The modern electrical grid system is designed to effectively serve large concentrations of people in specific populous areas. When many people are spread out over a vast area, the system is no longer efficient, and it becomes too expensive to extend power lines over the large distances between each home. In addition to being geographically isolated, much of the terrain of the Navajo Nation is rugged and without roads. This makes transporting the equipment to build new power lines very difficult, which further increases the cost of installing traditional infrastructure.

2.   Economic Issues

Although geographic isolation limits the Navajo Nation's access to energy, economics play a role as well. As noted above, the cost of extending power lines in the rugged terrain of the Navajo Nation is extremely high. The average cost to extend a line a single mile is about $27,000. Due to the isolated nature of many Navajo households the cost of the line extension cannot be split over many customers because any given line extension may only reach a few additional customers.

Additionally, despite the large reserves of natural resources for energy production located on the Navajo Nation, the Navajo Tribal Utility Authority ("NTUA") does not operate any of its own power plants, so it is required to purchase electricity from other utility providers. About fifty percent of NTUA's revenues go to purchasing electricity from other suppliers, increasing the cost to its consumers and limiting its funding for new power lines.

Cost is also an issue for households that want to use large-scale photovoltaic systems to generate electricity. Very few households on the Navajo Nation can afford the large up-front cost of a photovoltaic system. The NTUA has a leasing program for two-kilowatt photovoltaic systems, which generate enough electricity to power home lighting, television, and small appliances, but are not an equal replacement for grid electricity. Although this program exists, adoption has been extremely low. The monthly cost is still high, and the supply is relatively low. The program requires a fifteen-year lease at a rate of $95 per month, with an $85 initial fee. Only 200 households are currently leasing such systems.

3.   Legal/Political Issues

Legal issues have also slowed electricity development on the Navajo Nation. In 1966, a land dispute between the Navajo and Hopi tribes halted all development on over 1.5 million acres of land in the western portion of the Navajo Nation. During the "Bennett Freeze," no new housing could be built, no roads or schools could be constructed, and the building of electrical infrastructure was outlawed in that area. The development freeze was enacted to prevent either tribe from taking ownership of the land, but it also had the effect of forcing the residents of the area to live in poverty for the past forty years. They have been unable to develop any new infrastructure or even make repairs to their homes.

Although the ban was lifted in 2006, the damage done by the freeze remains. Of the 8,000 residents of the area, only ten percent have running water, and only three percent have electricity. The infrastructure needed to run power lines is largely lacking, as are roads needed for new construction. Although a bill was recently put before Congress to create a trust fund to help develop the former Bennett Freeze area, it will be years before the area can reach a level of home electrification even equal to the rest of the Navajo Nation.

Many elderly Navajo have lived their entire lives without electricity and with a constant promise from the NTUA that electricity will be coming soon. As a result, many people have lost hope that they will ever be provided electrical services. . . . Despite a clear wish for electrification, many Navajo communities have no choice but to burn kerosene and wait.

II.   BENEFITS OF SOLAR TECHNOLOGIES

Eagle Energy, operating under its original "Elephant Energy" brand, has been supplying affordable, small-scale solar lighting technologies to rural Namibians for the last three years. In both Namibia and the Navajo Nation, many homes lack electricity because they are located in rural areas where grid electrification does not make economic sense. Like Namibia, the Navajo Nation also has world-class solar energy resources, making it an ideal location for solar energy production. New Mexico and Arizona have abundant sunshine, and receive some of the highest levels of solar radiation in the United States.

Eagle Energy's small-scale solar technologies are ideal for Navajo Nation residents living in rural areas that are not likely to receive grid electricity in the near future. Eagle Energy is currently distributing six different solar lighting technologies on the Navajo Nation. . . . All of these technologies use small solar panels to charge rechargeable batteries that power LED bulbs. Some of the lights are designed as flashlights, some as lanterns, and some can also be used to charge cell phones.

These . . . provide a quality source of lighting, allowing people to work and learn when they previously were forced to live in the dark or pay a high price for illumination via kerosene or propane. At a cost of $25 to $35, Eagle Energy's lights are not much more expensive than a kerosene lantern, and incur no additional monthly cost after purchase. . . .

A.   Economic Benefits

Eagle Energy's solar-powered lights provide a distinct economic advantage compared to kerosene and propane-fueled lanterns because they do not require users to buy multiple replacement fuel canisters per month. Although solar-powered lights come with rechargeable batteries that must be replaced after one or two years, the five-dollar cost is negligible compared to replacement fuel canisters.

. . . .

B.   Health Benefits

Solar Lanterns also provide a health benefit over the kerosene lanterns commonly used by the Navajo Nation. Although the health impacts caused by using fuel lighting is an understudied field, a recent article . . . found that vendors using simple kerosene lanterns were exposed to particulate matter concentrations significantly greater than the amount present in the ambient air. Such exposure can present long-term health risks. The article concluded that the best solution to combat this problem is the use of solar LED lighting.

C.   Educational and Productivity Benefits

Solar lighting technologies also provide an increased quality of light, which can benefit educational quality. Candles and kerosene lanterns provide a low-quality light source, making it difficult for children to read and do homework. Eagle Energy's solar technologies provide high-quality light, allowing children to read and do schoolwork after dark. Additionally, children who grow up using solar lights may be more prone to learn about the technology and come up with innovative ideas and uses for it. Solar lighting technologies can also provide a benefit to people without electricity who work from home, allowing them to work after dark at a lower cost compared to kerosene lanterns.

D. CO_2 Emission Benefits

Kerosene lanterns also produce CO_2 emissions, causing harm to the environment. The average kerosene lantern, when used for four hours per night, produces over 100 Kg of CO_2 emissions per year. Assuming that each of the 18,000 households on the Navajo Nation has just one lantern and uses it for four hours per night, the net greenhouse gas emissions reduction from kerosene lanterns on the Navajo Nation would be over 1.8 million Kgs per year. For reference, this is equal to driving over four million miles in the average car. Replacing these lanterns with solar-powered lighting technologies would eliminate these harmful emissions.

MODEL LAW ON LIGHTING FOR DEVELOPING COUNTRIES

Lakshman Guruswamy et al.
44 DENV. J. INT'L L. & POL'Y 337, 337–38, 341–42, 348, 351–52 (2016)

A Bill

To promote the development and deployment of clean lighting to save lives, improve livelihoods, empower women, and combat global warming by creating a thriving global market for clean, affordable, and efficient household, commercial and community lighting, and for other purposes.

Be it enacted by the [legislative organ] of the [developed country] assembled,

Short Title

This Act may be cited as the *"Development and Dissemination of Clean Lighting* Act of [year].

Effective Date. This Act becomes effective on [*date*].

§ 1. Findings

(a) [*Name of country*] is a member of the community of nations that has accepted well-recognized principles of international law and policy establishing the right of developing countries to sustainable development.

(b) [*Name of country*] seeks to support sustainable development pertaining to energy poverty and access to safe and sustainable lighting products through this Act.

(c) It is estimated that of the 1.3 billion people worldwide without access to electricity, most rely on kerosene for illumination.

(d) The use of kerosene for lighting generates indoor air pollution, contributing to the deaths of 1.8 million people per year. Kerosene fires kill more than 1 million people per year.

(e) [*Number of people*] in [*name of country*] currently use kerosene for lighting.

(f) Kerosene fires and indoor air pollution cause the deaths of [*number of people*] in [*name of country*] per year.

(g) Children are disproportionately vulnerable to the dangers of kerosene. Accidental ingestion of kerosene leads to fever, cough, abdominal discomfort, or death.

(h) Light generated by kerosene lamps is poor and inefficient, rendering it virtually impossible for people, especially women and children, to accomplish household and social tasks, or engage in economic activity after nightfall.

(i) Lighting costs for kerosene are 325–1625 times higher than those for electric light bulbs, and are borne by some of the world's poorest people.

(j) Kerosene is fossil fuel-based, thus a nonrenewable energy source. Kerosene lamps consume an estimated 77 billion liters of fuel per year. Each year, the burning of kerosene for lighting emits 240 million tons of carbon dioxide into the atmosphere, thus contributing to global climate change.

(k) Safe, sustainable lighting positively impacts the quality of life and environment by:

(i) Allowing women, children, and men to engage in educational and economic endeavors after nightfall,

(ii) Promoting gender equality and women's empowerment,

(iii) Improving household health and safety,

(iv) Alleviating the financial burden presented by kerosene,

(v) Advancing environmental stability by reducing use of kerosene, and

(vi) Reducing contributions to global climate change.

§ 2. Policy

The House of Parliament hereby declares it is the national policy of [*name of country*] to:

(a) Appropriate financial resources towards the research and development of the most appropriate and sustainable energy technologies for improved indoor lighting products that advance the objectives of this Act in [*name of country*];

(b) Foster the growth of a domestic indoor lighting manufacturing industry by supporting entrepreneurs through tax incentives, loans, and micro- and other forms of financing that advance the objectives of this Act;

(c) Ensure that all indoor lighting products meet relevant standards for physical durability, product life-span, and light output;

(d) Install and distribute indoor lighting products in a matter that emphasizes accessibility while encouraging the recipient to contribute to the cost in currency, exchange, and/or sweat equity;

(e) Stimulate community participation in the financing, manufacturing, distribution, and promotion of the objectives of this Act;

(f) Seek the assistance, expertise, guidance, and experience of non-governmental organizations (NGOs) and community advocacy groups in all aspects of the implementation of the Act;

(g) Promote awareness and education about indoor air pollution caused by kerosene lamps and lanterns;

(h) Promote the involvement of current kerosene lamp and lantern users, *inter alia*, in the research, design, development, manufacturing, distribution, monitoring, maintenance, evaluation, and marketing of improved indoor lighting products; and

(i) Conduct training on use and maintenance to indoor lighting product users and community members. . .

. . . .

§ 6. Implementation and Administration

(a) Implementation

The Administrator shall . . . implement this Act by:

[(i)] Consulting and collaborating, with the Ministers of (1) Health and Human Wellness, (2) Energy, (3) Environment & Natural Resources, (4) Education, and (5) Industry & Commerce. . . .

(ii) Encourag[ing] public participation in the implementation of the provisions of this Act. . . .

. . . .

(iii) Where appropriate, seeking international aid assistance in the form of technological assistance and expertise for monitoring and evaluation from, *inter alia*, intergovernmental organizations, other states, NGOs, community advocacy groups, corporations, private individuals, and charitable trusts.

(iv) Creating and implementing a system whereby end users can acquire lighting products by sweat equity or exchange;

(v) Creating and implementing a program for recycling used batteries, which may require lighting product distributors, retailers, and charging stations to collect used batteries;

(vi) Using innovation, affordable and appropriate sustainable energy technologies, and/or techniques that provide greater economic benefits, at a limited cost to the end-user;

(vii) Using technologies and organizational methods, which have been successfully tried, tested, and demonstrated by other developing countries. . . .

. . . .

COMMENTARY

. . . .

The Model Law provides a series of findings and lays the foundation for establishing the programs to support the distribution and use of off-grid lighting products. . . .

. . . .

Providing lighting to developing countries can be a costly endeavor, even if the long-term benefits are shown to outweigh the initial costs. Extending and maintaining the main electrical grid out to remote rural areas is an expensive national undertaking. Even in India, one of the largest growing economies in the world, over 400 million people live in communities are lacking reliable electricity that can supply electricity for more than three hours per day. Solar lighting would at first seem like a cheaper solution, as much of India is located in a climate zone that receives, on average, at least eight hours of sunlight per day.

Thus, off-grid solar LED lights have been shown to be a relatively effective medium-term solution for areas that cannot be connected to the electrical grid. Again, to use the case studies in India as an example, a single solar LED light like the ones used in these studies can be purchased for, on average, about 549 Indian Rupees (nine US dollars at the time of the study), and has a warranty of six months. Assuming that a warranty of six months represents the *absolute minimum lifetime* of the product, this would mean that the maximum the household using this light could spend is about 1,098 Rupees (eighteen US dollars) in one year, all other factors being equal (although, in the final study, most of the lights actually exceeded the initial six month period, lasting the full year, and thus bringing the actual cost down to only 549 Rupees for most of the participating households). The same study found that the average rural Indian household in Madhya Pradesh spends 1,800 Rupees per year on kerosene for one lamp (and that excludes other factors such as the cost of the lamp itself, or the external costs to health resulting from burns and inhalation of smoke). Thus, even at its "most expensive" (*i.e.* assuming that each light needs to be replaced every six months), the use of off-grid solar lighting products was still proven to be more economical than kerosene lighting, saving each participating household at least 702 Rupees. In addition, each household would avoid the associated health risks of using kerosene lighting.

The solar lights in this study were all produced, tested, and certified within India, thereby cutting down on the costs associated with procurement and distribution. These Model Laws are drafted to allow and encourage the adopting countries to establish a similar lighting market. As discussed above, having a lighting market may address corruption and would also allow for easier distribution and replacement or repair or the lighting products.

QUESTIONS

1.   Identify at least four factors referenced in the Tarasi excerpt that have contributed to the problem of thousands of individuals living on Navajo Nation trust lands having homes that lack electricity service.

2.   Identify at least four characteristics of small-scale solar energy technologies referenced in the articles above that make these technologies a potentially appealing means of improving the quality of life for Navajos who presently lack access to grid-supplied electricity.

3.   Suppose you represented a solar energy policy advocacy group that sought to propose federal legislation capable of helping to accelerate the deployment of solar energy technologies on Navajo lands. Brainstorm at least three plausible policy strategies potentially capable of furthering that objective.

4.   Identify at least three substantial legal or policy obstacles to more widespread small-scale solar energy deployment in developing countries. How would a developing country's enactment of a version of the Model Law on Lighting excerpted above help to overcome each of the obstacles you identified?

CHAPTER 6

SOLAR ENERGY DEVELOPMENT

∎ ∎ ∎

As solar energy development has spread throughout the world in recent decades, its growth has given rise to a diverse array of complex property law, environmental law, and land use law issues. Neighbor disputes over the shading of solar panels have resurrected centuries-old debates about whether and to what degree landowners should have rights to prevent neighbors from shading their land. The growing presence of rooftop solar panels in urban and suburban neighborhoods has also sparked debates over the extent to which homeowner associations and local governments should be empowered to restrict solar energy installations for aesthetic reasons. The rapid emergence of utility-scale solar energy development has likewise challenged policymakers to craft policies that accommodate large solar farm installations while still protecting wildlife habitats, scenic view sheds, cultural resources, and other important features of rural land.

This chapter explores several property law, environmental law, and land use law issues arising in the context of solar energy development. It also introduces readers to some of the basic leasing, permitting, and financing work transactional lawyers do when representing clients on solar energy projects.

A. SOLAR ACCESS LAWS

The world's growing interest in rooftop solar energy has made the potential for neighbor disputes over shading greater than at any point in modern history. Solar energy systems must have direct access to sunlight to be fully productive and generate less electricity when a tree, building, or other structure is shading them. On the other hand, laws that prohibit or restrict reasonable land uses solely to prevent the shading of neighboring property can also impose significant costs on individuals and broader society. *Solar access* laws seek to balance the competing interests of landowners and their neighbors in conflicts over the shading or potential shading of solar energy systems. The relevance of solar access laws continues to increase as solar energy projects and devices become ever more commonplace in urban and suburban communities throughout the world. The following excerpt from a government-funded report provides a basic introduction to the solar access problem and explains how it can discourage individuals and businesses from adopting distributed solar energy technologies.

LEGISLATING FOR SOLAR ACCESS: A GUIDE AND MODEL ORDINANCE

Troy A. Rule
SolarTech Solar 3.0 Project, U.S. Dept. of Energy Award
No. DE-EE0005348/001, 6–8 (2012)

What is the Solar Access Problem?

The solar access problem is the possibility that trees or structures on neighboring property can shade a landowner's solar energy system and decrease the system's productivity. To be fully productive, rooftop solar panels and most other solar energy systems require un-shaded exposure to the sun's radiation during peak sunlight hours. As depicted in *Figure A* below, neighbors can sometimes grow trees or build structures on their properties capable of shading and thereby diminishing the effectiveness of a solar energy system.

Figure A: The Solar Access Problem

The Solar Access Problem

Solar Panels

Property Line

Neighbor   Solar User

How can solar access laws encourage solar energy development?

Solar access laws promote solar energy development by enabling landowners with solar energy systems to prohibit southerly neighbors from growing trees or erecting structures that could shade the systems. Even when a solar energy system is free from shade, it must typically generate power for several years before its owner can fully recoup its up-front cost. The risk that neighbors might shade the system in the future reduces the certainty that landowners will eventually recover their investments in small-scale solar energy systems and can thus deter solar energy installations. By reducing the risk of unwanted shading, solar access laws mitigate this additional source of financial uncertainty associated with distributed solar energy.

Why not rely solely on privately-negotiated easements to protect solar access?

The most straightforward way for a landowner to secure sunlight access for a solar energy system is to acquire solar access easements from neighbors. A solar access easement is an easement across the low-altitude airspace of a nearby parcel that is tailored to ensure delivery of direct sunlight onto the easement grantee's solar energy system. Solar access easements effectively prohibit easement grantors from growing vegetation or erecting structures in their airspace that shade the easement grantee's solar energy device. The neighboring airspace that is typically burdened under a solar access easement is represented by the shaded area in *Figure B* below.

Figure B: Airspace Burdened under a Typical Solar Access Easement

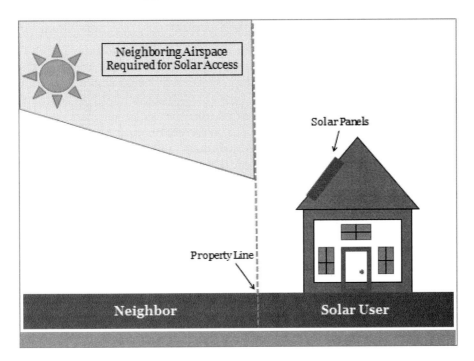

Numerous states have already enacted laws that recognize the validity of solar privately negotiated solar access easements. Unfortunately, some neighbors are unwilling to restrict the heights of trees and structures on their land under such easements, even in exchange for compensation. Landowners whose neighbors refuse to sell them solar access easements often have no other means of protecting their solar installations from shading. Fearful that neighbors will eventually grow trees or erect structures that shade their solar energy system, some such landowners may ultimately choose not to install a system at all.

––––––––––––

Modern solar access laws in the United States are not a uniform set of rules applied consistently across the country. Instead, they are a diverse conglomeration of common law doctrines, state statutes, and local government ordinances. The following materials describe the evolution and breadth of solar access laws in the United States and highlight some of the strengths and shortcomings of the various rules that comprise this increasingly important body of law.

1.   RIGHTS TO SUNLIGHT UNDER COMMON LAW

Centuries before solar panels started appearing on rooftops, courts and policymakers in some parts of the world had already begun developing laws to govern shading conflicts among neighbors. Laws in ancient Rome protected a landowner's right to a reasonable amount of sunlight on property. *See* Borimir Jordan & John Perlin, *Solar Energy Use and Litigation in Ancient Times*, 1 SOLAR L. REP. 583, 592–93 (1979). The English common law *doctrine of ancient lights* similarly provided protection to landowners against their neighbors' shading under certain circumstances. The doctrine of ancient lights was comparable to common law rules governing prescriptive easements on land. Under the doctrine, a landowner "acquired, after 20 years of uninterrupted use, an easement preventing a neighbor from building an obstruction that blocks light from passing through the landowner's window." *Ancient-Lights Doctrine*, BLACK'S LAW DICTIONARY 95 (10th ed. 2014).

The doctrine of ancient lights seemed focused primarily on protecting landowners' reasonable investments in the construction of buildings designed to make indoor use of natural light. Until the emergence of electric grids and Thomas Edison's incandescent light bulb in the late nineteenth and early twentieth centuries, such legal protections may have been justifiable because prior to that time many landowners relied on natural sunlight to illuminate building interiors. However, the need for those protections had diminished by 1959, when a major United States court considered whether landowners in this country held any common law protection against shading from neighbors. The *Fontainebleau* court surely had no idea its disposition of a dispute between neighbors over the shading of a hotel beach would continue to influence the evolution of solar energy law more than a half-century later.

FONTAINEBLEAU HOTEL CORP. V. FORTY-FIVE TWENTY-FIVE, INC.
District Court of Appeal of Florida, Third District, 1959
114 So.2d 357

PER CURIAM.

This is an interlocutory appeal from an order temporarily enjoining the appellants from continuing with the construction of a fourteen-story addition to the Fontainebleau Hotel, owned and operated by the appellants. Appellee, plaintiff below, owns the Eden Roc Hotel, which was constructed in 1955, about a year after the Fontainebleau, and adjoins the Fontainebleau on the north. Both are luxury hotels, facing the Atlantic Ocean. . . . The 14-story tower will extend 160 feet above grade in height and is 416 feet long from east to west. During the winter months, from around two o'clock in the afternoon for the remainder of the day, the shadow of the addition will extend over the cabana, swimming pool, and sunbathing areas of the Eden Roc, which are located in the southern portion of its property.

In this action, plaintiff-appellee sought to enjoin the defendants-appellants from proceeding with the construction of the addition to the Fontainebleau (it appears to have been roughly eight stories high at the time suit was filed), alleging that the construction would interfere with the light and air on the beach in front of the Eden Roc and cast a shadow of such size as to render the beach wholly unfitted for the use and enjoyment of its guests, to the irreparable injury of the plaintiff; further, that the construction of such addition on the north side of defendants' property, rather than the south side, [and] was actuated by malice and ill will on the part of the defendants' president toward the plaintiff's president. . . . It was also alleged that the construction would interfere with the easements of light and air enjoyed by plaintiff and its predecessors in title for more than twenty years and 'impliedly granted by virtue of the acts of the plaintiff's predecessors in title, as well as under the common law and the express recognition of such rights by virtue of Chapter 9837, Laws of Florida 1923 * * * .' Some attempt was also made to allege an easement by implication in favor of the plaintiff's property, as the dominant, and against the defendants' property, as the servient, tenement.

. . . .

The chancellor . . . entered a temporary injunction restraining the defendants from continuing with the construction of the addition. His reason for so doing was stated by him, in a memorandum opinion, as follows:

> 'In granting the temporary injunction in this case the Court wishes to make several things very clear. The ruling is not based on any alleged presumptive title nor prescriptive right of the plaintiff to light and air nor is it based on any deed restrictions nor recorded plats in the title of the plaintiff nor of the defendant nor of any plat of record. It is not based on any zoning ordinance nor on any provision of the building code of the City of Miami Beach nor on the decision of any court, *nisi prius* or appellate. It is based solely on the proposition that no one has a right to use his property to the injury of another. In this case it is clear from the evidence that the proposed use by the Fontainebleau will materially damage the Eden Roc. There is evidence indicating that the construction of the proposed annex by the Fontainebleau is malicious or deliberate for the purpose of injuring the Eden Roc, but it is scarcely sufficient, standing alone, to afford a basis for equitable relief.'

This is indeed a novel application of the maxim *sic utere tuo ut alienum non laedas*. This maxim does not mean that one must never use his own property in such a way as to do any injury to his neighbor. *Beckman v. Marshall*, Fla. 1956, 85 So.2d 552. It means only that one must use his property so as not to injure the lawful *rights* of another. *Cason v. Florida Power Co.*, 74 Fla. 1, 76 So. 535, L.R.A.1918A, 1034. In *Reaver v. Martin Theatres*, Fla.1951, 52 So.2d 682, 683, 25 A.L.R.2d 1451, under this maxim, it was stated that 'it is well settled that a property owner may put his own property to any reasonable and lawful use, so long as he does not thereby deprive the adjoining landowner of any right of enjoyment of his property *which is recognized and protected by law, and so long as his use is not such a one as the law will pronounce a nuisance.*' [Emphasis supplied.]

No American decision has been cited, and independent research has revealed none, in which it has been held that—in the absence of some contractual or statutory obligation—a landowner has a legal right to the free flow of light and air across the adjoining land of his neighbor. Even at common law, the landowner had no legal right, in the absence of an easement or uninterrupted use and enjoyment for a period of 20 years, to unobstructed light and air from the adjoining land . . . And the English doctrine of 'ancient lights' has been unanimously repudiated in this country. 1 AM. JUR., *Adjoining Landowners*, § 49, p. 533; *Lynch v. Hill*, 1939, 24 Del. Ch. 86, 6 A.2d 614, overruling *Clawson v. Primrose*, 4 Del. Ch. 643.

There being, then, no legal right to the free flow of light and air from the adjoining land, it is universally held that where a structure serves a useful and beneficial purpose, it does not give rise to a cause of action, either for damages or for an injunction under the maxim *sic utere tuo ut alienum non laedas*, even though it causes injury to another by cutting off the light and air and interfering with the view that would otherwise be available over adjoining land in its natural state, regardless of the fact that the structure may have been erected partly for spite. . . .

We see no reason for departing from this universal rule. If, as contended on behalf of plaintiff, public policy demands that a landowner in the Miami Beach area refrain from constructing buildings on his premises that will cast a shadow on the adjoining premises, an amendment of its comprehensive planning and zoning ordinance, applicable to the public as a whole, is the means by which such purpose should be achieved. . . . But to change the universal rule—and the custom followed in this state since its inception—that adjoining landowners have an equal right under the law to build to the line of their respective tracts and to such a height as is desired by them (in the absence, of course, of building restrictions or regulations) amounts, in our opinion, to judicial legislation. As stated in *Musumeci v. Leonardo, supra* [77 R.I. 255, 75 A.2d 177], 'So use your own as not to injure another's property is, indeed, a sound and salutary principle for the promotion of justice, but it may not and should not be applied so as gratuitously to confer upon an adjacent property owner incorporeal rights incidental to his ownership of land which the law does not sanction.'

. . . .

The record affirmatively shows that no statutory basis for the right sought to be enforced by plaintiff exists. . . . It also affirmatively appears that there is no possible basis for holding that plaintiff has an easement for light and air, either express or implied, across defendants' property, nor any prescriptive right thereto—even if it be assumed, arguendo, that the common-law right of prescription as to 'ancient lights' is in effect in this state. And from what we have said heretofore in this opinion, it is perhaps superfluous to add that we have no desire to dissent from the unanimous holding in this country repudiating the English doctrine of ancient lights.

. . . .

Since it affirmatively appears that the plaintiff has not established a cause of action against the defendants by reason of the structure here in question, the order granting a temporary injunction should be and it is hereby reversed with directions to dismiss the complaint.

Reversed with directions.

The *Fontainebleau* court's holding that land ownership conferred no legal protection against neighbors' shading began to take new relevance in the late 1970s and early 1980s, when a major oil embargo by the Organization of Arab Petroleum Exporting Countries (OPAEC) (now known as OPEC) and other factors sparked the nation's first period of significant interest in solar energy.[1] During that era, advancements in solar energy technologies and a strong national desire to promote energy independence and protect environmental resources prompted many to question whether the common law's existing lack of protections against shading still effectively served the interests of society. This sentiment was famously evident in *Prah v. Maretti*—a 1982 state supreme court case involving a dispute over a neighbor's potential shading of a passive solar energy system.

PRAH V. MARETTI

Supreme Court of Wisconsin, 1982
108 Wis.2d 223

ABRAHAMSON, J.

This appeal from a judgment of the circuit court for Waukesha county . . . was certified to this court by the court of appeals . . . as presenting an issue of first impression, namely, whether an owner of a solar-heated residence states a claim upon which relief can be granted when he asserts that his neighbor's proposed construction of a residence (which conforms to existing deed restrictions and local ordinances) interferes with his access to an unobstructed path for sunlight across the neighbor's property. This case thus involves a conflict between one landowner (Glenn Prah, the plaintiff) interested in unobstructed access to sunlight across adjoining property as a natural source of energy and an adjoining landowner (Richard D. Maretti, the defendant) interested in the development of his land.

The circuit court concluded that the plaintiff presented no claim upon which relief could be granted and granted summary judgment for the defendant. We reverse the judgment of the circuit court and remand the cause to the circuit court for further proceedings.

I.

According to the complaint, the plaintiff is the owner of a residence which was constructed during the years 1978–1979. The complaint alleges that the residence has a solar system which includes collectors on the roof to supply energy for heat and hot water and that after the plaintiff built

---

[1] The energy crisis of 1973 was precipitated by President Nixon's support for Israel during the 1973 Yom Kippur War between Egypt, Syria, and Israel. The subsequent oil embargo caused oil prices to quickly spike from $3 per barrel to $12. *See Energy Crisis (1970s)—Facts & Summary*, HISTORY.COM, http://www.history.com/topics/energy-crisis (last visited Sept. 23, 2017).

his solar-heated house, the defendant purchased the lot adjacent to and immediately to the south of the plaintiff's lot and commenced planning construction of a home. The complaint further states that when the plaintiff learned of defendant's plans to build the house he advised the defendant that if the house were built at the proposed location, defendant's house would substantially and adversely affect the integrity of plaintiff's solar system and could cause plaintiff other damage. Nevertheless, the defendant began construction. The complaint further alleges that the plaintiff is entitled to "unrestricted use of the sun and its solar power" and demands judgment for injunctive relief and damages.

After filing his complaint, the plaintiff moved for a temporary injunction to restrain and enjoin construction by the defendant. . . .

. . . Plaintiff's home was the first residence built in the subdivision, and although plaintiff did not build his house in the center of the lot it was built in accordance with applicable restrictions. Plaintiff advised defendant that if the defendant's home were built at the proposed site it would cause a shadowing effect on the solar collectors which would reduce the efficiency of the system and possibly damage the system. To avoid these adverse effects, plaintiff requested defendant to locate his home an additional several feet away from the plaintiff's lot line, the exact number being disputed. Plaintiff and defendant failed to reach an agreement on the location of defendant's home before defendant started construction. The Architectural Control Committee and the Planning Commission of the City of Muskego approved the defendant's plans for his home, including its location on the lot. After such approval, the defendant apparently changed the grade of the property without prior notice to the Architectural Control Committee. The problem with defendant's proposed construction, as far as the plaintiff's interests are concerned, arises from a combination of the grade and the distance of defendant's home from the defendant's lot line.

The circuit court denied plaintiff's motion for injunctive relief, declared it would entertain a motion for summary judgment and thereafter entered judgment in favor of the defendant.

. . . .

III.

. . . .

The plaintiff presents three legal theories to support his claim that the defendant's continued construction of a home justifies granting him relief: (1) the construction constitutes a common law private nuisance; (2) the construction is prohibited by sec. 844.01, Stats. 1979–80; and (3) the construction interferes with the solar easement plaintiff acquired under the doctrine of prior appropriation.

. . . .

We consider first whether the complaint states a claim for relief based on common law private nuisance. This state has long recognized that an owner of land does not have an absolute or unlimited right to use the land in a way which injures the rights of others. The rights of neighboring landowners are relative; the uses by one must not unreasonably impair the uses or enjoyment of the other. VI–A *American Law of Property* sec. 28.22, pp. 64–65 (1954). When one landowner's use of his or her property unreasonably interferes with another's enjoyment of his or her property, that use is said to be a private nuisance. . . .

The private nuisance doctrine has traditionally been employed in this state to balance the rights of landowners, and this court has recently adopted the analysis of private nuisance set forth in the Restatement (Second) of Torts. . . . The Restatement defines private nuisance as "a nontrespassory invasion of another's interest in the private use and enjoyment of land." RESTATEMENT (SECOND) OF TORTS sec. 821D (1977). The phrase "interest in the private use and enjoyment of land" as used in sec. 821D is broadly defined to include any disturbance of the enjoyment of property. . . .

. . . .

Although the defendant's obstruction of the plaintiff's access to sunlight appears to fall within the Restatement's broad concept of a private nuisance as a nontrespassory invasion of another's interest in the private use and enjoyment of land, the defendant asserts that he has a right to develop his property in compliance with statutes, ordinances and private covenants without regard to the effect of such development upon the plaintiff's access to sunlight. In essence, the defendant is asking this court to hold that the private nuisance doctrine is not applicable in the instant case and that his right to develop his land is a right which is *per se* superior to his neighbor's interest in access to sunlight. This position is expressed in the maxim "*cujus est solum, ejus est usque ad coelum et ad infernos*," that is, the owner of land owns up to the sky and down to the center of the earth. The rights of the surface owner are, however, not unlimited. *U.S. v. Causby*, 328 U.S. 256, 260–1, 66 S.Ct. 1062, 1065, 90 L.Ed. 1206 (1946). *See also* 114.03, Stats.1979–80.

The defendant is not completely correct in asserting that the common law did not protect a landowner's access to sunlight across adjoining property. At English common law a landowner could acquire a right to receive sunlight across adjoining land by both express agreement and under the judge-made doctrine of "ancient lights." Under the doctrine of ancient lights if the landowner had received sunlight across adjoining property for a specified period of time, the landowner was entitled to continue to receive unobstructed access to sunlight across the adjoining property. Under the doctrine the landowner acquired a negative prescriptive easement and could prevent the adjoining landowner from obstructing access to light.

Although American courts have not been as receptive to protecting a landowner's access to sunlight as the English courts, American courts have afforded some protection to a landowner's interest in access to sunlight. American courts honor express easements to sunlight. American courts initially enforced the English common law doctrine of ancient lights, but later every state which considered the doctrine repudiated it as inconsistent with the needs of a developing country. Indeed, for just that reason this court concluded that an easement to light and air over adjacent property could not be created or acquired by prescription and has been unwilling to recognize such an easement by implication. *Depner v. United States National Bank*, 202 Wis. 405, 408, 232 N.W. 851 (1930); *Miller v. Hoeschler*, 126 Wis. 263, 268–69, 105 N.W. 790 (1905).

Many jurisdictions in this country have protected a landowner from malicious obstruction of access to light (the spite fence cases) under the common law private nuisance doctrine. If an activity is motivated by malice it lacks utility and the harm it causes others outweighs any social values. . . . Shortly after this court upheld a landowner's right to erect a useless and unsightly sixteen-foot spite fence four feet from his neighbor's windows . . . the legislature enacted a law specifically defining a spite fence as an actionable private nuisance. Thus, a landowner's interest in sunlight has been protected in this country by common law private nuisance law at least in the narrow context of the modern American rule invalidating spite fences. . . .

This court's reluctance in the nineteenth and early part of the twentieth century to provide broader protection for a landowner's access to sunlight was premised on three policy considerations. First, the right of landowners to use their property as they wished, as long as they did not cause physical damage to a neighbor, was jealously guarded. *Metzger v. Hochrein*, 107 Wis. 267, 272, 83 N.W. 308 (1900).

Second, sunlight was valued only for aesthetic enjoyment or as illumination. Since artificial light could be used for illumination, loss of sunlight was at most a personal annoyance which was given little, if any, weight by society.

Third, society had a significant interest in not restricting or impeding land development. *Dillman v. Hoffman*, 38 Wis. 559, 574 (1875). This court repeatedly emphasized that in the growth period of the nineteenth and early twentieth centuries change is to be expected and is essential to property and that recognition of a right to sunlight would hinder property development. . . .

. . . .

Considering these three policies, this court concluded that in the absence of an express agreement granting access to sunlight, a landowner's obstruction of another's access to sunlight was not actionable. . . . These three policies are no longer fully accepted or applicable. They reflect factual circumstances and social priorities that are now obsolete.

First, society has increasingly regulated the use of land by the landowner for the general welfare. *Euclid v. Ambler Realty Co.*, 272 U.S. 365, 47 S.Ct. 114, 71 L.Ed. 303 (1926); *Just v. Marinette*, 56 Wis.2d 7, 201 N.W.2d 761 (1972).

Second, access to sunlight has taken on a new significance in recent years. In this case the plaintiff seeks to protect access to sunlight, not for aesthetic reasons or as a source of illumination but as a source of energy. Access to sunlight as an energy source is of significance both to the landowner who invests in solar collectors and to a society which has an interest in developing alternative sources of energy.

Third, the policy of favoring unhindered private development in an expanding economy is no longer in harmony with the realities of our society. *State v. Deetz*, 66 Wis.2d 1, 224 N.W.2d 407 (1974). The need for easy and rapid development is not as great today as it once was, while our perception of the value of sunlight as a source of energy has increased significantly.

Courts should not implement obsolete policies that have lost their vigor over the course of the years. The law of private nuisance is better suited to resolve landowners' disputes about property development in the 1980's than is a rigid rule which does not recognize a landowner's interest in access to sunlight. As we said in *Ballstadt v. Pagel*, 202 Wis. 484, 489, 232 N.W. 862 (1930), "What is regarded in law as constituting a nuisance in modern times would no doubt have been tolerated without question in former times.". . . .

. . . .

Yet the defendant would have us ignore the flexible private nuisance law as a means of resolving the dispute between the landowners in this case and would have us adopt an approach . . . of favoring the unrestricted development of land and of applying a rigid and inflexible rule protecting his right to build on his land and disregarding any interest of the plaintiff in the use and enjoyment of his land. This we refuse to do.

Private nuisance law, the law traditionally used to adjudicate conflicts between private landowners, has the flexibility to protect both a landowner's right of access to sunlight and another landowner's right to develop land. Private nuisance law is better suited to regulate access to sunlight in modern society and is more in harmony with legislative policy and the prior decisions of this court than is an inflexible doctrine of non-recognition of any interest in access to sunlight across adjoining land.

We therefore hold that private nuisance law, that is, the reasonable use doctrine as set forth in the Restatement, is applicable to the instant case. Recognition of a nuisance claim for unreasonable obstruction of access to sunlight will not prevent land development or unduly hinder the use of adjoining land. It will promote the reasonable use and enjoyment of land in a manner suitable to the 1980's. That obstruction of access to light might be found to constitute a nuisance in certain circumstances does not mean that it will be or must be found to constitute a nuisance under all circumstances. The result in each case depends on whether the conduct complained of is unreasonable.

Accordingly we hold that the plaintiff in this case has stated a claim under which relief can be granted. Nonetheless we do not determine whether the plaintiff in this case is entitled to relief. In order to be entitled to relief the plaintiff must prove the elements required to establish actionable nuisance, and the conduct of the defendant herein must be judged by the reasonable use doctrine.

. . . .

For the reasons set forth, we reverse the judgment of the circuit court dismissing the complaint and remand the matter to circuit court for further proceedings not inconsistent with this opinion.

. . . .

CALLOW, J. (dissenting).

The majority has adopted the Restatement's reasonable use doctrine to grant an owner of a solar heated home a cause of action against his neighbor who, in acting entirely within the applicable ordinances and statutes, seeks to design and build his home in such a location that it may, at various times during the day, shade the plaintiff's solar collector, thereby impeding the efficiency of his heating system during several months of the year. Because I believe the facts of this case clearly reveal that a cause of action for private nuisance will not lie, I dissent.

. . . .

It is a fundamental principle of law that a "landowner owns at least as much of the space above the ground as he can occupy or use in connection with the land." *United States v. Causby*, 328 U.S. 256, 264, 66 S.Ct. 1062, 1067, 90 L.Ed. 1206 (1946). . . . As stated in the frequently cited and followed case of *Fontainebleau Hotel Corp. v. Forty-Five Twenty-Five, Inc.*, 114 So.2d 357 (Fla. Dist. Ct. App. 1959), *cert. denied*, 117 So.2d 842 (Fla. 1960):

"There being, then, no legal right to the free flow of light and air from the adjoining land, it is universally held that where a structure serves a useful and beneficial purpose, it does not give rise to a cause of action, either for damages or for an injunction under the maxim *sic utere tuo ut alienum non laedas*, even though it causes injury to another by cutting off the light and air and interfering with the view that would otherwise be available over adjoining land in its natural state, regardless of the fact that the structure may have been erected partly for spite." *Id.* at 359 (emphasis in original).

See Venuto v. Owens-Corning Fiberglas Corp., 22 Cal.App.3d 116, 127, 99 Cal. Rptr. 350, 357 (1971). I firmly believe that a landowner's right to use his property within the limits of ordinances, statutes, and restrictions of record where such use is necessary to serve his legitimate needs is a fundamental precept of a free society which this court should strive to uphold.

As one commentator has suggested:

"It is fashionable to dismiss such values as deriving from a bygone era in which people valued development as a 'goal in itself,' but current market prices for real estate, and more particularly the premiums paid for land whose zoning permits intensive use, suggest that people still place very high values on such rights."

Williams, *Solar Access and Property Rights: A Maverick Analysis*, 11 CONN. L. REV. 430, 443 (1979) (footnote omitted). *Cf.* Goble, *Solar Access and Property Rights: Reply to a "Maverick" Analysis*, 12 CONN. L. REV. 270 (1980).

The majority cites two zoning cases, *Village of Euclid v. Ambler Realty Company*, 272 U.S. 365, 47 S.Ct. 114, 71 L.Ed. 303 (1926), and *Just v. Marinette County*, 56 Wis.2d 7, 201 N.W.2d 761 (1972), to support the conclusion that society has increasingly regulated private land use in the name of public welfare. *Supra*, at 189. The cases involving the use of police power and eminent domain are clearly distinguishable from the present situation as they relate to interference with a private right solely for the *public* health, safety, morals, or welfare. In the instant case, we are dealing with an action which seeks to restrict the defendant's private right to use his property, notwithstanding a complete lack of notice of restriction to the defendant and the defendant's compliance with applicable ordinances and statutes. The plaintiff who *knew* of the potential problem before the defendant acquired the land seeks to impose such use restriction to accommodate his personal, private benefit—a benefit which could have been accommodated by the plaintiff locating his home in a different place on his property or by acquiring the land in question when it was for sale prior to its acquisition by the defendant.

I know of no cases repudiating policies favoring the right of a landowner to use his property as he lawfully desires or which declare such policies are "no longer fully accepted or applicable" in this context. *Supra*, at 189. The right of a property owner to lawful enjoyment of his property should be vigorously protected, particularly in those cases where the adjacent property owner could have insulated himself from the alleged problem by acquiring the land as a defense to the potential problem or by provident use of his own property.

The majority concludes that sunlight has not heretofore been accorded the status of a source of energy, and consequently it has taken on a new significance in recent years. Solar energy for home heating is at this time sparingly used and of questionable economic value because solar collectors are not mass produced, and consequently, they are very costly. Their limited efficiency may explain the lack of production.

. . . .

I would submit that any policy decisions in this area are best left for the legislature. "What is 'desirable' or 'advisable' or 'ought to be' is a question of policy, not a question of fact. What is 'necessary' or what is 'in the best interest' is not a fact and its determination by the judiciary is an exercise of legislative power when each involves political considerations." *In re City of Beloit*, 37 Wis.2d 637, 644, 155 N.W.2d 633 (1968). . . .

. . . .

I conclude that plaintiff's solar heating system is an unusually sensitive use. In other words, the defendant's proposed construction of his home, under ordinary circumstances, would not interfere with the use and enjoyment of the usual person's property. *See* W. Prosser, *supra*, sec. 87 at 578–79. "The plaintiff cannot, by devoting his own land to an unusually sensitive use, such as a drive-in motion picture theater easily affected by light, make a nuisance out of conduct of the adjoining defendant which would otherwise be harmless." *Id.* at 579 (footnote omitted).

. . . .

I further believe that the majority's conclusion that a cause of action exists in this case thwarts the very foundation of property law. Property law encompasses a system of filing and notice in a place for public records to provide prospective purchasers with any limitations on their use of the property. Such a notice is not alleged by the plaintiff. Only as a result of the majority's decision did Mr. Maretti discover that a legitimate action exists which would require him to defend the design and location of his home against a nuisance suit, notwithstanding the fact that he located and began to build his house within the applicable building, municipal, and deed restrictions.

. . . .

I believe the facts of the instant controversy present the classic case of the owner of a solar collector who fails to take any action to protect his investment. There is nothing in the record to indicate that Mr. Prah disclosed his situation to Mr. Maretti prior to Maretti's purchase of the lot or attempted to secure protection for his solar collector prior to Maretti's submission of his building plans to the architectural committee. Such inaction should be considered a significant factor in determining whether a cause of action exists.

. . . .

Because I do not believe that the facts of the present case give rise to a cause of action for private nuisance, I dissent. . .

NOTES & QUESTIONS

1. How do you think the electrification of buildings in the early twentieth century and the widespread use of light bulbs for indoor lighting by the 1950s may have impacted the *Fontainebleau* court's analysis? If the court had heard the case 100 years earlier, how might such timing have affected the analysis, and why?

2. Solar access laws expose the inherent conflict between two well-known common law maxims. The first maxim, *sic utere tuo ut alienum non laedas*, provides a primary basis for modern nuisance law and the holding in *Fontainebleau*, and is secondarily cited in a dissenting opinion in *Prah*. The second maxim, *cujus est solum, ejus est usque ad coelum et ad infernos*, appears in *Prah* and is arguably implied in *Fontainebleau* as well.

     a. How do each of these maxims translate into English?

     b. How does the *Fontainebleau* court's interpretation of the *sic utero* maxim impact its holding?

     c. Suppose that all courts literally applied the second maxim (also known as the *ad coelum* rule) and interpreted it as always having priority over the *sic utero* maxim. If that were true, which party would have prevailed in *Fontainebleau*, and which would have prevailed in *Prah*? Why? If you represented a solar energy industry advocacy group, would you favor solar access laws based on such a strong application of the *ad coelum* rule? Why or why not?

3. Suppose a state legislator had proposed a bill directing courts to apply only common law nuisance doctrine to resolve all solar access conflicts and that your client was opposed to the bill. Craft a one-paragraph argument articulating at least three distinct reasons why private nuisance doctrine alone is an unsatisfactory means of governing solar access conflicts.

4. What are the three policy rationales the majority in *Prah* identifies that may have made former courts reluctant to embrace the doctrine of ancient

lights? On what basis does the *Prah* majority argue that these rationales are no longer as relevant or convincing as they were decades ago?

5.   The dissenting opinion in *Prah* contains language arguing that solar energy technologies are "sparingly used and of questionable economic value because solar collectors are not mass produced, and consequently, they are very costly." Is this statement more or less true today than it was in 1982? How, if at all, do you think the evolution of the rooftop solar energy industry since 1982 impacts the validity of the dissenting justice's argument?

6.   *The Limits of Landowners' Airspace Rights.* As suggested in the cases below, U.S. courts certainly do not interpret the *ad coelum* rule as literally giving landowners limitless rights in the airspace above their land. In the famous case of United States v. Causby, 328 U.S. 256 (1946), the United States Supreme Court made clear that landowners do not have property interests in the "navigable airspace" through which manned aircraft fly (which begins at 500 feet above ground in most of the country) because such space is a "public highway" for air travel. However, the *Causby* court made clear that a landowner does have a property interest in "at least as much of the space above the ground as he can occupy or use in connection with the land." *Id.* at 264. For a more detailed discussion of low-altitude airspace rights and of the role of airspace in renewable energy development and in other aspects of environmental sustainability movement, *see generally* Troy A. Rule, *Airspace in a Green Economy*, 59 UCLA L. REV. 270 (2011).

2.   STATE SOLAR ACCESS STATUTES

Recognizing that the common law afforded landowners little or no protection against solar panel shading, several states enacted solar access legislation during the late 1970s and early 1980s. Drafters of these state statutes sought primarily to help landowners better manage shading risks in hopes of encouraging more private investment in solar energy. Rather than adopting a single uniform statute, state legislatures during this period embraced a diverse range of approaches, a few of which are explored in the following materials.

a.   California's Solar Shade Control Act

California's Solar Shade Control Act was among several state solar access statutes enacted during the solar energy push of the late 1970s. Because of the Act's relative conciseness and simplicity, excerpts from the Act and the two cases below that interpret it provide a good introduction to this type of statute and valuable practice for readers seeking to hone their statutory interpretation skills.

SOLAR SHADE CONTROL ACT
CAL. PUB. RES. CODE §§ 25980–86 (West 2009)

. . . .

§ 25982. After installation of solar collector; placement or growth of tree or shrub on property of another

After the installation of a solar collector, a person owning or in control of another property shall not allow a tree or shrub to be placed or, if placed, to grow on that property so as to cast a shadow greater than 10 percent of the collector absorption area upon that solar collector surface at any one time between the hours of 10 a.m. and 2 p.m., local standard time.

§ 25982.1.   Solar shade control notice; requirements

(a) An owner of a building where a solar collector is proposed to be installed may provide written notice by certified mail to a person owning property that may be affected by the requirements of this chapter prior to the installation of the solar collector. If a notice is mailed, the notice shall be mailed no more than 60 days prior to installation of the solar collector and shall read as follows:

SOLAR SHADE CONTROL NOTICE

Under the Solar Shade Control Act (California Public Resources Code § 25980 et seq.) a tree or shrub cannot cast a shadow greater than 10 percent of a solar collector absorption area upon that solar collector surface at any one time between the hours of 10 a.m. and 2 p.m. local standard time if the tree or shrub is placed after installation of a solar collector. The owner of the building where a solar collector is proposed to be installed is providing this written notice to persons owning property that may be affected by the requirements of the act no more than 60 days prior to the installation of a solar collector. The building owner is providing the following information:

Name and address of building owner: _____

Telephone number of building owner: _____

Address of building and specific location where a solar collector will be installed (including street number and name, city/county, ZIP Code, and assessor's book, page, and parcel number):

_____

Installation date of solar collector: _____

_____

Building Owner, Date

. . .

§ 25983. Violations; private nuisance; written notice from owner of solar collector

A tree or shrub that is maintained in violation of Section 25982 is a private nuisance . . . if the person who maintains or permits the tree or shrub to be maintained fails to remove or alter the tree or shrub after receiving a written notice from the owner or agent of the affected solar collector requesting compliance with the requirements of Section 25982.

§ 25984. Application of chapter; exemptions

This chapter does not apply to any of the following:

(a) A tree or shrub planted prior to the installation of a solar collector.

(b) A tree planted, grown, or harvested on timberland as defined in Section 4526 or on land devoted to the production of commercial agricultural crops.

(c) The replacement of a tree or shrub that had been growing prior to the installation of a solar collector and that, subsequent to the installation of the solar collector, dies, or is removed for the protection of public health, safety, or the environment.

(d) A tree or shrub that is subject to a city or county ordinance.

§ 25985. Ordinance to exempt city or unincorporated areas from provisions of chapter; requirements

(a) A city, or for unincorporated areas, a county, may adopt, by majority vote of the governing body, an ordinance exempting their jurisdiction from the provisions of this chapter. The adoption of the ordinance shall not be subject to the California Environmental Quality Act (commencing with Section 21000).

(b) Notwithstanding the requirements of this chapter, a city or a county ordinance specifying requirements for tree preservation or solar shade control shall govern within the jurisdiction of the city or county that adopted the ordinance.

SHER V. LEIDERMAN

California Court of Appeal, Sixth District, 1986
181 Cal.App.3d 867

BRAUER, A.J.

Rudolph and Bonnie Sher appeal from a judgment against them in favor of P. Herbert and Gloria Leiderman following a court trial. Their appeal presents an issue of first impression in this state, namely, whether an owner of a residence designed to make use of solar energy can state a cause of action for private nuisance when trees on his neighbor's property interfere with his solar access. We determine that California nuisance law does not provide a remedy for blockage of sunlight, and, for reasons discussed below, we decline to expand existing law.

The Shers' appeal also includes claims that the California Solar Shade Control Act applies to give them a private cause of action against the Leidermans. . . .

The Facts

The extensive findings set forth in the trial court's statement of decision are not in dispute and form the basis for our factual summary.

In 1962 the Shers entered into a long term land lease with Stanford University. The lot they leased was located in a new residential development on the Stanford campus known as Pine Hill 2, one of five model planned subdivisions developed by Stanford for use by faculty and staff. All building and landscaping on subdivision lots was subject to Stanford's prior review and approval. Shortly after the Shers' plans were approved, the Leidermans leased an adjacent lot. They in turn obtained design approval for their home and proceeded with construction. Both families moved into their new homes in 1963 and have lived there ever since.

The Shers' lot fronts on Mayfield Avenue and is situated on the northeast slope of a hill. The Leidermans' lot is southwest of Shers' and occupies the upper slope and the crest of the hill, fronting on Lathrop Drive. The two lots share a common boundary along the Shers' southern—and the Leidermans' northern—property line.

The Shers' home was designed and built to take advantage of the winter sun for heat and light. The home is oriented on the lot so as to present its length towards the south. South-facing windows are relatively larger than others in the house. The south side of the house is also "serrated" to expose the maximum area to the sun. A large south-facing concrete patio operates to radiate sunlight into the home's interior. Skylights add to the light inside the house and an open floor plan in the common areas increases the general circulation of light and air. Roof overhangs are designed at an angle and length to block the hot summer sun while permitting winter sunlight to enter the house. Roof and walls are well insulated. Deciduous trees and shrubs along the southern side of the house aid in shading and cooling in the summer but allow winter sunlight to reach the house.

The trial court found that the Sher home is a "passive solar" home. The design features and structures identified above form a system intended to transform solar into thermal energy. The court also found that a concomitant design goal was to create a bright and cheerful living environment. Though the home includes many passive solar features, it does not make use of any "active" solar collectors or panels. Nor does it employ any "thermal mass" for heat storage and distribution. Building materials used throughout were typical and conventional for the time; the house does not contain any special materials primarily selected for effective thermal retention.

At the time the Shers and Leidermans designed and built their homes there were no trees on either lot. For that matter, this was true of all of Pine Hill 2. Over the years both parties, as well as their neighbors, landscaped their properties. As noted above, the Shers' landscaping was designed to enhance and complement their home's effectiveness as a solar system. The Leidermans' landscape plan was disapproved in part by the Stanford housing office, specifically in regard to a number of trees they proposed to plant within a 10 foot sewer easement along their northern property line bordering the Shers' lot. Despite the lack of approval, however, the Leidermans proceeded to implement their plan. Between 1963 and approximately 1976 they planted a large number of trees, including Monterey pine, eucalyptus, redwood, cedar and acacia. The trial court found that these trees were planted to beautify the appearance of the Leiderman property, to attract birds and other small creatures, and to provide shade and privacy. The court found no intent on the Leidermans' part to deprive the Shers of sunlight.

In 1972, the Shers discovered that certain trees on the Leiderman property cast shadows on the Sher house in the wintertime. The offending trees were topped the following spring and the cost was borne by the Shers. In 1977 several other Leiderman trees were removed because their continued growth in the sewer easement posed a threat to the sewer line. The cost of this removal was shared by the Shers and Stanford. Further tree work was done at the Shers' expense in the winter of 1979. The Leidermans themselves also engaged in certain tree trimming and removal over the years at a cost to them of approximately $4,000. Since 1979, however, the Leidermans have refused either to undertake any further trimming on their own or to cooperate with the Shers in this regard.

At time of trial trees on the Leiderman property completely blocked the sun to much of the Sher home in the winter months. From December 21 to February 10, the central portion of the Sher home was cast in shadow between 10:00 a.m. and 2:00 p.m. The Shers added a skylight over their kitchen area to help alleviate the problem, but now this too is largely shaded during the winter.

The shade problem has transformed the formerly cheerful and sunny ambience of the Sher home; the interior is now dark and dismal in the winter months. The shading has also had an adverse impact on the home's thermal performance. The Shers' expert testified that heat loss during the winter months amounted to an equivalent of approximately 60 therms of natural gas. This converts into $30 to $60 per season in heating costs. Two

experts testified that the loss of sunlight to the Shers' house has resulted
in a diminution of market value between $15,000 and $45,000. It appears,
however, that this loss of value is attributable more to the gloomy
atmosphere of the house than to its decreased effectiveness as a solar
system. . . .

In order to restore sunlight to the Shers' home during the winter
months it would be necessary to trim certain trees on the Leiderman
property, top others and remove those where topping would destroy the
character of the tree or possibly kill it. Annual trimming would also be
necessary.

. . .

Discussion

1. *Private Nuisance*

The trial court found that the relief requested by the Shers would
amount to burdening the Leiderman property with a permanent easement
for passage of light to the Sher property. It is well settled in California that
a landowner has no easement for light and air over adjoining land, in the
absence of an express grant or covenant. . . . Nuisance law is in accord:
blockage of light to a neighbor's property, except in cases where malice is
the overriding motive, does not constitute actionable nuisance, regardless
of the impact on the injured party's property or person. (*Haehlen v. Wilson*
(1936) 11 Cal.App.2d 437, 441, 54 P.2d 62.).

Only one court in the country, the Wisconsin Supreme Court, has
departed from established law in this field. (*Prah v. Maretti* (1982) 108
Wis.2d 223, 321 N.W.2d 182.). . . .

. . . .

Although obstruction of sunlight would appear to fall within this
concept of a private nuisance as "a nontrespassory invasion of another's
interest in the use and enjoyment of land" (Rest. 2d Torts, § 821), courts
have traditionally refused to consider a landowner's access to sunlight a
protected interest. . . .

. . . Most significant, however, as chronicled in depth in the Shers'
opening brief, is the recent public recognition of sunlight, not only for its
aesthetic value but also as an important alternative energy source, with
far-reaching economic impact. One has only to look at the proliferation of
legislation in recent years emanating from all levels of government to
realize that promotion of the use of solar energy is of paramount public
interest today.

Because of this inversion of social priorities over the years, it is urged
that interference with solar access should no longer be considered a "mere"
obstruction of light, as it once was; today it may in fact amount to

substantial and perceptible harm, certainly no less substantial than the harm caused by other recognized nuisances such as unpleasant odors, noise, smoke, vibrations or dust. . . .

. . . .

The Shers also point out that the statutory definition of nuisance in the California Civil Code, section 3479, as "anything" which is "an obstruction to the free use of property" so as to "interfere with the comfortable enjoyment of life or property" is broad enough to encompass a cause of action based on unreasonable obstruction of light. They can, however, cite us to no California case which has so applied section 3479.

. . . .

. . . [W]e take the position that it is solely within the province of the legislature to gauge the relative importance of social policies and decide whether to effect a change in the law. (*Bodinson Mfg. Co. v. California E. Com.* (1941) 17 Cal.2d 321, 109 P.2d 935.) The California legislature has already seen fit to carve out an exception to established nuisance law, in the form of the California Solar Shade Control Act. . . .

We are unwilling to intrude into the precise area of the law where legislative action is being taken. If the legislature intended to limit its protection of solar access to those situations circumscribed by the Solar Shade Control Act, our expansion of the nuisance law beyond those bounds would be unwarranted. On the other hand, the Solar Shade Control Act may well represent the initial phase of a more comprehensive legislative plan to guarantee solar access; in that case, judicial interference could undermine the orderly development of such a scheme.

In addition to these concerns, we are troubled by certain aspects of the Shers' thesis. Though the Solar Age may indeed be upon us, it is not so easily conceded that individual property rights are no longer important policy considerations. The Shers contend that the land use cases (*Village of Euclid, Ohio v. Amber Realty Co.* (1926) 272 U.S. 365, 47 S.Ct. 114, 71 L.Ed. 303, and progeny) and subsequent widespread use of zoning and other local regulation have eroded the vitality of these policies. As the dissent in *Prah v. Maretti, supra,* 108 Wis.2d. 223, 321 N.W.2d at p. 194 pointed out, however, expanded use of the police power and eminent domain only supports the conclusion that society has increasingly seen fit to regulate private land use for the *public* health, safety, morals, or welfare. The case before us concerns the imposition of restrictions on land use for a *private* benefit, a far different proposition in our view. A landowner's right to use his property lawfully to meet his legitimate needs is a fundamental precept of a free society. Though his use may be made subject to limitations for the sake of the public good, it cannot be said that his rights vis-a-vis adjoining owners are thereby diluted.

Moreover, established principles of due process and property law would seem to require that a property owner, or prospective purchaser, have notice of limitations on the use of his property. Zoning and other local ordinances provide such notice, as do the recording laws, while abatement through a nuisance action would not. . . .

. . . Since legislative solutions are feasible and since we believe that determination of policy is peculiarly a legislative function under the Constitution, we defer to that body, and affirm the trial court's judgment on this cause of action.

2. *The Solar Shade Control Act*

The Solar Shade Control Act ("the Act"), discussed briefly in the preceding section, provides limited protection to owners of solar collectors from shading caused by trees on adjacent properties. If a tree is allowed to grow to a point where it shades more than 10% of a neighbor's collector during certain hours of the day, the owner of the collector has recourse to the local city attorney or district attorney. The complainant must establish to the satisfaction of the prosecutor that the violation is occurring. If satisfied, the prosecutor then serves the owner of the offending tree(s) with a notice to abate the violation. If this is not accomplished within 30 days of receipt of the notice, the complainant can commence an action by filing an affidavit with the prosecutor. (Pub. Resources Code § 25983.)

The Shers applied to the Santa Clara County District Attorney's office pursuant to the above section. The Deputy District Attorney, however, after investigating the matter, determined that the Act did not apply to the Shers' situation and refused to issue a notice to abate.

The threshold issue is whether the definition of solar collector in section 25981 of the Act applies to a home such as the Shers'. . . .

. . . [W]e turn to the definition of solar collector contained in section 25981. This section reads: "As used in this chapter, 'solar collector' means a fixed device, structure, or part of a device or structure, which is used primarily to transform solar energy into thermal, chemical, or electrical energy. The solar collector shall be used as part of a system which makes use of solar energy for any or all of the following purposes: (1) water heating, (2) space heating or cooling, and (3) power generation." The trial court found that since the Shers' house contained no "solar collectors" the Act did not apply. The Shers argue that the Act was intended to give broad protection to both active and passive solar homes and that parts of the structure of their house qualify as solar collectors under the definition set forth above.

The Shers' argument is based on the words "structure, or part of a . . . structure . . . used as a part of a system which makes use of solar energy." They point out that the trial court specifically found that the design features of their house "were intended to transform solar energy into thermal energy, and are used as part of a system which makes use of solar energy for space heating and cooling." Their south-facing windows and skylights are clearly "parts of a structure" and form an integral part of their solar energy system.

This interpretation of the language of the statute, however, fails to take into account the modifying word "primarily." Though it may be true that the Shers' south-facing windows were intended to catch the rays of the winter sun and provide warmth to the interior of the house, it cannot be said that the *primary* function of a window is to convert solar into thermal energy.

Furthermore, the interpretation suggested by the Shers, if followed to its logical conclusion, would give rise to a host of other definitional problems. Does *any* south-facing window in *any* home qualify as a solar collector? What in fact is a "south-facing" window? The Shers' home, for example, is oriented approximately 45 degrees off the east-west axis; their windows actually face southwest. Would the 10% shading factor be calculated on all windows and skylights or on each separately? The Shers installed a concrete patio on the southern side of their home to radiate heat and light to the home's interior. Is this also a collector? Well insulated roof and walls are listed in the trial court's statement of decision as integral parts of the Shers' passive solar system. If these too are "parts of a structure" which make use of solar energy, then every square inch of the Sher home, and others like it, would be rendered immune from shading by the operation of the Act. This clearly extends the scope of the Act to absurd proportions. Moreover, we do not believe that the legislature could have intended to impose upon local law enforcement agencies the enormous task of making these factual determinations whenever a collector is not readily identifiable as such.

. . . .

In summary, we find that the Solar Shade Control Act was not intended to apply to provide protection from shading to exclusively passive solar homes. Since we decide the Shers' claim on this basis, we do not find it necessary to address the other issues raised in the briefs regarding the Act.

. . . .

Judgment as amended is affirmed.

ZIPPERER V. COUNTY OF SANTA CLARA

California Court of Appeal, Sixth District, 2005
133 Cal.App.4th 1013

MCADAMS, J.

Plaintiffs John and Cecilia Zipperer sued the County of Santa Clara on various theories, based on allegations that their solar home was malfunctioning as a result of shading from trees growing on defendant's adjoining property. The trial court sustained defendant's demurrer to plaintiffs' first amended complaint, without leave to amend. This appeal followed. For reasons explained in the opinion, we agree with the trial court's determination that plaintiffs have not stated any cause of action against defendant. . . . we therefore affirm.

FACTS

In the mid-1980s, plaintiffs built a solar home on their property in Los Gatos, after obtaining permits to do so from defendant.

In 1991, defendant acquired a parcel of land that adjoins plaintiffs' property, and defendant placed that land in a Parks Reserve. There is a grove of five or six trees growing on defendant's land. Since 1991, those trees have been growing at the rate of 10 to 15 feet per year. By 2004, the trees were about 100 feet taller than when defendant acquired the land.

In 1997, plaintiffs' solar system began to malfunction because the trees on defendant's land interfered with the sunlight reaching their solar panels. Despite numerous requests from plaintiffs, and notwithstanding verbal promises by "certain officials and certain individuals that this situation would be corrected," defendant did not trim or remove the trees.

PROCEDURAL HISTORY

. . . .

In May 2004, plaintiffs brought this action against defendant. . . . As to their negligence claim, plaintiffs alleged that defendant violated various statutes, including the Solar Shade Control Act.

In July 2004, defendant demurred to the complaint. . . .

. . . .

Following a hearing held in December 2004, the trial court entered its formal order sustaining defendant's demurrer without leave to amend. . . .

This appeal ensued.

. . . .

One essential element of a cause of action for negligence is a legal duty. (*Potter v. Firestone Tire & Rubber Co.* (1993) 6 Cal.4th 965, 984, 25 Cal.Rptr.2d 550, 863 P.2d 795.) "That duty may be imposed by law, be assumed by the defendant, or exist by virtue of a special relationship." (*Id.* at p. 985, 25 Cal.Rptr.2d 550, 863 P.2d 795.) In this case, plaintiffs base their negligence claim on the asserted breach of a statutory duty arising under the Solar Shade Control Act. (See Pub. Res. Code, §§ 25980–25986.)

Governing Substantive Law: The Solar Shade Control Act

"The Solar Shade Control Act . . . provides limited protection to owners of solar collectors from shading caused by trees on adjacent properties." (*Sher v. Leiderman, supra,* 181 Cal.App.3d at p. 880, 226 Cal.Rptr. 698.) Enacted in 1978, the Act has been described as "protecting active or passive solar energy systems (SES's) against obstruction by later-planted or later-grown trees and foliage. . . ." (*Kucera v. Lizza, supra*, 59 Cal.App.4th at p. 1152, 69 Cal.Rptr.2d 582, statutory citation omitted.)

In pertinent part, the Act provides: "After January 1, 1979, no person owning, or in control of a property shall allow a tree or shrub to be placed, or, if placed, to grow on such property, subsequent to the installation of a solar collector on the property of another so as to cast a shadow greater than 10 percent of the collector absorption area" during mid-day hours as specified in the statute. (§ 25982; see generally, 11 Witkin, Summary of Cal. Law, *supra*, Equity, § 137 p. 820.)

The Act permits local jurisdictions to exempt themselves from its operation. The exemption provision states: "Any city, or for unincorporated areas, any county, may adopt, by majority vote of the governing body, an ordinance exempting their jurisdiction from the provisions of this chapter . . ." . . . .

The Parties' Contentions

. . . .

The parties . . . disagree about the statutory exemption. Defendant asserts that it is exempt from the Act, having adopted an ordinance as authorized by section 25985. Plaintiffs argue against application of the exemption here, asserting "that there was already in existence a continuing duty on the part of the County" when it adopted the ordinance and a continuing breach of that duty when plaintiffs' solar system began to fail. Plaintiffs thus contend: "The County should be liable for any of the damages they had already caused." They characterize defendant's use of the exemption provision as "a quasi-ex post facto application on the part of the County." As we understand it, the essence of plaintiffs' argument on this point is that defendant's ordinance offends constitutional principles because it operates retroactively, defeating their preexisting damage claims. Defendant does not specifically meet that contention.

Analysis

As we now explain, plaintiffs' statutory claim cannot be maintained because defendant is exempt from the Solar Shade Control Act by virtue of its adoption of a qualifying ordinance, as permitted by section 25985. Given that determination, we need not address the parties' differing interpretations of other provisions of the Act.

. . . .

In this case, we conclude, the statutory right of action was eliminated by the exemption provision, which operated as a valid repeal method. Here, at the very time that the Legislature created the statutory right of action under the Solar Shade Control Act, it expressly empowered cities and counties to foreclose such actions against them. In this case, once defendant exercised that power, plaintiffs' statutory cause of action was abolished. . . . In short, we conclude, the exemption provision—put in place by the Legislature and adopted by defendant—is a valid mechanism for extinguishing a statutory claim under the Solar Shade Control Act.

To sum up, plaintiffs' statutory cause of action is abolished. Plaintiffs enjoyed no vested rights in this statutory claim, which was unknown at common law, and which was not pursued to final judgment before its elimination by defendant's use of the exemption provision. That exemption operated as a form of repeal when defendant adopted it, extinguishing plaintiffs' statutory right of action. Because the mechanism of repeal was authorized by the Legislature, the elimination of plaintiffs' claim under these circumstances does not implicate retrospectivity concerns. . . . we affirm.

NOTES & QUESTIONS

1.   Suppose that Alejandro and Belinda were next door neighbors living in the same county in California and that the county had not adopted any ordinance exempting it from California's Solar Shade Control Act. In 2009, Alejandro planted a small redwood tree in his backyard. In 2013, Belinda installed a PV solar panel array on her rooftop. At that time, Alejandro's tree was still small and seemed to pose no immediate shading threat to Belinda's panels. By 2018, however, Alejandro's redwood tree had grown so much that it had begun partially shading Belinda's solar panels during much of the year. Noticing that her solar panels were generating less electricity because of the shading, Belinda contacted Alejandro and asked him to cut back his tree to end the shading problem. Alejandro expressed sympathy for Belinda's plight but politely refused to trim back his tree, noting that none of the tree's branches overhung into the airspace above Belinda's property.

a.   Based on the facts above, does Belinda have a valid private nuisance or trespass claim against Alejandro? Why or why not?

b.   Does Belinda have a valid claim against Alejandro under the California's Solar Shade Control Act? Why or why not?

c.   Assume the same facts as above except one: suppose that, in 2014, the original redwood tree died so Alejandro replaced it with another redwood tree of similar size and this new tree was the one causing the shading in 2018. Does this change your answers to part a. or b.? Why or why not?

d.   Assume the same facts as in the original fact pattern above except one: suppose Alejandro had first planted his redwood tree in 2014 rather than 2009. Does this change your answers to part a. or b.? Why or why not?

2.   In what specific way does the *Sher* majority use the distinction between public and private benefits to support its holding that the facts in the case failed to give rise to a private nuisance claim?

3.   Suppose you were legal counsel for the plaintiff in *Sher*. Craft an argument that a public benefit was at stake in the case and therefore your client should be able to bring a nuisance claim.

4.   The court's analysis of the statutory claim in *Sher* turned on interpretation of the term "solar collector". What was the specific type of solar energy strategy at issue in the case? How did the court distinguish that solar energy use from other uses? What was the court's finding as to whether the use at issue constituted a "solar collector", and how did its finding impact the disposition of the case?

5.   In 2017, Tesla Motors announced plans to produce and sell solar PV rooftop shingles. These shingles would serve dual functions: to protect the building rooftops and to generate electric power. Tesla CEO Elon Musk promised that the shingles would cost "less than a traditional roof" after accounting for the value of the electricity they generated. *See* Vikram Aggarwal, *Tesla Roof Challenges Solar Panel Industry*, S.F. CHRON. (June 12, 2017), http://www.sfchronicle.com/opinion/openforum/article/Tesla-roof-challenges-solar-panel-industry-11214679.php. Will these shingles constitute "solar collectors" under California's Solar Shade Control Act? Why or why not? If nearly all new homes in California began using the Tesla solar shingles, how would that influence the impact and reach of the Act?

6.   In *Zipperer*, why was Santa Clara County able to avoid trimming its trees under the Solar Shade Control Act even though the trees were clearly shading the plaintiff's solar energy system? Do you think this is a fair outcome? Why or why not?

7.   *California's Softening of Solar Access Rights.* A strong political backlash following a highly-publicized neighbor dispute led the California

state legislature to amend the Solar Shade Control Act in 2008. The following is a brief summary of how and why legislators opted to amend the statute:

> Prior to its . . . amendment, California's Solar Shade Control Act used a public nuisance approach to protecting solar access. As originally enacted in 1978 . . . [i]f Neighbors violated the Act, Solar Users could sue to enjoin the shading as a public nuisance. Neighbors who were found guilty of violating the original statute could be cited with criminal fines of up to $1,000 per day until they removed the offending vegetation.
>
> Various shortcomings of the Solar Shade Control Act were eliminated by the California state legislature in 2008. Political support for the amendments arose after a highly publicized neighbor dispute involving the Act generated popular criticism toward some of its provisions. In December of 2007, a court convicted a couple of violating California's Solar Shade Control Act by allowing their trees to shade a neighbor's solar panel. After seven years of hearings and $37,000 in legal fees, the couple finally trimmed the trees. Under the amended statute, violators are no longer subject to criminal prosecution on a public nuisance theory and can only be civilly liable—likely in the form of damages . . . rather than injunctive relief . . .

Troy A. Rule, *Shadows on the Cathedral: Solar Access Laws in a Different Light*, 2010 U. ILL. L. REV. 851, 875–76 (2010).

For a more detailed description of the heated neighbor dispute that sparked the amendment and the individuals involved, see Felicity Barringer, *Trees Block Solar Panels, and a Feud Ends in Court*, N.Y. TIMES, Apr. 7, 2008, at A14.

b. Other State Solar Access Statutes

California is certainly not the only state with a solar access statute on the books. For example, as of 2017, at least 15 states had enacted laws expressly recognizing the validity of voluntarily-negotiated solar access easements between neighbors. Under these statutes, a landowner seeking protection against shading must first convince a neighbor to voluntarily agree to grant such an easement, typically in exchange for compensation. Once drafted and executed by the parties, the easement document memorializing the neighbors' agreement is then recorded against title in the real property records like any other easement. For a full listing of state statutes that expressly allow for solar access easements and links to each of those laws, visit http://www.solarresourceguide.org/solar-laws/ (last visited Sept. 23, 2017).

Still other states have enacted statutes that are comparable to California's Solar Shade Control Act in that they provide some level of protection against solar panel shading but are slightly different in various ways. For instance, some statutes go farther than California's Act—which only protects against shading from trees and other vegetation—by statutorily protecting solar energy users against shading from buildings as well. Unfortunately, like many other types of land use restrictions, solar access protection statutes can also impose significant costs on landowners and society by constraining other valuable land uses. Some of the strongest solar access statutes restrict uses of the airspace just above neighbors' property in ways that are arguably not always justifiable. The excerpt below frames solar access conflicts as conflicts over airspace and then describes some of the most controversial state-level strategies for addressing them. Portions of two solar access statutes referenced in the article then follow, along with questions crafted to highlight the perplexing policy tensions associated with these laws.

SHADOWS ON THE CATHEDRAL: SOLAR ACCESS LAWS IN A DIFFERENT LIGHT

Troy A. Rule
2010 U. ILL. L. REV. 851, 861–62, 875–78 & 891–92 (2010)

The legal entitlement at issue in the solar access context is not an entitlement to sunlight itself. Unlike water, oil, gas, or minerals, sunlight is not sufficiently "scarce" to warrant property right protection. On average, the earth receives enough sunlight in one hour to satisfy global energy needs for an entire year. The amount of sunlight reaching a given rooftop would not materially diminish even if solar panels were capturing solar energy from every other rooftop on the planet. Indeed, the non-scarcity of sunlight is largely what makes it such an attractive potential energy source. . . .

In contrast, exclusive *access* to the direct sunlight radiating onto a specific location is scarce. Typically, the surface of only one object may capture direct sunlight in any given location and moment. All items situated behind that object are in its shadow and do not receive direct radiation from the sun. Access to direct sunlight dramatically improves the energy productivity of PV cells and is thus of critical importance in solar energy development.

A landowner can exclude others from trespassing onto its land to shade solar collectors, thereby protecting solar access in some cases, but a landowner's right to exclude ends at the property boundary line with respect to shading. Often, solar panels are situated close enough to southerly property lines and the altitude of the sun at relevant hours of day is sufficiently low that there is a risk of shading by neighbors. A land-owner who is contemplating installing solar collectors thus often demands assurances that neighbors will not position structures or vegetation in their airspace that would shade the collectors. Owners of neighboring properties, however, are usually reluctant to agree to restrict their rights in the airspace above their land without receiving compensation in return.

Because solar access conflicts are ultimately disputes over use of *airspace*, not sunlight, the entitlement [associated with] these conflicts must be defined accordingly. Should landowners who have installed or seek to install solar panels on their property (Solar Users) be legally entitled to an easement or other restriction across their neighbor's airspace to protect solar access? Or, should owners of properties near a Solar User (Neighbors) be entitled to exercise rights in the airspace above their property without liability for shading nearby solar collectors?

. . . .

2.   *Permit-Based Statutes*

Statutes in Massachusetts and Wisconsin authorize municipalities to adopt ordinances under which they can grant "permits" that effectively create solar access easements across properties situated near Solar Users. . . . Permit-based solar access statutes generally prohibit Neighbors from obstructing any solar collectors described in Solar Users' permits. Neighbors have no right to compensation for their consequent loss of airspace rights.

. . . .

3.   *Prior Appropriation-Based Statutes*

[Solar access] statutes in New Mexico and Wyoming purport to use a "first-in-time" rule analogous to the prior appropriation doctrine in water law. . . .

In New Mexico and Wyoming, a landowner can unilaterally acquire solar access rights across Neighbors' airspace, without compensating Neighbors, by being the first to make "beneficial use" of the airspace. A landowner who installs a qualifying solar collector, records a valid solar right instrument or declaration with the county clerk, and satisfies statutory neighbor notice requirements under these statutes acquires "solar rights." Solar rights acquired under these statutes are not rights in sunlight itself or in some other scarce resource for which private property rights did not previously exist. The New Mexico and Wyoming statutes define a "solar right" as a property right "to an unobstructed line-of-sight path from a solar collector to the sun, which permits radiation from the sun to impinge directly on the solar collector." In essence, a solar right is an easement across a Neighbor's airspace for the specified purpose of solar access. New Mexico's statute even has language requiring that a solar right "be considered an easement appurtenant."

In solar access disputes in New Mexico and Wyoming, "priority in time" supposedly "[has] the better right." Unfortunately, solar access conflicts are rarely disputes over competing solar access easements in which one Solar User erects a solar collector in the solar access path of another Solar User. Instead, such disputes are almost always between Solar Users seeking to obtain or enforce solar access rights and Neighbors with no interest in installing solar collectors who seek only to preserve existing airspace rights. In nearly every circumstance, Neighbors were "first-in-time" with respect to the [airspace involved] because they hold title to the surface estate directly below the airspace at issue. Although the New Mexico and Wyoming statutes are a well-intended effort to innovatively promote solar access, they ignore Neighbors' existing airspace rights and misapply the prior appropriation doctrine. The statutes seem based on the presumption that neither Solar Users nor their Neighbors already possess rights in the airspace at issue. In truth, Neighbors of Solar Users do hold such rights under common law.

The New Mexico and Wyoming statutes are not the first-in-time rules they purport to be, but they do adjust or reallocate existing property rights among landowners based on priority in time of use. They can thus generate many of the same unintended consequences associated with first-in-time rules. California's Solar Shade Control Act and the Wisconsin and Massachusetts permit-based solar access statutes are like the New Mexico and Wyoming statutes in this regard. All of these statutes enable Solar Users to unilaterally acquire rights in or impose restrictions on Neighbors' airspace, but *only to the extent* that the airspace is not already occupied. Such approaches promote solar energy development by motivating Solar Users to install solar collectors quickly before Neighbors make use of the airspace needed for solar access. They may also, however, encourage opportunistic landowners to install solar panels with ulterior motives of acquiring a view easement across Neighbors' property or of preventing or delaying Neighbors' more productive uses. The rules might also motivate Neighbors to overdevelop their properties with trees or structures to avoid forfeiting their airspace rights to new Solar Users. Because they impose individualized burdens based on the needs of individual private landowners and without compensation, the rules are also more vulnerable to constitutional challenge.

. . . .

[4. *The Iowa Approach*]

In Iowa, prospective Solar Users have the right to acquire solar access easements from Neighbors at market value when voluntary bargaining proves unsuccessful. An Iowa landowner wishing to install solar collectors applies to a locally designated "solar access regulatory board" for an order granting a solar access easement. The easement application requires, among other things, legal descriptions of the dominant and servient estates and proposed easement area, names and addresses of the affected

Neighbors, and descriptions of the type, size, and proposed location of the solar collector. By requiring applicants to gather and provide the information relevant to the proposed easement, the statute helps to minimize the administrative burden imposed on local governments.

Iowa's solar access application also requires applicants to make certain affirmative statements aimed at minimizing abuses of the statute. For example, a statement by the applicant certifying that the solar collector's location and design reasonably minimize impacts on Neighbors' rights helps to deter requests for excessively broad easements. Similarly, a required statement affirming that the applicant has endeavored and failed to negotiate voluntary solar access easements with Neighbors encourages landowners to attempt voluntary Coasean bargaining before seeking government intervention.

Solar access regulatory boards in Iowa hold a hearing on each solar easement application, with notice to affected landowners, verifying among other things that the proposed easement has been tailored to minimize the impact on Neighbors and does not impair Neighbors' preexisting construction plans. Whenever the board enters an order authorizing the grant of a solar access easement, it must "determine the compensation that may be awarded to the servient estate owner if the solar access easement is granted." By requiring Neighbor compensation, the Iowa statute acknowledges Neighbors' entitlement to their airspace rights. . . .

SOLAR RIGHTS ACT (NEW MEXICO)
N.M. STAT. ANN. §§ 47–3–1–12 (West 2007)

§ 47–3–1.   Short title

Sections 47–3–1 through 47–3–5 NMSA 1978 may be cited as the "Solar Rights Act".

§ 47–3–2.   Declaration and findings

The legislature declares that the state of New Mexico recognizes that economic benefits can be derived for the people of the state from the use of solar energy. Operations, research, experimentation and development in the field of solar energy use shall therefore be encouraged. While recognizing the value of research and development of solar energy use techniques and devices by governmental agencies, the legislature finds and declares that the actual construction and use of solar devices, whether at public or private expense, is properly a commercial activity which the law should encourage to be carried out, whenever practicable, by private enterprise.

§ 47–3–3.   Definitions

As used in the Solar Rights Act:

A.   "solar collector" means a device, substance or element, or a combination of devices, substances or elements, that relies upon sunshine as an energy source and that is capable of collecting not less than twenty-five thousand British thermal units on a clear winter solstice day or that is used for the conveyance of light to the interior of a building. The term also includes any device, substance or element that collects solar energy for use in:

(1)   the heating or cooling of a structure or building;

(2)   the heating or pumping of water;

(3)   industrial, commercial or agricultural processes; or

(4)   the generation of electricity.

A solar collector may be used for purposes in addition to the collection of solar energy. These uses include, but are not limited to, serving as a structural member or part of a roof of a building or structure and serving as a window or wall; and

B.   "solar right" means a right to an unobstructed line-of-sight path from a solar collector to the sun, which permits radiation from the sun to impinge directly on the solar collector.

§ 47–3–4.   Declaration of solar rights

A.   The legislature declares that the right to use the natural resource of solar energy is a property right, the exercise of which is to be encouraged and regulated by the laws of this state. Such property right shall be known as a solar right.

B.   The following concepts shall be applicable to the regulation of disputes over the use of solar energy where practicable:

(1)   "beneficial use." Beneficial use shall be the basis, the measure and the limit of the solar right, except as otherwise provided by written contract. If the amount of solar energy which a solar collector user can beneficially use varies with the season of the year, then the extent of the solar right shall vary likewise;

(2)   "prior appropriation." In disputes involving solar rights, priority in time shall have the better right except that the state and its political subdivisions may legislate, or ordain that a solar collector user has a solar right even though a structure or building located on neighborhood property blocks the sunshine from the proposed solar collector site.

Nothing in this paragraph shall be construed to diminish in any way the right of eminent domain of the state or any of its political subdivisions or any other entity that currently has such a right; and

(3) "transferability." Solar rights shall be freely transferable within the bounds of such regulation as the legislature may impose. The transfer of a solar right shall be recorded in accordance with Chapter 14, Article 9 NMSA 1978.

C. Unless a singular overriding state concerns occur which significantly affect the health and welfare of the citizens of this state, permit systems for the use and application of solar energy shall reside with county and municipal zoning authorities. . .

§ 47–3–5.   Prior rights unaffected

Nothing in the Solar Rights Act shall be construed to alter, amend, deny, impair or modify any solar right, lease, easement or contract right which has vested prior to the effective date of the Solar Rights Act.

ACCESS TO SOLAR ENERGY (IOWA)
IOWA CODE ANN. §§ 564a.1–9 (1981)

564A.1. Purpose

It is the purpose of this chapter to facilitate the orderly development and use of solar energy by establishing and providing certain procedures for obtaining access to solar energy.

564A.2. Definitions

As used in this chapter, unless the context otherwise requires:

1. "Development of property" means construction, landscaping, growth of vegetation, or other alteration of property that interferes with the operation of a solar collector.

2. "Dominant estate" means that parcel of land to which the benefits of a solar access easement attach.

3. "Servient estate" means land burdened by a solar access easement, other than the dominant estate.

4. "Solar access easement" means an easement recorded under section 564A.7, the purpose of which is to provide continued access to incident sunlight necessary to operate a solar collector.

5. "Solar access regulatory board" means the board designated by a city council or county board of supervisors under section 564A.3 to receive and act on applications for a solar access easement or in the absence of a specific designation, the district court having jurisdiction in the area where the dominant estate is located. Notwithstanding chapter 602 the jurisdiction

of the district court established in this subsection may be exercised by district associate judges.

6. "Solar collector" means a device or structural feature of a building that collects solar energy and that is part of a system for the collection, storage, and distribution of solar energy. For purposes of this chapter, a greenhouse is a solar collector.

7. "Solar energy" means energy emitted from the sun and collected in the form of heat or light by a solar collector.

564A.3. Designation

The city council or the county board of supervisors may designate a solar access regulatory board to receive and act on applications for a solar access easement. The board designated by the city council may be a board of adjustment having jurisdiction in the city, the city council itself, or any board with at least three members. The board designated by the county board of supervisors may be a board of adjustment having jurisdiction in the county, the board of supervisors itself, or any other board with at least three members. The jurisdiction of a board designated by the city council extends to applications when the dominant estate is located in the city. The jurisdiction of a board designated by the county board of supervisors extends to applications when the dominant estate is located in the county but outside the city limits of a city. In the absence of the designation of a specific board under this section, the district court having jurisdiction in the area where the dominant estate is located shall receive and act on applications submitted under section 564A.4 and to that extent shall serve as the solar access regulatory board for purposes of this chapter. . . .

564A.4. Application for solar access easement

1. An owner of property may apply to the solar access regulatory board designated under section 564A.3 for an order granting a solar access easement. The application must be filed before installation or construction of the solar collector. The application shall state the following:

a. A statement of the need for the solar access easement by the owner of the dominant estate.

b. A legal description of the dominant and servient estates.

c. The name and address of the dominant and servient estate owners of record.

d. A description of the solar collector to be used.

e. The size and location of the collector, including heights, its orientation with respect to south, and its slope from the horizontal shown either by drawings or in words.

f.   An explanation of how the applicant has done everything reasonable, taking cost and efficiency into account, to design and locate the collector in a manner to minimize the impact on development of servient estates.

g.   A legal description of the solar access easement which is sought and a drawing that is a spatial representation of the area of the servient estate burdened by the easement illustrating the degrees of the vertical and horizontal angles through which the easement extends over the burdened property and the points from which those angles are measured.

h.   A statement that the applicant has attempted to voluntarily negotiate a solar access easement with the owner of the servient estate and has been unsuccessful in obtaining the easement voluntarily.

i.   A statement that the space to be burdened by the solar access easement is not obstructed at the time of filing of the application by anything other than vegetation that would shade the solar collector.

2.   Upon receipt of the application the solar access regulatory board shall determine whether the application is complete and contains the information required under subsection 1. The board may return an application for correction of any deficiencies. Upon acceptance of an application the board shall schedule a hearing. The board shall cause a copy of the application and a notice of the hearing to be served upon the owners of the servient estates in the manner provided for service of original notice and at least twenty days prior to the date of the hearing. The notice shall state that the solar access regulatory board will determine whether and to what extent a solar access easement will be granted, that the board will determine the compensation that may be awarded to the servient estate owner if the solar access easement is granted and that the servient estate owner has the right to contest the application before the board.

3.   The applicant shall pay all costs incurred by the solar access regulatory board in copying and mailing the application and notice.

4.   An application for a solar access easement submitted to the district court acting as the solar access regulatory board under this chapter is not subject to the small claims procedures under chapter 631.

564A.5. Decision

1.   After the hearing on the application, the solar access regulatory board shall determine whether to issue an order granting a solar access easement. The board shall grant a solar access easement if the board finds that there is a need for the solar collector, that the space burdened by the easement was not obstructed by anything except vegetation that would shade the solar collector at the time of filing of the application, that the proposed location of the collector minimizes the impact of the easement on

the development of the servient estate and that the applicant tried and failed to negotiate a voluntary easement. However, the board may refuse to grant a solar access easement upon a finding that the easement would require the removal of trees that provide shade or a windbreak to a residence on the servient estate. The board shall not grant a solar access easement upon a servient estate if the board finds that the owner, at least six months prior to the filing of the application, has made a substantial financial commitment to build a structure that will shade the solar collector. In issuing its order granting the solar access easement, the board may modify the solar access easement applied for and impose conditions on the location of the solar collector that will minimize the impact upon the servient estate.

. . . .

3.   The solar access regulatory board shall determine the amount of compensation that is to be paid to the owners of the servient estate for the impairment of the right to develop the property. Compensation shall be based on the difference between the fair market value of the property prior to and after granting the solar access easement. The parties shall be notified of the board's decision within thirty days of the date of the hearing. The owner of the dominant estate shall have thirty days from the date of notification of the board's decision to deposit the compensation with the board. Upon receipt of the compensation, the board shall issue an order granting the solar access easement to the owner of the dominant estate and remit the compensation awarded to the owners of the servient estate. The owner of the dominant estate may decline to deposit the compensation with the board, and no order granting the solar access easement shall then be issued.

4.   When the order granting the solar access easement is issued, the owner of the dominant estate shall have it recorded in the office of the county recorder who shall record the solar access easement and list the owner of the dominant estate as grantee and the owner of the servient estate as grantor in the deed index. The solar access easement after being recorded shall be considered an easement appurtenant in or on the servient estate.

QUESTIONS

1.   According to the excerpt above, why does sunlight itself arguably *not* warrant any property protection? What other scarce natural resource (rather than sunlight) is truly at stake in neighbor disputes over solar access?

2.   The relevance of the *ad coelum* rule in solar access conflicts was discussed earlier in this Chapter. Based on the *ad coelum* rule, which party

already holds a property interest in the airspace typically at issue in a neighbor dispute over the shading of solar panels: the solar user or the neighbor? Why?

3.   New Mexico's Solar Rights Act treats "solar rights" as akin to water rights. What water rights doctrine does New Mexico's Act attempt to apply to solar rights? Do you think this approach is an effective one? Why or why not? What are some potentially important differences between solar resources and water resources that warrant tailoring separate policies to specifically govern each of these resources?

4.   From the perspective of solar energy users and their neighbors, what is the most important difference between New Mexico's Solar Rights Act and Iowa's solar access statute? Why? Which statutory approach do you think is superior, and why?

3. LOCAL SOLAR ACCESS ORDINANCES

Although most municipalities have no solar access ordinance, a handful of municipal governments across the country have adopted local laws to govern solar access issues. Some local solar access ordinances mirror the state statutes described above by establishing new causes of action for solar panel shading. Others, however, take a different approach and impose land use controls to prevent solar access conflicts before they even arise. For instance, a handful of municipalities in the United States have adopted ordinances designed to ensure that all homes in new residential subdivisions have direct sunlight access and are therefore ready to host solar energy systems if the homeowners ever decide to install them. The City of Eugene, Oregon, is one locality that has embraced this approach. Portions of Eugene's solar setback ordinance are excerpted below, followed by a case interpreting a similar but more complicated solar setback ordinance adopted in Ashland, Oregon.

SOLAR STANDARDS (EUGENE, OREGON)
EUGENE CITY CODE §§ 9.2780 & 9.2795 (2015)

9.2780   Purpose of Solar Standards.

Solar standards are utilized to create lot divisions, layouts and building configurations to help preserve the availability of solar energy to one and two family dwellings.

9.2795   Solar Setback Standards.

(1) **Applicability.** These standards apply to all structures on R–1 and R–2 zoned lots, 4000 square feet or greater, with a minimum north-south dimension of 75 feet.

(2) **Solar Setback Requirements.** Buildings shall be setback from the northern property line according to the standards in this section. An applicant for a development permit for a building subject to this

section shall submit verification on a form approved by the city manager that shows either the solar setback or how the structure qualifies for an exemption. . .

(3) Exemptions to Solar Setback Requirements. A building is exempt from the solar setback standards when any of the following conditions exist:

(a) <u>Slopes</u>. The lot on which the building is located has an average slope of 20 percent or more in a direction greater than 45 degrees east or west of true north.

(b) <u>Existing Shade</u>. The building will shade an area that is already shaded by one or more of the following:

    1.   An existing or approved building or structure.

    2.   A topographic feature.

    3.   Coniferous trees or broadleaf evergreens that will remain after development of the site.

(c) <u>Insignificant Benefit</u>. The building will shade one or more of the following:

    1.   A non-developable area, such as designated open space, a public utility easement, street or alley.

    2.   The wall of an unheated space, such as a garage, excluding solar greenhouses and other similar solar structures.

    3.   The wall of a non-residential structure.

    . . . .

(d) <u>Neighbor Approval.</u> The owner of the abutting property to the north, for which a certificate of occupancy has been issued by the city, grants an exemption to the solar setback requirement on a form supplied by the city and subject to a fee set by the city manager.

SULLIVAN V. CITY OF ASHLAND

Court of Appeals of Oregon, 1994
130 Or.App. 480

HASELTON, J.

Petitioner City of Ashland (city) seeks review of [the Land Use Board of Appeals' (LUBAs')] remand of the city's determination of the "northern lot line" of certain property for purposes of the city's solar access ordinance. We reverse.

In 1993, respondent Sullivan's neighbor, Johnson, applied to the city for a permit to build a home on land south of Sullivan's property. In greatly simplified form, the Sullivan and Johnson properties, with the projected home site, were situated like this:[2]

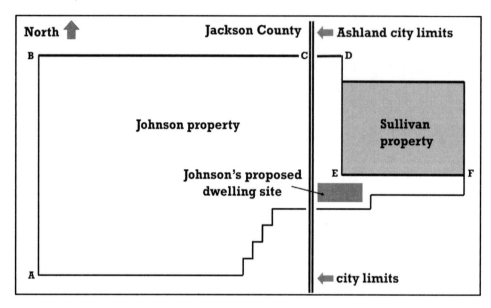

After the city's planning staff and planning commission approved Johnson's application, Sullivan appealed to the city council, arguing that the proposed structure did not conform to the setback requirements of Ashland's land use ordinance (LUO), with particular reference to the ordinance's solar access chapter. Under Ashland's solar access provisions, structures are required to be set back relative, in part, to a northern lot line. Sullivan asserted, in particular, that the staff and planning commission had incorrectly identified line "BCD" in the above illustration, rather than line "EF," as the operative "northern lot line" and had, thus, erroneously deprived her of part of her southern solar access.

Two provisions of Ashland's solar access chapter were especially pertinent to Sullivan's argument. Ashland's LUO 18.70.010 provides:

"The purpose of the Solar Access Chapter is to provide protection of a reasonable amount of sunlight from shade from structures and vegetation whenever feasible to all parcels in the city to preserve the economic value of solar radiation falling on

---

[2] The original diagram was not printable. This diagram is the author's own re-creation of the original.

structures, investments in solar energy systems, and the options for future uses of solar energy."

LUO 18.70.020.D, which defines "northern lot line," reads as follows:

"Any lot line or lines less than forty-five (45) degrees southeast or southwest of a line drawn east-west *and intersecting the northernmost point of the lot.* If the northern lot line adjoins any unbuildable area (*e.g.,* street, alley, public right-of-way, parking lot, or common area) other than a required yard area, the northern lot line shall be that portion of the northerly edge of the unbuildable area which is due north from the actual northern edge of the applicant's property." (Emphasis supplied.)

Before the city council, Sullivan did *not* argue that LUO 18.70.020.D was somehow ambiguous; *i.e.,* that its plain language could ever be interpreted in such a way that line "EF" could be a northern lot line. Instead, Sullivan argued that rote application of LUO 18.70.020.D in this case would, in her view, yield a result contradicting the policies expressed in LUO 18.70.010. Consequently, she reasoned, the former should give way to the latter, and line "EF" should be designated as the northern lot line most consistent with the solar access chapter's policies.

The city council rejected Sullivan's arguments:

"We specifically find that the northern lot line, as defined in [LUO] 18.70.020 D, is that lot line at the northernmost point of the lot or line BD * * *. We find that there is only one such northern lot line, and that the Staff used that line in the determination of the solar access calculations for the issuance of the building permit.

"* * * *

"It makes more sense, opponents would argue, to use line EF in the above diagram. Again, we find that staff made a correct determination. * * * We interpret the ordinance to not allow any discretion in the determination of the northern lot line. Line EF or any other line than the one staff determined to be correct cannot be the northern lot line applying the clear and objective standards of the ordinance.

"* * * [T]he intent and purpose of the solar access chapter as expressed in section 18.70.010 does not amend the unambiguous provisions of that chapter."

. . . .

On appeal, LUBA remanded, holding that the city's determination of the northern lot line lacked the "necessary interpretative findings." LUBA's remand turned on two premises. First, LUBA held that LUO 18.70.020.D is susceptible to an interpretation under which line "EF" could be a northern lot line:

> "[A]s petitioner points out, line 'EF' could also be considered a northern lot line, under the above quoted definition. While the LUO 18.70.020.D definition recognizes there can be more than one northern lot line on any given piece of property, the challenged decision simply contains a conclusory statement that 'there is only one such northern lot line [referring to line BD].' "

Second, given that "ambiguity," the city was obliged to interpret LUO 18.70.020.D by reference to the general purposes of the solar access ordinance, as set out in LUO 18.70.010:

> "Because it is unclear what lines constitute the northern lot line under LUO 18.70.020.D, it is appropriate to look to the purposes of the solar access ordinance * * * .
>
> "* * * *
>
> "Clearly, the purpose of the solar access ordinance is to protect solar access. The solar access setbacks are designed to protect a lot's southern exposure by requiring setbacks from northern lot lines. In view of this purpose for the city solar access ordinance and the ambiguous language of LUO 18.70.020.D, we remand the challenged decision for the city to supply the necessary interpretative findings. The city must either explain why it does not consider line EF to be a northern lot line or recalculate the subject property's northern lot lines to include line EF. * * *"

Both of LUBA's premises were wrong. There is no "possible, rational" application of LUO 18.070.020.D by which line "EF" could be a northern lot line.... This is a matter of simple and inalterable geometry. LUO 18.70.020.D requires that a northern lot line intersect "the northernmost point of the lot" at an angle of 45 degrees or less. As the city found, line "EF" does not intersect the northernmost point of Johnson's property *at all*. Only line "BCD" satisfies that express definitional requirement.

. . . .

Reversed and remanded.

NOTES & QUESTIONS

1.   Why do solar setback ordinances in the United States (including those in Eugene and Ashland) typically measure shade-based setback lines from the northern property line, rather than the southern property line? How, if at all, would you expect such ordinances to be different if adopted in Australia? Why?

2. Why do you think Eugene's solar setback ordinance allows for exceptions in some instances based on the steepness and direction of the slope on the lot where a new building is proposed?

3. Only a small handful of localities have ever adopted solar access-based setbacks. In the minds of many rooftop solar energy advocates, such setbacks can seem appealing because they effectively reserve space on each new residential rooftop for a future solar energy installation. On the other hand, these setbacks can also significantly constrain other uses of land and the space directly above it. The following excerpt elaborates on this point:

> At first blush, shade-based setbacks are appealing. . . . The rules apply uniformly within a given zone, like any ordinary setback or height restriction. They may also be less administratively burdensome . . . and may provide greater certainty to landowners.
>
> Nevertheless, statutes that impose shade-based setbacks on all properties within an area—not just those situated near solar panels—are probably not cost justified. . . . Less than 0.5% of residential rooftops in the United States presently hold solar panels. Thus, more than 99% of the time, Solar Users that [benefit] under these statutes do not exist. Until rooftop solar systems become far more prevalent, it seems a dubious presumption that the solar access protected under broad shade-based setbacks is of greater social benefit than the endless number of other legal uses of airspace within a jurisdiction that are prohibited by the setbacks.

Troy A. Rule, *Shadows on the Cathedral: Solar Access Laws in a Different Light*, 2010 U. ILL. L. REV. 851, 879–80 (2010).

The argument in the excerpt above hinges on the fact that only a small fraction of the nation's homeowners presently own or lease rooftop solar panels. Suppose you were a solar energy advocate and were lobbying for a shade-based setback ordinance in a major city. Craft a detailed response to the excerpted, arguing that shade-based setback requirements are a cost-justifiable and worthy policy strategy.

4. How do the Eugene solar setback ordinance's "Existing Shade" exceptions and "Neighbor Approval" section help to mitigate the concerns expressed in the quote in Problem 3 above?

5. Do you think the *Sullivan* court applied Ashland's solar setbacks ordinance in the way that was most consistent with the purposes of the ordinance? Why or why not?

6. Based on your reading of *Sullivan* above, how (if at all) would you recommend that the city of Ashland amend its solar setbacks ordinance?

7. *Other Solar Zoning Ordinances.* A handful of local ordinances in the United States go beyond imposing solar setbacks in their efforts to limit solar access conflicts in urban and suburban neighborhoods. The following excerpt

by Professor Sara Bronin highlights some of these other types of solar zoning ordinances:

> At their most basic . . . solar zoning ordinances could limit heights, restrict lot sizes, establish setback requirements . . . and create other rules that would facilitate solar access. . . . Perhaps the most sophisticated solar zoning ordinance in this country governs construction in Boulder, Colorado, which has created a system of "solar envelopes" and "solar fences," each of which function differently in different neighborhoods. The solar envelope . . . delineates a three-dimensional space over a parcel beyond which no construction or vegetation can occur without illegally interfering with the solar rights of neighbors. The solar fence represents a vertical plane along a property line that casts an imaginary shadow that cannot be exceeded in length by the shadows cast by any building or tree on the neighboring property. The Boulder solar ordinance divides the city into three zones, governed by area-wide rules establishing various solar envelope, solar fence, and other requirements. . . .

Sara C. Bronin, *Solar Rights*, 89 B.U.L. REV. 1217, 1246–47 (2009).

B. SOLAR RIGHTS LAWS

In addition to weighing the risk that a building or tree on neighboring property might shade their solar panels, landowners in urban and suburban settings must also consider whether installing a solar array on their property would violate applicable land use restrictions. Some municipal land use ordinances aggressively restrict solar panel installations within certain areas of town or heavily regulate where landowners may install solar panels on their land. Some private homeowners' associations across the country have also recorded Covenants, Conditions and Restrictions (CC&Rs) that regulate the location, visibility or appearance of solar energy systems. *Solar rights laws* are statutes that preempt or invalidate private or municipal restrictions on distributed solar energy development.

1. SOLAR RIGHTS VERSUS MUNICIPAL LAND USE RESTRICTIONS

Concerned that local governments will use land use controls to excessively restrict solar energy development, a handful of state legislatures have enacted solar rights statutes that preempt certain municipal restrictions on solar energy. For example, under one California statute:

> [a] city or county may not deny an application for a use permit to install a solar energy system unless it makes written findings based upon substantial evidence in the record that the proposed

installation would have a specific, adverse impact upon the public health or safety, and there is no feasible method to satisfactorily mitigate or avoid the specific, adverse impact.

CAL. HEALTH & SAFETY CODE § 17959.1(b) (West 2017). A similar statute in Nevada provides more detailed guidance to courts and stakeholders, preempting any municipal restriction on solar energy installations "which decreases the efficiency or performance of the system by more than 10 percent of the amount that was originally specified for the system." NEV. REV. STAT. § 278.0208 (2011).

In other states, however, the scope of state-level preemption of local restrictions on solar energy is less clear. The *Babb* case below illustrates how state and local laws can clash in the context of permit approvals for distributed solar energy systems in jurisdictions where there is no state-level preemption statute. When reading the *Babb* case, keep in mind that, in most municipalities (including the one in the case), citizens and business must first secure development permit approvals through their municipality's Planning and Zoning Commission. Then, they must separately get approval from the municipality's legislative body (the "Board of Aldermen" in this case) to receive their final permit.

BABB V. MISSOURI PUBLIC SERVICE COMM'N

Missouri Court of Appeals, W.D., 2013
414 S.W.3d 64

WITT, J.

The Board of Aldermen ("Board") for Clarkson Valley, Missouri ("City," collectively including the Board), denied the application of James and Frances Babb ("the Babbs") for a Special Use Permit ("SUP") for the installation of a solar energy system ("system") on their home. The Board denied the Babbs' application based on an ordinance addressing solar energy systems. The Babbs, along with the Missouri Solar Energy Industries Association ("MOSEIA"), filed suit alleging *inter alia* that the City's ordinance was preempted by the State's permissive regulations on renewable energy, specifically the "Electric Utility Renewable Energy Standard Requirements," 4 CSR 240–20.100. . . . The trial court granted partial summary judgment . . . based upon a finding that the City's ordinance regulating the grant of an SUP to the Babbs was preempted by the State's statutes and regulations and the ordinance was thus void. . . . Later, the Babbs . . . received an appealable final judgment. This appeal by the City follows.

In its . . . appeal, the City argues that the trial court erred in granting summary judgment because . . . the City's building ordinances do not actually conflict with the State's statutes and regulations. . . .

We affirm.

Factual and Procedural Background

In November of 2008, pursuant to an initiative petition, the voters of Missouri adopted Proposition C, the Missouri Clean Energy Initiative, which adopted, among other provisions the "Renewable Energy Standard" found in sections 393.1020–393.1030. Proposition C mandated that 15 percent of the electricity produced by Missouri investor-owned utilities come from renewable energy sources by the year 2021, with 2 percent of that coming from solar photovoltaics. Pursuant to Proposition C, the Public Service Commission ("PSC") in conjunction with the Department of Natural Resources ("DNR") adopted regulations regarding renewable energy sources. . . . Two regulations govern various aspects of how Missouri residents can utilize renewable energy, including solar, wind and other listed forms of renewable energy. . . . One governs how renewable energy systems are to be designed and approved for use. 4 CSR 240–20.065. The other governs how residents and electric utilities are able to receive credits on their electricity bills and Renewable Energy Tax Credits ("RECs"). . . .

After the passage of Proposition C, the Babbs began working on a plan to install a solar energy power system for their home. They completed an extensive application process as outlined in 4 CSR 240–20.065 and submitted it to the PSC and the local investor-owned utility company, Missouri Ameren ("Ameren"). Ameren approved the plan on October 12, 2011. On November 1, 2011, the Babbs submitted an application to the City for a building permit to construct the system. The original plan called for the installation of one hundred solar energy panels on the roof of their home. Although there were other homes that included solar energy panels within the City, the Babbs' plan called for more panels than anyone else had previously constructed. The plan, however, complied with the City's ordinances that were in effect at the time the plan was submitted in that "there were no requirements therein with respect to the installation or operation of solar energy systems at residential single-family dwellings." The same day that the Babbs' application for a building permit was filed, the City imposed a moratorium on the construction of solar energy systems within the City. From the record it is unclear which came first: the filing of the application or the adoption of the moratorium.

On January 3, 2012, while the Babbs' building permit application was pending but the moratorium was in effect, the Board adopted two new ordinances. The first changed the type of permit needed for solar energy systems from a building permit that the City's Planning and Zoning Commission ("P & Z") is authorized to issue, to an SUP that would require the final approval by the Board. . . . The second ordinance specifically addressed the requirements for installation of solar energy panels on or adjacent to a residence. . . . Upon learning that the type of permit required to construct the system had been changed, the Babbs filed an application for an SUP on January 5, 2012. On January 31, 2012, the local fire department, the Monarch Fire Department, approved the plans as required by the ordinance.

On February 3, 2012, the P & Z held a public hearing specifically on the Babbs' SUP application. Following the hearing, pursuant to concerns raised by the P & Z and the public, the Babbs modified the plan to reduce the number of solar panels on the roof of the residence from one hundred to forty-two. In conjunction with lessening the number of rooftop panels, the Babbs agreed to install the remaining panels on stand-alone poles on the ground on their property adjacent to their residence. At the conclusion of the hearing, the P & Z held a vote and it was indicated that the P & Z would recommend the Babbs' plan be approved if the number of roof-top panels were reduced as had been discussed. The Babbs then submitted a revised plan and revised SUP application consistent with their representations to the P & Z. Subsequently, the P & Z voted to recommend approval of the revised plan and the granting of an SUP. Shortly thereafter, but prior to final determination by the Board, on February 9, 2012, the Babbs signed a contract with Ameren to construct the system.

After the P & Z recommended approving the Babbs' plan, the Board held a meeting at which they reviewed the Babbs' SUP application. The Board voted 6–0 to deny the permit. The Board did not set forth the reasons for that denial.

The Babbs filed suit in the Circuit Court of Cole County alleging that the city ordinance was void by preemption because its proscriptions, as applied, prohibited the building of any rooftop solar energy system as permitted in the regulations and encouraged by the Missouri Renewable Energy Act of 2008. Their . . . petition sought a declaratory judgment against the PSC, the Board and City. Count I sought declaratory judgment that the City ordinance was in conflict with the statute and regulations and therefore void. . . .

One month after filing its petition, the Babbs moved for partial summary judgment. . . . On June 29, 2012, the trial court granted partial summary judgment. . . . The trial court ordered the City to issue a permit within one day of the court's order, and failing to do so, ordered that construction of the system could commence without a permit.

The City did not issue the permit, so the Babbs began construction without waiting for the judgment to become final. In November 2012, the Babbs completed construction of their solar energy system and also amended their petition, with leave of court. . . . On April 15, 2013, the trial court entered a final judgment that finalized its previous partial summary judgment. The City brings this appeal.

. . . .

. . . [T]he City argues that the trial court erred in granting summary judgment based on preemption because the ordinances do not conflict with the state statutes and regulations. It contends that its ordinances are merely regulatory, not prohibitive, such that there is no actual conflict. . . .

"A municipality derives its governmental powers from the state and exercises generally only such governmental functions as are expressly or impliedly granted it by the state." *City of Dellwood v. Twyford*, 912 S.W.2d 58, 59 (Mo. banc 1995) (citation omitted). A municipal ordinance that conflicts with the general law of the state is void. *Id.* (citing *Morrow v. City of Kansas City*, 788 S.W.2d 278, 281 (Mo. banc 1990)). A municipal ordinance must be in harmony with the general law of the state upon the same subject; otherwise, it is void. . . .

The Babbs argue that the state has preempted this area of regulation and therefore the City cannot further regulate solar power systems. . . . The Babbs argue that the state statutes and regulations preempt the ordinances because "the ordinances are inconsistent with and present an irreconcilable conflict with what is allowed by the PSC rule." The Babbs do not point to any express language in either the statute or regulation that expressly preempts local ordinances with regard to solar energy systems generated by a utility customer, and in fact the regulations on their face anticipate some authority by local entities to regulate various aspects of the systems. Thus, because there is no express language regarding preemption, we must review to see if the City's ordinance is in conflict with the state statutes and regulations.

. . . "If a local law either prohibits what state law allows, or allows what state law prohibits, then a local law is in conflict with the state law and, therefore, preempted." *Borron v. Farrenkopf*, 5 S.W.3d 618, 622 (Mo. App. W.D.1999) (citations omitted).

However, while preemption forbids a *conflict* with state law, it does not prohibit *additional regulations* by the locality. *State ex rel. Hewlett v. Womach*, 355 Mo. 486, 196 S.W.2d 809, 815 (1946). "The fact that an ordinance enlarges upon the provisions of a statute by requiring more than the statute requires creates no conflict therewith, unless the statute limits the requirements for all cases to its own prescriptions." *Id.* at 815 (citation omitted). When an ordinance simply adds to the statute, absent express language in the statute prohibiting such additional requirements, the ordinance is valid. *Id.* . . . .

Neither party questions the validity of the applicable state statute or state regulations. Therefore, we must compare the plain meaning of the applicable statutes and state regulations to the municipal ordinances to determine whether the ordinances are preempted or in conflict.

A. Statute Governing the Regulations

The state regulations at issue were promulgated under the authority of the Net Metering and Easy Connection Act, codified at section 386.890. . . .

. . . .

Notably, the statute requires that the system "meet all applicable safety, performance, interconnection, and reliability standards established by any local *code* authorities" and that the plans be approved by the "retail electric supplier." . . . .

B. Regulations Governing Customer-Generated Solar Energy Systems

Pursuant to the authority of the statute, two applicable state regulations that govern customer-generated solar energy systems have been adopted. . . . [T]he first establishes the process of how such systems are to be constructed while the second establishes how those systems can produce energy tax credits and rebates. The latter cross-references the former because the rebate legislation was adopted apparently to encourage the use of such systems.

The regulatory language of both regulations follows that of the statute. The PSC requires that the electric utility to which the private system will attach approve the plans and specifications of each proposed system. The first regulation, 4 CSR 240–20.065, implements the Net Metering and Easy Connection Act (section 386.890) and states, in relevant part, that:

> Each qualified electric energy generation unit used by a customer-generator shall meet *all applicable safety, performance, interconnection, and reliability standards established by any local code authorities*. . . .

4 CSR 240–20.065(6)(A) (emphasis added).

. . . .

The City points to language in one of three definitional sections that indicates a customer-generator system should meet "all applicable safety, performance, interconnection and reliability standards established by . . . *any local governing authorities*." 4 CSR 240–20.065(1)(C)6 (emphasis added). The City contends that this is a clear affirmation of its police power and argues that the statutory and regulatory schemes "expressly permit" the City to impose its own building and zoning code onto all customer-generated energy systems in addition to their regulation by the State. While this language does give some support for the City's position, we still must review the ordinance to see if it conflicts with the provisions of the statutes and regulations.

C. Local Ordinance Adds Prohibitive Restrictions

A portion of the new ordinance, section 500.020–M2300, "Solar Energy Systems," of the municipal code provides, in relevant part, that:

> C.2. Roof Mounted Solar Energy Systems shall be parallel to the plain [sic] of the roof and shall not extend more than six inches above the roof surface.

> C.3. A roof mounted system shall terminate at least three feet from the edge or ridge of the roof and one and one half feet from any valley.

In addition to these design specifications, the ordinance contains three pages of "General Requirements" for solar energy systems. . . . the Babbs point to no provisions that specifically conflict with the statutes or regulations. While it may be that some of these provisions either individually or in concert may be "inconsistent and irreconcilable" with the requirements of the statutes or the regulations in practical application, the motion for partial summary judgment failed to show how they were in conflict and therefore the grant of partial summary judgment on these grounds was in error.

. . . .

In essence, the City established an application process for its residents, which appears on its face to be consistent with the state statutes and regulations. . . . The Babbs have not established that the ordinance and statutes are in conflict or that the additional requirements of the ordinance make the construction of such a system within the City impossible or unreasonably restrictive, such that the ordinance in application keeps any such system from reasonably being located anywhere within the City, therefore making the ordinance inconsistent and irreconcilable with the state statutes and regulations.

"Local regulations may exceed state requirements, so long as they do not prohibit what state law permits." *Borron*, 5 S.W.3d at 623 (citations omitted). A city "may only enact ordinances 'in conformity' with state law on the same subject." *City of Kansas City v. Carlson*, 292 S.W.3d 368, 371 (Mo. App. W.D.2009). However, while the State may have no concern and therefore have no restrictions regarding the use of reflective materials that shine bright sunlight into a neighbor's window, or the way the solar panels may appear from the street or a neighboring property so as to devalue neighboring property, these are clearly areas of great concern to the City and the citizens thereof. These types of restrictions are within the police powers of the City.

We find that the trial court's grant of summary judgment to the Babbs and MOSEIA on Count I of the petition was error. Point One is granted. . . .

. . . .

All concur.

NOTES & QUESTIONS

1.   Why do you think the Missouri Solar Energy Industries Association joined the lawsuit in *Babb*?

2.   Based on the *Babb* opinion, what was arguably suspicious about the timing of the City's adoption of its moratorium on permits for solar energy systems? Why was the timing suspicious, and what might it suggest about the City's motivation for adopting the moratorium?

3.   Does Missouri's legislature possess authority to enact a statute that effectively preempts ordinances akin to the ordinance at issue in *Babb*? Why or why not?

4.   Suppose you are a hired advocate for a group representing the interests of local governments in Missouri, and that the state's legislature is considering a "solar rights" bill that would preempt all local ordinances that effectively prohibit solar energy installations. Craft a one-paragraph statement aimed at convincing legislatures to vote against the bill.

5.   *Calls for a Missouri Solar Rights Statute.* The *Babb* case prompted some Missouri legislators to propose a new state statute to clarify and strengthen protections for citizens against municipal restrictions on solar energy development. State Senator Jason Holsman proposed Senate Bill 579 in December 2013, which sought to provide those protections. However, the bill died before making it out of committee. *See also* Joyce LaFontain, *Show-Me the Sun: How Missouri Can Support Its Commitment to Renewable Source of Energy through Preemption of Local Zoning Ordinances*, 59 ST. LOUIS U. L.J. 617 (2015).

2. SOLAR RIGHTS VERSUS PRIVATE COVENANT RESTRICTIONS

Like municipal land use laws, private covenants can also restrict rooftop solar energy development. Numerous private homeowners' associations throughout the country have included provisions in their declarations of covenants, conditions, and restrictions (CC&Rs) prohibiting or restricting solar energy installations based on concerns about the potential adverse aesthetic impacts of rooftop solar panels within their neighborhoods. A declaration of CC&Rs is a document that is typically recorded in the real property records against every lot within a subdivision. The provisions found in CC&Rs are generally structured to benefit and burden all of the subdivision's lot owners. Among other things, provisions in CC&Rs often restrict potentially offensive or obnoxious land uses and protect property values and the quiet enjoyment of property within the subdivision.

Although the use of CC&Rs is generally a well-established and accepted means of preserving the character and feel of neighborhoods, private covenant restrictions on distributed solar energy have bred controversy in some states. Among other things, such provisions can contravene broader statewide public policy goals by hindering solar energy installations. Accordingly, as of 2017, at least 12 states (AZ, CA, CO, FL, HI, MD, MA, NV, NM, NC, OR & WI) had enacted solar rights statutes preempting and invalidating certain types of private covenant restrictions on solar energy development. When a homeowners' association in one of these states tries to prevent a homeowner from installing rooftop solar panels based on a private covenant provision, these statutes may entitle the homeowner to ignore the covenant and install panels anyway. The following case addresses a dispute over whether the private CC&Rs applicable in one Arizona neighborhood "effectively prohibited" residents from installing solar energy systems in violation of that state's solar rights statute.

GARDEN LAKES COMMUNITY ASS'N, INC. V. MADIGAN

Court of Appeals of Arizona, Div. 1, Dept. B, 2003
204 Ariz. 238

GEMMILL, J.

Homeowners in the Garden Lakes subdivision in Avondale, Arizona are members of the homeowners association known as the Garden Lakes Community Association, Inc. ("Association"). The Association issued architectural restrictions governing the construction and appearance of solar energy devices on homes within the subdivision. The appellee homeowners claimed that the restrictions were unenforceable under Arizona Revised Statutes ("A.R.S.") section 33–439(A)(2000) because the restrictions "effectively prohibited" the homeowners from installing or using solar energy devices. The trial court found in favor of the homeowners. We affirm.

FACTS AND PROCEDURAL HISTORY

William and Joan Madigan and Henry and LaVonne Speak owned homes in the Garden Lakes subdivision. To provide a general plan for the use and enjoyment of the planned community, the Association recorded a Declaration of Covenants, Conditions, Restrictions and Easements for Garden Lakes ("Declaration"). The Declaration applies to all owners of property within Garden Lakes who purchased a lot after the Declaration was recorded on January 28, 1986. The Madigans and the Speaks purchased their lots thereafter and accepted their deeds subject to the following provision in the Declaration:

No improvements, alterations . . . or other work which in any way alters the exterior appearance of any property or improvements thereon . . . shall be made or done . . . unless and until the Architectural Review Committee has, in each such case, reviewed and approved the nature of the proposed work, alteration, structure or grading and the plans and specifications therefor.

The Association established an architectural review committee ("ARC") and architectural review guidelines ("guidelines").

Guidelines were issued regarding the construction and appearance of solar panels and equipment:

1. All solar energy devices Visible from Neighboring Property or public view must be approved by the Architectural Review Committee prior to installation.

2. Panels must be an integrated part of the roof design and mounted directly to the roof plane. Solar units must not break the roof ridge line, must not be visible from public view and must be screened from neighboring property in a manner approved by the Board of Directors or its designee(s). Roof mounted hot water storage systems must not be Visible from Neighboring Property. Tracker-type systems will be allowed only when not Visible from Neighboring Property.

3. The criteria for screening set forth in Section III(M) "Machinery and Equipment", shall apply to solar panels and equipment.

(Original capitalization preserved). Under the "Machinery and Equipment" section, the guidelines provided:

[S]screening or concealment shall be solid and integrated architecturally with the design of the building or structure, shall not have the appearance of a separate piece or pieces of machinery, fixtures or equipment, and shall be constructed and positioned in such a manner so it is level and plumb with vertical building components and shall be structurally stable in accordance with sound engineering principles.

The Madigans and the Speaks installed solar energy devices ("SEDs") on the roofs of their respective homes without ARC or Association approval. These SEDs included solar panels to collect and transfer heat to their swimming pools. The Association sued the Madigans and the Speaks in separate actions, alleging failure to comply with the guidelines and breach of the Declaration. The Association sought permanent injunctions compelling the removal of the SEDs, monetary penalties, and attorneys' fees and costs. The Madigans and Speaks defended on the basis of A.R.S.

§ 33–439, arguing that subsection (A) rendered the guidelines void and unenforceable:

> Any covenant, restriction or condition contained in any deed, contract, security agreement or other instrument affecting the transfer or sale of, or any interest in, real property which *effectively prohibits* the installation or use of a solar energy device as defined in § 44–1761 is void and unenforceable.

ARIZ. REV. STAT. ("A.R.S.") § 33–439(A) (2000) (emphasis added).

The two actions were consolidated. Prior to trial, the Association waived the estimated $100,000 in fines allegedly owed by the Madigans and the Speaks. Also, William Madigan died before trial and Joan Madigan had the solar equipment removed from the roof of her home. . . .

During trial, the court granted judgment as a matter of law in favor of the Madigans. The Association's case against the Speaks was submitted to the advisory jury with special interrogatories.

After post-trial briefing, the trial court entered judgment in favor of the Speaks and Madigans. The court found that the Association's guidelines, combined with the Association's conduct, "effectively prohibited" the Speaks from placing solar energy devices on their residence. The court therefore concluded that, based on A.R.S. § 33–439(A), the Association was not entitled to an injunction enforcing the guidelines regarding solar energy devices. The court also awarded attorneys' fees and costs to the Speaks and Madigans.

The parties agree that the homeowners did not comply with the architectural guidelines of the Association and did not have the approval of the Association or its ARC for installation of their SEDs. The Association on appeal makes several arguments in support of its fundamental position that the trial court erred in concluding that the guidelines were unenforceable under A.R.S. § 33–439(A). . . .

. . . .

ANALYSIS

The Declaration constitutes a contract between "the subdivision's property owners as a whole and the individual lot owners." *Horton*, 200 Ariz. at 525, ¶ 8, 29 P.3d at 872 (citing *Ariz. Biltmore Estates Ass'n v. Tezak*, 177 Ariz. 447, 448, 868 P.2d 1030, 1031 (App.1993)). The Madigans and Speaks purchased their homes subject to the restrictions in the Declaration and the guidelines issued pursuant to the Declaration. . . . Restrictive covenants and architectural guidelines that are clear and unambiguous are generally enforceable against the individual homeowners within the association. . . . The Arizona legislature has carved out an exception to the enforceability of these contracts, however, for restrictions that "effectively prohibit" the installation or use of solar energy devices. A.R.S. § 33–439(A).

The Association argues that § 33–439(A) essentially means that covenants, restrictions, and conditions in deeds, along with guidelines promulgated under them, must lead to the "inevitable preclusion" of the installation of solar energy devices to render such limitations void and unenforceable. The Association contends that the Speaks had the burden of proving that the Declaration and guidelines "inevitably precluded" the installation of their solar heating unit and that they failed to meet that burden of proof. The Speaks respond that the evidence showed that the Association's requirements for installation of the solar heating device either could not be met or added so much cost to the installation that any homeowner would forego solar energy and opt instead for a gas or electric pool heater.

To decide this case, we must interpret A.R.S. § 33–439(A). Our goal in interpreting statutes is to fulfill the intent and purpose of the legislature. . . . We look first to the plain language of the statute as the most reliable indicator of its meaning. *State v. Williams*, 175 Ariz. 98, 100, 854 P.2d 131, 133 (1993). To assist in determining the legislative intent, we may also consider the statute's context, language, subject matter, historical background, effects and consequences, spirit and purpose. *Hayes v. Continental Ins. Co.*, 178 Ariz. 264, 268, 872 P.2d 668, 672 (1994).

. . . .

The statute at issue here, A.R.S. § 33–439(A), was enacted in 1980. The enactment of § 33–439(A) and other solar energy statutes reveals that the legislature sought to encourage the use of solar energy by offering incentives and limiting disincentives for the use of SEDs. The legislative history, however, does not reveal the precise meaning and application of the crucial phrase "effectively prohibits."

While it might be desirable to have a bright-line rule or formula to determine precisely whether a particular restriction effectively prohibits the installation or use of solar energy devices, the legislature has not chosen to provide guidance beyond the phrase "effectively prohibits." The legislature has instead adopted a practical, flexible standard that permits the many variations of restrictions and effects to be considered on a case-by-case basis. . . .

We disagree with the Association's argument that "effectively prohibit" must be interpreted as meaning that any restrictions on SEDs must "inevitably preclude" them before the restrictions should be deemed unenforceable. We decline the invitation to provide a new or alternative definition for the phrase "effectively prohibits." Whether a restriction effectively prohibits SEDs is a question of fact to be decided on a case-by-case basis.

To determine whether a deed restriction effectively prohibits the installation or use of an SED, numerous factors may be relevant. These factors include the content and language of the restrictions or guidelines; the conduct of the homeowners association in interpreting and applying the restrictions; whether the architectural requirements are too restrictive to allow SEDs as a practical matter; whether feasible alternatives utilizing solar energy are available; whether any alternative design will be comparable in cost and performance; the feasibility of making the required modifications; the extent to which the property at issue is amenable to the required changes; whether decisions previously made by the homeowner or a prior owner are responsible for limiting or precluding the installation of SEDs rather than the restrictions themselves; the location, type of housing, and value of the homes in the community; and whether the restrictions impose too great a cost in relation to what typical homeowners in the community are willing to spend. By providing this list of potentially relevant factors and by the comments that follow, we do not intend to predetermine relevancy in any particular case. We do intend, however, to provide general guidance to trial courts and parties involved in or anticipating litigation over restrictions affecting SEDs.

The Association correctly asserts that the burden of proof was on the homeowners to prove that the Declaration and guidelines effectively prohibited them from installing and using a solar energy device.... Applying the applicable standards of review ... we conclude that the homeowners met their burden of proof.

Much of the testimony at trial focused on two alternative designs that the Association argues were feasible and would comply with the guidelines. The Association produced expert testimony supporting the alternatives of constructing a patio cover on the Speaks' home and placing the solar panels on the top of the patio roof or building a screening wall around the existing panels on the roof.

Regarding the patio cover alternative, the evidence revealed two impediments. First, the Speaks' expert testified that a patio cover large enough to hold the Speaks' solar panels would have to be at least thirteen feet by forty feet. The Speaks' pool is about six feet from the back of their house. The proposed patio cover thus would cover part of the pool. Evidence was introduced that the City of Avondale does not allow patios to encroach into pool setback areas. Second, the Association's construction expert testified that the cost of building a patio cover for the Speaks would be nearly $5,000. The cost of installing the solar panels on the patio roof would be an additional expense.

The other solution suggested by the Association would require the building of an aesthetic screen forty-eight feet long by five feet high on the tile roof to hide the solar panels. The Association's expert opined that the screen could be constructed using louvers—analogous to venetian blinds—that could be adjusted to allow the sun to hit the panels. Even with the louvers, however, at some times of the year the screen would cause some shading on the solar panels, thereby decreasing solar efficiency. The vertical supports and other bracing materials would be constructed of wood painted to match the colors in the subdivision and the roof tile.

The Association's expert admitted that he had never seen this type of screening device on a residential roof. Two other witnesses testified that they had never seen a screen wall of the proposed size built on a residence. . . .

The court was entitled to consider the increased cost in reaching its conclusions. . . .

The cost necessary to comply with aesthetic and architectural restrictions is not, standing alone, dispositive. Because the cost of complying with some restrictions may be so expensive as to effectively prohibit SEDs, however, we conclude that cost is a factor to be considered. The focus of this part of the overall inquiry should be on the motivation of the average homeowner within the association community to install SEDs given the financial burden and potential loss of solar efficiency imposed by the restrictions. The location, type of housing, and value of the homes in the community may be relevant in this inquiry.

We believe that evidence of cost was properly presented in this case. A distributor of solar pool heaters in Arizona testified that in the Phoenix and Tucson markets, most people will not buy a solar system that costs more than $4,500. He explained that because solar systems generally cost more than gas and electric heating devices, solar companies must show consumers that they can recoup the difference in three to five years when the fuel costs for the other methods are considered. If the recoupment period goes beyond five years, most people will not purchase a solar system.

We conclude that substantial evidence supported the trial court's finding that the Association's guidelines effectively prohibited the installation and use of SEDs. The evidence is sufficient to support a finding that the patio cover was not a viable option for the Speaks because the added expense would have dissuaded homeowners in the community from undertaking the project and the size of the patio cover would have violated applicable city restrictions. The evidence also supports a finding that the proposed screen was no more than an idea that would not work in execution. The decreased solar efficiency and additional cost of the screening provide further support for the court's conclusion.

. . . .

Section 33–439(A) does not eliminate the power of a homeowners association to impose aesthetic and architectural restrictions on the installation and use of SEDs. But SEDs may not be explicitly prohibited or "effectively prohibited" by the guidelines of an association or by an association's interpretation and application of its guidelines.

Because there was substantial evidence supporting the trial court's ruling that the Association's restrictions effectively prohibited the installation and use of solar energy devices in violation of A.R.S. § 33–439(A), the restrictions as applied in this case are unenforceable and the Association is not entitled to relief. Accordingly, we affirm the judgment in favor of the homeowners.

The homeowners request an award of their attorneys' fees incurred in defending this appeal. The trial court granted an award of attorneys' fees to the homeowners under A.R.S. section 12–341.01(A) (Supp. 2000). We likewise, in our discretion, award fees to the homeowners under this statute. . . .

NOTES & QUESTIONS

1. What type of solar energy system was involved in the *Madigan* case? All else equal, do you think this specific type of system warrants *more* or *less* protection against private covenant restrictions than a residential solar PV array that generates electric power for onsite use? Why?

2. What were the two main "alternative designs" the homeowners' association offered to the landowners in *Madigan*? What specific reasons did the court give for finding that the association's restrictions did "effectively prohibit" the landowners' solar installations in spite of the availability of these alternatives?

3. When considering whether the proposed alternative designs were cost-prohibitive, do you think it was proper for the *Madigan* court to focus on the perspective of an "average" resident in the community rather than the perspective of the landowners directly involved in the claim? Why or why not?

4. How many specific factors did the *Madigan* court identify as being potentially relevant in determining whether a private covenant restriction "effectively prohibited" solar energy installations? Do you think this multi-factor approach is an effective and justifiable means of defining what "effectively prohibit" should mean under these statutes? Why or why not? Can you identify any potential alternative approaches that might be more effective?

5. *Rooftop Solar Installations on Historic Buildings.* One other class of land use restrictions that can complicate or impede rooftop solar energy are laws aimed at protecting historically significant buildings and neighborhoods. Owners of designated historic buildings often must navigate through additional regulatory requirements to secure permission to install rooftop solar panels. As important as promoting solar energy might seem to some,

preserving historic properties and resources is an important public policy goal as well. Sometimes, owners of historically significant buildings are able to gain permission to install PV systems in rooftop areas that are not visible to passers-by. However, in situations when hiding the panels is infeasible, landowners may be unable to secure the permits required for a solar installation. For a detailed discussion of some of the unique issues and challenges associated with solar PV installations on historic buildings and in designated historic districts, see generally A. KANDT ET AL., IMPLEMENTING SOLAR PV PROJECTS ON HISTORIC BUILDINGS AND IN HISTORIC DISTRICTS (2011), http://www.nrel.gov/docs/fy11osti/51297.pdf.

3.   COMMUNITY SOLAR ENERGY

One disadvantage of distributed solar energy technologies is that many citizens throughout the country do not own a rooftop on which to install a new solar array. Others may own a rooftop but cannot afford to purchase solar panels with cash and cannot qualify for a lease or financing for a new rooftop solar energy system. Community solar energy programs have emerged as one potential means of addressing this problem and making solar energy investment accessible to more Americans. Most community solar programs enable electric utility customers to purchase a small share or portion of a commercial-scale, locally-sited solar PV array. Often, customers can pay for their share of the array—which may be as small as a single solar panel—through charges on their monthly electric bills. As more customers opt to participate in these program, their organizers are able to install more and larger community solar energy systems around town, which feed their power onto the electric distribution grid for local use. In the words of one commentator:

> Community solar . . . encourages creative siting of solar projects, such as on landfills or otherwise blighted land, over parking lots, and on third-party roofs—such as schools and churches. This siting flexibility can also convey ancillary benefits, such as shade in parking lots. Similarly, the presence of solar panels on public buildings, like schools, can increase public awareness of clean energy, spur more community action, and confer educational benefits.
>
> . . . .
>
> . . . [C]ommunity solar [also] significantly reduces the barriers to entry traditionally imposed by the residential model, most prominently by minimizing both per-watt and total investment costs. . .

Samantha Booth, Comment, *Here Comes the Sun: How Securities Regulations Cast a Shadow on the Growth of Community Solar in the United States*, 61 UCLA L. REV. 760, 768–69 & 772 (2014).

As shown in Figure 6.1, community solar projects have rapidly emerged as a significant source of solar energy generating capacity. Increasingly, electric utilities and other entities are establishing and expanding community solar programs and thereby helping to drive the growth of this type of solar energy development.

Figure 6.1. Growth in U.S. Community Solar Generating Capacity

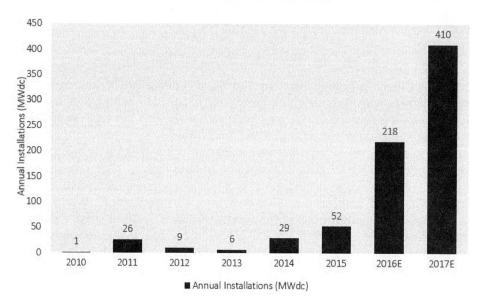

Source: Corey Honeyman, *U.S. Community Solar Outlook 2017*, GREENTECH MEDIA (Feb. 6, 2017), https://www.greentechmedia.com/ research/report/us-community-solar-outlook-2017

Although aggressive policies in California and Colorado have done much to drive community solar energy growth in those states, community solar development has expanded most rapidly in Minnesota in recent years. This growth has largely been attributable to Community Solar Gardens legislation enacted there in 2013 requiring the state's regulated utilities to generously offer community solar programs to their retail customers and to allow third-party developers to bid to provide the large solar arrays needed to support the program. The Minnesota statute creating the program is excerpted below.

COMMUNITY SOLAR GARDENS (MINNESOTA)
MINN. STAT. ANN. § 216B.1641 (West 2014)

(a) The public utility subject to section 116C.779 shall file by September 30, 2013, a plan with the commission to operate a community solar garden program which shall begin operations within 90 days after commission approval of the plan. Other public utilities may file an application at their election. The community solar garden program must be designed to offset the energy use of not less than five subscribers in each community solar garden facility of which no single subscriber has more than a 40 percent interest. The owner of the community solar garden may be a public utility or any other entity or organization that contracts to sell the output from the community solar garden to the utility under section 216B.164. There shall be no limitation on the number or cumulative generating capacity of community solar garden facilities other than the limitations imposed under section 216B.164, subdivision 4c, or other limitations provided in law or regulations.

(b) A solar garden is a facility that generates electricity by means of a ground-mounted or roof-mounted solar photovoltaic device whereby subscribers receive a bill credit for the electricity generated in proportion to the size of their subscription. The solar garden must have a nameplate capacity of no more than one megawatt. Each subscription shall be sized to represent at least 200 watts of the community solar garden's generating capacity and to supply, when combined with other distributed generation resources serving the premises, no more than 120 percent of the average annual consumption of electricity by each subscriber at the premises to which the subscription is attributed.

(c) The solar generation facility must be located in the service territory of the public utility filing the plan. Subscribers must be retail customers of the public utility located in the same county or a county contiguous to where the facility is located.

(d) The public utility must purchase from the community solar garden all energy generated by the solar garden. The purchase shall be at the rate calculated under section 216B.164, subdivision 10, or, until that rate for the public utility has been approved by the commission, the applicable retail rate. . . . A subscriber's portion of the purchase shall be provided by a credit on the subscriber's bill.

(e) The commission may approve, disapprove, or modify a community solar garden program. Any plan approved by the commission must:

    (1) reasonably allow for the creation, financing, and accessibility of community solar gardens;

    (2) establish uniform standards, fees, and processes for the interconnection of community solar garden facilities that allow the utility to recover reasonable interconnection costs for each community solar garden;

    (3) not apply different requirements to utility and nonutility community solar garden facilities;

    (4) be consistent with the public interest;

(5) identify the information that must be provided to potential subscribers to ensure fair disclosure of future costs and benefits of subscriptions;

(6) include a program implementation schedule;

(7) identify all proposed rules, fees, and charges; and

(8) identify the means by which the program will be promoted.

(f) Notwithstanding any other law, neither the manager of nor the subscribers to a community solar garden facility shall be considered a utility solely as a result of their participation in the community solar garden facility.

(g) Within 180 days of commission approval of a plan under this section, a utility shall begin crediting subscriber accounts for each community solar garden facility in its service territory, and shall file with the commissioner of commerce a description of its crediting system.

(h) For the purposes of this section, the following terms have the meanings given:

(1) "subscriber" means a retail customer of a utility who owns one or more subscriptions of a community solar garden facility interconnected with that utility; and

(2) "subscription" means a contract between a subscriber and the owner of a solar garden.

————————

Although Minnesota's largest investor owned utility, Xcel Energy, has generally been a willing supporter of and adherent to the state's community solar requirements, some issues have arisen over the scope of utilities' obligations under the statute. Among other things, most utilities would prefer to build and operate their own community solar gardens and do not want to be legally obligated to purchase large amounts of electricity from solar gardens developed by others. The following (unpublished) case examines one of the primary legal questions that arose as Minnesota's statute drove rapid community solar growth in the state: whether there was any limit on the number of third-party or "co-locator" community solar gardens a utility must accept and integrate into its electricity distribution system.

IN RE NORTHERN STATES POWER CO.

Court of Appeals of Minnesota, 2016
2016 WL 3043122

HALBROOKS, J.

Relator, a developer of solar-energy facilities, challenges an August 6, 2015 order issued by respondent Minnesota Public Utilities Commission (PUC), arguing that the PUC . . . acted in excess of its statutory authority by limiting relator's interconnection rights. We affirm.

FACTS

Minnesota's community solar garden (CSG) statute, MINN. STAT. § 216B.1641 (2014), was enacted in 2013 to promote solar growth in the state by providing individual customers and communities the opportunity to work together to have a community solar resource. Under this model, non-utility-scale customers who typically face economic barriers to participation in a solar program would purchase or lease a subscription at a central solar installation and receive a bill credit for the electricity generated in proportion to the size of their subscription. *See* MINN. STAT. § 216B.1641(a)-(b).

Under the statute, respondent Northern States Power Company d/b/a Xcel Energy was required to file a plan with the PUC outlining its proposed CSG program. MINN. STAT. § 216B.1641(a). Xcel met the statutorily defined deadline by submitting a proposed plan on September 30, 2013. The PUC received voluminous comments between October 4 and December 3, 2013, from various high-level stakeholders in the solar industry who provided input on Xcel's proposed plan. Based on this feedback, the PUC issued an order on April 7, 2014, rejecting Xcel's proposal and requiring the company to file a revised CSG plan. Xcel complied by filing a revised plan on May 7, 2014.

After additional stakeholder commentary, the PUC issued an order on September 17, 2014, approving Xcel's modified CSG plan. Both this order and the previous April 7 order permitted co-location of CSGs but were silent on the topic of co-location caps. The program launched on December 12, 2014, and Xcel began accepting applications from individuals and developers hoping to construct and operate CSGs. The overall response to the CSG program was unquestionably more positive than originally anticipated, and Xcel became concerned that utility-scale producers were taking advantage of the lucrative benefits provided by the program. Relator Sunrise Energy Ventures, LLC submitted 100 applications in the first hour of the program.

Xcel first raised the issue of utility-scale developers on January 13, 2015, in supplemental comments submitted to the PUC. Xcel urged the PUC to place limitations on co-located solar gardens in the CSG program for multiple reasons, including (1) possible complications created by interconnecting utility-scale solar projects to the distribution system, (2) the company's belief that permitting large-scale operations to participate in the program would run counter to legislative intent, and (3) potential rate impacts to non-participating customers.

Xcel requested that the PUC affirm its intention to process only those applications proposing CSGs of no more than 1 megawatt (MW) in size, meaning that co-located applications from a single developer would be processed so long as they, in the aggregate, did not exceed 1 MW. On June 22, 2015, Xcel entered into a partial settlement with several stakeholders in the solar industry. Sunrise was not part of this process. The agreement proposed to limit the aggregate capacity of co-located CSGs to 5 MW for applicants already in the approval queue and 1 MW for applications submitted after September 25, 2015, allowing Xcel to unilaterally scale down any larger CSGs and refund application deposits and fees associated with the scaled-down portions. . . .

The PUC approved a modified plan adopting portions of the partial settlement agreement, including the CSG co-location caps. Sunrise filed a petition for reconsideration with the PUC on August 26, 2015, that the commission denied on October 15, 2015. The PUC reiterated that its August 6, 2015 order modifying Xcel's plan to include co-limitation caps was based on its determination that "allowing unlimited co-location would render the 1 MW statutory limit superfluous, undermine the legislative intent to foster small, widely distributed solar gardens rather than utility-scale solar developments, and create a risk of significant rate increases to ratepayers." . . . . This certiorari appeal follows.

. . . .

III. INTERCONNECTION RIGHTS

Sunrise argues that the PUC violated the Public Utility Regulatory Policies Act of 1978 (PURPA) by allowing Xcel to refuse interconnection based on upgrade needs if the costs exceed $1 million. PURPA was enacted in late 1978 to address a nationwide energy crisis. . . . Congress granted the Federal Energy Regulatory Commission (FERC) exclusive jurisdiction over the regulation and sale of electric power at wholesale cost in interstate commerce. *Occidental Chem. Corp. v. La. Pub. Serv. Comm'n*, 494 F.Supp.2d 401, 406 (M.D. La. 2007). "[T]he FERC . . . promulgate[s] rules to encourage cogeneration and small power production, including rules requiring electric utilities to purchase electricity from, and sell electricity to, QF's." *Id.* PURPA was codified in Minnesota under MINN. STAT. § 216B.164, which enables the PUC to regulate the energy industry and implement PURPA's provisions.

Sunrise maintains that PURPA and Minnesota's implementing statutes do not permit caps as a basis to refuse interconnection. *See* 16

U.S.C. § 2621(d)(15) (2012) ("Each electric utility shall make available, upon request, interconnection service to any electric consumer that the electric utility serves."); MINN. STAT. § 216B.164. Because of this mandatory language, Sunrise argues that the PUC's $1 million interconnection cap as a basis for refusal is per se unlawful. Respondents assert that Sunrise's argument is misplaced. . . .

The entirety of Sunrise's PURPA argument rests on the contention that PURPA controls and, therefore, prohibits Xcel from denying a project on the basis of interconnection costs. But the CSG is an alternative program to the section 10 tariff that governs larger utility-scale projects because MINN. STAT. § 216B.164 already offers developers a vehicle for solar development.

We find it persuasive that the FERC recently addressed this question in another jurisdiction. Winding Creek Solar LLC filed a petition for enforcement against the California Public Utilities Commission, arguing that California's alternative-energy program is inconsistent with PURPA because of statewide caps on the obligation of utility companies under the statute. *Winding Creek Solar LLC*, 151 FERC ¶ 61,103 at *1 (2015). The FERC held that

> as long as a state provides QFs the opportunity to enter into long-term legally enforceable obligations at avoided cost rates, a state may also have alternative programs that QFs and electric utilities may agree to participate in; such alternative programs may limit how many QFs, or the total capacity of QFs, that may participate in the program.

Id. at *3. Here, Sunrise provides no evidence that it elected to be governed by PURPA instead of under the CSG statute, and this is likely due to the difference in rates that Sunrise would be subjected to under the different statutes. Sunrise would benefit economically by participating in this state's solar-power initiative through the CSG program rather than through the traditional competitive-bid process. Because the CSG program is an alternative to the statute governing the solar-power competitive-bid process, the PUC may lawfully place limitations on participation, including on interconnection costs, without violating state and federal law.

Affirmed.

NOTES & QUESTIONS

1.   Why do you think Xcel wants rights to limit the size and number of third-party community solar gardens that the utility must interconnect into its distribution system? What limits does Minnesota's Community Solar Garden

statute seem to place on utilities' obligations to accept and interconnect such facilities?

2.   What was the Minnesota PUC's role in the settlement process between third-party solar producers and Xcel related to caps on the Community Solar Garden Program?

3.   How does Sunrise try to use PURPA in its argument against Xcel in the *In re Northern States Power Co.* case? On what rationale does the court seem to reject this PURPA-based argument?

4.   *Continued Growth for Minnesota's Community Solar Gardens.* Although Minnesota's Community Solar Gardens statute had a somewhat rocky start, within a few years after its enactment the statute had become one of the primary drivers of solar energy development in that state. As of late 2017, more than 40 community solar gardens were operating in Minnesota. The projects had an aggregate generating capacity of over 100 MW, and Xcel energy predicted that projects totaling more than 200 MW of capacity would be operating in the state before the end of the year. Nearly 180 more community solar garden projects were in various phases of planning or construction. See Mike Hughlett, *Xcel's solar garden program passes milestone: 40 projects online*, MINNESOTA STAR TRIBUNE (Oct. 4, 2017), http://www.star tribune.com/xcel-s-solar-garden-program-passes-milestone-40-projects-online/ 449459783/.

C. UTILITY-SCALE SOLAR ENERGY

In recent years, the fastest growing segment of the solar energy industry has been utility-scale solar energy projects—massive solar farms sited in relatively remote rural areas. According to a 2017 study, utility-scale solar generating capacity in the United States grew at an average rate of 72% annually from 2010 to 2016. *See Utility-Scale Solar Has Grown Rapidly Over The Past Five Years*, U.S. ENERGY INFO. ADMIN. (May 4, 2017), https://www.eia.gov/todayinenergy/detail.php?id=31072. The appeal of utility-scale solar power is at least partly attributable to *economies of scale*—the lower per-unit costs of these projects resulting from efficiencies achieved due to the projects' large size. Utility-scale solar energy projects come in two primary varieties: (i) thermal or concentrating solar power plants (CSPs) and (ii) large ground-mounted PV arrays. One other new but promising approach to utility-scale solar energy generation, concentrated photovoltaics (CPVs), uses mirrors or lenses to concentrate sunlight onto high-efficiency PV cells.

Unlike utility-scale ground-mounted PV projects, which feature thousands of PV solar panels mounted across vast stretches of open land, CSP projects rely upon thousands of mirrors or other reflective devices to concentrate sunlight onto particular places and thereby generate intense thermal energy or heat. That heat ultimately boils water to produce steam, which spins electromagnetic turbines to generate electricity in the same basic way that coal- or gas-fired plants generate power. CSP projects are a type of *thermal solar* strategy because, unlike solar PV arrays, CSP projects generate electricity using heat and steam.

As concentrating solar technologies have matured in recent years, a variety of diverse CSP project designs have emerged. At tower-based CSP projects, thousands of reflective mirror-like *heliostats* concentrate sunlight onto one or more receivers perched atop tall towers. These heliostats are carefully calibrated and programmed to tilt slowly throughout the day to reflect as much light onto the receivers as possible. The intense heat resulting from this concentrated sunlight ultimately brings water in the receiver tower to a boil, producing steam and driving the generation of electric power.

One distinct advantage of tower-based CSP is the possibility of using molten salt to store heat on the project's receiver tower after the sun goes down. Because of the unique qualities of the molten salt, a tower-based CSP project that uses it can often continue to generate electricity for several hours after sunset when many utilities encounter periods of peak grid load demand. When available, this unique approach to energy storage can greatly mitigate the intermittency disadvantages of solar energy as an energy resource. *See* Knvul Sheikh, *New Concentrating Solar Tower Is Worth Its Salt with 24/7 Power*, SCI. AM. (July 14, 2016), https://www.scientificamerican.com/article/new-concentrating-solar-tower-is-worth-its-salt-with-24-7-power/. Chapter 7 of this Casebook includes more discussion of molten salt technologies' potential as an energy storage strategy.

As innovative and valuable as they are, tower-based CSP technologies also have some significant drawbacks. Their primary disadvantages relate to the project towers, which often stand 500 feet or more above the rural landscape and can tarnish pristine views for local residents and visitors. The towers can likewise interfere with military aircraft radar or otherwise conflict with military aviation activities in remote areas. However, the most notorious aspect of CSP towers is their potential to create hazards for migratory birds and other bird species, which can collide into them or suffer fatal burns when flying through the scorching heat that surrounds them during sunny daylight hours. For example, an estimated 6,000 birds die around the towers at California's Ivanpah CSP project each year alone, despite various efforts to deter birds from coming near the towers. Researchers continue to search for more effective ways of addressing this problem. *See* Louis Sahagun, *This Mojave Desert Solar Plant Kills 6,000 Birds A Year. Here's Why That Won't Change Any Time Soon*, L.A. TIMES (Sept. 2, 2016), http://www.latimes.com/local/california/la-me-solar-bird-deaths-20160831-snap-story.html. For more in-depth coverage of conflicts between CSP projects and birds, see the subsection on wildlife conservation found later in this Chapter.

Among other things, advancements in CSP technologies have led to an increasing number of CSP projects that feature no tall towers and consist instead of rows and rows of reflective "troughs." These troughs, which usually have a parabolic shape, concentrate sunlight on small metal tubes situated only a few feet above the troughs themselves. The tubes are filled with oil or some other heat transfer fluid, which reaches extremely high temperatures and then flows to a location on the project site where it boils water to generate steam. Although trough-based CSPs have less energy storage potential than tower-based CSPs, they tend to create comparatively fewer siting issues and are an increasingly cost-effective and popular strategy for utility-scale solar energy development.

Developers of utility-scale solar energy projects rarely encounter obstacles related to homeowners' association covenant restrictions or shading from trees or buildings on adjacent land because their projects tend to be sited in relatively remote, unpopulated areas. However, developers of these projects do face a wide range of other hurdles that often require the assistance of legal counsel. From the earliest stages of the utility-scale solar siting process until the day a giant new solar energy farm begins generating electric power, developers and their lawyers navigate countless legal and policy issues in this burgeoning area of legal practice. The following materials provide a general overview of some of these issues from a transactional lawyer's perspective.

1. FINDING AND LEASING A PROJECT SITE

Transactional lawyers routinely play numerous roles in the development of utility-scale solar energy projects. Most developers of these projects rely on legal counsel to assist in the negotiation and drafting of solar lease agreements, easements, and financing agreements that the project requires. Developers also often depend upon land use and environmental attorneys to assist with the laborious and potentially contentious process of securing all requisite government permits and approvals. Energy lawyers commonly help to negotiate and draft power purchase agreements (PPAs) with utilities and other anticipated off-takers of the project's generated power. And it is not uncommon for attorneys to assist with various other project-related tasks and issues, from construction contracting to corporate formation and structuring to tax strategies.

Much of the lawyering associated with utility-scale solar energy closely mirrors that covered in Chapter 4 of this Casebook's discussion of utility-scale wind energy development, so coverage of those items is not repeated in this Chapter. Like wind energy developers, utility-scale solar energy developers must consider a lengthy list of factors when searching for a project site. Once they find a site, utility-scale solar developers also resemble wind energy developers in that they typically lease (rather than purchase) the site, conduct a rigorous title and survey review of the site to identify and manage title-related risks and secure project financing, and comply with a seemingly endless list of permitting requirements. Chapter 4's materials on wind energy development would thus provide a useful introduction and primer for lawyers representing clients on utility-scale solar energy projects as well.

Despite its similarities to wind energy development work, siting and leasing activities for utility-scale solar energy development certainly involve some unique issues that are worthy of mention. The following excerpt from a publication produced by the law firm of Stoel Rives LLP identifies several similarities and differences between wind and solar energy development at the utility-scale from the developer's perspective. The excerpt also aptly highlights many important practical issues that can arise in the context of utility-scale solar energy development.

THE LAW OF SOLAR: A GUIDE TO BUSINESS AND LEGAL ISSUES—SOLAR PROJECT PROPERTY RIGHTS: SECURING YOUR PLACE IN THE SUN

Stoel Rives LLP, 5th Ed. (2017)

Developing and operating a successful solar energy project requires more than having the latest solar technologies. Low-maintenance, high-return projects start with securing long-term project site rights under leases or easements that ensure control of the land for all necessary uses, undisturbed access, exposure to solar rays, and flexibility for project modifications based on rapidly emerging technologies or market changes The form and substance of solar leases and easements vary based on the type of system (photovoltaic ("PV"), concentrated photovoltaic ("CPV"), or concentrated solar power ("CSP"), for example), the type of installation (rooftop or ground-mount), and the type of landowner or host (not-for-profit, commercial, residential, or utility-scale). . .

I.   Distinguishing Land Rights and Identifying Project Needs.

Among the first steps in developing a solar project is securing rights to the land needed to construct, operate, and maintain the project. Typically, site rights are established through a lease or easement agreement. In order to maintain the deductibility of land cost for federal income tax purposes, it is usually best that the project entity not acquire fee title to the land. For large, utility-scale CSP projects, however, purchasing fee title may have economic and water rights advantages. Project counsel should be mindful of the relative advantages and disadvantages of leases and easements in various states. These issues can range from differences in tax treatment to nonrecognition of easements for possessory uses. . . Project developers should examine their project needs in terms of unobstructed spatial requirements; exclusivity; the distribution, transmission, or use of the power generated by the project; energy storage; and resource demand (such as water, surplus power supply, and thermal energy storage). . .

A.   The Solar Project Property Agreement.

1.   The Purpose and Scope of the Interest. Lease agreements provide the broadest occupancy and use rights for a project site and are normally best for CSP and CPV projects and ground-mounted PV systems. A solar lease agreement should provide the developer with unrestricted access to and from the property and the exclusive right to use the leased property for solar energy development. Developers generally do not share the leased property with other occupants because, unlike wind energy projects that allow for compatible simultaneous uses of the land, solar projects are land-intensive and typically require that the developer have exclusive use of the property. While some sheep grazing may be possible and can be useful in managing vegetation among certain solar arrays that are four feet off the ground or higher, developers are generally well served to lease on an exclusive basis property that is wholly unoccupied. . .

Easements can be ideal agreements for rooftop and smaller-scale PV projects when the project developer and the project share a larger space with the landowner or third parties. An easement is a real property interest whereby the landowner grants to the developer a right to use the property for a specific purpose in a form that cannot be unilaterally revoked without cause and that can be pledged as security for financing. A typical rooftop shared space easement secures to the developer a right to the property and is defined by a scope of use, exclusivity (or nonexclusivity), a term, and certain responsibilities and rights of each party to the easement. A license or revocable permission to conduct an activity on the property is unsuitable for establishing most project site rights. . .

2.   The Scope of Property Subject to a Solar Project Property Agreement. A solar developer will want to ensure that it contracts for sufficient land to access, developer, and operate its project; to protect its project facilities from dust, dirt, debris, vandalism, shading, and other outside forces; and to provide flexibility in selecting the precise location for the system and any ancillary facilities. However, unlike wind projects and some ocean and tidal projects, solar projects are land-intensive, dense developments. A typical wind project uses, on average, one acre to produce one megawatt of energy. A wind developer might lease a 50-acre parcel and use 10 percent of it. In a typical wind project, the landowner may continue to use the remaining portion of the larger leased premises for agriculture or other uses while profiting from the wind power produced on the leased land. On the other hand, solar projects can require up to five acres for every megawatt produced, and the solar facilities usually occupy (or the

landowner is generally denied entry to) virtually the entire project site. . . .
Consequently, the landowner may have more concern for the location and
configuration of a project that uses less than all of the landowner's
contiguous lands to preserve access to and use of remaining areas that may
still be put to productive use by the landowner.

3.   **Potential Resolutions to the Scope of Land Requirements**. In
utility-scale solar projects, there are few alternatives to leasing or
otherwise acquiring secure control over those lands for the life of the
project. . . . [L]ands with low agricultural or mineral value are better
situated for lower land rents and to potentially allow a developer a better
marginal return. . . The savvy developer will research the value of the land
and its potential uses, and be prepared to negotiate an agreement that
provides an attractive income stream to the landowner in light of local
market conditions while maintaining profit margin for the prospective
project.

Regardless of any alternative-use value of a particular property,
reaching agreement on the amount of land subject to the agreement, the
payments and other terms and conditions of the agreement will involve a
number of factors. Most common payment terms are tied to the number of
acres of land under contract, the type(s) of improvements intended for the
particular site, the amount of energy produced by the project, and what
other interests or properties of the landowner may be disturbed or used in
the project for access, transmission, operation and maintenance, or other
facilities. In addition, a site-control agreement may give the landowner
comfort that the developer will minimize the project's impact on the land
and make available any unused space for other uses by the landowner. For
example, an agreement may provide:

- A minimum annual rent payment based on the amount of
  acreage under contract. In an agricultural area, this rent may
  be based on the land's agricultural value or other highest and
  best use value, whichever is greater.

- A power sale revenue-based payment to be made if and to the
  extent a negotiated percentage of the payments received by
  the developer from energy produced and sold by the project in
  a particular year exceeds the minimum annual rent payment
  for that year.

- An agreement by the developer to consult with the landowner
  during the project's scoping stage regarding the location of
  the project and its related facilities. Sometimes, certain
  sensitive areas of a larger parcel are made off-limits for
  certain types of development in the agreement itself or carved
  out of the land subject to contract in the first place.
  Consulting with landowners can give more comfort that their

concerns will at least be heard and considered in the siting process. Notwithstanding the consultation provision, the agreement will typically make clear that the developer is the final arbiter on where, whether, and when to locate project facilities within the project footprint.

. . .

B. Alternative Land Rights: Fee Interests; Federal and State Lands. Utility-scale CSP and PV systems are uniquely suited for large swaths of flat land. With current technology, the slope of most project sites should not exceed 1 percent. . . Relatively flat, wide open spaces in areas with plentiful sunshine call to mind the Southwest, the plains states, and inland rural areas of California. Ownership of these lands runs the entire range of private landowners; federal, state, or local governments; or Native American tribes.

State and federal lands are under the jurisdiction of the departments of state lands and the Bureau of Land Management (the "BLM"), respectively. Count[ies], cit[ies], and other state-subdivisions are governed by the applicable state statutes and local ordinances. Each state has a unique scheme for leasing or licensing the use of its public lands, as does the federal government. Many of these departments are well-acquainted with granting grazing or mineral rights but can be less familiar with the installation of large-scale solar projects. Developers should explore the various forms of land-control rights available from the state or federal government for the land at issue.

BLM regulations specify procedures for obtaining site rights, called right-of-way ("ROW") grants. The regulations allow resource assessment, construction, and project operations. They provide for project-specific rent (based on appraisal, with a phase-in period during project development) and terms of the grants (generally not to exceed 30 years, with an option to renew). For utility-scale solar projects, the BLM has created a separate Solar Energy Program. The purpose of the program is to support the responsible development of utility-scale solar energy projects on BLM-administered lands in the six southwestern states. Under the Solar Energy Program, the BLM has classified about 79 million acres of BLM lands that are excluded from solar energy development and also identified about 285,000 acres of BLM lands as priority areas, or Solar Energy Zones, that are suitable for utility-scale solar projects. So far, the BLM has approved 19 Solar Energy Zones across California, Nevada, Arizona, Colorado, Utah, and New Mexico and may identify new zones in the future. New applications for utility-scale solar projects are processed in accordance with the BLM's Record of Decision for the Solar Programmatic Environmental Impact Statement. Multiple applications for the same land can trigger a competitive process. The process includes BLM consideration and approval of a detailed Plan of Development for each project and full environmental review in compliance with the National Environmental Policy Act. . .

II. Overcoming Title Roadblocks.

Securing an interest in property for a solar project requires more than just a signed solar project property agreement. If a rooftop or utility-scale project site is encumbered by existing leases, easements, mineral rights, or other interests, the project developer takes its interest in the land or site subject to those existing rights. Unless discovered and dealt with early on, third-party rights that prohibit or potentially interfere with or limit the project can result in significant delays, liabilities, losses, and costs to the developer. Accordingly, the developer should obtain and carefully analyze a search and examination of the title to the project site along with a complete, detailed survey of the site and proposed location of project facilities, and purchase a policy of title insurance to help protect its investment in the project. These principles apply equally to a new acquisition (including acquisition of the equity interests in an existing project entity, where there are additional, special title insurance concerns) or the financing of an existing or to-be-constructed solar energy facility.

A. Title Review. It is fundamental that for a complete review of title, one must obtain all documents in the public record and off-record agreements relating to the proposed project lands to (1) determine the person(s) or entity(ies) vested with title, (2) determine whether the title is subject to liens or mortgages that create unacceptable risks to the solar project, and (3) discover all encumbrances, such as easements for utilities, road rights-of-way, mineral and timber rights, or other interests held by people or entities other than the landowner that might prevent, limit, or interfere with construction or operation of the project as planned. Beyond review of available documentation, a developer would be deemed to have notice of (and will take subject to) the rights of parties in possession of the subject property or whose rights could be ascertained from a visual inspection of the subject property. Such indicators of potential third-party rights could be a road or utility line crossing the subject property without a corresponding recorded easement (hence one aspect of the value of a complete survey), the actual physical presence of third parties on the land, or signage, vehicles, or the like on the land that indicates a third-party presence or interest. It is critical to obtain the title information as soon as possible and review it thoroughly to make certain that all interests of record and off-record are discovered, disclosed, and analyzed carefully. Insurable title to the lease and/or easement is a key factor in successfully financing, selling, or syndicating a project as well as a prudent precursor to any project development or purchase of a project or a project site control position.

B. Determining Whether to Undertake Curative Measures. Once all of the information contained in the preliminary title reports or commitments for title insurance, the survey(s), and all off-record agreements relating to the site have been reviewed, it is necessary to cull those title issues that must be corrected or cured from those that will not impair the vitality of the project and may be permitted to remain. If a leasehold or easement interest is obtained from someone claiming to own the land, when, in fact, the fee simple title of record is vested in another (or otherwise known to be vested in another, even if not of record), the title company will require correction of the title and/or the affected site control agreement before a policy can be issued. . . Most often, mortgages must be addressed in some manner that will permit the lender's interest to coexist with the project, while ensuring that the project is not subject to foreclosure by the prior mortgagee. Easements or rights-of-way can also be problematic—some must be adjusted or a side agreement entered with the easement holder to allow access to or construction and/or operation of the proposed project or related facilities or uses, whereas others may not create any risk to the project and need not be addressed. All such interests should be carefully reviewed and any potential problems dealt with before proceeding with any development on a project.

C. Curing Title Defects. After identifying potential title issues that need to be addressed, one must analyze the range of curatives to address the issue, determine the most efficient and effective means to that end, and negotiate appropriate documentation to resolve the matter. For existing mortgages, developers should work with their attorneys and the title company to evaluate whether a subordination agreement is required, which can be difficult or impossible to obtain from institutional and other lenders, or if a nondisturbance agreement will suffice. For existing easements, the developer should evaluate whether a consent and crossing agreement is necessary, or if the easement holder will modify its easement to allow the solar project or related facilities to cross or overlap the easement area or limit the area of a blanket easement to avoid overlapping any project facilities or access.

A utility, a lender, another landowner, or some other person with a pre-existing lien or encumbrance on or an interest in the project property may not always be interested in helping to solve the developer's title problem. Nevertheless it is often necessary to secure that person's cooperation and agreement to deal with the issue in the most effective and complete way. Parties with a legal interest in a project site may hold such interest for the long term. Initiation and maintenance of good relationships with such parties may help to resolve and avoid problems throughout the life of the project.

. . .

III. Other Potential Property and Land Issues. . .

A. Water Rights for Concentrated Solar Power Projects. Water rights can be a concern regardless of the type of solar project. Every project likely has a need for water at some point in its life span. Where a project site control agreement grants or includes water rights in the project rights and the agreement or applicable law disallows waste, the developer will have to figure out a way to keep the water right in effect without forfeiture or limitation and without using the water for purposes not allowed under the applicable water right. For instance, a water right for irrigation use on a particular area of the project site most likely cannot be used to support project activities or facilities, other than perhaps irrigation of vegetation in the prescribed area. . . Water requirements for CSP projects require careful consideration and planning. When a project is located in a semidesert or desert environment, solar radiation is plentiful, but water may be scarce or severely limited. Project developers should give early and careful consideration to the water requirements for the proposed CSP project and potential sources. A few of the critical questions to ask include:

- Is there a source of water currently in place on the property—a surface source (such as a river or canal), a municipal source, or a groundwater well?

- If there is no surface source, is water available from an aquifer or a local source?

- Do the available water rights allow the water to be used at the place(s), in the quantities, at the time(s), and for the purpose(s) desired by the developer?

- Are there available alternative uses that the developer can take advantage of to ensure that the full amount of water required to be used to preserve the right can be lawfully used and applied to avoid forfeiture or other penalty?

- If water rights must be acquired, are such rights available, both legally and physically? What is the process and timing to acquire and perfect those rights?

- What water laws and restrictions will affect the ability to obtain water for the project?

- If a well or surface diversion or any storage is required to bring water to or store water for the project, what water rights or permits and easements are needed, and how much time is needed to obtain those rights?

- What are the ramifications of water use for permitting and environmental review of the project?

A clear understanding of a project's water needs, the availability of water at a project site, and the time and cost involved in obtaining water is essential to establishing a project's construction and operation timeline, budget, output, and, ultimately, feasibility. . .

———————

NOTES AND QUESTIONS

1.   Based on the excerpted article above, identify at least two differences between utility-scale wind energy development and utility-scale solar energy development that require developers and their lawyers to take different approaches when siting and securing property rights for these projects. What different approaches does solar energy development require, and why?

2.   According to the article excerpt above, why are easements potentially more advantageous than leases for securing property rights in the context of large commercial rooftop solar projects than in the context of ground-mounted projects in rural areas?

3.   Why would securing a *license* (i.e., permission to use a rooftop) from a rooftop owner be a risky and unsatisfactory approach for a developer seeking to site and developer a large commercial rooftop solar array?

4.   Why is the availability of significant water resources crucially important in the context of some types of utility-scale solar energy projects but not others?

5.   Based on the excerpted article above, what does it mean to "cure" title defects, and why might a developer's efforts to cure any such defects be crucial to the success of a utility-scale solar energy project?

6.   *Solar over Water Projects.* In recent years, as climate change and population growth have caused water resources to become even more valuable in some arid regions of the world, there has been growing interest in installing solar PV panels over canals or floating panels atop reservoirs. Such "solar over water" projects not only generate clean renewable power without occupying the surface of land; they can also reduce evaporation so that more stored water ultimately reaches end users. In 2017, China completed the world's largest floating solar PV array—a 40 MW facility in the city of Huainan that can power thousands of homes and businesses. See Simon Brandon, China just switched on the world's largest floating solar power plant, weforum.org (June 2, 2017), https://www.weforum.org/agenda/2017/06/china-worlds-largest-floating-solar-power/. Such so-called *floatavoltaic* solar projects are likely to become even more common as floating solar technologies progress in the coming decades.

2.   SOLAR PROJECTS ON TRIBAL ANCESTRAL LANDS

As mentioned in the article above and elsewhere in this Casebook, much of the land in the desert Southwest has excellent solar resources and other characteristics that make it an attractive region for utility-scale solar energy development. However, most of this desert Southwest land is also the *ancestral land* of one or more Indian tribes, meaning that the tribes were actively occupying or using the land before European explorers arrived. In the United States today, many tribes have rights to occupy and use only a small fraction of their ancestral lands as *Indian trust lands* (also commonly known as *reservation lands*). The majority of these tribes' ancestral land is now privately owned or is designated as ordinary state or federal public lands. However, many tribes still attach great significance to all of their ancestral lands—including off-reservation lands. Accordingly, tribes often have strong concerns about the potential for land development to harm sacred burial grounds, artifacts, or other cultural resources.

In recent decades, wind and solar energy development projects on remote public lands in the Southwest have triggered numerous conflicts between developers and Indian tribes in that region. As described in the case below, the National Historic Preservation Act requires that government officials "consult" with a tribe when engaging in significant land development on its ancestral lands, even when those lands are not within the boundaries of the tribe's reservation lands. Unfortunately, tribes and developers often disagree about what developers must do to satisfy this consultation requirement.

QUECHAN TRIBE OF FORT YUMA INDIAN RESERVATION v. U.S. DEPT. OF INTERIOR

United States District Court, Southern District of California, 2010
755 F.Supp.2d 1104

BURNS, D.J.

On October 29, 2010, Plaintiff (the "Tribe") filed its complaint, alleging Defendants' decision to approve a solar energy project violated various provisions of federal law. On November 12, the Tribe filed a motion for preliminary injunction, asking the Court to issue an order to preserve the status quo by enjoining proceeding with the project, pending the outcome of this litigation. After the motion was filed, Imperial Valley Solar LLC intervened as a Defendant.

On Monday, December 13, the Court held a[n] oral argument at which the parties appeared through counsel. After the parties were fully heard, the Court took the matter under submission, with the intent to rule within two days.

Background

The Quechan Tribe is a federally-recognized Indian tribe whose reservation is located mostly in Imperial County, California and partly in Arizona. A large solar energy project is planned on 6500 acres of federally-owned land known as the California Desert Conservation Area ("CDCA").

The Department of the Interior, as directed by Congress, developed a binding management plan for this area.

The project is being managed by a company called Tessera Solar, LLC. Tessera plans to install about 30,000 individual "suncatcher" solar collectors, expected to generate 709 megawatts when completed. The suncatchers will be about 40 feet high and 38 feet wide, and attached to pedestals about 18 feet high. Support buildings, roads, a pipeline, and a power line to support and service the network of collectors are also planned. Most of the project will be built on public lands. Tessera submitted an application to the state of California to develop the Imperial Valley Solar project. The project is planned in phases.

After communications among BLM, various agencies, the Tribe, and other Indian tribes, a series of agreements, decisions, and other documents was published. The final EIS was issued some time in July, 2010. . . . On September 14 and 15, certain federal and state officials, including BLM's field manager, executed a programmatic agreement (the "Programmatic Agreement") for management of the project. The Tribe objected to this. On October 4, 2010, Director of the Bureau of Land Management Robert Abbey signed the Imperial Valley Record of Decision ("ROD") approving the project, and the next day Secretary of the Interior Ken Salazar signed the ROD. The ROD notice was published on October 13, 2010.

The area where the project would be located has a history of extensive use by Native American groups. The parties agree 459 cultural resources have been identified within the project area. These include over 300 locations of prehistoric use or settlement, and ancient trails that traverse the site. The tribes in this area cremated their dead and buried the remains, so the area also appears to contain archaeological sites and human remains. The draft environmental impact statement ("EIS") prepared by the BLM indicated the project "may wholly or partially destroy all archaeological sites on the surface of the project area."

The Tribe believes the project would destroy hundreds of their ancient cultural sites including burial sites, religious sites, ancient trails, and probably buried artifacts. Secondarily, it argues the project would endanger the habitat of the flat-tailed horned lizard, which is under consideration for listing under the Endangered Species Act and which is culturally important to the Tribe. The Tribe maintains Defendants were required to comply with the National Environmental Policy Act (NEPA), the National Historical Preservation Act (NHPA), and the Federal Land Policy and Management Act of 1976 (FLPMA) by making certain analyses and taking certain factors into account deciding to go ahead with the project. The Tribe now seeks judicial intervention under the Administrative Procedures Act (APA).

. . . .

The parties agree that, under NHPA Section 106 (16 U.S.C. § 470f) and its implementing regulations, the Bureau of Land Management (BLM) is required to consult with certain parties before spending money on or approving any federally-assisted undertaking such as the project at issue here, and that the Tribe is one of those parties. The Tribe maintains BLM didn't adequately or meaningfully consult with them, but instead approved the project before completing the required consultation. According to the Tribe, BLM simply didn't consider what the tribe had to say before approving the project.

The Court finds this to be the strongest basis for issuance of injunctive relief and therefore focuses on it.

NHPA Consultation Requirements

The NHPA's purpose is to preserve historic resources, and early consultation with tribes is encouraged "to ensure that all types of historic properties and all public interests in such properties are given due consideration. . . ." *Te-Moak Tribe v. U.S. Dept. of Interior*, 608 F.3d 592, 609 (9th Cir. 2010) (quoting 16 U.S.C. § 470a(d)(1)(A)). The consultation process is governed by 36 C.F.R. § 800.2(c)(2), one of Section 106's implementing regulations. Under this regulation, "[c]onsultation should commence early in the planning process, in order to identify and discuss relevant preservation issues . . . ." § 800.2(c)(2)(ii)(A). The Ninth Circuit has emphasized that the timing of required review processes can affect the outcome and is to be discouraged. *Id.* (citing *Pit River Tribe v. U.S. Forest Serv.*, 469 F.3d 768, 785–86 (9th Cir. 2006)). The consultation requirement is not an empty formality; rather, it "must recognize the government-to-government relationship between the Federal Government and Indian tribes" and is to be "conducted in a manner sensitive to the concerns and needs of the Indian tribe." § 800.2(c)(2)(ii)(C). A tribe may, if it wishes, designate representatives for the consultation. *Id.*

The Section 106 process is described in 36 C.F.R. §§ 800.2–800.6. After preliminary identification of the project and consulting parties, Section 106 requires identifying historic properties within a project's affected area, evaluating the project's potential effects on those properties, and resolving any adverse effects. The Tribe insists this consultation must be completed at least for Phase 1 of the project, before construction begins.

Throughout this process, the regulations require the agency to consult extensively with Indian tribes that fall within the definition of "consulting party," including here the Quechan Tribe. Section 800.4 alone requires at least seven issues about which the Tribe, as a consulting party, is entitled to be consulted before the project was approved. Under § 800.4(a)(3), BLM is required to consult with the Tribe identify issues relating to the project's potential effects on historic properties. Under § 800.4(a)(4), BLM is required to gather information from the Tribe to assist in identifying properties which may be of religious and cultural significance to it. Under § 800.4(b), BLM is required to consult with the Tribe to take steps necessary to identify historic properties within the area of potential effects. Under § 800.4(b)(1), BLM's official is required to take into account any confidentiality concerns raised by tribes during the identification process. Under § 800.4(c)(1), BLM must consult with the Tribe to apply National Register criteria to properties within the identified area, if they have not yet been evaluated for eligibility for listing in the National Register of Historic Places. Under § 800.4(c)(2), if the Tribe doesn't agree with the BLM's determination regarding National Register eligibility, it is entitled to ask for a determination. And under § 800.4(d)(1) and (2), if BLM determines no historic properties will be affected, it must give the Tribe a report and invite the Tribe to provide its views. Sections 800.5 and 800.6 require further consultation and review to resolve adverse effects and to deal with failure to resolve adverse effects.

Furthermore, under § 800.2, consulting parties that are Indian tribes are entitled to *special consideration* in the course of an agency's fulfillment of its consultation obligations. This is spelled out in extensive detail in § 800.2(c). Among other things, that section sets forth the following requirements:

> (A) The agency official shall ensure that consultation in the section 106 process provides the Indian tribe ... a reasonable opportunity to identify its concerns about historic properties, advise on the identification and evaluation of historic properties, including those of traditional religious and cultural importance, articulate its views on the undertaking's effects on such properties, and participate in the resolution of adverse effects. ... **Consultation should commence early in the planning process, in order to identify and discuss relevant preservation issues and resolve concerns about the confidentiality of information on historic properties.**

> (B) The Federal Government has a unique legal relationship with Indian tribes set forth in the Constitution of the United States, treaties, statutes, and court decisions. **Consultation with Indian tribes should be conducted in a sensitive manner respectful of tribal sovereignty. ...**

> (C) **Consultation with an Indian tribe must recognize the government-to-government relationship between the Federal Government and Indian tribes. The agency official shall consult with representatives designated or identified by the tribal government. ... Consultation with Indian tribes ... should be conducted in a manner sensitive to the concerns and needs of the Indian tribe. ...**

(D) When Indian tribes ... attach religious and cultural significance to historic properties off tribal lands, section 101(d)(6)(B) of the act requires Federal agencies to consult with such Indian tribes ... in the section 106 process. **Federal agencies should be aware that frequently historic properties of religious and cultural significance are located on ancestral, aboriginal, or ceded lands of Indian tribes ... and should consider that when complying with the procedures in this part.**

36 C.F.R. § 800.2(c)(2)(ii)(A)-(D) (emphasis added). . . .

. . .

The Tribe's Evidence and Arguments

In support of its point that Defendants failed to adequately consult, the Tribe cites its letter to BLM's Field Manager on February 4, 2010, in which it expressed concern that the schedule for issuance of the ROD didn't allow enough time for adequate consultation, and that the required consultation was being inappropriate deferred. . . . This letter says the Tribe had informally learned that a Programmatic Agreement was being developed, which BLM intended to approve by September, 2010. It also expressed the concern that, if the project were ultimately approved in spite of the presence of cultural resources, the quick schedule wouldn't allow enough time for BLM to consult with the tribe to develop a plan to avoid harming the sites.

By itself, this letter suggests the Tribe was consulted late in the planning process, wasn't being consulted when it wrote the letter, and was concerned about the lack of consultation. It also suggests the time frame for consultation was compressed. The Tribe also cites other later documents, showing that it expressed its dissatisfaction to the Department.

At oral argument, the Tribe admitted BLM engaged in some communication and did some consulting, but described the purported consulting as cursory and inadequate, consisting mostly of informational meetings where the Tribe's opinions were not sought, rather than government-to-government consultation.

Defendants' Evidence and Arguments

In response, Defendants provide string citations to materials in the record which they say document "extensive consultation with tribes, including Plaintiff." (Opp'n to Mot. for Prelim. Inj. at 4:18–5:2). This description of the documents is general and cursory, and sheds little light on the degree to which BLM consulted with the Tribe, or whether the consultation was intended to comply with NEPA or NHPA. First, the documentation includes consultations with other tribes, agencies, and with the public. While this other consultation appears to be required and serves other important purposes, it doesn't substitute for the mandatory consultation with the Quechan Tribe. In other words, that BLM did a lot of consulting in general doesn't show that its consultation with the Tribe was adequate under the regulations. Indeed, Defendants' grouping tribes together (referring to consultation with "tribes") is unhelpful: Indian tribes aren't interchangeable, and consultation with one tribe doesn't relieve the BLM of its obligation to consult with any other tribe that may be a consulting party under NHPA. . . .

. . . .

Analysis of Documentary Evidence

Preliminarily, several points bear noting. First, the sheer volume of documents is not meaningful. The number of letters, reports, meetings, etc. and the size of the various documents doesn't in itself show the NHPA-required consultation occurred.

Second, the BLM's communications are replete with recitals of law (including Section 106), professions of good intent, and solicitations to consult with the Tribe. But mere *pro forma* recitals do not, by themselves, show BLM actually complied with the law. As discussed below, documentation that might support a finding that true government-to-government consultation occurred is painfully thin.

At oral argument, the Tribe described the meetings as cursory information sessions and the reports and other communications as inadequate. Its briefing also argues that Defendants have confused "contact" with required "consultation." Defendants In response, Defendants argue that the Tribe "has been invited to government-to-government consultations since 2008" "BLM began informing the Tribe of proposed renewable energy projects within the California Desert District as early as 2007," and "[s]ince that time BLM has regularly updated the Tribe on the status of the [Imperial Valley Solar] project." (Opp'n, 5:26–6:3.)

The Tribe's first document contact with BLM was the tribal historical preservation officer's letter of February 19, 2008. That letter put BLM on notice that the historical and cultural sites within the project area would be considered important to the Tribe. It also asked BLM to provide a survey of the area and to meet with the Tribe's government, which would have constituted government-to-government consultation. BLM could not have provided the survey at that time, and apparently also didn't comply with the meeting request, because the historic preservation officer re-sent the letter the next month. In fact, the documentary evidence doesn't show BLM ever met with the Tribe's government until October 16, 2010, well after the project was approved. All available evidence tends to show BLM repeatedly said it would be glad to meet with the Tribe, but never did so.

Although BLM invited the Tribe to attend public informational meetings about the project, the invitations do not appear to meet the requirements set forth in 36 C.F.R. § 800.2(c)(2)(ii). This is particularly true because the Tribe first requested a more private, closed meeting between BLM and its tribal council. In later communications, the Tribe continued to request that BLM meet with its tribal council on the Tribe's reservation. In addition, the Tribe repeatedly complained that the properties hadn't been identified, and asked for a map showing where the identified sites were, requests that apparently went unanswered at least as late as June, 2010. The Tribe's letter of August 4, 2010 apparently acknowledges receipt of maps, but asks for an extension of the deadline so it could review them before responding.

The documentary evidence also confirms the Tribe's contention that the number of identified sites continued to fluctuate. . . . And Defendants have admitted the evaluation of sites eligible for inclusion in the National Register hasn't *yet* been completed.

BLM's invitation to "consult," then, amounted to little more than a general request for the Tribe to gather its own information about all sites within the area and disclose it at public meetings. Because of the lack of information, it was impossible for the Tribe to have been consulted meaningful as required in applicable regulations. The documentary evidence also discloses almost no "government-to-government" consultation. While public informational meetings, consultations with individual tribal members, meetings with government staff or contracted investigators, and written updates are obviously a helpful and necessary part of the process, they don't amount to the type of "government-to-government" consultation contemplated by the regulations. This is particularly true because the Tribe's government's requests for information and meetings were frequently rebuffed or responses were extremely delayed as BLM-imposed deadlines loomed or passed.

No letters from the BLM ever initiate government-to-government contact between the Tribe and the United States or its designated representatives. . . Rather, the Tribe was invited to attend public informational meetings or to consult with two members of her staff, an archaeologist and a person identified only as a "point of contact." The BLM in fact rebuffed the Tribe's August 4 request that the BLM meet with the tribal council on its reservation, proposing instead that the tribal council call BLM staff.

. . . .

Defendants have emphasized the size, complexity, and expense of this project, as well as the time limits, and the facts are sympathetic. Tessera hoped to qualify for stimulus funds under the American Recovery and Reinvestment Act of 2009 by beginning construction no later than the end of this year, which is about two weeks away. To that end, BLM apparently imposed deadlines of its own choosing. Section 106's consulting requirements can be onerous, and would have been particularly so here. Because of the large number of consulting parties (including several tribes), the logistics and expense of consulting would have been incredibly difficult. None of this analysis is meant to suggest federal agencies must acquiesce to every tribal request.

That said, government agencies are not free to glide over requirements imposed by Congressionally-approved statutes and duly adopted regulations. The required consultation must at least meet the standards set forth in 36 C.F.R. § 800.2(c)(2)(ii), and should begin early. The Tribe was entitled to be provided with adequate information and time, consistent with its status as a government that is entitled to be consulted. The Tribe's consulting rights should have been respected. It is clear that did not happen here.

The Court therefore determines the Tribe is likely to prevail at least on its claim that it was not adequately consulted as required under NHPA before the project was approved. Because the project was approved "without observance of procedure required by law," the Tribe is entitled to have the BLM's actions set aside under 5 U.S.C. § 706(2)(D).

NOTES & QUESTIONS

1.   In the case above, why was the Quechan Tribe strongly concerned about the development of the Imperial Valley Solar Project, even though the project was no being sited on the tribe's Indian trust (reservation) lands?

2.   Describe the difference between the BLM's view of the NHPA Section 106 consultation requirement and the tribe's view of that requirement. Which view did the *Quechan Tribe* court seem to embrace, and why?

3.   According to the *Quechan Tribe* opinion, why was the BLM apparently seeking to hurriedly expedite the permitting of its utility-scale solar energy project?

4.   *The Importance of Due Diligence.* When pursuing large development projects, developers and their lawyers often encounter pressure to try to save time and money by cutting small corners in their evaluation of potential issues at project sites. In 2016, municipal officials in Santa Clara County, California were reminded of the potential hazards of such an approach when they learned that they had sited a ground-mounted solar PV array atop a known burial ground of the Ohlone Indian tribe. Fortunately, it appeared that the solar project had not disturbed human remains or other major cultural resources at the site. See Julia Baum, *San Jose: Solar panels built on Ohlone burial ground near Highway 87*, THE MERCURY NEWS (Aug. 9, 2017), http://www.mercury

news.com/2016/08/09/san-jose-solar-panels-built-on-ohlone-burial-ground-near-highway-87/.

3. UTILITY-SCALE SOLAR AND WILDLIFE PROTECTION

Like wind farms, utility-scale solar energy projects often occupy remote rural areas and can therefore potentially harm wildlife habitats and populations in those areas. The impacts of large solar energy projects tend to be quite different from those of wind farms, where bats and birds can fall victim to enormous turbine blades. However, utility-scale solar energy development certainly can still have significant adverse impacts on wildlife populations. As described above, most solar energy farms occupy very large tracts of rural land. When developers site a project on land that serves as critical habitat for a threatened or endangered animal species, practical and legal challenges often arise.

a. Concentrating Solar Projects and Birds

The most dramatic clash between wildlife and solar energy involves concentrating solar plants, which use mirrors to reflect light toward towers where intense heat makes steam and ultimately generates electricity. As mentioned earlier in this Chapter, on sunny days the airspace near these towers can reach extremely high temperatures and pose a lethal hazard to birds flying in the area. The following excerpt is one commentator's description of this hazard at California's Ivanpah Solar Electric Generating System (ISEGS)—a large concentrating solar plant developed by the private developer BrightSource Energy, Inc.

A LESSON FROM ICARUS: HOW THE MANDATE FOR RAPID SOLAR DEVELOPMENT HAS SINGED A FEW FEATHERS

Morgan Walton
40 VT. L. REV. 131, 135–36, 138–41 (2015)

. . . The ISEGS is located in San Bernadino County, California, 4.5 miles southwest of Primm, Nevada. The facility contains three separate solar thermal collection towers with adjacent mirror fields built from 2010 to 2013. Combined, the facility uses over 300,000 heliostat mirrors to track the sun and reflect sunlight to boilers atop three 459-foot tall collection towers (one for each mirror field). The equipment is activated each morning and is run until the evening. Electricity is generated by concentrated sunlight hitting the boiler pipes and superheating the water inside to create steam. That steam is pumped to spin the turbines, which creates up to 400 MW of electricity. Electricity is delivered via three supply lines to a substation that is owned and operated by Southern California Edison (SCE). The stored energy then provides power to over 140,000 homes in Southern California.

Several federal and state agencies have been involved in the approval, planning, construction, and operation of the solar power facility. For instance, the California Energy Commission (CEC) and the U.S. Fish and Wildlife Service (USFWS) both played crucial roles in approving the project. The USFWS's contributions were of particular importance in consulting with developers about the biological impact to species in the area, with special focus on the desert tortoise population. In addition to these agencies, the [U.S. Bureau of Land Management (BLM)] was significantly involved in the initial process because the power plant was to be built on federal public land managed by the agency. It was therefore the BLM's responsibility to evaluate the overall environmental impact, consider the alternatives, and release a Final [Environmental Impact Statement (EIS)] before the project could be approved.

The BLM prepared the EIS according to [National Environmental Protection Act (NEPA)] requirements in cooperation with other state and federal agencies. The Final EIS addresses multiple areas of potential impact including: effects to air, soil, and water; biological resources; cultural resources; public health and safety; socioeconomics; visual resources; and recreation. The Final EIS concluded that the proposed project would have both beneficial and adverse impacts on different areas. The project would have the maximum benefit to the socioeconomic, greenhouse gas, and air pollutant impacts. In contrast, the plan would have the greatest adverse impact on biological resources, soil and water resources, and visual resources, all of which could not be completely mitigated. . . .

. . . .

After the ISEGS began producing energy on February 13, 2014, workers quickly noticed "smoke plume[s]" caused by birds igniting in midair when they flew over the solar mirrors. These "streamers," as the workers called them, drew national attention starting in August 2014, but the deaths were first noticed early in the project's operation. In April of 2014, the U.S. Fish and Wildlife's Office of Law Enforcement (OLE) sent scientists from their Forensics Laboratory to investigate 233 bird deaths (71 different species) related to solar facilities, and published a report on their findings. The study investigated all incidents of avian mortality at three different sites, including the ISEGS. Each project used a different form of solar technology (photovoltaic, trough, and solar power tower systems), and bird deaths were documented at all three sites. The study concluded that there were three main causes of death: "impact trauma, predation and solar flux," where birds at all three sites were killed by impact trauma and predation, and only birds at the ISEGS were killed by solar flux.

While trauma was the leading cause of death at all three sites, trauma and solar flux were the two major causes of death in Ivanpah. Solar flux is "intense radiant energy focused by the mirror array on the power-generating tower" creating extreme heat, which the birds fly through. In the solar flux deaths, the investigators found:

> Exposure to solar flux caused singeing of feathers, which resulted in mortality in several ways. Severe singeing of flight feathers caused catastrophic loss of flying ability, leading to death by impact with the ground or other objects. Less severe singeing led to impairment of flight capability, reducing ability to forage and evade predators, leading to starvation or predation.

The investigators discovered that the solar sites killed 71 different species. The species covered an ecologically diverse range of characteristics including: size variance (from hummingbirds to pelicans); raptors; aerial, aquatic, and ground feeders; nocturnal and diurnal species; and resident and non-resident (migratory) species. The results indicated that 47 deaths, of the 141 carcasses collected, were from solar flux exposure. Additionally, investigators found a significant number of dead insects that led to the theory that the intense light from the mirror field acts as a "mega-trap" by "attracting insects which in turn attract insect-eating birds, which are incapacitated by solar flux injury, thus attracting predators and creating an entire food chain vulnerable to injury and death."

Unable to obtain technical data on the solar flux temperature at Ivanpah, investigators gathered data from other solar power tower style plants. In these other projects, when the mirrors directed concentrated solar light to the power tower, the beams could "multiply the strength of sunlight by 5000 times" and generate "temperatures in excess of 3600 degrees Fahrenheit." Usually only a fraction of the mirrors are directed at the power tower at any given time, which creates an optimal functioning temperature of 900° F around the tower. The Fish and Wildlife investigators observed that most of the "streamer" events occurred near the tower in the field where the solar flux temperatures would be the highest. The investigators then conducted studies to determine that feathers can burn or singe at an air temperature of 752° F, which they concluded must have at least been the minimum temperature in the solar flux when the birds would have flown through. During their time in Ivanpah, the investigators observed an average of one "streamer" every two minutes.

The Fish and Wildlife study recommends several ways to mitigate the bird deaths caused by solar flux. But the agency's main suggestion is to monitor the situation and conduct daily observations to study the full impact on avian wildlife for a two-year period. Some mitigation measures include: clearing [the] area around the towers to decrease the habitat attractiveness; suspending "power tower operation during peak migration" periods; placing "perch deterrent devices . . . on tower railings near the flux field"; and employing other exclusionary measures. The investigators emphasize a lack of knowledge regarding the scope of avian mortality at these facilities, and limited data exists about how solar flux fully affects birds and insects. But they do admit that "[t]he numbers of dead birds are likely underrepresented, perhaps vastly so."

However, not all interested parties agree with the findings of the USFWS investigators. BrightSource's own investigators estimate that the number of bird deaths from solar flux is more in the range of 1,000 birds per year. A recent report estimates the number of deaths to be above 3,500, but even that number is fiercely debated. One expert with the Center for Biological Diversity estimates the number closer to 28,000 birds killed per year. Both BrightSource and the Center have opposed interests and the radical difference in estimates reflects each group's priorities: BrightSource wants to diminish the ecological impact, but also stay on pace to build future projects; the Center for Biological Diversity wants to decrease the adverse impact to wildlife. While BrightSource admitted that they want to reduce avian impacts and use technology to detect, monitor, and deter bird movement around the solar facilities; they also reiterated their larger mission to provide renewable energy and fight climate change, and that such goals often come with necessary trade-offs to succeed.

QUESTIONS

1.   What is "solar flux", and why does it occur more commonly at CSP plants than at other types of utility-scale solar energy facilities?

2.   What is the "necessary trade-off" mentioned in the excerpt above? What are some factors that make it difficult to accurately measure and find the optimal balance in this trade-off for any given solar energy project?

3.   What "mitigation measures" are mentioned in the excerpt that might help to reduce avian deaths at the Ivanpah solar project site? Why do you think regulators failed to expressly require the developer and operator of the plant to institute these measures as part of the project approval process?

b.   Solar Energy and Other Protected Species

Although the potential hazards of CSPs to birds are dramatic, the majority of the nation's disputes related to the wildlife impacts of utility-scale solar farms have centered on other animals. The protected animal species that has seemingly generated the most obstacles for utility-scale solar projects in recent years is the desert tortoise. The growing presence of human activity in desert regions of the Southwest has caused wild populations of the desert tortoise to decline precipitously over the past half century. The desert tortoise is a threatened species under the ESA today, which affords it various legal protections that impede numerous types of development in remote areas of the nation's desert Southwest region, including solar energy development. For more thorough background information on the desert tortoise, its population range, and efforts to limit solar farms' impacts on the species, see generally Philip J. Murphy et al., SOLAR ENERGY AND THE MOJAVE DESERT TORTOISE (2013), http://www. energy.ca.gov/2014publications/CEC-500-2014-011/CEC-500-2014-011.pdf.

The following case addresses one recent legal dispute between a developer and wildlife conservation advocates over a proposed solar energy project and its potential impacts on desert tortoise habitat areas in southern Nevada. The case also provides a useful explanation of the ESA and how it impacts large solar energy projects sited in or near the habitats of endangered or threatened species.

DEFENDERS OF WILDLIFE V. ZINKE
United States Court of Appeals, Ninth Circuit, 2017
856 F.3d 1248

M. SMITH, C.J.

This case arises from the Bureau of Land Management (BLM)'s approval of a right-of-way on federal lands in Nevada for the construction of an industrial solar project, known as Silver State South, and the project's possible impact on the desert tortoise. Plaintiff Defenders of Wildlife (DOW) contends that the Department of the Interior, the U.S. Fish and Wildlife Service (FWS), and the BLM (collectively, the Federal Defendants) violated the requirements of the Endangered Species Act (ESA), 16 U.S.C. § 1531, et seq., and the Administrative Procedures Act (APA), 5 U.S.C. § 706, by issuing a Biological Opinion (BiOp) analyzing the effect of Silver State South on the desert tortoise that was arbitrary, capricious, and an abuse of discretion, and subsequently relying on the BiOp to grant the right-of-way. The district court concluded that the BiOp fully complied with both the ESA and APA, and granted summary judgment for the Federal Defendants and Intervenor-Defendants Silver State Solar Power South, LLC and Silver State South Solar, LLC (collectively, Defendants). We affirm.

BACKGROUND

I.   Statutory Framework

"The Endangered Species Act of 1973, 16 U.S.C. § 1531, et seq., 'is a comprehensive scheme with the broad purpose of protecting endangered and threatened species.'" *Conservation Cong. v. U.S. Forest Serv.*, 720 F.3d 1048, 1050–51 (9th Cir. 2013) (quoting *Ctr. for Biological Diversity v. U.S. Bureau of Land Mgmt.*, 698 F.3d 1101, 1106 (9th Cir. 2012)). The ESA tasks the Secretary of the Interior and the Secretary of Commerce with identifying and maintaining a list of endangered and threatened species. 16 U.S.C. § 1533(a)(1)–(2). Endangered species are those "in danger of extinction throughout all or a significant portion of its range." *Id.* at § 1532(6). Threatened species are those "likely to become an endangered species within the foreseeable future." *Id.* at § 1532(20). The Secretary of the Interior is additionally charged with designating "critical habitat" for each listed species. *Id.* at § 1533(a)(3)(A)(i). Critical habitat is defined as (a) "specific areas within the geographical area occupied by the [endangered] species . . . on which are found those physical or biological features (I) essential to the conservation of the species and (II) which may require special management considerations or protection," *id.* at § 1532(5)(A)(i), and (b) "specific areas outside the geographical area occupied by the species . . . [that] are essential for the conservation of the species," *id.* at § 1532(5)(A)(ii). However, critical habitat generally does "not include the entire geographical area which can be occupied by the threatened or endangered species." *Id.* at § 1532(5)(C).

Section 7(a)(2) of the ESA "affirmatively commands each federal agency to 'insure that any action authorized, funded, or carried out' by the agency 'is not likely to jeopardize the continued existence of any endangered species . . . or result in the destruction or adverse modification of habitat of such species.' " *Or. Nat. Res. Council v. Allen*, 476 F.3d 1031, 1033 (9th Cir. 2007) (quoting 16 U.S.C. § 1536(a)(2)). To comply with Section 7(a)(2), an agency proposing an action (the action agency) must first determine whether the action "may affect" an endangered or threatened species or its critical habitat. 50 C.F.R. § 402.14(a) (2016). If the action agency determines that its proposed action "may affect" an endangered species or its critical habitat, the action agency must initiate formal consultation with either the FWS or the National Marine Fisheries Service (NMFS), as appropriate (collectively, the consulting agency). . . .

. . . [I]f formal consultation is required, "the consulting agency must prepare a biological opinion that advises the action agency as to whether the proposed action, alone or 'taken together with cumulative effects, is likely to jeopardize the continued existence of listed species or result in the destruction or adverse modification of critical habitat.' " *Conservation Cong.*, 720 F.3d at 1051 (quoting 50 C.F.R. § 402.14(g)(4)). Jeopardy to the continued existence of a listed species (jeopardy) "means to engage in an action that reasonably would be expected, directly or indirectly, to reduce appreciably the likelihood of both the survival and recovery of a listed species in the wild by reducing the reproduction, numbers, or distribution of that species." 50 C.F.R. § 402.02. Destruction or adverse modification of critical habitat (adverse modification) "means a direct or indirect alteration that appreciably diminishes the value of critical habitat for both the survival and recovery of a listed species." *Id.* (2014). . . .

If the consulting agency determines that a proposed action *is* likely to result in jeopardy or adverse modification, the consulting agency must suggest "reasonable and prudent alternatives, if any" that avoid jeopardy or adverse modification. 50 C.F.R. § 402.14(h)(3). If there are no alternatives, then any "take" of the listed species resulting from the proposed action will violate Section 9 of the ESA, which prohibits the taking of any member of an endangered or threatened species. *Ctr. for Biological Diversity*, 698 F.3d at 1106–07 (citing 16 U.S.C. § 1538(a)(1)(B)). Violations of Section 9 can result in "substantial civil and criminal penalties, including imprisonment." *Id.* at 1107 (internal quotation marks omitted).

If the consulting agency concludes that the proposed action is *not* likely to result in jeopardy or adverse modification, but the project nevertheless results in takings of a listed species that "result from, but are not the purpose of, carrying out" the requested agency action, the consulting agency must include an incidental take statement in the biological opinion. 50 C.F.R. § 402.02. The incidental take statement "(1) specif[ies] the impact of the incidental taking on the species; (2) specif[ies] the 'reasonable and prudent measures' that the FWS considers necessary or appropriate to minimize such impact; (3) set[s] forth 'terms and conditions' with which the action agency must comply to implement the reasonable and prudent measures . . . ; and (4) specif[ies] the procedures to be used to handle or dispose of any animals actually taken." *Or. Nat. Res. Council*, 476 F.3d at 1034. . . . Compliance with the terms of an incidental take statement "exempts the action agency from the prohibition on takings found in Section 9 of the ESA." *Nat'l Wildlife Fed'n v. Nat'l Marine Fisheries Serv.*, 524 F.3d 917, 924–25 (9th Cir. 2008). . . .

II. The Desert Tortoise

The desert tortoise is a reptile native to the Mojave and Sonoran deserts in southern California, southern Nevada, Arizona, and the southwestern tip of Utah. In 1990, the FWS listed the desert tortoise as "threatened[ ]". . . . In 1994, the FWS divided the entire range of the desert tortoise into six recovery units to "conserve the genetic, behavioral, morphological, and ecological diversity necessary for long-term sustainability of the entire [desert tortoise] population." The FWS then designated a total of 6.4 million acres of land within the six recovery units as the desert tortoise's critical habitat. . . . One of the six recovery units, the Eastern Mojave Recovery Unit, is at issue here.

III. The Silver State South Project

In 2008, NextLight Renewable Power, LLC submitted right-of-way applications to the BLM for the construction of two solar power facilities, Silver State North and Silver State South. It proposed to locate both project sites on unincorporated public lands in the Ivanpah Valley. Although the proposed project sites fell within the Eastern Mojave Recovery Unit, both were outside the designated critical habitat for the desert tortoise within this recovery unit. However, Silver State South would be located within a corridor between Silver State North and the Lucy Gray Mountains, which is currently the geographical linkage that provides "the most reliable potential for continued population connectivity [of the desert tortoise] throughout the Ivanpah Valley." Connectivity is the "degree to which population growth and vital rates are affected by dispersal" and "the flow of genetic material between two populations." Connectivity promotes stability in a species by "providing an immigrant subsidy that compensates for low survival or birth rates of residents" and "increasing colonization of unoccupied" habitat.

In October 2010, the BLM approved the application for Silver State North but deferred approval of the application for Silver State South. The BLM explained that the deferral of Silver State South was in part due to the "higher density of [desert] tortoise that reside in that portion of the project area," which "requires additional wildlife consideration and potentially further consultation with the [FWS]."

In October 2012, the BLM issued a draft Supplemental Environmental Impact Statement (SEIS) that evaluated three alternative layouts for Silver State South. In response to the SEIS, the Nevada field office of the FWS recommended that the BLM reject all three layouts and choose a "No Action" alternative. The FWS expressed concern over Silver State South's potential impact on habitat fragmentation and genetic isolation of the desert tortoise and noted that the proposed layouts would reduce the existing width of the corridor between Silver State North and the Lucy Gray Mountains to .02 miles, .03 miles, or 1 mile. In the alternative, the FWS recommended that the BLM create a new proposal that would keep the corridor [wider]. . . . The FWS also recommended the adoption of additional mitigation measures to offset any reductions in the linkage and monitoring studies to track impact on population demographics and genetic stability.

On February 11, 2013, the BLM initiated formal consultation under the ESA for Silver State South. The consultation process among the BLM, the FWS, and Silver State Solar Power South, LLC . . . resulted in a new proposal (the BLM-preferred alternative) that was authorized by the BLM in 2014. The BLM-preferred alternative reduced the size of the project from 3,881 acres to 2,427 acres, and left a 3.65 mile long corridor between Silver State South and the Lucy Gray Mountains with a width ranging from 1.39 to 2 miles. The BLM-preferred alternative also incorporated measures to minimize adverse effects on the desert tortoise, such as the translocation of desert tortoises found within the project site, and measures to offset the loss of the desert tortoise habitat, primarily consisting of the Silver State South applicants funding the BLM's conservation activities.

Of particular importance to this case, the Silver State South applicants agreed to fund a monitoring program jointly developed by the U.S. Geological Survey and the BLM (the USGS monitoring study) that would track the regional desert tortoise populations for changes in demographic and genetic stability. . . .

IV. The Biological Opinion

On September 30, 2013, the FWS issued the BiOp, which formally reviewed the BLM-preferred alternative. The BiOp selected the entire Ivanpah Valley as the "action area" for Silver State South, because of the "potential effects . . . on connectivity for the desert tortoise within the entire valley."

The BiOp first concluded that Silver State South would be "not likely to adversely affect the critical habitat of the desert tortoise," because "the proposed actions would not occur within the boundaries of critical habitat of the desert tortoise or directly or indirectly affect the primary constituent elements of critical habitat" ("no adverse modification" determination).

The BiOp next concluded that Silver State South was unlikely to appreciably diminish the reproduction, numbers, or distribution of the desert tortoise in the action area ("no jeopardy" determination). The BiOp found no long term effects on the reproductive rates of tortoises that live adjacent to the project site or of tortoises that would be translocated. It estimated that few tortoises would be harmed or killed because of the proposed translocation of tortoises found in the project site and fencing to be built around Silver State South. It also acknowledged that the habitat loss of 2,388 acres "will reduce connectivity between the southern and northern ends of Ivanpah Valley," but explained that the proposed mitigation measures would "offset, to some degree, the decrease in the width of the linkage." The BiOp therefore expressed "uncertain[ty] as to whether the reduced width of the corridor between the Silver State South Project and the Lucy Gray Mountains would cause demographic or genetic instability." But, the BiOp reasoned, should Silver State South ultimately degrade connectivity, the USGS monitory survey would be able to detect any change and "the long generation time [of the tortoise] and re-initiation requirements of section 7(a)(2) would enable [the BLM] to undertake correction actions on the ground to bolster connectivity."

The BiOp also concluded that Silver State South would not appreciably impede the long-term recovery of the desert tortoise. . . . The BiOp again noted that the USGS monitoring study would detect any changes to connectivity, which would allow for imposition of remedial measures.

V. The BLM Approval of the Right-of-Way for Silver State South

In February 2014, the BLM issued a Record of Decision, and granted the requested right-of-way for Silver State South. The Record of Decision specifically approved the BLM-preferred alternative for Silver State South and noted that the "reasonable and prudent measures contained in the [BiOp] significantly minimize and/or mitigate environmental damage and protect resources." Construction of Silver State South has now been completed.

VI. Procedural History

On March 6, 2014, DOW sued the Federal Defendants to enjoin construction of Silver State South. Silver State Solar Power South, LLC and Silver State South Solar, LLC, another subsidiary of the original project applicant, subsequently intervened as defendants. The district court denied DOW's request for a preliminary injunction, concluding that DOW could not show a likelihood of success on the merits of their claim that the BiOp's "no jeopardy" determination was arbitrary or capricious. *Defs. of Wildlife v. Jewell*, No. CV 14–1656–MWF, 2014 WL 1364452, at *14 (C.D. Cal. Apr. 2, 2014).

The parties subsequently cross-moved for summary judgment. The district court denied DOW's motion and granted summary judgment for the various Defendants. . . . The district court . . . concluded that the BiOp fully complied with both the ESA and the APA, and that the BLM permissibly relied upon the BiOp in authorizing Silver State South. DOW timely appealed on May 28, 2015.

STANDARD OF REVIEW

We review de novo a district court's grant of summary judgment. . .

"Agency decisions under ESA are governed by the Administrative Procedure Act, which requires an agency action to be upheld unless it is found to be 'arbitrary, capricious, an abuse of discretion, or otherwise not in accordance with law.' " *Pac. Coast Fed'n of Fishermen's Ass'ns, Inc. v. Nat'l Marine Fisheries Serv.*, 265 F.3d 1028, 1034 (9th Cir. 2001) (quoting 5 U.S.C. § 706(2)(A)). . . .

ANALYSIS

I. Jeopardy Analysis

DOW first argues that the BiOp's determination that Silver State South would not result in jeopardy to the desert tortoise impermissibly relied upon unspecified remedial measures. DOW cites the BiOp's conclusion, which states:

> To summarize, we concluded that the proposed actions are not likely to appreciably diminish reproduction, numbers, or distribution of the desert tortoise in the action area, or to appreciably impede long-term recovery of the desert tortoise. *Integral to that conclusion* is our expectation that the reduction in the width of habitat east of the Silver State South Project is *either*

unlikely to degrade demographic or genetic stability in Ivanpah Valley *or* that we will be able to detect degradation of those values and implement remedial actions, if necessary.

(Emphasis added). DOW interprets this second sentence to indicate that the BiOp's "no jeopardy" determination was dependent on the ability to detect future demographic or genetic degradation and implement remedial measures. And, because the BiOp did not identify specific remedial actions to combat these future effects, DOW argues that BiOp's "no jeopardy" determination was arbitrary and capricious.

DOW's objection to the BiOp's "no jeopardy" determination fails for two reasons. First, the BiOp did not rely on mitigation measures to make its "no jeopardy" determination. Throughout the BiOp, the FWS expressly stated that it was uncertain if the reduced width of the corridor between Silver State South and the Lucy Gray Mountains would cause genetic or demographic instability. This uncertainty reflected the lack of a scientific consensus regarding the requisite corridor width necessary to support connectivity for the desert tortoise. In the face of such uncertainty, the FWS permissibly concluded that the reduced width of the corridor would not result in jeopardy. . . .

Second, our precedents do not require mitigation measures to be identified or guaranteed when the mitigation measures themselves may be unnecessary. . . . DOW cites no authority for the proposition that an agency must . . . identify and guarantee mitigation measures that target uncertain future negative effects. As aptly noted by the district court, "[t]he FWS cannot be expected to respond to data that is not yet available to surmise potential mitigation actions that are not needed under the agency's current interpretation of the data."

Here, although the BiOp repeatedly emphasized that monitoring would allow the FWS to detect any future genetic or demographic degradation and implement responsive mitigation measures, the BiOp ultimately found these potential harms to be uncertain. As such, even the sentence of the BiOp upon which DOW relies acknowledges that the need for future mitigation measures is similarly uncertain, by explaining that the implementation of remedial actions will only be done "if necessary." Because the BiOp did not rely upon these potential remedial measures to target a certain or existing harm that would be caused by Silver State South, the BiOp was not obligated to identify or guarantee these future remedial measures. Accordingly, the BiOp's "no jeopardy" determination was neither arbitrary nor capricious.

II. Adverse Modification Analysis

The BiOp concluded that Silver State South would be "not likely to adversely affect critical habitat of the desert tortoise," because "the proposed actions would not occur within the boundaries of critical habitat of the desert tortoise or directly or indirectly affect the primary constituent elements of critical habitat." The BiOp therefore did not analyze whether Silver State South would adversely modify the critical habitat within the Ivanpah Valley. . . .

. . . .

Although the construction of Silver State South was not to occur on any critical habitat, DOW argues that the BiOp was obligated to perform an adverse modification analysis because evidence in the record indicated that the construction of Silver State South would narrow the corridor between two critical habitats, and thus adversely affect the connectivity of the desert tortoise. DOW contends that this reduction in connectivity constitutes adverse modification of critical habitat because it is an impact to the critical habitat's recovery value.

. . . .

We agree with Defendants that the plain language of the ESA requires that an adverse modification of critical habitat consists of two elements: (1) a "modification" of the habitat that is (2) "adverse." 16 U.S.C. § 1536(a)(2). Both the 1986 and 2016 definitions reflect that understanding by defining adverse modification as a "direct or indirect *alteration*" that "appreciably diminishes the value of the critical habitat." 50 C.F.R. § 402.02 (2014) (emphasis added); 50 C.F.R. § 402.02 (2016) (same). . . .

. . . .

With this proper understanding of "adverse modification" in mind, we conclude that reduced connectivity resulting from the narrowing of the corridor between Silver State South and the Lucy Gray Mountains cannot constitute adverse modification because the construction of Silver State South would not have resulted in any alteration to the critical habitat of the desert tortoise. It is undisputed that the corridor itself is not critical habitat and the construction of Silver State South would not have taken place on any critical habitat within the Ivanpah Valley. Nor can reduced connectivity itself serve as the alteration; reduced connectivity can lead to a change in the desert tortoise's genetic health, which is an alteration to the species, not its critical habitat. Accordingly, the BiOp's determination that Silver State South was "not likely to adversely affect the critical habitat of the desert tortoise," which permitted the FWS to forego an adverse modification analysis, was neither arbitrary nor capricious.

. . . .

V.   The BLM's Reliance on the BiOp

Because the BiOp was neither legally nor factually flawed, the BLM permissibly relied upon the BiOp in approving of the right-of-way for Silver State South. . . .

CONCLUSION

For the foregoing reasons, the district court's grant of summary judgment to the Defendants is AFFIRMED. . . .

NOTES & QUESTIONS

1.   What specific statutory obligation did the BLM have under the ESA in connection with its decision of whether to approve the right-of-way for the solar project?

2.   Why were a formal consultation with the FWS and a biological opinion necessary in connection with the BLM's approval of the Silver State South project, even though the project was not altering desert tortoise critical habitat?

3.   What is a "no jeopardy" determination under the ESA, and why was DOW challenging the "no jeopardy" determination issued in connection with Silver State South? What did the court hold on this issue?

4.   What is an "adverse modification" analysis, and on what ground did DOW argue the BLM was required to conduct such an analysis in conjunction with its disposition of the Silver State South right-of-say application? What was the court's determination with respect to this issue?

5.   Do you agree with the *Zinke* court's holding and arguments? Why or why not?

6.   *Other Protected Species Potentially Impacted by Utility-Scale Solar Projects.* In addition to birds and the desert tortoise, a handful of other ESA-listed species have created obstacles to utility-scale solar energy development in recent years. For instance, wildlife conservation advocates have also recently challenged utility-scale solar energy development in portions of California that serve as important habitat for the blunt-nosed leopard lizard, San Joaquin kit fox, and giant kangaroo rat. *See, e.g., Defenders of Wildlife v. U.S. Fish*, 2016 WL 4382604 (2016) (denying a request for preliminary injunction to stop development of a utility-scale solar PV project in the Panoche Valley of California). Other species potentially creating challenges for utility-scale solar energy developers in desert regions of the Southwest include the Mojave ground squirrel, Mojave fringe-toed lizard, and flat-tailed horned lizard. *See* Amy Wilson Morris & Jessica Owley, *Mitigating the Impacts of the Renewable Energy Gold Rush*, 15 MINN. J.L. SCI. & TECH. 293, 298 (2014). Regardless of whether they are ultimately successful, such challenges can significantly delay solar energy development in remote rural areas.

Having concluded its coverage of legal and policy topics specific to wind and solar energy development, this Casebook turns its attention in Chapter

7 to various strategies for integrating intermittent renewables into the electric grid and to some of the complex policy challenges that these strategies are generating across the country.

CHAPTER 7

ENERGY STORAGE, SMART GRIDS, AND DEMAND-SIDE MANAGEMENT

■ ■ ■

As highlighted earlier in this Casebook, the intermittent nature of wind and sunlight continues to constrain their ability to serve as energy sources. Most electricity customers expect their utility to reliably supply them as much power as they reasonably need, regardless of the hour of day or time of year. Obviously, when the sun is not shining and the wind is not blowing solar panels and wind turbines cannot dependably meet that demand. Accordingly, most utilities continue to rely on electricity generated from fossil fuels or nuclear power to supply the majority of their baseload power needs and on expensive natural gas-fired "peaker" plants to help them avoid major load imbalances. The unpredictability of electricity generation at most wind and solar farms limits their capacity to serve these valuable functions.

Fortunately, a wide range of innovations are emerging that seek to address the intermittency challenges of wind and solar power so that these resources can play larger roles in meeting global energy needs. For instance, improvements in energy storage technologies are enabling utilities, businesses, and individuals to more efficiently and affordably store wind- and solar- generated electricity for later use. These technologies—ranging from utility-scale bulk energy storage facilities to much smaller home battery systems—enhance the flexibility of a grid's electricity supply by enabling grid operators, utilities, and customers to store power during periods of excess supply and then quickly dispatch it when it is needed later. Such flexibility is increasingly important as utilities seek to integrate more wind and solar energy sources into the electricity system.

In addition to energy storage and other supply-side technologies, numerous other innovations are increasingly improving grid flexibility on the demand side as well. Various *demand-side management* systems and policies are emerging that apply scientific innovation, digital technologies and basic microeconomics principles to make grid load demand more responsive to fluctuations in electricity supply. At the wholesale level, grid operators are increasingly incentivizing utilities and other large electricity users to become more flexible in their demand for wholesale power. Meanwhile, at the retail level, utilities are using smart meter technologies and time-based pricing to send more accurate price signals to customers about variations in the true cost of their electricity consumption across time. In response, many retail customers are voluntarily adjusting their electricity consumption habits to save money on their electricity bills. Efforts to make buildings more energy efficient—especially during the hottest and coldest times of the year—are likewise helping to increase the flexibility of electricity demand. The greater flexibility made possible through the gradual emergence of these various demand-side management strategies is progressively helping the electricity system to accommodate increased amounts of wind and solar power.

Smart grid systems and devices have a crucial role to play in helping grid operators to fully harness the benefits of load balancing strategies such as energy storage and demand side management. Smart grid systems use computers, the Internet, and sophisticated digital platforms to facilitate near-instantaneous two-way communication between electricity producers and consumers. The information sharing, signaling, and automated response capabilities achievable through these technologies are helping to facilitate unprecedented levels of investment in renewables, energy storage, and demand-side management, but they are also raising new legal issues that stakeholders are only beginning to address.

The various policies and government programs that are evolving to govern technologies such as energy storage, demand-side management strategies, and smart grids comprise another important area of renewable energy law. Although some of these issues were covered briefly in Chapters 1 and 2, this Chapter examines them in more detail and highlights how they are impacting renewable energy development across the country.

A. ENERGY STORAGE

Inadequate energy storage technologies are arguably the single greatest impediment to transitioning the world's energy systems to run primarily on renewable energy resources. Fortunately, governments and private companies throughout the world are investing billions of dollars annually in energy storage research and development to overcome this hurdle, and there are growing signs that their collective investment is paying off. The per-unit costs for many types of energy storage are steadily declining and appear poised to fall much further in the coming years. As energy storage systems and devices become more economical and effective throughout the 21st century, their role within the energy sector is certain to expand.

1. WHAT IS ENERGY STORAGE?

Before delving too deeply into the legal and policy issues associated with energy storage technologies, it is worthwhile to clarify what the term "energy storage" generally means within energy industry circles. In a very broad sense, even fossil fuels such as coal and petroleum are technically forms of energy storage. The energy in fossil fuels first entered the earth's atmosphere as solar energy millions of years ago. Plants initially captured and stored that energy over several years in plants through photosynthesis, and natural processes eventually condensed and stored the energy in underground deposits. When fossil fuels burn, they quickly release much of that stored energy. Of course, in modern energy law and policy the term *energy storage* typically excludes fossil fuels. The term generally encompasses only facilities, systems, and devices that store previously-generated *electric* energy. The Federal Energy Regulatory Commission defines "energy storage" as

> . . . property that is interconnected to the electrical grid and is designed to receive electrical energy, to store such electrical energy as another energy form, and to convert such energy back to electricity and deliver such electricity for sale, or to use such energy to provide reliability or economic benefits to the grid.

Third-Party Provision of Ancillary Services; Accounting and Financial Reporting for New Electric Storage Technologies, 144 FERC ¶ 61,056, at 172 (July 18, 2013).

The California Public Utilities Commission has offered a slightly different definition for energy storage, describing it as:

> . . . a set of technologies capable of storing previously generated electric energy and releasing that energy at a later time. EES technologies may store electrical energy as potential, kinetic, chemical, or thermal energy, and include various types of batteries, flywheels, electrochemical capacitors, compressed air storage, thermal storage devices and pumped hydroelectric power.

POLICY PLANNING DIV. STAFF, CAL. PUB. UTILS. COMM'N, ELECTRIC ENERGY STORAGE: AN ASSESSMENT OF POTENTIAL BARRIERS AND OPPORTUNITIES 2–3 (2010).

Unfortunately, as subsidy and incentive programs for energy storage expand, controversies over what qualifies as an energy storage system under these programs are multiplying as well. Although the definitions above seem relatively inclusive, they are arguably too narrow to include some valuable types of energy storage strategies. Consider, for example, Nevada's 110 MW Crescent Dunes molten salt solar heat storage. This system, which uses concentrated sunlight to heat molten salt on tall towers, retains thermal energy so well that it continues to generate electric power for several hours after the sun goes down. *See* Knvul Sheikh, *New Concentrating Solar Tower Is Worth Its Salt with 24/7 Power*, SCI. AM. (July 2016), https://www.scientificamerican.com/article/new-concentrating-solar-tower-is-worth-its-salt-with-24-7-power/. However, since the thermal energy stored in hot molten salt has never been converted into electricity, one could argue that it falls outside the definitions of energy storage set forth above. Policymakers will increasingly have to grapple with questions about what qualifies as energy storage as they seek to promote greater investment in energy storage strategies in the coming years.

One other important distinction in energy storage policy is the difference between distributed energy storage and bulk energy storage. *Distributed energy storage* systems are relatively small systems designed primarily to store electricity for later use by a single onsite residential or commercial landowner. Presently, most owners of distributed energy storage systems remain connected to the electric grid and continue to rely on their electric utility to supply them power during certain periods. However, as the efficiency and affordability of distributed energy storage improves, so does its potential to enable landowners with rooftop solar to go "off grid" and no longer require any grid-supplied electricity service. The possibilities of these distributed energy storage technologies obviously present a growing threat to the conventional centralized utility model.

Bulk energy storage systems differ from distributed energy storage systems in that they are generally much larger and store much greater quantities of electric power for eventual dispatch to numerous offsite electricity customers. The distinction is worth noting in part because utilities tend to be more supportive of bulk energy storage development than distributed energy storage. A utility that builds its own bulk energy storage facility can usually include the capital costs of the new facility into its rate base and improve the reliability of its grid operations. By contrast, retail utility customers with solar panels who purchase distributed energy storage systems, become less dependent on grid-supplied power and often end up paying smaller monthly electricity bills.

Bulk energy storage technologies have tremendous potential and could soon have transformative impacts on the electricity industry, so attorneys entering the practice of energy law today are almost certain to encounter issues related to them during their careers. A general understanding of the primary types of energy storage technologies and of the regulatory structures that are beginning to emerge around them is therefore valuable for any new energy lawyer. In the excerpt below, Professor Amy L. Stein describes several basic types of bulk energy storage and their potentially transformative impacts on the modern electricity industry.

RECONSIDERING REGULATORY UNCERTAINTY: MAKING A CASE FOR ENERGY STORAGE

Amy L. Stein

41 FLA. ST. U. L. REV. 697, 705–16 (2014)

Bulk energy storage consists of a suite of technologies used to hold the energy from previously generated electricity at times of low demand until demand is high or transmission lines are freed up to transmit the electricity. Bulk energy storage in the United States is dominated by pumped-storage hydropower (PSH), a century-old technology that uses cheaper off-peak electricity to pump water from a lower to an upper reservoir and then releases the water to turn turbines to generate electricity during on-peak hours. Although it has the capacity to provide price advantages, PSH has generated its share of controversy over the years, with critics pointing to energy inefficiencies and adverse environmental impacts of damming water. There are approximately twenty-two gigawatts (GW) of PSH deployed in the United States across forty sites, much of which was built between 1970 and 1990. Pumped storage developers have refined the technology to increase efficiency, and the international interest in PSH is growing. Nevertheless, this form of storage is geographically constrained.

The next generation of grid-scale energy storage includes compressed air energy storage (CAES), a technology that uses off-peak energy to drive compressors that inject air into an underground storage cavern. The air heats as it is compressed, and this heat energy is later released to turn turbines and generate electricity back onto the grid during on-peak hours. Only one large CAES 110 megawatt (MW) commercial facility has been constructed in the United States in McIntosh, Alabama, but it is leading the way for future projects. CAES projects are planning to move forward in both Ohio and Texas, and Nebraska may not be far behind. Recent demonstration projects are even trying to break CAES free from its geological shackles by storing air in existing pipelines and steel air storage tanks instead of underground, an advance that would render CAES much more mobile.

Other storage generally takes three additional forms: (1) electro-chemical (batteries), (2) mechanical (flywheels), and (3) thermal energy. Batteries can take many forms (Li-ion, NaS, NiCd, Metal Air, lead acid, liquid, etc.), each with their own strengths and weaknesses depending on whether they are evaluated based on energy, power, or dischargeability. But many other types are racing to the commercial finish line. The primary limitations associated with batteries, however, are the costs and the size of the battery required to store a meaningful amount of electricity. One of the world's largest battery storage facilities is operating in Fairbanks, Alaska. The Alaskan battery is larger than a football field, yet can only provide enough electricity for 12,000 residents for seven minutes.

Efforts to develop smaller, more effective batteries are slowly taking hold. Duke Energy has installed a thirty-six MW advanced-lead acid battery at the Notrees Wind Farm in Texas, connecting to Texas' grid operator, Electric Reliability Council of Texas (ERCOT). AES Energy Storage owns and operates an eight MW lithium-ion battery plant in Johnson City that provides rapid frequency regulation services to New York's grid operator, New York Independent Service Operator (NYISO) and the world's largest lithium-ion battery farm (thirty-two MW) in West Virginia... Similar discussions surround fuel cells, a technology that functions like batteries through electrochemical processes. Battery storage is expanding on an international level as well, with Japan, India, and China coupling storage with telecommunications towers.

Flywheels reflect yet another form of energy storage. Flywheels accelerate a rotor to a very high speed and maintain the energy in the system as rotational energy—energy that is available instantly when needed by slowing down the flywheel. New York is home to the first flywheel storage plant. With help from the New York State Energy Research and Development Authority (NYSERDA), Beacon Power has developed a [20] MW flywheel energy storage plan in Stephentown, New York. . . .

A last form of energy storage, generally not used for bulk system storage, is thermal energy storage. A common thermal energy storage system "chills a storage medium [usually water, ice, or a phase-change material] during periods of low cooling demand and then uses the stored cooling later to meet air conditioning load or process cooling loads." California, for instance, recently began installing fifty-three MW in distributed ice storage across rooftops. Although it is unclear which form of "new generation" energy storage will ultimately prevail for widespread commercialization, it is becoming clear that some form of energy storage is on the horizon.

[ ] Value of Energy Storage

Energy storage has varied benefits, depending on its type and purpose. Many types of energy storage are able to provide multiple services, and therefore yield multiple benefits. A productive economy requires significant amounts of electricity, and demand is only projected to increase in the future. Nearly every modern convenience—like computers, cell phones, machinery, and lights—is at the mercy of adequate electricity flows. . . . [I]nvestors should take confidence in the government's recognition of the four primary categories of energy storage benefits. . . . : (1) reliability, (2) lower costs, (3) efficient production, and (4) environmental benefits.

1. Reliability

A first benefit of energy storage is its ability to enhance the reliability of the grid. These reliability benefits can come in the form of backup electricity in times of power outages, enhanced power quality to prevent outages, and frequency regulation that adjusts for differences between grid operators' predictions and actual demand.

Backup Electricity. The concept of backup electricity is far from novel. Hospitals and other emergency service providers have been relying on back-up generators for many years. Santa Rita jail in California, one of the largest inmate facilities, has taken steps to insulate itself from the risk of power outages by being one of the first microgrids capable of isolating itself from the traditional grid, in part based on the energy storage onsite. This type of distributed storage also is particularly useful in times of power outages due to weather-related disruptions, which are often sporadic and short-lived. For instance, Hurricane Sandy provided a platform for a few energy storage facilities operating in New York to demonstrate their success.

Power Quality. Energy storage also can assist in a general class of services referred to as power quality and system stability. The National Renewable Energy Laboratories describes it well:

> Power quality refers to voltage spikes, sags, momentary outages, and harmonics. Storage devices are often used at customer load sites to buffer sensitive equipment against power quality issues. Electric power systems also can experience oscillations of frequency and voltage. Unless damped, these disturbances can limit the ability of utilities to transmit power and affect the stability and reliability of the entire system. System stability requires response times of less than a second, and can be met by a variety of devices including fast-responding energy storage.

Frequency Regulation. Grid operator projections of supply and demand do not always mirror reality. In fact, most days require some last-minute injections or withdrawals to correct for the gaps between supply and demand. . . .

Maintaining the frequency of the transmission system within an acceptable range is critical to reliable operations. When generation dispatch does not equal actual load and losses on a moment-by-moment basis, the imbalance will result in the grid's frequency deviating from the standard (sixty Hertz). Minor frequency deviations affect energy consuming devices; major deviations cause generation and transmission equipment to separate from the grid, in the worst case leading to a cascading blackout.

. . . Although fossil fuel generators have traditionally been used to regulate or correct frequency deviations, energy storage can join other emerging technologies like demand response to help provide this service. The faster a resource can ramp up or down, the more accurately it can respond to the correction signal, which places these emerging technologies at a distinct technological advantage over fossil fuel generators.

2.   *Lower Costs*

A second benefit of energy storage is its ability to reduce electricity prices. Electricity prices vary depending on its time of use, and prices are generally highest during "on-peak" periods, when the majority of our population is awake and "plugged in." Where energy storage can reduce the amount of peak electricity needed, costs are projected to decrease. Although these on-peak periods represent only a small proportion of the total time electricity is needed, resource planners cannot base their decisions on the average load. Instead, energy resources are developed based on the peak loads. Generation, transmission, and distribution systems also must be sized for peak demand; as demand grows, new systems (both lines and substations) must be installed, often only to meet the peak demand for a few hours per year. Without wide scale energy storage, these peak demands are addressed primarily through peaker power plants. Peaker plants are those generators that are able to ramp up and down rapidly to respond to a need from the grid operator. Furthermore, peaker plants also bring with them significant capital cost requirements, additional emissions, and usually a need to construct additional transmission lines to connect to the existing grid. Instead of building additional generation to satisfy peak loads, energy can be generated and stored during off-peak periods and discharged during peak periods to satisfy increased load.

In addition to ensuring adequate on-peak resources and reducing or eliminating the need for peaking facilities, this type of action also could reduce the need to construct additional transmission and distribution lines. New lines may be difficult or expensive to build, often involving high capital costs and generating significant siting controversy. These expenses and controversies can be avoided or deferred by deploying energy storage located near the load. Bringing the energy storage closer to the source also may alleviate the high line-loss rates that occur during peak demand. Energy storage may be able to reduce or eliminate some of these costs, reducing rates for consumers. . . .

3.   *Efficiency*

A third benefit of energy storage lies in its ability to address potential over-generation during off-peak periods. Under the current constraints requiring instantaneous electricity use, significant amounts of electricity are wasted. This waste occurs for a number of reasons, including the generation of electricity during off-peak hours without demand to satisfy the supply and constraints along transmission lines. Renewable resources like wind, for instance, are generally strongest during winter, off-peak hours. This disconnect between supply and demand can result in excess electricity that could be captured through energy storage.

For example, the Bonneville Power Association (BPA) has been faced with "too much of a good thing" with ample wind resources and water flows for hydropower. Its transmission lines can only transmit so much electricity, and this has forced the agency to choose between providing wind or hydropower to the grid. Were BPA to allow the excess water to spill over the dams, it would send hyper-oxygenated water into the Columbia River's vital salmon runs, subjecting it to potential Clean Water Act violations. Consequently, BPA agreed to supply the power obligations of their thermal generators without charge, a plan that was not as appealing to wind generators, who were not concerned with saving fuel costs and were instead concerned with generating wind to obtain the useful production tax credits (PTCs) and Renewable Energy Credits (RECs) associated with wind generation. The dispute resulted in a FERC order requiring a new BPA curtailment protocol in which BPA agreed to compensate the wind generators for any PTC and unbundled RECs lost due to non-generation.

Energy storage would have alleviated this problem, allowing for the electricity generated from both wind and hydropower to eventually make it to the grid. Additional energy storage would minimize the curtailment of renewable energy during these times of generator or transmission constraints, improve the capacity factors of generators, and reduce the pressure on minimum load requirements for conventional generators. . . .

4. *Environmental*

A fourth benefit of energy storage is found in the reduced environmental impact that is realized by relying on more renewable energy to supply our nation's increasing electricity demand. Fossil fuel combustion is the number one contributor of our nation's greenhouse gas (GHG) emissions, as well as a number of other air pollutants. Renewable energy by itself is not interchangeable with the baseload sources of fossil fuel energy like coal. Yet, by pairing energy storage with renewable energy, it firms the renewable energy generation, and may be able to displace some fossil fuel generators, as well as avoid their corresponding GHG and pollution emissions. More precisely, it could displace polluting peaker plants and the ancillary services that are traditionally provided by fossil fuel generators. . . .

The use of energy storage to provide energy services as opposed to traditional fossil fuel generation will also minimize the market risks associated with different primary fuel sources. Natural gas looks quite attractive at the present time, with vast shale discoveries and low natural gas prices. But an adjustment of our energy economy away from coal towards natural gas will result in a less diversified supply than presently exists, increasing the risk of supply disruptions due to future congestion in natural gas pipelines or price increases.

————————

QUESTIONS

1.   Professor Stein suggests that pumped-hydro energy storage is "geographically constrained." Identify at least two specific attributes of pumped-hydro energy storage development that inherently limit the locations where developers can plausibly site these projects and explain how they impact project siting decisions.

2.   Why do you think utilities considering whether to build bulk energy storage facilities often compare the per-kW cost of building these projects to that of developing a new gas-fired "peaker" plant?

3.   Why are bulk energy storage plants potentially valuable to electricity providers like the Bonneville Power Administration, which Stein described as having "too much" power during certain windy periods?

4.   *Slow Progress for Compressed Air Energy Storage (CAES)*. At the time of the Stein article's publication in 2014, developers were exploring several promising CAES projects. The excerpt specifically mentions projects under consideration in Ohio, Texas, and Nebraska. Unfortunately, as of late 2017, no major new CAES projects had come online in those states or anywhere else in the country. However, multiple companies were still actively developing CAES technologies that they believed would be able to dispatch stored power at per-unit costs that are on par with those of new peaker plants. *See, e.g.,* Peter Maloney, *Hydrostor Comes Ashore to Turn Old Coal Plants Into Compressed-Air Storage*, UTIL. DIVE (Apr. 25, 2017), http://www.utilitydive. com/news/hydrostor-comes-ashore-to-turn-old-coal-plants-into-compressed-air -storage/441017/; Joshua S. Hill, *EU Scientists Propose Air As World's Next Big Energy Storage Option*, CLEAN TECHNICA (Mar. 29, 2017), https://clean technica.com/2017/03/29/eu-scientists-propose-air-worlds-next-big-energy- storage-option/. Only time will tell whether these next-generation CAES technologies are truly capable of delivering cost-effective bulk energy storage.

5.   *The Push for Affordable Distributed Energy Storage*. Although bulk energy storage development has predominated the nation's fledgling energy storage market, distributed energy storage technologies are rapidly improving and becoming more cost effective. One 2016 report predicted that the nation's behind-the-meter distributed energy storage capacity would exceed the nation's bulk energy storage capacity by the year 2020. *See* Stephen Lacey, *How Distributed Battery Storage Will Surpass Grid-Scale Storage in the US by 2020*, GREENTECH MEDIA (Mar. 10, 2016), https://www.greentechmedia.com/ articles/read/how-distributed-battery-storage-will-surpass-grid-scale-storage- in-the-us-b. Tesla Motors Inc. and other large companies have been aggressively developing and improving energy storage products for homes and

businesses for years and, in a few regions where policies are favorable, retail demand for these products is steadily growing. See, e.g., Peter Maloney, *California's SGIP opens to strong demand for storage incentives*, UTILITYDIVE.COM (May 5, 2017), http://www.utilitydive.com/news/californias-sgip-opens-to-strong-demand-for-storage-incentives/442022/.

6. *Storing Energy for a Solar Eclipse.* In August of 2017, a total solar eclipse temporarily darkened skies across the United States. In California, where there is over 10,000 MW of installed solar generating capacity, grid operators predicted that the eclipse would substantially impact grid load balances even though only a partial eclipse would occur in that state. Fortunately, the state's roughly 3,000 MW of energy storage capacity played a role in helping to keep the lights on in California as solar panel productivity dipped. This very rare instance gave CAISO, California's primary grid operator, an opportunity to showcase the value of energy storage as a means of overcoming the intermittency-related challenges of solar power. See Andy Colthorpe, *3,000MW of California Energy Storage Will Ramp to Deal With Solar Eclipse*, PV TECH (Aug. 17, 2017), https://www.pv-tech.org/news/3000 mw-of-california-energy-storage-will-ramp-to-deal-with-solar-eclipse.

2. ENERGY STORAGE INCENTIVE POLICIES

As Professor Stein described above, energy storage systems serve unique load balancing functions that could be ultimately be instrumental in helping the nation's electricity grid transition toward greater reliance on clean, sustainable energy sources. Recognizing that low-cost energy storage technologies are the holy grail of the modern energy industry, governments at all levels are seeking ways to accelerate their development. The following materials highlight some of the primary government policies aimed at promoting investments in energy storage.

a. Federal Investment Tax Credits

The federal government has been slower to promote energy storage technologies than it has been to promote wind energy, solar energy, and many other renewables. However, Congress and other federal policymakers have established a few influential energy storage incentives policies. For instance, many citizens that purchase new distributed energy storage systems can at least partially qualify for the federal Investment Tax Credit (ITC), which was described in Chapter 5 of this Casebook as a solar energy policy incentive program. As highlighted in that chapter, the ITC is a 30% tax credit on the purchase of qualifying energy systems and is claimed over a five-year period. As of 2017, there were two main limitations on energy storage systems' eligibility for the ITC. First, the credit is available only if at least 75 percent of the energy stored on the energy storage system in each of its first five years of use is generated from onsite solar energy resources. Second, taxpayers can claim the credit only to the extent that energy stored on it is generated from onsite solar. *See*

NAT'L RENEWABLE ENERGY LAB., FEDERAL TAX INCENTIVES FOR BATTERY STORAGE SYSTEMS (2017), https://www.nrel.gov/docs/fy17osti/67558.pdf. These conditions prevent citizens from claiming the ITC for purchases of energy storage products that they use solely to exploit arbitrage opportunities under time-based retail electricity pricing and net metering programs.

A numeric example can illustrate how behind-the-meter energy storage systems potentially create arbitrage opportunities for retail electricity customers under time-based pricing plans. Suppose Aisha is a residential retail electricity customer of PowerCo, an electric utility. Under PowerCo's time-of-use pricing structure, PowerCo charges Aisha $0.30 per kWh during a designated peak period running from 3:00PM to 7:00PM on weekdays and charges just $0.10 per kWh at all other times. Suppose further that Aisha purchased a home battery system and small rooftop solar array in 2017 and participates in PowerCo's retail net metering program, which credits her at the applicable retail rate for any power she feeds onto the electric grid. Aisha could engage in arbitrage by charging up her home battery system at a cost of $0.10 per kWh during off-peak hours and then feeding that stored power back onto the grid during the designated peak period for a credit of $0.30 per kWh. This simple practice could theoretically generate $0.20 per kWh in income or credit for Aisha, which could quickly add up to several hundred dollars per year.

The ITC's eligibility criteria do not prohibit the type of arbitrage practices described in the example above, but they do disqualify energy storage system owners from claiming the ITC to the extent that the systems are storing grid-supplied power rather than power produced using onsite solar panels. For example, suppose that only 60% of the power that Aisha stored on her home battery system in 2017 was generated by her rooftop solar array and that the other 40% was purchased via the grid. Aisha would not qualify for *any* ITC because less than 75% of the energy stored on her system was generated by solar onsite. On the other hand, if exactly 80% of the power Aisha stored on her battery system in each of the first five years after she purchased it was generated by her solar panels, she would be eligible for 80% of the applicable ITC. For instance, if her storage system cost $10,000 she could claim a 30% ITC calculated on amount equal to 80% of the $10,000 purchase price. Specifically, her total claimable ITC over five years would be $8,000 × 0.30 = $2,400.

It's worth pointing out that Aisha's total tax credit would be even smaller if she purchased her home battery system sometime after 2017 because (as described in Chapter 5) the amount of the ITC is scheduled to gradually decline and then drop to 0% for residential projects by 2024. On the other hand, some have suggested that ITCs for energy storage systems could eventually become more generous because of growing bipartisan support for energy storage incentives. *See, e.g.*, Peter Maloney, *With Tax*

Reform on the Table, Senators Prepare Second Push for Energy Storage Incentives, UTIL. DIVE (Feb. 7, 2017), http://www.utilitydive.com/news/with-tax-reform-on-the-table-senators-prepare-second-push-for-energy-stora/43 5595/.

b. State Energy Storage Mandates and Targets

Over the past decade, a handful of states have also enacted laws aimed specifically at encouraging energy storage development within their boundaries. For instance, a few states have promoted in-state energy storage investment by imposing mandates or legislating targets modeled after renewable portfolio standard (RPS) programs. California's legislature led the way with this approach in 2013 by enacting AB 2514, a bill establishing the state's Energy Storage Procurement Framework and Design Program. The statute requires California's three major investor-owned utilities to collectively install at least 1,325 of MW of energy storage capacity in various forms by the year 2024. *See* CAL. PUB. UTIL. CODE §§ 2835 *et seq.* (2013). Pursuant to language in the statute, the state's Public Utilities Commission (CPUC) ultimately divided this obligation among the three utilities and added "procurement" targets for each even year through 2020. *See* CAL. PUB. UTIL. COMM'N, D.13–10–040 (2013).

In 2016, the California legislature built further upon AB 2514 by enacting AB 2868, which requires the state's three largest investor-owned utilities to propose projects or initiatives for adding at least 500 MW of *distributed* energy storage in the state. *See* CAL. PUB. UTIL. CODE §§ 2838.2–.3 (2016). In 2017, the CPUC interpreted this bill as essentially amending the state's original AB 2514 target, meaning that the utilities were obligated to collectively add 500 MW of distributed storage capacity within their territories as part of compliance with the collective 1,325 MW target. *See* Buck Endemann et al., *CPUC Requires Additional 500 MW of Energy Storage from California IOUs*, K&L GATES: GLOBAL POWER L. & POL'Y (May 3, 2017), https://www.globalpowerlawandpolicy.com/2017/05/cpuc-requires-additional-500-mw-of-energy-storage-from-california-ious/#_ftnref1.

By mid-2017, a small handful of other state legislatures had followed California's lead and enacted energy storage targets or mandates. Oregon's legislature enacted a modest energy storage mandate in 2015. Under Oregon's statute, each of the state's two largest utilities, Portland General Electric and PacifiCorp, must have at least 5 MW of energy storage capacity by the year 2020. *See* Peter Maloney, *Oregon PUC Release Guidelines for Energy Storage Mandate*, UTIL. DIVE (Jan. 6, 2017), http://www.utilitydive.com/news/oregon-puc-release-guidelines-for-energy-storage-mandate/433462/. As directed under a new Massachusetts state statute, regulators in that state set an energy storage target in 2017 for utilities to have of 200 MWh of collective installed energy storage capacity by the year 2020. *See* Press Release, Mass. Office of Energy and Envtl. Affairs, *Baker-Polito Administration Sets 200 Megawatt-Hour Energy Storage Target* (June 30, 2017), http://www.mass.gov/eea/pr-2017/ doer-sets-200-megawatt-hour-energy-storage-target.html. New York's legislature likewise passed a law in June of 2017 directing state regulators to establish energy storage capacity targets. See Peter Maloney, *New York Expected to Set High Bar for Energy Storage After Target Bill Passage*, UTIL. DIVE (June 27, 2017), http://www.utilitydive.com/news/new-york-expected-to-set-high-bar-for-energy-storage-after-target-bill-pass/445845/. This growing list of state with energy storage mandate and target programs suggests that such programs could eventually be among the most impactful policy strategies for promoting energy storage investment, much like RPS standards have been for wind and solar power.

c. State-Level Rebates and Tax Credits

Another increasingly popular way to promote energy storage investment at the state level has been to offer rebates or tax credits on purchases of distributed energy storage systems. Such rebates and tax credits function as direct subsidies, essentially discounting the cost of new energy storage equipment to make it more appealing to consumers. These programs are already helping to accelerate energy storage development in states that have adopted them.

As of 2017, the most aggressive state-level distributed energy storage incentive policy was the California Public Utility Commission's Self-Generation Incentive Program (SGIP)—a program originally launched in 2001. The CPUC reopened its SGIP in 2017 by authorizing to $448 million in "incentives" or rebates for installations of qualifying behind-the-meter distributed energy storage systems. Under this revamped program, the CPUC was directed to make the $448 million in incentives available incrementally across five "Steps", with the magnitude of the incentive declining after each step. For instance, when Step One of the updated SGIP opened in May of 2017 it offered incentives of up to $500 per kWh to qualifying purchasers of new home battery installations. The incentive was so popular that it quickly sold out: applicants claimed nearly all the program's roughly $50 million in Step One funds in less than 24 hours. Because Step One sold out in less than ten days, the program rules required the CPUC to reduce the Step Two incentive amount to just $400 per kWh. *See* CAL. PUBLIC UTIL. COMM'N, SELF GENERATION INCENTIVE PROGRAM HANDBOOK 22 (2017), http://www.cpuc.ca.gov/sgip/. Still, even this $400/kWh incentive was large enough to offset as much as half of the cost of a new home battery system and continued to drive high numbers of home battery installations across the state.

Maryland has also enacted legislation in 2017 providing for direct state subsidies on private purchases of distributed energy storage systems.

Maryland's SB 758 created the nation's first state-level tax credit program for energy storage investments. The program offers a generous 30% state income tax credit for qualifying energy storage installations, capped at $5000 for residential energy storage and $75,000 for commercial energy storage installations. However, the program also has an overall cap of just $750,000 per year that could greatly limit its impact as energy storage systems become more popular in the state over the coming years. *See* Peter Maloney, *Maryland Passes 30% Energy Storage Tax Credit for Residential, C&I Installations*, UTIL. DIVE (Apr. 13, 2017), http://www.utilitydive.com/news/maryland-passes-30-energy-storage-tax-credit-for-residential-ci-installa/440363/.

d. Hawaii's Customer Self-Supply (CSS) Option

Hawaii is likely to be another hotbed for early adoptions of distributed energy storage systems because of the unique market conditions there and the Hawaii Electric Co. (HECO) "Customer Self-Supply" (CSS) option. As of 2017, HECO customers in certain designated geographic areas of the utility's service area could exercise this CSS option and receive expedited permitting for combined solar and distributed storage systems. In exchange for these expedited permitting privileges, CSS customers must agree to feed very little excess power onto the grid and to receive no compensation for that excess power. *See Customer Self-Supply and Grid-Supply Programs*, HAWAI'IAN ELECTRIC, https://www.hawaiianelectric.com/clean-energy-hawaii/producing-clean-energy/customer-self-supply-and-grid-supply-programs (last visited Aug. 11, 2017).

Even though HECO's CSS option does not offer customers any subsidies for purchasing home battery systems, it is still likely to encourage many behind-the-meter energy storage installations in that state. HECO's retail prices for grid-supplied electricity have long been among the highest in the nation, so many HECO customers who don't already have a rooftop solar energy system are interested in getting one. Because rooftop solar is so popular in the state, HECO had previously eliminated its net metering program and taken other actions that made it difficult for customers to interconnect new solar PV systems into the grid. HECO's CSS option is thus one of few remaining avenues for HECO customers to secure approvals for new rooftop solar arrays. *See* Eric Wesoff, *Rooftop Solar in Oahu Crashes with Loss of Net Metering, Lack of Self-Supply Installs*, GREENTECH MEDIA (Feb. 7, 2017), https://www.greentechmedia.com/articles/read/rooftop-solar-in-hawaii-crashes-with-loss-of-net-metering-lack-self-supply.

QUESTIONS & NOTES

1.   Victor, a resident of Florida, purchased and installed a home battery system and rooftop solar array for his residence in 2017. For the succeeding five years, 90% of the power stored on his battery system was generated by his solar panels and at least 75% of the power stored was from his panels in each of those five years. The battery system cost a total of $20,000. Based on the facts above, calculate Victor's total claimable ITC.

2.   As described in the materials above, California's SGIP program offers energy storage system rebates that are made available in "Steps". Under the program, the most generous rebates are given to applicants who purchase energy storage systems in the earliest Steps. If funds allocated for paying out rebates under a previous Step dry up very quickly, the rebates available in the subsequent Step are much smaller. Why do you think California regulators structured the SGIP program in this way? Can you think of other renewable energy policies that might be more effective if they adopted a similar approach?

3.   What does Hawaii's experience with HECO's CCS option suggest about the potential long-term market and policy landscape for distributed energy storage systems? Do you think subsidies will always be required to persuade individuals and business to invest in distributed energy storage technologies? Why or why not? Do you think subsidizing purchases of these technologies in the short term is justifiable as a policy matter? Why or why not?

B. DEMAND-SIDE ENERGY MANAGEMENT

In addition to energy storage technologies, there are numerous other strategies capable of helping grid operators and utilities to more smoothly integrate intermittent renewable energy sources into the electricity system. Many of these other technologies and programs enlist the help of utility customers to keep electricity loads balanced. For instance, some strategies focus on increasing the energy efficiency of the most energy-intensive devices and equipment, such as heating, ventilation and air conditioning (HVAC) systems or lighting systems in large industrial buildings. Designing such systems to be more energy-efficient can help to "flatten" peaks in grid load demand during periods of extreme outdoor temperatures in the summer or winter months. Other initiatives focus on designing new HVAC, lighting, and other high-electricity-use systems to automatically respond to grid load fluctuations if programmed to do so. In industry jargon, these and other programs and technologies that promote greater flexibility and reliability on the demand side of the grid are collectively known as *demand-side management* strategies.

1. RETAIL DEMAND RESPONSE

One of the most promising components of modern demand-side management is a subset of innovations and policies known as *demand response* programs. Demand response programs help and encourage electricity customers to more swiftly and dependably adjust their electricity use when there is too much or not enough power on the grid. The sudden and unpredictable fluctuations in production that characterize wind turbines and solar panels make grid reliability more difficult in regions that depend heavily on wind- and solar-generated energy sources. Ideally, in such settings, retail electricity customers would be willing and able to promptly respond to sudden decreases in electricity supply by temporarily scaling back their electricity use. Utilities with an ability to reliably field such responses from their customers are spared from having to build and operate as many peaker plants and can thus more affordably and easily use intermittent renewable energy resources.

Unfortunately, customers who are unaware of temporary grid load imbalances and have no incentive to care about them are not likely to increase or decrease their electricity use when imbalances arise. Creating demand flexibility within a grid system thus requires at least two basic things: (1) a way to quickly and clearly communicate with customers about temporary changes in grid balances; and (2) a way to incentivize customers to modify their electricity use in response to those signals. As intermittent wind and solar energy resources assume ever-larger roles in generating the nation's electric power, industry stakeholders are increasingly considering how demand response strategies might help grid systems and operators to adapt to these changes. The following excerpt from a 2014 Hawaii Public Utilities Commission Policy Statement provides a more details on demand response programs and their growing importance in balancing loads on electricity grids.

POLICY STATEMENT AND ORDER REGARDING DEMAND RESPONSE PROGRAMS
Hawaii Public Util. Comm'n (Apr. 28, 2014)
2014 WL 2448810

In this Policy Statement and Order, the commission sets forth policy guidelines for the continued operation and expansion of demand response programs, and orders the [Hawaiian Electric Company (HECO)] Companies to respond to a number of commission directives in furtherance of these guidelines. The commission strongly supports the use of cost-effective and efficiently run demand response programs. Such programs have assisted electric utilities in meeting system reserve requirements, deferring the need for future capacity additions, and promoting the reliable and economical operation of the electrical grid. However, demand response can—and should—also be used to provide ancillary-services and to assist with the integration of additional renewable energy resources. Furthermore, given the high costs of petroleum-based fuels, demand response programs may offer a more economical alternative to the traditional creation of new generating capacity, and may also provide customers with an additional option to manage their energy costs.

. . . .

Nationwide, demand response programs have grown dramatically over the past several years. . . . Demand response should be considered and used as another essential tool in the generation tool kit.

. . . .

. . . [D]emand response refers to a consumer's change in electricity consumption, relative to the expected levels, in response to an inverse change in the price of electric energy or to incentive payments designed to induce a change in consumption.

The commission reiterates that as demand response programs have evolved, so has their use such that these programs are no longer simply considered methods to decrease consumption during peak periods, but are also methods to assist in balancing system operations and in the integration of renewable energy resources. Hence, it is more appropriate to view demand response programs not only as peak reduction programs, but as programs designed to modify customer use of electricity so as to permit the most efficient and cost-effective operation of the electrical system.

Demand response programs can be further classified by describing the basic mechanisms that can be used to encourage changes in consumption patterns; that is, whether the mechanism is a (1) time-based pricing program or an (2) automated or manual control program.

There are three basic types of time-based pricing that can be used to encourage modifications in customer use of electricity. First, on-peak/off-peak pricing sets two prices: one for on-peak usage and one for off-peak usage. The on-peak/off-peak periods are established according to the load characteristics of each utility. Second, time-of-use pricing is similar to on-peak/off-peak pricing, but applies to several different time periods within a day. Time-of-use pricing can also be used to encourage the use of energy at a reduced price to customers that can increase loads at the time of a potential curtailment of certain renewable energy supply sources, such as wind and solar. Third, real time pricing reflects prices on an hourly basis, with some limited notice of the changes to the customer. . . .

Likewise, there are various types of automated or manual control programs where the system operator either (1) asks a customer to take a previously agreed-upon curtailment action when the operator requires such a response for either operational or economic reasons or (2) a customer is automatically curtailed by a previously agreed-upon amount by way of equipment that either permits the system operator to reduce or terminate load, and to restore the previous levels, or that operates autonomously (based on system frequency deviations, for example). These programs are sometimes described as "incentive based" programs, as they generally provide participants a credit or payment for taking the prescribed action. . . .

In addition to these time-of-use or manual/automatic demand response programs, there is a potential for customer-side implementation of demand response. For example, customers may provide demand-response through use of their generating and storage resources, provided that the generators and storage resources can be controlled by the system operator or by autonomous operation of on-site distributed energy equipment such as by a smart inverter.

Demand response programs can also be used to provide ancillary services. These ancillary services include, but are not limited to, the provision of spinning reserves to defer or avoid higher cost generating unit operation, frequency management (such as droop response and regulation), provision of a "bridge" for the time period between a sustained ramp down of renewable energy sources and when additional quick-start generation can be brought on line, or other system needs. Demand response can be faster and more accurate than generation response and can respond autonomously to frequency deviations as well as to system operator commands.

2. TIME-BASED RETAIL ELECTRICITY PRICING

One of the most basic ways a utility can influence their customers' demand patterns is to charge electricity prices that vary based on the time of year and time of day. The growing adoption of smart meter technologies across the country has made time-based differential electricity pricing more feasible today than ever before. These technologies and the need for greater demand flexibility to accommodate renewables on the grid are causing many utilities to consider adopting more time-based retail electricity rate structures.

The general concept of charging customers different prices at different times is certainly nothing new. Producers of a wide range of products and services routinely charge prices that vary based on time, helping them to even out customer demand across longer time periods and thereby enhance their profitability. For example, many restaurants offer special happy hour discount pricing to increase business during the mid-afternoon gap between lunchtime and the evening dinner rush. Movie theaters often use matinee discount pricing to motivate people with flexible schedules to go to movies earlier in the day when theaters tend to be less crowded. And airlines charge prices that vary widely depending on the time departure as a means of expanding their customer base, filling airplane seats, and collecting additional revenues from customers who are willing to pay extra to fly at certain high-demand times. Using time-based pricing strategies can offer similar benefits to utilities, boosting electricity demand during certain times and reducing it at other times. This ability to manipulate aggregate load demand through simple price variations can help utilities and grid operators to more easily manage load imbalances caused by intermittent electricity supplies or other factors.

In recent years, electric utilities have introduced a wide array of time-based pricing schemes into their rate structures. Although utilities often market time-based rate plans to retail customers as money-saving voluntary programs, a growing number of utilities are making them the "default" plan and requiring customers to proactively opt out of them. A few electric utilities have made time-based retail rate structures mandatory. Basic microeconomics principles arguably support this transition toward more time based pricing. Customers tend to make more economically efficient electricity use decisions if the prices they pay across time vary based on variations in the costs of supplying them power. Those efficiency gains increase as time-based fluctuations in retail prices become more closely aligned with time-based fluctuations in utilities' costs.

Figure 7.1 illustrates the idea of dynamic cost alignment in retail electricity pricing by placing several time-based electricity pricing structures onto a spectrum. Those on the left are the least closely aligned with fluctuations in utilities' marginal costs of supplying power across time. At the far left end of the spectrum are *unitary or "flat" rate plans*— plans that charge customers the same price per kWh for electricity regardless of the time of day or year. At the far right are *perfectly dynamic pricing* plans, which would price power at different rates in real time based on supply and demand—much like shares of stock on the New York Stock Exchange during trading hours. The following are brief discussions of other pricing schemes found in the middle of these two extremes.

Figure 7.1. Potential Retail Electricity Pricing Schemes

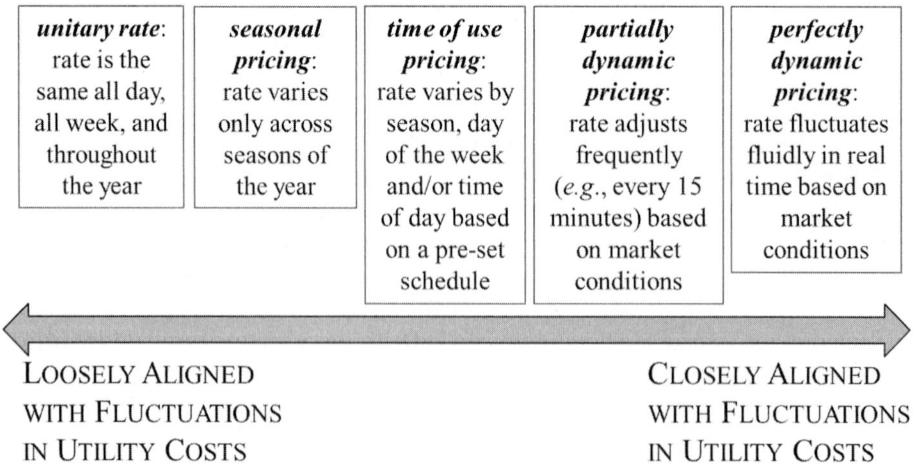

| *unitary rate*: rate is the same all day, all week, and throughout the year | *seasonal pricing*: rate varies only across seasons of the year | *time of use pricing*: rate varies by season, day of the week and/or time of day based on a pre-set schedule | *partially dynamic pricing*: rate adjusts frequently (*e.g.*, every 15 minutes) based on market conditions | *perfectly dynamic pricing*: rate fluctuates fluidly in real time based on market conditions |

LOOSELY ALIGNED
WITH FLUCTUATIONS
IN UTILITY COSTS

CLOSELY ALIGNED
WITH FLUCTUATIONS
IN UTILITY COSTS

Seasonal Pricing. Near the left end of the spectrum on Figure 7.1 are *seasonal pricing* programs. This type of pricing scheme can help to smooth out predictable seasonal variations in load demand. In warmer climates, load demands tend to be higher during the summer months because of greater-than-average usage of air conditioning systems. Historically, many utilities have built costly additional peaker plants or purchased expensive peak wholesale power to meet customers' elevated demand during these periods. Seasonable pricing programs are one potentially low-cost alternative to that approach. For example, a utility might charge a residential retail rate of 12 cents per kWh for electricity during the months of June, July and August and charge only 10 cents per kWh during the other nine months of the year. Utilities can implement this type of seasonable pricing even with customers who do not have smart meters and thus have their meters manually read just once per month.

By charging higher retail per-kWh prices for power during the summer, utilities are better able to recoup their higher costs of supplying wholesale peak power during those periods. Charging higher retail prices during peak seasons also sends more accurate signals to customers that can incentivize them to conserve electricity during those times and to invest in energy efficiency upgrades to moderate air conditioner usage. Although retail electricity prices that vary by season are only slightly more dynamically aligned with utility costs than unitary rates, they can be a worthwhile first step toward more time-based pricing models.

Time of Use Pricing. Several electric utilities have introduced *time-of-use (TOU) pricing* programs in recent decades. These programs often involve far more time-based price variation than is available under mere seasonal pricing plans. Although enrollment in TOU pricing programs is optional among most utilities that offer these programs, some utilities are beginning to make TOU rates their default retail price structure or are considering making TOU rates mandatory for all customers. Under most TOU pricing programs, per-kWh retail electricity rates increase during certain predetermined times of the day and week when the utility anticipates experiencing a high load demand. To offset these higher *peak rates*, utilities often offer reduced *off-peak rates* to their customers.

Again, a numeric example is useful in illustrating how these rate structures typically work. Suppose that PowerCo's unitary flat rate is 10 cents per kWh. However, under its optional TOU pricing plan, customers can agree to pay a higher peak rate of 30 cents per kWh from 3:00pm to 6:00pm on weekdays in exchange for the privilege of paying a lower off-peak rate of just 5 cents per kWh during all other times of the week. This two-tiered price structure incentivizes customers enrolled in the plan to shift their most flexible electricity consumption (running the laundry machine, running the dishwasher, etc.) to non-peak times, which can help to flatten the utility's aggregate load demand across the day and week.

Most utility customers who enroll in TOU plans must adjust their electricity consumption habits to see significant savings under these plans. Another simple numeric example helps to emphasize this point. Suppose that Carlos—a hypothetical PowerCo retail customer—typically consumes 2000 kWh per month and that 400 kWh of that consumption typically occurs on weekdays between 3:00pm and 6:00pm. Assuming for simplicity that PowerCo imposes no fixed fees or charges, would Carlos be wise to enroll in PowerCo's TOU pricing plan? Under the utility's ordinary flat-rate pricing structure, the amount due on Carlos' electricity bill would be:

2000kWh × $0.10/kWh = $200.00.

If, Carlos had enrolled instead in PowerCo's TOU pricing plan, his total due would have been:

(charges for off-peak power) + (charges for peak power)

= (1600kWh × $0.05/kWh) + (400kWh × $0.30/kWh)

= $80.00 + $120.00 = $200.00.

Based on these calculations, Carlos would save no money under the TOU plan. However, Carlos could see significant savings if he were to shift some of his electricity consumption to off-peak times. For instance, suppose he avoided running his home's dishwasher and clothes dryer during peak hours and programmed his home's thermostat to automatically shut off during those hours. If, through these modest changes, Carlos were to shift just 100 kWh of his power consumption from peak periods to off-peak periods, his bill under the TOU pricing structure would be:

(charges for off-peak) + (charges for peak)

= (1700kWh × $0.05/kWh) + (300kWh × $0.30/kWh)

= $85.00 + $90.00 = $175.00.

This suggests that switching to a TOU plan and making those changes could save Carlos an average of $25 per month. Indeed, well-structured TOU pricing plans can be a win-win for utilities and for customers who are willing and able to adjust their consumption habits. By shifting load demand to off-peak times, such plans can likewise help utilities to integrate more intermittent electricity sources such as wind or solar power into their energy resource mix.

Partially and Perfectly Dynamic Pricing. On the far right of the spectrum in Figure 7.1 are dynamic pricing schemes. Unlike the other pricing strategies on the spectrum, dynamic pricing generally does not involve electricity rates set months or years in advance. Instead, customers pay rates that fluctuate daily, hourly or even more frequently based on fluctuations in wholesale electricity market prices or grid load conditions. For example, if the hourly wholesale price for power in ElectriCo's area at a given moment is four cents per kWh, the utility might charge customers eight cents per kWh. If, two hours later, the hourly rate has climbed to six cents per kWh, the utility might increase its retail price to ten cents. Then, if later that evening the wholesale rate available to ElectriCo has dropped to just two cents per kWh, the utility might drop its retail rate to six cents per kWh.

If the administrative and equipment costs associated with dynamic pricing were low enough, perfectly dynamic pricing could theoretically have some great advantages. Perfectly dynamic electricity pricing is appealing from an economics perspective because it facilitates the continuous flow of clear and accurate price signals among electricity producers and consumers. Such signals are necessary to drive electricity use patterns that optimally respond to current market conditions.

As of 2016, multiple utilities in Illinois were offering dynamic pricing programs for retail electricity. As the technology necessary to support dynamic pricing improves and grows more affordable, more and more utilities could begin considering it for their own customers. Among other things, smart appliances and thermostats are increasingly available that can receive real-time information from utilities about fluctuations in electricity prices and automatically shut off or otherwise adjust to price changes. By helping load demand to more effectively respond to fluctuations in electricity supplies, these sorts of technologies and programs could help wind and solar resources to be more central energy sources in decades to come despite their intermittent nature.

QUESTIONS & NOTES

1. Suppose that Dana's utility, ElectriCo, has just introduced an optional TOU pricing program for its residential customers. Customers who enroll in the program get to pay just six cents per kWH for power during most of the week (which is much lower than the flat 12-cent-per-kWh that is currently charged). However, in exchange for this lower off-peak rate they must agree to pay 20 cents per kWh for electricity used during peak hours. ElectriCo charges no other retail fees or charges.

   a.   Dana wants to know whether she would save money if she were to enroll in ElectriCo's TOU pricing program without making any change to her electricity consumption habits. Assume for simplicity that Dana presently consumes exactly 1000 kWh of power per month during hours that would be considered off-peak under the TOU program and that she consumes 500 kWh of power per month during hours that would be considered on-peak. Would she save money by enrolling in the TOU pricing program? Why or why not?

   b.   Suppose Dana knows that, by running her washer and dryer during off-peak times, she could shift 200 kWh of her on-peak electricity consumption per month to off-peak hours. If Dana were to make those chances, would she save money by switching to ElectriCo's TOU pricing program? If so, by how much? If not, how much would she save by keeping her flat-rate plan?

2.   *Free Electricity.* Utilities and other power producers sometimes allow wholesale energy prices to become negative, signaling a willingness to *pay* others in the wholesale market to take their excess electricity off of the grid. In Texas, several utilities have also tried offering free electricity to retail customers during certain hours of the day as a way to dispose of excess electric power. For instance, under TXU's free overnight plan, customers accept slightly higher retail electricity prices during peak times in exchange for a zero-cents-per-kWh nighttime rate. *See* Clifford Krauss & Diane Cardwell, *A Texas Utility Offers a Nighttime Special: Free Electricity*, N.Y. TIMES (Nov. 8, 2015), http://www.nytimes.com/2015/11/09/business/energy-environment/a-texas-utility-offers-a-nighttime-special-free-electricity.html?_r=0.

3. WHOLESALE DEMAND RESPONSE

Demand response programs are not only appealing strategies at the retail level; federal regulators have also pursued them at the wholesale level in recent years. Most notably, FERC issued an Order (No. 745) in 2011 that essentially required operators of wholesale electricity markets to promote demand response in those markets by treating it as a valuable commodity equivalent to additional units of generated power. However, some electricity producers strongly objected to demand response rules shortly after FERC established them. Among other things, opponents argued that the rules unfairly favored demand response over electricity generation. The United States Supreme Court ultimately ruled on these issues in 2016 in *FERC v. EPSA*. The majority opinion, excerpted below, helped to further clarify the delineation between state and federal regulatory authority over the electricity industry. By creating greater certainty about the enforceability of FERC Order No. 745, the case also helped to solidify the role of demand response in wholesale electricity markets.

FERC v. ELECTRIC POWER SUPPLY ASS'N
Supreme Court of the United States, 2016
136 S.Ct. 760

KAGAN, J.

The Federal Power Act (FPA or Act), 41 Stat. 1063, as amended, 16 U.S.C. § 791a *et seq.*, authorizes the Federal Energy Regulatory Commission (FERC or Commission) to regulate "the sale of electric energy at wholesale in interstate commerce," including both wholesale electricity rates and any rule or practice "affecting" such rates. §§ 824(b), 824e(a). But the law places beyond FERC's power, and leaves to the States alone, the regulation of "any other sale"—most notably, any retail sale—of electricity. § 824(b). That statutory division generates a steady flow of jurisdictional disputes because—in point of fact if not of law—the wholesale and retail markets in electricity are inextricably linked.

These cases concern a practice called "demand response," in which operators of wholesale markets pay electricity consumers for commitments *not* to use power at certain times. That practice arose because wholesale market operators can sometimes—say, on a muggy August day—offer electricity both more cheaply and more reliably by paying users to dial down their consumption than by paying power plants to ramp up their production. In the regulation challenged here, FERC required those market operators, in specified circumstances, to compensate the two services equivalently—that is, to pay the same price to demand response providers for conserving energy as to generators for making more of it.

Two issues are presented here. First, and fundamentally, does the FPA permit FERC to regulate these demand response transactions at all, or does any such rule impinge on the States' authority? Second, even if FERC has the requisite statutory power, did the Commission fail to justify adequately why demand response providers and electricity producers should receive the same compensation? The court below ruled against FERC on both scores. We disagree.

I

A

Federal regulation of electricity owes its beginnings to one of this Court's decisions. In the early 20th century, state and local agencies oversaw nearly all generation, transmission, and distribution of electricity. But this Court held in *Public Util. Comm'n of R.I. v. Attleboro Steam & Elec. Co.*, 273 U.S. 83, 89–90, 47 S.Ct. 294, 71 L.Ed. 549 (1927), that the Commerce Clause bars the States from regulating certain interstate electricity transactions, including wholesale sales (*i.e.,* sales for resale) across state lines. That ruling created what became known as the "*Attleboro* gap"—a regulatory void which, the Court pointedly noted, only Congress could fill. *See id.* at 90, 47 S.Ct. 294.

Congress responded to that invitation by passing the FPA in 1935. The Act charged FERC's predecessor agency with undertaking "effective federal regulation of the expanding business of transmitting and selling electric power in interstate commerce." *New York v. FERC*, 535 U.S. 1, 6, 122 S.Ct. 1012, 152 L.Ed.2d 47 (2002). . . . Under the statute, the Commission has authority to regulate "the transmission of electric energy in interstate commerce" and "the sale of electric energy at wholesale in interstate commerce." 16 U.S.C. § 824(b)(1).

In particular, the FPA obligates FERC to oversee all prices for those interstate transactions and all rules and practices affecting such prices. The statute provides that "[a]ll rates and charges made, demanded, or received by any public utility for or in connection with" interstate transmissions or wholesale sales—as well as "all rules and regulations affecting or pertaining to such rates or charges"—must be "just and reasonable." § 824d(a). And if "any rate [or] charge," or "any rule, regulation, practice, or contract affecting such rate [or] charge[,]" falls short of that standard, the Commission must rectify the problem: It then shall determine what is "just and reasonable" and impose "the same by order." § 824e(a).

Alongside those grants of power, however, the Act also limits FERC's regulatory reach, and thereby maintains a zone of exclusive state jurisdiction. As pertinent here, § 824(b)(1)—the same provision that gives FERC authority over wholesale sales—states that "this subchapter," including its delegation to FERC, "shall not apply to any other sale of electric energy." Accordingly, the Commission may not regulate either within-state wholesale sales or, more pertinent here, retail sales of electricity (*i.e.*, sales directly to users). *See New York,* 535 U.S., at 17, 23, 122 S.Ct. 1012. State utility commissions continue to oversee those transactions.

Since the FPA's passage, electricity has increasingly become a competitive interstate business, and FERC's role has evolved accordingly. Decades ago, state or local utilities controlled their own power plants, transmission lines, and delivery systems, operating as vertically integrated monopolies in confined geographic areas. That is no longer so. Independent power plants now abound, and almost all electricity flows not through "the local power networks of the past," but instead through an interconnected "grid" of near-nationwide scope. *See id.* at 7, 122 S.Ct. 1012 ("electricity that enters the grid immediately becomes a part of a vast pool of energy that is constantly moving in interstate commerce," linking producers and users across the country). In this new world, FERC often forgoes the cost-based rate-setting traditionally used to prevent monopolistic pricing. The Commission instead undertakes to ensure "just and reasonable" wholesale rates by enhancing competition—attempting, as we recently explained, "to break down regulatory and economic barriers that hinder a free market in wholesale electricity." *Morgan Stanley Capital Group Inc. v. Public Util. Dist. No. 1 of Snohomish Cty.,* 554 U.S. 527, 536, 128 S.Ct. 2733, 171 L.Ed.2d 607 (2008).

As part of that effort, FERC encouraged the creation of nonprofit entities to manage wholesale markets on a regional basis. Seven such wholesale market operators now serve areas with roughly two-thirds of the country's electricity "load" (an industry term for the amount of electricity used). . . . Each administers a portion of the grid, providing generators with access to transmission lines and ensuring that the network conducts electricity reliably. . . . And still more important for present purposes, each operator conducts a competitive auction to set wholesale prices for electricity.

These wholesale auctions serve to balance supply and demand on a continuous basis, producing prices for electricity that reflect its value at given locations and times throughout each day. Such a real-time mechanism is needed because, unlike most products, electricity cannot be stored effectively. Suppliers must generate—every day, hour, and minute—the exact amount of power necessary to meet demand from the utilities and other "load-serving entities" (LSEs) that buy power at wholesale for resale to users. To ensure that happens, wholesale market operators obtain (1) orders from LSEs indicating how much electricity they need at various times and (2) bids from generators specifying how much electricity they can produce at those times and how much they will charge for it. Operators accept the generators' bids in order of cost (least expensive first) until they satisfy the LSEs' total demand. The price of the last unit of electricity purchased is then paid to every supplier whose bid was accepted, regardless of its actual offer; and the total cost is split among the LSEs in proportion to how much energy they have ordered. So, for example, suppose that at 9 a.m. on August 15 four plants serving Washington, D.C. can each produce some amount of electricity for, respectively, $10/unit, $20/unit, $30/unit, and $40/unit. And suppose that LSEs' demand at that time and place is met after the operator accepts the three cheapest bids. The first three generators would then all receive $30/unit. That amount is (think back to Econ 101) the marginal cost—*i.e.,* the added cost of meeting another unit of demand—which is the price an efficient market would produce. . . FERC calls that cost (in jargon that will soon become oddly familiar) the locational marginal price, or LMP.

As in any market, when wholesale buyers' demand for electricity increases, the price they must pay rises correspondingly; and in those times of peak load, the grid's reliability may also falter. Suppose that by 2 p.m. on August 15, it is 98 degrees in D.C. In every home, store, or office, people are turning the air conditioning up. To keep providing power to their customers, utilities and other LSEs must ask their market operator for more electricity. To meet that spike in demand, the operator will have to accept more expensive bids from suppliers. The operator, that is, will have to agree to the $40 bid that it spurned before—and maybe, beyond that, to bids of $50 or $60 or $70. In such periods, operators often must call on extremely inefficient generators whose high costs of production cause them to sit idle most of the time. . . . As that happens, LMP—the price paid by *all* LSEs to *all* suppliers—climbs ever higher. And meanwhile, the increased flow of electricity through the grid threatens to overload transmission lines. . . . As every consumer knows, it is just when the weather is hottest and the need for air conditioning most acute that blackouts, brownouts, and other service problems tend to occur.

Making matters worse, the wholesale electricity market lacks the self-correcting mechanism of other markets. Usually, when the price of a product rises, buyers naturally adjust by reducing how much they purchase. But consumers of electricity—and therefore the utilities and other LSEs buying power for them at wholesale—do not respond to price signals in that way. To use the economic term, demand for electricity is inelastic. That is in part because electricity is a necessity with few ready substitutes: When the temperature reaches 98 degrees, many people see no option but to switch on the AC. And still more: Many State regulators insulate consumers from short-term fluctuations in wholesale prices by insisting that LSEs set stable retail rates. . . . That, one might say, short-circuits the normal rules of economic behavior. Even in peak periods, as costs surge in the wholesale market, consumers feel no pinch, and so keep running the AC as before. That means, in turn, that LSEs must keep buying power to send to those users—no matter that wholesale prices spiral out of control and increased usage risks overtaxing the grid.

But what if there were an alternative to that scenario? Consider what would happen if wholesale market operators could induce consumers to refrain from using (and so LSEs from buying) electricity during peak periods. Whenever doing that costs less than adding more power, an operator could bring electricity supply and demand into balance at a lower price. And simultaneously, the operator could ease pressure on the grid, thus protecting against system failures. That is the idea behind the practice at issue here: Wholesale demand response, as it is called, pays consumers for commitments to curtail their use of power, so as to curb wholesale rates and prevent grid breakdowns. . . .

These demand response programs work through the operators' regular auctions. Aggregators of multiple users of electricity, as well as large-scale individual users like factories or big-box stores, submit bids to decrease electricity consumption by a set amount at a set time for a set price. The wholesale market operators treat those offers just like bids from generators to increase supply. The operators, that is, rank order all the bids—both to produce and to refrain from consuming electricity—from least to most expensive, and then accept the lowest bids until supply and demand come into equipoise. And, once again, the LSEs pick up the cost of all those payments. So, to return to our prior example, if a store submitted an offer *not* to use a unit of electricity at 2 p.m. on August 15 for $35, the operator would accept that bid before calling on the generator that offered to produce a unit of power for $40. That would result in a lower LMP—again, wholesale market price—than if the market operator could not avail itself of demand response pledges. See ISO/RTO Council, Harnessing the Power of Demand: How ISOs and RTOs Are Integrating Demand Response Into

Wholesale Electricity Markets 40–43 (2007) (estimating that, in one market, a demand response program reducing electricity usage by 3% in peak hours would lead to price declines of 6% to 12%). And it would decrease the risk of blackouts and other service problems.

Wholesale market operators began using demand response some 15 years ago, soon after they assumed the role of overseeing wholesale electricity sales. Recognizing the value of demand response for both system reliability and efficient pricing, they urged FERC to allow them to implement such programs. . . . And as demand response went into effect, market participants of many kinds came to view it—in the words of respondent Electric Power Supply Association (EPSA)—as an "important element[ ] of robust, competitive wholesale electricity markets." App. 94, EPSA, Comments on Proposed Rule on Demand Response Compensation in Organized Wholesale Energy Markets (May 12, 2010).

Congress added to the chorus of voices praising wholesale demand response. In the Energy Policy Act of 2005, 119 Stat. 594 (EPAct), it declared as "the policy of the United States" that such demand response "shall be encouraged." § 1252(f), 119 Stat. 966, 16 U.S.C. § 2642note. In particular, Congress directed, the deployment of "technology and devices that enable electricity customers to participate in . . . demand response systems shall be facilitated, and unnecessary barriers to demand response participation in energy . . . markets shall be eliminated." *Ibid.*

B

Spurred on by Congress, the Commission determined to take a more active role in promoting wholesale demand response programs. In 2008, FERC issued Order No. 719, which (among other things) requires wholesale market operators to receive demand response bids from aggregators of electricity consumers, except when the state regulatory authority overseeing those users' retail purchases bars such demand response participation. . . .

Concerned that Order No. 719 had not gone far enough, FERC issued the rule under review here in 2011, with one commissioner dissenting. See *Demand Response Competition in Organized Wholesale Energy Markets*, Order No. 745, 76 Fed. Reg. 16658 (Rule) (codified 18 CFR § 35.28(g)(1)(v)). The Rule attempts to ensure "just and reasonable" wholesale rates by requiring market operators to appropriately compensate demand response providers and thus bring about "meaningful demand-side participation" in the wholesale markets. 76 Fed. Reg. 16658, ¶ 1, 16660, ¶ 10; 16 U.S.C. § 824d(a). The Rule's most significant provision directs operators, under two specified conditions, to pay LMP for any accepted demand response bid, just as they do for successful supply bids. . . . In other words, the Rule requires that demand response providers in those circumstances receive as much for conserving electricity as generators do for producing it.

. . . .

The Rule rejected an alternative scheme for compensating demand response bids. Several commenters had urged that, in paying a demand response provider, an operator should subtract from the ordinary wholesale price the savings that the provider nets by not buying electricity on the retail market. Otherwise, the commenters claimed, demand response providers would receive a kind of "double-payment" relative to generators. . . But FERC explained that, under the conditions it had specified, the value of an accepted demand response bid to the wholesale market is identical to that of an accepted supply bid because each succeeds in cost-effectively "balanc[ing] supply and demand." *Id.,* at 16667, ¶ 55. And, the Commission reasoned, that comparable value is what ought to matter given FERC's goal of strengthening competition in the wholesale market: Rates should reflect not the costs that each market participant incurs, but instead the services it provides. . . Moreover, the Rule stated, compensating demand response bids at their actual value—*i.e.*, LMP—will help overcome various technological barriers, including a lack of needed infrastructure, that impede aggregators and large-scale users of electricity from fully participating in demand response programs. . . .

The Rule also responded to comments challenging FERC's statutory authority to regulate the compensation operators pay for demand response bids. Pointing to the Commission's analysis in Order No. 719, the Rule explained that the FPA gives FERC jurisdiction over such bids because they "directly affect [ ] wholesale rates." *Id.,* at 16676, ¶ 112. . . . Nonetheless, the Rule noted, FERC would continue Order No. 719's policy of allowing any state regulatory body to prohibit consumers in its retail market from taking part in wholesale demand response programs. . . . Accordingly, the Rule does not require any "action[ ] that would violate State laws or regulations." 76 *id.* at 16676, ¶ 114.

C

A divided panel of the Court of Appeals for the District of Columbia Circuit vacated the Rule as "*ultra vires* agency action." 753 F.3d 216, 225 (2014). The court held that FERC lacked authority to issue the Rule even though "demand response compensation affects the wholesale market." *Id.* at 221. The Commission's "jurisdiction to regulate practices 'affecting' rates," the court stated, "does not erase the specific limit[ ]" that the FPA imposes on FERC's regulation of retail sales. *Id.* at 222. And the Rule, the court concluded, exceeds that limit: In "luring . . . *retail* customers" into the wholesale market, and causing them to decrease "levels of *retail* electricity consumption," the Rule engages in "direct regulation of the retail market." *Id.* at 223–224.

The Court of Appeals held, alternatively, that the Rule is arbitrary and capricious under the Administrative Procedure Act. . . .

Judge Edwards dissented. He explained that the rules governing wholesale demand response have a "direct effect . . . on wholesale electricity rates squarely within FERC's jurisdiction." *Id.* at 227. . . .

We granted certiorari, 575 U.S. ___, 135 S.Ct. 2049, 191 L.Ed.2d 954 (2015), to decide whether the Commission has statutory authority to regulate wholesale market operators' compensation of demand response bids and, if so, whether the Rule challenged here is arbitrary and capricious. We now hold that the Commission has such power and that the Rule is adequately reasoned. We accordingly reverse.

II

Our analysis of FERC's regulatory authority proceeds in three parts. First, the practices at issue in the Rule—market operators' payments for demand response commitments—directly affect wholesale rates. Second, in addressing those practices, the Commission has not regulated retail sales. Taken together, those conclusions establish that the Rule complies with the FPA's plain terms. And third, the contrary view would conflict with the Act's core purposes by preventing all use of a tool that no one (not even EPSA) disputes will curb prices and enhance reliability in the wholesale electricity market.

A

The FPA delegates responsibility to FERC to regulate the interstate wholesale market for electricity—both wholesale rates and the panoply of rules and practices affecting them. As noted earlier, the Act establishes a scheme for federal regulation of "the sale of electric energy at wholesale in interstate commerce." 16 U.S.C. § 824(b)(1); *see supra*, at 767. . . . FERC has the authority—and, indeed, the duty—to ensure that rules or practices "affecting" wholesale rates are just and reasonable.

Taken for all it is worth, that statutory grant could extend FERC's power to some surprising places. As the court below noted, markets in all electricity's inputs—steel, fuel, and labor most prominent among them— might affect generators' supply of power. . . . We cannot imagine that was what Congress had in mind.

For that reason, an earlier D.C. Circuit decision adopted, and we now approve, a common-sense construction of the FPA's language, limiting FERC's "affecting" jurisdiction to rules or practices that "*directly* affect the [wholesale] rate." *California Independent System Operator Corp. v. FERC*, 372 F.3d 395, 403 (2004) (emphasis added). . . .

Still, the rules governing wholesale demand response programs meet that standard with room to spare. In general (and as earlier described), wholesale market operators employ demand response bids in competitive auctions that balance wholesale supply and demand and thereby set wholesale prices. . . . The operators accept such bids if and only if they bring down the wholesale rate by displacing higher-priced generation. And when that occurs (most often in peak periods), the easing of pressure on the grid, and the avoidance of service problems, further contributes to lower charges. . . . Wholesale demand response, in short, is all about reducing wholesale rates; so too, then, the rules and practices that determine how those programs operate.

And that is particularly true of the formula that operators use to compensate demand response providers. As in other areas of life, greater pay leads to greater participation. If rewarded at LMP, rather than at some lesser amount, more demand response providers will enter more bids capable of displacing generation, thus necessarily lowering wholesale electricity prices. Further, the Commission found, heightened demand response participation will put "downward pressure" on generators' own bids, encouraging power plants to offer their product at reduced prices lest they come away empty-handed from the bidding process. 76 Fed. Reg. 16660, ¶ 10. That, too, ratchets down the rates wholesale purchasers pay. Compensation for demand response thus directly affects wholesale prices. Indeed, it is hard to think of a practice that does so more.

B

The above conclusion does not end our inquiry into the Commission's statutory authority; to uphold the Rule, we also must determine that it does not regulate *retail* electricity sales. That is because, as earlier described, § 824(b) "limit[s] FERC's sale jurisdiction to that at wholesale," reserving regulatory authority over retail sales (as well as intrastate wholesale sales) to the States. *New York*, 535 U.S., at 17, 122 S.Ct. 1012 (emphasis deleted). . . .

Yet a FERC regulation does not run afoul of § 824(b)'s proscription just because it affects—even substantially—the quantity or terms of retail sales. It is a fact of economic life that the wholesale and retail markets in electricity, as in every other known product, are not hermetically sealed from each other. To the contrary, transactions that occur on the wholesale market have natural consequences at the retail level. And so too, of necessity, will FERC's regulation of those wholesale matters. . . . When FERC regulates what takes place on the wholesale market, as part of carrying out its charge to improve how that market runs, then no matter the effect on retail rates, § 824(b) imposes no bar.

And in setting rules for demand response, that is all FERC has done. . . .

. . . .

. . . Nothing in § 824(b) or any other part of the FPA suggests a more expansive notion, in which FERC sets a rate for electricity merely by altering consumers' incentives to purchase that product. . . .

Consider a familiar scenario to see what is odd about EPSA's theory. Imagine that a flight is overbooked. The airline offers passengers $300 to move to a later plane that has extra seats. On EPSA's view, that offer adds $300—the cost of not accepting the airline's proffered payment—to the price of every continuing passenger's ticket. So a person who originally spent $400 for his ticket, and decides to reject the airline's proposal, paid an "effective" price of $700. But would any passenger getting off the plane say he had paid $700 to fly? That is highly unlikely. And airline lawyers and regulators (including many, we are sure, with economics Ph.D.'s) appear to share that common-sensical view. It is in fact illegal to "increase the price" of "air transportation . . . after [such] air transportation has been purchased by the consumer." 14 CFR § 399.88(a) (2015). But it is a safe bet that no airline has ever gotten into trouble by offering a payment not to fly.

And EPSA's "effective price increase" claim fares even worse when it comes to payments not to use electricity. In EPSA's universe, a wholesale demand response program raises retail rates by compelling consumers to "pay" the price of forgoing demand response compensation. But such a consumer would be even more surprised than our air traveler to learn of that price hike, because the natural consequence of wholesale demand response programs is to bring *down* retail rates. Once again, wholesale market operators accept demand response bids only if those offers lower the wholesale price. . . . And when wholesale prices go down, retail prices tend to follow, because state regulators can, and mostly do, insist that wholesale buyers eventually pass on their savings to consumers. EPSA's theoretical construct thus runs headlong into the real world of electricity sales—where the Rule does anything but increase retail prices.

EPSA's second argument that FERC intruded into the States' sphere is more historical and purposive in nature. . . .

. . . Demand response, then, emerged not as a Commission power grab, but instead as a market-generated innovation for more optimally balancing wholesale electricity supply and demand. . . .

. . . [N]othing supports EPSA's more feverish idea that the Commission's interest in wholesale demand response emerged from a yen to usurp State authority over, or impose its own regulatory agenda on, retail sales. In promoting demand response, FERC did no more than follow the dictates of its regulatory mission to improve the competitiveness, efficiency, and reliability of the wholesale market.

Indeed, the finishing blow to both of EPSA's arguments comes from FERC's notable solicitude toward the States. As explained earlier, the Rule allows any State regulator to prohibit its consumers from making demand response bids in the wholesale market. . . . And that veto gives States the means to block whatever "effective" increases in retail rates demand response programs might be thought to produce. Wholesale demand response as implemented in the Rule is a program of cooperative federalism, in which the States retain the last word. That feature of the Rule removes any conceivable doubt as to its compliance with § 824(b)'s allocation of federal and state authority.

III

These cases present a second, narrower question: Is FERC's decision to compensate demand response providers at LMP—the same price paid to generators—arbitrary and capricious? . . .

. . . .

. . . The Commission, not this or any other court, regulates electricity rates. The disputed question here involves both technical understanding and policy judgment. The Commission addressed that issue seriously and carefully, providing reasons in support of its position and responding to the principal alternative advanced. In upholding that action, we do not discount the cogency of EPSA's arguments. . . . Nor do we say that in opting for LMP instead, FERC made the better call. It is not our job to render that judgment, on which reasonable minds can differ. Our important but limited role is to ensure that the Commission engaged in reasoned decisionmaking—that it weighed competing views, selected a compensation formula with adequate support in the record, and intelligibly explained the reasons for making that choice. FERC satisfied that standard.

IV

FERC's statutory authority extends to the Rule at issue here addressing wholesale demand response. The Rule governs a practice directly affecting wholesale electricity rates. And although (inevitably) influencing the retail market too, the Rule does not intrude on the States' power to regulate retail sales. FERC set the terms of transactions occurring in the organized wholesale markets, so as to ensure the reasonableness of wholesale prices and the reliability of the interstate grid—just as the FPA contemplates. And in choosing a compensation formula, the Commission met its duty of reasoned judgment. FERC took full account of the alternative policies proposed, and adequately supported and explained its decision. Accordingly, we reverse the judgment of the Court of Appeals for the District of Columbia Circuit and remand the cases for further proceedings consistent with this opinion.

It is so ordered.

JUSTICE ALITO took no part in the consideration or decision of these cases.

[JUSTICES SCALIA and JUSTICE THOMAS dissented from the majority opinion].

NOTES & QUESTIONS

1.   According to *FERC v. EPSA*, how has the scope of the federal government's regulatory jurisdiction over electric utilities under the Commerce Clause evolved over time?

2.   What is the specific FERC rule that EPSA is challenging in *FERC v. EPSA*? What appears to be the purpose of the rule?

3.   From the perspective of regional grid operators, in what sense is a kWh of demand response equivalent to kWh of additional generated power? Do you think it's appropriate for wholesale electricity markets to price these two units in the same way? Why or why not?

4.   On what specific ground did EPSA assert in *FERC v. EPSA* that FERC had exceeded its regulatory authority in issuing Order No. 745? How did the Court respond to this argument?

5.   Does the majority's holding in *FERC v. EPSA* benefit and strengthen the nation's wind and solar energy industries, or does it harm? Defend your answer.

6.   *Proposed Grid Resiliency Pricing Rule.* In late 2017, the DOE issued in a Notice of Proposed Rulemaking (NOPR) a rule that would effectively favor nuclear and coal energy sources over demand response and renewables in wholesale markets. *See* Grid Resiliency Pricing Rule, 82 FR 46940–01, 2017 WL 4481523(F.R.) (Oct. 10, 2017). The NOPR would require FERC to issue a new tariff rules for wholesale electricity markets that would compensate nuclear and coal-fired power generators for the supposed "resilience attributes" of those energy sources. *Id.* at 46941. In essence, the NOPR asserted that coal and nuclear power generators that are able to a "90-day fuel supply on site" are able to provide additional resilience benefits to the grid and should be guaranteed compensation for these benefits. *Id.* at 46945. Accordingly, the NOPR would create special tariffs for these energy sources—artificially high prices utilities and other wholesale purchasers would be required to pay.

Opponents of the NOPR noted that demand response, wind energy, and energy storage systems often provide even greater resilience benefits than coal plants and nuclear plants. For instance, on frigid winter days some thermal generating facilities cannot operate because of extremely cold temperatures but wind farms and demand response programs are able to continue operating. Nonetheless, the NOPR would exclude these other energy sources from the tariff benefits. The NOPR's proposed tariffs would surely benefit some coal and nuclear energy generators that increasingly struggle to remain price-competitive in wholesale markets against other energy sources such as renewables, demand response, and energy storage. However, the tariffs would also interfere with valuable competition and could ultimately destabilize some wholesale electricity markets. See Robbie Orvis & Mike O'Boyle, *DOE rulemaking threatens to destroy wholesale markets with no tangible benefit*, UtilityDive.com (Oct. 2, 2017), http://www.utilitydive.com/news/doe-rulemaking-threatens-to-destroy-wholesale-markets-with-no-tangible-bene/506289/.

C. SMART METERS AND THE SMART GRID

A crucial component of any retail demand-side management strategy is the widespread deployment of smart grids and smart meters that are advanced enough to support it. The following materials provide basic introductory information about smart grid technologies and smart meters and highlight some of the primary legal and policy issues arising as grid operators and utilities integrate these innovations into the electricity system.

1. SMART METER TECHNOLOGIES

For most of the electricity era, utilities have used simple analog meters to measure customers' electricity use and calculate their monthly bills. Utilities that use these basic meters typically send out employees monthly to physically visit each home and business in their service territory and record the total number of kWhs showing on the meters, which are generally affixed to a building's exterior wall. The utility then determines the total number of kWhs consumed during that month by subtracting the newest meter reading from the previous month's reading. For example, if a customer's meter had a reading 47,021 kWh on January 1 and 48,021 kWh on February 1, the utility would charge the customer for 1000 kWH of electricity on the next electricity bill.

The practice of measuring customers' electricity consumption with analog meters has largely worked for most of the last century. However, reliance on analog meters is increasingly undesirable because it fails to provide information that could enable utilities to better operate grids and more accurately price electric power. For instance, analog meters do not measure the specific times of the day or month when customers consume power, making it impossible for utilities to charge higher prices during peak use periods when it is particularly costly to supply electric power. Analog meters are also generally unable to support solar net metering programs like those described in Chapter 5. They only measure the flow of electricity *into* a customer's building and typically cannot measure the amounts of excess electric power that customers with distributed energy systems feed onto the electric grid.

Smart meters and smart grid technologies can facilitate far more detailed and instantaneous communication about customers' electricity use than was ever possible with conventional analog meters. Unfortunately, transitioning to smart metering technologies is also very expensive. In the words of one pair of energy law scholars:

> The distribution system ... was not designed for the kinds of bidirectional power flows that significant deployment of distributed energy resources such as rooftop solar and storage require. ... [W]e really do need a different type of infrastructure,

and we need it in thousands of local distribution systems across the country. Modernizing this part of the grid will require significant investment in overhauling existing infrastructure and deploying new technologies to enhance the intelligence of the system . . . enable two-way communications between customers and their electricity providers, which is critical for time-variant pricing, and to accommodate the growth and increasing diversity of customer-side generation and storage. One recent estimate put the range of total investment needed in the distribution and consumer segments of the system to achieve a fully functioning "smart grid" at $255 to $385 billion.

William Boyd & Ann E. Carlson, *Accidents of Federalism: Ratemaking and Policy Innovation in Public Utility Law*, 63 UCLA L. REV. 810, 855–56 (2016).

Despite the relatively high cost of converting the nation's tens of millions of analog meters to smart meters, utilities throughout the country are increasingly doing it. As of 2016, American utilities had installed roughly 65 million smart meters, with about 88% of those installations done on residential homes. *See Frequently Asked Questions: How Many Smart Meters Are Installed in the United States, and Who Has Them?*, ENERGY INFO. ADMIN., https://www.eia.gov/tools/faqs/faq.php?id=108&t=3 (last visited Aug. 9, 2017). That said, as shown in Figure 7.2, some utilities are far ahead of others in their embracing of smart meter technologies. Some large utilities have achieved "full deployment" of smart meters, meaning that nearly every customer now has one. In contrast, some other major electric utilities have installed almost no smart meters in their service territories.

Figure 7.2. Aggregate Smart Meter Installations by State (as of 2015)

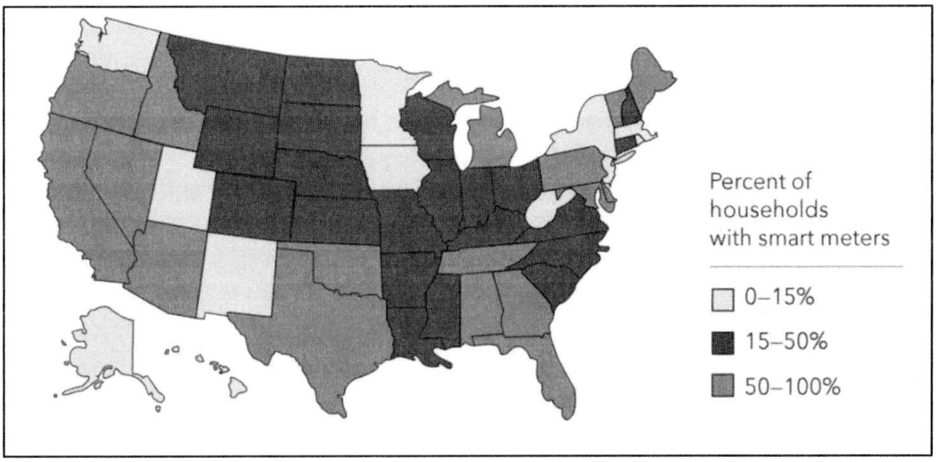

Source: Inst. for Electric Innovation

Although cost barriers partly explain some utilities' delay in transitioning to smart meters, they are not the only obstacle standing in the way. In many regions of the country, vocal minorities of utility customers have vigorously objected to smart meter installations on their homes and businesses. A few have objected to smart meter installations based on fears that electromagnetic signals associated with the meters could have adverse impacts on their health. However, most objectors resist smart meter installations on the ground that the meters would allow utilities or governments to collect information about their electricity use in ways that violate their constitutional privacy rights. In the *Naperville* case that follows, a court analyzes and ultimately rejects one advocacy group's claim that smart meters violate customers' privacy rights. Despite the holding in *Naperville*, several unanswered questions remain regarding the constitutional limits on utilities gathering and use of smart meter data.

NAPERVILLE SMART METER AWARENESS V. CITY OF NAPERVILLE

United States District Court, N.D. Illinois, Eastern Division, 2015
114 F.Supp.3d 606

LEE, D.J.

Naperville Smart Meter Awareness ("NSMA"), an Illinois not-for-profit corporation, has sued the City of Naperville ("the City") over the installation of smart meters in its members' homes. NSMA has moved for leave to file its Third Amended Complaint for Injunctive Relief in accordance with Federal Rule of Civil Procedure 15(a)(2). NSMA reasserts its claims pursuant to 42 U.S.C. § 1983, alleging violations of its members' rights to freedom from unreasonable search under the Fourth Amendment (Count I), and equal protection of the laws under the Fourteenth Amendment (Count III). NSMA also alleges violations of its members' rights to privacy and freedom from unreasonable search under the Illinois Constitution (Count II). For the following reasons, the Court grants in part and denies in part NSMA's motion for leave to file its Third Amended Complaint.

Factual Background

What follows is a brief summary of the allegations set forth in the proposed Third Amended Complaint.

NSMA is an Illinois not-for-profit corporation whose stated mission is to "educate, engage and empower families, friends and neighbors to advocate for a fiscally responsible and safe utility meter solution in Naperville, Illinois." 3d Am. Compl. ¶ 8. In Naperville, all residential electrical utility services are provided by the Department of Public Utilities-Electric, a company owned and operated by the local city government. . . . In January 2012, the Naperville Department of Public

Utilities-Electric began replacing its customers' analog electricity meters with smart meters as part of a local program called the Naperville Smart Grid Initiative. . . . The Naperville Smart Grid Initiative is funded in part by the U.S. Department of Energy, which received $4.5 billion of federal tax dollars under the American Recovery and Reinvestment Act of 2009 for the purpose of modernizing the nation's electrical power grid. . . .

Like analog meters, smart meters can measure customers' total residential usage for monthly billing purposes. . . . Unlike analog meters, smart meters are also equipped with wireless radio transmitters that, when activated, send usage data via radio-frequency waves to nearby neighborhood "network access points," which then relay usage data to Naperville's Department of Public Utilities-Electric. . . . While analog meters are capable of measuring only total accumulated consumption of energy ("total kilowatt hours used over a month"), smart meters measure aggregate electricity usage much more frequently—in intervals of fifteen minutes. . . . Smart meters have the ability to collect data consisting of "granular, fine-grained, high-frequency type of energy usage measurements" (so-called "Interval Data") totaling to "over thousands of intervals per month." *Id.* ¶¶ 35, 43.

NSMA alleges that Interval Data allows the City to collect more than just the aggregate data necessary for billing purposes previously available through analog meters. . . . The City also collects Interval Data from participants who voluntarily choose to partake in the Demand Response Program, which promotes the use of less electricity during periods of high demand. . . .

As an alternative to having new smart meters installed in their homes, Naperville residents may opt to have their old analog meters replaced with "non-wireless meters." *Id.* ¶ 148. These "non-wireless meter alternatives" are essentially smart meters with their radio transmitters deactivated so that they emit no radio-frequency waves and must be read manually by a reader meter each month. *See id.* ¶ 149. Non-wireless meters are able to collect "the same highly detailed Interval Data" as smart meters. *Id.* Residents who choose the non-wireless meter alternative must pay a one-time installation fee of $68.35, plus an additional monthly fee of $24.75. . . . NSMA describes the non-wireless meters as a "marginally lesser harm from among the two unsatisfactory alternatives." *Id.* ¶ 152.

NSMA asserts a number of concerns arising from the implementation of smart meters. Most notably, because smart meters are capable of taking data measurements in frequent, discrete increments, NSMA alleges that the smart meters present privacy risks that analog meters do not. . . . Specifically, NSMA claims that a home's smart meter data history is capable of revealing "intimate details about the personal lives and living habits of NSMA members" and that an inspector of this detailed history can determine "when [residents] are away from home or asleep . . . and [when they are using] different appliance[s]." *Id.* ¶¶ 74, 88, 90. NSMA posits that through the use of mechanisms such as "energy disaggregation software" and "intuitive observation," the City—and by extension law enforcement personnel—is capable of conducting an "intrusive search of the intimate details of NSMA members' in-home activities" that goes beyond assumptions or guesses. *Id.* ¶¶ 64, 78, 81. NSMA also alleges that the radio-frequency waves that smart meters emit present health risks to Naperville residents. In support, it claims that radio-frequency waves have been "known to cause headaches, heart palpitations, ringing in the ears, anxiety, sleep disorders, depression, and other symptoms, particularly in individuals who suffer from electromagnetic sensitivity." *Id.* ¶ 123.

Earlier in this litigation, the Court granted the City's motion to dismiss NSMA's First Amended Complaint with leave to amend some of the counts therein. After so amending, the City again moved to dismiss the claims in the Second Amended Complaint. The Court granted in part and denied in part the City's second motion to dismiss NSMA's Second Amended Complaint.

NSMA now moves for leave to file a Third Amended Complaint. In Count I, NSMA alleges the City's collection of detailed smart meter data constitutes an unreasonable search of information under the Fourth Amendment. . . . In Count II, NSMA also alleges that the City's collection of detailed smart meter data constitutes an unreasonable search and invasion of privacy under Article I, § 6 of the Illinois Constitution of 1970. . . . In Count III, NSMA alleges that the City has violated its members' right to equal protection both by singling out NSMA members for an additional level of unequal treatment stemming from retaliatory motives, as well as by denying requests by NSMA members to retain analog meters for medical reasons while granting similar requests made by non-members. . . . NSMA seeks an injunction ordering the City to make analog and non-wireless meters available at no additional cost upon customer request. . . . Because the City does not oppose the motion with regard to Count III, the Court will solely address Counts I and II.

    . . . .

Analysis

I.   **Fourth Amendment Claim (Count I)**

In the proposed Third Amended Complaint, NSMA seeks to remedy the defects that had caused the Court to dismiss the past two attempts to allege Fourth Amendment violations. . . .

In its prior order granting the City's motion to dismiss NSMA's First Amended Complaint, the Court held that NSMA members have no reasonable expectation of privacy under the Fourth Amendment in the aggregate measurements of their electrical usage—regardless of whether that aggregate usage is measured monthly, weekly, daily, hourly, or in fifteen-minute increments. *See Naperville Smart Meter Awareness*, No. 11–C–9299, 2013 WL 1196580, at *12 (N.D. Ill. Mar. 22, 2013). The Court found that NSMA's "assertions [did] not support a reasonable inference that the type of nonaggregate information purportedly capable of being collected by smart meters [was] actually being captured by [the City]." *Id.* at *13. NSMA, nevertheless, in its Second Amended Complaint, insisted that data showing aggregate residential power usage in fifteen-minute intervals reveals "intimate details about [residents'] personal lives and living habits." *Naperville Smart Meter Awareness*, No. 11–C–9299, 69 F.Supp.3d 830, 2014 WL 4783823, at *6 (N.D. Ill. Sept. 25, 2014). The Court, however, in granting in part and denying in part the City's motion to dismiss NSMA's Second Amended Complaint, held, once again, that the aggregate data measured in fifteen-minute intervals is not entitled to protection under the Fourth Amendment. *See id.* The Court found that "[a]ny imagined explanation for [a] peak [in total power usage] necessarily relies on nothing more than guesses and assumptions, [as] the electrical usage data itself does not provide any information confirming how many or what types of household appliances or devices are in use at any time." *Id.*

NSMA now alleges the availability of new "energy disaggregation" software technology "allows for the breakdown of Interval Data collected via a smart meter into appliance-level itemized consumption," enabling the City to garner information beyond the aggregate data to which its members have consented. 3d Am. Compl. ¶ 75. NSMA further asserts that, while the City has chosen to collect data on the 15-minute interval, the smart meter is capable of collecting Interval Data in 5, 15, 30, or 60-minute intervals. *Id.* ¶ 38. Therefore, at least according to NSMA, because smart meters can now accumulate "a history of energy, power, and reactive power over thousands of intervals per month . . . , there is far more information here than an analog meter is capable of providing via its single monthly reading of energy." *Id.* ¶ 43. With these additional allegations, NSMA again alleges that the installation and use of smart meters by the City amounts to an unreasonable search of its members' homes under the Fourth Amendment.

The Fourth Amendment provides that "[t]he right of the people to be secure in their persons, houses, papers, and effects, against unreasonable searches and seizures, shall not be violated," and it has been held to guarantee individual privacy from some forms of government intrusion. . . . However, "a person has no legitimate expectation of privacy in information he voluntarily turns over to third parties." *Smith v. Maryland*, 442 U.S. 735, 743–44, 99 S.Ct. 2577, 61 L.Ed.2d 220 (1979). . . . To state a Fourth Amendment violation, NSMA must allege—beyond mere capability—that the City has gathered more than just aggregate measurements of electrical usage.

After reviewing the proposed Third Amended Complaint, the Court concludes that NSMA still falls short of alleging a legally cognizable Fourth Amendment claim. Even if smart meters are capable of capturing more than the aggregate data previously presented, as NSMA alleges, NSMA still has not alleged that the City is *actually* collecting and using the data in a way that would amount to an unreasonable search or invasion of privacy. . . .

   . . . .

In an attempt to fill this lacuna, NSMA claims that, using "disaggregation algorithms" currently available in the marketplace, the City could ascertain the level of detail that NSMA fears. 3d Am. Compl. ¶ 81. NSMA alleges there is "no restriction . . . to prevent the City from utilizing a disaggregation service . . . [which] would allow an even more intrusive search of the intimate details of NSMA members' in-home activities." *Id.* ¶ 78. But the fact that the City theoretically could employ this technology (if indeed it can) to glean more detailed information about a user's personal life does not in and of itself constitute an allegation—or lead to a reasonable inference—that the City is doing that here. . . .

   . . . .

NSMA's attempt to hinge a Fourth Amendment claim on theoretic possibilities without presenting any allegations about what the City is actually doing with the data is futile. Because NSMA has failed to allege that smart meters are relaying detailed information beyond aggregate data about members' electricity usage to the City and that the City is disaggregating the data to analyze the private lives of its residents, there is no cognizable claim upon which relief can be granted.

Some final points, NSMA's claim that its members have not consented to the "two-way, real-time communication between NSMA members and the City through use of smart meters" is a moot point. *Id.* ¶¶ 91–105. NSMA members are deemed to have consented through their usage of electricity services knowingly supplied by the City. . . . Lastly, the City's Demand Response Program does not change the above finding of consent as it is solely a voluntary program, and does not collect any information beyond Interval Data measurements. *Id.* ¶¶ 56–58.

For these reasons, the Court concludes that NSMA has failed to satisfy the Rule 12(b)(6) pleading requirements with respect to the Fourth Amendment claim (Count I), and thus the motion for leave to file the Third Amended Complaint with respect to that claim is denied.

II. Article I § 6, Illinois Constitution Claim (Count II)

NSMA also alleges that the City's installation of smart meters capable of capturing Interval Data constitutes an unreasonable search and invasion of privacy under the Illinois Constitution of 1970. Article I, § 6 of the Illinois Constitution provides that: "The people shall have the right to be secure in their persons, houses, papers and other possessions against unreasonable searches, seizures, invasions of privacy or interceptions of communications by eavesdropping devices or other means." Ill. Const. art. I, § 6. NSMA alleges that, because the Illinois Constitution contains an express privacy clause, it should not be considered co-extensive with the Fourth Amendment claim. 3d Am. Compl. ¶ 210.

NSMA's Fourth Amendment and Illinois Constitution claim, however, both hinge on the same factual core: that the information gathered and analyzed by the City through smart meters is more than just the aggregate measurements of electricity usage. . . . Because the NSMA has failed to point to any new valid factual allegations to support that there has been a search of its members' homes or an impermissible invasion of privacy through the City's use of smart meters, NSMA's motion to file leave to assert a claim under the Illinois Constitution likewise is denied.

. . . .

Conclusion

The Court grants in part and denies in part NSMA's motion for leave to file a Third Amended Complaint [102]. NSMA's motion for leave to file a Third Amended Complaint asserting an unreasonable search and invasion of privacy claim under the U.S. Constitution (Count I) and the Illinois Constitution (Count II) is denied with prejudice. Because the City did not oppose the motion with regard to NSMA's equal protection claim, the Court grants the motion solely as to Count III.

QUESTIONS & NOTES

1.   According to NSMA, how did the City's installation of smart meters on residential homes violate citizens' Fourth Amendment rights?

2.   According to NSMA, how did the potential availability of "disaggregation algorithms" strengthen its claim against the City? On what ground did the *Naperville* court reject this argument?

3.   Suppose the Naperville Police Department suspected that a household was growing several unauthorized marijuana plants in its basement and using lamps to provide light to the plants during certain hours of the day. Suppose further that a police officer obtained the household's disaggregated smart meter records from the city's utility department showing an unusually high degree of energy use at unusual times of day and sought to submit these records as evidence in a criminal case against individuals living in the home. Based on *Naperville*, do you think such use of smart meter records would constitute an unreasonable search in violation of the Fourth Amendment? Why or why not?

4.   *Potentially Valuable Uses of Smart Meter Data.* Despite some customers' concerns about invasions of privacy, there have been growing calls in recent years for more collection and open disclosure of smart meter data. Advocates of greater energy use data disclosure emphasize the data's potential value in efforts to increase efficiency and drive innovation. For a thorough examination of this issue, see Alex Klass & Elizabeth Wilson, *Remaking Energy: The Critical Role of Energy Consumption Data*, 104 CAL. L. REV. 1095 (2016).

5.   *Smart Meters as Health Hazards.* NMSA is just one of numerous opponents of smart meters that have resisted them by asserting that electromagnetic field (EMF) radiation associated with the devices poses health and safety risks. In response to these concerns, researchers have extensively investigated the impacts of low-level EMF radiation on the human body. As of 2017, no major study had uncovered evidence that EMF radiation from smart meters caused any significant adverse health effects. *See, e.g.*, ALAN RIVALDO, HEALTH AND RF EMF FROM ADVANCED METERS (2012), http://www.puc.texas. gov/industry/electric/reports/smartmeter/smartmeter_rf_emf_health_12-14-20 12.pdf; ARIZ. DEP'T OF HEALTH SERVS., PUBLIC HEALTH EVALUATION OF RADIO FREQUENCY EXPOSURE FROM ELECTRONIC METERS (2014), http://www.azcc.gov/ 11-4-14smartmeters11-0328.pdf.

2.   GRID-LEVEL SMART TECHNOLOGIES

Like smart meters, smart grid equipment and devices incorporate countless digital and Internet-based technologies to enhance the efficiency and responsiveness of electric grids. The U.S. Department of Energy's Office of Electricity Delivery and Energy Reliability website describes the potential benefits of smart grids as follows:

> The Smart Grid represents an unprecedented opportunity to move the energy industry into a new era of reliability, availability, and efficiency. . . . The benefits associated with the Smart Grid include:
>
> - More efficient transmission of electricity
> - Quicker restoration of electricity after power disturbances
> - Reduced operations and management costs for utilities, and ultimately lower power costs for consumers
> - Reduced peak demand, which will also help lower electricity rates
> - Increased integration of large-scale renewable energy systems
> - Better integration of customer-owner power generation systems, including renewable energy systems
> - Improved security

. . . A smarter grid will add resiliency to our electric power System and make it better prepared to address emergencies. . . . Because of its two-way interactive capacity, the Smart Grid will allow for automatic rerouting when equipment fails or outages occur. . . . In addition, the Smart Grid will take greater advantage of customer-owned power generators to produce power when it is not available from utilities. By combining these "distributed generation" resources, a community could keep its health center, police department, traffic lights, phone System, and grocery store operating during emergencies. In addition, the Smart Grid is a way to address energy efficiency, to bring increased awareness to consumers about the connection between electricity use and the environment. And it's a way to bring increased national security to our energy System. . . .

What is the Smart Grid?, SMARTGRID.GOV, https://www.smartgrid.gov/the_smart_grid/smart_grid.html (last visited Sept. 28, 2017).

Not surprisingly, a utility's enthusiasm for smart grid technologies often depends on how they will likely impact the utility's bottom line. The excerpt below explains why utilities' degree of support of smart grid development sometimes diverges from that of broader society.

ENVISIONING THE SMART GRID: NETWORK ARCHITECTURE, INFORMATION CONTROL, AND THE PUBLIC POLICY BALANCING ACT

Elias L. Quinn & Adam L. Reed
81 U. COLO. L. REV. 833, 837–40, 842–43, 852–53 & 873–74 (2010)

. . . [D]espite the projected cost of developing a national smart grid, the efficiencies it is expected to create should more than compensate for the initial investment. . . An upgraded electrical grid is its own source of savings, as the grid would operate more efficiently, would need less maintenance and large-scale infrastructural investment, and would fall victim to fewer "power disturbances" such as outages and overloads that impose significant costs on the U.S. economy. By most accounts, these efficiency savings swallow smart grid technology costs. Accordingly, investing in efficiency promises more handsome returns than investing in renewable energy generation (to say nothing of its being something of a prerequisite), and the smart grid is a key enabler of a number of efficiency measures.

But in addition to these static efficiency concerns, there is also a dynamic efficiency story to tell. Simply put, the upgraded grid is necessary to facilitate broad-scale renewable electricity generation. Integrating electricity from variable input sources such as wind farms and solar arrays requires accurate, real-time information about the supplies and demands influencing the grid at any given time, as well as mechanisms to balance loads with generation. From this dynamic efficiency perspective, investing in the smart grid is critical to the feasibility and utilization of other energy-related investments.

The overhaul of the nation's electricity grid and the development of the smart grid may well deserve its reputation as the next great source of innovation and economic growth. However, a lot of work remains between the present state of affairs and the smart grid promised land. This infrastructure will not spring wholly formed from utility installation trucks. Many decisions regarding its network architecture—the actors, physical means, and legal entitlements by which data is collected, aggregated, analyzed, utilized, provided, or sold to interested parties (be they consumers, utilities, data brokers, or others)—are not yet standardized, and in many cases these decisions are almost entirely unformed.

A more pressing question for smart grid proponents is but a new variation on an age-old philosophical conundrum: which comes first, the network or the regulatory controls? The problem of the smart grid's network architecture poses a classic chicken-or-egg dilemma that should be addressed early and head-on in the grid overhaul process. The regulatory structure surrounding the grid will inform how it develops and the shape it takes in the process. Questions as to who controls which parts of the grid, what their rights are, and to whom they answer will inform investment decisions, directing grid development in much the same way zoning influences residential development. However, physical aspects of the network's architecture, such as the data pathway to the first aggregator of consumer usage data, will largely determine which regulatory schemes bear on its operation. Such regulatory schemes would determine whether, for instance, state public utility commissions are the ultimate regulatory authority on the network, or if the federal government's authority may be in play on the grid—be it through the Department of Energy, the Federal Energy Regulatory Commission, the Federal Trade Commission, the Federal Communications Commission, or even some (perhaps synergistic) combination thereof.

. . . Of course, with smart grid technology rapidly evolving (and, for that matter, redefining itself), policymakers cannot hope to fully design the grid's network architecture in advance of its development. Nor would such an outcome even be desirable. Rather, the challenge for regulators in the face of such protean technology is the creation of a consistent, multi-jurisdictional regulatory architecture to scaffold the development of network architecture. That regulatory architecture must be determinate enough to support network investment, and yet ought to remain flexible enough to spur continuing innovation. In doing so, it must balance a number of public policy considerations associated with the smart grid: cost savings versus emissions reductions; consumer privacy versus information access and innovation; and improved utility returns versus viable new business models.

. . . .

. . . The economic regulation of utilities and the legal principles that govern that system largely determine both the utility's investment decisions and its fundamental identity as, above all else, a generator and seller of electricity. These facets of utility decision-making are critical to the deployment of smart grid technologies for two reasons. First, the smart grid represents a type of investment very different from the investments historically made by utilities, because it attempts to control and shape demand rather than simply satisfying it with generation. Second, many potential functions of the smart grid—such as total demand reduction through in-home feedback displays or the derivation of consumer behavioral trends from detailed usage information—may be seen by utilities as outside their historical role of generating, transmitting, and selling electricity at rates sufficient to recoup costs. Such non-traditional functions may be marginalized in the development of regulations because utilities have a financial interest in promoting a vision of the smart grid that meets their needs while ignoring visions that do not. Thus, absent modifications to the regulatory environment, smart grid functions focusing on cost reduction and load shifting through dynamic pricing, facilitation for plug-in vehicles, and other clearly revenue-positive actions tend to place higher on the list of utility priorities than smart grid functions leading to enhanced consumer awareness of environmental footprint, true demand reduction, or opportunities for innovative use of detailed data. This dynamic is captured nicely in Xcel Energy's definition of the smart grid:

> [T]he general definition of a smart grid is an intelligent, auto-balancing, self-monitoring power grid that accepts any source of fuel (coal, sun, wind) and transforms it into a consumer's end use (heat, light, warm water) with minimal human intervention.

This statement defines the core of the smart grid, as the utility views it, according to two fundamental characteristics. First, the smart grid's mission is fundamentally about the efficient delivery of electricity, the utility's primary product. Second, the defining methodology of that mission is automation, so as to minimize the need to rely on the actions of people. . . .

. . . .

. . . Utilities are not profit-maximizing firms in the traditional sense. Their returns are largely pre-determined (and largely guaranteed) by regulators, and they attract capital by serving as low-risk tranches within capital market portfolios. As such, utilities have very little incentive to examine new business models, products, or ideas outside their core competency of selling electricity to consumers. Indeed, utilities must be careful not to engage in behavior that would be perceived as risky or speculative by regulators or, worse, ratepayers and their advocates, as higher risks and higher costs are ultimately borne by the ratepayer. This risk-intolerance shadows utilities' deployment of smart grids because they represent new investment risks that are not yet fully understood and may affect both investors' perceptions of regulatory and market risk in the electric utility sector and ratepayers' concerns about the effects of smart grid investment on their monthly energy bills.

None of this implies that utilities will not invest in smart grid technologies. Rather, the danger is more subtle: that the regulatory and legal architecture that defines the concerns and proper roles of the utility may ultimately define the concerns and proper roles of the smart grid in a way that limits its potential and creates difficulties for non-utility smart grid applications, particularly those focused on consumers rather than utilities. It is not surprising, given this regulatory and legal edifice, that utility-driven conceptions of the core of the smart grid's potential—cost savings from load shifting, reduced administrative costs from replacing meter-readers with automated communication, and improved integration of variable renewable generation assets, to name a few—are overwhelmingly preoccupied with functions that affect the utility's supply-side costs in a favorable manner, with interaction from consumers only where necessary to achieve such objectives.

. . . .

Moreover, traditional rate-of-return regulation creates incentives in many ways antithetical to the modern project of electricity reform. Especially when framed as a means to reduce electricity consumption, a smart grid is, under the existing regulatory lens, hardly more than a huge capital expense focused on minimizing profits. For a utility to hasten to deploy such smart grid technologies is, therefore, economically irrational under existing incentive structures. Of course, existing incentives could prompt utilities to deploy some smart grid components—for example, advanced metering and home automation for time-shifting of demand— that reduce costs while otherwise maintaining existing sales levels. But demand-reducing smart grid technologies that are less friendly to utility profitability may be marginalized in the process unless utilities are compensated in some way for the lost electricity sales. Moreover, because utilities have an extensive pre-existing relationship with regulators, a failure to deliberately account for the needs of other players in the emerging smart grid marketplace may result in a "default" regulatory and network architecture for a smart grid that is excessively utility-centric.

[ ] Consumer Privacy

The backbone of the smart grid is the collection of information. Depending on the grid architecture, information about customer electricity consumption could be collected in a number of ways, and at many levels of granularity. Early smart metering systems collected information about usage in half-hour increments. Newer models often default to five-minute collection, but can in fact be used to measure usage at resolutions of less than a second. The available information determines the kinds of analysis that are available: with finer-grained information, specific appliance events can be deciphered from the user's load profile and a consumer's daily activities can be determined with surprising (and potentially disturbing) levels of detail. This information could be of interest to a host of potential actors, some relatively benign (market researchers interested in the number of times a person makes tea throughout the workday), some more questionable (insurance companies using intimate personal information to identify risky behavior and thus adjust premiums), and some downright monstrous (criminals examining usage information to determine when the user is not home—or is home alone).

Protecting consumers from dangerous and unauthorized disclosure of their personal information requires careful thinking about who may collect the information, who owns the information, how the physical network collecting the information is protected against attack, and how to ensure that users authorized by consumers to use the data guard it from inadvertent disclosure to unauthorized parties.

QUESTIONS

1.   In the excerpt above, Quinn & Reed argue that utilities tend to support only certain types of smart grid development. Why are they willing to support some types but not others?

2.   Which of the seven bulleted benefits associated with smart grids listed in the smartgrids.gov excerpt above would you expect utilities to be *most* interested in promoting and which would you expect them to be *least* interested in promoting, and why?

3.   What is the potential chicken-and-egg problem Quinn & Reed highlight in the regulation of smart grids? What are some approaches policymakers could take to mitigate that problem?

4.   Based on the Quinn & Reed excerpt, why are regulated utilities typically more risk-averse than ordinary corporations, and how does that risk aversion potentially impact utilities' willingness to voluntarily invest in smart grid technologies?

5. What are the potential uses for electricity consumption data mentioned in the Quinn & Reed article?

6. Do you think utilities should be permitted to sell electricity consumption data gathered via smart grid devices to third parties? Why or why not? If so, under what conditions?

3. MICROGRIDS

One other group of smart grid technologies worthy of mention in this Chapter are those related to *microgrids*: grid systems with sufficient electricity generation and storage resources to operate independently from a larger grid. As distributed energy, energy storage, smart metering, and smart grid technologies advance and become more affordable, microgrids could become increasingly common—especially in geographically remote areas. The most familiar function of microgrid technologies has historically been that of supplying reliable power to areas that are disconnected from the larger grid. However, microgrids can also serve valuable purposes in urban settings that are already in close proximity to the conventional grid system. The excerpt below more thoroughly describes microgrids, their potential uses, and their possible impacts on the electricity markets and regulation.

THE URBAN MICROGRID: SMART LEGAL AND REGULATORY POLICIES TO SUPPORT ELECTRIC GRID RESILIENCY AND CLIMATE MITIGATION

Kevin B. Jones et al.
41 FORDHAM URB. L.J. 1695, 1702–13, 1753–1756 (2014)

A microgrid is able to operate independently from the larger system because it is composed of an energy supply source and electric infrastructure to distribute energy from its generation sources. This independent generation and distribution system is a *power island*: "an energized section of circuits separate from the larger system." When the area disconnects from the centralized grid, the islanded area transitions from redundant infrastructure to the primary power source for all consumers connected to the islanded area. Once islanded, the system maintains its own frequency and voltage. The ability of a small power network to remain operational when disconnected from the centralized grid is a major benefit during extreme weather. When connected to the centralized grid, the microgrid is a secondary electricity system that complements centralized operations. . . .

Microgrids are used in one of two ways: "(1) [s]ystems that are intended to always be operated in isolation from a large utility grid[; and] (2) [s]ystems that are normally connected with a larger grid." . . .

In its most elegant form, a microgrid is the ultimate implementation of the smart grid, and one that has a great deal of consumer appeal. The ideal microgrid would feature a digital control system that could integrate solar photovoltaics (PV), efficient combined heat-and-power (CHP) generators, battery storage, thermal storage, demand response, and electric vehicle charging. This system would intelligently manage both supply and demand resources in a manner that ensures high reliability, reduces carbon emissions, and saves consumers money. The microgrid could operate disconnected from the utility system or could reconnect and sell any excess resources back to the interconnected grid.

Many market and technological trends suggest that the microgrid era could be on the not-too-distant horizon. Declining costs for solar PV, low natural gas prices, abundant biofuels, advances in distributed storage alternatives, and the rapid development of energy management technologies suggest a bright future for microgrid development. There are even predictions that a microgrid industry is not only on the rise, but that "just like the independent power industry did for generation, microgrids could break the seal on the utility compact, introducing competition into the energy industry's last great monopoly—the electric distribution business."

II. THE MICROGRID CASE STUDIES

The early focal points of microgrid development are rural village electrification, university campuses, military bases, and, more recently, critical community facilities during emergencies. University campuses and military facilities are a natural fit for microgrid development because their electric loads come from multiple buildings, which are often centrally arranged on a common footprint and often have their own electric distribution facilities. Universities are a niche microgrid market both for their physical as well as intellectual architecture. A university campus is the ideal physical setting given the multiple building loads, favorable infrastructure for CHP, the usual presence of back-up generators, the increasingly common solar PV systems, the presence of campus sustainability plans, and an island-like setting where the university often owns all of the electric distribution system on its side of the utility transformer. On campuses there are also diverse intellectual resources and research budgets to support microgrid development. Military bases, for a number of similar reasons, are also well suited for microgrid development. . . .

A. An Urban Microgrid Serving a Common Footprint: UCSD and the Philadelphia Navy Yard

[University of California, San Diego (UCSD)] has one of the most advanced microgrids in the country. It operates under a strategic partnership with the local utility, San Diego Gas and Electric (SDG&E),

and uses engineering and information technology firms to test and implement state-of-the-art technology. Through testing advanced technologies, UCSD's microgrid has proven to be extremely efficient. It serves as an example of the economic, reliability, and environmental benefits that cutting edge technologies can achieve.

1.   *UCSD's Microgrid Facility*

UCSD's current microgrid started in 2006 when the University began making aggressive plans to reduce its carbon footprint and become a self-sustaining campus. Since 2008, UCSD's microgrid has received $4 million in funding from the California Energy Commission and another $4 million in public and private funding. It serves around 45,000 students, faculty, and employees on the 1200 acre campus. UCSD owns a 69 kilovolt (kV) substation, ninety-six 12 kV underground feeder circuits, and four 12 kV distribution substations. This infrastructure provides UCSD with an ideal framework for its 42 megawatt (MW) microgrid. UCSD's distributed resources include a 30 MW cogeneration system containing two gas turbines and a steam turbine, a 3.8 million gallon thermal energy storage system that aids in campus cooling, 3.0 MW of solar PV covering close to 100% of usable rooftop space, and a 2.8 MW fuel cell powered by biogas from the city sewage treatment plant. UCSD is also becoming a leader in energy storage and electric vehicle charging technology.

The University is in the process of installing a diverse portfolio of energy storage that will be integrated with its PV generation and will soon have installed approximately fifty electric vehicle charging stations. UCSD's diverse distributed resources are optimized by a master controller that monitors and controls the real-time operation of the microgrid, which allows UCSD to "self-generate ninety-two percent of its own annual electricity and ninety-five percent of its heating and cooling load." . . .

. . . .

UCSD's microgrid uses an array of advanced technologies to produce, distribute, monitor, and store energy. UCSD uses a mix of solar PV and concentrating PV system (CPV) at both on and off campus locations. Every single architecturally and structurally available on-campus rooftop has PV installations. UCSD's CPV panel is mounted on a movable platform atop a metal pole at its East Campus Energy Complex and was installed by Concentrix Solar, a German CPV technology manufacturer. The CPV technology has an average efficiency of 27.2%, or nearly twice that of conventional PV technology. To better integrate the intermittent solar energy into the system, UCSD has developed solar forecasting optimization algorithms. Every minute, two sky-imaging systems look for clouds over the university campus and forecast the clouds' positions with respect to the PV systems on campus from one to fifteen minutes into the future. The system also forecasts the next day's weather by running high-resolution models of the atmosphere over southern California and the Pacific Ocean to forecast the burn-off time of the marine-layer clouds and project other weather events. The forecasts are then blended and optimized to estimate electricity output from PV systems and make charge and discharge decisions for energy storage.

UCSD has the most diversified energy storage system of any university campus in the world. It has a 3.8 million gallon thermal energy storage system, a 2.8 MW fuel cell powered by biogas from a local sewage treatment plant, and seven energy storage systems with a total capacity of 2.7 MW and 5 MWh. The seven battery storage systems are primarily used to integrate the school's PV generation. The school is also testing used electric vehicle (EV) storage batteries of 108 kW and 180 kWh lithium-ion batteries to demonstrate the usefulness of used batteries.

UCSD's microgrid has many benefits for the school, the local utility, and others. Through its microgrid, the school saves more than $800,000 a month when compared to buying all of its energy from the grid. Much of the microgrid relies on smart grid data analytics that present real improvements in energy efficiency and reductions in energy cost. The smart technologies ultimately make the production, monitoring, distribution, and use of energy more efficient and reduce the need for investing in additional physical infrastructure.

Furthermore, UCSD's microgrid supports the reliability of San Diego's electric grid. The school provides nearly all of its energy needs, which reduces the demand placed on San Diego's transmission and distribution system (T&D) and helps defer SDG&E's need to expand its T&D infrastructure in the future. In the event of a power outage in San Diego, the microgrid can run in islanded mode and can provide "black start" service to the main distribution grid. A facility with black start service has the ability to assist an electric system in restoring power from collapse to normal operation; this is necessary to reestablish power in the event of grid failure. UCSD's microgrid can help energize the local distribution grid when such an event occurs. UCSD has also been able to create a strong relationship with SDG&E.

UCSD's integration of efficient CHP and renewable energy into its microgrid has reduced its GHG emissions. The school's CHP plant is roughly fifty percent more efficient and produces about seventy-five percent fewer emissions than a conventional natural gas plant. As a result of its energy management efforts, the school is working towards a climate action plan of reducing GHGs to 1990 levels by 2020 and achieving climate neutrality by 2025.

2.   Current California Policies Affecting Microgrids

UCSD's microgrid benefits from California's energy and environmental goals, which are some of the most progressive in the nation. . . . In order to achieve the state's progressive goals by 2020, the California Public Utility Commission (CPUC) has created several regulations and financial incentives to promote distributed generation.

CPUC defines the scope and authority of public utilities and electrical corporations, but it also lists many exemptions for distributed generation. The CPUC states: " '[p]ublic utility' includes every . . . electrical corporation . . . where the service is performed for, or the commodity is delivered to, the public or any portion thereof." Further, if the electrical corporation receives compensation or payment of any kind for its services, the electrical corporation "is a public utility subject to the jurisdiction, control, and regulation of the commission." Lastly, the CPUC states:

> When any person or corporation performs any service for, or delivers any commodity to, any person, private corporation, municipality, or other political subdivision of the state, that in turn either directly or indirectly, mediately or immediately, performs that service for, or delivers that commodity to, the public or any portion thereof, that person or corporation is a public utility subject to the jurisdiction, control, and regulation of the commission and the provisions of this part.

However, the CPUC has created many regulations that exempt distributed generation from being regulated as electric corporations. According to Section 218 of the California Public Utility Code, electrical generators are exempt from status as a corporation when:

> (1) The producer generates or distributes electricity "through private property solely for its own use or the use of its tenants and not for sale or transmission to others."

> (2) The producer generates and sells electricity to no more than two other corporations or persons who are located on the property where the electricity is generated or on the adjacent property. However, if there is an intervening public road between the two properties, and the two properties are not under common ownership or the tenants are not affiliates or subsidiaries of the generator, then the producer is not exempt from being an electrical corporation.

> (3) The producer sells or transmits electricity "to an electrical corporation or state or local public agency, but not for sale or transmission to others."

Thus, California's regulations support microgrid implementation as long as the microgrid is located on a single piece of property, does not sell electricity to more than two tenants on its property, and does not sell electricity to others outside of its property other than electric corporations or state agencies. Section 218 specifically states that cogeneration, landfill gas, digester gas, solar energy, and small power producers are not considered electrical corporations as long as they meet the criteria set forth in the section.

. . . .

Through these regulations, the CPUC has made it possible for individuals, businesses, universities, hospitals, or others to create their own microgrids without being considered "electrical corporations," as long as they follow statutory provisions. . . .

However, while many regulations and incentives support microgrid implementation, certain regulations limit the potential physical expansion of microgrids. If, for example, UCSD wanted to expand its microgrid to include a neighboring hospital or other critical community facility not affiliated with UCSD, the construction would violate CPUC Section 218 because a public street divides UCSD and the hospital. Accordingly, neighboring critical community facilities would not be able to connect to and become part of UCSD's microgrid unless current regulations change to allow microgrids to cross public streets onto property owned by others. An additional restriction prevents a microgrid from selling power to more than two tenants on a property. Property owners with numerous tenants, such as apartment complexes, malls, commercial office parks, or other businesses, could not sell electricity to more than two tenants, eliminating the incentive for property owners to invest in a microgrid. Thus, these regulations, while supporting microgrids in certain situations, limit their growth in others.

. . . .

III. ADVANCING URBAN MICROGRID POLICY

. . . .

Front and center to the legal and regulatory challenges facing microgrids is their unclear legal definition. Case study examples lack a cohesive legal definition of what a microgrid is, or, possibly more importantly, is not. Developing a clear statutory and regulatory definition of a "microgrid" would significantly refine public policy and incent a market reaction. Central to this definition is clarifying whether a microgrid is or is not an electric corporation similar to a standard distribution utility, and, if it is not, in what ways does the microgrid legally differ from the electric corporation. . . . Subjecting a microgrid owner to the same rules and regulations as an electric distribution utility that is subject to rate and service quality regulation by the state regulatory commission could likely stifle microgrid development given the significant costs and overheads that public utility regulation creates. On the other hand, not being subject to the same regulatory scheme as an electric corporation suggests that microgrid owners will have significantly reduced scope and authority compared to a fully regulated distribution utility given that the current regulatory regime exists for established policy reasons. Clearly resolving the legal definition of a microgrid is a necessary starting point.

Another big picture legal issue involves opening access to public rights of ways. . . . On the other hand, increasing the footprint of single site microgrids will accelerate concerns over utility revenue adequacy embodied in the expansion of distributed energy resources, and possibly lead to redundant or stranded utility distribution system resources. Defining clear public policies around the definition and authority of microgrids, as well as the related utility franchise rights, in a holistic manner that considers all utility customers, is a vital first step in microgrid policy development.

. . . .

While a key feature of an urban microgrid is its ability to island during outages caused by severe weather events, an equally important feature is for microgrid customers to share the benefits of the utility network. Critical to sharing utility network benefits is the ability to increase microgrid efficiency by selling excess energy from the microgrid back to the utility or wholesale market and at other times purchasing network energy services for peak and back-up service when microgrid resources are physically or economically unavailable to serve load within the microgrid. Balancing the microgrid's contribution to network benefits is another challenging issue that must be resolved in a manner that is just and reasonable for all customers. . . .

As microgrids expand to more complex configurations serving multiple customers, policymakers will also have to grapple with a multitude of consumer protection issues such as service quality and customer data privacy. . . Today's regulatory compact between the public utility and state regulatory authority has developed with rather sophisticated (some might say burdensome) processes for measuring and incenting service quality. Meanwhile, today's smart grid technologies are capable of collection, storage, and analysis of large amounts of customer data. When non-utility parties have access to detailed customer data, and likely in a more lightly-regulated environment, customer data privacy issues will grow in significance. . . .

QUESTIONS & NOTES

1. How might microgrid technologies pose a threat to utilities' existing monopolies over electricity distribution within their service territories?

2. Why is the issue of whether laws classify microgrid operators as electric corporations comparable to ordinary distributed electric utilities an important factor in the long-term growth of microgrids in the United States?

3.   What specific regulatory exemptions have enabled college campuses like UCSD managed to develop and operate microgrids in California? How, if at all, would you recommend that these exemptions be expanded to accommodate additional types of microgrid development?

4.   How could microgrid technologies help to bring electricity service to remote villages and communities that are situated great distances away from major electric grid systems?

5.   *Blockchain-Based Community Microgrids.* One type of urban microgrid that has garnered growing attention in recent years uses blockchain technologies to enable peer-to-peer sharing of electricity. Blockchain, which supports Bitcoin currency trading, is a secure, distributed digital database capable of processing and recording an enormous volume of transactions in rapid succession. Recently, some companies have begun operating blockchain-supported microgrids. These innovative microgrids allow connected participants within a community—including owners of distributed solar or distributed energy storage systems—to buy and sell dynamically-priced power in fluid local markets without directly involving any centralized utility in the transactions. As blockchain-based microgrid technologies mature, they could further threaten traditional centralized electric utility models by eliminating the need utilities to serve as middlemen between producers and sellers of power.

Policymakers in some states are actively encouraging blockchain-based microgrid development, in part because of the additional resiliency benefits the microgrids can bring to larger grid systems. For instance, regulators in New York, who are hoping to be better prepared in the future for major storms comparable to Superstorm Sandy, have been fairly supportive of blockchain-based microgrid development projects in that state. A highly-publicized blockchain microgrid project in Brooklyn already had 50 connected participants as of early 2017. *See* Diane Cardwell, *Solar Experiment Lets Neighbors Trade Energy Among Themselves*, N.Y. TIMES (Mar. 13, 2017), https://www.nytimes.com/2017/03/13/business/energy-environment/brooklyn-solar-grid-energy-trading.html?mcubz=1.

D. ENERGY EFFICIENCY AND CONSERVATION

Along with demand response, energy efficiency and conservation comprise the other primary components of demand-side energy management. The "duck curve" problem discussed in Chapter 5 of this Casebook provides a useful background for highlighting the potentially positive impacts of energy efficiency and conservation in demand-side management. As the duck curve aptly conveys, electric utilities in sunny regions where lots of customers have rooftop solar panels commonly experience sharp spikes in grid load demand on hot summer evenings. During summer afternoons, many customers are running air conditioning units to keep buildings cool but their rooftop solar panels are producing electricity that offsets much of that air conditioning use and helps to keep utilities' electricity demand relatively low. Unfortunately, shortly after the sun goes down, it is still very hot outside but customers' solar panels are producing far less power. Consequently, the demand for grid-supplied electricity rapidly increases and utilities must scramble to meet that spiking demand. These daily spikes become increasingly severe as more and more utility customers get their own rooftop solar arrays.

Initiatives aimed at increasing the energy efficiency of building HVAC systems and other major building appliances are an additional means of combatting the duck curve and many other intermittency-related grid balancing problems. Designing HVAC systems and certain other major appliances to require less electricity on extremely hot days helps to partially flatten peaks in load demand on those days because such systems require less peak power to operate. Programs that educate utility customers about electricity conservation and encourage or support them in engaging in it can likewise have load-flattening effects. Through these and other benefits, energy efficiency and conservation initiatives can help grid operators and utilities to more easily integrate intermittent renewables into their grid systems.

1. STATE ENERGY EFFICIENCY PROGRAMS

For decades, state governments throughout the country have offered a wide range of tax credits or rebates to customers to incentivize them to purchase energy efficiency-enhancing appliances or products. However, some states have gone one step further and required *utilities* to develop and implement programs to promote energy efficiency and conservation within their territories. Of course, aggressive energy efficiency and conservation programs are not always appealing to electric utility companies because those companies are in the business of selling electricity. A successful energy efficiency or conservation policy causes declines in total electricity consumption and can thereby reduce utility revenues. In that sense, backing such programs can arguably go directly against a utility's core business interests. Recognizing this problem, some state policymakers have sought to structure their energy efficiency or conservation policies such that utilities have sufficient incentives to support them. Although some policies aimed at persuading utilities to genuinely promote energy efficiency and conservation have been effective, others have not. The following Arkansas case involves issues surrounding the structuring of such policies in that state.

ARKANSAS ELEC. ENERGY CONSUMERS, INC.
V. ARKANSAS PUBLIC SERVICE COMM'N

Court of Appeal of Arkansas, 2012
410 S.W.3d 47

ROBBINS, J.

As part of a larger effort to establish energy-efficiency policies and requirements for Arkansas utilities, the Arkansas Public Service Commission opened Docket No. 08–137–U to consider innovative approaches to utility regulation necessitated by the shift toward energy conservation. In doing so, the Commission issued Orders 15 and 18, which approved a general policy to award incentives to utilities for their achievement in delivering essential energy-conservation services. The Commission also established specific goals to be used as standards for awarding or not awarding the incentives during the 2011–13 program years. Appellants Arkansas Electric Energy Consumers, Inc., and Arkansas Gas Consumers, Inc., appeal from Orders 15 and 18, arguing that the incentives were not authorized by law and constituted an improper abandonment of traditional ratemaking practices. We affirm the Commission's orders.

To place the Commission's ruling in context, we begin with the passage of the Energy Conservation Endorsement Act (ECEA) almost thirty-five years ago during the oil crisis of the 1970s. *See* Act 748 of 1977, codified at ARK. CODE ANN. §§ 23–3–401 to –405 (Repl. 2002). The ECEA declared that the United States was confronted with a "severe and very real" energy crisis; that the demand for fuels was outstripping supplies; that enormous amounts of energy were being wasted due to inadequate insulation and other inefficiencies; and that the President of the United States had established energy conservation as a high-priority national goal. ARK. CODE ANN. § 23–3–402. In light of these considerations, our General Assembly determined that a "proper and essential function" of regulated utilities was to engage in energy-conservation programs, projects, and practices. ARK. CODE ANN. § 23–3–404. The ECEA defined "energy conservation and program measures" as including, but not limited to, insulation programs; programs that improved load factors and contributed to reductions in peak power demands; and programs that encouraged the use of renewable energy technologies or sources. ARK. CODE ANN. § 23–3–403.

In section 405, the ECEA established the authority of the Public Service Commission to "propose, develop, solicit, approve, require, implement, and monitor" energy-conservation measures that caused utility companies to incur "costs of service and investments." ARK. CODE ANN. § 23–3–405(a)(1). The Commission was granted the power to approve such programs and measures, following proper notice and hearings, and to order them into effect if it determined that they would be "beneficial to the ratepayers of such public utilities and to the utilities themselves." ARK. CODE ANN. § 23–3–405(a)(2). In those instances, the Commission was required to declare that the costs of such conservation measures were proper costs of providing utility service. Further, once the programs or measures were approved or ordered into effect, the Commission was required to

> order that the affected public utility company *be allowed to increase its rates or charges as necessary to recover any costs incurred by the public utility company* as a result of its engaging in any such program or measure.

ARK. CODE ANN. § 23–3–405(a)(3) (emphasis added). The italicized portion of the statute is a primary point of controversy in this appeal, as is the following, final provision of the ECEA:

> Nothing in this subchapter shall be construed as limiting or cutting down the authority of the commission to order, require, promote, or engage in other energy conserving actions or measures.

ARK. CODE ANN. § 23–3–405(b).

For reasons best left explained by history, the ECEA did not spark a large, concerted effort toward energy-conservation programs in the decades that followed, either by the utilities or the Public Service Commission. Between 2006 and 2008, however, the utility-regulatory field in Arkansas saw a significant increase in energy-conservation activity, whereby the Commission not only ordered utilities to implement energy-efficiency programs but developed rules that required utilities to submit their programs for approval and explain the anticipated benefits. The Commission also opened numerous dockets to address and explore energy efficiency in all areas of utility use. Included among those dockets was No. 08–137–U. . . In its first order in Docket 08–137–U, the Commission noted the following:

> [W]ithin the national public utility regulatory dialogue there is a growing level of references to and discussion of shifting regulatory paradigms which may necessitate innovative approaches to the traditional ratebase rate of return regulation which for decades has governed the setting of revenues and rates for electric and gas public utilities.

More specifically, the Commission recognized that the increased emphasis on energy efficiency would decrease usage by consumers and could compromise revenue recovery by the utilities. The Commission therefore invited input regarding these concerns from its staff; from the Attorney General; from public utilities; and from appellants.

The vast majority of those that filed testimony and comments agreed that the current regulatory framework did not promote energy efficiency and that implementation of energy-efficiency programs warranted adjustments to the traditional ratemaking process. Witnesses explained that a utility is an investor-owned business and entitled to a financial return for its shareholders. They observed that this return, combined with a utility's general cost of doing business, ordinarily formed the basis for establishing consumer rates under traditional rate base/rate of return regulation. They stated, however, that the traditional ratemaking paradigm emphasized increased consumer usage and increased utility investment in physical plant (generation, transmission, and distribution) as means of producing revenue for the utility and providing a basis for investors to receive a return. Energy-conservation measures, they said, upset this paradigm by decreasing consumer usage and decreasing the need for investment in physical plant, thereby reducing the utility's ability to recover its fixed costs and provide a return to its shareholders.

Based on these observations, several parties proposed that three mechanisms were necessary for a beneficial energy-efficiency program: 1) recovery of the program costs incurred by the utility in implementing energy-efficiency measures; 2) recovery of the utilities' lost contribution to fixed costs (LCFC) occasioned by the drop in consumer revenue; and 3) financial incentives paid to the utility in order to either provide a return to shareholders or to promote exemplary performance of conservation programs... The staff cautioned, however, that incentives should be awarded only in those instances where the utility could demonstrate that its programs met or exceeded performance goals set by the Commission.

By the time of the final hearing, the Commission had approved a bill rider that allowed utilities to recover their program costs and LCFC. Those charges are not at issue on appeal. The need and methodology for incentives, however, continued to be debated. Several witnesses testified that, because energy-efficiency programs cause utility shareholders to forego the traditional means of earning a return on investment, some type of incentive is necessary to promote meaningful performance and to motivate utilities to reject their usual patterns of usage and plant acquisition as a means of generating a return. There was also testimony that incentive plans in which utilities and consumers share the savings engendered by energy conservation programs constitute "good public policy" and serve to align utility and consumer interests, being beneficial to both. . . .

Appellants opposed the use of incentives, arguing that the Commission did not have the authority under the ECEA to award them. Appellants relied on that portion of the Act that allows a utility to recover its "costs" resulting from a conservation program. ARK. CODE ANN. § 23–3–405(a)(3). Appellants contended that incentives could not be defined as costs.

In Order No. 15, the Commission determined that it possessed the authority under both the ECEA and general ratemaking statutes to award incentives. The Commission declared that the ECEA allowed utilities to recover "any costs" resulting from conservation programs, a broad term that included incentives. It also ruled that incentives were necessary to meet the statutory mandate in Arkansas Code Annotated section 23–3–405(a)(2) that energy-conservation programs must benefit both consumers and the utility. Further, the Commission noted that Arkansas Code Annotated section 23–3–405(b), which provides that *7 "nothing in this subchapter shall be construed as limiting or cutting down the authority of the commission to order, require, promote, or engage in other energy conserving actions or measures," permitted the award of incentives. The Commission therefore approved a general policy to grant incentives to utilities "to reward achievement in the delivery of essential energy conservation services."

As proposed, the incentives covered years 2011–13 but would not be awarded contemporaneously during the efficiency program year. Rather, they would be awarded, if at all, only "after the fact" based on a "robust" evaluation, measurement, and verification analysis. . . . The utility, however, was entitled to no benefits at all unless it achieved eighty percent or more of the specific savings goals established by the Commission. The Commission declined to impose a penalty on those utilities that did not meet the savings goals but reserved the right to revisit that question at a later time.

Appellants filed a timely petition for rehearing from Order No. 15. . . . They reiterated that the Commission lacked the statutory authority to award incentives, and additionally argued that an award of incentives constituted abandonment of traditional ratemaking practices. The Commission rejected appellants' arguments in Order No. 18, which led to this appeal.

I.   *Commission's Statutory Authority to Award Incentives*

Appellants argue first that the ECEA does not clothe the Commission with the authority to award incentives to a utility for implementing energy-efficiency programs. They contend that Arkansas Code Annotated section 23–3–405(a)(3) provides only for a utility's recovery of "costs," which they interpret to mean the actual, out-of-pocket expenses incurred by the utility relative to its energy-efficiency programs. Appellees respond that incentives fall within the meaning of that phrase "any costs" as used in section 405(a)(3) because incentives operate as a substitute for the return on investment that shareholders traditionally receive, which is considered a cost of service. . . . Appellees also argue that incentives represent the "opportunity cost" of the utilities' forgone investment in physical plants, which has historically yielded a return to shareholders. . . .

We note at the outset that appellants do not argue that the Commission lacked substantial evidence to award incentives. Rather, their challenge is to the Commission's legal authority. The issue before us is therefore one of law. . . We need only determine whether the Commission possessed the authority to award incentives based on our de novo interpretation of the applicable statute. . . In doing so, we observe that the interpretation of a statute by the agency charged with its execution is highly persuasive, and, while not binding on this court, will not be overturned unless it is clearly wrong. . . .

. . . .

Upon viewing the ECEA in its entirety, we conclude that the question of whether incentives are recoverable as "costs" under section 23–3–405(a)(3) need not be reached. Instead, we look to section 23–3–405(b), which provides that nothing in the subchapter—a phrase that includes the Commission's authority to award costs—shall be construed as limiting the authority of the Commission to, among other things, promote or engage in other energy conserving acts or measures. Keeping in mind that statutes pertaining to utility regulation must be strictly construed . . . , the intent of subsection 405(b) could not be clearer. The statutory scheme ensures that the utilities recover the costs they incur in engaging in conservation programs; but . . . the "cost" provision is not intended as a limitation on the Commission's ability to pursue other means of promoting energy efficiency. The incentives in this case were approved by the Commission in large part to promote the utilities' pursuit of energy conservation. We acknowledge that the ECEA does not expressly mention the Commission's authority to award incentives. But, even in 1977, there would have been an obvious impracticability in attempting to create an exhaustive list of devices that the Commission might employ to carry out its energy-conservation duties. The legislature obviously foresaw that the Commission would need some measure of flexibility to meet energy-conservation challenges not only in the reduced-supply years of the 1970s but in whatever conservation needs might arise in the future. Thus, the passage of section 405(b).

We therefore affirm the Commission's authority to award incentives under the ECEA. . . .

II. *Abandonment of Traditional Ratemaking Practices*

Appellants' final argument is that the Commission's use of incentives amounted to an abandonment of traditional ratemaking practices. By "traditional," appellants mean the method by which the utilities' rates are set, during a rate case, based on their costs and the rate of return applied to their rate base.

The Commission has broad discretion in choosing an approach to rate regulation and is free, within its statutory authority, to make any reasonable or pragmatic adjustments that may be called for under particular circumstances. . . . Our courts are not generally concerned with the method used by the Commission to establish components of rate regulation. . . .

. . . .

There is no doubt that the Commission undertook a new direction in this case, as evidenced by the purpose of this docket, which was to explore innovative ratemaking. The Commission's use of incentives, however, is more in the nature of a pragmatic adjustment, necessitated by the practical considerations of requiring utilities to pursue energy conservation. No assets were removed from the rate base . . . and the Commission emphasized that the rate base/rate of return method is still the practice in Arkansas. . . .

As for appellants' concern that incentives lead to a windfall and over-earning by the utilities, we note that the utilities are awarded incentives only if they save costs and achieve extraordinary performance in those savings. At that point, they receive a small percentage of those savings with consumers retaining the remainder. . . . Further, the Commission expressly stated that incentives would be awarded only after a "robust" review conducted by the Commission. . . .

Based on the foregoing, we affirm Commission Orders 15 and 18 in Docket 08–137–U.

Affirmed.

QUESTIONS

1. Why do you think the plaintiffs—advocacy groups representing the interests of Arkansas retail electric and gas utility ratepayers—would be motivated to challenge the incentive policies at issue in this case? In other words: how might these incentive policies potentially harm retail electricity customers?

2. Neither of the parties in *Arkansas Electric Energy Consumers* contested that utilities were entitled under the statute at issue to fully recover the costs of any implemented energy efficiency and conservation programs. Why, then, did those who provided testimony in Commission hearings believe it was justifiable to also provide financial incentive payments to utilities for achieving energy efficiency and conservation goals?

3. What specific statutory language did the majority in *Arkansas Electric Energy Consumers* cite in support of its conclusion that the Commission was empowered to award incentives to utilities for reaching energy efficiency and conservation goals? Briefly explain the court's rationale on this issue in your own words.

4.   Under the policy at issue in *Arkansas Electric Energy Consumers*, utilities received incentive payments only *after* achieving specific goals and undergoing a robust regulatory review. Suppose you were a utility advocate in Arkansas. Why might providing *ex post facto* awards reduce some utilities' interest in adopting efficiency and conversation programs? What specific changes would you recommend for these policies to address that problem?

2. GREEN BUILDING POLICIES AND PROGRAMS

Construction companies and manufacturers of major appliances and HVAC systems are also capable of advancing energy efficiency and conservation goals and thereby easing the nation's transition toward more renewable energy sources. Improving the efficiency of energy-intensive systems and devices in homes and commercial buildings could greatly reduce the nation's carbon footprint. The greatest potential efficiency gains in this area relate to building heating, cooling, and lighting. For example, those three categories account for between 54 and 71 percent of a typical office building's energy use. *See* NAT'L GRID, MANAGING ENERGY COSTS IN OFFICE BUILDINGS (2002), https://www9.nationalgridus.com/non_html/ shared_energyeff_office.pdf.

Recognizing that a large proportion of the nation's energy consumption relates to buildings, governments have sought for decades to incentivize greater energy efficiency in buildings and major appliances. For instance, most Americans have seen the United States Environmental Protection Agency (EPA) Energy Star program logo on major appliances or in buildings. The Energy Star program is a voluntary standardized labeling program that helps consumers identify energy-efficient buildings and appliances and compare energy efficiency attributes when making purchasing decisions. According to the EPA's Energy Star website, the program has saved more than $430 billion in utility bills and reduced greenhouse gas emissions by more than 2.8 billion tons since its inception in 1992. *See Energy Star Overview*, ENERGY STAR, https://www.energystar. gov/about (last visited Sept. 28, 2017).

A large non-governmental organization, the United States Green Building Council (USGBC), has also greatly influenced the evolution of energy efficiency policy for buildings. Established in 1993, the USGBC describes itself as an organization "focused on the transformation of the built environment at the national, state and local level through the engagement of our local communities, membership (organizations and individuals) and national stakeholders." U.S. GREEN BLDG. COUNCIL, 2017–2019 STRATEGIC PLAN 2 (2017), https://slideblast.com/2017-2019-strategic-plan-amazon-web-services_59548c511723ddd9c007c1e0.html. The LEED green building certification program is one of the chief ways that the USGBC furthers its mission. "LEED" stands for "Leadership in Energy and Environmental Design."

Under the LEED program, USGBC-authorized and trained professionals examine buildings to determine whether they qualify for LEED silver, gold, or platinum certification. These privately employed professionals determine whether a building qualifies for certification primarily based upon a points system that rewards various types of energy-efficient and environmentally friendly building features. Based on one study, LEED-certified buildings generated 34% fewer carbon dioxide emissions and consumed 25% less total energy than non-certified buildings. *See* KIM FOWLER ET AL., RE-ASSESSING GREEN BUILDING PERFORMANCE: A POST OCCUPANCY EVALUATION OF 22 GSA BUILDINGS (2011). As of 2017, more than 38,000 commercial buildings and more than 131,000 homes had earned LEED certification. *See USGBC Statistics*, U.S. GREEN BUILDING COUNCIL (July 1, 2016), https://www.usgbc.org/articles/usgbc-statistics (current as of July 2017) (last visited Sept. 28, 2017).

Although most energy-related green building practices focus on reducing a building's energy consumption, some practices focus on building-related renewable energy: building features that generate electric power for onsite use. In the following excerpt, Professor Sara Bronin explains more of the basics of LEED certification and green building and also uses a case study to highlight how laws and special interest politics can impede progress toward more energy-sustainable development.

BUILDING-RELATED RENEWABLE ENERGY
AND THE CASE OF 360 STATE STREET
Sara C. Bronin
65 VAND. L. REV. 1875, 1876–1932 (2012) (excerpts)

Currently, our buildings consume 40% of our energy, use two-thirds of our electricity, and emit 40% of our greenhouse gases. To reduce this negative environmental impact, public policymakers and advocates have encouraged demand reductions, while private industry has made building systems more efficient. Yet, with population growth and the expansion of human activity, energy consumption shows no sign of abating. Thus, while continuing demand-side, consumption-reduction strategies, it will be important to develop and facilitate supply-side solutions, including the construction of building-related renewable energy ("BRRE"). . . . Because most human activity takes place in buildings, a well-conceived policy approach to BRRE could transform the American energy landscape.

. . . .

This Article uses a case study—the 360 State Street project, a mixed-use LEED® Platinum project in downtown New Haven, Connecticut—to illustrate the barriers to maximizing the operating capacity of BRRE. . . .

. . . .

Building-related renewable energy is renewable energy—primarily solar, wind, geothermal, and fuel cell technologies—incorporated into inhabited structures and used by those structures' occupants. The definition encompasses both small-scale and midsized generating facilities.

"Small-scale" means individual distributed generation: the production of electricity by a small-scale source located at or very near the end user it serves. Examples of small-scale projects include a rooftop solar collector, a homeowner's geothermal well, or a set of small wind turbines on a commercial building.

"Midsized" means BRRE projects that serve one or more buildings featuring multiple occupancy types, multiple users, and/or large square footages. These projects can serve large, single-owner real estate developments with one or many users, such as 360 State Street, a mixed-use complex with approximately 420,000 occupiable square feet and more than 500 unique users. That complex uses a fuel cell that captures waste heat to serve the heating needs of occupants (an arrangement known as combined heat and power). Midsized projects may also cross property lines and serve different property owners. . . .

B.   Reducing the Negative Impact of Buildings

To repeat the startling statistics mentioned above: our buildings consume 40% of our energy, use two-thirds of our electricity, and emit 40% of our greenhouse gases. These numbers, which present the impact of buildings in relative terms, are expected to keep growing. In the United States, the building and appliance sector is expected to see an average of 2% growth in greenhouse gas emission rates annually between 2006 and 2030—a higher growth rate than any other sector. Global consumption trends suggest that demand for energy will increase 2.2% annually each year until 2020, and there is no reason to believe that the U.S. building and appliance sector will not either match or outstrip this level of growth.

Reducing the current and projected negative environmental impacts of buildings can be achieved most effectively in two ways: energy efficiency and BRRE.

1.   Energy Efficiency

One way to reduce the negative environmental impact of buildings is to make them more efficient—that is, to address their demand for energy. Energy efficiency is commonly called a "fifth fuel," next to coal, nuclear, petroleum, and renewable energy, and the measure of wattage saved by energy-efficient technology has been termed a "negawatt." The idea behind these terms—and many of the policies supporting energy efficiency—is that increases in efficiency reduce overall usage.

. . . Federal incentives for energy efficiency have been robust. State legislatures have also provided a range of incentives for energy efficiency, including personal and corporate tax deductions and credits, sales tax exemptions, property tax benefits, rebates, grants, loans, and bonds.

To some extent, and perhaps spurred by these incentives, a transformation in energy efficiency has already occurred. . . . The nonprofit organization American Council for an Energy-Efficient Economy ("ACEEE"), for example, has studied the impact of appliance, equipment, and lighting standards. It has concluded that, since the time of the Council's inception through the year 2035, such standards will have saved consumers more than $1.1 trillion cumulatively, with a reduction in energy use by the equivalent of two years of total U.S. energy consumption. . . .

Voluntary labeling programs that go beyond minimum standards have also helped popularize and improve energy efficiency. Programs such as the U.S. Green Building Council's LEED Green Building Rating System (a whole-building labeling program) require certain energy-efficiency benchmarks (for example, ensuring that the building is 30% more energy efficient than the building code requires) to be met by a project before it can be certified as "sustainable" under the system. . . . The voluntary labeling of common household appliances (and now homes) through the Energy Star® program allows consumers to estimate energy use over time and make choices accordingly.

Despite these gains, many have begun to doubt the impact of energy efficiency. . . . *The Economist* in 2008 surmised that "[i]n the eyes of many consumers, electricity and fuel are often too cheap to be worth saving, especially in countries where their prices are subsidised." And finally, scholars have raised serious concerns about end-user motivation to do anything that would require specific actions. It is difficult for most people to make a proactive, sustained choice to be energy efficient—say shutting off lights when leaving a room, or measuring the temperature of a hot shower. It is much easier to be efficient when the user has no choice, which is the direction that technology may need to go to ensure serious gains in energy efficiency.

While energy efficiency has become more popular and should continue to be incorporated into whole-building and appliance design, it is necessary to address the supply side of the energy equation to ensure real reductions of the negative environmental impacts of the built environment.

2.   BRRE

With demand showing no signs of abating, a second way to reduce the negative environmental impact of buildings is to make the buildings themselves the source of clean energy production. Incorporating building-related renewable energy into new or existing structures targets the supply side of the energy equation. . . .

. . . .

All types of BRRE have significant costs during their usable lives. Three key areas of state law affect whether these costs can be recouped by an owner or operator of BRRE from multiple end users: submetering, net metering, and rates being paid by or to the owner of the BRRE. . . .

1.   Submetering

Submetering refers to the measurement and billing of energy (electricity or heat) usage of individual users within a multiuser property or development. Submetering is thus relevant to midsized BRRE projects where multiple users (tenants, neighbors, BRRE co-owners, or others) are involved. . . .

How does submetering work? When a project is connected to infrastructure owned or controlled by a public utility, submetering occurs "after" the point of connection to the utility infrastructure. There may be one master meter at this point of connection, meaning that one party (presumably the owner of the project) will receive bills for overall usage from the utility company. That party will then obtain information through the submetering monitoring equipment (the meters) for the same period and pass bills reflecting respective shares, based on usage, to the other users. . . . When a project is not connected to such infrastructure and is "off the grid," submetering occurs within the project boundaries. The end users pay the owner of the BRRE pursuant to rules established by the state. In either form, bills can be read through wired or wireless communication systems, and many companies offer reliable technologies and services for bill collection and processing.

Submetering has many benefits for the owner of a project incorporating BRRE. Most significantly, it allows her to recoup the costs of operating the BRRE by charging end users for their use of the energy produced by BRRE. Submetering also benefits the tenants themselves. Instead of being billed by square footage or number of occupants, they are billed for their usage. . . . And overall, there are environmental benefits associated with reductions in usage that submetering generally inspires. For these reasons and more, in 2011, a multiagency federal task force issued a report recommending submetering in building design and retrofits wherever there is economic justification.

    . . . .

Despite . . . the potential benefits of submetering, submetering is prohibited, in whole or in part, in many states. . . . Utility companies often lobby against submetering legislation for fear that liberalizing submetering rules will result in less revenue and less demand for their services. In some states, their views have been held up in court under the theory that state policy intended to create an electricity monopoly by designating public utilities in the first place.

Consumer groups have different concerns about submetering. They view the manipulation of usage data as a real possibility, since in the past, technology has not been good enough to accurately monitor usage, and some property owners have been unscrupulous. Consumer groups also worry about the effect of submetering on low-income populations, especially in a situation where a building is being shifted from a master-metered building to a submetered one. . . . Defective meters, poorly installed equipment, or unfair distribution of nonmetered costs also present concern.

In my opinion, the benefits of submetering far outweigh potential concerns, and regulations (especially if modeled after those of New York State, a pioneer in submetering) can address many concerns by placing limitations on billing procedures, billable costs, and rates. . . .

. . . .

IV. INSTALLATION AND OPERATION OF BRRE AT 360 STATE STREET

With this background in mind, I turn now to the case study, 360 State Street. This complex, mixed-use project, located in downtown New Haven, Connecticut, was completed in October 2010. It incorporates a four hundred-kilowatt fuel cell that has the capacity to meet nearly all energy and electricity needs of users. . . .

. . . .

The story of the disposition of the 360 State Street site (the "Site") provides some important context. The Site, at the corner of Chapel and State Streets, is comprised of 1.605 acres on about a third of a city block. It is one block away from the New Haven Town Green, which is the heart of the city. . . .

1. Site History

For decades, the Site was part of a bustling, primarily commercial core with retail shops, company offices, and service providers of various types and sizes. By the early twentieth century, the Shartenberg-Robinson department store occupied most of the Site's frontage along Chapel Street. . . . The store's fortunes depended on a vibrant, well-populated urban core. The city's population peaked between 1920 and 1950. . . . But by the middle of the twentieth century, "white flight" to the suburbs had begun in earnest.

To try to stem the tide, New Haven decisionmakers implemented "urban renewal" strategies that other cities had experimented with around the country. . . . As part of an anticipated urban renewal effort along State Street, the city razed the Shartenberg-Robinson department store and every other building on the Chapel and State Street sides of the block some time in the 1960s.

... By the time the Site was slated for disposition to a private owner in 2006, it had been operated as surface parking for at least three decades.

2.   Picking a New Owner

In 2006, the City of New Haven announced a request for proposals ("RFP") for private parties' purchase and redevelopment of what it called "the former Shartenberg Site." ...

. . . .

... After a five-month review process involving many stakeholders, the City announced the selection of Becker + Becker ("B+B"), a Connecticut-based architecture, planning, and development firm. . . .

. . . .

... Of the requirements imposed on the developer, the most relevant to this question is contained in section 6.4(A)(iv) of the development agreement, in which B+B agreed to design the project to be certified under the U.S. Green Building Council's LEED Green Building Rating System. Because of the way the LEED program is set up, B+B had to select and register for a rating program before construction began. In 2007, when B+B was making this choice, two rating systems were possible options. The first was the LEED for New Construction rating system, which required a building to achieve a certain minimum level of energy efficiency for it to be considered certifiable at all. Up to fourteen additional points (out of sixty-nine available) could be obtained through various energy-efficiency and renewable energy measures. A building had to achieve twenty-six points to be certified. The second rating system, the LEED for Neighborhood Development ("LEED-ND") program, was in "pilot" mode. The LEED-ND program had no energy-performance requirement, focusing instead on the location of the building and its impact on its immediate surroundings. To be certified in the pilot program, a project had to achieve 40 points (out of a possible 106). The project could obtain up to nine points for energy-efficiency and renewable energy measures. Regardless of which of the two programs B+B chose, neither explicitly required BRRE to be installed at 360 State Street.

After doing an assessment of costs required to comply with each program, B+B chose to register with the LEED-ND program, targeting Platinum (the highest level) certification. . . .

. . . .

After reviewing the significant demands on the grid that the building would impose and the immense carbon footprint of designing the building in a conventional way, B+B decided to explore the possibility of incorporating BRRE into 360 State Street. B+B believed that a local BRRE system could meet 100% of the owner's energy needs and most of the energy needs of its diverse group of tenants. In addition, by using BRRE and increasing the building's LEED rating, the developer could become eligible to qualify for programs, such as a then-pending state green building tax credit, that would help to subsidize the costs of constructing BRRE.

In addition to analyzing the costs of installing BRRE, B+B also analyzed the costs of operating it. B+B recognized at the outset that it could not afford to incorporate BRRE unless it could also engage in submetering tenants' usage and charge tenants for their use of the energy produced by the BRRE that B+B would eventually choose. . . .

. . . .

During the course of the design, B+B considered all four primary alternatives for BRRE at 360 State Street: geothermal wells, wind energy, solar energy, and a fuel cell. These technologies could have been used individually or together in a variety of configurations, but their suitability depended on many factors, ranging from soil conditions to wind patterns to cost effectiveness. Ultimately the developer chose to incorporate only a fuel cell, which, at least in terms of installation costs, was the best value to the owner.

. . . .

. . . If designed properly, a fuel cell could meet all or nearly all of the energy needs of every occupant of 360 State Street. B+B worked with its mechanical, electrical, and plumbing engineers to design an integrated combined heat and power system using a four hundred-kilowatt, natural gas-fed fuel cell from United Technologies. Relative to conventional generation, the 360 State Street configuration eliminates 99.8% of pollution and triples the efficiency of production and delivery. As built and operating at full capacity, the fuel cell can meet 88% of occupants' electric needs and nearly all of their heating and hot water needs. In March 2009, B+B received a grant from a state clean energy fund for installation costs of up to $985,000. Other incentives, including a federal tax credit, brought the payback period for the fuel cell installation costs (which totaled $3.5 million) to 3.5 years.

The installation of the fuel cell alone would arguably have made 360 State Street one of the greenest buildings in the country (and the first multifamily application of a fuel cell). But the property owner also invested in nearly twenty energy-efficiency measures that have reduced the building's energy usage by more than 50% above conventional construction. Thus, the demand from occupants of the 360 State Street project could be more economically met by a smaller BRRE system than a conventional building of the same size would have required.

. . . .

. . . [T]he . . . most time-consuming, expensive, and contentious legal issues involving the project have related to the operation of the fuel cell. Outlining these legal issues—with the background of the program, design, and technology of BRRE at the project in mind—is the purpose of this final Part of this Article.

Simply put, Connecticut state law prevents real estate developers and property owners from recouping the costs of installing and operating BRRE. The biggest barrier in the case of 360 State Street has been the state's prohibition on submetering in residential applications. . . [S]ubmetering allows the owners of an energy source to recoup operating costs by charging third-party end users for their usage. At 360 State Street, the inability to recoup operating costs from third-party end users (and in particular the residential tenants) means the project's fuel cell has only been operating to the extent necessary to meet the needs of the owner and the commercial tenants (that is, the retail stores and the parking garage). All of the tenants of the five hundred rental apartments are using conventional electricity from the local public utility instead of clean energy from the on-site fuel cell.

. . . .

Having the ability to submeter individual apartment units would [have] allow[ed] the project to break even on the operation side. Instead, the fuel cell, which was installed at a great cost to the development team, idles at just half of its available capacity. Ironically, the state of Connecticut subsidized the purchase of the fuel cell but fails to make it financially feasible for its owner to fully utilize it.

. . . .

. . . [T]hese descriptions highlight how difficult it is for developers of midsized BRRE, especially BRRE with many different end users, to navigate entrenched bureaucracies and understand rights ex ante. . . .

Second, and relatedly, these descriptions underscore the immense power of utility companies, both at state legislatures and before industry regulatory bodies. As the case of 360 State Street reveals, utility companies may see submetering and midsized BRRE as threats. Well-equipped with legal departments, budgets for outside counsel, and time, public utilities clearly have the upper hand in preventing changes to the legal status quo. Figuring out a way to either neutralize or combat (with education) the influence of utility companies should be a key consideration for advocates of BRRE.

QUESTIONS & NOTES

1. What is *submetering*, and how did the unavailability of submetering in Connecticut adversely impact the energy sustainability of the 360 State Street building?

2. What are some ways that the LEED certification process, as described in the Bronin excerpt, differs from the typical municipal permitting process for new buildings?

3. What are at least two ways that green building standards and codes help to promote renewable energy development?

4. *Submetering at 360 State Street Finally Allowed.* After several years of negotiations and public debate, Connecticut's governor and the state's Department of Energy & Environmental Protection finally agreed to allow electrical submetering in the 360 State Street project. As of 2016, submetering was finally enabling full use of the property's impressive fuel cell system. *See* Dan Millstein, *Submetering Savings, Step by Step*, MULTIHOUSING NEWS (May 8, 2017), https://www.multihousingnews.com/post/the-energy-conservation-potential-of-a-submetering-system/.

5. *Fuel Cells as Renewable Power.* Instead of relying on wind, solar, or geothermal resources for renewable energy, 360 State Street used fuel cells. See Chapter 8 of this Casebook for more information on how fuel cells work and on their strengths and limitations as a renewable energy source.

3. THE PREEMPTION DEBATE OVER GREEN BUILDING STANDARDS

As suggested above, many state or local government entities have sought to promote greater energy efficiency in buildings and appliances over the years. However, the patchworks of disparate requirements that can result from state and local government level building code regulation sometimes frustrate builders and manufacturers, who would often prefer to be able to operate anywhere in the country under a single set of uniform national standards. As described in the two cases below, Congress enacted the Energy Policy and Conservation Act (EPCA) in 1975 with the aim of promoting greater energy efficiency in building design. Unfortunately, the EPCA sometimes does the opposite and actually helps developers avoid having to comply with stricter state and local building energy efficiency standards. These developers' desire for uniformity is understandable, but it can slow progress toward greater energy efficiency whenever the federal efficiency standard is less stringent than a state or local one. The following cases grappled with the issue of federal preemption of local building energy efficiency standards. Although several states and municipalities have developed sustainability-oriented land use and building standards, concerns about the potential for federal preemption continue to hinder some state and local governments' efforts to increase the energy efficiency of buildings in their jurisdictions.

AIR CONDITIONING, HEATING AND REFRIGERATION INSTITUTE V. CITY OF ALBUQUERQUE

United States District Court, District of New Mexico, 2008
2008 WL 5586316

VÁZQUEZ, C.J.

THIS MATTER comes before the Court on Plaintiffs' Motion for Preliminary Injunction, filed August 29, 2008. . . . The Court, having considered the briefs, relevant law, the evidence presented at the hearing held on October 1, 2008, and being otherwise fully informed, finds that Plaintiffs' motion is well-taken and will be **GRANTED**.

BACKGROUND

Plaintiffs, local and regional distributors of heating, ventilation, air conditioning, and water heating products and three national trade associations that represent the manufacturers, contractors, and distributors of these products, assert that certain portions of three City of Albuquerque ordinances that impose minimum energy efficiency standards for commercial and residential buildings are preempted by the Energy Policy and Conservation Act ("EPCA"), 42 U.S.C. 6201, et seq., as amended by the National Appliance Energy Conservation Act ("NAECA"), Pub. L. No. 100–102 (1987), and the Energy Policy Act of 1992 ("EPACT"), 42 U.S.C. §§ 6311–17. In the instant motion, Plaintiffs seek a preliminary injunction prohibiting the City of Albuquerque from enforcing the challenged sections of the regulations until this case is resolved.

I.   Energy Policy and Conservation Act and the Energy Policy Act of 1992

The EPCA was designed, in part, to reduce the United States' "domestic energy consumption through the operation of specific voluntary and mandatory energy conservation programs." S. Rep. No. 94–516, at 117 (1975). . . . Part of EPCA's energy conservation program was to "authorize energy efficiency standards for major appliances." *Id.* at 118. . . . The EPCA, as amended by the NAECA and the EPACT, establishes nationwide standards for the energy efficiency and energy use of major residential and commercial appliances and equipment, including heating, ventilating, and air conditioning ("HVAC") products and water heaters. Principal responsibility for maintaining, and, if necessary, amending these standards was given to the U.S. Department of Energy ("DOE").

The EPCA, as amended, contains a preemption provision that prohibits state regulation "concerning" the energy efficiency, energy use, or water use of any covered product with limited exceptions. 42 U.S.C.

§ 6297(c). A "state regulation" is defined as any "law, regulation, or other requirement of a State and its political subdivisions." 42 U.S.C. § 6297(a)(2)(A). EPCA provides a number of exceptions from federal preemption. *Id.* at § 6297(f). The only exception relevant to this case applies when the regulation is in a building code for new construction and certain conditions are met. 42 U.S.C. § 6297(f)(3).

EPACT expanded the EPCA's federal appliance program to include energy efficiency standards for commercial and industrial appliances. . . . EPACT incorporated the preemption provisions of 42 U.S.C. § 6297, with a few distinctions that are not relevant to this case. . . .

II. City of Albuquerque's Energy Conservation Code

In 2007, the Mayor of Albuquerque formed the Green Ribbon Task Force to develop and implement changes to the City's building regulations to significantly reduce carbon dioxide and greenhouse gas emissions while providing industry with the flexibility to use innovative designs and techniques to achieve the effective use of energy. The Green Ribbon Task Force was composed of builders, developers, architects, unions and various companies, organizations and individuals. After months of consideration, the Green Ribbon Task Force proposed a combination of performance-based and prescriptive options to achieve increased energy efficiency in the building industry. The City's Green Building Manager then drafted Volumes I and II of the Albuquerque Energy Conservation Code ("Code") based on the options developed by the Green Ribbon Task Force. At the time the Code was drafted, the Green Building Manager, by his own admission, was unaware of federal statutes governing the energy efficiency of HVAC products and water heaters and the City attorneys who reviewed the Code did not raise the preemption issue. The Code was approved by the City Council and became effective on October 1, 2008.

A. Volume I of the Albuquerque Energy Conservation Code

Volume I of the Code applies to commercial and multi-family residential buildings. Volume I adopts and incorporates by reference the American Society of Heating, Refrigeration, and Air Conditioning ("ASHRAE") Standard 90.1–2004, with a few amendments. Volume I applies to new buildings, additions to existing buildings, and alterations of existing buildings. It does not apply to repairs, provided that there is no increase in the annual energy consumption of the equipment following the repair. Volume I also addresses the replacement of HVAC equipment in existing buildings. In single unit replacements, building owners who replace an existing HVAC unit with a unit that meets federal energy efficiency requirements must replace or modify other components in the building to make up for the energy efficiency loss resulting from the decision not to use a higher efficiency unit.

Consistent with the Green Ribbon Task Force's recommendations, Volume I provides two performance-based paths to compliance—LEED certification at the silver level and 30% efficiency improvement—as well as a prescriptive option.

The LEED rating system was devised by the United States Green Building Council. In the context of new construction and major renovations, LEED evaluates buildings in six areas: sustainable sites, water efficiency, energy and atmosphere, materials and resources, indoor environmental quality, and innovation and design process. LEED provides four progressive levels of certification: certified (26–32 points), silver (33–38) points), gold (39–51 points) and platinum (52–69 points). The Code requires LEED certification at the silver level for buildings covered by Volume I.

In addition to LEED, the Code provides a second performance-based option. . . .

. . . .

B. Volume II of the Albuquerque Energy Conservation Code

Volume II of the Code applies to one and two family detached dwellings and townhouses. Volume II applies to new construction, additions, alterations and renovations. It does not apply to repairs; the replacement of furnaces and air conditioners before July 1, 2009; and the replacement of an existing furnace where such replacement would require "extensive revisions" to other systems or elements of a building.

Volume II adopts and incorporates by reference the 2006 International Energy Conservation Code ("IECC"). Volume II contains the same two performance-based options as Volume I—LEED silver certification and 30% energy reduction option (referred to as Section 405)—as well as two additional performance-based options. . . . In order to take advantage of any of the performance-based options, the owners must comply with certain mandatory requirements such as caulking and sealing around doors, adequately supporting the joints in the ductwork, and other construction quality issues.

In addition to the four performance-based options, Volume II also contains a prescriptive option. The prescriptive option provides for energy efficiency standards for HVAC and water heating products in excess of federal standards.

C. The High Performance Building Ordinance

In 2007, the Albuquerque City Council adopted the Albuquerque High Performance Buildings Ordinance ("Ordinance"), which applies to new buildings and existing buildings undergoing alteration when the work area of the alteration exceeds 50% of the building area. The Ordinance sets several prescriptive standards for energy efficiency that are in excess of federal standards. In addition, the Ordinance requires the Green Building Manager to "establish alternative performance-based criteria for overall building energy conservation which may be used for compliance in lieu of standards prescribed therein." *See* Ordinance at § 3(A)(2). Mr. Bucholz, the current Green Building Manager, interprets this provision as requiring compliance with Volumes I and II of the Code.

LEGAL ANALYSIS

I.   Ripeness

As an initial matter, Defendant asserts that Plaintiffs' claims are not ripe because the Code has not yet gone into effect, much less been applied to Plaintiffs. . . .

Plaintiffs are making a challenge to the facial validity of the Code and Ordinance, which are predominantly legal questions. When a question is "predominantly legal," there is generally no need to await further factual development. . . . Because the issues raised in this case are predominantly legal, Plaintiffs' facial challenge is ripe for review.

II. PRELIMINARY INJUNCTION

. . . .

D. Success on the Merits

The fourth prerequisite for obtaining a preliminary injunction is a showing of a likelihood of success on the merits. . . .

Preemption can occur in one of three ways: express preemption by statute, occupation of the field, or conflict between state and federal regulation. . . . This case presents a question of express preemption. An express preemption analysis turns on the interpretation of the statutory provision that allegedly preempts state law. . . . Consequently, the Court begins with the text of the provision in question and then moves on to the structure and purpose of the act in which it occurs. . . .

Section 6297 contains a "general rule of preemption," which states that, subject to certain specified exceptions, when a federal energy conservation standard is established for a covered product, "no State regulation concerning the energy efficiency, energy use, or water use of such covered product shall be effective with respect to such product." 42 U.S.C. § 6297(c). The use of the word "concerning" suggests that Congress intended the preemption provision to be expansive.

"Concerning" is defined as "relating to." Black's Law Dictionary 289 (6th ed. 1990). The Supreme Court has repeatedly emphasized that the words "relating to" express a broad pre-emptive purpose. . . .

The legislative history makes it clear that the purpose behind § 6297's broad preemption provision was to eliminate the systems of separate state appliance standards that had emerged as a result of the DOE's "general policy of granting petitions from States requesting waivers from preemption," that caused appliance manufacturers to be confronted with "a growing patchwork of differing State regulations which would increasingly complicate their design, production and marketing plans." S. Rep. No. 100–6, at 4. Congress intended that § 6297 would "preempt[ ] State law under most circumstances." H.R. Rep. 100–11 at 19. There is no doubt that Congress intended to preempt state regulation of the energy efficiency of certain building appliances in order to have uniform, express, national energy efficiency standards.

The legislative history of NAECA provides insight on Congress's purpose in including the "building code" exception for residential products at § 6297(f)(3). The House Report states that the building code exception was intended to "prevent[ ] State building codes from being used as a means of setting mandatory State appliance standards in excess of the Federal Standards." H.R. Rep. 100–11 at 26. The building code exception was intended to give states flexibility, but this flexibility was "limited" to "ensure that performance-based codes cannot expressly *or effectively* require the installation of covered products whose efficiencies exceed . . . the applicable Federal standard . . ." H.R. Rep. 100–11 at 26 (emphasis added). . . .

The Court must now consider whether the City's Code and Ordinance are "regulation[s] concerning the energy efficiency, energy use, or water use" of a covered product and, if so, if the Code and Ordinance qualify for an exemption from the preemption provision.

1. The Code is a regulation concerning the energy efficiency, energy use, or water use of covered products.

Defendant first argues that Plaintiffs are unlikely to succeed on the merits because the prescriptive standards within the Code are optional avenues for compliance, not mandatory requirements, and the EPCA preemption provision only applies to mandatory requirements. . . .

There is no question that the prescriptive alternatives, which explicitly require covered products in excess of federal standards, are regulations that "concern" the energy efficiency of covered products. The performance-based alternatives, while not as obvious, are also regulations that, directly or indirectly, concern the energy efficiency, energy use, or water use of covered products. . . . The fact that the Code imposes additional expenses if federally-compliant products are used strongly suggests that the Code "concerns" the energy efficiency of covered products. Consequently, the Code, and each of the alternatives within the Code, are preempted by EPCA and EPACT unless they qualify for a preemption exception.

2.   Is the Code excepted from preemption under EPCA and EPACT?

. . . .

The EPCA provides an exemption from preemption for residential building codes that meet certain requirements. . . .

. . . .

Based on the limited evidence before the Court, it appears that every performance-based option in Volume II of the Code fails to meet at least one of the seven requirements for an exemption from preemption.

Plaintiffs are likely to prevail on their challenge to the portions of the Code that explicitly require the use of appliances with standards in excess of federal efficiency standards. . . . Plaintiffs are also likely to prevail on their challenge to the portions of the Code that address renovations and replacements because § 6297(f)(3) only provides an exemption for building codes for new construction. While it is less clear that Plaintiffs will prevail on their challenge to the performance-based options, Plaintiffs, at a minimum, have raised questions that are "serious, substantial, difficult and doubtful."

. . . .

The City's goals in enacting Albuquerque's Energy Conservation Code and the Albuquerque High Performance Buildings Ordinance are laudable. Unfortunately, the drafters of the Code were unaware of the long-standing federal statutes governing the energy efficiency of certain HVAC and water heating products and expressly preempting state regulation of these products when the Code was drafted and, as a result, the Code, as enacted, infringes on an area preempted by federal law. The extent to which the Code and the Ordinance are preempted will be determined after development of a full record.

CONCLUSION

IT IS THEREFORE ORDERED that Plaintiffs' Motion for Preliminary Injunction, filed August 29, 2008, is **GRANTED.** Defendant City of Albuquerque is hereby enjoined from enforcing Volumes I and II of the Albuquerque Energy Conservation Code and the High Performance Building Ordinance pending resolution of this case. If there are portions of the Albuquerque Energy Conservation Code that are not implicated by the claims in this case, the parties are encouraged to submit an agreed order narrowing the scope of this preliminary injunction.

BUILDING INDUSTRY ASS'N OF WASHINGTON V. WASHINGTON STATE BUILDING CODE COUNCIL

United States Court of Appeals, Ninth Circuit, 2012
683 F.3d 1144

SCHROEDER, C.J.

The Energy Policy and Conservation Act of 1975 ("EPCA"), 42 U.S.C. § 6295 et seq., as amended, establishes nationwide energy efficiency standards for certain residential home appliances, and expressly preempts state standards requiring greater efficiency than the federal standards. It nonetheless exempts from preemption state building codes promoting energy efficiency, so long as those codes meet certain statutory conditions. § 6297(f)(3).

This case is a challenge to the State of Washington's Building Code, see WASH. ADMIN. CODE § 51–11–0100 et seq., brought by the Building Industry Association of Washington ("BIAW"), along with individual builders and contractors. The impetus for this challenge is the State's 2009 requirement that new building construction meet heightened energy conservation goals. This is the first case at the appellate level to consider EPCA's preemption-exemption provision. Plaintiffs-Appellants ("Plaintiffs") argue that the Building Code does not satisfy EPCA's conditions for exemption. The district court, however, held that Washington had satisfied EPCA's conditions, and therefore was not preempted. We affirm.

To escape preemption, a state's building code must satisfy the seven conditions codified in 42 U.S.C. § 6297(f)(3). The two at issue here are § 6297(f)(3)(B) and (C). . . .

. . . .

BACKGROUND

The Federal Regulatory Framework

Congress enacted EPCA as a comprehensive federal regime regulating energy and water conservation standards for certain consumer appliances. Congress gave [the United States Department of Energy ("DOE")] primary responsibility for promulgating regulations prescribing a "minimum level of energy efficiency or a maximum quantity of energy use" for the covered consumer products. 42 U.S.C. § 6291(6)(A); see § 6295.

. . . Consumer products covered by EPCA's energy-efficiency provisions are identified in § 6292, and include durable goods such as refrigerators, air conditioners, water heaters, furnaces, dishwashers, clothes washers and driers, kitchen ranges and ovens, faucets, and showerheads. § 6292(a). These covered consumer products are typically installed in new home construction.

As initially enacted in 1975, EPCA provided that federal energy efficiency standards be established for covered products, and it preempted all state "efficiency standard[s] or similar requirement[s]" for covered products. . . . Congress modified the blanket preemption in 1987, when it amended EPCA to carve out an explicit exemption from preemption for certain efficiency standards in state and local building codes. . . . EPCA thus now expressly exempts from preemption any regulation or other requirement contained in a state or local building code for new construction concerning the energy efficiency or energy use of covered products, but only if the provisions of the code satisfy seven statutory conditions. 42 U.S.C. § 6297(f)(3). . . .

        . . . .

. . . As long as a state building code meets these conditions, the state does not need to petition for the DOE's approval to enforce its building code. *See* § 6297(f)(4)(A).

Behind the 1987 preemption exemption lies Congressional recognition that state and local building codes have a major impact on energy consumption. Buildings, and the fixtures installed in them, make up a large proportion of energy and electricity use throughout the country. See 2010 Buildings Energy Data Book *1–2, 1–6 (DOE 2010), online at http://buildingsdatabook.eren.doe.gov/docs/DataBooks/2010_BEDB.pdf (nearly 40% of energy use, and over 70% of electricity use) (accessed June 18, 2012). Buildings and fixtures tend to have long lifespans, so choices made at the outset during construction are likely to have far-reaching future effects on energy consumption. It is for this reason that Congress, in EPCA, has permitted states some limited means of regulating these choices. Federal regulations promulgated under EPCA provide minimum standards for the energy efficiency of such fixtures . . . and the federal statute preempts state attempts to impose minimum standards greater than the federal law. . . . States thus cannot, for example, require that any water heater sold or installed in the state meet energy-efficiency requirements more stringent than federal requirements. States seeking to implement energy conservation goals through their building codes must therefore ensure that the code satisfies the conditions established in EPCA for exemption from federal preemption. . . .

The Washington State Building Code

Washington's legislature has opted to use its regulatory police power to enact a statewide code for building construction to promote, inter alia, energy efficiency goals. The development of the code before us reveals the State's sensitivity to EPCA's conditions. The Washington legislature identified energy consumption patterns in new building construction as an area in which it could create incentives for energy efficiency, and enacted a regulatory regime that meets specific efficiency goals over the next two decades. The legislature explained that it enacted energy conservation mandates to balance "flexibility in building design" against "the broader goal of building zero fossil-fuel greenhouse gas emission homes and buildings by the year 2031." REV. CODE WASH. § 19.27A.020(2)(a); *see also id.* § 19.27A.130 ("Washington can spur its economy and assert its regional and national clean energy leadership by putting efficiency first.").

While the legislature has mandated the goals, it has delegated authority to Defendant-Appellee Washington State Building Code Council ("Council"), to promulgate and update the statewide building code. . . . The Council must review and may amend the state Building Code periodically . . . and between 2013 and 2031 it will have to amend the Code progressively to implement the legislature's mandated goals. . . . The Building Code that will be effective in 2031 will have to achieve a "seventy percent reduction in annual net energy consumption" compared to the Building Code effective in 2006, the baseline year. § 19.27A.160(1).

The Council amended the Code effective in 2009 to implement a 15% reduction in new buildings' energy consumption, compared to the 2006 baseline. The 2009 amendments . . . are the subject of Plaintiffs' challenge here.

In the 2009 Code, the Council offered builders three methods, termed "pathways," for achieving the 15% reduction in energy consumption. Each such pathway to compliance is codified under one of three chapters of the Code. . . . A builder who elects the Chapters 5 or 6 pathways will not fully achieve the 15% reduction in energy consumption. The Building Code therefore requires a builder electing Chapters 5 or 6 to earn one "credit" under Chapter 9, which provides alternative methods for further reducing energy consumption by the necessary amount. . . . [T]he options set forth in Chapter 9 address different ways of achieving more efficient residential building energy use, by addressing the "efficiency of a building's shell," or "efficiency of a home's heating equipment," or "efficiency of other energy consuming devices." The credit system in Chapter 9 is the subject of the preemption challenge in this case, because some of its provisions involve use of EPCA covered products.

. . . Chapter 9 contains a menu of options, "Table 9–1," from which each builder can choose how best to secure its required one credit. Wash. Admin. Code § 51–11–0900. Some options are worth one credit, while others are worth half, one-and-a half, or two credits each. . . .

The Council's 2009 proposed changes that added Chapter 9 were controversial from the beginning. . . . In a letter to the Council in November 2009, for example, the Air Conditioning, Heating, and Refrigeration Institute said that unless the Council supplemented Table 9–1 with additional options, Chapter 9 "could indirectly force homebuilders to install high efficiency HVAC and water heating equipment" in order to earn the required credit. . . . Citing the importance of the construction industry to the recovery of the state's economy during a time of deep recession, the Governor asked the Council to delay implementing the amendments from July 2010 until April 2011. The Council filed an emergency rule delaying the effective date, but only until October 29, 2010. . . . Plaintiffs determined litigation was necessary.

This Litigation

Plaintiffs filed this action in May 2010 in the Western District of Washington. In their complaint, Plaintiffs alleged their businesses would be harmed if the 2009 revisions to the Building Code were allowed to go into effect, because the revisions would increase costs of installing appliances and thereby reduce demand for new home construction. Plaintiffs sought declaratory and injunctive relief on their claim that the Building Code was expressly preempted by EPCA, and they argued it did not satisfy the statutory conditions that provide a safe harbor from preemption under § 6297(f)(3). Environmental groups supportive of the 2009 revisions moved to intervene on behalf of the Council. In July 2010, the district court granted a motion to intervene filed by the Northwest Energy Coalition, Sierra Club, Washington Environmental Council, and Natural Resources Defense Council.

Defendants and intervenors (collectively "Defendants") then filed a joint motion for summary judgment, arguing that the Washington Building Code met all seven statutory conditions for exemption from preemption. . . .

. . . .

Plaintiffs cross-moved for summary judgment, arguing that Chapter 9 failed to satisfy four of the seven statutory conditions. *See* § 6297(f)(3)(B), (C), (E), (F). In addition to challenging compliance with conditions (B) and (C), they also argued before the district court that Chapter 9 failed conditions (E) and (F), but Plaintiffs do not pursue those latter challenges on appeal.

The district court disagreed with Plaintiffs and granted summary judgment to Defendants. . . .

Plaintiffs timely appeal.

DISCUSSION

. . . .

Subsection B

Plaintiffs argue that the Building Code's Chapter 9 does not satisfy EPCA subsection (B), which provides in relevant part that, to survive preemption, the Building Code cannot "require that the covered product have an energy efficiency exceeding the applicable energy conservation standard" established under federal law. 42 U.S.C. § 6297(f)(3)(B). Several options under Chapter 9 call for higher efficiency covered products (options 1a, 2, 5a, and 5b), and the remaining options do not. Builders can choose. They do not have to use higher efficiency products.

Plaintiffs acknowledge that Chapter 9 does not legally mandate use of higher efficiency covered products. Their contention is, rather, that the other options are so costly that builders are economically coerced and hence "required" to select the higher efficiency options. Defendants counter that an economic incentive is not a requirement. We agree that allowing less expensive, more efficient options does not require builders to use more efficient products within the meaning of the federal statute. . . .

Congress's use of the word "require" in the statutory text of § 6297(f)(3)(B) indicates it intended compulsion backed by force of law. The dictionary definition of the verb "require" is to "impose a compulsion or command upon (as a person) to do something; demand of (one) that something be done or some action taken; enjoin, command, or authoritatively insist (that someone do something)." Webster's Third New International Dictionary 1929 (1971). This definition leaves no room for the Plaintiffs' argument that cost considerations outside the Building Code itself force them to select higher efficiency options and hence "require" those options. . . . We thus must conclude that Chapter 9 satisfies subsection (B) in that it does not require such options.

. . . .

The state would effectively require higher efficiency products, in violation of subsection (B), if the code itself imposed a penalty for not using higher efficiency products. This is what a building code ordinance for the city of Albuquerque, New Mexico did. The federal district court for the District of New Mexico therefore granted a preliminary injunction against enforcing that ordinance. *See Air Conditioning, Heating, and Refrigeration Institute v. City of Albuquerque*, 2008 WL 5586316 (D.N.M. 2008). That court held, in relevant part, that the ordinance did not satisfy EPCA's subsection (B), because the ordinance itself had created a situation in which the builder had no choice. Albuquerque's ordinance imposed costs, as a matter of law, on builders who installed certain covered products meeting federal standards, by requiring the builder to install additional products that would compensate for not using a higher efficiency product. *Id.* at *2. As the court explained, "if products at the federal efficiency standard are used, a building owner must make other modifications to the home to increase its energy efficiency." *Id.* at *9. The Albuquerque ordinance thus effectively required use of higher efficiency products by imposing a penalty through the code itself.

Here, by contrast, the Washington Building Code itself imposes no additional costs on builders. . . . We hold the Washington Building Code complies with subsection (B) because it does not create any penalty or legal compulsion to use higher efficiency products.

. . . .

Subsection C

Plaintiffs' challenge to the Washington Building Code's compliance with § 6297(f)(3)(C) is more factual. That subsection of the federal law authorizes a state or local building code to allow builders to meet energy efficiency objectives through a system of credits for alternative methods to reduce energy use. Subsection (C) provides that where two options reduce energy use by equivalent amounts, the building code must provide credits to those options on a "one-for-one" basis. § 6297(f)(3)(C). To survive preemption, Washington's Building Code must therefore give credits in proportion to energy use savings without favoring particular products or methods.

Plaintiffs argued to the district court that Chapter 9 does not satisfy subsection (C), because the state has assigned the same value to several options that do not reduce energy use by equivalent amounts. In support of their motion for summary judgment, Plaintiffs offered a declaration purporting to show that the state had assigned credit values that were incorrect or not equivalent. Ted Clifton, a builder affiliated with one of the Plaintiff corporations, submitted the declaration. . . . He opined that the computer models the State used to estimate and assign credit values were "inconsisten[t]," used "rough approximations and rounding," and were based on "flawed" assumptions.

Defendants, by contrast, offered evidence to show that the Council used computer models to assign credit values proportional to the equivalent amount by which each Chapter 9 option would reduce the building's energy use. . . . According to the State's declarations, that model, known as SEEM, has been used since 1982 by entities such as the Northwest Power and Conservation Council ("NWPCC"), and is described as "the industry standard."

To explain the use of the model, Defendants provided the declaration of Tom Eckman, manager of conservation resources at NWPCC and chair of the Regional Technical Forum. . . . According to Eckman, the SEEM model allows the Council to determine how installing different components and products in the new building will affect its energy use in many situations. It therefore also allows the State to isolate the energy-reducing effect of any given component, and assign a credit value to that component.

The district court, in rejecting Clifton's declaration, ruled correctly that Clifton had established no qualifications to provide expert testimony about the accuracy of the SEEM model. . . . There was no abuse of discretion in rejecting the declaration.

Defendants, on the other hand, offered expert declarations that explained the quantitative computer models used in assigning credit values. The district court considered the Defendants' evidence after it found Eckman qualified to offer expert opinion regarding energy efficiency modeling. It also concluded that the data that went into the SEEM model was shown to be accurate. . . . This finding is supported by the expert declarations and is not clearly erroneous.

Plaintiffs are thus left to quibble over whether the credit values for Chapter 9's options are sufficiently proportional to the amount by which the State's numbers indicate they reduce energy use. . . .

Any credit-based system that involves comparing different methods of reducing energy, however, may seem like comparing apples and oranges. Option 1b, geothermal heat pump, uses the ground to help heat or cool the house in different seasons. Option 4a, ventilator system, supplies an otherwise well-sealed house with fresh air, while avoiding using energy unnecessarily to maintain internal climate control. It is unsurprising that these methods do not produce identical results in energy savings.

Indeed, in EPCA, Congress recognized that some variation will be inevitable, for it speaks in terms of equivalencies. The statute in subsection (C) requires that the credits be awarded "one-for-one" where different options bring about savings in "equivalent energy use or equivalent cost." § 6297(f)(3)(C). The covered consumer products differ in many ways, including in the kind of energy used—such as gas, electricity, or geothermal heat. Therefore reductions of energy consumption in different contexts can be compared meaningfully only through quantitative estimates. . . .

The district court correctly ruled that the credit values in Chapter 9 are closely proportional to the average reduction in equivalent energy use across a variety of climatic and other environmental situations. . . In requiring that credits be awarded on a one-for-one equivalent energy use basis, Congress intended not mathematical perfection, but rather preventing the building code from discriminating between products and building methods. Chapter 9 of the 2009 Washington Building Code achieves this objective. . . .

CONCLUSION

The district court did not err in granting summary judgment to Defendants. The Washington Building Code satisfies the conditions Congress set forth in EPCA for exemption from federal preemption.

AFFIRMED.

QUESTIONS

1.   How would you expect the optimal building code standards for energy efficiency for homes in Alaska to differ from those for homes in Arizona? How might laws preempting all state and local building code energy efficiency standards and imposing a single, uniform nationwide standard potentially produce sub-optimal policy outcomes?

2.   Why do you think commercial builders and manufacturers of home fixtures and building materials would prefer for the federal government to establish a single set of nationwide uniform standards related to energy efficiency that preempts all state and local building energy efficiency laws?

3.   How did the *Building Industry Association of Washington* court distinguish the building code provisions at issue in that case from those challenged in *City of Albuquerque*? Do you believe this is a useful means of distinguishing between these cases? Why or why not?

––––––––––––

Having concluded its coverage of energy storage and demand-side management, this Casebook now proceeds to its final chapter. Chapter 8 examines legal and policy issues related to several renewable energy strategies other than wind and solar energy. Many of these other strategies, such as geothermal energy, biomass and biofuels, and wave energy, suffer from limitations that have heretofore prevented them from playing major roles in the modern energy industry. However, they all have the potential to mature into important renewable energy sources in the decades to come.

CHAPTER 8

OTHER RENEWABLE ENERGY STRATEGIES

∎ ∎ ∎

In addition to wind and solar energy, several other types of renewable energy strategies are a part of the global transition toward a more sustainable energy system. Each of these other types of energy strategies has promise but also has disadvantages that have historically limited its use. For instance, geothermal energy facilities can generate clean, low-cost renewable power but are presently developable in only in a few geographic locations where geothermal resources are sufficiently close to the earth's surface. Biomass and biofuels are also renewable and non-intermittent energy resources, but the financial and environmental costs of producing and transporting them have historically limited their usefulness. Hydropower has long been a valuable type of renewable energy, but most of the nation's best hydropower sites are already developed and future hydropower development will be difficult due to environmental concerns and other constraints. Electric vehicle technologies show increasing potential to dethrone petroleum as the world's primary transportation energy source, but high battery costs and other constraints have heretofore prevented them from achieving that goal. And wave energy technologies could someday generate large quantities of emissions-free renewable power for major load centers in the nation's densely-populated coastal areas, but they have not yet matured to a point of being economically viable.

Despite the shortcomings of the additional renewable energy strategies just described, innovation and significant investment in each of these strategies continues and they all warrant coverage in this Casebook. This chapter examines each of the less-prominent types of renewable energy strategies mentioned in the preceding paragraph and explores some of the laws and policies that are emerging to govern them.

A. GEOTHERMAL ENERGY

Geothermal energy is one type of renewable energy strategy with limitations that have thus far precluded it from playing a major role in the global energy system. Utility-scale geothermal energy facilities use heat originating deep within the earth's crust to rotate turbines and thereby generate electric power. There are three primary types of geothermal electricity plants: flash steam plants, dry steam plants, and binary cycle plants. Flash steam plants convert hot water from deep beneath the earth into steam. Dry steam plants use naturally-heated geothermal steam itself to drive turbines and generate power. Binary cycle plants use geothermally-heated water to heat some other liquid with a lower boiling point and make steam that way, allowing the plant to generate steam using a lower-temperature geothermal resource.

In places where they are affordably accessible from the surface, geothermal energy resources are among the most ideal energy resources in the world. Geothermal power plants occupy relatively small land footprints, require little or no external fuel, produce minimal carbon dioxide emissions, and generate reliable supplies of totally renewable electric current. The non-intermittent nature of geothermal resources could allow them to serve as valuable sources of clean, renewable baseload power to complement wind and solar energy resources.

Although utility-scale geothermal power technologies are relatively new, humans have been using geothermal energy resources for thousands of years. According to the U.S. Department of Energy:

> Archaeological evidence shows that the first human use of geothermal resources in North America occurred more than 10,000 years ago with the settlement of Paleo-Indians at hot springs. The springs served as a source of warmth and cleansing, their minerals as a source of healing.

A History of Geothermal Energy in America, DEP'T ENERGY, https://energy. gov/eere/geothermal/history-geothermal-energy-america#1901 (last visited July 24, 2017). By the late 1800s, a growing number of hot springs sites in the United States were no longer used solely for bathing and cleaning; some cities in Oregon and Idaho had begun pumping hot springs water through pipes into communities to heat homes and other buildings. Then, in 1904, the Italian businessman Prince Piero Ginori Conti developed the world's first geothermal electricity generating system at the Lardarello dry steam field in Tuscany, Italy, ushering in the era of geothermal power. *See id.*

Geothermal power technologies gradually improved throughout the twentieth century, causing geothermal energy development to slowly expand across the globe. That growth accelerated in the early twenty-first century as various aggressive government-supported renewable energy incentive programs drove even greater investment in geothermal power. As of late 2015, a total of 13.3 GW of geothermal generating capacity had been installed in 24 countries throughout the world, with 12.5 GW more in various stages of development. *See* BENJAMIN MATEK, 2016 ANNUAL U.S. & GLOBAL GEOTHERMAL POWER PRODUCTION REPORT 4 (2016), http://geo-energy.org/reports/2016/2016%20Annual%20US%20Global%20Geothermal %20Power%20Production.pdf. The United States has long been among the world's leaders in geothermal energy development, having roughly 3.7 GW of installed geothermal generating capacity as of that time.

Despite its abundant advantages, utility-scale geothermal energy development suffers from one primary constraint that has historically hindered its growth: geothermal resources are largely inaccessible in much of the country. Most of the Midwest and Eastern United States lacks geothermal resources that are commercially developable with current technologies. Although there is plenty of subsurface geothermal heat in these regions, it is situated too far below the ground to be reachable at a manageable cost. As of early 2017, the world's deepest geothermal well was only about three miles below the surface. *See* Jeremie Richard & Gael Branchereau, *Iceland Drills 4.7 km Down into Volcano To Tap Clean Energy*, PHYS.ORG (May 5, 2017), https://phys.org/news/2017-05-iceland-drills-km-volcano-energy.html. Humankind's inability to affordably drill deeper into the earth's crust presently keeps much of the planet's geothermal resources out of reach.

As shown in Figure 8.1, accessible geothermal resources are more prevalent in the Western United States than in the rest of the country. However, even in regions where geothermal energy resources are comparatively close to the surface, geothermal power development in most areas remains impractical with existing technologies. Accordingly, there are relatively few operating geothermal electric generating facilities in the United States today. The pace of geothermal development in the United States has also been significantly slower than that of wind or solar power in recent years.

Figure 8.1. United States Geothermal Resources Map

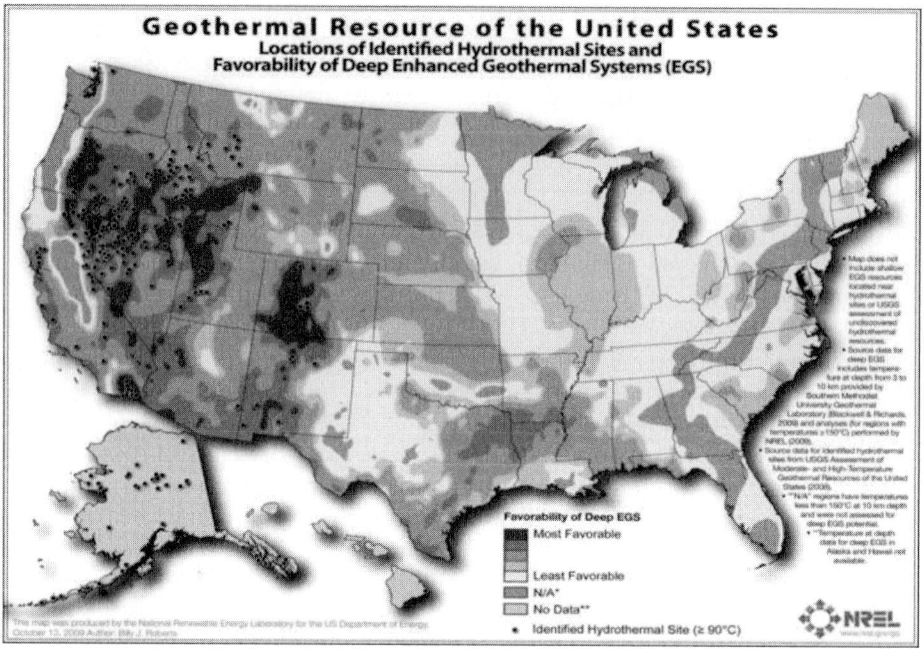

Source: Nat'l Renewable Energy Lab

Figure 8.2 below shows the quantity of installed and planned geothermal generating capacity by state across the United States as of 2015. As illustrated in the map, California and Nevada are unquestionably the nation's leaders in geothermal energy production and few other states generate any significant geothermal power. However, as technologies enabling deeper well drilling or the generation of power using lower-temperature geothermal resources advance further, geothermal energy development could someday emerge as a major renewable energy source on par with wind and solar power. In a small handful of countries around the world that have particularly favorable geothermal resources, geothermal power plants are already beginning to play a primary role in meeting electricity demand.

Figure 8.2. Geothermal Power Development by State

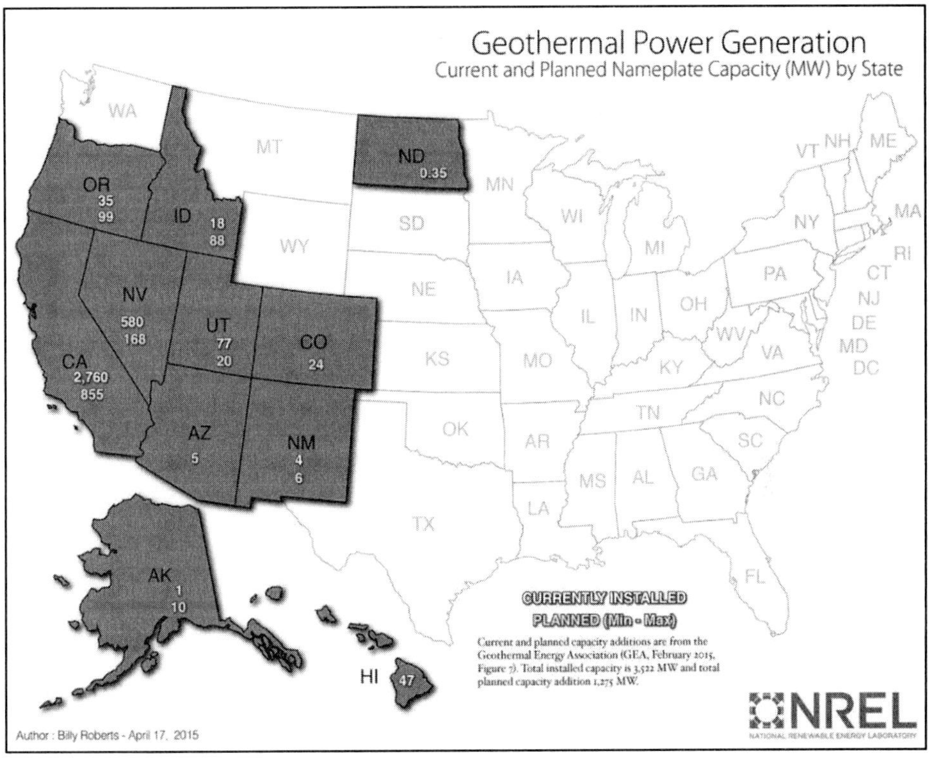

Source: Nat'l Renewable Energy Lab

Advancements in *deep enhanced geothermal system* (EGS) technologies hold the greatest promise for transforming geothermal energy into a primary baseload energy source in the coming decades. EGS generally involves the drilling of very deep wells into hot, dry subsurface rock. Operators then inject cold water into these deep wells with very high pressure to enhance the permeability of the rock. As geothermal heat originating deep underground heats this injected water, some of it resurfaces and is usable to generate electric power.

Even if improvements in EGS technologies ultimately make it easier and less expensive to access deep geothermal resources, concerns about triggering earthquakes could impede extensive geothermal development in some regions. For example, one 2013 study found that fluid removal and reinjection by geothermal power plants near California's Salton Sea was causing increased seismic activity in that area. *See* Emily E. Brodsky & Lia J. Lajoie, *Anthropogenic Seismicity Rates and Operational Parameters at the Salton Sea Geothermal Field*, 341 SCIENCE 543 (2013). Still, geothermal energy is already an important type of renewable energy development in some parts of the country, so it's worthwhile to have a basic understanding of the unique practical and legal issues surrounding geothermal energy projects.

1. WHO OWNS GEOTHERMAL RESOURCES?

Like property rights in wind and sunlight, private interests in geothermal resources have not historically been precisely defined or delineated under property law. However, as innovation and other factors have increased the commercial value of geothermal resources in recent decades, neighbor disputes over their use have become more common. This trend is gradually compelling courts and policymakers to confront complex questions about the allocation of property interests in geothermal heat and steam.

Because of the distinct characteristics of geothermal resources, various stakeholders could conceivably claim that the law should allocate property interests in geothermal resources to *them*. For example, mineral rights holders might argue that geothermal steam is a type of "mineral" and is therefore included in their minerals estate because it is a usable resource found in the subsurface of land like coal or oil. On the other hand, surface rights holders might alternatively assert that laws should allocate rights in geothermal heat and steam to them under the *ad coelum* rule because these resources reside in empty space below the ground and are not tangible, extractable mineral resources. Some groundwater rights holders might likewise try to claim interests in geothermal resources based on the notion that geothermal steam necessarily includes groundwater. And one could even argue that deep geothermal resources should be public trust or *commons* resources shared by all since they originate so far below the surface.

Legal questions about property ownership in geothermal resources made their way into the courts relatively quickly after the first major geothermal electric generating facilities began sprouting up in the United States in the 1960s. The federal government was often a party in these early disputes because it had reserved mineral rights under land patents when initially conveying much of the land in the Western United States to private homesteaders. However, over the years some surface owners and water rights holders have questioned the federal government's claims to geothermal rights based on mineral rights reservations. As highlighted in the two cases below, over the past half-century legislators and courts have cleared up some issues regarding the ownership of geothermal resource rights but other issues are still partially unresolved.

UNITED STATES V. UNION OIL CO. OF CALIFORNIA

United States Court of Appeals, Ninth Circuit, 1977
549 F.2d 1271

BROWNING, C.J.

This is a quiet title action brought by the Attorney General of the United States pursuant to section 21(b) of the Geothermal Steam Act of 1970, 30 U.S.C. s 1020(b), to determine whether the mineral reservation in patents issued under the Stock-Raising Homestead Act of 1916, 43 U.S.C. § 291 et seq., reserved to the United States geothermal resources underlying the patented lands. The district court held that it did not. 369 F.Supp. 1289 (N.D. Cal. 1973). We reverse.

Various elements cooperate to produce geothermal power accessible for use on the surface of the earth. Magma or molten rock from the core of the earth intrudes into the earth's crust. The magma heats porous rock containing water. The water in turn is heated to temperatures as high as 500 degrees Fahrenheit. As the heated water rises to the surface through a natural vent, or well, it flashes into steam.

Geothermal steam is used to produce electricity by turning generators. In recommending passage of the Geothermal Steam Act of 1970, the Interior and Insular Affairs Committee of the House reported: "(G)eothermal power stands out as a potentially invaluable untapped natural resource. It becomes particularly attractive in this age of growing consciousness of environmental hazards and increasing awareness of the necessity to develop new resources to help meet the Nation's future energy requirements. The Nation's geothermal resources promise to be a relatively pollution-free source of energy, and their development should be encouraged." H.R. REP. No. 91–1544, 91st Cong., 2d Sess., *reprinted at* 3 U.S. Code Cong. & Admin. News 5113, 5115 (1970).

Appellees are owners, or lessees of owners, of lands in an area known as "The Geysers" in Sonoma County, California. Beneath the lands are sources of geothermal steam. Appellees have developed or seek to develop wells to produce the steam for use in generating electricity. The lands were public lands, patented under the Stock-Raising Homestead Act. All patents issued under that Act are "subject to and contain a reservation to the United States of all the coal and other minerals in the lands so entered and patented, together with the right to prospect for, mine, and remove the same." Section 9 of the Act, 43 U.S.C. § 299. The patents involved in this case contain a reservation utilizing the words of the statute. The question is whether the right to produce the geothermal steam passed to the patentees or was retained by the United States under this reservation.

There is no specific reference to geothermal steam and associated resources in the language of the Act or in its legislative history. The reason is evident. Although steam from underground sources was used to generate electricity at the Larderello Field in Italy as early as 1904, the commercial potential of this resource was not generally appreciated in this country for another half century. No geothermal power plants went into production in the United States until 1960. Congress was not aware of geothermal power when it enacted the Stock-Raising Homestead Act in 1916; it had no specific intention either to reserve geothermal resources or to pass title to them.

It does not necessarily follow that title to geothermal resources passes to homesteader-patentees under the Act. The Act reserves to the United States "all the coal and other minerals." All of the elements of a geothermal system—magma, porous rock strata, even water itself—may be classified as "minerals." When Congress decided in 1970 to remove the issue from controversy as to future grants of public lands, it found it unnecessary to alter the language of existing statutory "mineral" reservations. It simply provided that such reservations "shall hereafter be deemed to embrace geothermal steam and associated geothermal resources." Geothermal Steam Act of 1970, 30 U.S.C. § 1024. Thus, the words of the mineral reservation in the Stock-Raising Homestead Act clearly are capable of bearing a meaning that encompasses geothermal resources.

The substantial question is whether it would further Congress's purposes to interpret the words as carrying this meaning. The Act's background, language, and legislative history offer convincing evidence that Congress's general purpose was to transfer to private ownership tracts of semi-arid public land capable of being developed by homesteaders into self-sufficient agricultural units engaged in stock raising and forage farming, but to retain subsurface resources, particularly mineral fuels, in public ownership for conservation and subsequent orderly disposition in the public interest. The agricultural purpose indicates the nature of the grant Congress intended to provide homesteaders via the Act; the purpose of retaining government control over mineral fuel resources indicates the nature of reservations to the United States Congress intended to include in such grants. The dual purposes of the Act would best be served by interpreting the statutory reservation to include geothermal resources.

Events preceding the enactment of the Stock-Raising Homestead Act contribute to an understanding of the intended scope of the Act's mineral reservation. Prior to 1909, public lands were disposed of as either wholly mineral or wholly nonmineral in character. *United States v. Sweet*, 245 U.S. 563, 567–68, 571, 38 S.Ct. 193, 62 L.Ed. 473 (1918). This practice led to inefficiencies and abuses. In 1906 and again in 1907, President Theodore Roosevelt pointed out that some public lands were useful for both agriculture and production of subsurface fuels, and that these two uses could best be served by separate disposition of the right to utilize the same land for each purpose. The President called the attention of Congress "to the importance of conserving the supplies of mineral fuels still belonging to the Government." 41 CONG. REC. 2806 (1907). To that end, the President recommended "enactment of such legislation as would provide for title to and development of the surface land as separate and distinct from the right to the underlying mineral fuels in regions where these may occur, and the disposal of these mineral fuels under a leasing system on conditions which would inure to the benefit of the public as a whole." *Id.*

. . . .

This background supports the conclusion, confirmed by the language of the Stock-Raising Homestead Act, the Committee reports, and the floor debate, that when Congress imposed a mineral reservation upon the Act's land grants, it meant to implement the principle urged by the Department of Interior and retain governmental control of subsurface fuel sources, appropriate for purposes other than stock raising or forage farming.

We turn to the statutory language. The title of the Act "The Stock-Raising Homestead Act" reflects the nature of the intended grant. The Act applies only to areas designated by the Secretary of Interior as "stock-raising lands"; that is, "lands the surface of which is, in his opinion, chiefly valuable for grazing and raising forage crops, do not contain merchantable timber, are not susceptible of irrigation from any known source of water supply, and are of such character that six hundred and forty acres are reasonably required for the support of a family. . ." 43 U.S.C. § 292. The entryman is required to make improvements to increase the value of the entry "for stock-raising purposes." *Id.* § 293. On the other hand, "all entries made and patents issued" under the Act must "contain a reservation to the United States of all the coal and other minerals in the lands," and such deposits "shall be subject to disposal by the United States in accordance with the provisions of the coal and mineral land laws." *Id.* § 299. The subsurface estate is dominant; the interest of the homesteader is subject to the right of the owner of reserved mineral deposits to "reenter and occupy so much of the surface" as reasonably necessary to remove the minerals, on payment of damages to crops or improvements. *Id.*

The same themes are explicit in the reports of the House and Senate committees. The purpose of the Act is to restore the grazing capacity and hence the meat-producing capacity of semi-arid lands of the west and to furnish homes for the people, while preserving to the United States underlying mineral deposits for conservation and disposition under laws appropriate to that purpose. . . .

Commenting upon the mineral reservation, the House report states:

It appeared to your committee that many hundreds of thousands of acres of the lands of the character designated under this bill contain coal and other minerals, the surface of which is valuable for stock-raising purposes. The purpose of (the provision reserving minerals) is to limit the operation of this bill strictly to the surface of the lands described and to reserve to the United States the ownership and right to dispose of all minerals underlying the surface thereof. . . .

H.R. REP. NO. 35, *supra*, at 18.

The floor debate is revealing. The bill drew opposition because of the large acreage to be given each patentee. . . . In response, supporters emphasized the limited purpose and character of the grant. They pointed out that because the public lands involved were semi-arid, an area of 640 acres was required to support the homesteader and his family by raising livestock. . . . They also pointed out that the grant was limited to the surface estate, and they emphasized in the strongest terms that all minerals were retained by the United States.

. . . .

Appellees argue that references in the Congressional Record to homesteaders' drilling wells and developing springs indicate that Congress intended title to underground water to pass to patentees under the Act. These references are not to the development of geothermal resources. As we have seen, commercial development of such resources was not contemplated in this country when the Stock-Raising Homestead Act was passed. Moreover, in context, the references are to the development of a source of fresh water for the use of livestock, not to the tapping of underground sources of energy for use in generating electricity.

This review of the legislative history demonstrates that the purposes of the Act were to provide homesteaders with a portion of the public domain sufficient to enable them to support their families by raising livestock, and to reserve unrelated subsurface resources, particularly energy sources, for separate disposition. This is not to say that patentees under the Act were granted no more than a permit to graze livestock, as under the Taylor-Grazing Act, 43 U.S.C. §§ 315 et seq. To the contrary, a patentee under the Stock-Raising Homestead Act receives title to all rights in the land not reserved. It does mean, however, that the mineral reservation is to be read broadly in light of the agricultural purpose of the grant itself, and in light of Congress's equally clear purpose to retain subsurface resources, particularly sources of energy, for separate disposition and development in the public interest. Geothermal resources contribute nothing to the capacity of the surface estate to sustain livestock. They are depletable subsurface reservoirs of energy, akin to deposits of coal and oil, which it was the particular objective of the reservation clause to retain in public ownership. The purposes of the Act will be served by including geothermal resources in the statute's reservation of "all the coal and other minerals." Since the words employed are broad enough to encompass this result, the Act should be so interpreted.

Appellees assert that the Department of Interior has expressed the opinion that the mineral reservation in the Act does not include geothermal resources, and that this administrative interpretation is entitled to deference... The documents upon which appellees rely do not reflect a contemporaneous construction by administrators who participated in drafting the Act to which courts give great weight in interpreting statutes. Nor is this a case in which Congress has approved an administrative interpretation, explicitly or implicitly. On the contrary, Congress noted the Department of Interior's interpretation, observed that a contrary view had been expressed, concluded that "the opinion of the Department is not a conclusive determination of the legal question . . . ," and provided for "an early judicial determination of this question (upon which the committee takes no position)." H.R. REP. NO. 91–1544, 91st Cong., 2d Sess. . . .

Appellees contend that enactment of the Underground Water Reclamation Act of 1919, 43 U.S.C. §§ 351 et seq., three years after passage of the Stock-Raising Homestead Act, indicates that Congress did not consider subsurface water to be a "mineral." We disagree; indeed the more reasonable implication seems to us to be to the contrary.

. . . .

Reversed and remanded.

ROSETTE INC. V. UNITED STATES
United States Court of Appeals, Tenth Circuit, 2002
277 F.3d 1222

BRISCOE, CIRCUIT JUDGE.

Plaintiffs Rosette Incorporated, et al. (Rosette), appeal from the district court's grant of summary judgment in favor of the United States as to the ownership of geothermal resources on property obtained pursuant to patents issued under the Stock Raising Homestead Act of 1916 (SRHA), 43 U.S.C. § 291 et seq.; 42 Stat. 1445 (repealed 1976); 39 Stat. 862–64, 65 (repealed 1976). We affirm, agreeing with the district court that the geothermal resources at issue in this case are "minerals" within the reservation of the patents.

I.

Rosette is a collection of related corporations controlled by Dale Burgett or members of his immediate family. Rosette owns the surface estate to certain real property in Section 7, Township 25 South, Range 19 West, Hidalgo County, New Mexico, by virtue of patents issued in 1933 and 1935 under the SRHA. The SRHA permitted any person qualified to acquire land to make a stockraising homestead entry on lands designated by the Secretary of the Interior. 43 U.S.C. § 291. Such designated lands were to be lands the surface of which is, in [the Secretary of the Interior's] opinion, chiefly valuable for grazing and raising forage crops, do not contain merchantable timber, are not susceptible of irrigation from any known source of water supply, and are of such character that six hundred and forty acres are reasonably required for the support of a family.

43 U.S.C. § 292.

Under the SRHA, a homesteader could obtain a patent on the land if he resided for three years thereon and made permanent improvements tending to increase the value of the land for stockraising purposes. 43 U.S.C. § 293. However, the SRHA required that the patent issued be "subject to and contain a reservation to the United States of all the coal and other minerals in the lands so entered and patented, together with the right to prospect for, mine, and remove the same." 43 U.S.C. § 299. Rosette's patents contained a reservation of mineral rights by the United States consistent with 43 U.S.C. § 299.

Several wells were drilled in Section 7 in the 1940s and 1950s, one of which encountered water as hot as 240 degrees Fahrenheit. In 1970, Congress enacted the Geothermal Steam Act (hereinafter Steam Act), which granted the Secretary of the Interior the authority to lease geothermal resources, including steam, hot water and hot brines, heat from geothermal foundations and byproducts of geothermal foundations, owned or reserved by the United States. 30 U.S.C. § 1001 *et seq.* The Secretary of the Interior leased the geothermal rights to Section 7 to Amax Exploration, Inc., and later to Lightning Dock Geothermal, Inc. Rosette is a designated operator under the lease through agreements with the various leaseholders, and pays royalties. The lease agreement does not permit Rosette to drill deeper than 1,000 feet without prior written consent.

Rosette is in the business of growing roses in greenhouses for commercial distribution. The roses are planted in the ground. Rosette uses the heat in water from five wells located in Section 7 to heat its greenhouses, after which the water is discharged. No heat is transported off of the surface estate or used to generate other energy. Rosette uses water from wells outside Section 7 for irrigation purposes.

In 1993 Rosette filed an action for quiet title, ejectment, declaratory judgment and permanent injunction against the United States, arguing that geothermal resources are not reserved minerals under the SRHA. The United States filed a counterclaim for past-due royalties and seeking to enjoin Rosette. The district court dismissed Rosette's claims as barred by the statute of limitations, and this court affirmed. *Rosette, Inc. v. United States*, 141 F.3d 1394 (10th Cir. 1998).

Rosette reopened and installed a pump on a capped well, Well 55–7, located in Section 7, intending to use water from that well for the heating of the greenhouse. The depth of Well 55–7 exceeded 1,000 feet. Rosette did not seek permission from the geothermal leaseholder or the United States to utilize the well. As a result of Rosette's actions in reopening Well 55–7, the United States filed its second amended counterclaim to enjoin Rosette from using geothermal resources on its lease located deeper than 1,000 feet. Rosette's answer asked the district court to quiet title as to the geothermal resources against the United States.

The district court heard the second amended counterclaim on cross-motions for summary judgment after the parties had stipulated to numerous facts. . . . The district court . . . found that title to the geothermal resources in Section 7 was vested in the United States as a matter of law, and issued a preliminary and permanent injunction prohibiting Rosette from utilizing the geothermal resources located deeper than 1,000 feet without authorization from the United States and the lessee. The court further ordered Rosette to remove its pump and recap Well 55–7. The parties stipulated as to damages.

II.

Rosette argues that the district court erred in finding that the United States has title to the geothermal resources under Section 7. Rosette's argument essentially advances three points: 1) Geothermal resources as a whole are not "minerals" under the SRHA; 2) even if geothermal resources as a whole may be "minerals" under the SRHA, the particular geothermal resources under Section 7 do not constitute "minerals" under the SRHA; and 3) even if the geothermal resources under Section 7 are "minerals" under the SRHA, Rosette still has the right to use the resources as surfaceholder to advance the purposes of Rosette's homestead.

. . . .

Geothermal resources as minerals under the SRHA

The determination of whether geothermal resources are minerals under the SRHA requires interpretation of that Act. . . .

The United States Supreme Court examined the scope of the mineral reservation in the SRHA in *Watt v. Western Nuclear, Inc.*, 462 U.S. 36, 103 S.Ct. 2218, 76 L.Ed.2d 400 (1983). The question at issue in that case was whether gravel extracted from the ground of a patented site was a "mineral" and thus the property of the United States. The Court reasoned that, for a substance to be a mineral reserved under the SRHA, it must not only be a mineral within one or more familiar definitions of that term, but also the type of mineral that Congress intended to reserve to the United States in lands patented under the SRHA. *Id.* at 44, 103 S.Ct. 2218. The Court stated that Congress' underlying purpose in severing the surface estate of lands patented from the mineral estate was to facilitate the concurrent development of both surface and subsurface resources, and that while Congress expected homesteaders to use the surface of land for stockraising and raising crops, it sought to ensure that valuable subsurface resources would remain subject to development by other developers who would be more likely to make use of the resources. *Id.* at 47, 103 S.Ct. 2218.

Given the underlying purpose of the SRHA, the Court stated that "the determination of whether a particular substance is included in the surface estate or the mineral estate should be made in light of the use of the surface estate that Congress contemplated," that is, stockraising and the raising of forage crops. *Id.* at 52, 103 S.Ct. 2218. The Court concluded that in order to qualify as a "mineral" under the reservation of the SRHA a substance must be 1) mineral in character, i.e. inorganic, 2) removable from the soil, 3) usable for commercial purposes, 4) and of such a character that there was no reason to suppose Congress intended it to be included in the surface estate. *Id.* at 53, 103 S.Ct. 2218. The Court determined that gravel came under this definition. . . . [T]he Court recited the established rule that land grants are construed favorably to the Government, and nothing passes except what is conveyed in clear language, with any doubts resolved in favor of the Government. *Id.* at 59–60, 103 S.Ct. 2218.

We have found no decisions since *Western Nuclear* addressing the question of whether geothermal resources are minerals under the SRHA. The issue was squarely addressed in an earlier case decided by the Ninth Circuit. See *United States v. Union Oil Co. of California*, 549 F.2d 1271 (9th Cir. 1977). In *Union Oil*, the court applied an analysis substantially similar to that used in *Western Nuclear*. The court first determined that geothermal resources are actually the result of a process in which magma heats water contained in porous rock strata, and that, at a general level, all of the elements involved in the process, including water itself, could properly be classified as minerals. . . .

. . . .

Geothermal resources as mineral in character

The first step in the *Western Nuclear* analysis is to determine whether geothermal resources in general are minerals in character, that is, inorganic. *Western Nuclear*, 462 U.S. at 53, 103 S.Ct. 2218. Rosette argues the substance in question is the heat from the water, and that heat itself cannot properly be classified as inorganic. Rather, according to Rosette, heat is properly found in plants and animals and is one of the properties, in addition to light and air, which is appurtenant to the property. However, as recognized in *Union Oil*, geothermal resources are not isolated substances and are dependent upon heat from magma being transmitted to water contained in porous rock strata. 549 F.2d at 1273. There is no question that both magma and rock are inorganic in character.

Rosette contends that water cannot be a "mineral," citing *Andrus v. Charlestone Stone Products Co.*, 436 U.S. 604, 98 S.Ct. 2002, 56 L.Ed.2d

570 (1978). In *Andrus*, the Court held that water was not a "valuable mineral deposit" within the scope of the federal mining statute. However, *Andrus* is not applicable here. . . . In *Union Oil*, the court determined that water could be classified as a mineral. The court pointed to a wide variety of sources, including mining treatises and texts on mineralogy in making this determination. *See* 549 F.2d at 1273, n. 5.

We conclude that the geothermal process as a whole is inorganic within the definition set forth in *Western Nuclear*, and thus may be classified as generally mineral in character.

Geothermal resources as removable from soil and usable for commercial purposes

The parties do not dispute that geothermal resources as a whole are removable from the soil and usable for commercial purposes. Therefore, these two parts of the *Western Nuclear* test are satisfied.

Geothermal resources as included by Congress in surface estate

The final requirement is whether "there is no reason to suppose" that Congress intended geothermal resources to be included within the surface estate. . . .

It is fairly certain that, at the time of the passage of the SRHA, Congress did not specifically intend that geothermal resources as such be retained by the federal government. *See Union Oil,* 549 F.2d at 1273 (noting that although steam had been used to generate electricity in Italy as early as 1904, no geothermal power plants went into production in the United States until 1960). However, the question is not what Congress intended to reserve, but rather what Congress intended to give away in its grant to the landholder in the SRHA. . . .

As noted by the courts in *Western Nuclear* and *Union Oil*, the purpose of the SRHA was to open up lands suitable for development for ranching and the planting of forage crops, with the understanding that the farmer-stockman who would be a tenant would be unlikely to want to develop the underlying resources. *Western Nuclear*, 462 U.S. at 53–56, 103 S.Ct. 2218; *Union Oil*, 549 F.2d at 1276–79. The question, then, is whether the farmer-stockman contemplated by Congress to be a patent holder would want to develop geothermal resources.

Rosette contends that geothermal resources are, in their essence, hot water, and that the water is useful in the farming and ranching context. . . .

It is highly unlikely that Congress intended that homesteaders taking patent to the surface area develop geothermal resources. Certainly, it would be difficult for such homesteaders to utilize geothermal steam or even hot water for use in the production of forage crops and the raising of livestock.

. . . .

Based on the application of the *Western Nuclear* test, we conclude that geothermal resources in general are in fact "minerals" under the SRHA. The components of the process, including magma, rock, and water, are minerals in the general sense that they are inorganic. The product of the process, whether steam or hot water, may be extracted from the soil and is usable for commercial purposes. Further, there is no reason to suppose that Congress intended that the geothermal resources be included in the surfaceholder's patent given the stated purpose of the patent to promote the raising of livestock and forage crops. The next question is whether the geothermal resources in the case at hand are so unusual as to take them outside this definition.

Geothermal resources in Well 55–7 as minerals under the SRHA

Rosette argues even if geothermal resources in a general sense are "minerals" under the SRHA, the particular geothermal resources used by Rosette do not fall under this definition. Rosette argues that, in the Steam Act, Congress recognized that not all geothermal resources were reserved to the federal government under the SRHA, that the particular nature of the hot water used by Rosette takes it outside the definition of a mineral under the SRHA because it was essentially potable water that could be used for stockraising and the planting of forage crops, and further that the water is not hot enough for commercial use.

. . . .

Nature of geothermal resources

Rosette argues the geothermal resources in question in this case are not salt water and geothermal steam, as was the case in *Union Oil*, but rather potable heated water containing less than 1,400 milligrams per liter of solids. According to the stipulated facts, beneficial use of the groundwater in Section 7 has been made for irrigation of field crops, stock watering, and various domestic uses, including drinking water. Rosette contends this is strong evidence that the geothermal rights should remain with it as the surfaceholder, as the water would be useful for the stockraising and forage crop producing activities contemplated in the SRHA. However, the geothermal resources in question in this case are from Well 55–7, which was an exploratory well drilled deeper than 1,000 feet. The temperature of the water from the well was at 232.9 degrees Fahrenheit. The well was drilled in the 1980s and was never used as a source for irrigation. It is unlikely Congress, in passing the SRHA, contemplated that the surfaceholder would have the inclination and the expertise to develop geothermal resources at that temperature for the purpose of irrigation of forage crops and watering of stock. Although Rosette argues it could use the water for irrigation, its roses are irrigated from wells in an adjacent section.

There simply is no reason to suppose that Congress intended a geothermal well such as the one at issue be included within its grant of land to homesteaders under the SRHA. Given the characteristics of the well, Rosette's argument that the geothermal resources are included within its surfaceholder rights is not persuasive.

Temperature of geothermal resources

Rosette's next argument is that the temperature of the well is not sufficient to feasibly produce electrical energy. Rosette argues the temperature of the water renders it useless under the Steam Act, and further prevents it from being removable from the soil for purposes of the definition of a mineral under the SRHA. Both parties acknowledge the question of whether the temperature in Well 55–7 is hot enough for commercial generation of electricity is a disputed question of fact, which, if material, would require a remand. The district court found that the question was not material, and we agree.

. . . .

. . . Rosette argues that, 1) since removal and utilization are one process in connection with geothermal resources, then 2) geothermal resources must be converted to electricity in order to be utilized and removed; and if 3) the geothermal resources cannot be feasibly converted into electricity, then 4) they cannot be removed, and 5) therefore they are not minerals under the SRHA.

. . . Even if the temperature of the geothermal resources in question does not allow them feasibly to be converted into electricity, this does not prevent them from being removed from the soil and utilized for commercial purposes. They may, for example, be removed by the mineral holder and sold to the surfaceholder for the heating of greenhouses or other surface structures on the property. The mineral rights may also be leased by the federal government directly to the surfaceholder for such purposes. In either case, the minerals are being removed from the soil and used for commercial purposes. Nor is the production of electricity the only purpose for which the geothermal resources can be used under the Steam Act. Although the Steam Act is generally geared toward the production of energy, it also encompasses other commercial uses for geothermal power. . . .

Whether or not the temperature of the geothermal resources in Well 55–7 is high enough to allow it to be used to generate electricity is immaterial to its status as a mineral under the SRHA.

Entitlement to use of geothermal resources notwithstanding reservation clause

Rosette's final argument is that, even if the geothermal resources under Section 7 are minerals under the SRHA, Rosette still has the right to use the resources as surfaceholder to advance the purposes of the homestead. Rosette contends it has a permit to utilize the water rights in the section to develop the homestead, and that use could not be infringed by the federal government.

It is undisputed that Rosette has the right to beneficial use of 450 acre feet of water per annum issued by the New Mexico State Engineers Office. It is further undisputed that these rights predate the passage of the Steam Act. However, the rights do not predate the SRHA, and therefore, Rosette's rights to the use of the water are governed by its rights under its patents and the reservation of mineral rights by the federal government.

Rosette argues it is utilizing the geothermal resources in question to further its crop-raising activities, and that it has a right to do so in connection with its homestead. . . .

. . . .

. . . The purpose of the SRHA was to encourage settlement of the land for use in stockraising and the raising of forage crops. See *Western Nuclear*, 462 U.S. at 53, 103 S.Ct. 2218. Webster's Third New International Dictionary defines forage as "vegetable food (as hay, grain) for domestic animals." *Webster's Third New International Dictionary* 886 (1993). Other definitions are similar. *See, e.g.*, 40 C.F.R. Pt. 158, App. A (1999) (listing forage crops as typical annual and perennial grasses, corn, sorghum, small grains for forage and perennial legumes). These definitions would not encompass the commercial raising of roses.

. . . .

. . . Thus, while Rosette might be able to use the heated water from geothermal resources under its property for use in watering livestock or irrigating forage crops and remain within the patent, the commercial activity of heating greenhouses to produce roses for sale falls outside the patent. Therefore, Rosette, by virtue of being the surfaceholder, does not acquire the right to use the geothermal resources in Well 55–7 for use in providing heat for its commercial greenhouse operation. The right to the resources remains in the federal government.

AFFIRMED.

———————

NOTES & QUESTIONS

1.   In the *Union Oil* case, the court described geothermal resources as "depletable subsurface reservoirs of energy, akin to deposits of coal and oil." Do you agree with that characterization? Why or why not? Why do you think the court chose to describe geothermal resources with that language?

2.   Suppose your client owned land originally patented to her under the Homestead Act of 1862, a federal land patent act distinct from the SRHA that patented land to citizens who built a home and cultivated an agricultural crop on eligible land. The patent deed associated with her land reserved all minerals to the United States with the same reservation language quoted from the patent in *Rosette* above. Suppose further that your client operated a rose-growing business identical to that of the landowner in *Rosette* and wanted to use the land's geothermal resources (which were very similar to those at issue in *Rosette*) in the same way that the *Rosette* landowner sought to use them (to heat greenhouses). Craft a one-paragraph statement that distinguishes your client's case from *Rosette* and argues that your client is legally entitled to use the geothermal resources to heat the greenhouses on her land. Do you think your argument would succeed in court? Why or why not?

3.   *Similar Conflicts over Subsurface Pore Space.* Another potentially environmentally-beneficial use of subsurface resources in the Western United States is for the storage of carbon dioxide gas captured at fossil fuel-fired power plants. After a mineral rights holder completes oil and gas extraction at a given site, an enormous volume of *pore space*—tiny holes in deep subsurface rock where oil or gas used to reside—remains. Landowners seeking to use this pore space to store carbon dioxide (or natural gas, in some cases) have had disputes with the federal government that closely resemble the one in *Rosette*. In essence, landowners in these cases have argued that the mineral rights reservations in their land patents under the Stock-Raising Homestead Act of 1916 did not reserve subsurface pore space. For a more complete introduction to these issues, see generally Kevin L. Doran & Angela M. Cifor, *Does the Federal Government Own the Pore Space under Private Lands in the West?*, 42 ENVTL. L. 527 (2012).

2.   POLICIES PROMOTING GEOTHERMAL ENERGY

Given the tremendous advantages of geothermal energy generation, it is no surprise that policymakers have sought to encourage private investment in geothermal energy research and project development over the years. Geothermal power could still have a very bright future as a major renewable energy resource if researchers ever develop an affordable way to tap into geothermal resources situated much deeper below the surface. The following excerpt describes and analyzes some ongoing policy efforts to overcome existing technological barriers and ultimately facilitate more widespread use of geothermal resources.

CAPTURING THE HEAT OF THE EARTH: HOW THE FEDERAL
GOVERNMENT CAN MOST EFFECTIVELY ENCOURAGE
THE GENERATION OF ELECTRICITY
FROM GEOTHERMAL ENERGY

Ben Tannen
37 ENVIRONS: ENVTL. L. & POL'Y J. 133, 136–38, 140–45, 159–61 & 164 (2014)

Increased reliance on geothermal energy could transform the landscape of American energy use, particularly in the electricity-generation sector. Geothermal resources are extremely abundant. If fully used, the United States' geothermal resources could generate well over three-quarters of the country's current electrical capacity. Additionally, unlike many renewable energy sources, geothermal power plants could meet baseload, or everyday, demand, since geothermal plants can produce electricity almost constantly. This reliability stands in stark contrast to wind and solar power, which depend on the amount of wind or sunshine present on a given day. . . . Finally, geothermal energy is extremely clean, with power plants emitting less than one percent of the carbon dioxide of a typical fossil fuel plant and low levels of traditional air pollutants. Geothermal energy is thus a plentiful, reliable, and potentially cheap domestic source of energy that could help slow climate change.

Given this technology's potential, the sluggish pace of geothermal electricity development over the first decade of the new millennium is puzzling. During this time period, geothermal electricity generation in the United States remained fairly constant at 0.4 percent of total generation while electrical capacity of other renewable sources like wind increased dramatically. A major reason for this lack of progress is that geothermal regulation over the past four decades by all levels of government has insufficiently addressed geothermal-specific project constraints. Geothermal power plants differ from many other commercially available renewable and conventional power plants since the viability of some aspects of geothermal technology still depends heavily on further research and development (R&D) efforts, capital costs of the plants are extremely high and uniquely structured, and prime geothermal resources are overwhelmingly located on federal lands. Since policymakers can only properly address most of these geothermal-specific needs with substantial funds or federal permits, federal action and inaction, rather than state policy, determine the course of geothermal development even more so than for other sources of renewable energy. . . .

. . . .

Conventional geothermal electricity generation is . . . the overwhelmingly dominant form of geothermal power generation today. . . .

Even more promising is [enhanced geothermal system (EGS) technology], a comparatively new technology. . . .

While EGS technology is still in an experimental phase, it is slowly but surely moving towards commercialization. DOE research into EGS began decades ago and today several test EGS plants exist worldwide and, for a time, one commercial EGS plant operated. The technology continues to face sizeable challenges, ranging from drilling issues to excessive water loss within the magma. Nevertheless, the potential payoff is enormous, as the USGS has estimated that thirteen Western states alone could provide 345,100 MW to 727,900 MW of new EGS electrical capacity. Developers will only realize the promise of both hydrothermal and EGS technologies, however, if a regulatory scheme conducive to their success is in place.

. . . .

2.   Recent Geothermal Legislation

The American Jobs Creation Act of 2004 (Jobs Act), a broad tax statute, was the first piece of federal legislation to have a major impact on geothermal policy in the new millennium. The Jobs Act expanded the production tax credit (PTC) to include geothermal energy technologies. This statute thus enabled geothermal developers to take advantage of a major tax incentive for renewable energy development, in existence since 1992 but which heretofore had only applied to wind and certain types of biomass technologies.

One year later, the massive Energy Policy Act of 2005 (EPAct) dramatically changed the American geothermal landscape. Provisions of the Act that encouraged renewable energy generally also boosted geothermal development, such as the creation of a federal loan guarantee program for projects using "new or significantly improved [renewable energy] technologies." EPAct's Title II, Subtitle B was entirely dedicated to geothermal energy. This subtitle restructured the process for leasing public land for geothermal development and mandated a new federal survey of geothermal resources to replace the most recent one from 1978. Other scattered provisions explicitly affected geothermal energy, such as Section 322's exemption of fluids used in hydraulic fracturing related to geothermal activities from regulation under the Safe Drinking Water Act.

The Energy Independence and Security Act of 2007 (EISA) was yet another major recent piece of geothermal legislation. Like EPAct, EISA has an entire subtitle, Title VI, Subtitle B, devoted to geothermal energy. It mostly encouraged educational and R&D efforts, such as a government partnership with industry to develop advanced drilling technologies and the establishment of a centralized repository of information about geothermal technology at a university. EISA also required DOE to study a variety of peculiar applications of geothermal technology, such as its ability to help produce hydrogen and biofuels. Perhaps most importantly, EISA appropriated $90 million annually from fiscal years 2008 to 2012 for DOE to carry out the Act's geothermal-specific provisions. This appropriation was the first major infusion of federal funds into geothermal technology in decades.

Finally, the American Recovery and Reinvestment Act of 2009 (ARRA) was the most recent federal statute to have a huge impact on geothermal development. It dramatically increased federal geothermal R&D support, allocating $16.8 billion to DOE for "energy efficiency and renewable energy" projects, of which $400 million was devoted to the Geothermal Technologies Program (GTP), DOE's geothermal research arm. ARRA also provided developers with financial support by extending the PTC's expiration date for geothermal energy from January 1, 2011 to January 1, 2014 and by allowing developers to take a Treasury Department grant in place of the PTC or ITC for projects beginning before the end of 2011 under certain circumstances.

. . . .

A.   Geothermal Projects' Reliance on Federal Lands

The vast majority of American geothermal resources are on public lands, making federal lands leasing policy critical to geothermal development. The DOI's Bureau of Land Management (BLM) administers geothermal leases on BLM and USFS lands, which account for forty percent of the United States' current geothermal capacity. The importance of federal leasing policy will only grow, as ninety percent of all geothermal resources exist on federal land. The overwhelming concentration of geothermal resources on public lands stands in stark contrast to other renewable energy resources, for which federal lands leasing policy is far less important. . . .

. . . .

In 2005, EPAct dramatically altered the three-and-a-half decades-old federal lands geothermal leasing process. EPAct . . . require[s] competitive leasing in all circumstances except for a few rarely applicable exceptions. Developers nominate desirable lands for which BLM then assigns leases through competitive bidding. In order to reduce delays, the statute requires BLM to conduct auctions at least once every two years in states with pending nominations. . . .

. . . .

. . . [W]hile EPAct has improved the public lands leasing process for geothermal development, the restoration of a noncompetitive leasing option and the designation of a lead agency for the leasing process could further promote geothermal development on public lands.

NOTES & QUESTIONS

1.   Identify at least five different types of government incentives for geothermal energy development referenced in the excerpt above.

2.   Tannen suggests that governments have under-invested in geothermal energy technology research. Do you agree? Why or why not? What sort of analysis or process would you recommend that governments use to determine how to allocate scarce research dollars among various types of energy technologies?

3.   From the perspective of developers, what seem to be the primary advantages and disadvantages of a mandatory competitive bidding process for geothermal leases? Do you think those perceived advantages or disadvantages are likely different from the perspective of the general public? Why or why not? If so, how are they different?

4.   *Two Federal Tax Credits.* When aggregated, the federal tax credits available for geothermal energy development are among the most generous offered for any energy strategy. As of 2017, under § 48 of the Internal Revenue Code (IRC) geothermal energy projects could qualify for a federal investment tax credit (ITC) of up to 10 percent of the project's cost. New geothermal power projects could *also* qualify for the per-kWh production tax credit (PTC) scheduled to gradually phase out through the year 2019. As suggested above, however, despite these general tax credit programs, geothermal energy development growth in the United States has been slow compared to that of wind and solar energy over the past decade.

5.   *Ground Source Heat Pump Systems.* One of the most promising types of energy strategies using a subsurface heat source involves no electricity generation at all. Ground source heat pump systems utilize pumps to heat or cool buildings or water with warm or cool air from underground. The recent interest of some major tech companies in these systems suggests these technologies may finally be maturing to a point of economic viability on a widespread scale. For instance, Google X unveiled a startup company in 2017 called Dandelion that seeks to use new drilling technologies to install affordable subsurface geothermal "ground loop" pipes near buildings. According to the company, these ground loop systems would retail for between $20,000 and $25,000, and would help to cool homes during summer months and heat them during the winter. *See* Kaya Yurieff, *Google's New Startup Uses Energy from Your Lawn to Heat Your Home,* CNNMONEY (July 7, 2017), http://money.cnn.com/2017/07/07/technology/google-dandelion/index.html; https://dandelionenergy.com/.

B. BIOMASS

Biomass and biofuel technologies comprise another important category of renewable energy strategies. Biomass and biofuels are *biogenic* materials—typically plant-based materials or animal waste—burned to produce usable energy. Biomass in various forms has long served as an important type of renewable energy resource throughout the world. Technically, even an ordinary wood fireplace is a biomass energy device because the wood burned inside it is a type of biomass and burning the wood produces valuable heat energy. In that sense, humans have been using biomass for energy since pre-historic times and billions still rely on it today as a primary energy source for cooking, lighting, heating indoor spaces, and various other functions.

In recent years, government incentive policies aimed at promoting renewable energy development have driven an unprecedented degree of interest in biomass energy technologies. As Figure 8.3 shows, roughly 46% of all renewable energy consumption in the United States was attributable to biomass as of 2016—more than wind, solar and geothermal energy combined. Biofuels accounted for nearly half of that figure. Unquestionably, biomass in all of its forms is a major component of the nation's renewable energy portfolio.

Figure 8.3. U.S. Energy Consumption by Energy Source (2016)

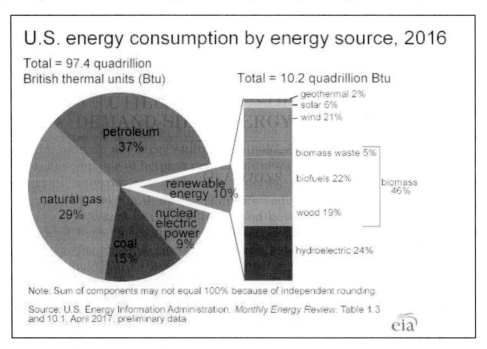

Recent technological advancements that have made the process of converting biomass to electric power more efficient and cost-effective are helping to drive significant growth in today's biomass energy industry. Many of the same government programs that have spurred the expansion of the nation's wind and solar energy industries are propelling investment in biomass energy as well. In some forested regions that lack developable wind energy resources, electric generating facilities fueled partially or entirely with biomass are becoming increasingly common. Unlike wind and sunlight, biomass energy resources do not suffer from intermittency problems. Electric generating facilities that use biomass supply dispatchable baseload power throughout the day and on almost any day of the year.

Despite the advantages of biomass energy, some stakeholders and policymakers have questioned whether it warrants the same favorable policy treatment that wind and solar energy receive. A major downside of biomass electricity generation is that it involves the burning of carbon-based material, which emits carbon dioxide into the atmosphere and contributes to global warming. When the emissions associated with harvesting, processing, and transporting biomass are considered, biomass electricity generation often is not *carbon neutral*: the carbon dioxide emissions attributable to it often accelerate rather than decelerate the pace of global warming. Some biomass energy strategies likewise threaten precious forest resources that would otherwise help to slow the pace of climate change by sequestering atmospheric carbon dioxide. Numerous factors, including the type of biomass involved, how and where biomass is grown or collected, how far it travels before it is burned, and the combustion process itself all affect the net environmental benefits or costs of any given biomass energy strategy. This wide variance in environmental impacts can add complexity and controversy to policymaking efforts aimed at promoting the development and adoption of biomass energy technologies.

1. DEFINING BIOMASS ENERGY UNDER INCENTIVE POLICIES

Distinguishing among various types of biomass energy strategies and ensuring that government-provided benefits flow only to those strategies that warrant them is often an expensive and arduous task. As the following cases show, ambiguous "gray areas" continue to complicate the crafting of effective biomass-related programs and policies. Each of the two cases below confronts difficult questions about whether and to what extent certain biomass energy strategies should qualify for favorable treatment under state renewable energy policies. The first case addresses the question of whether "primary harvest whole trees"—entire trees cut down for the sole purpose of helping to fuel electricity production—qualify as biomass under North Carolina's RPS standard. The second case considers whether residual wood waste from saw mills that is sold as "hog fuel"—a fuel product commonly used in *cogeneration* facilities that generate both heat and electricity—qualifies as biomass under an Oregon biomass tax credit statute.

STATE EX REL. UTILITIES COMM'N V. ENVIRONMENTAL DEFENSE FUND

Court of Appeals of North Carolina, 2011
214 N.C. App. 364

STEELMAN, J.

. . . .

North Carolina's Renewable Energy and Energy Efficiency Portfolio Standard ("REPS"), N.C. GEN. STAT. § 62–133.8(b), requires electric public utilities to meet renewability and efficiency standards beginning in 2012. If a utility does not meet this requirement, the Commission can impose a penalty up to $1,000 for each violation. . . .

Any electric utility that wants to generate tradable Renewable Energy Certificates ("RECs"), which can be used to comply with REPS, must register its facility as a "renewable energy facility" with the North Carolina Utilities Commission ("Commission"). . . . Facilities that generate electric power using a "renewable energy resource" are considered renewable energy facilities. N.C. Gen. Stat. § 62–133.8(a)(7). The statute defines "renewable energy resource" to include "a biomass resource, including agricultural waste, animal waste, wood waste, spent pulping liquors, combustible residues, combustible liquids, combustible gases, energy crops, or landfill methane." § 62–133.8(a).

On 1 March 2010[,] Duke Energy Carolinas, LLC ("Duke") applied to the Commission to register two of its thermal electric generating stations, Buck Steam Station ("Buck") and Lee Steam Station ("Lee"), as renewable energy facilities. Duke had conducted production trials at both stations in which a blend of wood chips and coal was used as fuel.

The Commission determined that wood derived from whole trees in primary harvest is a "biomass resource" and thus a "renewable energy resource" within the meaning of the statute and approved Duke's applications for the Buck and Lee stations.

. . . .

Appellants contend that the Commission erred in its conclusion that wood fuel from primary harvest whole trees is a "biomass resource" and thus a "renewable energy resource" within the meaning of N.C. Gen. Stat. § 62–133.8(a). We disagree.

. . . .

When construing a statute, the court looks first to its plain meaning. . . . The court must give effect to the plain meaning as long as the statute is clear and unambiguous. *State v. Jackson*, 353 N.C. 495, 501, 546 S.E.2d 570, 574 (2001).

The statute at issue in the instant case is not ambiguous because all wood fuel is encompassed by the meaning of the term "biomass." Since the statute does not specifically define "biomass," we look to its ordinary meaning. *The New Oxford American Dictionary* defines "biomass" as "organic matter used as fuel." *The New Oxford American Dictionary* 166 (Elizabeth J. Jewell et al. eds., 2d ed.2005). A report produced by the North Carolina Biomass Council defines biomass as "any organic matter that is available on a renewable or recurring basis, including *agricultural crops and trees, wood and wood wastes and residues,* plants (including aquatic plants), grasses, residues, fibers, animal wastes, and segregated municipal waste." Ben Rich, North Carolina Biomass Council, *The North Carolina Biomass Roadmap: Recommendations for Fossil Fuel Displacement through Biomass Utilization 4 (2007),* http://www.ncsc.ncsu.edu/bioenergy/docs/NC_Biomass_Roadmap.pdf (emphasis added). The Commission applied the definition from *The Biomass Roadmap* in considering whether a particular type of fuel is a "biomass resource." . . .

All wood fuel is clearly encompassed by each of these definitions. Not only is wood listed as an example of a biomass in *The Biomass Roadmap,* wood is also organic and renewable, which are the criteria encompassed by the definitions. Therefore, wood fuel from primary harvest whole trees is a biomass resource within the meaning of the statute.

Appellants argue that not all biomass is a biomass resource within the meaning of the statute. Appellants advance two theories to support this argument. First, that the list of biomass resources provided in the statute is an exhaustive list; and second, that the doctrine of *ejusdem generis* limits the term "biomass resources" so that it only includes biomass material of the same type as the listed resources. The plain meaning of the statute does not support either theory.

First, the language of the statute indicates that the legislature did not intend to limit the term "biomass resources" to only include the resources listed in the statute. *The New Oxford American Dictionary* defines the word "including" to mean "containing as part of the whole being considered." *The New Oxford American Dictionary, supra* at 854. Similarly, *Black's Law Dictionary* explains, "The participle including typically indicates a partial list." *Black's Law Dictionary* 831 (9th ed.2009). Both of these definitions suggest that a list introduced by the word "including" would be illustrative, rather than exhaustive. . . . We hold that the list provided by the legislature is not an exhaustive list of all of the biomass materials included in the broad term "biomass resources."

Second, the term "biomass resources" is not limited by the doctrine of *ejusdem generis.*

> " '[T]he *ejusdem generis* rule is that where general words follow a designation of particular subjects or things, the meaning

of the general words will ordinarily be presumed to be, and construed as, restricted by the particular designations and as including only things of the same kind, character and nature as those specifically enumerated.' "

State v. Lee, 277 N.C. 242, 244, 176 S.E.2d 772, 774 (1970) (internal citations omitted).

North Carolina courts have followed this explanation of how the doctrine of *ejusdem generis* should be applied by employing the doctrine when a list of specific terms is *followed* by a general term. *See. . . . Lee,* 277 N.C. at 244, 176 S.E.2d at 774 (interpreting the phrase "or other like weapons" to be limited to automatic or semiautomatic weapons, where the phrase followed a specific list of automatic and semiautomatic weapons).

The provision at issue here does not fit the doctrine as described in *Lee* because the general phrase "biomass resources" *precedes* the list of specific examples.

. . . .

Even assuming *arguendo* that the doctrine of *ejusdem generis* can be applied when the general term precedes the specific, the rule would not apply in the instant case because the specific terms do not have a unifying characteristic. "The rule does not apply to restrict the operation of a general expression where the specific things enumerated have no common characteristic, and differ greatly from one another." *State v. Fenner,* 263 N.C. 694, 698, 140 S.E.2d 349, 352 (1965). . . .

Any resource that can be considered a biomass because it is organic and renewable is a biomass resource within the plain meaning of the statute. All wood fuel meets these criteria and thus is a "biomass resource" and a "renewable energy resource."

Appellants' arguments are without merit.

AFFIRMED.

WARRENTON FIBER COMPANY V. DEPARTMENT OF ENERGY
Court of Appeals of Oregon, 2016
283 Or. App. 270

FLYNN, J.

This case arises out of a decision by the Oregon Department of Energy (ODOE)'s decision that Warrenton Fiber is not eligible for a biomass tax credit for tree bark that it stripped from pulp logs at its mill and then sold as "hog fuel." Warrenton sought review of that decision in the circuit court, which concluded that ODOE relied on an invalid rule in rejecting Warrenton's application for a tax credit certification. ODOE challenges that determination, contending that it had authority to enact the challenged rule, which excluded from the definition of biomass "[s]awdust or other residual wood waste from mill operations." OAR 330–170–0040(1)(c) (Nov. 2, 2010). We conclude that the rule is valid and, thus, reverse and remand the trial court's grant of summary judgment to Warrenton and denial of summary judgment to ODOE. . . .

I. BACKGROUND

We begin by explaining the statutory context out of which the parties' dispute arises. Under Oregon's biomass tax credit program, an "agricultural producer" or "biomass collector" is allowed a tax credit for the "production" or "collection" of "biomass in Oregon that is used, in Oregon, as biofuel or to produce biofuel." ORS 315.141(3)(a). The legislature has charged the ODOE with the task of establishing procedures and criteria for determining the amount of the credit, and with providing "written certification to taxpayers that are eligible to claim the credit[.]" ORS 315.141(5)(a). As pertinent to this appeal, the legislature has defined "biomass," as

"organic matter that is available on a renewable or recurring basis and that is derived from:

"(A) Forest or rangeland woody debris from harvesting or thinning conducted to improve forest or rangeland ecological health and reduce uncharacteristic stand replacing wildfire risk[.]"

ORS 315.141(1)(d). At the time that Warrenton sought the disputed certification, OAR 330–170–0040(1) provided, as pertinent:

"For the purposes of these rules biomass does not include:

"* * * *

"(c) Sawdust or other residual wood waste from mill operations[.]"

Warrenton purchased pulp logs, which it hauled to its facility, stripped off the bark, and turned the remaining portion of logs into wood chips. Warrenton sold some of the stripped bark as "hog fuel" and sought a biomass tax credit certification from ODOE for $ 97,690.70 against the taxes due for its sale of the hog fuel. ODOE denied the application on the basis of OAR 330–170–0040(1)(c). . . .

II. DISCUSSION

In reviewing an agency order. . . . we consider whether the rule exceeds ODOE's statutory authority. In this context, our review of the rule's validity is limited to "the wording of the rule itself (read in context) and the statutory provisions authorizing the rule." *Wolf v. Oregon Lottery Commission*, 344 Or. 345, 355, 182 P.3d 180 (2008).

There is no dispute that ODOE is generally authorized to "[a]dopt rules and issue orders to carry out the duties of the director and the State

Department of Energy," and those duties specifically include certifying biomass tax credits. ORS 469.040(1)(d). . . . Warrenton argues, however, and the trial court agreed, that the rule exceeds ODOE's authority because it excludes from the definition of "biomass" material to which the legislature intended to extend the tax credit. We disagree.

The parties' dispute primarily turns on whether the rule is consistent with ORS 315.141(1)(d)(A), which—as quoted above—defines "biomass" to include:

> "organic matter that is available on a renewable or recurring basis and that is derived from:
>
> "(A) Forest or rangeland woody debris from harvesting or thinning conducted to improve forest or rangeland ecological health and reduce uncharacteristic stand replacing wildfire risk[.]"

As construed by ODOE, that definition is consistent with OAR 330–170–0040(1)(c) because the statute identifies woody debris biomass according to the direct source of the debris, and "residual wood waste from mill operations" describes a different source than "[f]orest or rangeland woody debris from harvesting or thinning." Warrenton urges us to construe the statutory definition as reaching woody residue created from mill operations if the trees used in those mill operations originally came "from harvesting or thinning conducted to improve forest or rangeland ecological health and reduce uncharacteristic stand replacing wildfire risk."

. . . .

B.   Statutory Construction

As indicated above, the question for the court when reviewing an agency's construction of inexact statutory terms is whether that construction is consistent with the legislature's intent. *Coast Security Mortgage Corp.*, 331 Or. at 354, 15 P.3d 29. Determining the meaning of the statute is a question of law, ultimately for the court. *Springfield Education Assn*, 290 Or. at 224, 621 P.2d 547. As with other questions of statutory construction, in determining the scope of an agency's statutory authority, "we seek to discern the legislature's intent by examining the text and context of the relevant statutes and, if useful to the analysis, pertinent legislative history." *Assn. of Acupuncture*, 260 Or. App. at 678, 320 P.3d 575. . . . Here, the text and context of ORS 315.141(1)(d)(A) lead us to conclude that the legislature intended to make the biomass tax credit available when woody debris is removed from the forest *as debris* and sold for biofuel.

1.   Textual analysis of ORS 315.141(1)(d)(A)

First, we agree with ODOE that the text—"[f]orest or rangeland woody debris from harvesting or thinning"—suggests a legislative intent to identify woody biomass according to the method by, and location at which, the debris is created. Rather than extend the definition of biomass to all woody debris, the legislature limited the category according to the location of the debris—"[f]orest or rangeland"—and the process by which the debris is created—"from harvesting or thinning." The legislature did not define the term "debris," and it is not a legal or technical term, so we look to the plain and ordinary meaning of the term. . . . The ordinary meaning of "debris" is "the remains of something broken down or destroyed." *Webster's Third New Int'l Dictionary* 582 (unabridged ed. 1993). The qualification that this woody debris (or remains) must be "forest or rangeland" debris suggests that the location of the debris must be a forest or rangeland. And the further qualification that the remains must be "from harvesting or thinning" suggests a direct connection to those activities. *See Webster's* at 913 (as pertinent, defining "from" as "a function word" used "to indicate the source or original or moving force of something"). Thus, the text suggests a legislative intent to allow a biomass tax credit for woody remains that are located in the forest or rangeland and directly related to a harvesting or thinning operation.

   2.   *Statutory context*

   That construction is also suggested by the context, which can include other provisions of the bill originally approved by the legislature, although codified in different chapters or sections of the Oregon Revised Statutes. . . . When the legislature adopted the biomass tax credit, it also specified the credit rates for each type of biomass. Or. Laws 2007, ch. 739, § 5. That provision described the credit for "woody biomass" in terms of the location from which the biomass is collected:

> "For woody biomass *collected from* nursery, orchard, agricultural, forest or rangeland property in Oregon, including but not limited to prunings, thinning, plantation rotations, log landing or slash resulting from harvest or forest health stewardship, $ 10.00 per green ton."

Or Laws 2007, ch. 739, § 5 (*Former* ORS 469.790 (2007); *renumbered as* ORS 469B.403(6) (2011)) (emphasis added). None of the other tax credit rates would cover wood waste collected from a mill. *See* ORS 469B.403. The legislature's description of the woody biomass credit rate with reference to the location from which it has been collected, in combination with the text of ORS 315.141(1)(d)(A) persuades us that the legislature intended "forest or rangeland woody debris" to mean debris collected, as debris, from the forest or rangeland.

   Warrenton argues that extending the tax credit to mill waste would be consistent with a general statement of legislative policy, adopted in 2005, which encourages the Department of Forestry to promote biofuel in conjunction with forest health. *See* ORS 526.277(3) (2005), *amended by* Or.

laws 2011, ch. 276, § 4 ("The development of biomass markets, including energy markets, that use forest biomass unsuitable for lumber, pulp and paper products as a primary source of raw material may assist in the creation of a sustainable, market-based model for restoring complexity and structure to Oregon's forests."). Warrenton may be correct that a broader range of woody biomass would be consistent with the general policy described in ORS 526.277, but that does not persuade us that the 2007 legislature intended a meaning for ORS 315.141(1)(d)(A) other than what the text and closely related statutory context suggest. . . .

3. *Legislative history*

Neither party has identified legislative history that resolves the narrow question of statutory construction at issue in this case, and we have found none. However, the limited history regarding the language of ORS 315.141(1)(d)(A) is consistent with the construction we have identified. ORS 315.141 was enacted in 2007 as part of House Bill (HB) 2210, a comprehensive biofuel bill. . . . As originally drafted, the definition of "biomass" in HB 2210 included "organic matter * * * that is derived from wood, forest, or field residues," a definition that might have reached wood waste from mill operations. . . . The ultimate language used in ORS 315.141(1)(d)(A) is the product of amendments added by the House Energy and the Environmental Committee. . . . While the bill was pending before the House Energy and the Environment Committee, the committee received written testimony from Ronald Suppah, Tribal Council Chair for the Confederated Tribes of the Warm Springs Reservation of Oregon, in support of the tax credit. . . . Suppah described the tribe's existing biomass operation, and emphasized that "a significant purpose of the biomass project is to improve forest health by providing a market for the small diameter biomass by-product from forest health projects." *Id.* However, he explained that "[f]orest health projects will typically be a more expensive source of biomass than urban wood or mill wood waste residuals because of transportation costs and because it involves intensive hand and mechanical treatments." *Id.* As a result, Suppah explained, "[i]f the Project were operated to maximize profit, the Project would use exclusively sawmill residuals and urban wood which would mean that there would not be any forest health benefits." *Id.* Thus, to allow projects "to operate profitably and at the same time maximize the forest health benefits," the Tribe recommended "market incentives in the form of tax credits, grants, green market credits which help to lower the overall cost of the Project." *Id.* We recognize that this legislative history represents the testimony of only one committee witness, but we highlight Suppah's testimony because it may explain why the legislature intended to extend the tax credit only to woody debris collected in the forests and rangelands.

III. CONCLUSION

Thus, we conclude that the legislature intended the biomass category of "[f]orest or rangeland woody debris from harvesting or thinning" to mean organic material that is debris when collected from the forest or rangeland. That definition is consistent with the challenged rule, which categorizes "residual wood waste from mill operations" as not biomass.

. . . Because we conclude that the rule is valid, we reverse.

NOTES & QUESTIONS

1. Compare the holding in the *State ex rel. Utilities Commission* with that of *Warrenton Fiber*. In *State ex rel. Utilities Commission*, wood from trees chopped down for the sole purpose of generating electricity was deemed to be biomass for purposes of North Carolina's RPS program. In *Warrenton Fiber*, residual bark from a saw mill was deemed not to be biomass under Oregon's biomass tax credit statute. As between the state statutes analyzed in these two cases, which do you think is more protective of environmental resources? Why? How (if at all) would you reconcile these two cases?

2. What is a potentially adverse unintended impact of North Carolina's biomass statute on the state's forests? How would you recommend amending the state's statute to avoid that impact?

3. The *Warrenton Fiber* court quoted testimony from a local tribal council representative as being supportive of the court's interpretation of "biomass" under the statute at issue in the case.

a. How did the representative's testimony allegedly support the court's holding?

b. Suppose you were an Oregon legislator proposing a bill that would amend Oregon's biomass tax credit statute to include coverage for sawmill byproducts. Craft an argument for why the tribe's testimony should not be viewed as persuasive on this issue.

4. *Biomass Energy Incentives and Sustainable Forest Management*. As suggested in the questions above, one argument made against the inclusion of some types of woody biomass in renewable energy incentive policies is that such inclusion might inadvertently promote deforestation. Professor Jody Endres has described this risk as follows:

Deforestation . . . accounts for seventeen percent of the world's yearly total emissions of CO_2. The onslaught of new forest biomass demand created by renewable energy policies could result in further direct and indirect conversion, releasing copious amounts of carbon into the atmosphere. This scenario calls into question the accuracy of various renewable energy policies' accounting for GHG emissions. . .

Jody Endres, *Barking Up the Wrong Tree? Forest Sustainability in the Wake of Emerging Bioenergy Policies*, 37 VT. L. REV. 763, 765 (2013). As the global demand for woody biomass grows, the tension between forest conservation and renewable energy production could potentially escalate as well.

2. BIOMASS-FUELED COGENERATION

The cases above illustrate how the characteristics of some biogenic materials make it difficult to determine to what extent they should qualify as renewables under state renewable energy policies. Similar controversies have arisen regarding certain types of energy facilities that use both biomass and non-renewable energy resources. For example, suppose operators of an existing coal-fired power plant mix biomass pellets into the coal they feed into the plant and thereby reduce the plant's coal consumption by 10 percent. Should the operators should qualify for any subsidies or credits on that basis?

Biomass-fueled *cogeneration* facilities are another type of biomass-related energy strategy that has raised controversial eligibility questions under renewable energy incentive programs. Biomass cogeneration facilities use heat generated from the burning of biomass to generate electric power while simultaneously serving one or more other functions. As shown in the case below, when developers of these facilities seek tax credits or other government benefits, courts and policymakers often must delve deeply into the details of the plant's operations to determine whether and to what degree they qualify.

W.E. PARTNERS II, LLC v. UNITED STATES
United States Court of Federal Claims, 2015
119 Fed. Cl. 684

WHEELER, D.J.

This case arises under Section 1603 of the American Recovery and Reinvestment Act of 2009, Pub. L. No. 111–5, 123 Stat. 115, 364 ("Section 1603"). Plaintiff W.E. Partners II, LLC ("WEP II") funded the construction of an open-loop biomass facility in Lewiston, North Carolina next to a Perdue chicken rendering plant to which it provides steam. The facility was designed and now operates to meet Perdue's steam needs for the chicken rendering processes. The facility includes a steam-turbine generator to produce electricity from the steam before it passes through to process the chicken. The electricity generation allows the plant to qualify for state and federal renewable energy incentives. Section 1603 provides for reimbursement of a portion of the costs incurred for "a facility using open-loop biomass to produce electricity." Internal Revenue Code ("I.R.C.") § 45(d)(3) (2012). The question presented is whether WEP II is entitled to reimbursement of a percentage of the total cost of the facility ($9,037,769), or only of the lesser costs associated with the portion of the facility necessary to produce electricity. At the prescribed 30 percent reimbursement rate, WEP II claims entitlement to $2,711,331, whereas the Department of Treasury has allowed only $943,754. The difference, $1,767,577, is in dispute. The issue is before the Court on cross-motions for summary judgment.

The question to be resolved is primarily one of statutory interpretation. While the language of the statute, if read without context or reference to agency guidance, might suggest that reimbursement based on total cost is mandatory whenever a facility uses open-loop biomass to generate electricity, the Court does not agree with such an outcome. When read in conjunction with the applicable Internal Revenue Service ("IRS") Notice and Treasury Department Guidance, the Court finds that Section 1603 requires only reimbursement for the portion of the cost that is fairly allocable to the production of electricity. Accordingly, the Court grants summary judgment in favor of Defendant.

Background

A. *W.E. Partners II and the Biomass Facility*

Plaintiff WEP II is a single-purpose limited liability company formed in 2010 to design, construct, and operate a biomass boiler facility at a Perdue chicken rendering plant in North Carolina. This biomass facility burns forest products waste (e.g., limbs, bark, sawdust, shavings) and agricultural residue (e.g., peanut and soybean hulls, cotton gin residue) to produce steam. The steam is then used for industrial manufacturing processes, to produce electricity, or both. Boiler facilities that produce steam for industrial processes are known as process steam plants, and boilers used for electrical generation are known as power generation plants. Boilers that utilize steam for both industrial processes and energy generation are known as cogeneration plants. The WEP II biomass facility is a cogeneration plant. In this cogeneration plant, the steam from a biomass boiler is routed through an electricity generating turbine before being used for other industrial processes, such as for the chicken rendering plant. The amount of electricity generated is a function of the steam flow, temperature, and pressure of the steam passing through the turbine. Pressure and temperature drop while passing through the turbine, while the steam flow remains constant. Increased steam flow or drops in temperature or pressure across the turbine increases the amount of electricity generated.

The WEP II facility uses three boilers, each with a heat input of 29.4 million Btu (mmBtu), a steam flow of 20,700 pounds per hour (pph), and a pressure of 325 pounds per square inch (psi). All steam produced by the boilers passes through a 495 kilowatt (kW) turbine that generates electricity and releases the steam at a pressure of 135 psi. This lower pressure steam can then be used in the chicken rendering plant. In total, 2.2 percent of the useful energy that the WEP II facility produces is electrical energy, and 97.8 percent is thermal energy.

B.   *Section 1603 of the American Recovery and Reinvestment Act of 2009*

President Obama signed the Recovery Act into law on February 17, 2009. Although a detailed discussion of the statute is not necessary here, the purpose of the Act was to create jobs and promote economic recovery, in part by spurring investments in specified technologies. . . .

Section 1603 of the Recovery Act permits investors in qualifying renewable energy property to apply for a reimbursement of costs in lieu of a tax credit. 123 Stat. at 364. Section 1603(a) provides that the Secretary of the Treasury "shall, subject to the requirements of this section, provide a grant to each person who places in service specified energy property to reimburse such person for a portion of the expense of such property as provided in subsection (b)." *Id*. at 364. Section 1603(b) provides that "[t]he amount of the grant . . . shall be the applicable percentage of the basis of such property." *Id*. The applicable percentage is contingent on the type of energy property placed into service. *Id*. at 364–65. Section 1603(d)(1), which is applicable here, includes "[a]ny qualified property (as defined in section 48(a)(5)(D) of the Internal Revenue Code of 1986) which is part of a qualified facility (within the meaning of section 45 of such Code)." *Id*. at 365. Section 1603(d)(1) allows a cost reimbursement of 30 percent. *Id*. at 364–65. Section 1603 uses the definitions of "qualified property" and "qualified facility" from Sections 45 and 48 of the Internal Revenue Code to describe the energy properties eligible for a 30 percent reimbursement. *Id*. at 365. . . . Section 1603 also gives the Treasury Department the authority to "recapture [ ] the appropriate percentage of the grant . . . as the Secretary of the Treasury determines appropriate" if the property "ceases to be a specified energy property." 123 Stat. at 365.

I.R.C. Section 48 provides that "the term 'qualified property' [includes] . . . (I) tangible personal property, or (II) other tangible property (not including a building or its structural components), but only if such property is used as an integral part of the qualified investment credit facility." I.R.C. § 48(a)(5)(D). As provided in Section 1603, qualified property under I.R.C. Section 48 must also be part of a qualified facility under I.R.C. Section 45. 123 Stat. at 365. For the facility at issue here, Section 45 provides that a qualified facility is "a facility using open-loop biomass to produce electricity . . . the construction of which begins before January 1, 2014." I.R.C. § 45(d)(3)(a). Qualified property of an open-loop biomass facility under Section 45 is further defined by I.R.S. Notice 2008–60:

(1) *In general.* For the purposes of § 45(d)(3), an open-loop biomass facility is a power plant consisting of all components

necessary for the production of electricity from open-loop biomass (and, if applicable, other energy sources). Thus, a qualified open-loop biomass facility includes all burners and boilers (whether or not burning open-loop biomass), any handling and delivery equipment that supplies fuel directly to and is integrated with such burners and boilers, steam headers, turbines, generators, and all other depreciable property necessary to the production of electricity. . . .

I.R.S. Notice 2008–60 § 3.01(1), 2008–30 I.R.B. 178.

The Treasury Department also promulgated guidance for Section 1603 applications, explaining that "Qualified Facility Property is property that is an integral part of a qualified facility described in IRC section 45(d) . . . (1) . . . [and for open loop biomass facilities] uses open-loop biomass to produce electricity." . . .

. . . .

C. *The Treasury Department's Review of the WEP II Section 1603 Application*

The National Renewable Energy Laboratory (NREL), a Department of Energy laboratory, assists the Treasury Department in reviewing Section 1603 applications for reimbursement. In its assessment of WEP II's Section 1603 application, the NREL calculated that a biomass boiler with a heat input of 8.4 to 11.2 mmBtu would be sufficient to power a 495 kW turbine. Thus, one of WEP II's three 29.4 mmBtu boilers would be more than sufficient to power the facility's 495 kW turbine. Accordingly, the NREL determined that one-third of the WEP II facility's costs could be attributed to electrical production and it recommended an eligible cost basis that included all costs associated with the turbine and one third of all other costs. The revised calculations indicated an eligible cost basis of $3,145,847 and a Section 1603 reimbursement of $943,754.

D. *History of Proceedings*

On June 25, 2012, WEP II submitted a Section 1603 reimbursement application for the biomass facility. WEP II claimed an eligible cost basis of $9,037,769 and requested reimbursement of $2,711,331 (30 percent of the cost basis). On December 9, 2012, the Treasury Department issued an award letter approving a reimbursement of only $943,754, which represented the cost of the turbine and one-third of all other costs, including the boilers. On December 21, 2012, WEP II sent a protest email to the Treasury Department program indicating its disagreement with the reduced award.

WEP II filed its complaint in this Court on January 22, 2013, asserting that the Government violated its mandatory obligation to award reimbursement grants in the amount of 30 percent of the eligible cost basis of a biomass facility. WEP II further asserted that the Treasury's evaluation of its application and failure to provide the 30 percent reimbursement were arbitrary and capricious. The Government answered that WEP II is not entitled to any further recovery because the reduced reimbursement correctly reflects a commensurate reduction in the facility's eligible cost basis under Section 1603. With the issues joined, WEP II filed a motion for summary judgment on June 13, 2014, and the Government filed a cross-motion for summary judgment. . . .

. . . .

. . . As a threshold matter, although neither the Government nor WEP II challenges the validity of the agency's interpretation of I.R.C. Section 45, the Court must determine whether the IRS Notice and the Treasury Guidance demand deference as agency interpretations of Section 1603.

. . . .

. . . [T]he Court finds that the Treasury Department's interpretation of Section 1603 is entitled to considerable weight as a reasonable interpretation of the statute and a reasonable limitation consistent with the intent of Congress. The Treasury Guidance properly restrains the broad language of Section 1603. Thus, under Section 1603 and the applicable guidance, the Court must determine (1) whether the WEP II facility is a "qualified facility" for Section 1603 reimbursement, (2) if the WEP II facility is a qualified facility, what property is qualifying, and (3) of the qualifying property, what costs are eligible for reimbursement.

2.   *Qualifying Facilities*

To qualify for a Section 1603 reimbursement, a facility must be a "qualifying facility" as defined in I.R.C. Section 45. § 1603(d)(1), 123 Stat. at 365. Qualifying open-loop biomass facilities include "a facility using open-loop biomass to produce electricity . . . the construction of which begins before January 1, 2014." I.R.C. § 45(d)(3)(A). The WEP II facility began construction prior to January 1, 2014 and burns biomass to produce electricity. Although there is some ambiguity as to whether Section 1603 applies to cogeneration facilities that do not qualify as combined heat and power facilities under Section 1603(d)(7), the Government does not seriously contest this issue. *See* 123 Stat. at 365. Thus, WEP II is a qualifying facility under Section 45.

3.   *Qualifying Property*

Within a qualified facility, only qualified property is eligible for Section 1603 reimbursement. Section 1603(d)(1) uses the definition of qualified property contained in I.R.C. Section 48. § 1603(d)(1), 123 Stat. at 365. The provision at issue here provides that qualified property means "tangible personal property" or "tangible property (not including a building or its structural components), but only if such property is used as an integral part of the qualified investment credit facility." I.R.C. § 48(a)(5)(D). I.R.S. Notice 2008–60 further defines qualifying property as all "components necessary for the production of electricity from open-loop biomass." § 3.01(1). Finally, the Treasury Guidance defines qualifying property as "property that is an integral part of a qualified facility." Treasury Guidance at 12–13.

WEP II asserts there is no evidence that "the facility must be one whose 'primary function' is to produce electricity." Pl.'s Mot. Summ. J. 5. However, as clarified by Notice 2008–60, only those components necessary for the production of electricity are qualified property. . . .

The Government contends that not all components of the WEP II facility are qualifying property because WEP II is primarily a steam facility and includes boilers that are not necessary for the production of electricity. The Government bases this conclusion on its calculation that 495 kW of electricity could be produced with a heat input of 8.4 to 11.2 mmBtu, or approximately one-third of the heat produced by WEP II's three-boiler system. The Government does not, however, identify any property in the WEP II facility that remains unused in the production of electricity. . . . [A]lthough the WEP II facility's boilers produce both nonqualifying thermal energy and qualifying electrical energy, all steam produced by the boilers and passing through the turbine contributes to the generation of electricity. Therefore, every part of the facility is qualifying property necessary to the production of that electricity. . . . All three boilers send steam through the turbine, and thus all three boilers are necessary to the production of electricity generated therefrom.

. . . Thus, all of the WEP II property is qualifying property. Nonetheless, as described below, only a portion of the qualifying property's costs are eligible for Section 1603 reimbursement.

4. *Eligible Cost Basis*

. . . .

. . . Pursuant to the Treasury Guidance, the Treasury Department determined that 8.4 and 11.2 mmBtu of steam would be sufficient to generate 495 kW, the amount produced by WEP II's turbine. Thus, one of WEP II's three 29.4 mmBtu boilers reasonably could be allocated to the qualifying activity of generating electricity. Based on these calculations, the Treasury Department awarded WEP II a 30 percent reimbursement for the full cost of the turbine and one-third of all other costs. In light of the WEP II facility's substantial thermal energy production and comparatively small electrical generation, the Court concludes that the Treasury Department's determination of the WEP II facility's eligible cost basis is a reasonable allocation of the costs between the generation of qualifying electrical energy and nonqualifying thermal energy.

Conclusion

For the reasons set forth above, the Court finds in favor of the Defendant. Plaintiff's motion for summary judgment is DENIED, and Defendant's cross-motion for summary judgment is GRANTED. . . .

────────────

NOTES & QUESTIONS

1.   Under what theory did WEP II believe it was entitled to reimbursement of a greater percentage of the cost of its biomass cogeneration facility?

2.   Why do you think the Treasury Department enlists NREL officials for help in reviewing Section 1603 tax reimbursement applications, even though the NREL has no expertise in tax policy? Why do you think the court deferred to the Treasury's determinations regarding WEP II's qualifying reimbursement amount rather than making its own judgment on the issue?

3.   Suppose WEP II had no biomass facility and therefore produced all of the steam for its chicken rendering plant with an electric water heating system that ran solely on power generated at a nearby coal-fired power plant. Would reliance on that electric water heating system instead of the WEP II biomass facility have resulted in just $1/3$ more coal-generated electricity generation, or would it have resulted in even more coal-fired power generation than that? Building on your answer, craft a policy argument on behalf of WEP II that *all* of its biomass facility (not merely $1/3$ of it) should qualify under the Section 1603 30% reimbursement provisions.

3.   WASTE-TO-ENERGY FACILITIES

Trash is a unique class of partially-biogenic material that, like wood or grass, is capable of being burned to generate electric power. Supplies of garbage are arguably "renewable" in the sense that incinerating them rather than dumping them into landfills does not generally reduce the quantity of future garbage available for such uses. Still, certain adverse environmental impacts of *waste-to-energy* (WTE) facilities—power plants that burn trash to generate electricity—make WTE a controversial practice. The excerpt below describes WTE facilities, the ways that state governments across the United States presently treat them, and some common objections to this controversial type of renewable energy strategy. Following the article is a case addressing a dispute between an environmental advocacy group and Arizona energy regulators over the proper classification of a WTE facility under a renewable energy policy in that state.

GARBAGE, POWER, AND ENVIRONMENTAL JUSTICE: THE CLEAN POWER PLAN RULE

Ana Israel Baptista & Kumar Kartik Amarnath
41 WM. & MARY ENVTL. L. & POL'Y REV. 403, 404–07, 411–13 & 418–21 (2017)

The environmental justice ("EJ") movement in the United States is intimately tied to the siting of waste disposal facilities like hazardous waste landfills, trash transfer stations, and municipal solid waste incinerators. Since watershed moments like the Warren County landfill protests, where an African-American community resisted the waste industry's targeting tactics to the infamous leaked Cerrell memo in California, the concentration and co-location of waste-related activities in communities of color and low income communities has largely defined the relationship between waste, class, and race. Garbage incinerator facilities follow a similar trajectory of other waste-related proposals in that they are often sited in close proximity to communities of color and low-income communities, thereby contributing to an already disproportionate environmental burden for these communities.

Waste incineration has taken many forms over the last thirty years. In the 1960s and 1970s, as federal and state regulations around waste disposal into landfills became more stringent and landfill space was becoming increasingly limited, incinerators became perceived as a viable alternative for waste disposal. In the 1990s, the deregulation of interstate waste exportation further fueled the creation of larger regional waste facilities controlled by private companies who sought to rebrand themselves as "Waste-to-Energy" ("WTE") facilities rather than "resource recovery facilities." . . . These facilities attracted trash from a larger regional waste-shed and aggressively pursued new opportunities for federal and state subsidies related to renewable energy. These facilities have been marketed and sold to municipalities and the public as technologically advanced approaches to handling all manner of solid waste with the added bonus of producing energy from the steam generated by burning garbage. But incinerator facilities in fact produce large amounts of air pollution such as nitrogen oxides ("NOx"), particulate matter ("PM"), dioxin, furans, as well as carbon dioxide ("CO_2"). . . .

. . . .

Although local opposition to new incinerator proposals in the last twenty years has been largely successful, this industry continues to evolve new mechanisms to capture financial incentives and secure waste contracts that maintain their dominance in local and regional waste management systems. Recent proposals for incinerator facilities in places like Baltimore, Maryland, and Arecibo, Puerto Rico, demonstrate the continued targeting of low income and communities of color for new facility siting. The incineration industry continues to seek inclusion into state Renewable

Portfolio Standards ("RPS") where they can capture renewable energy subsidies. There are currently twenty-one states where incinerators are considered "renewable energy" under state RPS programs. . . .

> . . . .

. . . The U.S. EPA suggests that biomass and biogenic derived CO_2 should be considered carbon neutral because it is a part of the existing carbon cycle that releases CO_2 naturally. This rationale is countered by various stakeholders that point to the problem of time scales related to the carbon cycle. . . .

> . . . .

. . . The United Nations Environment Programme ("UNEP") diverges from the U.S. EPA in its analysis of the life cycle logic of biogenic CO_2:

> Climate change is time-critical—it is widely accepted that immediate reductions in global GHG emissions are essential to reduce the impact of climate change. The atmosphere does not differentiate between a molecule of biogenic CO_2 and a molecule of fossil-derived CO_2, therefore it appears logical that immediate efforts should be made to minimize emissions of all CO_2 regardless of source.

Additionally, combustion of MSW and biomass releases more carbon dioxide than coal and natural gas on a per kilowatt-hour basis. The U.S. EPA estimates incinerators emit more CO_2 per unit of electricity (2,988 lbs/MWH) than coal-fired power plants (2,249 lbs/MWH). . . . This makes waste a very poor fuel source for power generation. . . .

> . . . .

While estimates vary on the exact proportion of MSW waste that is considered biogenic, generally non-biogenic waste, particularly plastics, have increased as a proportion of total waste over the last two decades in the U.S. . . .

Estimates from the EIA suggest that 50–60% of municipal solid waste is biogenic and that "[t]he biogenic material in MSW contributed about 52% of the energy from MSW that was burned in electricity generating waste-to-energy facilities." But the heat content of the many types of biogenic waste varies widely as does the overall biogenic proportion of the waste stream. For example, increased packaging in materials discarded during periods of high consumption (e.g., Christmas) and the uneven diversion rates of organics across regions can significantly diverge from averages reported annually or statewide. . . .

There are currently eighty-four WTE facilities in the US across twenty-one states. Some of the recent battles over new incinerator development proposals are located in low income and communities of color in Puerto Rico and Maryland where they have been opposed by local communities invoking environmental injustice.

SIERRA CLUB—GRAND CANYON CHAPTER V. ARIZONA CORP. COMM'N

Court of Appeals of Arizona, Div. 1, 2015
354 P.3d 1127

OROZCO, J.

This appeal concerns the development of a proposed "waste-to-energy" (WTE) facility, which would generate electricity by burning landfill waste, and the classification of electrical power that would be produced by the proposed facility. The Arizona Constitution grants the Arizona Corporation Commission (the Commission) broad power to "prescribe just and reasonable" classifications and rates for services rendered by public service corporations. Ariz. Const. art. 15, § 3. We review the scope of that authority and the deference due a Commission decision, later vacated by the superior court, granting approval for the proposed WTE facility. For the reasons that follow, we reverse the superior court's decision and reinstate the Commission's decision to the extent it grants an application by Mohave Electric Cooperative, Inc. (Mohave) for a waiver to the Renewable Energy Standard and Tariff (REST) rules.

FACTS AND PROCEDURAL BACKGROUND

Arizona public utility corporations providing electricity are subject to the REST rules promulgated in Arizona Administrative Code (A.A.C.) sections R14–2–1801, *et seq.* These rules require affected corporations "to satisfy an Annual Renewable Energy Requirement by obtaining Renewable Energy Credits [(Credits)] from Eligible Renewable Energy Resources." A.A.C. R–14–2–1804.A. A Credit is obtained for each kilowatt-hour "derived from an Eligible Renewable Energy Resource." A.A.C. R14–2–1803.A. Although specific Eligible Renewable Energy Resources are listed in the rules, the Commission "may adopt pilot programs in which additional technologies are established as Eligible Renewable Energy Resources." A.A.C. R14–2–1802.D. The Commission also "may waive compliance with any provision of [the REST rules] for good cause." A.A.C. R14–2–1816.A.

Mohave filed an application asking the Commission to either (1) recognize a proposed WTE facility as a "pilot program," or (2) waive the REST rules for the proposed facility "to the limited extent necessary to recognize energy produced [by the] facility as an 'Eligible Renewable Energy Resource.'" Mohave's application stated that Reclamation Power Group, LLC (RPG), which intended to develop, own, and operate the proposed WTE facility in Maricopa County, could not provide "economically viable" power unless the Commission classified the municipal solid waste that would be used as fuel by the facility as a Credit-eligible "Renewable Energy Resource." Appellee, Sierra Club-Grand Canyon Chapter (Sierra Club) successfully intervened to oppose Mohave's application.

The Commission's Utilities Division (Staff) produced a report on Mohave's application and drafted a recommended decision. The report stated that Mohave had provided Staff with a "breakdown, by category" of a waste sample from a landfill that Mohave claimed was representative of the waste composition the WTE facility would burn as fuel if the facility became operational. The report discussed how the Mohave "breakdown" showed ninety-five percent of the waste consisted of "biogenic material." The Staff report concluded that burning waste of this composition would mean "the biogenic material contributes about [ninety-one] percent of the energy to the process while non-biogenic materials contribute about [nine] percent[.]" The report suggested that the ninety-one percent figure was high in relation to the results of other studies. As a result, Staff recommended that the Commission not grant "pilot program" status and instead grant a good-cause waiver of the REST rules to allow seventy-five percent of the kilowatts produced by the facility to be Credit-eligible "as being produced by an Eligible Renewable Energy Resource."

Both Mohave and Sierra Club filed exceptions to the Staff recommendation. Following an open meeting, the Commission held a three-day evidentiary hearing before an administrative law judge (ALJ). . . . Following the evidentiary hearing, the Commission adopted most of the Staff findings and recommended decision, with two important changes: the Commission (1) granted the WTE facility "pilot program" status under the REST rules . . . and (2) granted Credits for ninety percent of the kilowatt hours that would be produced by the facility.

Sierra Club petitioned for a rehearing, which the Commission granted. . . . Following the rehearing, the Commission affirmed its initial decision "in its entirety." The Commission denied Sierra Club's petition for rehearing on that decision.

Sierra Club then sought review of the Commission's decision in superior court. . . . Following briefing and oral argument, the superior court vacated the Commission's decision, stating that "the authorities and arguments provided by [Sierra Club] are well-taken, and this Court adopts those authorities and arguments in support of its decision." The superior court further awarded Sierra Club its attorney fees and costs. After entry of judgment by the superior court, this timely appeal followed. . . .

      . . . .

In entering judgment in favor of Sierra Club, the superior court made the following determinations:

1. The Corporation Commission's [REST] rules do not allow [m]unicipal [s]olid [w]aste . . . as an eligible renewable energy resource and, therefore, waste-to-energy facilities using [municipal solid waste] are not eligible as a pilot program under the rules;

2. The proposed [WTE] facility does not qualify for a waiver from the requirements of the REST rules because good cause was not established for a waiver and a waiver would be inconsistent with the exclusion of [municipal solid waste] as an eligible renewable resource under the rules; and

3. There was no credible evidence to support the Commission's determination that 90% of the electricity from the proposed [WTE] facility would come from biogenic sources.

We analyze these conclusions in turn.

A.   The Superior Court's Interpretation of the REST Rules

The superior court's first two conclusions construe and interpret the REST rules. We therefore review them de novo to the extent necessary to resolve this appeal. . . .

As previously noted, the REST rules require affected utility corporations "to satisfy an Annual Renewable Energy Requirement by obtaining [Credits] from Eligible Renewable Energy Resources." A.A.C. R14–2–1804.A. The rules generally define "Eligible Renewable Energy Resources" as "applications of . . . technologies that displace Conventional Energy Resources that would otherwise be used to provide electricity to an Affected Utility's Arizona customers[.]" A.A.C. R14–2–1802.A. A "Conventional Energy Resource" is defined as "an energy resource that is non-renewable in nature, such as natural gas, coal, oil, and uranium, or electricity that is produced with energy resources that are not Renewable Energy Resources." A.A.C. R14–2–1801.C. By express provision in the REST rules, "[t]he Commission may waive compliance with any provision of [the REST rules] for good cause." A.A.C. R14–2–1816.A.

Sierra Club asserts the superior court correctly found that good cause for a waiver was not established. . . .

. . . .

Although the Commission granted Mohave's application for pilot program status, the Commission also acknowledged that an "independent and alternative basis" existed to grant Mohave a waiver of the REST rules. This conclusion was consistent with the Staff recommendation that the Commission grant Mohave a waiver. In its recommendation, Staff

700 OTHER RENEWABLE ENERGY STRATEGIES CH. 8

emphasized the experimental nature of WTE facilities and concluded that "the potential benefits [of a WTE facility] outweigh the potential consequences, especially when compared to the alternative of landfilling [municipal solid waste]." Staff maintained this position throughout the Commission's proceedings.

On this record, we cannot conclude that Sierra Club showed by clear and satisfactory evidence that good cause for a waiver was not established. Much of the evidence presented to the Commission may be characterized as a debate over the degree to which municipal solid waste used as fuel for WTE facilities may be considered "renewable." Given the Commission's constitutional authority over these matters, the Commission is ultimately charged with evaluating such issues and, as such, is the best-equipped branch of government to do so. Although meaningful judicial review requires that courts make their own legal determinations, courts properly must exercise a more deferential review towards discretionary matters "constitutionally entrusted to the Commission." *See U.S. W. Commc'n, Inc. v. Ariz. Corp. Comm'n,* 185 Ariz. 277, 280, 915 P.2d 1232 (App. 1996).

Irrespective of whether the use of municipal solid waste as fuel makes a WTE facility eligible for pilot program status, the REST rules do not explicitly exclude energy produced from municipal solid waste, or at least those portions that may be considered "renewable," from being considered Credit-eligible if the Commission waives the REST rules for good cause. To the extent this involves construing the REST rules, we conclude only that the Commission retained the discretion to issue a good cause waiver of the rules. The Staff report and testimony stating that a WTE facility could provide substantial benefit to Arizona's utility infrastructure provided sufficient good cause to issue such a waiver. The superior court's conclusion that the Commission could not waive the REST rules because it "would be inconsistent with the exclusion of [municipal solid waste] as an eligible renewable resource under the rules" is neither supported by the plain language of the REST rules nor by clear and satisfactory evidence in this record.

B. The Superior Court's "No Credible Evidence" Conclusion

We next turn to the superior court's conclusion that no credible evidence supported the Commission's determination allowing ninety percent of the municipal solid waste that will be used as fuel by the WTE facility to be considered a "renewable energy source." Because this conclusion "disturbed" the Commission's decision, we must determine whether the superior court's conclusion is supported by "clear and satisfactory evidence." *See Tucson Elec. Power Co.,* 132 Ariz. at 243, 645 P.2d 231.

Similar to an appellate court's general deference to trial courts on credibility determinations and the weighing of evidence, the Commission is also entitled to deference when "the [C]ommission's ultimate conclusion or findings of facts [are] supported by substantial evidence, is not arbitrary or is not otherwise unlawful." *Simms v. Round Valley Light & Power Co.*, 80 Ariz. 145, 154, 294 P.2d 378 (1956). . . .

The two evidentiary hearings before the Commission involved significant amounts of live testimony as well as written exhibits. Seven witnesses testified at the first hearing and nine at the second. In its initial recommendation, Staff stated that data received from Mohave, which was considered in formulating the Staff recommendation, showed the municipal solid waste that would be used by the proposed WTE facility would be composed of an estimated ninety-five percent biogenic (renewable) material. Staff deduced that burning municipal solid waste of such composition would mean ninety-one percent of the energy produced by the facility would be produced by renewable sources. However, Staff also noted that the ninety-five percent figure submitted by Mohave was high in relation to data about waste composition collected from other WTE facilities throughout the United States. Staff thus recommended seventy-five percent of any energy produced by the WTE facility be deemed Credit-eligible.

After Mohave filed exceptions to the Staff recommendation, one Commissioner proposed an amendment that generated the ninety percent figure, with an additional provision that could reduce the percentage based on what Staff might discover from Mohave's mandatory semi-annual reports. At the first evidentiary hearing, a Staff representative testified that Staff had recommended the seventy-five percent figure because "we feel, since [the WTE facility] is an experiment or pilot . . . you might want to choose the more conservative estimate of the [seventy-five] percent. But that's, obviously . . . a call for the Commission." At the second evidentiary hearing, a different Staff representative testified that the ninety percent figure was "within the range . . . calculated based on the samples provided by Mohave" and that "it would be a reasonable starting figure," as would Staff's recommendation of seventy-five percent.

At the second evidentiary hearing, Ronald Blendu testified about the data Mohave submitted to Staff. Blendu stated that the data was generated from 15,300 pounds of trash collected from a municipal area in western Maricopa County. The trash was sorted "into various categories" to give RPG an idea of "what the fuel supply would [be to] go into the [WTE facility]." . . .

Given this evidence in the Commission record, the superior court improperly reweighed the evidence in concluding no credible evidence existed to support the ninety percent figure adopted by the Commission . . . Sierra Club contends that the Commission's decision was based on speculative evidence that "defied credibility." But in doing so, Sierra Club merely claims the data produced by Mohave and relied upon by Staff is an apparent outlier among similar data collections around the United States. . . .

. . . By establishing procedures to report on the actual composition of municipal solid waste used as fuel once the WTE facility became operational, the Commission implicitly acknowledged that future Credit eligibility may require adjustment depending on the data collected. Because the facility is not operational, no data on its fuel consumption currently exists, and the Commission was faced with deciding Mohave's application using projections and historical data from other facilities across the country. . . . without new evidence showing Mohave was deceptive in producing its data or it was impossible, not just improbable, that the proposed WTE facility would produce ninety percent of its power from a renewable energy source, the superior court was bound by the Commission's factual findings.

CONCLUSION

We conclude the Commission was acting within the REST rules' purview by granting a waiver to Mohave for the WTE facility. We also conclude substantial evidence supported the Commission's determination that ninety percent of energy produced by the WTE facility would be eligible for Credits, contingent upon the reporting requirements and adjustments required by the Commission's decision. Accordingly, we reverse the judgment of the superior court and reinstate the Commission's decision as necessary to be consistent with this decision. Because we reverse the superior court's judgment, we set aside the award of attorney fees to Sierra Club.

NOTES & QUESTIONS

1.   What is *environmental justice*, and on what ground do the authors of the article excerpt above believe Waste-to-Energy facilities create environmental justice concerns?

2.   How do the EPA and UNEP differ in their views about the carbon neutrality of biomass and other biogenic materials? Whose views do you think are most correct, and why?

3.   How do the Energy Information Administration's estimates (cited in the article excerpt above) regarding the proportion of landfill waste that is biogenic differ from the utility-provided estimates in *Sierra Club—Grand Canyon*? How would you defend this difference if you represented the utility in that case?

4.   In *Sierra Club-Grand Canyon*, why was it so important to the utility that its waste be classified as renewable under Arizona's REST standard?

What would have likely happened to the landfill waste at issue in the case if the utility had lost the lawsuit and none of the waste had been deemed eligible under the REST standard? Do your answers affect your view of whether the case was rightly decided? Why or why not?

5.   *Landfill Methane as a Renewable Resource.* A somewhat less controversial waste-to-energy strategy involves the capturing of methane gas from landfills and burning that gas to generate electricity. Landfills emit large amounts of methane gas as trash deteriorates over time. These emissions are especially troubling because the adverse greenhouse effects of methane emissions are far more severe than those of carbon dioxide emissions. According to the EPA's website, municipal solid waste is the third-largest source of anthropogenic methane gas emissions in the country. *See Basic Information about Landfill Gas*, US EPA, https://www.epa.gov/lmop/basic-information-about-landfill-gas#two-a (last visited Oct. 1, 2017). Fortunately, a growing number of landfills in the United States are capturing methane gas and burning it to generate energy. As of June 2017, there were already landfill gas energy projects at more than 60% of the nation's 1000+ landfill sites. *See id.* As of that time, developers of landfill gas energy projects could also qualify for federal production tax credits and for credits under renewable portfolio standards in dozens of states across the country. *See Resources for Funding Landfill Gas Energy Projects*, US EPA, https://www.epa.gov/lmop/resources-funding-landfill-gas-energy-projects (last visited July 31, 2017).

C.   RENEWABLE ENERGY IN TRANSPORTATION

Yet another important strategy for helping the nation transition toward a more sustainable energy system is to promote greater use of renewables in the transportation sector. Transportation activities account for more than a quarter of all energy consumption in the United States each year. For over 100 years, the vast majority of those transportation activities have involved automobiles and other vehicles that run primarily on petroleum-based products such as gasoline or diesel fuel.

As concerns grow about the climate change impacts, smog problems, national security risks, and other adverse consequences of the transportation sector's dependence on petroleum, support for cleaner and more renewable transportation energy strategies is growing as well. The nation is gradually shifting away from petroleum as its primary transportation energy source and legislators, lawyers, and courts are slowly tackling the myriad legal and policy issues arising from this transition. The following materials focus on just a few of the numerous thorny questions associated with this progression toward cleaner, more sustainable sources of transportation energy.

1. TRANSPORTATION POWERED BY BIOFUELS AND BIOGASES

The most prominent sources of renewable transportation energy today are biofuels and biogases. *Biofuels* are liquid fuels originating from recently-living organisms and include ethanol, algae fuel, and other biogenic liquids. For reasons explained below, corn-based ethanol has long been the most substantial source of renewable transportation energy in the United States. *Biogases* are gases produced from the breakdown of sewage, manure, food, or other recently-generated organic waste. Refined biogases are increasingly fueling vehicles designed to run on compressed natural gas.

Since the earliest days of the automobile, engineers have been producing demonstration vehicles that run on renewable liquid or gaseous energy sources instead of conventional petroleum products such as diesel fuel or unleaded gasoline. Policymakers have also been heavily subsidizing the biofuels industry for roughly half a century in hopes of accelerating the advancement of biofuel technologies and enabling the nation to become less dependent on foreign oil. These investments by governments and private companies have enabled biofuels to become a substantial source of renewable transportation energy throughout the country.

The most common type of biofuel in the world is corn-based ethanol. Ethanol is generally considered a renewable energy product because most ethanol fuel products are derived from corn—a fast growing and widely-available agricultural crop. Nearly every gasoline-powered vehicle on the road in the United States today is running at least partially on ethanol. Most of the unleaded gasoline products sold throughout the country are "E10" fuels, meaning they are comprised of roughly 10% ethanol and 90% gasoline. The engines of most automobiles sold in the United States are designed to operate on this mix of ethanol and gas. Unquestionably, the federal government policies that have led to the predominance of E10 unleaded gasoline have made the nation's transportation energy mix more renewable.

In recent years, some policymakers have advocated for even greater use of ethanol in gas-powered vehicles. For instance, a growing number of Americans own flex fuel cars, which are specially designed to run on fuel that consists of up to 85% ethanol and as little as 15% gasoline, and some government programs encourage the purchase and use of such vehicles. In 2011, the EPA also approved the use of 15% ethanol (or "E15") gasoline products in most automobiles with model years of 2001 or newer. However, not all stakeholders are in favor of expanding the use of ethanol in automobiles. In fact, some have argued that E15 gasoline may actually harm many of the vehicles for which it the EPA approved its use.

At times, the federal government's subsidization and favorable treatment of biofuel producers has drawn criticism from stakeholders, politicians and the public. Subsidies and other programs that increase demand for corn-based ethanol are among the most common targets of these critics. Despite the billions of dollars in subsidies that governments have paid to biofuels researchers and producers over the years, most of the nation's transportation activities still run on fossil fuels. To some, continuing to heavily subsidize the nation's corn-based ethanol industry is no longer justifiable given that decades of favorable policy treatment have produced only modest successes.

In 2015, the EPA drew strong opposition when it interpreted provisions of the Energy Policy Act as allowing the agency to soften certain federal renewable fuel targets in ways that seemingly treated corn-based ethanol as the only viable type of renewable vehicle fuel. This EPA action generated significant controversy and ultimately resulted in litigation over the scope of the agency's discretionary authority in this area of the law. In the following excerpt, Professor Arnold Reitze describes the nation's federal biofuel policies and ultimately argues that such policies have been excessively favorable to agricultural interests. Following the article is a case analyzing a legal challenge to the EPA's 2015 regulatory action.

BIOFUEL AND ADVANCED BIOFUEL
Arnold W. Reitze
33 UCLA J. ENVTL. L. & POL'Y 309, 310–63 (2015) (excerpts)

I. INTRODUCTION

Early in the 20th Century, it was recognized that ethanol was not just for drinking, but could be used to power vehicles. In 1908, ethanol was used to fuel the Model T Ford. In 1925, Henry Ford called ethyl alcohol the fuel of the future. He also believed converting corn into alcohol would help ease the economic crisis for farmers that would later morph into the Great Depression. Thus began the concept of using motor vehicle fuel policy to subsidize farmers. . . .

In 1973 the Arab members of the Organization of Petroleum Exporting Countries (OPEC) imposed an embargo on petroleum exports to the United States. This led to Congress developing an interest in supporting a renewable fuel industry. Renewable fuel is defined as "fuel that is produced from renewable biomass and that is used to replace or reduce the quantity of fossil fuel present in a transportation fuel," or "in home heating oil or jet fuel." In 1974 the Solar Energy Research Development and Demonstration Act provided support for research and development of conversion of cellulose into fuel. The Clean Air Act (CAA) Amendments of 1977 expanded EPA's authority to regulate fuels. In the 1980s, however, nearly all the limited federal support went to incentivize ethanol production from corn.

This resulted in a rapid expansion of ethanol production with over 100 corn alcohol production plants by the mid-1980s. Subsequently, most ethanol plants closed due to a worldwide over supply of petroleum at a relatively low price.

The CAA Amendments of 1990 provided a boost for ethanol production, by requiring the use of oxygenated fuels during the winter in 39 carbon monoxide nonattainment areas. Additional oxygen in fuel, which alcohol can supply, improves combustion. The 1990 CAA Amendments also required the production of reformulated gasoline (RFG) that met specified chemical requirements, including having an oxygen content equal to or greater than two percent by weight. RFG was to be used in nine specified severe ozone nonattainment areas and in other severe ozone nonattainment areas that might be subsequently designated.

II.   RENEWABLE REQUIREMENTS

The Energy Policy Act of 2005 (2005 EPAct) was the first federal law that required motorists to purchase first generation renewable biofuel blends (RFS1), which used corn and soybeans as the feedstock. The EPAct also amended CAA § 211(k) to eliminate the oxygenate requirement for RFG, but added renewable fuel requirements that were codified in a new CAA § 211(*o*). On May 1, 2007, EPA promulgated regulations to implement the 2005 EPAct. The Energy Independence and Security Act of 2007 (EISA) significantly modified the EPAct's renewable fuel requirements. EISA increased the mandatory use of renewable fuel. The renewable fuel volume requirements were expanded to include all transportation fuel except fuel for ocean-going vessels. . . .

. . . .

The renewable fuel requirements call for 4 billion gallons of renewable fuel to be used in gasoline in 2006 and the amount increases in steps each year to 36 billion gallons in 2022. Thereafter EPA will set the applicable annual volumes. Renewable fuels include ethanol produced from grain, starch, oilseeds, vegetable, animal or fish materials, sugarcane, sugar beets, sugar components, tobacco, potatoes, or other biomass. Renewable fuels also include natural gas from biogas sources, cellulosic ethanol, and biodiesel from plant or animal wastes. EPA periodically approves feedstock and processes that can be used to produce renewable fuel that satisfies the requirements of CAA section 211(*o*). For example, on December 17, 2012, EPA approved ethanol from grain sorghum as a renewable fuel, and if approved processes are used, it qualifies as an advanced biofuel. Approved fuels and processes are codified at 40 C.F.R. § 80.1426.

. . . .

III. THE ADVERSE EFFECTS OF USING ETHANOL AS FUEL

Modern monoculture agriculture provides the benefits of increased yields and economies of scale, but it also entails adverse environmental impacts. Using corn and other food crops for biofuel and biodiesel production exacerbates the adverse environmental impacts that are associated with commodity crop agriculture. Much of the adverse environmental impact of ethanol use is attributable to corn production, which is discussed below. However, since neither farmers nor food consumers pay for these negative externalities, there is little incentive to effectively control them. The 2013 corn crop of 13.99 billion bushels set a new production record that was 700 million bushels higher than the previous record set in 2009. An estimated 4.9 billion bushels of corn was used to produce about 13.8 billion gallons of ethanol, which is about one-third of the crop. The ethanol industry, however, says that on a net basis only 22 percent of the crop is used for ethanol because ethanol production results in the production of a high-energy animal feed byproduct. In 2014, corn production increased again with an estimated 14.2 billion bushels. Five million bushels of corn were used to produce ethanol fuel, which is claimed to be enough food to feed the entire population of the Western Hemisphere outside the United States.

. . . .

The United States in 2014 produced more than 58 percent of the world's ethanol and Brazil produced about 25 percent. Ethanol production dominates biofuel production in the U.S. through 187 cornstarch processing facilities, located primarily in Iowa, Nebraska, Minnesota, Indiana, and Illinois. . . .

. . . .

B. *Net Energy*

A theoretical benefit from the use of renewable fuel is that its combustion leads to lower GHG emissions, particularly CO_2, than combustion of fossil fuel having equivalent energy. Ethanol has about two-thirds the energy of an equal volume of gasoline, so more of it needs to be combusted to power motor vehicles. The lower energy content therefore results in a ten percent ethanol blend having a two to three percent decrease in miles per gallon (mpg) compared to pure gasoline.

A CO_2 reduction benefit is dependent on renewable energy having significantly more energy than the fossil fuel energy used to produce it. For ethanol, its input carbon from corn produces no net atmospheric CO_2 increase when combusted. But, the fossil fuel energy used to produce ethanol releases CO_2 that nullifies GHG reduction benefits. However, some ethanol plants purify their CO_2 emissions and sell them to the carbonated beverage industry or to food processors for flash freezing. Output-input studies are used to evaluate the net energy from using ethanol as fuel. These studies are heavily influenced by assumptions concerning corn yields per acre, the energy requirements for fertilizer manufacture, the amount of fertilizer applied to corn fields, the energy embodied in farm machinery, the efficiency of the ethanol conversion process selected, and the energy inputs attributable to the co-products produced.

. . . .

C.   *Water*

The increasing demand for ethanol will require expanding the use of scarce water resources if increased production is to be achieved. Nearly 60 percent of the world's water is used for agriculture; adding water for crops to be used as fuel stresses this limited resource. It requires as much as 30 gallons of water to produce enough corn ethanol to drive an average car one mile. The petroleum industry argues that to produce a barrel of ethanol from corn requires about 50,000 gallons of water, but producing a barrel of oil using fracking technology requires 50 gallons. . . .

. . . .

D.   *Land Use*

Agricultural land devoted to corn production has increased substantially due to the demand created by CAA mandates as well as by federal and state subsidies. In 2014, 91.6 million acres of corn and 84.1 million acres of soybeans were planted, up 11 percent in one year. In 2000, 72.7 million acres were harvested for corn and 72.7 million acres were harvested for soybeans.

. . . .

E.   *Cost of Food*

The mandated use of ethanol for fuel and the billions of dollars provided in government subsidies benefits the corn producers and to a lesser extent soybean farmers, but livestock and poultry farmers complain that the demand for corn-based ethanol increases their costs for feed corn. Some food consumer groups also believe ethanol production raises food prices. The National Council of Chain Restaurants in 2012 claimed the renewable fuel standard costs restaurant chains up to $3.2 billion a year. Restaurant owners have joined the petroleum industry in calling for a repeal of the renewable fuel standard. . . .

. . . .

IV.   ADVANCED BIOFUELS

. . . .

Advanced biofuel is a subset of renewable fuel. It is ethanol not derived from corn that has fifty percent or less lifecycle greenhouse gas (GHG) emissions than the gasoline or diesel it is replacing. Advanced biofuel can be produced from sugarcane, sugar beets, raw sugar, cane molasses, other molasses, wheat grain, sweet sorghum, Jerusalem artichokes, and other grains. It also may include ethanol produced from waste, biomass-based diesel, biogas from renewable biomass, butanol or other alcohols produced from renewable biomass, and fuel derived from cellulosic ethanol. . . .

. . . .

Ethanol produced from cellulose or other non-food inputs is a promising source of biofuels. . . Fast growing woody crops such as hybrid willow and poplar have the potential to be feedstock for cellulosic fuel. Another potential feedstock is perennial grass, such as switchgrass or Giant Miscanthus. Switchgrass is a perennial Midwest and Southeast grass with nearly three times the yield of hay. . . .

An advantage of using cellulosic feedstock is that it can be grown on marginal or degraded land that can provide increased regional agricultural income without utilizing land used for food production. Moreover, cellulosic feedstocks require less pesticides and fertilizer than corn-based ethanol. However, demand for cellulosic ethanol could result in adverse impacts on forests if they were cut to produce fuel or converted to plantations of fast growing trees. Other environmental concerns include the potential for soil erosion, soil quality degradation, loss of wildlife habitat, the introduction of non-native plant species, and nutrient releases to water bodies. . . .

. . . .

One of the more promising feedstocks for long-term biofuel development is simple-cell algae. Algae requires little land to produce commercial quantities of oil compared to other feedstock, and it can produce 55 times the oil produced by soybeans from a given acreage. To meet half the nation's transportation fuel requirements from soybean-based biodiesel would require three times the arable land in the United States, but algae-based biodiesel could produce the same amount with less than three percent of the land. A significant limitation on the use of this technology will be its requirements for water. Algae produced in an open pond can require up to 3,650 gallons of water for each gallon of gasoline-equivalent fuel as well as needing inputs of large quantities of nitrogen and phosphorus. The water could be recycled wastewater, however, which could also provide needed nitrogen and phosphorus. The conversion process uses carbon dioxide as a nutrient, which could be an input from electric power plants or other industrial sources for commercial levels of algae biofuel production. . . In the short-term, commercialization of algae based fuel will be limited due to its cost. The biofuel industry, however, believes the cost to produce algae-based fuel will be competitive with petroleum-based fuel by 2020.

VI. BIOFUEL SUBSIDIES

To create an ethanol market, federal, state, and local governments provide subsidies to the ethanol industry. The first federal tax exemption for mixtures of gasoline and ethanol (gasohol) was provided by the Energy Tax Act of 1978. The first tax credit for biodiesel was enacted in 2004. Since 1978, the tax benefits provided to the biofuel industry have been modified many times. . . .

Although the biofuel subsidies have cost billions of dollars, it is difficult to precisely quantify them because both the recipients and Congress benefit from keeping subsidies hidden from budgetary scrutiny and obscuring who receives the benefits. . . .

These subsidies go primarily to the largest corporations producing ethanol. The five largest ethanol producers were responsible for more than 40 percent of the 13.8 billion gallons of ethanol produced in 2011. . . .

. . . .

In addition to tax benefits, Congress provides grants, loans, and loan guarantees to the biofuel industry. . . .

The most important subsidy for the biofuel industry is the existence of a legal mandate that requires their products to be purchased. CAA section 211(*o*), discussed above, requires renewable fuel, primarily ethanol, to be blended into gasoline in large quantities. This is the most important part of the industry's three-part biofuel business plan: (1) use a proven technology that has been used for more than two thousand years; (2) use government subsidies to build capacity and improve efficiency while lowering the cost of production; (3) use the power of government to force consumers to buy their product. While most businesses presumably would like to have a government-backed mandate that requires consumers to buy their product, other industries have not yet persuaded Congress to provide a guaranteed market.

AMERICANS FOR CLEAN ENERGY V. EPA

United States Court of Appeals, District of Columbia Circuit, 2017
864 F.3d 691

KAVANAUGH, C.J.

The Clean Air Act's Renewable Fuel Program requires an increasing amount of renewable fuel to be introduced into the Nation's transportation fuel supply each year. *See* 42 U.S.C. § 7545(*o*). By mandating the replacement—at least to a certain degree—of fossil fuel with renewable fuel, Congress intended the Renewable Fuel Program to move the United States toward greater energy independence and to reduce greenhouse gas emissions.

EPA is the federal agency primarily responsible for implementing the Renewable Fuel Program's requirements. Congress has directed EPA to annually publish renewable fuel requirements that apply to certain participants in the transportation fuel market. In 2015, EPA promulgated a Final Rule setting several renewable fuel requirements for the years 2014 through 2017. In this set of consolidated petitions, various organizations, companies, and interest groups challenge that EPA Final Rule on a number of grounds. Some argue that EPA set the renewable fuel requirements too high. Others argue that EPA set the renewable fuel requirements too low.

We reject all of those challenges, except for one: We agree with Americans for Clean Energy and its aligned petitioners (collectively referred to as "Americans for Clean Energy") that EPA erred in how it interpreted the "inadequate domestic supply" waiver provision. We hold that the "inadequate domestic supply" provision authorizes EPA to consider *supply-side* factors affecting the volume of renewable fuel that is available to *refiners, blenders, and importers* to meet the statutory volume requirements. It does not allow EPA to consider the volume of renewable fuel that is available to ultimate *consumers* or the *demand-side* constraints that affect the consumption of renewable fuel by consumers. . . .

I

A

In 2005, Congress passed and President George W. Bush signed the Energy Policy Act. Pub. L. No. 109–58, 119 Stat. 594 (2005). Among other things, that Act established the Clean Air Act's Renewable Fuel Program. . . . In 2007, Congress and President Bush amended the Renewable Fuel Program as part of the Energy Independence and Security Act. . . . As amended, the Renewable Fuel Program requires that increasing volumes of renewable fuel be introduced into the Nation's supply of transportation fuel each year. Congress enacted those requirements in order to "move the United States toward greater energy independence and security" and "increase the production of clean renewable fuels." . . .

. . . .

The Renewable Fuel Program statute contemplates that certain participants in the transportation fuel market—namely, "refineries," "blenders," and "importers"—will be required to satisfy annual "renewable fuel obligation [s]." 42 U.S.C. § 7545(*o*)(3)(B)(ii). To date, however, EPA has applied the renewable fuel obligations only to refiners and importers—not to blenders. . . When we refer to "obligated parties" in this opinion, we are referring to refiners and importers. To satisfy the renewable fuel obligations, each refiner and importer must ensure that a certain amount of renewable fuel is introduced into the Nation's transportation fuel supply. Each refiner and importer's renewable fuel obligation varies depending on how much fossil-based gasoline or diesel fuel it produces or imports.

The renewable fuel obligations applicable to refiners and importers mandate the introduction of four categories of renewable fuel into the transportation fuel supply. . . .

EPA has the responsibility to promulgate rules informing obligated parties (refiners and importers) of their annual renewable fuel obligations. . . . To do so, EPA first determines the annual volume requirement—also known as the "applicable volume"—for each category of renewable fuel. *Id.* § 7545(*o*)(2)(B). The annual volume requirement represents the total volume of renewable fuel that must be sold or introduced into the Nation's transportation fuel supply in a given year. . . .

The statute contains tables that set forth the annual volume requirements for each category of renewable fuel. . . .

Several statutory provisions guide EPA's determination of the annual renewable fuel volume requirements. Some provisions either require or allow EPA to lower the statutory volume requirements in specified circumstances. . . .

. . . [T]he "general waiver provision" allows EPA to reduce the statutory volume requirements in two circumstances. EPA may invoke the general waiver provision (i) if EPA determines that "implementation of the requirement would severely harm the economy or environment of a State, a region, or the United States" or (ii) if EPA determines that "there is an inadequate domestic supply." *Id.* § 7545(*o*)(7)(A).

. . . .

After EPA determines the volume requirements for the various categories of renewable fuel, it has a "statutory mandate" to "ensure[ ]" that those requirements are met. *Id.* § 7545(*o*)(3)(B)(i). . . .

. . . .

Once EPA issues a rule informing obligated parties (refiners and importers) of their renewable fuel obligations, it is up to the obligated parties to comply with the statute. But obligated parties need not themselves introduce renewable fuel into transportation fuel to comply with their renewable fuel obligations. Rather, to facilitate flexible and cost-effective compliance with the Renewable Fuel Program's requirements, Congress directed EPA to establish a "credit program" through which obligated parties can acquire and trade credits and thereby comply with the statute. . . .

. . . .

B

In December 2015, EPA promulgated the Final Rule that is under review in this case. *See Renewable Fuel Standard Program: Standards for 2014, 2015, and 2016 and Biomass-Based Diesel Volume for 2017*, 80 Fed.

Reg. 77,420 (Dec. 14, 2015) (hereinafter Final Rule). The Final Rule, which followed a proposed rule issued by EPA in June 2015, established volume requirements and the resulting percentage standards for the years 2014, 2015, and 2016 for all four categories of renewable fuel. . . .

EPA began its analysis in the Final Rule by explaining the competing concerns implicated by the Renewable Fuel Program's requirements. EPA noted that the "fundamental objective" of the Renewable Fuel Program "is clear: To increase the use of renewable fuels in the U.S. transportation system every year through at least 2022." *Id.* at 77,421. According to EPA, Congress's decision in the statute "to mandate increasing and substantial amounts of renewable fuel" use "clearly signals" that Congress intended "to create incentives to increase renewable fuel supplies and overcome constraints in the market." *Id.* at 77,423.

EPA noted that the Renewable Fuel Program's requirements were "readily achieved" in the few years after Congress created the program in 2005 and amended it in 2007. *Id.* That was due in large part to the fact that the industry had the capacity to produce—and the market had the capacity to consume—increasing quantities of ethanol. *Id.* But by 2014, ready compliance with the statutory volume requirements was no longer possible. That is because the industry hit the "E10 blendwall": an "infrastructure and market-related constraint on ethanol demand" that "arises because most U.S. vehicle engines were not designed to handle gasoline consisting of more than 10 percent ethanol." *Monroe Energy*, 750 F.3d at 913–14. Put differently, a few years into the amended Renewable Fuel Program, the supply of ethanol was much greater than the demand in the market.

Citing the E10 blendwall problem, EPA explained that obligated parties must increasingly rely on "sustained growth in the development and use of advanced, non-ethanol renewable fuels" (referred to as advanced biofuels) to meet their renewable fuel obligations. Final Rule, 80 Fed. Reg. at 77,423. However, EPA further noted that there were significant "real-world constraints" on the market's ability to consume increasing volumes of advanced biofuel. *Id.* at 77,422. Those constraints, according to EPA, meant that "the amount of renewable fuel that can be produced and imported is larger than the volume that can be consumed." *Id.* at 77,423. EPA cited those demand-side constraints as evidence that "[t]rying to force growth" at the rates set by the statutory volume requirements would "prove infeasible." *Id.*

In the Final Rule, EPA therefore adopted an approach that it believed properly balanced its statutory duty to "drive growth" in the supply of renewable fuels with the "real-world constraints" on the market's ability to produce and consume renewable fuels. *Id.* at 77,422–23.

. . . .

. . . For purposes of determining the available supply of renewable fuel, EPA considered only the actual volumes of renewable fuel both introduced and available for compliance with the statutory requirements in a given year. . . .

Applying that approach, EPA concluded that "the volumes for advanced biofuel and total renewable fuel specified in the statute cannot be achieved in 2014, 2015, or 2016." *Id.* at 77,431. EPA therefore relied upon its (i) cellulosic waiver authority and (ii) general waiver authority to reduce the volume requirements for total renewable fuel and advanced biofuel.

. . . .

. . . EPA concluded that the phrase "inadequate domestic supply" is best read to refer to "the adequacy of supply of renewable fuel" available to "the ultimate consumer[s]" of renewable fuel blended into transportation fuel. *Id.* at 77,436. EPA also concluded that its authority to determine the adequacy of the renewable fuel "supply" allowed the agency to look not only to supply-side factors in the market for renewable fuel—such as constraints on the production or import of renewable fuel—but also at factors affecting *demand for renewable fuel by consumers*—such as vehicle engine warranties and the effectiveness of those businesses marketing renewable fuel products. . . . Analyzing those factors, EPA concluded that the available supply of total renewable fuel still fell short of the statutory volume requirements. . . . EPA therefore relied on the "inadequate domestic supply" waiver provision to further reduce the 2014, 2015, and 2016 total renewable fuel volume requirements.

Below is a table summarizing the total renewable fuel volume requirements (in billions of gallons) issued by EPA in the Final Rule. For each year, the table lists the statutory volume requirements; the reduction to those statutory requirements attributable to EPA's use of the cellulosic waiver provision [a different statutory waiver provision, which was upheld in this case] and the general waiver provision; the final volume requirements set by EPA; and the total reduction to the statutory volume requirements made by EPA through use of its waiver authorities.

Table 1.1—Total Renewable Fuel Volume
Requirements (in billions of gallons)

Total Renewable Fuel Volume Requirements					
Year	Statute	Cellulosic Waiver Reduction	General Waiver Reduction	EPA Rule	Total Reduction from Waivers
2014	18.15	1.08	.79	16.28	1.87
2015	20.15	2.62	.95	16.93	3.57
2016	22.25	3.64	.5	18.11	4.14

. . . .

C

Following EPA's issuance of the Final Rule in December 2015, a number of parties filed petitions for review in this Court. Two petitions—one filed by National Biodiesel Board and the other filed by a group of petitioners including Americans for Clean Energy—challenge EPA's Final Rule for setting the renewable fuel volume requirements at too low a level. . . .

We now consider those petitions and the issues they present. . . .

. . . .

II

We first address whether EPA permissibly interpreted the "inadequate domestic supply" prong of its general waiver authority when lowering total renewable fuel volume requirements for the years 2014, 2015, and 2016. Americans for Clean Energy argues that EPA's interpretation of the phrase "inadequate domestic supply," under which EPA considered *demand-side* factors affecting the amount of renewable fuel available to *consumers*, is inconsistent with the statute. We agree with Americans for Clean Energy.

. . . .

A

1

The Renewable Fuel Program requires increasing volumes of renewable fuel to be introduced into the Nation's transportation fuel market. That market consists of a number of actors that play a part in delivering transportation fuel to consumers for use in their vehicles. There are refiners and importers, who manufacture and import conventional fossil-based gasoline and diesel fuels. In addition, there are biofuel producers, who manufacture the various categories of renewable fuel mandated by the Renewable Fuel Program. There are fuel blenders, who purchase fossil-based fuels and renewable fuels and mix the two together to create blended transportation fuels. There are retail fueling stations, who purchase blended transportation fuels and sell those fuels to consumers. And there are the consumers, who purchase transportation fuels for use in their vehicles. Although some market participants are vertically integrated—a refining company may also operate blending facilities or fueling stations, for example—many are not.

In enacting the Renewable Fuel Program, Congress chose not to place any compliance burdens on the fueling stations or consumers of transportation fuel. Instead, the statute allows EPA to designate three categories of upstream market participants—"refineries," "blenders," and "importers"—as "obligated parties" responsible for ensuring that the renewable fuel volume requirements are met. 42 U.S.C. § 7545(o)(3)(B)(ii)(I). To date, EPA has applied the renewable fuel obligations only to refiners and importers of fuel—not to blenders. . . . By requiring upstream market participants such as refiners and importers to introduce increasing volumes of renewable fuel into the transportation fuel supply, Congress intended the Renewable Fuel Program to be a "market forcing policy" that would create " 'demand pressure' to increase consumption" of renewable fuel. Final Rule, 80 Fed. Reg. at 77,423. . . .

. . . .

2

Although the Renewable Fuel Program statute establishes the annual volume requirements for the different categories of renewable fuel, Congress also granted EPA "waiver" power to reduce the statutory volume requirements in certain circumstances. Here, we consider the statute's "inadequate domestic supply" waiver provision. . . . The provision gives EPA discretion to "waive" the statutory requirements applicable to obligated parties "in whole or in part" by "reducing the national quantity of renewable fuel required under paragraph (2) . . . based on a determination by the Administrator, after public notice and opportunity for comment, *that there is an inadequate domestic supply*." 42 U.S.C. § 7545(o)(7)(A) (emphasis added).

. . . In the 2015 Final Rule, EPA relied on that provision to reduce the total renewable fuel volume requirements for the years 2014, 2015, and 2016. . . . In so doing, EPA issued its first-ever interpretation of the term "inadequate domestic supply" for the purposes of establishing a renewable fuel volume requirement. . . .

EPA began by noting its view that the statutory phrase "inadequate domestic supply" is ambiguous. . . . Having concluded that the phrase "inadequate domestic supply" is ambiguous, EPA stated that it had interpretive authority to adopt a reading of the waiver provision that would best align with "the overall policy goals" of the Renewable Fuel Program. . . . That "best" reading has two important elements that we consider here. . . .

First, EPA concluded that the best reading of the "inadequate domestic supply" provision is that it refers to the supply of renewable fuel available to *consumers* for use in their vehicles—not to the supply of renewable fuel available to *refiners, blenders, and importers* for use in meeting the statutory volume requirements. . . . Under that interpretation, EPA considered all factors that would affect the amount of renewable fuel available for sale to consumers including, among other things, the capacity and incentives of transportation fuel distributors and retail gas stations to distribute and sell blended transportation fuel. . . .

Second, EPA concluded that the "inadequate domestic supply" waiver provision grants it authority not only to consider supply-side constraints affecting the availability of renewable fuel—such as renewable fuel production or import capacity—but also to consider *demand-side* factors affecting consumers' desire or ability to consume renewable fuels. . . . Those demand-side factors included, among other things, the "existence of and expansion of" vehicles and engines "capable of using" renewable fuel; the number of "retail outlets that offer renewable fuels blends"; "the attractiveness" of renewable fuel blends "to consumers"; and the "marketing effectiveness" of those promoting renewable fuel products. . . .

An example helps crystallize the effects of EPA's interpretation. Suppose four things for a given year: (i) the statutory volume requirement is 10 million gallons; (ii) a supply of 10 million gallons of renewable fuel is available for use by refiners, blenders, and importers to meet the statutory volume requirement; (iii) due to distribution constraints, fuel retailers can make nine million gallons of renewable fuel available to consumers; and (iv) consumers can use—and therefore demand—eight million gallons of renewable fuel. Under EPA's interpretation of the "inadequate domestic supply" provision, EPA would be authorized: (i) to reduce the statutory volume requirement by one million gallons based on the distribution constraints that limit the amount of fuel offered by fuel retailers to consumers and (ii) to further reduce the volume requirement by an additional one million gallons to reflect consumer *demand* for renewable fuel. Those reductions could be made, according to EPA, notwithstanding the fact that the renewable fuel *supply* of 10 million gallons would be adequate to allow refiners, blenders, and importers to introduce enough renewable fuel into the Nation's fuel supply to meet the statutory volume requirement.

3

Americans for Clean Energy argues that EPA's interpretation of the phrase "inadequate domestic supply" is inconsistent with the text, structure, and purpose of the Renewable Fuel Program. According to Americans for Clean Energy, the scope of EPA's "inadequate domestic supply" waiver authority is clear: It authorizes EPA to consider *supply-side* factors affecting the volume of renewable fuel that is available to *refiners, blenders, and importers* to meet the statutory volume requirements. It does not, according to Americans for Clean Energy, allow EPA to consider factors, such as distribution capacity, affecting the supply of renewable fuel available to ultimate *consumers* for use in their vehicles. Nor does it allow EPA to consider *demand-side* constraints on the consumption of renewable fuel when determining the available renewable fuel supply.

We agree with Americans for Clean Energy that EPA's interpretation of the "inadequate domestic supply" waiver provision is inconsistent with the statute. . .

. . . .

The "inadequate domestic supply" provision authorizes EPA to "reduc[e] the national quantity of *renewable fuel* required" by the statute "based on a determination by" EPA "that there is an inadequate domestic supply." 42 U.S.C. § 7545(*o*)(7)(A) (emphasis added). Reading the "inadequate domestic supply" provision together with the section it modifies, the only reasonable interpretation is that the "product" at issue is the only product referenced in the provision: "renewable fuel."

Nor is the "inadequate domestic supply" waiver provision ambiguous with respect to the "person" at issue. Recall that the statute allows EPA to apply the annual renewable fuel obligations to three kinds of entities— refiners, blenders, and importers. *See id.* § 7545(*o*)(3)(B)(ii)(I). As discussed. . . . it is the *refiners, blenders, and importers*—not consumers— who must "use" the statutorily required volumes of renewable fuel by incorporating that fuel into the Nation's supply of transportation fuel. It follows that it is the *refiners, blenders, and importers*—not consumers— who must have access to an adequate "supply" of renewable fuel in order to meet the Renewable Fuel Program's statutory volume requirements. When the supply of renewable fuel is "inadequate" to allow refiners, blenders, and importers to introduce enough renewable fuel to meet the statutory volume requirements, the "inadequate domestic supply" waiver provision allows EPA to reduce those requirements to reflect that fact. That reduction, in turn, benefits obligated parties—not consumers.

In other words, the "inadequate domestic supply" waiver provision is just that: a waiver provision. It authorizes EPA to ease the Renewable Fuel Program's requirements when complying with those requirements would be infeasible. With that understanding of how the "inadequate domestic supply" provision operates in the statutory scheme, EPA's reading of the provision makes little sense: Whether consumers have an adequate supply of renewable fuel to fill their cars is not relevant to whether refiners, blenders, and importers have an adequate supply of renewable fuel to meet the statutory volume requirements. For purposes of measuring available "supply," the "persons" at issue are refiners, blenders, and importers.

. . . .

. . . As even EPA concedes, the "common understanding" of the term "supply" is "an amount of a resource or product that is available for use by the person or place at issue." *Id.* at 77,435; *see also id.* at 77,435 n.32 (collecting dictionary definitions); THE AMERICAN HERITAGE DICTIONARY OF THE ENGLISH LANGUAGE (5th ed. 2017 online) (an "amount available or sufficient for a given use"). When it comes to the "inadequate domestic supply" provision, we have already established: (i) that the "resource or product" is renewable fuel; (ii) that the "use" is compliance with the statute; and (iii) that the "persons" "at issue" are refiners, blenders, and importers. Putting that together, "supply" as used in the "inadequate domestic supply" provision refers to the "amount" of renewable fuel that is "available for use" by refiners, blenders, and importers in meeting the statutory volume requirements.

Importantly, whether a thing is "available" to someone has nothing to do with whether he or she decides to use it. (The fact that a person is on a diet does not mean that there is an inadequate supply of food in the refrigerator.) So too here: Whether there is an adequate amount of renewable fuel available to allow refiners, blenders, and importers to meet the statutory volume requirements has little to do with how much renewable fuel that refiners, blenders, and importers—much less consumers at the pump—ultimately decide to use.

. . . .

. . . [T]he Renewable Fuel Program's increasing requirements are designed to force the market to create ways to produce and use greater and greater volumes of renewable fuel each year. EPA's interpretation of the "inadequate domestic supply" provision flouts that statutory design: Instead of the statute's volume requirements forcing demand up, the lack of demand allows EPA to bring the volume requirements down. . . .

In short, applying the "traditional tools" of statutory interpretation, we conclude that the "inadequate domestic supply" waiver provision refers to the supply of renewable fuel available to refiners, blenders, and importers to meet the statutory volume requirements. *Chevron,* 467 U.S. at 843 n.9, 104 S.Ct. 2778. . . .

. . . .

We agree with Americans for Clean Energy that the statute forecloses EPA's reading of the "inadequate domestic supply" waiver provision. We therefore grant Americans for Clean Energy's petition for review of the 2015 Final Rule, vacate EPA's decision in the Rule to reduce the total renewable fuel volume requirements for 2016 through use of the "inadequate domestic supply" waiver authority, and remand the rule to EPA for further consideration in light of our interpretation.

We have considered all of the parties' other arguments and have found them to be without merit. We deny the remainder of the petitions for review.

So ordered.

NOTES & QUESTIONS

1.   According to Professor Reitze, why is it so difficult to determine the lifecycle greenhouse gas savings associated with fueling vehicles with ethanol instead of fossil fuels?

2.   What are the primary advantages and disadvantages of algae-based fuels over other types of biofuels? Based on these factors, what regions of the country do you think would be best suited for producing these fuels?

3.   Based on the Reitze article, describe in detail how a doubling of subsidies for corn-based ethanol would be likely to impact at least five (5) other industries within the United States economy.

4.   Based on the Reitze article, how have politics influenced the development of U.S. federal policies related to biofuels?

5.   According to *Americans for Clean Energy*, what is the "E10 blendwall problem" and how has it slowed the demand growth for renewable fuels in the United States?

6.   According to *Americans for Clean Energy*, what was incorrect about the EPA's interpretation of the Energy Policy Act's "inadequate supply waiver" provision?

7.   *Potential Impacts on the Trump Administration's Energy Policy Agenda.* Less than one month before the D.C. Circuit released its decision in *Americans for Clean Energy*, the Trump administration had issued a proposal to further soften the Energy Policy Act's renewable fuel standard requirements. By refusing to uphold the EPA's interpretation of the Renewable Fuel Program statute's "inadequate domestic supply" provision, the court in *Americans for Clean Energy* likely made it more difficult for the Trump administration to implement and enforce its proposal. *See, e.g.*, Mario Parker et al., *Trump May Have to Boost Biofuel after Court Deals Blow to Oil*, BLOOMBERG (July 28, 2017), https://www.bloomberg.com/news/articles/2017-07-28/epa-s-move-to-cut-2016-renewable-fuel-volume-rejected-by-court.

8.   *Renewable Natural Gas (Biomethane).* In addition to ethanol and other *liquid* biofuels, some renewable fuels in *gaseous* form are also increasingly used to power motor vehicles. These gaseous fuels are sometimes

collectively categorized as *renewable natural gas* or *biomethane* gas products. Renewable natural gas products most commonly originate as methane generated from decomposing waste in landfills, livestock operations, or wastewater treatment plants. Properly-refined renewable natural gas products can safely substitute for ordinary natural gas as fuel at many gas-fired power plants and in many vehicles designed to run on compressed natural gas (CNG). Because renewable natural gas products also qualify under the federal Renewable Fuels Standard described above, they could grow in importance as companies scramble to comply with these standards in the coming years. For additional information about renewable natural gas, see *Renewable Natural Gas (Biomethane) Production*, U.S. DEP'T ENERGY, https:// www.afdc.energy.gov/fuels/natural_gas_renewable.html (last visited Oct. 1, 2017).

2. ELECTRIC VEHICLES

An entirely different strategy for increasing the use of renewable energy in the nation's transportation sector is to design vehicles to run on electric power and then use wind, sunlight, and other renewable resources to generate that power. Ironically, many of the world's first manned vehicles were designed to fun on electricity rather than gasoline. However, the high cost and short range of electric vehicles soon persuaded engineers to favor petroleum-driven motor vehicles over electric ones. Within just a couple of decades, gasoline products thus emerged as the fuels of choice for the nation's burgeoning fleet of automobiles. For decades, technological constraints and political factors have perpetuated the transportation industry's heavy reliance on petroleum despite its adverse environmental and other impacts. The thousands of gas stations dotting the nation's landscape today add to the convenience of gasoline have helped to solidify petroleum's position as the nation's dominant transportation energy source.

After relying almost exclusively on petroleum for nearly a century, stakeholders in the automobile industry are now showing unprecedented levels of interest in helping electricity to become a primary source of transportation energy. Incentivized or compelled to do so under various state and federal policies, many of the nation's largest auto makers now manufacture and sell multiple models of passenger cars that run entirely or partially on electric power. Transitioning toward electric-powered vehicles could greatly enhance the energy sustainability of the nation's transportation sector if most of the electricity powering these cars were to come from wind, sunlight, or other renewable energy sources. On the other hand, if coal-fired power plants supply much of that electricity, the net environmental benefits of electric vehicles will be far less clear. The following excerpt describes the remarkable rise of electric vehicles over the past decade and governments' involvement in driving that growth. The article then introduces and explores some of the most important policy questions that have arisen as mass-produced electric vehicles have finally become economically viable in recent years.

LIFE CYCLE ANALYSIS AND TRANSPORTATION ENERGY

Alexandra B. Klass & Andrew Heiring
82 BROOK. L. REV. 485, 511–21 & 523–27 (2017)

Many of the same concerns that led to . . . federal biofuels policies . . . (e.g., achieving energy security, ensuring sufficient domestic oil and gas reserves, reducing GHG emissions from the transportation sector) have also led to federal and state policies that promote the development and sale of alternative vehicles to reduce the use of gasoline in the transportation sector. These alternative vehicles include hybrid electric vehicles (HEVs) such as the Toyota Prius, partial hybrid electric vehicles (PHEVs) such as the Chevy Volt, and all-electric vehicles such as the Tesla Model S and the Nissan Leaf. All of these alternative vehicles boast a much higher rate of fuel efficiency than traditional internal combustion engine vehicles (ICEVs). Nevertheless, fluctuating gasoline prices, consumer wariness of new technology, and the difficulty of creating the electric charging station infrastructure necessary for widespread use of EVs has made broad adoption of all of these technologies slower than many desire. The U.S. Energy Information Administration (ELA) estimates that by 2040, all forms of alternative vehicles will make up approximately 13% of the nation's automotive stock. But, as discussed below, some life cycle analysis studies call into question whether, at the present time, EVs are superior to ICEVs because, in many parts of the United States, electricity is generated primarily by coal-fired power plants, resulting in GHG emissions and adverse health effects that exceed those of ICEVs. Despite these studies, policymakers should look beyond these life cycle assessments and consider the benefits that EVs can provide as the nation moves away from coal-fired power toward more renewable electricity resources. . . .

A.   *Federal and State Mandates and Incentives to Reduce GHG and Other Air Emissions from Vehicles and Promote the Use of EVs*

Congress, EPA, and many states have implemented mandates and programs to reduce CO2 and other air emissions in the transportation sector through new vehicle efficiency standards that apply to all vehicles, including ICEVs, as well as specific mandates and tax incentives for EVs. For instance, since 2010, EPA and the National Highway Traffic Safety Administration (NHTSA) have engaged in several joint rulemaking proceedings imposing significantly higher corporate average fuel economy (CAFE) standards as well as limits on GHG emissions.

These standards impose an equivalent of 35.5 miles per gallon (mpg) for light duty model year 2016 vehicles and, after a landmark rulemaking in 2012, up to 54.5 mpg for light duty model year 2025 vehicles. NHTSA and EPA have also enacted heightened CAFE standards and GHG emission standards for heavy-duty trucks. Auto manufacturers that fail to meet the CAFE standards are subject to a civil penalty of $5.50 per each tenth of a mile per gallon under the target value multiplied by the total volume of vehicles manufactured for a model year for sale in the United States if the fleet fails to achieve the standard.

Among the states, California has always been a national leader in setting stringent vehicle emissions standards and was the first to incentivize the production, marketing, and use of EVs, creating a Zero-Emission Vehicle (ZEV) program in 1990. The program was designed to be technology-forcing and was initially successful, but modifications to the program creating ZEV credits for cleaner conventional vehicles and low-emission vehicles diminished its success. In recent years, however, [the California Air Resource Board] has substantially strengthened the program, with a mandate that requires 22% of cars with a model year of 2025 or later to be ZEVs.

California also worked with EPA and the NHTSA to harmonize their vehicle emissions standards, resulting in the 2012 joint rulemaking discussed above. As of 2015, approximately one third of the nation's new car sales occurred in a state governed by the ZEV rule. Minnesota took a unique approach to incentivize EV use and passed a law requiring utilities to discount electricity used for charging EVs, and mandated an opportunity to use renewable energy resources for charging.

Beyond the mandate in some states that car manufacturers and dealers offer EVs for sale, there are federal and state tax incentives to encourage the purchase of EVs. At the federal level, there is a federal tax credit of up to $7500 for the purchase of an EV or PHEV. Many states have additional tax incentives ranging from $1000 to $6000 to encourage the purchase of EVs for private and corporate use, and some states have mandated that state agencies purchase EVs or other lower emission vehicles. These subsidies increase demand for EVs by lowering their net costs, while state ZEV mandates create a market for EVs and force automakers to participate in it. . . .

. . . A more complicated question is whether the use of EVs, at least at the present time, results in clear environmental benefits over ICEVs.

EVs have no tailpipe emissions, so EVs will always be environmentally superior to ICEVs if those are the only emissions that are considered in the comparison. But once the focus expands beyond tailpipe emissions to include the emissions associated with the production and transportation of the energy resources necessary to produce electricity to power EVs, the emissions associated with the generation of electricity, and the emissions associated with EV battery production and disposal, the benefits of EVs become more questionable. Numerous experts have undertaken studies, some with a full life cycle analysis, to answer these questions.

B.   Life Cycle Studies of EVs and ICEVs

Scientists have undertaken a variety of life cycle analysis studies comparing EVs with ICEVs. These studies, described in more detail below, fall into three broad categories based on their scope: (1) tailpipe-to-tailpipe comparisons; (2) "use phase" studies, some of which consider solely the emissions from power plants and vehicle tailpipes and others which also consider emissions associated with the extraction and transportation of oil, gas, and coal energy resources; and (3) broader life cycle analyses that also consider battery and vehicle production and disposal.

1.   Tailpipe Studies

Tailpipe studies focus exclusively on the air emissions associated with driving the vehicle. In direct comparison to tailpipe emissions, EVs are always superior in terms of air pollution reduction to ICEVs, as EVs are virtually emission-free at the tailpipe level. This compares to the U.S. Department of Energy's Office of Energy Efficiency and Renewable Energy's estimate of national average annual emissions of an ICEV of approximately 11,500 pounds of CO_2 equivalent GHG emissions. Nevertheless, virtually no EV proponents rely solely on tailpipe emissions to support arguments in favor of EVs, recognizing that the air emissions and environmental impacts of electricity production must be included in any comparison of EVs and ICEVs. Use phase studies more accurately compare the total impacts of EVs and ICEVs.

2.   Use Phase Studies

A use phase analysis goes beyond tailpipe emissions and considers a broader suite of vehicle-related impacts. For EVs, this includes (1) the emissions associated with the extraction and transportation of coal, natural gas, nuclear, wind, hydropower, and solar energy resources used to produce electricity; and (2) the emissions associated with converting those energy resources into the electricity needed to charge the EV, such as the emissions from a coal-fired power plant or a natural gas-fired power plant. For ICEVs, a use phase analysis considers the environmental impacts of producing oil and biofuels, transporting those fuels to refineries and blending facilities, refining and blending those fuels to turn them into gasoline and other vehicle fuels, and the tailpipe emissions from the combustion of these fuels to drive the ICEV.

Once these factors are considered as part of the environmental impact of each type of vehicle, the environmental benefits of EVs as compared to ICEVs are decidedly more mixed. For instance, coal-fired electricity, which constitutes approximately one-third of electricity generation nationwide, emits substantial amounts of criteria pollutants such as nitrogen oxides, sulfur dioxides, and particulate matter; toxic emissions such as mercury; as well as CO_2 and other GHG emissions that contribute to climate change. Thus, a major question with regard to EVs is whether the decrease in tailpipe emissions compared to ICEVs can overcome the increase in electricity generation-related emissions and other use phase emissions. Taking the average mix of generation sources for U.S. electricity, the U.S. Department of Energy found that average annual GHG emissions are lower for EVs, HEVs, and PHEVs. However, the wide variety of energy resources used to produce electricity among the various states means that focusing on national averages is not always useful.

A 2015 study by economists Stephen P. Holland, Erin T. Mansur, Nicholas Z. Muller, and Andrew J. Yates sought to better understand how the geographical differences in electricity generation mix impacted the emissions of EVs across the country, and consequently whether existing federal and state subsidies for EVs were appropriate. . . . The researchers compared pollution rates from ICEVs and EVs for every county in the United States to determine and compare the environmental harm associated with each type of vehicle.

To conduct this comparison, the researchers converted pollution statistics to dollar-cost impacts and charted damage amounts across the United States. The researchers focused on five major pollutants: carbon dioxide, sulfur dioxide, mono-nitrogen oxides, particulate matter, and volatile organic compounds. ICEV costs were fairly variable across states and counties, with particularly high damage calculations in dense, more polluted urban centers, such as Los Angeles, Atlanta, New York, and Chicago. Damage in these environments is predominately due to non-GHG criteria pollutants, which cause localized harm. Even in these areas, the marginal cost of pollution from driving an average ICEV one mile was under five cents. By contrast, damage calculations for EVs varied widely, based on the primary energy sources used to generate electricity from state to state. In the coal-heavy Midwest, marginal damage estimates were nearly five cents per mile driven. In the Southeast and Texas, which rely on a larger proportion of nuclear, hydropower, and wind resources to generate electricity, marginal damage estimates were less than three cents per mile. The western states have the cleanest energy grids and thus had the lowest estimated marginal costs, at approximately one cent per mile. Overall, this study suggests that electricity generation emissions cause marginal costs as high [as] or higher than ICEV emissions in U.S. states east of the Rocky Mountains. Only in the western states, and in high-density urban areas in the East, were EVs equal to or better than ICEVs, in terms of costs associated with emissions.

Based on these data on the marginal costs of pollution from EVs and ICEVs, Holland et al. addressed the economic value of subsidizing EVs. Where lifetime environmental impacts for EVs are less than ICEVs, they concluded that a subsidy is justified in the amount by which the EV incurs fewer costs. Vice versa, where lifetime impacts are higher, a tax was justified to recoup the additional environmental costs the EV produced. The study concluded that subsidies are justified across the western states, portions of Texas, and Orlando, Atlanta, and New York. In the remainder of the country, the authors concluded that EVs should be taxed, often quite heavily, at over $5000 per car in most of the Midwest. By geographically breaking down where EVs are more environmentally than ICEVs, Holland et al. challenged the blanket assurances that EVs are preferable everywhere.

. . . .

Notably, the study assumed that any retired coal-fired power plants in the United States would be replaced exclusively by natural gas facilities. As a result, it did not consider the impact of replacing coal-fired generation with wind, solar, or hydropower resources, even though much of the coal-fired power that has been retired in the past ten years has been replaced in part by renewable resources in many states. . . [T]he trend in electricity generation is toward less carbon-intensive sources, which substantially improves the environmental prospects for EVs across the country. A myopic focus on how EVs interact with the present electricity generation mix risks eliminating both the present benefits of EVs in those areas with greener grids, and the future benefits in other areas with greening grids. . . .

3.   Broader Life Cycle Analyses: Localized Gasoline Impacts, Battery Impacts and Charging Programs

Although use phase analyses evaluate a broader range of environmental impacts than tailpipe emissions, they cannot fully evaluate the relative environmental impacts of EVs and ICEVs. For example, on the component side, EV batteries are significantly different than ICEV batteries, requiring different material components and manufacturing processes, and potentially resulting in different disposal impacts. To account for these aspects, plus others, researchers have performed life cycle analysis studies examining environmental consequences of EVs at the manufacturing and disposal phases as well as the use phase. Several of these studies are discussed below, many of which find a more positive environmental impact associated with EVs than the Holland, et al. study.

. . . .

A study by James Archsmith, Alissa Kendall, and David Rapson adds an additional factor to the assessment of EVs by noting the effects of ambient climate on EV efficiency. Both hot and cold temperatures substantially affect the range of an EV (due primarily to diversion of energy from propulsion to in-car climate controls), which requires more frequent charging (and thus, more kilowatt-hours consumed per mile). In areas with coal-dependent electricity generation and relatively extreme climates (e.g., the Midwest), use of EVs can substantially increase GHG emissions. The study concludes that, on average, most regions would see GHG reductions when comparing ICEVs to EVs, but states in the Midwest, South Central, and Mid-Atlantic regions might see increases. . . .

Other studies focus on the environmental impacts of the EV battery. Overall, EV vehicle production represents about "2–15% of total life cycle environmental impact," and battery production is the largest factor. Most EVs use a lithium-ion (Li-ion) battery to increase stored energy and range of the vehicle. In 2013, EPA concluded a life cycle analysis of Li-ion batteries to "identify the materials or processes within a battery's life cycle that are likely to pose the greatest impacts to both public health and the environment, and to evaluate nanotechnology innovations in advanced Li-ion batteries for electric vehicles that may enhance battery performance." . . . The study found that upstream, material-sourcing impacts differed based on the chemical composition of the battery, with rarer and more toxic metals increasing health-related and environmental costs. Batteries that used higher amounts of aluminum showed higher potential for ozone depletion simply because of the high amount of chlorofluorocarbon emissions required in the aluminum smelting process. . . .

With regard to battery disposal, the relative novelty of EVs in any substantial number has so far impeded life cycle analysis of battery disposal. EV Li-ion batteries cannot be disposed of in the same away as ICEV lead-acid batteries, and thus are worthy of separate consideration. An EPA study of Li-ion batteries concluded that their recycling potential was high, with only 3% of the original battery materials (measured by weight) going to landfill. The study cites the presence of valuable metals, including cobalt, lithium, and nickel, in the batteries as rendering recycling cost effective. . . .

C. *Policy Implications for EV Life Cycle Analyses*

The life cycle analysis studies discussed above reveal that despite the complete lack of tailpipe emissions associated with EVs, the use of coal in the electric grid can significantly compromise the environmental benefits of EVs as compared with ICEVs. This calls into question the federal and state programs that incentivize the purchase and use of EVs.

. . . It may very well be the case that today's EVs are not superior to ICEVs in certain parts of the country. But, that does not mean that EV incentives should be abandoned. First, there are areas of the country where EVs already produce lower emissions than ICEVs—where the grid is relatively clean—and incentives should certainly continue to operate in those regions. Second, the electric grid in the United States and across the world is in a state of transition, with an increasing focus on green technologies and renewable fuels. In 2015, coal accounted for only 34% of U.S. electricity generation—its lowest share since EIA recordkeeping began—as compared with 50% of total U.S. electricity generation as recently as 2005.

. . . As the grid improves, EVs will become increasingly able to reach their potential. While the environmental benefits of EVs may not be significant in all parts of the country, the electric grid is evolving to resemble those areas where EVs are manifestly beneficial. Though it may take decades for the most coal-dependent grids to embrace renewables, the benefits of EVs on grids powered by natural gas, hydropower, and renewable energy are already a reality. Decreasing or eliminating EV incentives for failure to provide immediate benefit would be shortsighted and ultimately harmful. Life cycle analysis tends to describe the world as it is, and it is a mistake to eliminate EV incentives in reliance on studies that show no environmental improvement over ICEVs. The greening of the electricity grid is still a relatively recent phenomenon and has significant potential for GHG reduction that would be left partially unrealized by continued reliance on gasoline-powered vehicles.

NOTES & QUESTIONS

1.   What is a *life cycle study* in the context of debates over the net environmental benefits of electric vehicles?

2.   How can the type of life cycle study performed impact conclusions regarding the relative net environmental benefits of electric vehicles over internal combustion engine vehicles?

3.   What does the Klass & Heiring article suggest about variations in the net environmental benefits of electric vehicles across regions of the United States? In what specific ways should these insights affect the crafting of incentives and other programs seeking to increase the adoption of electric vehicle technologies?

4.   *Electric Vehicles as Tools to Help Balance Grid Loads.* Another benefit of electric vehicle technologies is their potential to help to balance grid loads. If electric vehicles became sufficiently commonplace, their large batteries could eventually serve as an impactful source of short-term energy storage. Time-based retail electricity rate structures designed to influence when customers charge their electric vehicles could similarly help to smooth out peaks in electricity demand throughout the day. To quote one group of commentators:

> The emissions reduction potential and cost of operating electric vehicles depend heavily on when individuals choose to charge those vehicles. Drivers are most likely to plug in their vehicles when they return home in the evening. This timing coincides with peak-load energy use in the late afternoon and evening, when less efficient sources of electricity generation are used to meet peak load demands.

Depending on the mix of generating sources (coal, nuclear, gas, or renewable sources), recharging during peak periods may substantially increase the carbon emissions and costs associated with electric vehicles. Recharging during peak periods also could increase the costs and intrusiveness of power lines and other aspects of electric transmission systems. In short, recharging at the most convenient times could make the electric car policy less efficient than it would otherwise be, or worse, less efficient than other entirely different regulatory choices. . . . If instead agency officials could devise a policy to induce individuals to charge their vehicles during off-peak hours (e.g., midnight to 7 a.m.) in many regions of the United States, they may increase the environmental benefits of an electric vehicle fleet, decrease the costs, or both.

Michael P. Vandenbergh et al., *Regulation in the Behavioral Era*, 95 MINN. L. REV. 715, 767–68 (2011).

5.   *The Charging Station "Chicken and Egg" Problem.* One major obstacle to the widespread adoption of electric vehicles is the lack of a robust network of electric vehicle charging stations in much of the country. As of 2017, many electric vehicles had a relatively short "range" of roughly 100 miles or less. Given that there are far fewer electric vehicle charging stations than gas stations in most of the United States, it can difficult for drivers of these vehicles to find convenient places to charge them. Some electric car companies such as Tesla have their own charging station networks, but even those are limited in many geographic areas. Many electric vehicle advocates argue that, until charging stations become more ubiquitous, lots of would-be electric vehicle drivers are likely to continue driving gasoline-powered cars. *See* Brittany Patterson, *Electric Car Owners Struggle to Find a Charge*, SCI. AM. (July 16, 2015), https://www.scientificamerican.com/article/electric-car-owners-struggle -to-find-a-charge/; Christopher Mims, *The Problem with Electric Cars? Not Enough Chargers*, WALL STREET J. (Aug. 6, 2017), https://www.wsj.com/ articles/the-problem-with-electric-cars-not-enough-chargers-1502017202.

6.   *Hydrogen Fuel Cell Electric Vehicles.* Hydrogen fuel cell technologies represent one other possible means of powering transportation with renewable energy resources. These innovative technologies could potentially provide some of the advantages of both biofuels and ordinary electric cars. Like electric vehicles, hydrogen-powered cars ultimately run on electricity and produce zero emissions. For that reason, hydrogen fuel cell vehicles are often classified together with electric vehicles. However, many new hydrogen-powered vehicles have ranges exceeding 300 miles—ranges that are far greater than many electric vehicles and more akin to the ranges of vehicles running on biofuels. Hydrogen-powered car owners can also refuel their vehicles in just a few minutes, which is far less time than required to fully recharge most electric vehicles.

Hydrogen-powered cars typically use fuel cells to convert the chemical energy in compressed hydrogen gas to electricity that drives the vehicle forward. The fuel cells combine hydrogen with oxygen to produce water and electric current, with no emissions of carbon dioxide or other undesirable emissions. Unfortunately, hydrogen-powered vehicles resemble ordinary electric vehicles in that their net environmental impacts depend largely on the origin of the energy that powers them. Producing compressed hydrogen gas is itself an energy-intensive process. Although it is possible to produce hydrogen using electricity from renewables such as wind and sunlight, much of the world's hydrogen supplies are presently produced using natural gas. It will be impossible to fully harness the environmental and other benefits of hydrogen fuel cell technologies until affordable, cleanly-manufactured hydrogen gas becomes available at thousands of fueling stations throughout the country.

In the meantime, hydrogen fuel cell vehicles do generally qualify as "zero emissions vehicles" under most government incentive programs for alternative vehicles and thus usually get comparable favorable treatment under such programs. For more on the basics of hydrogen fuel cell technologies and policies aimed at promoting their development, visit the U.S. Department of Energy's *Alternative Fuels Data Center* at https://www.afdc.energy.gov/fuels/hydrogen_basics.html (last visited Aug. 29, 2017).

D. HYDROELECTRIC POWER

Hydropower facilities are a type of renewable energy source that already supplies much of the nation's renewable electricity. As shown on Figure 8.3 earlier in this chapter, in 2016 hydroelectric facilities generated 24% of the nation's renewable energy—more than the nation's aggregate production of wind-generated electricity and four times that of solar power. Hundreds of hydroelectric power stations are presently generating electricity across the United States. Figure 8.4 is a map produced by the Energy Information Administration showing operating hydroelectric facilities throughout the nation. Larger circles on the map denote those facilities with the largest generating capacity. As the map illustrates, major hydroelectricity facilities are most heavily concentrated in West coast states but play significant roles in meeting electricity demand in much of the country.

Figure 8.4. Hydroelectric Power Plants in the United States

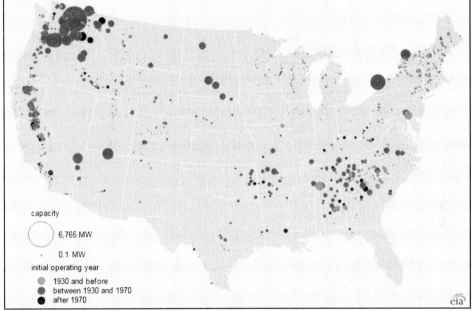

Source: U.S. Energy Info. Admin.

Given hydropower's important existing role as a renewable energy resource, one might wonder why laws and policies related to hydropower don't occupy at least one entire chapter of this Casebook. The reason is that, like coal and nuclear energy, hydropower's share of the nation's energy portfolio is gradually declining. Less than 1% of the electric generating capacity added in the United States between 2007 and 2016 was attributable to new hydropower. See *Hydroelectric Generators Are Among the United States' Oldest Power Plants*, U.S. ENERGY INFO. ADMIN. (Mar. 13, 2017), https://www.eia.gov/todayinenergy/detail.php?id=30312. Moreover, the average age of nation's existing fleet of hydroelectric plants is 64 years, so these plants tend to generate relatively few legal issues. In short, the typical modern energy lawyer in the United States is more likely to encounter issues related to wind and solar energy development than issues related to hydropower. Accordingly, the following materials provide only a basic overview of hydropower, the policies that govern it, and a brief discussion of small hydropower—the hydropower energy strategy that seemingly has the greatest potential to significantly expand within the next few decades.

1. HYDROPOWER'S HISTORY

Until the early 2000s, hydropower was the only significant source of renewable electric power in the United States. In fact, hydropower has long been among the world's most well-established strategies for generating electricity. The U.S. Energy Information Administration reports that hydropower accounted for 6.5% of all electricity generated in the country in 2016, making it the most productive renewable electricity source in that year. *See Frequently Asked Questions: What Is U.S. Electricity Generation By Energy Source?*, U.S. ENERGY INFO. ADMIN., https://www.eia.gov/tools/faqs/faq.php?id=427&t=3 (last visited Aug. 29, 2017).

One major distinction between hydropower and wind and solar power is that federal laws (rather than state laws) have closely regulated most of the nation's hydropower development for nearly a century. Given the massive scale of major hydroelectricity facilities and their heavy reliance on major waterways, it is understandable these projects have long involved heavy federal government involvement. However, as developers become increasingly interested in siting smaller-scale hydropower facilities, this history of strong federal jurisdiction over hydroelectricity project development may now be impeding hydropower's growth. In the following excerpt, Professor Gina Warren briefly describes the history of hydropower as an electricity source in the United States.

HYDROPOWER: IT'S A SMALL WORLD AFTER ALL
Gina Warren
91 NEB. L. REV. 925, 928–37 (2013)

As early as 31 B.C., Greeks and Romans used the watermill as a means of harnessing power—mostly the power to grind grain into flour. The mechanics of a watermill are simple. Running water flows over a paddle wheel that is connected to a drive shaft. The drive shaft then moves a piece of machinery—historically a saw, a grinder, or a pump. By the early eleventh century, the use of watermills was so widespread that in England one count estimated approximately one watermill per 350 people. By the eighteenth century, water mills were widely used in England to run factories that created textiles, tools, and other commodities. . . . When early Americans settled in the United States, they did so along the great New England rivers. . . . As Americans desired to become independent from England—and as the population grew—many saw dams as a means of harnessing more power to increase productivity. Water would gradually be released from a reservoir located above the dam to allow a stronger, more consistent flow of water to run over the paddles, resulting in a continuous and even operation of the watermill and around-the-clock harnessing of energy. While reservoir and dam construction resulted in increased productivity and bolstered industry, this "advancement" resulted in significant legal and environmental issues that have persisted to this day. Due to the artificial routing and blocking of the water, property upstream and downstream to the dams would be susceptible to flooding or drought, depending on the dam operation. Mill acts were introduced throughout the northeastern states. . . Most mill acts gave dam builders authorization to construct and maintain a watermill, dam, and reservoir on a river or stream so long as they paid complaining property owners—generally farmers—for flood damage.

These acts preempted common law damage claims and, in some states, allowed a specific amount of compensation to be paid to the injured party on an annual basis. . . . This was the beginning of a tug-of-war . . . between development (and the harnessing of power) and protection of private rights, public and private lands, and the environment.

A. Hydropower for Generation of Electricity

. . . .

Hydropower generation is similar to watermills, but instead of turning a paddle wheel, flowing water turns turbine blades, which then spin a generator to produce electricity. The Vulcan Street Plant was arguably the first hydroelectric power plant to begin operation in the United States on September 30, 1882. The electricity powered three buildings—two paper mills owned by Appleton Paper & Pulp Company and a residence. By 1889, there were two hundred hydropower facilities in the United States providing power on a small, local scale. In 1896, the scale of hydropower use expanded considerably with Nikola Tesla's work on alternating currents, which allowed hydroelectric power to be distributed from a Niagara Falls power plant in New York to the public in Buffalo some twenty-six miles away. Thereafter, in the late nineteenth and early twentieth centuries, hydropower flourished. According to the U.S. Department of Interior: Bureau of Reclamation, "By the early 1900's, hydroelectric power accounted for more than 40 percent of the United States' supply of electricity."

Regulation of hydroelectric power was mostly left to the individual states until Congress passed the Rivers and Harbors Acts of 1890 and 1899. The Acts made it illegal to construct bridges, causeways, dams, or dikes on or over navigable waters without the consent of Congress, which required approval by the Secretary of Transportation (for bridges or causeways) or the Chief of Engineers and Secretary of the Army (for dams or dikes). . . .

B. Hydropower Regulation Under the Federal Power Act

The Federal Water Power Act of 1920 (enacted in 1920, amended in 1935 and 1986, and renamed the Federal Power Act) (FPA) was the first national policy for the regulation of hydropower development. The purpose of the FPA was to set forth a comprehensive plan for development of the

Nation's water resources that were within the jurisdiction of the federal government. . . . It created a new commission—the Federal Power Commission, now known as the Federal Energy Regulatory Commission (FERC)—with the exclusive regulatory and licensing authority over hydropower facilities. Under the FPA, licenses are required for all new and already-built hydroelectric facilities located within the Act's jurisdiction. The Act's jurisdiction includes all navigable waters or waters that affect interstate commerce, dams or reservoirs that occupy federal land, or dams that utilize surplus water or water power from a government dam. When enacted, the FPA was thought to be a detailed and comprehensive plan, which left "no room or need for conflicting state controls." Provisions of the Clean Water Act, discussed in detail infra, somewhat altered this view. Nevertheless, the Commission remains the preeminent regulatory body, deciding whether development should occur and if so, by whom and how.

The Act authorizes the Commission to grant a fifty-year license to a hydropower operator as long as the project is: (1) in the public interest and (2) "best adapted to a comprehensive plan for improving or developing a waterway." . . . [T]he FPA was later amended to require the Commission to "give equal consideration to the purposes of energy conservation, the protection, mitigation of damage to, and enhancement of, fish and wildlife (including related spawning grounds and habitat), the protection of recreational opportunities, and the preservation of other aspects of environmental quality." In short, the Commission must now weigh the need for hydropower energy development within a national waterway against (1) the availability of alternative sources of power; (2) other potential uses of the river, including recreational uses; and (3) the protection of the environment, fish, and wildlife. Unfortunately, the statute provides the Commission little guidance—and allows for significant leeway—in balancing these values.

The FPA provides for a two-fold preference for public over private development of hydropower. First, it allows states and municipalities to have a preference for licensing if their plans are "equally well adapted . . . to conserve and utilize . . . the water resources of the region" as compared to the private hydropower developer's plans. . . . Second, it gives the federal government the right to take over the project and develop it or to take over the project after the license has expired.

While the Commission had exclusive authority to license and regulate private and municipal hydropower facilities, federally-owned hydropower facilities could be constructed and operated outside the FPA. In the mid-twentieth century, the U.S. Army Corps of Engineers (Corps) and the U.S. Bureau of Reclamation worked together to build the largest dams in the United States . . . including the well-known Hoover Dam. Construction of the Hoover Dam (originally known as the Colorado River's Boulder Dam) began in 1931 with the first electric generation from the facility occurring in 1936. Construction on the dam continued until 1961. As completed, Hoover Dam is 726.4 feet high and 1,244 feet long, containing a total of 7.65 million cubic yards of concrete. According to the Bureau of Reclamation, Hoover Dam generates an average of four billion kilowatt-hour[s] (kWh) of electricity annually, making it one of the largest electric power generating facility[ies] in the world. It remains the "highest and third largest concrete dam in the United States."

III. A FALL FROM GRACE

Following the big dam era, hydropower project construction began to see a decline in the United States with fewer and fewer licenses being sought and issued. The industry received a brief boost in the 1970s and 80s after Congress enacted the Public Utility Regulatory Policies Act (PURPA) of 1978 in response to the energy crises of the 1970s, but this boost was short-lived. PURPA encourages (1) energy conservation; (2) "optimization of the efficiency of use of facilities and resources by electric utilities"; and (3) equitable customer electricity rates, through among other things, development of small hydropower dams.53 In essence, the Act provides financial incentives for independent hydropower development by requiring utility companies to purchase power from independently owned hydropower producers at full "avoided cost" rates. [Today], [t]he usefulness of the Act for promotion of hydropower development has seemingly [ended]. The majority of the contracts executed in the 1980s have, or will soon, expire. . . .

Development as a whole has been on the decline with FERC issuing fewer and fewer licenses for new hydropower projects over the last several decades. . . Federal projects (non-FERC licensed projects) have similarly decreased. As of 2011, the median age of Corps hydropower facilities was forty-seven years, and 90% of Corps projects are thirty-four years or older. . . .

————————————

NOTES & QUESTIONS

1. Based on Professor Warren's excerpts above, why do you think hydroelectric energy development is governed more at the federal government level than is wind energy or solar energy development?

2. Describe in your own words the analysis that federal laws require FERC to conduct when considering whether to grant a license for a large hydroelectric project.

3. In what sense is the federal government itself a major producer of hydroelectric power? How has federal law helped to enable the federal government to take on this role? Do you think the federal government's

substantial involvement in the development of hydroelectric generating facilities is justifiable on policy grounds? Why or why not?

4. *Multi-Purpose Dams.* It is worth noting that the federal government constructed many of the hydroelectric facilities in the Western United States to serve multiple purposes and not solely to generate electric power. As the nation's appetite for electricity has grown over the past half century, the proportional share of electricity coming from these large hydropower projects has declined. To quote Professor Dan Tarlock,

> From the 1930s to the 1960s, hydroelectric generation became an integral part of many of the large publically financed multiple-purpose dams in the West. Hydro revenues helped to finance subsidized irrigation and free flood-control projects. Today, dams operated by the Tennessee Valley Authority, the Corps of Engineers, and the Bureau of Reclamation primarily on the Colorado, in Columbia, Missouri, and in California generate 51% of the nation's hydro. When other public dams are added, the figure jumps to 71%. However, even as large federal dams were being built, hydro's share of energy supply progressively declined as coal, oil, and gas came to dominate the electricity energy market outside of the Pacific Northwest and California. As nuclear plants began to come online in the 1960s, hydro's share further declined.

Dan Tarlock, *Hydro Law and the Future of Hydroelectric Power Generation in the United States*, 65 VAND. L. REV. 1723, 1733 (2012).

2. HYDROPOWER AND THE ENVIRONMENT

Although hydropower has several characteristics that make it a desirable source of renewable energy, it also creates environmental hazards that have increasingly limited its growth over the past few decades. The massive dams associated with large hydropower projects often intentionally flood millions of acres of valuable land, destroy precious wetland areas, and constrain the nation's use of its scarce water resources. However, hydropower's most notorious shortcoming is its potential hazards to wild fish populations. One pair of commentators highlighted this weakness of hydropower as follows:

> [W]hy don't all states utilize hydropower to help meet their renewable goals? Although it is a plentiful, carbon-free fuel, concerns remain over its environmental footprint. Damming rivers forever alters a region's geologic landscape, and a hydroelectricity facility's turbines often kill the fish that get caught in the plant. In the Pacific Northwest, hydroelectric plant operators routinely stop producing electricity during salmon spawning seasons and must take careful steps to reduce their impact on the fish population. Although these necessary steps

prevent massive fish kills and protect crucial species, they limit the efficiency and effectiveness of the hydropower facilities.

David C. Coen & Robert J. Thormeyer, *Should Large Hydroelectric Projects Be Treated as Renewable Resources?*, 32 ENERGY L.J. 541, 543–44 (2011).

The following excerpts from the background section of a 1997 Ninth Circuit Court case aptly illustrate the inherent tension between hydroelectric energy and fish conservation in the Pacific Northwest. The analysis and conclusion sections of the case centered on technical procedural issues and are thus intentionally omitted to ease reading.

AMERICAN RIVERS V. NATIONAL MARINE FISHERIES SERVICE

United States Court of Appeals, Ninth Circuit, 1997
126 F.3d 1118

FERGUSON, C.J.

Environmental and commercial fishing organizations (collectively "American Rivers"), appeal the district court's denial of their motion for summary judgment and its grant of defendants' cross-motion for summary judgment. The defendants are the National Marine Fisheries Service ("NMFS") and the federal agencies that operate the Federal Columbia River Power System ("River Power System"). American Rivers contends that the federal agencies violated § 7(a)(2) of the Endangered Species Act, 16 U.S.C. § 1536(a)(2), because the operation of the River Power System jeopardizes the existence of the Snake River salmon and adversely modifies the salmon's critical habitat. Specifically, American Rivers challenges the federal agencies' decision to use transportation measures—moving juvenile salmon downstream in trucks and barges—to avoid a determination that the operation of the River Power System jeopardizes the existence of the salmon.

I.   *Background*

A.   Factual Background

1.   Basic Facts

"Salmon and hydropower are the two great natural resources of the Columbia River Basin." *Northwest Resource Info. Ctr., Inc. v. Northwest Power Planning Council*, 35 F.3d 1371, 1375 (9th Cir. 1994), *cert. denied*, 516 U.S. 806, 116 S.Ct. 50, 133 L.Ed.2d 15 (1995) (hereinafter *Northwest Power*). The present case involves the continuing conflict between these two important resources.

Snake River sockeye and chinook salmon are anadromous fish—they hatch and spend their first years in fresh water, reach mature size while rearing in the Pacific Ocean, and return to their natal streams and lakes to spawn and die. Anadromous fish runs in the Columbia River Basin have dwindled as a result of human activities since the European settlement of the Northwest. *Northwest Power*, 35 F.3d at 1376. The decline of these stocks of salmon has been caused by over-harvest, habitat degradation, predation, poor ocean rearing conditions, and the construction and operation of over 200 dams in the Columbia River Basin. 57 Fed. Reg. 14,654, 14,660, 14,661.

In 1991, National Marine Fisheries Service listed the Snake River sockeye salmon as an endangered species. 56 Fed. Reg. 58,619. The following year, NMFS listed the Snake River spring/summer and fall chinook as threatened species. . . On December 28, 1993, NMFS designated the critical habitat for these three species, which encompasses the Snake River and Columbia River migratory corridor. 58 Fed. Reg. 68,544. Despite the salmon's listed status, only one Snake River sockeye returned to spawn in the Snake River in 1994. In 1995, only 1,800 Snake River spring/summer chinook and 350 Snake River fall chinook returned to the river to spawn. These numbers demonstrate that the listed salmon continue their march toward extinction.

The present controversy between salmon and hydropower concerns the downstream migration of juvenile salmon or "smolts" in the Columbia River Basin. Once the salmon hatch in the upstream areas of the Columbia River Basin, the smolts travel downstream to the Pacific Ocean. During this downstream migration the smolts pass eight of the dams and reservoirs that are part of the River Power System. The Bureau of Reclamation and the Corps of Engineers operate these hydroelectric, flood control, and water storage projects. The importance and magnitude of the River Power System is demonstrated by the fact that it generates approximately half of the electricity used in the Pacific Northwest.

All parties agree that the existence of the River Power System impedes the migration of salmon. At present, there are four ways in which the salmon migrating downstream may pass the eight mainstream Columbia and Snake River hydroelectric projects. The salmon may: (1) spill over the dams; (2) pass through the power turbines; (3) bypass to transportation facilities, including barges or trucks; or (4) bypass back into the river. . . . Each of these methods is subject to scientific debate as to its effectiveness and benefit to the listed salmon. . . .

Regardless of how the smolts pass the dams, the operation of the River Power System causes mortality to the smolts during their downstream migrations. The dams reduce water flow through reservoirs which slows the salmon's passage and contributes to salmon mortality. The salmon's slow passage through these reservoirs increases the exposure time of the juvenile salmon to: (1) predation; (2) higher water temperatures which make the salmon more susceptible to disease; and (3) water quality problems including dissolved gas supersaturation which causes gas bubble disease in juvenile and adult salmon. Moreover, during downstream migration some of the smolts pass through the hydroelectric turbines and emerge injured or disoriented, rendering them easy prey for squawfish. Furthermore, smolts that are diverted through the bypass systems at the dams may suffer descaling, disorientation, and stress.

The gravity of the salmon mortality problem is illustrated by NMFS's own estimate of cumulative passage mortality, which was as high as ninety-one percent for spring/summer chinook passing the mainstream hydroelectric projects. . . .

2.   The Smolt Transportation Program

In 1968, NMFS first experimented with transportation as a means of facilitating the smolts downstream migration. Snake River smolts have been transported from Lower Granite, Little Goose, and McNary Dams since the 1970s and from Lower Monumental Dam since 1993. Today the smolt transportation program entails removing the migrating juvenile salmon from the river, transporting them around the dams, and then releasing them back into the Columbia River below Bonneville Dam to continue their journey to the Pacific Ocean.

The Corps of Engineers operates the transportation program during the juvenile migration season. All four dams involved in the transportation program have mechanical bypass systems that divert a portion of the juvenile salmon away from the power house turbines and into vertical gatewells. From the gatewells, the salmon pass through small orifices into bypass channels which run the length of the power house. The salmon then enter a primary dewatering facility, and then a high velocity pipe or flume that carries them to the transportation facility where they are separated, sorted, marked, and examined. The salmon then are held in raceways and from these raceways they are loaded into tanker trucks or barges. The transportation barges are specially equipped to circulate river water into the holding tank. It takes approximately forty hours for a barge to travel to the release site below the Bonneville Dam. Once the salmon are released, they continue their migration for another 140 miles to the Pacific Ocean.

As with the other methods of passage around the dams, transportation also causes mortality. American Rivers contends that transportation results in the following negative impacts on the juvenile salmon: (1) stress and physical injury which accompanies bypass and handling; (2) predation and disease transmission during holding and transport; (3) predation at the point of release; and (4) homing impairment of returning adults. At this point in time, scientific research is inconclusive regarding the ability of the transportation program to improve the survival of the salmon. Although the efficacy of the transportation program has been questioned, scientific evidence suggests that it is more probable than not that transportation improves the relative survival of juvenile salmon under certain hydroelectric operational scenarios and flow regimes.

B. Statutory Framework

The Endangered Species Act ("ESA"), 16 U.S.C. §§ 1531–1543, has both substantive and procedural provisions designed to protect endangered species and their habitat. These provisions are triggered when a species is listed as endangered or threatened. 16 U.S.C. § 1533. Section 7(a)(2) of the ESA requires federal agencies to "insure that any action authorized, funded, or carried out by such agency . . . is not likely to jeopardize the continued existence of any endangered species or threatened species. . . ." 16 U.S.C. § 1536(a)(2). If a contemplated agency action may affect a listed species, then the agency must consult with the Secretary of the Interior, either formally or informally. 50 C.F.R. § 402.14(a); 16 U.S.C. § 1536(a)(4). The agency first prepares a biological assessment, in which it evaluates the potential effects of an action on the listed species and its critical habitat. 50 C.F.R. § 402.12(a). If the agency discovers that its action may affect a listed species or its critical habitat, the agency must initiate formal consultation with NMFS. 50 C.F.R. § 402.14(a). In formal consultation, NMFS must prepare a biological opinion evaluating the effects of the action. NMFS determines whether the action will jeopardize a listed species. 16 U.S.C. § 1536(b)(3)(A); 50 C.F.R. § 402.14(h)(3). If NMFS makes a jeopardy finding, then it may also suggest reasonable and prudent alternatives to the proposed action. *Id.* By definition, the reasonable and prudent alternatives may not jeopardize the listed species or result in the destruction or adverse modification of its critical habitat. *Id.*

QUESTIONS

1.   Describe in one paragraph in your own words how hydroelectric dams interfere with the life cycle of salmon in the Columbia River Basin.

2.   Describe specific strategies the Army Corp of Engineers and NMFS have employed to protect salmon populations in the Columbia River Basin from hazards associated with hydroelectric dams in the region.

3.   Suppose that it was determined that, even if operators employed every plausible mitigation strategy, there was a 90% chance that continued operation of the five largest hydroelectric dams in the Columbia River Basin would eliminate all remaining wild salmon populations in the Basin within 50 years.

a.   Based on the (hypothetical) information above, draft a one-paragraph argument in favor of shutting down these five hydroelectric dams within the next decade.

b.   Based on the (hypothetical) information above, draft a one-paragraph argument in favor of keeping the five massive hydroelectric facilities open indefinitely with regular monitoring.

c.   Which of these two positions do you believe is most convincing, and why?

4.   *Proposals to Privatize Hydropower Transmission Infrastructure.* In 2017, the Trump administration released a proposal for the federal government to sell certain public power operators' assets to private parties. Among the assets listed on the proposal were billions of dollars in Bonneville Power Administration (BPA) transmission lines and facilities. This transmission infrastructure has long supported a massive network of hydropower facilities in the Northwest, including Bonneville Dam (described in *American Rivers* above).

Supporters of a private sale of BPA's transmission assets argue that the agency has long been mired in inefficiency and bureaucracy and that privatizing the assets would mitigate those problems. Critics of the proposal worry about such an action's long-term impacts on water management, environmental protection, and the interests of Native American tribes and small municipalities in the region. See Kirk Johnson, *Down the Mighty Columbia River, Where a Power Struggle Looms*, N.Y. TIMES (July 28, 2017), https://www.nytimes.com/interactive/2017/07/28/us/columbia-river-privatization.html.

3.   SMALL HYDROPOWER

Over the next century, one of the more promising areas of potential growth in the U.S. hydropower industry is in the development of smaller-scale hydroelectricity projects. As of 2015, there were 1,640 hydropower plants in the United States with generating capacities of 10 MW or less, and these plants had a combined generating capacity of roughly 3,670 MW. *See* Kurt Johnson & Boualem Hadjerioua, *Small Hydropower in the United States* 5 (2015), https://info.ornl.gov/sites/publications/Files/Pub56556.pdf. However, more than one third of those 1,640 facilities were developed in the 1980s and the pace of development has steadily declined since that decade. *Id.* at 6. Still, some believe an increasingly favorable policy environment and additional technological advancements could eventually enable small hydropower to emerge as a major electricity source.

Small hydropower is viewed as less harmful to the natural environment and other waterway uses than large-scale hydropower, and policymakers are beginning to recognize that distinction when crafting laws. For instance, as of 2017, 25 of the 29 U.S. states with RPS policies included language specifying that only small hydropower projects (defined as facilities with maximum generating capacities of between 5MW and 30 MW) qualified as renewable energy sources under those programs. *See*

Steven Ferrey, *Moving the Needle of Western Climate and Energy Options*, 8 SAN DIEGO J. CLIMATE & ENERGY L. 129, 148–49 (2017).

In the following excerpt, Professor Gina Warren explains the basics of small hydropower, emphasizes the unique advantages of this type of energy strategy, and suggests some additional policy changes capable of helping to spur greater small hydropower investment in the coming years. The case that follows Professor Warren's excerpt highlights some ways that FERC licensing requirements have impeded small hydropower development projects in the United States, including some renovations of existing small hydropower facilities.

SMALL HYDROPOWER, BIG POTENTIAL: CONSIDERATIONS FOR RESPONSIBLE GLOBAL DEVELOPMENT

Gina Warren
53 IDAHO L. REV. 149, 152–53, 168–70, 172 & 174–76 (2017)

. . . Untapped small hydropower potential exists worldwide and could deliver upwards of 173 gigawatts (GW) of new energy. . . . Hydropower is created by the flow of water over a turbine or water wheel that is connected to an alternator or generator, which in turn generates electricity. The electricity can be used onsite, directed into the transmission grid for utility-scale distribution, or stored in batteries for later use. While there is no international definition of small hydropower, most concur that small hydropower generators are those that produce up to 10 megawatts (MW); however, this threshold is by no means a universal consensus. For example, for regulatory purposes, India draws the line at 25MW, China at 50MW, and the United States at 30MW.

A facility producing less than 1MW is generally labeled mini-hydropower; less than 100 kilowatts (kW) is generally labeled micro-hydropower; and less than 5kW is generally labeled pico-hydropower. Small and mini facilities usually contribute electricity to the regional or national grid, while pico and micro facilities are generally used for isolated individuals and villages. This article will focus on mini, small, and medium hydropower up to 30MW, referring generally to them as "small hydropower."

Small hydropower is flexible and can be located on rivers, in canals, locks, pipes, lakes, or just about any running waterway without the need to install elaborate or expensive dams. It can also be placed on existing infrastructure, such as an existing dam or other flood-control mechanism. This specific placement maximizes efficiency and minimizes environmental harm. . . .

. . . .

IV. CONSIDERATIONS FOR RESPONSIBLE SMALL HYDROPOWER DEVELOPMENT

If small hydropower is to become a larger part of our clean energy future, a stable, but flexible, development model is needed. A proper framework would include, at the very least: competent and thorough information gathered about the proposed site, facility, and output; and a simple, yet flexible, governance structure that utilizes the principles of subsidiarity.

A. Information

To reliably develop small hydropower, stakeholders will need an accurate and thorough understanding of multiple factors, including the feasibility of the specific site and the technological advancements available to generate a sufficient amount of electricity to offset any potential human or nature impacts of development at the location.

1. Site Feasibility Studies

Through years of mistakes in hydropower development, we now understand that not all sites can or should be developed.

Instead, it is important to study potential sites, looking for locations with the highest energy value and the least environmental and human impacts. For example, in 2006 the U.S. Department of Energy conducted a series of feasibility studies for small hydro development within the United States. It determined that 500,000 sites exist that are suitable for small or low-flow hydropower. Of those 500,000 sites, roughly 130,000 sites were determined to be feasible for immediate development. Of those 130,000 sites, however, 5,400 sites were determined to yield the highest potential output, potentially increasing United States' hydropower generation by 50%.

The feasibility study looked at criteria such as land and environmental sensitivities, existing infrastructure, access, transmission proximity, customer base proximity, financial viability, and hydropower potential. The vast majority of the best sites are those that can be located on existing infrastructure, near transmission and a customer base. . . . .

. . . .

2. Technology and Project Design

Smaller hydropower projects can be designed in a way to cater to the specifications of the exact location. Engineers can study the site and determine maximum generation output depending on the design of the turbine and the desired water flow. Because of technological enhancements and the nature of small hydropower, it can be designed so that it does not kill all aquatic creatures. . . .

Furthermore, small hydropower can be flexibly located on waterways *without* indigenous fish species, thereby significantly reducing environmental harm. . . .

. . . .

For effective development, small hydropower needs a flexible, but stable, information-based governance structure. The framework should be simple, expeditious, and economically viable so that the costs and complications do not outweigh the benefits. One way to help ensure this is through subsidiarity—by granting authority for licensing to the least (or lowest) centralized authority capable of undertaking the licensing.

In the United States this means that states and local governments would oversee licensing of more small, qualifying facilities. States could then screen the projects; ensuring the applications are complete by identifying any necessary consultations and studies so as to satisfy all licensing requirements, and finally, issuing the licenses if all requirements have been met. For other nations, their local and regional governing units could do the same. If properly implemented, this bottom-up approach could decrease costs, increase efficiency, and provide incentive for local governmental units to promote small hydropower development while still empowering them to protect their natural resources, fish, wildlife, and recreational opportunities. Immediate stakeholders could look at the specific facility, its local generation potential, and its specific environmental impact potential to the surrounding area when determining whether it is the best use of the waterway.

. . . .

. . . Likewise, all small hydropower projects should include, within their initial licensing, the requirement for frequent facility monitoring. Once a project is licensed, it should undergo frequent inspections and monitoring to ensure it does not cause unforeseen damage. Unlike large hydropower where, once it is put into place, it is extremely difficult to change or remove (even after more information surfaces as to its potential damaging impacts), small hydropower is more flexible because of its smaller physical size and cost. Reasonable monitoring should occur to prevent unintended or unforeseen consequences.

For example, one unintended consequence can come from placing multiple small facilities on one waterway, which can heighten the potential of negative cumulative impacts. Once small hydropower facilities are put into place, any additional facilities on the same waterway will need to be studied to ensure that the cumulative impacts do not outweigh the benefits. It is possible that cumulative impacts of several small projects could be even greater than the impacts of one large facility with the same energy output.

L.S. STARRETT CO. V. FERC

United States Court of Appeals, First Circuit, 2011
650 F.3d 19

TORRUELLA, C.J.

L.S. Starrett Company ("Starrett") appeals from two orders by the Federal Energy Regulatory Commission ("FERC" or "Commission"). The Commission concluded that Starrett would be required to seek licensing pursuant to Section 23(b) of the Federal Power Act ("FPA") if it proceeded with certain proposed changes to its Crescent Street Dam Project ("the Project"), a hydroelectric generating facility. Under Section 23(b), Starrett must seek licensing if (1) its facility is located on a stream over which Congress has Commerce Clause jurisdiction, (2) its proposed changes constitute "post-1935 construction" within the meaning of the FPA, and (3) the proposed modifications will affect the interests of interstate or foreign commerce. *See* 16 U.S.C. § 817(1). For the reasons below, we conclude that we have no choice but to affirm.

I. *Background*

The Project is located on the non-navigable Millers River in Athol, Massachusetts, on property that belongs to Starrett. It consists of (1) an 87-acre-foot reservoir; (2) a 20-foot-high, 127-foot-long concrete gravity dam; (3) two powerhouses, one at each end of the dam; and (4) various appurtenant facilities. The turbine generator in the powerhouse on the right side of the dam ("the right-side generator") currently has an installed capacity of 250 kW and an actual capacity of 80 kW. The turbine generator in the powerhouse on the dam's left side ("the left-side generator") had an installed and actual capacity of 112 kW until 2006, when it failed. Prior to the failure of the left-side generator, the combined installed capacity for the Project was 362 kW. This installed capacity was memorialized in a 1992 FERC order, which concluded that the Project did not require FERC licensing because there had been no post-1935 construction. *See L.S. Starrett Co., 61 FERC ¶ 62,200 (1992)* ("*Starrett I*"). The facility, however, could only actually produce 192 kW of electricity, even prior to the failure of the left-side generator, because of the physical limitations of the site.

After the left-side generator failed, Starrett began to investigate its options for replacement or repair. In early 2007, Starrett retained GZA GeoEnvironmental, Inc. ("GZA"), which prepared a feasibility study that examined the financial costs and benefits of repairing the left-side generator. The study concluded that it would be cost effective to use hydropower generated by a new left-side turbine generator ("the new left-side generator"). The new left-side generator's installed and actual capacity would be 198 kW. Installing the new left-side generator would increase the Project's combined installed capacity approximately 24%, to 448 kW, and its total actual capacity approximately 45%, to 278 kW. The total *actual* capacity of the Project, however, would remain less than the previous total *installed* capacity (i.e., 362 kW, the capacity documented in *Starrett I*), a point that Starrett now emphasizes.

In September 2008, believing that it did not require FERC licensing in order to proceed with its proposed changes, Starrett ordered a new cross-flow turbine generator and began the preparatory work for its installation inside the left powerhouse. According to Starrett, replacing the left-side generator required the following: (1) lowering the floor inside the powerhouse by approximately 5 feet; (2)(a) improving the plunge pool within the building footprint by mounting the draft tube below the turbine generator, and (b) widening the outlet portal from under the powerhouse to the river from approximately 4 to 17 feet, both in order to improve outlet hydraulics and project efficiency; (3) excavating approximately 10 cubic yards of bedrock from the bottom of the Millers River, again in order to improve outlet hydraulics and project efficiency; and (4) installing a transition piece to connect the existing penstock to the new turbine.

In March 2009, as Starrett was working to replace its left-side generator, the U.S. Fish and Wildlife Service ("USF & WS") wrote to the Commission to request that the Commission investigate the work occurring at the Project. The USF & WS had become aware that Starrett planned to install higher capacity machinery, and was concerned that the increased capacity at the Project would negatively impact migratory fish.

On May 4, 2009, the Commission notified Starrett that its proposed work would increase the capacity of the Project and would be considered post-1935 construction, thus triggering the Commission's licensing jurisdiction. The Commission asked Starrett to submit various details about its dam and the proposed changes. Starrett provided the requested details but maintained that its proposed work would not lead to an increase in capacity above the 362 kW total memorialized in *Starrett I* because only the installed capacity, not the actual capacity, would be over 362 kW. After reviewing these materials, the Commission issued an order finding that licensing of the Project was required. *See L.S. Starrett Co., 129 FERC ¶ 62,053 (2009)* ("*Starrett II*"). Following Starrett's request for rehearing, the Commission issued an order denying rehearing. *See L.S. Starrett Co., 130 FERC ¶ 61,112 (2010)* ("*Starrett III*").

II. *Discussion*

We are now required to review the Commission's determination that the Project fell within its jurisdiction under Section 23(b) of the FPA. Under that section, a hydroelectric project "without a valid pre-1920 permit" is subject to the Commission's licensing jurisdiction if it

(1)   is located on a navigable water of the United States;

(2)   occupies lands of the United States;

(3)   utilizes surplus water or water power from a government dam or

(4)   [a] is located on a stream over which Congress has Commerce Clause jurisdiction, [b] is constructed or modified on or after August 26, 1935, and [c] affects the interests of interstate or foreign commerce.

Starrett II, 129 FERC ¶ 62,053, at 64,160; *see also* 16 U.S.C. § 817(1). The Commission concluded that Starrett's dam was subject to licensing under the fourth criterion. We lay out the governing standard of review, and then address each of the three prongs of the fourth criterion.

A.   Standard of Review

Reviewing the Commission's orders under the Administrative Procedures Act, we "must reverse an agency action that is 'arbitrary, capricious, an abuse of discretion, or otherwise not in accordance with law.'" *Knott v. FERC*, 386 F.3d 368, 372 (1st Cir. 2004). . . .

"We review FERC's findings of fact for 'substantial evidence,' and if so supported, such findings are conclusive." *Knott*, 386 F.3d at 371. . . . "We 'defer to the agency's expertise . . . so long as its decision is supported by "substantial evidence" in the record and reached by "reasoned decisionmaking," including an examination of the relevant data and a reasoned explanation supported by a stated connection between the facts found and the choice made.'" *Id.* . . .

. . . .

B.   A "Commerce Clause Stream"

Section 23(b) requires us to ask whether L.S. Starrett's dam is on "a stream over which Congress has Commerce Clause jurisdiction," *see* 16 U.S.C. § 817(1), i.e., a "Commerce Clause stream." The Commission concluded, and L.S. Starrett does not dispute on appeal, that the Millers River is a "Commerce Clause stream." . . .

C.   Post-1935 "Construction"

In 1935, Congress amended the FPA "to require that persons *'intending to construct* a dam or other project works' on *nonnavigable* streams obtain a license." . . . . Thus, if post-1935 work constitutes "construction" within the meaning of the FPA and the other two prongs of Section 23(b) are met, a facility will be subject to the Commission's licensing jurisdiction.

The Commission argues that, because Congress has not spoken on the precise question at issue here—which it frames as "what constitutes 'construction'"—we need only determine if its interpretation of Section 23(b) was unreasonable. *See . . . Chevron* [*v. United States*], 467 U.S. at 844, 104 S.Ct. 2778 (explaining that when Congress implicitly delegates a question to an administrative agency, "a court may not substitute its own construction of a statutory provision for a reasonable interpretation made by the administrator of an agency"). The Commission contends that it was reasonable for it to determine that Starrett's proposed work would constitute post-1935 construction because the work would increase the Project's installed capacity. In addition, it notes that the Commission also found that the installation of the new generator would increase *actual* capacity, another indication that the proposed work constituted post-1935 construction. Alternatively, the Commission argues that it was reasonable for it to conclude that the proposal would result in post-1935 construction because it would increase the Project's "head."

Starrett, on the other hand, argues that Congress has addressed the precise question at issue here by limiting the Commission's jurisdiction to post-1935 "construction." Starrett contends that because the proposed work was merely a repair, and would not increase *actual* capacity beyond the 1992 *installed* capacity, it was not post-1935 construction.

1.   Standard of Review

We must first determine whether Congress unambiguously expressed an intent about the precise question at issue here. If we conclude that Congress did unambiguously express such an intent, our analysis ends there. If we conclude that Congress did not unambiguously express an intent on the precise question here, we must analyze whether the Commission's conclusion that the work here constituted jurisdictional construction was unreasonable.

. . . .

a.   Language of the Statute

. . . .

Black's Law Dictionary defines "construction" as "[t]he act of building by combining or arranging parts or elements." *Black's Law Dictionary* 355 (9th ed. 2009). Another dictionary defines "construction" as "the act of putting parts together to form a complete integrated object," and the verb "construct" as "to form, make, or create by combining parts or elements." *Webster's Third New International Dictionary* (Philip Babcock Gove et al. eds., 1971). These definitions do not suggest that "construction" has "a plain and unambiguous meaning with regard to the particular dispute" here. *Duckworth* [*v. Pratt & Whitney*], 152 F.3d at 5. . . . Rather, "construction" "is a chameleon, capable of taking on different meanings, and shades of meaning, depending on the subject matter and the circumstances of each particular usage." *Strickland v. Comm'r, Me. Dep't of Human Servs.*, 48 F.3d 12, 19 (1st Cir. 1995).

b. Statute as a Whole

If we conclude that the "plain language of the statute, standing alone, is ambiguous," the next step is to "ask whether this ambiguity can be resolved by looking to the 'specific context in which [the] language is used, and the broader context of the statute as a whole.'" *Perez-Olivo [v. Chavez]*, 394 F.3d at 49. . . . The parties have not called to our attention, and we have not found in our review of the FPA, any clues about the meaning of the word "construction" as it applies here. Therefore, we move on to the second stage of the *Chevron* analysis.

2. Reasonableness

The Commission argues that its conclusion here—i.e., that Starrett's proposed work would constitute jurisdictional construction—was reasonable because the proposed changes involved (1) an increase in installed capacity and (2) an increase in head. Responding to the Commission's argument about increased capacity, Starrett contends that the Project's new *actual* capacity (278 kW, up from 192 kW) would remain below the 1992 installed capacity (362 kW), and thus the Commission should not have exercised its jurisdiction. We conclude that the Commission's determination was reasonable because there is no doubt that, under Starrett's plan, there would be an increase in capacity no matter how the capacity was measured; both the actual and the installed capacities would be greater than their respective 1992 values. For this reason, we need not analyze the head issue or resolve any of the factual disputes related to that issue.

. . . .

The cases that Starrett cites to support its position are distinguishable because they did not involve increases in capacity. . . .

In short, we conclude that the Commission's determination that Starrett's facility met the second required prong was not unreasonable.

D. The Effect on Interstate Commerce

Before allowing the FERC to exert its licensing jurisdiction over projects involving post-1935 construction, Section 23(b) requires the Commission to "find that the interests of interstate or foreign commerce would be affected by [the] proposed construction." 16 U.S.C. § 817(1). The Commission argues that Starrett's construction meets the interstate commerce requirement because its dam is a member of a class of small hydroelectric projects that collectively have a substantial impact on interstate commerce because they produce power that would otherwise have to be produced elsewhere on the interstate grid. Starrett responds that (1) it is improper for the Commission to rely on this "cumulative effect" theory because it leaves the Commission's Commerce Clause jurisdiction without boundary; and (2) in any case, the Commission has not shown that

Starrett's facility belongs to a class of small hydroelectric projects that collectively affect interstate commerce.

We first address whether it was unreasonable for the Commission to consider the cumulative effect on commerce of many small hydroelectric facilities, and then address whether there was substantial evidence that Starrett's dam, in conjunction with others, actually has a significant impact on interstate commerce. . . .

1.   The "Cumulative Effect" Theory

The Supreme Court has noted that the language of the FPA "strongly implies that Congress drew upon its full authority under the Commerce Clause" in enacting the statute. [*Federal Power Commission v.*] *Union Elec. Co.*, 381 U.S. at 96, 85 S.Ct. 1253 [1965]. "Full authority under the Commerce Clause includes the power to reach a local activity whose effect on commerce, 'taken together with that of many others similarly situated, is far from trivial.'" *Habersham* [*Mills v. FERC*], 976 F.2d at 1384. . . . Assuming there was substantial evidence supporting the Commission's factual findings, it would not be unreasonable for the Commission to regulate Starrett's dam because "a small hydroelectric project that affects commerce only slightly" can "still be subject to congressional regulation if it is part of a class with a significant cumulative effect." *Habersham*, 976 F.2d at 1384. We thus turn to the second part of our analysis and ask whether the Commission's conclusion that Starrett's dam is part of a class of projects that, in the aggregate, have the required effect on interstate commerce "is supported by substantial evidence." *City of Centralia* [*v. FERC*], 661 F.2d at 792.

2.   Substantial Evidence

Starrett contends that its situation is comparable to the one in *City of Centralia,* where the Ninth Circuit concluded that the record failed to support the Commission's conclusion that a hydroelectric project either (1) itself had a substantial effect on commerce, 661 F.2d at 792; or (2) was part of a class of projects that, cumulatively, had a substantial effect on interstate commerce, *id.* at 793. We agree with the Commission that this case is more comparable to *Habersham,* where the Eleventh Circuit concluded that two small dams did meet the interstate commerce requirement because the Commission presented evidence that (1) by supplying power to a factory, the two hydroelectric projects "effectively displace[d] electricity that the factory otherwise would draw from the interstate grid," 976 F.2d at 1384; and (2) the Commission referred to two FERC reports that "indicate[d] that the small [hydroelectric] projects [around the nation] collectively account for a substantial portion of the nation's hydroelectric generating capacity," *id.* at 1385. Here, the Commission (1) explained that Starrett's dam produces power that Starrett would otherwise receive from the interstate grid, a point supported by the record; and (2) cited *Habersham*—which in turn, as noted above, cited two FERC studies—to support the proposition that small hydroelectric projects that displace power from the national grid can have a significant cumulative effect on interstate commerce.... We believe that there was substantial evidence to support the factual findings underlying the Commission's interstate commerce conclusion.

III. *Conclusion*

For the reasons stated, we affirm.

NOTES & QUESTIONS

1.   According to Professor Warren, what are some distinct advantages of small hydropower that could enable it to play a much larger role in supplying the nation's baseload power?

2.   Which levels of government does Professor Warren suggest are best suited to govern small hydropower development, and why?

3.   Based on the industry definitions provided in the Warren excerpt, was the hydroelectric plant at issue in *Starrett* a pico-, micro-, mini-, or small-hydropower facility?

4.   What is the "cumulative effect theory" and how did it affect the analysis in *Starrett*? From purely a policy perspective, do you think this theory requires that all hydropower facility licensing (including licensing for small hydropower facilities) be conducted at the federal government level? Why or why not?

5.   How did the developer in *Starrett* attempt to use the distinction between "installed" and "actual" generating capacity in its argument for exemption from FERC licensing requirements? How did the court respond to this argument? Do you agree with the court's treatment of the "installed" vs. "actual" distinction in the case? Why or why not?

6.   *Expanding FERC Licensing Exemptions.* The Hydropower Regulatory Efficiency Act of 2013 helped to simplify the licensing of some small hydroelectric projects. Among other things, the Act amended the definition of "small hydroelectric power projects" in Section 405 of the Public Utility Regulatory Policies Act of 1978 to cover all projects having an installed generating capacity of less than 10 MW. This broader definition generally exempts projects up to that size from the Federal Power Act's costly and time-consuming FERC licensing requirements. It remains to be seen whether these changes will spur any significant uptake in small hydropower development.

7.   *Pumped Storage Facilities.* Another facet of the hydropower industry that is predicted to see some growth in the coming decades is the development of pumped storage facilities. During periods of low electricity demand on the grid, pumped storage facilities use electricity to pump water from a lower-

elevation reservoir to a higher-elevation reservoir. When electricity demand is high, operators release water from the higher reservoir through hydroelectric turbines and back into the lower reservoir to generate power. According to the Energy Information Administration, as of 2013 there were only about 40 pumped storage facilities operating in the United States. However, these 40 facilities collectively represented more than 22 GW of energy storage capacity, or roughly 2% of the nation's total generating capacity. *See Pumped Storage Provides Grid Reliability Even with Net Generation Loss*, U.S. ENERGY INFOR. ADMIN., https://www.eia.gov/todayinenergy/detail.php?id=11991 (last visited Aug. 4, 2017). See Chapter 7 of this Casebook for a more detailed discussion of laws and policies related to pumped storage as a type of energy storage strategy.

8. *Incentivizing Investments in "Incremental" Hydropower.* As mentioned earlier in this chapter, most states with RPS policies do not give utilities credit toward their RPS goals for adding large hydropower projects to their energy portfolios. However, at least a couple of state RPS statutes do include provisions that reward utilities for increasing the efficiency or productivity of existing large hydroelectric plants. For example, Washington's RPS gives credit for "[i]ncremental electricity produced as a result of efficiency improvements completed after March 31, 1999, to hydroelectric generation projects owned by a qualifying utility and located in the Pacific Northwest . . . where the additional generation . . . does not result in new water diversions or impoundments. . . ." WASH. REV. CODE § 19.285.030(10) (2012). California's RPS program also gives credit for qualifying "incremental generation" from existing hydroelectric facilities. *See* EDMUND G. BROWN, JR., RENEWABLES PORTFOLIO STANDARD ELIGIBILITY 17–18 (2015) http://www.energy.ca.gov/2015publications/CEC-300-2015-001/CEC-300-2015-001-ED8-CMF.pdf.

E. OCEAN WAVE AND TIDAL ENERGY

Although the vast majority of the world's facilities that convert hydrokinetic energy into electricity reside on river dams, other promising strategies are emerging that seek to harness the kinetic energy in moving ocean water to generate electric power. The planet's waves, tides, and ocean currents contain tremendous amounts of energy that could eventually serve as major renewable energy sources. Although much of the law and policy related to marine hydrokinetic energy remains undeveloped, it may only be a matter of time before lawyers and policymakers begin actively confronting the unique issues associated with these promising technologies. The following is a short excerpt from a law journal article describing some of the basics of tidal, ocean current, and wave energy technologies and the general legal questions related to them.

HARNESSING THE OCEAN'S POWER: OPPORTUNITIES IN RENEWABLE OCEAN ENERGY RESOURCES

Todd J. Griset

16 OCEAN & COASTAL L.J. 395, 401–04, 423–24 & 431–32 & 434 (2011)

While offshore wind projects capture energy from winds located over the ocean's waters, marine hydrokinetic technologies capture energy from moving water itself. United States offshore hydrokinetic energy resources have the potential to provide a significant amount of power. These resources include the harnessable power of ocean currents, tides, and waves.

Tidal and marine current power projects use the mechanical energy of moving water to generate electricity. Because water is approximately 835 times denser than air, a given flow of water contains a great deal more energy than the same volume of air flowing at the same speed. Humans have long recognized the power of tides to perform useful work; as early as AD 1066, tidal energy was used mechanically to power grist mills in England. This technology crossed the Atlantic shortly after European colonists; by 1640, Captain William Traske had developed a "tyde mill" near the mouth of the North River in Salem, Massachusetts to grind corn. These historical tidal projects generally incorporated moving gates that allowed water to flow in during high tides; after the tide dropped, the impounded water was allowed to flow out through a water wheel or similar device to convert the power to usable mechanical energy.

Similar to conventional hydroelectric dams, modern barrage-based tidal projects rely on an improved version of the ancient tide mill technology, impounding water at high tide behind a barrage or dam and allowing it to flow through turbines to generate electricity. For example, the Rance Tidal Power Plant was constructed in France in 1966 and has a generating capacity of 240 megawatts. In North America, the Annapolis Royal Generating Station . . . has 20 megawatts of installed capacity. Despite the proven success of such technologies, barrage-based tidal projects have not been widely developed, partly because barrages affect other uses of coastal areas such as navigation, fisheries, and habitat for wildlife.

Other tidal energy projects do not use dams, but instead use other technology to convert the mechanical energy of moving water into electrical energy. Tidal in-stream energy conversion devices generate power without impoundments, generally with blades similar to windmills or revolving doors. A preliminary evaluation of the potential tidal in-stream generation capacity . . . suggests an average annual power potential of at least 1,600 megawatts. In-stream tidal energy conversion has great potential, but is not widely deployed in the United States; indeed, commercial-scale projects do not exist. In 2010, Maine-based Ocean Renewable Power Company installed a 60 kilowatt tidal turbine in Cobscook Bay to provide power for a United States Coast Guard search and rescue boat. As of February 2011, the Federal Energy Regulatory Commission (FERC) had issued twenty-six preliminary permits for tidal hydrokinetic projects with a total projected capacity of approximately 2,292 megawatts.

Marine currents similarly contain harnessable power. Through technology akin to tidal in-stream energy conversion, the kinetic energy of water flowing in a current can be used to generate electricity. The total worldwide power embodied in ocean currents is estimated to be about 5,000 gigawatts, with perhaps 70 gigawatts of potential capacity in the United States.

In addition to the energy embodied in water flowing due to tides and currents, power can be extracted from moving water in the form of waves. Looking strictly at coastal regions with a mean wave power density greater than 10 kilowatts per meter, the United States may have a total wave power flux of 2,100 terawatt-hours per year. This figure is more than half of the entire United States electric power industry's recent annual generation. Unfortunately, practical considerations significantly limit the ability to extract usable power from wave energy. For example, more than half of this estimated total wave power flux falls on the southern coast of Alaska and the Aleutian island chain, areas generally remote from significant load centers. . . . Furthermore, wave power devices fall short of 100 percent efficiency. However, extracting just 15 percent of this total flux and converting the power to electricity with an efficiency of 80 percent would yield 252 terawatt-hours per year, about 6 percent of the nation's current electricity consumption. As of February 2011, FERC had issued ten preliminary permits for marine wave hydrokinetic projects with a total projected capacity of 3,446 megawatts. Although wave energy is an immature technology, the sheer magnitude of energy embodied in waves nevertheless offers great potential as a future electricity resource.

. . . .

[A] tool to incentivize offshore renewable energy development is the enactment of a statute requiring utilities to purchase a specified amount of offshore energy through a long-term contracting procedure. Securing long-term contracts for the purchase of the power and associated commodities produced by renewable power projects is key to project finance and development. This has proved particularly true in recent years, where biomass and wind energy facilities have tended to be developed not by utilities but as merchant plants selling their output pursuant to power purchase agreements. For example, in 2010, the Maine Legislature enacted "An Act To Implement the Recommendations of the Governor's Ocean Energy Task Force." The Act includes an official policy statement supporting the development of deepwater offshore wind and marine hydrokinetic energy projects in waters off Maine:

> It is the policy of the State to encourage the attraction of appropriately sited development related to tidal and wave energy, including any additional transmission and other energy infrastructure needed to transport such energy to market, consistent with all state environmental standards; the permitting and siting of tidal and wave energy projects; and the siting, permitting, financing and construction of tidal and wave energy research and manufacturing facilities.

The Act further directs the Maine Public Utilities Commission to conduct a competitive solicitation for "deep-water offshore wind energy pilot projects" and "tidal energy demonstration projects" by September 1, 2010, using a modified version of Maine's existing statute for long-term contracting for renewable resources. The Commission is authorized to direct one or more of Maine's transmission and distribution utilities to purchase up to "30 megawatts of installed capacity and associated renewable energy and renewable energy credits from" such ocean energy resources, including up to 5 megawatts being provided by tidal energy demonstration projects. The Commission may order such contracts to have a term of up to twenty years. This is meant to enable project developers to obtain financing for their projects.

Notably, shallow-water offshore wind projects do not qualify for this incentive under Maine law. . . .

. . . .

Whether renewable ocean energy development will occur in U.S. waters on a commercial scale remains to be seen. The potential environmental impact of individual units remains largely unknown, let alone the impacts of build-out and development on a larger scale. The slate of technologies available for extracting usable energy from the sea is promising, but most—and particularly those with the greatest potential— remain in an immature state. As interest in refining these technologies continues, mechanisms for converting the oceans' energy into usable power are improving in efficiency and cost-effectiveness. Regulatory regimes applicable to renewable ocean energy continue to evolve as well. . . .

. . . .

Congressional action could further streamline the regulatory framework applicable to renewable ocean energy projects. Providing a stable structure for the development of the oceans' renewable energy potential would reduce the capital cost required to develop a given project. By providing a clear and consistent legal path for project developers to follow, such legislation would enable the best ocean energy projects to become more cost-competitive. . . .

Our oceans hold vast promise. The opportunity to transform that potential into usable energy is significant. Whether developing that potential into commercial-scale energy production is a reasonable choice remains to be seen. If renewable ocean energy resources are to be developed, promoting regulatory certainty would do much to promote their cost-effective development.

———————

QUESTIONS & NOTES

1.   In the excerpt above, Griset argues that "Congressional action could further streamline the regulatory framework applicable to renewable ocean energy projects." Suppose you were serving in Congress from a coastal state and were interested in promoting greater investment in ocean wave and tidal energy technologies. Develop and defend at least three plausible federal-level policy proposals for inclusion in a hypothetical bill aimed at promoting ocean wave and tidal development in the United States.

2.   *Ongoing Progress and Innovation.* In recent years, significant progress has been made in developing marine and hydrokinetic energy technologies in the United States. For example, engineers brought the nation's first grid-connected wave energy system online in 2015 off the island of Oahu in Hawaii. The system, which involves buoys anchored less than one mile off of the coast, generates enough electricity to power less than 20 homes but is nonetheless a promising start toward more efficient and productive projects. *See* AP, *Wave-powered Electricity Makes U.S. Debut in Hawaii*, CBS NEWS (Sept. 19, 2016), http://www.cbsnews.com/news/wave-powered-electricity-makes-us-debut-hawaii/. The U.S. Water Power Technologies Office has also collaborated with Oregon State University to build the nation's premier wave energy test facility off the coast of Oregon. Based on its design as of 2016, the facility would allow testing for up to 20 wave energy devices at any given time, which could help to accelerate innovation in the wave industry. *See* Press Release, Or. State Univ., Wave Energy Center Receives $40 Million to Construct World's Premier Test Facility (Dec. 12, 2016), http://oregonstate.edu/ua/ncs/archives/2016/dec/wave-energy-center-receives-40-million-construct-world%25E2%2580%2599s-premier-test-facility.

3.   *Utility-Scale Tidal Energy.* Some European countries are already far ahead of the United States in their deployment of marine and hydrokinetic energy technologies. One example is the MeyGen tidal stream project—a tidal energy farm in Scotland that touts itself as the world's first utility-scale tidal energy system. The project, which is heavily subsidized by the Scottish government, uses underwater turbines resembling wind turbines to harness energy in tidal streams. When fully constructed, the project is slated to have a generating capacity of up to 398MW—enough to meet the electricity needs of

as many as 175,000 homes. *See* Nikola Sturgeon, *World's First Large-scale Tidal Energy Farm Launches in Scotland*, GUARDIAN (Sept. 12, 2016), available at https://www.theguardian.com/uk-news/2016/sep/12/worlds-first-large-scale-tidal-energy-farm-launches-scotland.

4. *Additional Information on Marine and Hydrokinetic Energy.* Numerous resources are available online for further exploration of the possibilities of marine and hydrokinetic energy and the policy issues these technologies raise. The U.S. Department of Energy has produced a list of websites with more detailed information on this unique and emerging energy source. *See generally* Fact Sheet, U.S. Dep't of Energy, Marine and Hydrokinetic (MHK) Databases and Systems, https://energy.gov/sites/prod/files/2015/01/f19/MHK_DBsystems1pager.pdf (last visited Aug. 4, 2017).

CONCLUSION

A NEW ERA FOR ENERGY LAW

■ ■ ■

As described throughout this Casebook, an unprecedented transition is occurring in energy markets in the United States and throughout the world. For the first time since the dawn of the industrial revolution, economies across the planet are increasingly turning to renewable energy resources rather than to fossil fuels or nuclear power to meet their energy needs. Although this transition is still in its embryonic stages, it appears poised to permanently improve how humankind produces and uses energy.

Lawyers have important roles to play in the energy industry's shift toward renewable energy resources. Although the continued work of inventive engineers and scientists is needed to develop and improve renewable energy technologies and the devices and infrastructure to support them, scientific efforts and achievements alone are not enough to integrate sustainable energy technologies into modern society. Many of the laws that govern the energy industry today were adopted in former eras and are ill-suited to effectively govern emerging renewable energy markets and activities. Incumbent stakeholders such as coal companies, oil companies, investor-owned electric utilities, and manufacturers of gasoline-powered vehicles also often have incentives to slow the adoption of certain sustainable energy technologies within their markets. Effectively addressing these challenges will require law and policy innovation that is as inventive as the hard science energy research helping to drive it. To be successful, lawyers involved in this effort will need to be familiar with the most important emerging energy industries and equipped to analyze their economic, social, and environmental impacts.

This Casebook provides only a basic introduction to some of the most salient legal and policy issues surrounding the global transition toward a sustainable energy system. Its contents barely scratch the surface of what is rapidly becoming its own distinct and rich body of law and policy. Hopefully, those who study it will gain a deeper appreciation for the fascinating array of concepts and questions that comprises renewable energy law.

INDEX

References are to Pages